THE BRITISH EMPIRE
AND THE SECOND WORLD WAR

The British Empire
and
The Second World War

Ashley Jackson

hambledon
continuum

Hambledon Continuum
A Continuum imprint

The Tower Building,
11 York Road,
London SE1 7NX, UK

80 Maiden Lane,
Suite 704,
New York, NY 10038
USA

First Published 2006

ISBN 1 85285 417 0

A description of this book is available from the
British Library and from the Library of Congress.

Typeset by Carnegie Publishing, Lancaster.
Printed in the United Kingdom by MPG Books Ltd, Cornwall.

Contents

Illustrations

To my grandmother

Pauline Vivienne Townshend

One of the many millions of British women who worked in a war industry in a blitzed city whilst her fiancé fought with imperial forces overseas

Preface

The British Empire defined Britain's war between 1939 and 1945. It was a war fought in imperial theatres by imperial forces, all of which were dependent upon sea power and Britain's capacity to move food, goods, munitions and troops from one side of the world to the other. The campaigns in the Mediterranean and in Malaya were fought because of Britain's imperial heritage in these regions. Because of the Empire, events in Europe, such as the fall of France and Italy's declaration of war, had ramifications for Britain throughout the world. Imperial forces, in turn, contributed significantly to the Allied defeat of Italy and Germany in Europe, as well as to the fighting in theatres such as East Africa and the Levant. In Burma and India the British Empire and Commonwealth made a remarkable contribution to the defeat of Japan by killing over 200,000 enemy soldiers. Britain's historic dependence upon its Empire for imports and exports inevitably also decided the way in which Britain's enemies sought to defeat it, most notably by seeking to cut the sea routes on which Britain depended.

London, the nerve centre of a global Empire, had to coordinate the war effort of over sixty countries. It did so in a stunningly successful example of what today would be called coalition warfare. Bringing shared experiences to people across the world by virtue of the bonds of Empire, the war was one of the most significant globalizing experiences of the twentieth century. It nevertheless hastened the end of the Empire, as Britain's financial sacrifices brought about its precipitate economic decline. During the war Britain was also forced to champion the ideology of liberation, in order to trump Nazism and Japan's call for Asian solidarity, at the same time as it had to place unprecedented pressure upon colonial collaborators. In return, the latter demanded a firmer grip of their own on the reins of power. Although victory in 1945 saw the Empire at its apogee, the war was the key to the United States becoming a superpower, eclipsing Britain in Europe and in its former imperial strongholds.

The British Empire and the Second World War seeks to place the British Empire at the centre of our understanding of the Second World War. It is an account of how the British Empire as a whole fought the war. It shows, for example, what bound the war history of Malta to that of Hong Kong; how the Battle of the Atlantic affected the defence of British Borneo; and how German domination in Europe threatened the security of Australia and Malaya. It is not a campaign history, though it places the major and minor campaigns of the Second World

War within an imperial context, integrating well-known campaigns, with lesser-known operations. It also demonstrates that many of the features of the British home front were shared by Britain's subjects from Trinidad to Tasmania.

I am grateful to the Imperial War Museum for permission to reproduce illustrations. While preparing this book, Mansfield College, Oxford, and the Joint Services Command and Staff College, Defence Academy United Kingdom, Shrivenham, proved excellent places at which write. I am indebted to a number of previous authors for their work on and insights into Britain's imperial war: Judith Brown, I. C. B. Dear, Sir John Keegan, William Roger Louis, James Lunt and John Shuckburgh. Mark Bidgood, Neville Brown, James Noble and Ian Phimister supplied valuable information and read drafts of chapters. Toby Spanier gave me a computer. I would like to thank my publishers, Tony Morris and Martin Sheppard, for their help during the writing of this of this book. My wife, Andrea, and the other members of my family, have been encouraging and supportive throughout, both with the book and with many other things.

Woodstock, Oxfordshire

Note on the British Empire and Commonwealth

Place names are rendered as they were known to the British at the time of the Second World War. Thus 'Bechuanaland' not 'Botswana', 'Bombay' not 'Mumbai'. The terms 'the British Empire' or 'the Empire' are used where appropriate, though the sophistication 'the Empire and Commonwealth' is used when writing specifically of the Dominions as well as the rest of the Empire. This is for the sake of easy reading and is not intended to overlook the fact that the Dominions were autonomous states. 'The Commonwealth' refers to Britain and the Dominions of Canada, South Africa, Australia and New Zealand. The Irish Free State was also a Dominion, though not one usually bracketed with Britain and the other Dominions in discussions about imperial defence and imperial policy. It was a reluctant member of the Commonwealth and insisted on remaining neutral during the war. The 'Empire and Commonwealth' refers, therefore, to the four older Dominions together with India and the territories of the Colonial Empire – in other words, the entire 'red on the map', formal Empire. The term 'the Colonial Empire' refers, generally, to the Empire ruled by the Colonial Office – in other words, the entire British Empire *minus* the four Dominions, India and Burma (which was administered by India until 1937, and thereafter by a separate Burma Office). Aden was also separated from India in 1937, though it became a Colonial Office responsibility and thus a part of the Colonial Empire. This Colonial Empire consisted primarily of Crown Colonies and Protectorates.

India was a separate imperial entity, an empire within an empire, ruled by a Viceroy and the India Office in London, and responsible for maintaining numerous 'British' interests in areas such as Burma, the Persian Gulf, Nepal and Tibet. Southern Rhodesia was in a category all of its own, a self-governing colony. In theory, this made it subject to the Colonial Office, though in practice it was as politically autonomous as regards internal affairs as the Dominions. In Southern Africa, Bechuanaland, Basutoland and Swaziland were run like colonies but were in fact the responsibility of the Dominions Office, being ruled through Britain's High Commissioner to South Africa.

Further complicating the map of British power and influence in the world, there were other categories. Newfoundland was a lapsed Dominion, under direct British rule at the time of the Second World War, but soon thereafter to become a province of the Dominion of Canada. The Sudan was officially a Condominium jointly ruled by the British and the Egyptian governments. In practice, it was a British colony, but not one ruled by the Colonial Office. It was administered by the Foreign Office and a specialist Sudan Political Service. The New Hebrides was a Condominium jointly ruled by Britain and France, with an appointee of the King of Spain refereeing disputes between the two. Throughout the Middle East, Britain was the holder of certain League of Nations 'Mandates', territories of the defunct Ottoman Empire that Britain ruled or influenced, officially on behalf of that international body. These included Palestine and Trans-Jordan. Others, like Iraq, were officially independent nation states, though accommodating significant British military bases and by treaty obliged to allow British forces access and transit rights in times of war. They were therefore not fully sovereign and were very much a part of the British world system. Egypt, an unofficial British territory since 1882, was made a British Protectorate in 1914, though in 1922 it became independent. The British, nevertheless, maintained in the Suez Canal Zone, by treaty, the largest military installation in the world.

There were yet more Mandates, such as Southern Cameroon and Tanganyika, though they were ruled by the Colonial Office. The Dominions themselves had also acquired League of Nations Mandates following the First World War and the dismemberment of the German Empire. Thus South Africa ruled South-West Africa, and Australia ruled former German territories including northern New Guinea and the Bismarck Archipelago. The Dominions in the Pacific were also responsible for certain islands that had been transferred from British rule. Different again, there were some territories, like Tonga, that were independent but in special treaty relations with Britain.

The term 'informal empire' is generally used by imperial historians to describe the parts of the world which Britain did not formally rule but which nevertheless were heavily influenced by British military, commercial, economic and cultural power. Thus there is some coverage here of places in South America and China, including Argentina and Shanghai, that were certainly not 'red on the map' but in which Britain historically wielded influence and which figured in the British war effort of 1939–45. To these corners of the earth must be added Antarctica, a vast region that Britain sought to dominate in an imperial fashion, even if rival claimants refused officially to recognize Britain's claims. Nevertheless, the war saw British forces active in the region, and set the foundation stones of today's British Antarctic Survey and Territory.

Finally, during the war the territories administered by the British, and for which they held ultimate responsibility, grew significantly. This was either a result of enemy territory being conquered and held by British forces, or of the territory of allies or friendly governments being used as military bases from which better to prosecute the war. These occupations could last for years. Conquered enemy territories were usually administered by British Military Administrations. In this category were countries such as Italian Somaliland, Libya, Madagascar and Syria.

The Commander-in-Chief of Allied Forces in the Mediterranean, General Sir Harold Alexander, became Governor of Sicily; Gerneral Sir Henry Maitland Wilson earlier in the war became Military Governor of Cyrenaica. Southern Persia was occupied by the British, and bases were established in territories such as Iceland, the Faroe Islands and the Azores. At the end of the war Admiral Lord Louis Mountbatten's South East Asia Command was made responsible for the reoccupation of the Dutch East Indies and French Indo-China.

Population figures, where given, are taken from the *Concise Oxford Atlas* (Oxford, 1958), using figures taken from 1951 to 1955. Population figures are therefore not accurate but provide an approximate guide to the war period.

Abbreviations

AACC	Anglo-American Caribbean Commission
ABDA	Australian-British-Dutch-American Command
AFLOC	African Line of Communication
AIF	Australian Imperial Force
AL	Arab Legion
AMC	Armed Merchant Cruiser
ANZAC	Australia and New Zealand Army Corps
AOC	Air Officer Commanding
APC	African Pioneer Corps
APL	Aden Protectorate Levies
ARP	Air Raid Precautions
BAAG	British Army Aid Group
BEATS	British Empire Air Training Scheme
BNA	Burma National Army
BPF	British Pacific Fleet
BR	Burma Rifles
BIA	Burma Independence Army
CAM	Catapult Armed Merchant Ship
CBME	Combined Bureau Middle East
CGA	Ceylon Garrison Artillery
CIGS	Chief of the Imperial General Staff
CLT	Colonial and Locally Raised Troops
CMF	Citizens Military Force
CNVF	Ceylon Naval Volunteer Force
CSF	Caribbean Sea Frontier
DEMS	Defensively Equipped Merchant Ship
EAC	East Africa Command
EAC	Eastern Air Command (India)
EAMLS	East African Military Labour Service
EGSC	Eastern Group Supply Council
FAA	Fleet Air Arm
FECB	Far East Combined Bureau

FMF	Fiji Military Force
GDP	Gross Domestic Product
GHQ	General Headquarters
HAA	Heavy Anti-Aircraft
HCT	High Commission Territories
HKSRA	Hong Kong and Singapore Royal Artillery
HMAS	His Majesty's Australian Ship
HMIS	His Majesty's Indian Ship
HMNZS	His Majesty's New Zealand Ship
HMS	His Majesty's Ship
HMSAS	His Majesty's South African Ship
HSBC	Hongkong and Shanghai Banking Corporation
ICS	Indian Civil Service
ILL	Indian Independence League
INA	Indian National Army
INC	Indian National Congress
ISLD	Inter-Service Liaison Department (MI6)
KAAU	Kenya African Air Unit
KAR	King's African Rifles
LRDG	Long Range Desert Group
LRP	Long Range Penetration Force (Chindits)
LSSP	Lanka Sama Samajist Party (Ceylon)
MCP	Malayan Communist Party
MEC	Middle East Command
MESC	Middle East Supply Centre
MNBDO	Mobile Naval Base Defence Organization
MCP	Malayan Communist Party
MPAJA	Malayan People's Anti-Japanese Army
NCAC	Northern Combat Area Command (Burma–China)
NCO	Non Commissioned Officer
NEF	Newfoundland Escort Force
NMC	Native Military Corps
NRR	Northern Rhodesia Regiment
NZEF	New Zealand Expeditionary Force
OB	Ossewa Brandwag
OCT	Officer Commanding Troops
OKW	Oberkommando der Wehrmacht (German High Command)
OSS	Office of Strategic Services (American)
OUT	Operational Training Unit
RAAF	Royal Australian Air Force
RAF	Royal Air Force
RAMC	Royal Army Medical Corps

RAN	Royal Australian Navy
RAR	Rhodesia Africa Rifles
RAOC	Royal Army Ordinance Corps
RASC	Royal Army Service Corps
RCAF	Royal Canadian Air Force
RCN	Royal Canadian Navy
RFA	Royal Fleet Auxiliary
RIAF	Royal Indian Air Force
RIN	Royal Indian Navy
RNVR	Royal Naval Volunteer Reserve
RNZAF	Royal New Zealand Air Force
RNZN	Royal New Zealand Navy
RNVR	Royal Naval Volunteer Reserve
RNVR-SA	Royal Naval Volunteer Reserve South Africa
RPC	Royal Pioneer Corps
RWAFF	Royal West African Frontier Force
SAAF	South African Air Force
SANF	South African Naval Force
SAS	Special Air Service
SBS	Special Boat Service
SCC	Somali Camel Corps
SDF	Seaward Defence Force (South Africa)
SDF	Sudan Defence Force
SEAC	South East Asia Command
SIS	Secret Intelligence Service (MI6)
SOE	Special Operations Executive
SPA	South Pacific Area
SPS	Sudan Political Service
STS	Special Training School (SOE)
SWPA	South West Pacific Area
TJFF	Trans-Jordan Frontier Force
UDF	Union Defence Force
ULTRA	Intelligence material derived from Enigma decrypts
UKCC	United Kingdom Commercial Corporation
USAAF	United Stated Army Air Force
VLR	Very Long Range
WAAF	Women's Auxiliary Air Force
WAC	West Africa Command
WDAF	Western Desert Air Force
WEC	Wireless Experimental Centre (Delhi)
WESC	West African Supply Centre
WRNS	Women's Royal Naval Service

Let us therefore brace ourselves to our duties and so bear ourselves that if the British Empire and its Commonwealth last for a thousand years men will still say, 'This was their finest hour'.

Winston Churchill, 18 August 1940

1

Prologue

The image of Britain standing alone after the fall of France in June 1940 is embedded in the public awareness of the Second World War, epitomized by New Zealander David Low's famous *Evening Standard* cartoon of the defiant Tommy standing on the cliffs looking towards the Continent and resolutely saying, 'Very well, then, alone!' But Britain was by no means alone: as one incoming telegram reassured the British public in September 1939, 'Don't worry; Barbados is with you'. A *Punch* cartoon by Fougasse, published on 17 July 1940, had a different take on Low's theme. Two soldiers are pictured looking out to sea. 'So our poor Empire is alone in the world', remarks the first soldier. 'Aye, we are', replies the second, 'the whole five hundred million of us.'[1]

In Britain the war is primarily remembered as a European struggle, an understandable perspective born of geography and the close proximity of would-be invaders. This is not to say that some of the war's imperial landmarks are not recognized. The fighting role of imperial forces such as the Canadians at Dieppe and the pan-Commonwealth Eighth Army are well remembered. The role of Malta, a tiny but priceless launch-pad for operations against Axis forces and convoys in the Mediterranean, is also well known. The fall of Singapore remains perhaps the most widely remembered imperial feature of the Second World War, and the Fourteenth Army in Burma is paradoxically remembered as the 'Forgotten Army'. These imperial features, however, tend to be recalled in isolation, or to be viewed, as in the case of the war in the Mediterranean and the Western Desert, as extensions of the European conflict.

This view is a parochial one. The war ought to be recognized as a global struggle, and particularly as an *imperial* one, in which apparently disparate British battles and strategic concerns formed part of one interconnected whole, and in which every campaign that the British fought was fought alongside imperial allies for imperial reasons. Who, as well as where, Britain fought was to a large extent dictated by Empire; there would have been no quarrel with Italy or Japan if it had not been for two centuries of British overseas expansion on their doorsteps. The battlefields themselves were decided by Britain's imperial history, whether on the sea routes of the Atlantic and the Indian Ocean, in the skies above Iraq and Malta, the deserts of North Africa, the mountains of Abyssinia and north-east India, or the jungles of Borneo, Burma and Malaya. An imperial perspective helps connect all of these scenes of Second World War action to the

European war, as well as providing a perspective on how features of that European struggle, such as the German conquest of France, had ramifications throughout the world.

The story of Malta and the war in the Western Desert is part of our appreciation of the European and Mediterranean war, but it is equally valid to see them as the result of Britain's imperial status in the Middle East and the Far East. They are also illustrations of Britain's dependence upon imperial bases and resources in order to fight the war. Malta had been a British colony since the Revolutionary and Napoleonic Wars, and the Mediterranean had been a major bastion of British imperial power since the eighteenth century. A third of the Tobruk garrison captured in June 1942 was South African, and the Eighth Army of which it was a part was the most ethnically varied army to assemble in modern history because of its imperial composition. In late 1941 the Eighth Army was a quarter British and three-quarters imperial. It included not just men from Australia, Britain, India, New Zealand, South Africa and Southern Rhodesia, but also men from Basutoland, Bechuanaland, Ceylon, Cyprus, the Gambia, the Gold Coast, Kenya, Mauritius, Nigeria, Palestine, Rodrigues, Sierra Leone, the Seychelles, Swaziland, Tanganyika and Uganda. Further east, the war against Japan was not just an American conflict, despite Hollywood's colonization of that particular theatre. The territories of the Empire and Commonwealth played a notable part in fighting the Japanese and aiding American forces. The Fourteenth Army, which consisted of Indians from every corner of the Raj, Gurkhas from Nepal, Kenyans, Nigerians, Rhodesians and Somalis, as well as men from Kent and Cumberland, killed more Japanese soldiers than any other Allied formation in the war. By the summer of 1945 58 per cent of Admiral Lord Louis Mountbatten's South East Asia Command's personnel were Indian, and 25 per cent were African. This reflected the scale of India and Africa's manpower contribution to the imperial war effort.*

The Australians played a key role in the war against the Japanese in New Guinea, particularly in the early stages before American power and resources had been fully mobilized and deployed to the South-West Pacific. Many British territories in the Pacific as well as in South-East Asia fell to the Japanese, and, though tied down in other theatres, the British had every intention of returning to

---

*   When considering the ethnic composition of the 'British' forces that took the field against enemy units around the world, it is also worth remembering the disproportionate role played by Scotsmen. For over two centuries Scottish scientists, missionaries, politicians, explorers and soldiers had played a prominent role in British overseas expansion. The Second World War was again to see men from north of the border to the fore on battlefields from Europe to Egypt to Hong Kong, as well as imperial units with distinctly Scottish lineage such as South Africa's Transvaal Scottish Regiment. Scottish ports and naval bases, like Glasgow and Scapa Flow, were integral to the functioning of British maritime security, convoys and trade during the war. Even Ireland, a reluctant British Dominion that insisted on remaining neutral throughout the conflict, furnished over 43,000 men for service with British forces, whilst Ulster participated loyally as a part of the United Kingdom.

reconquer them. To this end the British Pacific Fleet was formed in 1944 to operate from Sydney alongside American naval task forces, and plans were made to base British soldiers in Australia and RAF bombers on Okinawa so that Britain could contribute to the invasion of the Japanese home islands. As it happened, the atomic bombs dropped on Hiroshima and Nagasaki curtailed the realization of this major British commitment, but it was British forces that took the surrender in Hong Kong and Singapore, Australians who rounded up the Japanese in Borneo and Sarawak, and Anglo-Indian divisions that arrived to supervise the Japanese surrendering in the Dutch East Indies and French Indo-China.

British Empire and Commonwealth forces fought a host of subsidiary military campaigns and obscure operations launched from little-known imperial bases. The names of Alamein and Malta, Singapore and Tobruk are familiar, but there were also imperial campaigns in Abyssinia, Borneo, Iran, Iraq, Java, Kenya, Madagascar, New Guinea, Iran, Somaliland, the Sudan, Sumatra and Syria. The Indian Ocean, as much as the Mediterranean and Atlantic, was the scene of significant naval operations and was a major naval battlefield by virtue of its vital sea routes. These connected Britain to Australasia and the major theatres of conflict in the Middle East and South Asia.

The air and naval forces of the Dominions, India and the Colonial Empire, in supplementing British and American forces, also deserve greater attention. Commonwealth airmen formed nearly one half of Bomber Command's strength in Europe. In the Mediterranean Australian warships made an important contribution, as did South African minesweepers, bombers and fighter aircraft. The Royal Canadian Navy expanded to become the third largest navy in the world and played a key role in the Battle of the Atlantic, and by the end of the war the Indian-officered Royal Indian Air Force had 30,000 personnel and nine squadrons of fighter aircraft engaged in the war against Japan. The British Empire Air Training Scheme prepared 130,000 airmen for war in training schools in Australia, Canada, South Africa and Southern Rhodesia. Places such as Assam and the Gold Coast became air bases of great importance to the fighting fronts in the Middle East, Burma and China.

As well as furnishing barracks for hundreds of thousands of soldiers, the Empire was the site of countless airstrips, aerodromes, Royal Naval Air Stations and flying boat anchorages used by the squadrons of the RAF and the Fleet Air Arm, together with the air forces of America, the Dominions, India and other allies. Many international airports, including those in Bahrain, Ceylon, the Maldives, Malta and Mauritius, began life during the war as RAF aerodromes. Tiny specks in vast oceans could become important bases, such as the Cocos Islands, a busy base for RAF aircraft attacking Japanese shipping, supplying behind-enemy-lines units fighting in Malaya and dropping supplies to liberated prisoner-of-war camps. With the assault on Britain's global communications network presented by the war, diversions had to be arranged in some parts of the world. Thus to supply the Middle East with sufficient aircraft, an air supply route was developed across the African continent because of the risks involved in shipping or flying large numbers of aircraft via the Axis-infested Mediterranean.

As in the air, so too at sea. Imperial ports and naval shore bases provided a global network for the warships of the fleets and squadrons that had historically policed the world, from the South Atlantic Station to the Mediterranean Fleet and from the China Station to the Eastern Fleet. All over the world imperial ports were used to the full by warships and merchantmen, as they travelled in convoys, and facilities were extended or created anew, particularly to compensate for the loss of bases in Singapore and the Far East. Thus Addu Atoll in the Maldives was developed as a major fleet base to supplement facilities at Trincomalee and Colombo in the light of the loss of Singapore. Ports such as Freetown and Halifax became essential convoy assembly points, and Durban acted as the base for the invasion of Madagascar. As a global economic community, the transfer of resources by sea was the lifeblood of the British Empire, in war as in peace. In war, the sea lanes of the world were also vital for the movement of martial resources to and from Britain, North America and the Empire's many overseas battle fronts.

The Empire defined Britain's participation in a global war that was an experience of profound significance for colonial societies and economies the world over. The reason why this was so is not difficult to discern. The British war effort was global because Britain ruled a quarter of the world's land surface, influenced much of the rest of it and had historically dominated its oceans. It was only because of Empire that Britain fought Italy and Japan at all; Pearl Harbor would have had little significance for Britain had it not been for its status as an Asian and Pacific power responsible for the safety of millions, looked to by both Chiang Kai-shek and the Governor-General of the Dutch East Indies for succour in the face of Japanese hostility. Unlike its enemies, Britain was obliged to fight both a European and an Asian war simultaneously after 1941, and all of its overseas territories were called upon to help defeat the powers that sought to overturn the international system of which Britain had been the prime creator and guarantor. Until the Second World War, Britain was the world's only superpower, and it was to Britain that countries such as Abyssinia and China looked in the 1930s when they were confronted by the aggression of the dictators.[2] In 1939 America was not a global power in terms of military strength, international diplomacy, reputation and overseas presence in the way that Britain was, despite the republic's phenomenal wealth and potential. The fact that America had risen to global pre-eminence by 1945, and Britain had been eclipsed, is a measure of the war's impact on the world order.

The Second World War was fought throughout the world and touched the lives of all people living in it. Given that a quarter of those people were British subjects, the study of the British Empire and Commonwealth at war is a highly important but neglected one. Britain's war cannot be properly understood without due weight being given to its imperial responsibilities and its imperial strategic vision and ambitions, and to the aid given by the far-flung territories of the Empire in its prosecution. Not only did Empire dictate where and how Britain fought the war, it also dictated how Britain's enemies sought to defeat British power. Naturally, Britain's enemies furthered their cause against Britain by attacking its Empire. For Italy and Japan, if less so for Germany, the main dispute with Britain was over access to the imperial fruits overfilling the British basket. Mussolini could not realize his ambitions for Italy if Britain continued to be the dominant imperial power in the region of the Suez Canal and eastern Mediterranean, and Emperor Hirohito's military government could not secure Japan's rightful place in the world if Britain continued to dominate Shanghai and monopolize so much of the treasure of South-East Asia.

In seeking to counter the mortal threat posed in every region of the world by the enmity of industrialized and militaristic enemies, Britain's capacity to wage war relied upon imperial bases and imperial resources both for defence and for the projection of military power. Territories such as Australia, Ceylon, Egypt, Fiji, India, Kenya and Mauritius became springboards for offensive Allied operations in neighbouring regions and bases for special forces engaged in espionage, sabotage and operations behind enemy lines. Familiar features of the British war effort, such as the intelligence-gathering operations centred on Bletchley and the activities of the Special Operations Executive (SOE), also depended on base facilities in the Empire and the wider world.

British imperial forces – properly so called because nowhere did British soldiers, sailors or airmen fight without men from the territories of the Empire and Commonwealth either by their side or forming the vital rear echelon units supporting them – fought major campaigns in regions where the Empire had grown and therefore had to be defended. New territorial responsibilities were taken on as enemy colonies were conquered, making it more accurate to describe the British Empire as being at its greatest territorial extent not in the wake of its post-First World War gains but in 1945, when Britain had reconquered its own colonies lost earlier to the Japanese and the Italians, and had acquired new territories as a result of the defeat of its enemies. British military administrations were established in Italian Somaliland, Libya, Madagascar, Sicily and Syria. Southern Iran was also invaded and taken over in order to prevent a German invasion from the north, to guard Britain's precious oil reserves and to maintain an Anglo-American supply link with Russia. British power was also extended into entirely new regions for strategic reasons, as when British armed forces took over the defence of Iceland in order to help prosecute the Battle of the Atlantic. At the end of the war Britain also became responsible for the Dutch East Indies and French Indo-China, as well as a sizeable chunk of Germany.

Given the huge importance of imperial forces, resources and bases for the British war effort, the wartime alliance that defeated the dictators needs to be better understood. The ubiquitous term 'the Allies' has come to stand as shorthand for Britain and America's deservedly celebrated war-time partnership, with

France and Russia somewhat uncomfortably tagged on as well. Many people at the time, however, emphasized Britain's alliance with its fellow white Commonwealth countries, India and the Colonial Empire. This is not surprising, given the lengthy delay before Britain's great power allies came onto the scene. For nearly two years the American alliance remained strictly non-combatant and, after a little over six months of war, the ally on which Britain had based all of its pre-war defence plans, France, was out for the count and its Vichy government and empire added to the list of likely enemies. At the start of the war Russia was in a pact with Nazi Germany, and from April 1941 with Japan. An unlikely set of allies, one might think.

In sharp contrast, within a week of the expiry of Neville Chamberlain's ultimatum to Hitler on 3 September 1939, the entire British Empire was at war. For many people at the time, the fact that the British Empire and Commonwealth stood united against the dictators was a source of pride and comfort. This heterogeneous unit of over fifty territories supported Britain's declaration of war because of the imperial nexus, and contributed during six years of global struggle to the defeat of Germany, Italy, Japan and their allies.*

The war dramatically affected home fronts throughout the Empire because of its demands, as the need for labour remained constant at a time of global food and raw material shortage, and as countries unprepared for conflict became war zones. All the stops were pulled out to increase agricultural production, to produce more raw materials and minerals, and to construct the air strips, barracks, bases, hospitals, internee camps, port facilities, roads and railways necessary for colonies to become effective military installations. A million Indians built airstrips and installations in Bengal and Assam, as the region became the great military encampment and supply dump from which the Japanese were to be pushed out of Burma and South-East Asia. Mauritian sugar planters turned their estates into vegetable gardens as the island faced starvation when import sources and the ships that delivered them dried up. Tasmanian women enrolled as factory workers when private companies turned their hand to the manufacture of high-technology weapons components. The Sultan of the Maldives ordered his people to aid the Royal Navy and RAF to build bases in their islands, and West Indian men and women found employment on new American bases constructed in their homelands, in the agricultural industry of America itself, and as labourers in Britain.

All of this, of course, was achieved whilst the colonial homelands were themselves under threat or actually experiencing direct attack. Few parts of the

---

* In addition, some of the 'lesser allies' who fought so bravely alongside British forces (and established their governments-in-exile in London) also aided Britain in imperial theatres. The Dutch contributed significantly, if vainly, to the defence of Malaya and British Borneo; Polish servicemen fought in Iran, Iraq, West Africa and the Western Desert, as well as in the Battle of Britain; and Free French forces fought with the Eighth Army in the Middle East and the French battleship *Richelieu* reinforced Britain's Eastern Fleet in Ceylon.

Empire escaped enemy attention, whether in the form of an occasional raid, propaganda broadcasts or leaflet drops, reconnaissance or bombardment, coastal minefields, the activities of secret agents, repeated bombing or years of enemy occupation. The use of colonies as bases for Allied military operations was a form of transformational 'friendly' occupation in itself, affecting people's lives on many levels. And of course, had Britain been defeated, every territory of the Empire would have changed hands and fallen under the sway of new imperial masters, as the largest imperial estate in history went under the auctioneer's hammer.

Different colonies were affected at different times and by different factors during the war, and to a greatly varying extent. For example, the entry of Italy brought colonies in the eastern Mediterranean and East Africa into the front line; and the rise of Japan brought the war suddenly to the doorstep of Ceylon and engulfed Malaya and the great 'fortress' of Singapore, in which so many hollow inter-war security hopes had reposed. Losses to Japan also escalated the demand for production in places such as West Africa, necessitating conscription to provide the cotton, food, rubber, sisal, tin and other products that the imperial treasure trove contributed to the global economy in war as in peace. The physical impact of the war also varied from one territory to another. Some islands in the Solomon and the Gilbert and Ellice Groups saw fierce fighting and some territories in the Far East endured three years of Japanese occupation. The Indian province of Assam witnessed devastating battles between imperial and Japanese forces in 1944. Senior officers visiting Malta often recalled personal memories of the horrors of the Western Front in the First World War to convey the extent of the bomb damage inflicted on the island. Other territories, too, were bombed, including Aden, Burma, Ceylon, Cyprus, Gibraltar, Hong Kong, Malaya, Palestine and Singapore. Scorched earth policies brought destruction to numerous imperial territories as Allied forces retreated, blowing up bridges and firing oil wells, as did fighting later in the war when Allied forces advanced. Submarine attacks affected Caribbean territories, and at a stroke, on the fall of France in June 1940, Britain's West African colonies were surrounded by hostile Vichy territory requiring a massive defensive concentration.

The Second World War, notwithstanding the Eurocentric manner in which it is often remembered, was viewed at the time as an imperial struggle, not only by the politicians and senior servicemen responsible for grand strategy, but also by many ordinary people around the world.[3] The British Empire and Commonwealth's war was fought by air marshals, admirals, generals, politicians and civil servants who had an imperial world view and an imperial strategic vision – unlike their adversaries in Germany, Italy and Japan. British imperial forces, though stretched to the limit as a result of the Empire's overwhelming inter-war focus on peace, disarmament and the global status quo, were dispersed throughout the world to counter the threat of enemies bent on British defeat. At the time of the Second World War, Britain and the Empire and Commonwealth were governed by men steeped in the imperial tradition, from the highest reaches of the departments of state in Whitehall down to the level of district commissioners living in remote corners of the Empire and supervising the day to day business of imperial government. At the summit of this vast and sprawling system of global rule was the King-Emperor George VI, an imperial monarch whose image was known throughout the world. Royal tours of the Empire and Commonwealth had been commonplace since the death of Queen Victoria, becoming part of the pageant of Empire as well as its high-level diplomacy, strengthening the bonds between Britain and its far-flung territories and ensuring that monarchs were very much aware of Britain's overseas connections and responsibilities. King George (along with his brother, Edward VIII, during his short reign), had pioneered royal touring since his youth and visited all of the Dominions as well as dozens of the colonies before war broke out.

Many of the men who served as British government ministers during the Second World War also had direct experience of the Empire and its people. Neville Chamberlain, Prime Minister at the outbreak of war, was the son of the most ardent imperialist Cabinet minister of the late nineteenth century, Joseph Chamberlain, and had run his father's plantation in the Bahamas in the 1890s. Winston Churchill, not surprisingly, had more imperial experience than any of his colleagues. The young Churchill saw action on the North-West Frontier in India, and in 1898 rode in the British Army's last cavalry charge at Omdurman in the Sudan. After observing the Spanish counter-insurgency at close quarters in Cuba, Churchill travelled to South Africa during the Anglo-Boer War as a war correspondent. In the Liberal government of Herbert Asquith, he served as Parliamentary Under-Secretary of State for the Colonies. His imperial vision was given full reign in 1911 when he was made First Lord of the Admiralty, master of the most powerful weapon on earth. In Lloyd George's post-war Cabinets, Churchill served as Secretary of State for War and Air, and as Secretary of State for the Colonies. Even when out of office in the inter-war years, Churchill remained a powerful imperial politician, particularly in the 1930s when he was the most vocal critic of the National Government's India policy.

Churchill's war-time administrations contained other men with significant imperial experience. Leo Amery, Clement Attlee, William Beaverbrook, Stafford Cripps, Anthony Eden and Harold Macmillan all had experience of living and working in the Empire, or of holding political positions that gave them an intimate knowledge of its affairs. Politicians from the Dominions were also naturally experienced in the affairs of Empire. Jan Christian Smuts of South Africa, the only Dominions politician to whom Churchill paid much attention, was a noted imperial statesman. He had been a member of the Imperial War Cabinet in the First World War, and played an important role in the Second World War in framing British policy in Africa and the Middle East. Robert Menzies, the Australian Prime Minister in the early stages of the war, was even touted as a potential rival for the British Prime Ministership when Churchill endured a torrid time in 1941 as a result of military reverses overseas. Peter Fraser, the Prime Minister of New

Zealand, born in Scotland, had lived in London until his mid-twenties, being typical of the many people in the Dominions who comfortably divided their loyalties between their country and the Empire to which it belonged.

As with the politicians, Britain's senior soldiers, sailors and airmen all tended to be old Empire hands in one respect or another, or to be themselves citizens of the Dominions. All of Britain's wartime Chiefs of Staff, for example, had extensive imperial experience, as did the majority of Britain's senior theatre commanders.* Generals like Alan Brooke, Claude Auchinleck, Bernard Montgomery, William Slim and Archibald Wavell had decades of imperial service between them, as had admirals Andrew Cunningham, Dudley Pound and James Somerville. The same was true of the RAF, in the shape of its most senior commanders, Arthur Tedder and Charles Portal. At the operational level, many senior British commanders of the Second World War were from the Dominions, including the Australian general Thomas Blamey, the New Zealand general Bernard Freyberg (who nearly became Commander-in-Chief Middle East in August 1940), and the New Zealand air marshals Arthur Coningham and Keith Park.

The Empire was a global community embracing millions of people around the world, particularly those in Britain and the Dominions bound by the thread of common racial heritage. The Empire was a given in the lives of many people, as much a fact of life as the European Union or America is today. This was reinforced in many ways. Stage productions, literature and popular songs such as 'There'll Always Be an England' made reference to imperial themes. The *Daily Mail* bore the words 'For King and Empire' beneath its title each day, and BBC radio broadcasts went out to 'Listeners here, and in the Empire and the United States of America'. References to the Empire and Commonwealth were frequent features of Churchill's speeches and radio broadcasts. Schools also helped embed the Empire as a fixture in the world view of the British people and their cousins in the Dominions. To give one example out of millions, Al Deere grew up in New Zealand and as a young man fought in the Battle of Britain as a pilot in No. 54 Squadron. 'In my generation', he explained, 'as schoolboys we always thought of [Britain] as the home country, always referred to it as the Mother Country. That was the old colonial tie ... There was no question that if this country was threatened, New Zealanders wouldn't go to war for Britain.'[4] Schools developed imperial consciousness in Britain too. In the film *Hope and Glory* a schoolteacher points to various parts of the world on the once-ubiquitous classroom wall map, and says

'Pink. Pink. Pink. Pink. What are all the pink bits?'
'They're ours, Miss', replies Rowan.

---

* The Chiefs of Staff were the three most senior representatives of the British Army, the Royal Navy and the RAF. They sat in committee with the Prime Minister and decided British strategy.

'Yes', says the teacher. 'The British Empire. What part of the world's surface is British?'

'Two-fifths, Miss', answers Jennifer Baker.

'Yes. Two-fifths – ours. That's what this war is all about. Men are fighting and dying to save all the pink bits for you ungrateful little twerps.'[5]

From the British West Indies, Connie Macdonald joined the Auxiliary Territorial Service (Jamaica) to work in the British Military Hospital at Kingston. As she recalled:

> We were British! England was our mother country. We were brought up to respect the Royal family. I used to collect pictures of Margaret and Elizabeth, you know. I adored them. It was the British influence. We didn't grow up with any Jamaican thing – we grew up as British.[6]

A general awareness of the Empire was common to all Britons, even if it had little direct significance or meaning for many of them. As the war progressed, more Britons had cause to contemplate the Empire, as sons or husbands wrote from distant jungles or islands, as children were evacuated to Canada, as hundreds of thousands of colonial subjects arrived in Britain as servicemen or labourers, and as food parcels marked 'From the Australian Food Front' appeared on the kitchen table. When Malaya fell to the Japanese there was panic buying of hot-water bottles. As one housewife in Birmingham put it in her diary, 'you won't be able to buy one until we get our rubber back', referring to the well-known fact that Malaya, recently taken by the Japanese, was the Empire's greatest producer of that precious commodity.[7]

In mobilizing the Empire for this extraordinary global war effort, a massive strain was placed on the imperial system and upon the fundamental bulwark of local political cooperation and popular acquiescence on which the Empire had come to rest. It was always likely, once Germany, Italy and Japan attacked Britain's global position simultaneously, that the costs of defending the Empire would outweigh the price that the Empire was capable of paying. In defending the Empire and using it as a strategic asset, the rising power of America was invited into many parts of the world that until the outbreak of war had been exclusive British fiefs, and indigenous peoples were brought into closer contact than ever before with the intrusive power of a modern imperial state. Still, the achievements and coordination of this global war effort was nothing short of miraculous.[8]

2

The Approach of War

It was not because of any criminal oversight that Britain was so poorly placed to meet the challenges presented by Germany, Italy and Japan. It was just that, as a sated power, recovering from the First World War and the effects of the depression, with a population that would not hear of another war and that elected governments only too pleased to translate this into cost-cutting action, Britain was simply in no position to fight a global war for national and imperial survival. Unfortunately, this peace-craving country, disarming rapidly for reasons of economy, domestic politics and international stability, was faced in Europe and Asia by three authoritarian states bent on military and territorial expansion. Put simply, Britain had peace as a national interest, and it had pared its armed forces both to reflect this and, it hoped, *encourager les autres*. The leaders of Germany, Italy and Japan, on the other hand, had decided that war and expansion were in their nations' interests. To achieve their several aims, Britain's naval power had to be crippled, and its Empire fundamentally weakened and at least partially dismantled. Germany would then emerge as an overwhelmingly powerful European superpower, with a vast new empire in the east and overseas colonies plucked from its prostrate enemies. Italy would be master of the Mediterranean and Middle East, at least in terms of the size of its territorial holdings, once it had been able to appropriate British and French territories. Japan's resource-rich eastern empire would stretch from northern China to South-East Asia and the East Indies, built on the wreckage of centuries of British, Dutch, French, and, latterly, American empire-building. If Britain was lucky and escaped the war as an independent nation state, it might retain an imperial rump, though this would be at the dictators' pleasure.

Hitler had predicted the demise of the British Empire during a speech in 1937, listened to, without interruption, by an uneasy audience comprising the Commanders-in-Chief of the three armed services, the War Minister and the Foreign Minister. According to the Führer, the signs of disintegration were already there, particularly in Egypt, India and Ireland. Internal disintegration would be compounded by the external threats of Japan in the Far East and Italy in the Mediterranean, which together would doom the Empire. Despite this pessimistic assessment of the Empire's survival chances – even without a war against Germany – Hitler was more than once to pledge to uphold the integrity of the British Empire in the months before the outbreak of war in September 1939, though any action to this effect was never likely to outdistance political expediency. Well aware of the likely result of embracing such a protector, the British government emphatically declined the final German offer to defend the Empire on 28 August 1939.

In the run up to the European war and the global conflict that it soon spawned, the great democracies of the day proved ill-equipped to meet the violent challenge of states that played outside the rules of international relations as those great democracies had framed them, and that sought so significantly to alter the map of the world. As Sir Halford Mackinder, a pioneer of geopolitics, predicted, a democracy 'refuses to think strategically unless and until compelled to do so for the purposes of defence'. It was therefore no surprise that, following the First World War, Britain sought to return to the world of 1914 and to shed its military surfeit as soon as possible. Rapid army demobilization and decades of naval disarmament followed the Armistice. The Western Front millions, and their comrades who had fought in imperial theatres such as East Africa and the Sinai peninsula, went back to civvie street and the British Army returned to its traditional role as an imperial garrison and police force numbering less than 200,000, with a third of its strength permanently based in India. Reflecting Britain's strategic heritage and the role allotted to its army in times of war, its standing expeditionary force was designed to be sent to Egypt, not Europe. The Indian Army, about the same size as the British Army, returned to its pre-war role as guardian of the North-West Frontier and as an imperial rapid response force for military undertakings from Asia to the Middle East. In 1939, therefore, Britain wielded two professional armies, small by the standards of those that opposed to them though capable of fast expansion. As well as their limited size, these armies were beset by significant frailties vis-à-vis their opponents, particularly the armies of Germany and Japan. The Indian Army, for instance, only began modernizing in the 1930s, and the British Army's tanks and tank tactics were markedly inferior to those of the Germans on the outbreak of war, despite Britain having led the field in terms of mechanization in the 1920s.

The Royal Navy was also reduced in size after the First World War, and the inter-war years saw attempts to use treaties to limit the size of the navies of potential aggressors in order to avoid an expensive arms race. Needless to say, Britain stuck scrupulously to the limitations imposed by these treaties. Meanwhile the Germans ignored the terms of the treaties, and proceeded to build the enormous *Bismarck* and *Tirpitz*, as did the Japanese, who proceeded to build the world's largest ever capital ships, the 'Yamato' class displacing over 70,000 tons and mounting 18.1 inch guns. A crucial concession came at the 1930 London Naval Conference when Britain lost its capital ship advantage over the Japanese. By agreeing a moratorium on capital ship building, the ratio of British to Japanese capital ships fell from 20:10 to 15:9. Working with these figures, if Britain had to retain six battleships in home waters to deal with the German threat, there would only be nine to send to deter Japan in the Far East – the same number as the

THE APPROACH OF WAR

Japanese would have available. Not only did this sum offer the Royal Navy no chance of superiority over the Japanese, it assumed that there would be no requirement for capital ships to keep Italy in check in the Mediterranean, a strategic luxury that the British were not permitted in 1941.

Whilst naval disarmament saw the size of warships limited and their numbers cut, the RAF was by the 1930s being prioritized by politicians increasingly concerned about the potential of enemy bombers to wreak havoc on Britain's major ports and cities, though it had of course shed most of the squadrons that in 1918 had given it a front-line strength of over 1500 machines. The money afforded the RAF in the 1930s did not mean, however, that there was sufficient construction undertaken to provide key imperial strongholds like Singapore with adequate modern aircraft cover. The first two and a half years of war were to show how important air power had become to imperial security, or rather its absence to the lack of it.

Inter-war Britain, still mighty at sea and the world's greatest trading nation and investor, *could* have found the money with which to pay for the two-hemisphere navy that might have dealt with Germany and Italy in Europe, and with Japan in the Far East, simultaneously. But politically Britain was not in a position to devote massive sums to rearmament at a time when it was supposed to be setting a global example in the other direction. It was heads or tails, and Britain's side of the coin happened to land face down. Disarmament and appeasement had not increased world security as had been hoped, and Britain's pursuit of these policies left it in a poor position when the guns opened fire. The limitations imposed by the Washington Naval Conference of 1935 further eroded the Royal Navy's capacity to protect the Empire, as policy came to focus firmly on the threat to Britain itself. What planning there was for the defence of the Eastern Empire came to revolve around the multi-million pound construction of naval facilities on the island of Singapore, a dubious investment from the start, though one founded upon the unspoken understanding that the chances of war with Japan were extremely remote.

With its great battleships the Royal Navy ruled the ocean waves and guaranteed not only British security but that of the entire Empire and the seaborne trade of the world.[1] So the theory went, even as late as 1939. The old precepts of imperial defence, founded on supremacy at sea, were still the basis of British defence policy. But this was simply unrealistic in a world where other powers had sophisticated navies. While Britain was disarming, new weapons, particularly land- and carrier-based aircraft, were rendering the battleship obsolete as the world's main index of military might. It was extremely unlikely that in a war against first-class powers the Royal Navy would be able to protect all of Britain's interests and territories across the globe. After a pioneering start, by 1939 Britain also lagged behind America and Japan in torpedo and carrier aircraft technology and doctrine. Air power – though being built up in Britain during the 1930s for fear of the bomber – was wholly inadequate across the Empire, and when the storm broke in the East, obsolete aircraft instead of the latest Spitfires took off to meet the advanced fighters of the Japanese. Even the Mediterranean theatre had to make do with Hurricanes battered in the fighting over Britain and France.

By 1939 there was an alarming lack of armed force to protect what was still the largest conglomeration of political and economic interests and commitments in the world. In fact there was not one adequately defended base throughout the entire Empire when judged against the scale of likely attack using modern weapons. Yet the maintenance of naval supremacy, and the consequent protection this afforded to all British territories against invasion from the sea, was still accepted as the basis of the total system of imperial defence. The gap between theory and actuality was now enormous, though there was nothing meaningful that could be done about it.[2] It was a classic case of imperial overstretch.

There was also an element of extremely bad luck in play against Britain during the Second World War. As was often the case, Churchill described the situation perfectly:

> There has never been a moment, there never could have been a moment, when Great Britain or the British Empire, single handed, could fight Germany and Italy, could wage the Battle of Britain, the Battle of the Atlantic and the Battle of the Middle East – and at the same time stand thoroughly prepared in Burma, the Malay peninsula, and generally in the Far East.[3]

The first element of bad luck was that it transpired that Britain was to face the simultaneous aggression of all three militaristic powers; there was to be no chance of dealing with one, regrouping and turning to meet another, though the Chiefs of Staff hoped that this might be possible. Calculations in February 1939 acknowledged the need to knock Italy out of the war early so that the fleet would be available for dispatch to the Far East if Japan declared war. Unfortunately for the British, although Italy was being destroyed as a political and military power in Africa during the winter of 1940–41, when chances of an early knockout looked reasonable, the Germans intervened in the theatre in spring 1941 and prolonged the war in the Mediterranean region by over two years. So there was no chance of Japan being met by a sizeable force built around battleships and carriers transferred from the Mediterranean Fleet. A second element of bad luck was that Britain, completely unexpectedly, was bereft of powerful allies. No one had conceived as possible, let alone planned for, the calamitous collapse of France in 1940, the power that was supposed to be Britain's closest ally if war with Germany were to break out. Everything had depended on the French alliance; particularly the British government's belief that time was on its side in a war with Germany. The French would hold Germany up in the west, allowing the Allies to use their command of the sea to garner international resources and build up their economies to a war-time pitch sufficient to overwhelm Germany. Other potential great power allies stood aloof from the struggle. Russia, unexpectedly and shockingly, entered into a pact with Germany and later with Japan, and America remained in military isolation, although it supported the British war effort in other ways, and itself suffered a catastrophic early reverse at Pearl Harbor that queered the pitch of British Far Eastern and Pacific defence planning.

Alongside this prediction deficit – the fact that no political or military preparation, understandably, was made against these seemingly unlikely possibilities – one must set a contemporary intelligence and attitude failure that directly and adversely affected Britain's capacity to defend its Empire. It is astounding to consider the ignorance in Britain and America – at the policy-making level, let alone the level of public opinion – about the advanced technological capacity of Japan's armed forces. The quality of the Japanese Empire's carriers, fighter aircraft, battleships and tactics were not commonly known about, and reports of them were discounted, or kept secret, because there was nothing that could be done about them as the clock counted down to December 1941. What made this ignorance fatal was the fact that it was a commonly held view that the Japanese – regardless – would be no match for European forces if they were rash enough to go to war. Defeat by these rather laughable Asiatics was simply inconceivable, and attitudes in Malaya, even as the Japanese transports made for the peninsula's eastern coast, reflected the sheer ignorance in the colonial world concerning the actual state of affairs. Churchill was completely wrong to believe that the sight of HMS *Prince of Wales* and *Repulse* would scare off the Japanese, just as Admiral Sir Tom Phillips was wrong to believe that battleships could not be sunk by aircraft. With such attitudes on the part of their leaders, it was no wonder that British citizens and servicemen around the world didn't give the Japanese much of a chance if war came.

Though politicians and service chiefs in Britain and the Dominions were well aware of Britain's limited capacity to resist aggression from three powerful sources at once, the public was less prepared. Few people appreciated the yawning gap between defence theory, on the one hand, and actual power, on the other. Although this gap had been widening since the late nineteenth century, the illusion of *Pax Britannica* and the grey guardians roaming the sea lanes of the world was still etched on Britain's national conscience, and on that of its Empire. Even as war descended on a world that Britain had done so much to shape in its own image and for its own ends, the Movietone newsreels broadcast reassuring images of soldiers, anti-aircraft guns and battleships just itching to have a go at anyone who dared to try and turn it all upsidedown. The image of Britain's nineteenth-century world power remained in the minds of people in Britain and throughout the world. Britain was the inter-war superpower on which the world, not just the Empire, depended for its general security. France helped in this undertaking, as the two great European powers sought together to safeguard the world system that they had forged, though in the 1930s the gaze of France was transfixed by the German threat across the border. Other powers with global potential, notably America and Russia, did not pretend to be interested in taking on the role of world policeman, and the only meaningful international body that existed, the

League of Nations, could only act successfully if its chief member, Britain, threw its weight behind its resolutions. It is one of the tragedies of the 1930s that those who suffered from the aggression of the Germans, Italians and Japanese still looked to Britain before anyone else for protection. Unfortunately, it was beyond Britain's capacity, given its global strategic balancing act in the face of so many potential aggressors, to go to the aid of Abyssinians, Czechoslovaks or Chinese when called upon to do so.

Because Britain's capabilities could not match its commitments if they all had to be defended at once, Britain had to use diplomacy as a supplement to actual armed power, and in the East as a substitute for it. 'Appeasement' was the order of the day, though the word gained pejorative associations that obscured the fact that it had been one of the central planks of British policy for centuries, rather than the preserve of a few powerful but guilty men in the 1920s and 1930s, intent upon ignoring the soothsayers' calls and stubbornly refusing to prepare Britain for the conflagration that loomed. Appeasement was a strategic imperative, not a diplomatic tool chosen hastily and in preference to a range of other options. Keeping the balance of power finely adjusted in Europe enabled Britain to concentrate on its major interests – its Empire and its connections with the wider world. But Neville Chamberlain's predecessors had two distinct advantages: they had been able to maintain a level of military power sufficient to deter rivals; and those rivals – France and Russia – had not sought to blow the international system apart.[4] At Munich, Chamberlain had his eye firmly on the imperial implications of European peace, and he had tried for years to neutralize the threat posed by Mussolini in the Mediterranean. Mussolini's policies and his armed forces – whose might was overestimated by Britain at the time – meant that the Mediterranean Fleet was kept at a strength that left the security of British possessions in the Indian Ocean and the Pacific fundamentally weakened. Singapore was there, but the battle fleet to operate from it did not exist. In the light of these insuperable force dispersal dilemmas, appeasement was an obvious diplomatic policy seeking to keep the peace and keep Britain's global interests out of the mire.

Germany, Italy and Japan all wanted empire for reasons of prestige and economic gain, as well as to relieve domestic political pressure. All had reason to resent the provisions of the Treaty of Versailles and the world order that the victorious powers had established following the First World War, and their ruling regimes had to varying degrees hitched their credibility to their capacity to revise the international system. All three Axis powers sought to challenge or supplant British authority in the three regions that British strategic planning sought to protect: in descending order, the British Isles and their home waters; the Mediterranean and Middle East; and Asia and the Far East. In absolute contrast to Germany, Italy and Japan, Britain had more to lose than any other country if war escaped its regional boundaries and disrupted the international order. Apart from being responsible for the defence of hundreds of millions of subjects scattered across the globe, Britain had played a leading role in fostering, protecting and lubricating the global economy. In 1939 Britain was still the world's greatest trading nation, living on global trade and foreign investments that depended on peace and the freedom of the world's major sea routes. War was a disaster for global commerce and exchange. Production was redirected to war, the merchant marine was depleted, consumers were severed from sources of supply, and overseas assets were liquidated.

All of the Axis powers had imperial ambitions. Japan's shopping list included the Dutch East Indies, the Philippines and Malaya, and Italy cast covetous eyes on Britain's prime position in the Mediterranean and Middle East. To Germany's ambitions in eastern and western Europe must be added plans for a return to the international colonial stage, particularly in Africa, where dreams of a German *Mittelafrika* stretching from the Atlantic to the Indian Ocean had not faded. Indeed, the uniforms worn by General Erwin Rommel's Afrika Korps, when it landed in Libya in early 1941 to stiffen Mussolini's forces, had been designed and manufactured for use by a new German colonial army that it was thought would soon be needed when French and British colonies began to fall like ripe fruits from the African empire tree.[5] The British government even considered handing over some African colonies to Germany as part of its policy of appeasement and as restitution for what it considered to be the harsher aspects of the Treaty of Versailles (though naturally Britain preferred any such territorial gifts to be excised from the French Empire). Furthermore, the Germans expected to scoop the Middle Eastern oil wells by virtue of a successful push across Russia and Egypt.

Britain's great strategic problem was that it could not face with adequate military deterrents the threat from three enemy states all at once. The rise of Italian military power, and the apparent readiness of Mussolini to unleash it, was a real threat to Britain's imperial communications and entire system of imperial defence. Italy, in a move redolent of European behaviour during the scramble for Africa, invaded Abyssinia in 1935, as Mussolini sought to build a new Roman Empire. Naturally Abyssinia looked to the League of Nations' two leading powers, Britain and France, for protection from Italy's blatantly illegal aggression. Britain could not respond effectively, however, simply for fear that Italian ill will would threaten prime imperial interests in the eastern Mediterranean, and perhaps lead to the loss of capital ships too precious to be risked and that might be needed at any moment to sail east in order to deter Japan. So Abyssinia was left to fend for itself because Britain – a military power of the first order – had too many imperial defence commitments. Continued Italian belligerence, however, caused this equation to work in reverse as well. The situation in the Mediterranean hamstrung British policy in the Far East, when it came to finding an adequate response to Japan's growing threat to British interests. If the Mediterranean Fleet was stripped of battleships in order to send a strong message to the Japanese, it might tempt Mussolini. But of course, by not moving any, the Far East was bereft of capital ships and Japan was similarly tempted. It was most infuriating: the

Royal Navy was quite capable of pulverizing the Italian navy, and, by closing the Suez Canal to Italian vessels, Britain could have destroyed Italy's ability to reinforce and supply its army in Abyssinia. There was, however, the threat of Italian retaliation to any such move, a particular nightmare being an air attack damaging or sinking capital ships in Malta or Alexandria. If RAF reinforcements were sent in anticipation of any such move, it would be at the cost of weakening Britain's defences against possible Luftwaffe attack and making even more likely the utter devastation of British cities that experts thought would be the outcome if a bombing war were to begin. The snakes outnumbered the ladders in this maddening game of imperial defence in the 1930s, leaving the aggressors to make all of the opening moves.

Britain was no longer a military power of the first order in the Far East, despite the propaganda surrounding its Singapore naval base. This was a huge problem, because, although militarily it had slipped down the ranks, Britain was still the major imperial power in the region and had the biggest commercial and financial stake there. This waning of British military power in the Far East was not a recent thing. In 1902 a naval alliance with Japan had been necessary to secure British possessions in the region, as the Royal Navy was obliged to concentrate major fleet units in home waters to meet the threat of the German High Seas Fleet. From that date, the security of Britain's Far Eastern holdings, including the two great antipodean Dominions, had been underwritten by Japan, a fact that pleased neither Australia nor New Zealand. America had also been unhappy about it, and put pressure on Britain not to renew the treaty. Britain duly obliged shortly after the First World War; but it never redeployed sufficient naval strength in the region to make good the loss. As Japan began to look increasingly like an enemy waiting to happen, there was nothing to provide a counterweight to its burgeoning naval power or to curb its growing sense of wounded pride.

Britain's failure to persuade America of the benefits of resolute joint action to warn Japan off from its belligerent course meant that it had little choice but to endure the calculated humiliations, simply because it did not have available in the area the kind of serious military power which alone would have made the Japanese sit up and take stock. In submitting to this, Britain earnestly hoped to keep the areas of major British interest (Shanghai and the Yangtse valley) out of the Sino-Japanese conflict, and made an effort not to provoke Japan, whilst trying to do at least something to help China. This of course was a tightrope in itself, as aid to China, such as supplying arms via Hong Kong or the newly-opened Burma Road, deeply offended the Japanese. As with the situation in the Mediterranean, it was infuriating: Britain had to stand by impotently, even when the car carrying the British Ambassador was strafed by a Japanese fighter whilst it was clearly displaying the Union Flag. As had been the case with Abyssinia, the League of Nations provided no succour for the Chinese, and again it was largely Britain – as the only League member with the requisite naval capability to take on Japan – that was left carrying the can. No proper sanctions or military measures could be taken without full American support, however, and this America was not willing to give. Britain's position was therefore dependent upon diplomacy alone, but, as in the European case, aggressive, militaristic, authoritarian states simply would not be talked out of a position considered wholly unreasonable by the democracies.

Imperial considerations, as well as those concerning the European balance of power and the geostrategic imperatives of Empire and global economy, shaped British foreign and defence policy in the pre-war period. Indeed imperial concerns, particularly the need to ensure imperial unity should war come, were paramount influences upon British policy. Britain's apparent vacillation and weakness in the face of persistent German, Italian and Japanese aggression and trouble-making were determined by imperial defence concerns and the unwill-ingness of the Dominions to join Britain in what they considered to be premature or avoidable conflict. It was considered vital by the British government that, if war came, the Commonwealth should go to war unanimously. Dominion opinion was therefore a major factor in British diplomacy and in Britain's reactions to the twists and turns of the dictators. In the mature union of politically independent countries that the Commonwealth had become by the 1930s, only the people of the Dominions themselves could decide for or against war, and it was important for Dominions leaders to show their people that the decision to go to war – if it came to that – was theirs and not Britain's, taken for their own safety and secu-rity not just for that of distant central Europeans or even just for the security of the British Isles.

Securing the assent of the Dominions, considered essential if Britain was to embark upon a war with Germany, was not easy. Since the early twentieth century the Dominions had become increasingly preoccupied with regional security concerns and Britain's increasing inability to meet them – whatever the promise of battle fleets and fortress bases. Since the end of the First World War the Dominions had also shown a marked reluctance to back Britain on policies that might lead to another European war. Though the Dominions supported the British and League of Nations policy of sanctions against Italy in 1935–36, at the Dominions Conference of 1937 South Africa favoured neutrality in a future war and Canada remained isolationist. Only New Zealand seemed happy to follow Britain's lead, even if this might mean war. The conference reinforced Neville Chamberlain's determination to pursue peace in Europe at almost any cost. 'Appeasement' was a rational policy to pursue, given Britain's traditional view of the European balance of power and its uniquely imperial economic, military and political orientation. Appeasement also, of course, bought priceless time for rear-mament, and for the education of public opinion at home and in the Commonwealth.

Right up until the eve of war South Africa and Canada remained non-committal. From May 1939 the Committee of Imperial Defence planned on the assumption that at least one of the Dominions would remain neutral when war came. The imperial unity considered so necessary an aspect of British foreign policy had been achieved, however, when Prime Minister Neville Chamberlain made his melancholy broadcast announcing war with Germany on 3 September 1939, though with only a whisker to spare. Whilst the Dominions would not have gone to war over Czechoslovakia in 1938, by the time of Hitler's invasion of Poland the following year they had concluded that Hitler was not to be appeased, and that he posed a threat to an imperial world in which the Dominions had found security and prosperity.

For the rest of the Empire, however, war came on Britain's say so. Thus in September 1939 the entire Indian subcontinent went to war with Germany at the stroke of an ultimatum's expiration in Berlin and an announcement from the British Viceroy. Similar announcements were made throughout the Colonial Empire, from Aden to Cyprus, Fiji to Sarawak, from the Seychelles to Tobago, where the local potentates who administered the colonies alongside British district officials were summoned to meetings by their respective Governors. There they were told of the war and of its likely local manifestations, and were invited to reaffirm their allegiance to an imperial monarch in whose name they and their people were soon to be called to bear the multifarious burdens of global, industrialized warfare.

3

Imperial War

From an ivory tower in Cambridge, Sir John Seeley, one of the founding fathers of British imperial scholarship, set down a Palmerstonian phrase now hackneyed as a description of the piecemeal, unplanned manner in which Britain had gained history's largest Empire. In his lectures on *The Expansion of England*, Seeley pronounced that 'the British Empire was acquired in a fit of absence of mind'. His point was that there was no central blueprint for Empire, no 'Plan of Global Dominance' mulled over and then approved by a British Cabinet, just continual growth on the peripheries. British interests kept stumbling into things and as often as not the result was imperial expansion.*

A striking feature of the Second World War was that this rag-tag British Empire, this conglomeration born of disparate motives sprawled pink across the maps of the world, fought as a unit, and a streamlined one at that. Presence of mind was uppermost, and Empire was most imperial when Britain was engaged in global conflicts, from the eighteenth to the twentieth century. Nowhere is the sense of the Empire acting as a unit better illustrated than in the history of the Second World War. For the first time in its history, the centre *did* have a plan, as well as the conviction, the technology and the need to carry it through and make every single part of the Empire jump to its tune. The war was something of an imperial heyday, though it is more often remembered as the swansong of Empire. During the war, the Empire approached the otherwise elusive status of a formidable, efficient and effective power system, prepared to exploit its

---

*   Sir John Seeley, *The Expansion of England: Two Courses of Lectures* (1883). In contrast, Harry Flashman, the philandering, gutless, though unfortunately fictional Victorian soldier-hero of George MacDonald Fraser's remarkable novels, had quite a different perspective on British imperial expansion, expressed in typically coarse fashion. 'Absence of mind, my arse', he declares. 'We *always* knew what we were doing; we just didn't always know how it would pan out.' His was the view from the colonial front, the view of the empire-builder not the armchair observer. Flashman's point was that it was '*presence* of mind' on the part of Britons overseas that led to imperial expansion, even if they could not foresee where their actions would lead. Presence of mind, but also 'countless other things, such as greed and Christianity, decency and villainy, policy and lunacy, deep design and blind chance, pride and trade, blunder and curiosity, passion, ignorance, chivalry and expediency, honest pursuit of right, and determination to keep the bloody Frogs out'. George MacDonald Fraser, *Flashman and the Mountain of Light* (1990). As a summary of the motive forces of British imperial expansion, MacDonald Fraser's list is hard to better.

apparently limitless resources, and able to deploy large-scale fighting forces simultaneously throughout the world.[1] After victory had been won in 1945, Churchill told a London audience that 'the British Commonwealth and Empire stands more united and more effectively powerful than at any time in its long romantic history'. This was indeed true, though the effort to reach that pitch of power, led ultimately to the Empire's demise.

The British Empire had had opportunities to rehearse for truly global warfare on numerous occasions since the Seven Years' War, and to develop an administrative, military and economic system to meet it. In doing this, the metropole shared its organizational role with other centres of imperial power. By the middle of the twentieth century the Empire was strong enough at the periphery – in power centres such as Cairo, Canberra, Delhi and Ottawa – to be capable of helping London orchestrate a massive, global war effort. During the war, Britain put new and unparalleled demands upon its Empire. It was to be used as a strategic asset, a battlefield, a manpower reservoir and a warehouse of industrial, agricultural and mineral resources. Connecting the demand for soldiers, tanks and food were the ships of the Merchant Navy and the Royal Navy, criss-crossing the world's oceans and steaming into the ports upon which the very survival of the British cause and the independence of the British people rested.

In 1939 most Britons saw the Empire as a source of strength, as the very essence of Britishness, and as a vital buttress of the civilized world. In *1066 And All That* parlance, the Empire was a Good Thing, just as much as Nazism was a Bad Thing.[2] And because the Empire existed, British soldiers fought in the Malayan jungle, Indians fought in Iraq, New Zealanders attempted to repel German paratroops in Crete, Scottish troops looked out upon Japanese positions on the Chinese mainland, Canadian seamen hunted U-boats off Iceland, and Basotho muleteers brought wounded Australians down from inaccessible mountain ranges in Italy. They were all *imperial* soldiers, summoned to arms by the needs of a far-flung Empire and its constituent parts, just like the Roman legionaries on top of Hadrian's Wall hundreds of years before.

All the territories of the British Empire mobilized fully for war, not just the self-governing Dominions of Australia, Canada, New Zealand and South Africa. (The exception was the Irish Free State, a Dominion in name at least, which remained neutral.)[3] The Indian Raj was a linchpin of the war in the East, the colonies of tropical Africa and South-East Asia were key providers of men and materials and became battle zones themselves, and the galaxy of islands and enclaves over which the Union Flag flew in the Pacific, the Indian Ocean, the Mediterranean, the Caribbean and the Atlantic all put men into British uniforms and dug for victory on the home front.

The Empire provided many bases. India was a launch-pad for the war against the Japanese army in Burma; Australia became home to hundreds of thousands of American troops, as the war raged in nearby Pacific territories; and Ceylon became a surprisingly important base for operations in the Indian Ocean and

South-East Asia following the loss of Singapore. Other bases, however, were not a part of Britain's domains. Egypt was an independent nation state, neutral until two months before the end of the war, yet housed Britain's largest overseas concentration of military power. Numerous other countries not officially part of the Empire also supplied major military resources. Iraq and Iran were independent countries that Britain invaded in order to strengthen its position against the Germans, to defend essential oilfields and refineries, and to enable Anglo-American supplies to reach Russia. Apart from Hong Kong Island and the New Territories, there were no formal British imperial holdings in China, yet British influence in Shanghai and the Yangtse valley amounted to a quasi-imperial presence that was deeply affected by the course of the war. The territory over which Britain ruled actually grew during the war, as enemy colonies, including Eritrea, Italian Somaliland, Lebanon, Libya, Madagascar and Syria, were conquered and occupied. British bases and military power were also established in other new areas, for example in the French Comoros Islands off the African coast, in Iceland, the Faroe Islands and the Azores. At the end of the war, Britain was responsible for the Dutch East Indies and French Indo-China until the former colonial powers could muster the strength to return.

The war effort of India and the Dominions dominate accounts of the Second World War that give space to the imperial contribution. This is not surprising. Their contribution to the war effort, by virtue of their size and resources, was the greatest. A truly imperial perspective must also consider, however, the war of the sixty million people of the Colonial Empire – the red-on-the-map *not* including the Dominions and the Raj. Sparsely populated rural districts in Africa, as well as tiny islands in the Indian Ocean and Pacific, were a part of the British war effort, often performing vital roles. Even the polar ice caps were not immune from military operations during this six year imperial war. Britain sent warships to protect its claims in Antarctica and obliterate sovereignty markers left by Nazi ships.

Though they were nowhere near as powerful as America or Russia, the Empire and Commonwealth's contribution to the British war effort was of real importance. In the long months before American military exports to Britain and the provisions of the Lend-Lease Bill came fully on stream in 1941, Commonwealth production was invaluable, and throughout the war troops, food and raw materials from across the Empire and Commonwealth were a key feature of Britain's war machine. The Dominions and India in particular produced significant amounts of military hardware, from armoured cars in India and South Africa to bombers in Canada, Bren gun carriers in New Zealand and minesweepers in Australia. Early in the war these imperial sources of armaments were vital at 'a time when a few million rounds of small arms ammunition from India or Australia meant more to us than all the later billions from North America'.[4] Britain, however, remained the centre of the Empire and Commonwealth's production of military hardware, supplying 70 per cent of the munitions available to imperial forces, a figure that stood at over 90 per cent during the crucial first fifteen months of the war. Nevertheless, it is not an exaggeration to say that the contribution of the overseas Commonwealth was indispensable to survival between 1939 and 1941.[5]

Whilst focusing on the war effort of the Empire it must nor be forgotten that other allies, great and small, contributed much to ultimate victory. Polish troops as well as Polish airmen served in numerous imperial theatres, and imperial troops fought alongside Free French forces. It goes without saying that the contribution of America and Russia was pivotal, in the case of America both before and after it became embroiled in hostilities with Germany and Japan. In almost every theatre, and in Britain itself, American supplies and American forces were ubiquitous. In policing the Atlantic against U-boats and delivering supplies to Russia via Iran, as well as to the imperial forces in the Middle East via the Horn of Africa and the Red Sea ports, Americans were involved and active on Britain's side, even though their country was officially at war with no one. In the Western Desert campaign, often seen as the last great single-handed British victory, American military hardware was important in achieving the famed victory of Alamein, and large American forces joined the British for the final push to eject the Axis from Africa.

The armoured divisions of the Empire and Commonwealth, whether fighting in Libya, Italy or Burma, rode into battle not just in British tanks but in American Honeys, Grants, and most famously, Shermans. British imperial force received about 30 per cent of all American tank production, as well as 86,000 jeeps. Elsewhere, the carrier USS *Saratoga* served for a time with the British Eastern Fleet, and the carrier USS *Wasp* was loaned at the personal request of Churchill to ferry Spitfires for the defence of Malta. The American-built Catalina flying boat was a mainstay of ocean patrolling by British forces in the Atlantic and the Indian Ocean, and in India and Burma the Fourteenth Army relied for its supplies on American-built Dakota transport aircraft. The Fleet Air Arm received 38 per cent of its aircraft over the course of the war from American factories. On the high seas many of the 2700 Liberty ships built in American shipyards joined the Merchant Navy and transported goods around the Empire, and nearly forty American-built escort carriers loaned to the Royal Navy gave Britain a surfeit of vessels in that class by the end of the war. In all America supplied Britain with ninety-nine escort vessels, excluding the fifty old destroyers exchanged in 1941 for Caribbean base facilities. On top of this, 391 major and 2004 minor landing craft were delivered to Britain under Lend-Lease. Over 36,000 American aircraft were delivered to British imperial forces, 20 per cent of their wartime supply. By 1944 America was also supplying Britain with 28 per cent of its munitions. To facilitate this enormous transfer of military hardware from America to Britain and the various fighting fronts, a large supply organization – 'an overseas Whitehall' – was established in Washington, alongside one for the Commonwealth.[6]

This massive American input into imperial fighting theatres inevitably brought political and economic involvement in its wake that was rarely conducive to a post-war return to settled and solitary British rule, including a presidential foray into Indian politics that elicited a volcanic response from Churchill.[7] The longer the war lasted, the more Britain found itself leaning on American aid, and between 1942 and 1945 American economic aid represented about 9 per cent of Britain's total war expenditure.[8] By 1945 Britain had received $270,000 million in Lend-Lease assistance. (British assistance in the other direction, often overlooked, amounted to nearly a quarter of this figure, and a further $2,074,000,000 of British aid was sent to Russia.) America's stake in the bankrolling of the war, and its superiority in certain areas of war production, enhanced the weight of its voice in the higher councils of Allied war planning. (For example, America's virtual monopoly in the production of landing craft decided when and where they were to be used for large-scale amphibious assaults.) Like grass coming through concrete, American personnel, money and influence kept cropping up, and a major Colonial Office initiative was launched to defend the Empire from American encroachment and to persuade Americans that the British Empire was not a nefarious threat that needed to be swept away along with the dictators.[9] The wartime extension of American influence contributed to its rise to the status of a truly global military and economic power.

Though Americans in general were unwilling to take action to support what they considered to be the 'imperialist' features of Britain's war effort, many Americans identified with Britain's cause long before their country entered the war, some to the extent of joining the British armed forces. American pilots were to be found flying in Malta and Singapore as well as in the Battle of Britain, and in Burma an American Volunteer Group threw its Tomahawks into the ring in defence of the Burma Road and its precious supply cargoes trucking overland to China. In September 1942 the three pioneering American Eagle squadrons serving with the RAF in Britain were transferred to the United Stated Army Air Force. Elsewhere, American forces and merchant vessels worked alongside British forces before December 1941, for example in patrolling the Atlantic and in shipping supplies around the Cape to the ports of the Sudan and Egypt. American forces took over the operation of air bases in British West Africa, and released British forces for fighting duties, when, in the summer of 1941, they took over an increased share of the running of the Iranian transport network following the Anglo-Soviet invasion.

The men who directed the British war effort from London were alive to the opportunities and risks that Britain's imperial status presented as they sought to defeat its enemies. The Chief of the Imperial General Staff confided to his diary how annoyed he was that the First Lord of the Admiralty, Admiral of the Fleet Sir Dudley Pound, kept nodding off during Chiefs of Staff meeting when major decisions were being made about 'the biggest Imperial war that we are ever likely to be engaged in'.[10] The most prominent Briton of the Second World War was never blind to the importance of the Empire during the war, or of the war's significance for the Empire's future. Winston Churchill was acutely aware of the imperial nature of Britain's fight, and the Empire was rarely far from his mind, as was shown repeatedly in his speeches and broadcasts. He understood that British world power depended upon the Empire and that Britain – unique among the Great Powers of the world – was an imperial state.

Churchill's experience over five decades as a parliamentarian, soldier, journalist, historian and Cabinet Minister contributed to his emergence as the greatest imperial statesman of his age, breathing imperial rhetoric as second nature; no speech-writers were needed to prompt Churchill to be more inclusive when it came to the overseas branches of the British world. If talking about a chip shop in Salford, Churchill would find a way to mention how important its chips were to the Empire. 'Hold Calais for the good of the British Empire', he signalled the commander during the evacuation of Dunkirk, and on the fall of Singapore he told the people of Australia that it was 'a British and an imperial defeat'. Perhaps most famously, on 18 August 1940, with the Battle of Britain raging in the skies above, Churchill said that upon the outcome of the Battle of Britain 'depends our own British life and the long continuity of our institutions and our Empire ... If the British Empire and its Commonwealth last for a thousand years, men will still say, "This was their finest hour"'. For Churchill, the British Empire was central to Britain's greatness. He had not become 'the King's First Minister in order to preside over the liquidation of the British Empire', he thundered in the Commons in late 1941. This was a warning and a pledge aimed at America, but also at the enemies of the Empire, at that moment in late 1941 threatening or overrunning its soil from the Mediterranean to the Pacific. Realizing that the security of Britain and its vital trade routes was the key to imperial survival, he put their defence ahead of the defence of imperial possessions in the Far East, a painful but necessary strategic prioritization. The British Empire would continue to fight without Singapore, and even, God forbid, without Australia, but it would die if Britain was overrun or the lifeline of the Atlantic bridge was severed.

Hitler also appreciated the significance of the British Empire, at least to the extent that he admired it and wished Germany to possess foreign holdings itself. In July 1940 a new 'Peace Offensive' saw Hitler guarantee the territorial integrity of the British Empire if Britain accepted Germany's European conquests. But by then it was far too late. France had fallen and Britain stood alone, with the five hundred million people of the Empire mobilizing across the globe. Hitler was genuinely shocked by Britain's determination to continue the war. In the Reichstag on 19 July 1940 he said that:

> it almost causes me pain to think that I should have been selected by Fate to deal the final blow to the structure which these men have already set tottering ... Mr Churchill ought perhaps, for once, to believe me when I prophesy that a great Empire will be destroyed – an Empire which it was never my intention to destroy or even harm.[11]

With the British still stubborn in their refusal to see sense, in November 1940

Hitler determined that, after Russia had been conquered, he would turn his attention to the partition of the British Empire. In doing so he would ensure the exclusion of America, so that the other great Anglo-Saxon power would not have the chance to set itself up as Britain's successor. Others also stood to benefit from the partition of the British Empire. The Japanese and Italians, in particular, could not see a way forward for their own nations without a downsizing of British territory. Russia, too, had grand designs on Britain's Empire, particularly in the Persian Gulf and Indian Ocean. In October 1940, even as it was planning the annihilation of Russia, the German government was discussing the delimitation of spheres of influence across the world with Russian officials in Berlin.

The Empire and Commonwealth was the world's largest political, economic and military unit, and it went to war as one. In 1939 it was Britain's responsibility to defend every inch of the Empire and Commonwealth. This was why the failure to do so in the East was so bad for British prestige. Furthermore, it was the imperial link that was the direct cause of the participation of each colony in the war, with London utilizing the resources of each colony to the greatest extent possible. Events in one theatre affected those in another, particularly in the realm of human and material resource provision. When, for example, the Mediterranean was secured by Allied naval and air power and by victories in the North Africa desert warships became more readily available for the build up of naval forces for the war against Japan.

The Empire was often the very reason for British military and naval campaigns. Even in the Pacific – where British power was crippled and America dominated the Allied war effort – the war was still fought out in British colonies (the Gilbert and Ellice Islands, the Solomon Islands) The Australasian Dominions also played a significant part in the fighting and in providing base facilities for American forces. Iran was invaded in order to shore up Britain's position in the Middle East and secure the oil supplies upon which its war effort depended. The British government and its web of overseas officials expected the Empire to pull together in one direction, and made every effort to ensure that this was the case.

A global strategic awareness was second nature to British political and military policy-makers because of the country's imperial heritage. Further down the chain from the strategists in Whitehall, British officers and colonial administrators on the ground, from school to the university and staff college, were versed in the basic tenets of imperial defence and what frequently-reprinted textbooks termed 'imperial military geography'. Imperial awareness was developed through literature, art and the stage, education, newspaper and radio coverage of imperial affairs, royal tours and sporting events. There was also extensive movement of people to and from different parts of the Empire, be they soldiers, migrants, missionaries, administrators or traders.

Lord Baden-Powell, founder of the Boy Scout movement, illustrated this imperial strategic awareness and the method in which it was passed on to children through popular literature. Writing of a tour of Scout centres in British Africa during the 1930s, Baden-Powell's account includes numerous throwaway lessons in imperial defence. 'A great British man-of-war – the *Barham* – lay before us as we came to the mouth of the Suez Canal at Port Said.' Nearby was a steamer full of Italian soldiers off to Abyssinia. Baden-Powell told his young audience that Italy had nearly gone to war with Britain because of the latter's opposition to Mussolini's Abyssinian invasion:

> Had she done so, we should have stopped her ships going through the Canal, and the *Barham* was there, like a traffic policeman, to stop them if necessary. Also the Mediterranean Fleet was close by, in Alexandria, like a lot more policemen in a police-station, ready to come out if wanted.[12]

Baden-Powell was writing in a decade when the theory of imperial defence still remained clear and uncluttered by the problem of too many enemies and insufficient forces. Continuing his African progress, Baden-Powell travelled on to the Red Sea, to call at Port Sudan and Aden before heading off to British East Africa. Here he drew his readers' attention to a tiny volcanic island in the Bab el Mandeb Straits where the Red Sea meets the Gulf of Aden.

> These straits are a narrow waterway about eight miles across, with the island of Perim in the middle. If that island were armed with any big guns or warships it could prevent enemy's ships passing in or out of the Red Sea, just as Gibraltar with its guns and warships can stop ships using the Mediterranean. But Perim *has* got guns, and they are British guns! Also, as our ship rounded the corner of the island, there we saw, above the roofs of the village and the barracks, the towering upper works of two British men-of-war anchored in the inner harbour behind them. But you must not think that Britain holds these posts from any wish to go to war; quite the opposite: Britain has become a sort of policeman of the world and aims to prevent other nations fighting.[13]

The British Empire was a thalassocracy, a sea-based world power. The Royal Navy and the Merchant Navy (and imperial offshoots like the Royal Australian Navy and the Canadian Merchant Navy) were inextricably bound up with the British Empire. This was particularly the case during the Second World War. Previous wars had seen the British attack and be attacked across the world's oceans. Britain isolated enemies using seapower, and its enemies attempted to strip Britain of its naval power as a prelude to invasion, or to starve it by sinking its merchant vessels. The protection of the British Empire's commerce was the main task of the Royal Navy, along with dealing with enemy battlefleets, transporting military forces and blockading enemy territories. The system of imperial trade defined the British Empire and sustained Britain and most of the Empire's component territories, and it was as a trade defence force that the navy earned its bread and butter.[14] The thousands of vessels of the Merchant Navy and the hundreds of warships of the Royal Navy traversed the world's sea lanes and loaded, unloaded, refuelled, repaired and revictualled at the many ports and harbours of the Empire and the wider world.[15] The Merchant Navy was a multinational force, standing at nearly 200,000 men in 1938. Of these 70 per cent were British and 5 per cent foreign; the remaining quarter were Lascars, mainly natives of India and East Africa. Naval bases such as Aden, Alexandria, Bermuda, Cape Town, Colombo, Gibraltar, Halifax, Hong Kong and Singapore were part of the British world.

Britain's enemies were well aware of how important this global network was, hence their attempt to disrupt imperial trade using U-boats, surface raiders and other forms of offensive naval warfare. As the Royal Navy staggered under the weight of too many enemies at once, convoys became vital to imperial exchange and military supply, and self-sufficiency became the overriding preoccupation of colonial governments the world over. The shipyards of America, Australia, Britain and Canada worked tirelessly to build merchant ships as losses mounted, and to augment the stock of warships most intimately connected with convoy defence, corvettes and destroyers.[16] Puny these ships may have appeared when measured against the destructive might and huge deadweight of battleships, but they were crucial in defending convoys, a role in which battleships were powerless, given their lack of anti-submarine warfare capabilities. Ancient destroyers, such as the fifty given by America to Britain in exchange for base rights in the Caribbean, and new corvettes were the guardian angels of British convoys all over the world.[17] Corvettes were a major item on the production list of Canadian shipyards. Australia built them as well, and South Africa built minesweepers and converted whalers and trawlers to serve as escort vessels. Like the little boats that saved the British Expeditionary Force at Dunkirk, it was the smaller vessels of the Royal Navy and its partners, some converted from civilian working vessels, which protected the mighty convoys upon which the survival of the Empire depended.

Beyond corvettes and destroyers, the Admiralty procured warships of all descriptions in its desperate attempt to defend British trade, and that of neutrals. If these could not be built in time, existing ships were converted for offensive purposes – a cruiser laid down but not yet complete might become an escort carrier, or an existing merchant ship might find itself transformed into a weapon of war as naval guns were added to turn it into an Armed Merchant Cruiser (AMC). All sorts of measures were taken to protect the precious merchant ships: AMCs met an urgent need after the Royal Navy had initially requisitioned fifty cargo and cargo-passenger liners for conversion, Many of those not so converted nevertheless had four-inch guns or twelve-pounders bolted on. These measures were taken because of the acute shortage of available cruisers. Some merchantmen even had a single aircraft mounted on them to create what were known as Catapult Armed Merchant ships (CAMs). Service personnel trained merchant seamen as part of the Defensively Equipped Merchant Ship (DEMS) organization to man guns on merchant vessels. This organization was strengthened by the addition of soldiers, and in May 1941 the War Office regularized the position and created the Maritime Anti-Aircraft Regiment of the Royal Artillery (Maritime Royal Artillery from November 1942). It served all over the world and peaked at 13,000 members in 1944. By 1944 there were 35,000 military personnel on board merchant ships. There were even *merchant* aircraft carriers, as the Admiralty did everything it could to meet the insatiable demand for trade protection at sea in the face of a new generation of submarines and torpedoes. In winning the war against the submarine, air power was crucial. This was provided both by carrier-borne aircraft and particularly by long-range ones such as the Shorts Sunderland and the American-built Liberators and Catalinas, often flying as a part of RAF's Coastal Command. By 1945 RAF Coastal Command had 784 aircraft, 511 dedicated to anti-submarine warfare, the remainder to the campaign against German shipping.[18]

In war as in peace, Britain's global marine had to be plotted, scheduled and marshalled. Operational control of all merchant shipping was handed directly to the Admiralty, and responsibility for the loading and unloading of all merchant ships was handed to the Ministry of Shipping (Ministry of War Transport from May 1941). The shipper Alfred Holt's Blue Funnel Line, for instance, comprising eighty-seven ships at the outbreak of war, was duly taken over by the authorities. Headquartered at India House in Liverpool, the fleet had forty other ships (including captured enemy vessels) handed over to it for management during the course of the war.[19]

Protected points around the globe were needed in which to gather the thousands of vessels plying the Empire's trade and nourishing the war theatres with fresh drafts of men, mail, rifles, tanks, bully beef and beer. Major ports in Ceylon, Egypt, Gibraltar, Sierra Leone, South Africa, the Sudan and Trinidad became assembly points for ships and their escorts waiting to form into convoy. The famous 'HX' (Halifax) Atlantic and 'WS' ('Winston's Specials') convoys shunted vital supplies around the world (the former to Britain, the latter to the Middle East via the Cape), whilst Mediterranean operations like 'Pedestal' and its many predecessors were mounted at great cost to keep Malta in the fight and to shuttle supplies from Gibraltar to Alexandria. From September 1939 convoys began to sail homeward from Gibraltar and Sierra Leone, outward and homeward to and from Bergen in Norway, and outward into the Atlantic by the North Channel, around the south of Ireland or through the English Channel. Along the world's convoy routes imperial bases helped vessels along the way. RAF bases in Arabia, for example, providing cover in the Arabian Sea, British and American aircraft operating from Ascension Island and Iceland offered extra cover to convoys in mid-Atlantic, and flying boats from Diego Garcia shepherded vessels travelling across the Indian Ocean to or from Ceylon.

Second only to the Atlantic bridge convoy routes connecting Britain with America and Canada were the 'WS' convoy routes connecting Britain with Suez via the Cape and the Indian Ocean. By March 1941 643,198 imperial servicemen had been escorted across the waters guarded by the ships of the East Indies Station, along with millions of tons of supplies, as the Middle East, the Persian Gulf, India, Singapore, and Australasia were kept in touch across the waters of the Indian Ocean. British-controlled trooping fleets also brought American soldiers to Europe, and in the first months of 1942 they conveyed 16,500 Americans to the Far East. Tens of thousands of Canadians were brought to Britain, and Lend-Lease was delivered to Russia via Archangel and the Persian Gulf. This, indeed, was the mobility of manpower and resources conferred by seapower. Upon it depended a complex system of global exchange and interdependency, an exercise in imperial housekeeping that ensured that during the war both butter *and* guns were supplied and delivered.

A particular war-time concern was the transport of oil products.[20] The main British oil companies, Royal Dutch Shell and Anglo-Persian, owned 336 tankers between them, and the American company Standard Oil owned eighty-three British-flagged tankers. Britain controlled the fleet and was therefore able to oblige sterling countries to cut their consumption. Huge new military demands for oil products now had priority over domestic consumption, with the build up, for example, of imperial forces in India and the arrival of tens of thousands of Americans in Australia. From February 1941, the massive withdrawal of vessels from the eastern cross-trades to the British supply routes led to a rapid fall of stocks in countries bordering the Indian Ocean. Sixty-eight British tankers were sunk in the Atlantic area in the first half of 1942. The Persian Gulf region was crucial in providing the oil for the forces in the Middle East, and in 1940 about a third of Britain's aviation spirit imports were being shipping from Caribbean refineries.

Supply and logistics were key aspects of the imperial war effort, spreadeagled as its territories and its fighting fronts were. By September 1943 Ferry Command had brought 2241 aircraft from North America to Britain via Gander airport in the colony of Newfoundland. With the virtual closure of the Mediterranean to merchant shipping, the British were obliged to make use of the longest supply route in the history of war, taking supplies and soldiers from Britain to the Middle East via the Cape and the Red Sea. Thousands of aircraft were delivered to the Western Desert by the trans-African Takoradi air route and the Burma Road delivered supplies to Chiang Kai-shek's beleaguered Chinese forces. The railways, roads and waterways of Iran delivered Lend-Lease goods to Stalin, and the African Line of Communication (AFLOC) funnelled the produce of East Africa towards the hungry mouths of the million imperial servicemen fighting in the Middle East.[21] In announcing the fall of Singapore to the Commons in a secret session, Churchill revealed that, since the start of hostilities with Japan, over 300,000 men had been moved from Britain and the Middle East to South-East Asia and South Asia, 'and we have over 100,000 on salt water at the present time'. This massive transfer of resources had been affected with little loss of life. As Churchill concluded: 'I regard this as a prodigy of skill and organization on the part of all those responsible for it.'[22] This might stand as an epigraph for the entire imperial war effort.

Britain had never really contemplated the enormous scale of the war effort that it would demand from the Empire, because it had never really contemplated, and certainly not planned for, the disastrous situation in which it found itself following the fall of France and the entry of Italy and Japan into the war. The Great Power ally on which so many calculations in the event of war with Germany had rested fell at a stroke, and Hitler was able to charge Göring with the destruction of the RAF from bases across the Channel in northern France, as a prelude to Operation Sealion, the invasion of Britain itself. Five immediate imperial ramifications of the fall of France were the loss of French naval power in the western Mediterranean; the establishment of U-boat bases on the Atlantic coast that greatly enhanced Germany's ability to make war on the Atlantic convoys; the surrounding of poorly defended British West African colonies by hostile Vichy territories; the loss of Syria as a base for potential air operations against hostile forces in the Caucasus; and the use of Indo-China as a base for Japan's attack on British South-East Asia. Similarly, the temporary eradication of American naval power in the Pacific after Pearl Harbor was a bolt from the blue, and Russia's official neutrality – towards both Germany and Japan – further loaded the dice against the Empire and Commonwealth.

In mobilizing the Empire for the total war effort that these misfortunes were to demand, British colonial officials and their indigenous collaborators capitalized on a degree of acceptance and legitimacy that British rule had fostered over the years by accident as much as design, a degree of acceptance and legitimacy that is often overlooked today because it does not sit comfortably with the common view of imperial rule as something that was ceaselessly contested by colonial populations. In actual fact, the mass of the Empire's population in 1939 was in no way engaged in activities calculated to cast off British rule, and lived lives in which the direct, quotidian British presence was strictly limited. For the British, of course, this had its drawbacks when it came to getting people to identify with a cause that seemed far distant and barely comprehensible. As the Resident Commissioner of the Bechuanaland Protectorate ruefully noted whilst on a recruiting tour of the Okavango Delta in 1940, 'people here don't know what government is or why anyone is fighting at all'.[23]

In mobilizing colonial populations for war, British officials worked closely, with the indigenous political elites and their chains of command, from emirs, princes and chiefs to sub-chiefs, native tribunal clerks and village headmen. Officially at least, the Empire went to war because it was called to do so by an imperial cause in the name of good against evil, with the imperial monarchy – to which all subjects of the Empire owed allegiance – as its focal point. In some parts of the Empire elements of specific communities, like Jews in Palestine and Muslims in India, were also supportive of the war effort for their own political reasons. In Malaya the Chinese community had good reason to side with the British against the Japanese; educated West Africans hoped that loyalty during the war would lead to political advances from which they would profit; and the kings of Basutoland and Swaziland calculated that sending men to war would remove the threat of their territories being transferred from British to South African rule.

The British Empire also had to be mobilized at the ideological level, a new departure for a colonial system that had never before had the same pressing need to *talk* to its subjects to elicit their support and sustain their morale. In one of many examples of the colonial world reflecting developments in Britain, government information offices were created, and radio, newspapers and posters were used to inform, educate and encourage the public. A great deal of effort in Whitehall and colonial administrations overseas went into getting across the right messages to colonial subjects as well as to allies and enemies.[24] War mobilization was followed closely by a perceived need to begin shaping the post-war colonial world as a motive for this war-time glut of official information and propaganda indulgence. Outfits like the Ministry of Information's Empire Division and Empire Informa-tion Service were to the fore in this operation. There were many other official and semi-official organizations doing the same thing, including the BBC's Empire Service, the British Overseas Wireless Service and regional newspapers and radio stations throughout the Empire. BBC and government broadcasts were increas-ingly important in war-time Africa. The general newsreel *British News* was sent to twenty-eight colonies each week and the Colonial Film Unit made fortnightly African news films. (Typical titles were *Barbados Day in Portsmouth, These are London Firemen, English and African Life, Our Indian Soldiers* and *This is an Anti-Aircraft Gun*. 140,000 Africans saw the unit's films each week.) In Britain, with a host of dwellings and facilities developed for the thousands of imperial subjects who lived or temporarily resided in Britain, efforts were also made. The Colonial Office, for example, financed a Moslem centre in Cardiff, a mosque in East London and a seamen's hostel in North Shields for West Indians and Africans.

The Empire was brought to war by utilizing the global networks of institutions and personnel, built up in some cases over centuries, from the officials in White-hall, to the young district commissioners and wily chiefs out in the colonies.[25] Harold Macmillan's task when he joined the Colonial Office was 'the mobilization of all the potential resources of the Colonial Empire, both of men and of mate-rials, for the purposes of war'.[26] This required an immense amount of work, and in 1944 the Colonial Office received 81,000 telegrams, a leap from the 15,500 in 1937. This was handled with traditional Whitehall *sangfroid*.[27] London was a unique global capital, home to the offices of state that ran the Empire and to imperial representatives from around the world in the form of High Commis-sioners, visiting chiefs and itinerant Dominions Prime Ministers.[28] The city was also home to many Allied governments that had lost their lands to the conquering Nazis. Should Britain also fall, there were plans for the evacuation of the British government and the Royal Family, the former to India and the latter to Canada. The Royal Navy planned to continue the fight from Halifax. Overseas, Whitehall established regional organizations for the coordination of the war effort, such as the Middle East Supply Centre, opened a satellite organization in Washington, and sent Cabinet Ministers to reside in key imperial cities, such as Accra, Cairo and Singapore.

If the enemies of the British Empire and Commonwealth were counting on the 'subject races' rising up in great numbers, they were to be sorely disappointed. Though unbridled loyalty was not the order of the day, though the British media was shocked at the indifference displayed by the people of Malaya to Britain's military fate in the region, and though many Britons were saddened by the opposition of Indian political leaders to the war effort, British rule had at least created enough goodwill, political alliances and simple acquiescence to ensure that the Empire was a use rather than a hindrance to the war effort and that rebellion was the exception not the norm. Churchill's rhetoric positioned the Empire unequivocally behind the cause of democracy and freedom, and there was an extraordinary general acceptance and even enthusiasm for the war effort across the Empire. 'The nature of British imperialism, with its peace-time free press, civil rights, habeas corpus, the cultivation of elites, and promises – however vague – of ultimate self-government, paid enormous dividends during the war.'[29] In June 1944 the Colonial Secretary, Oliver Stanley, paid tribute in the House of Commons to the 'profound loyalty' of the Solomon Islanders, who had displayed 'not just a mere passive loyalty, not merely a failure to betray, but active help in extremely dangerous operations'.[30] Some colonial subjects identified with the British cause in the hope of reward, though a sense of loyalty was alive and kicking throughout the British imperial world. The 'colonial nationalist' was a remote and subterranean figure in the war period in most parts of the Empire. It was not difficult for colonial leaders in the colonies to identify with the British stand against the dictators, and to encourage their people to support the war effort, even if they did not relish the prospect of continued British overlordship. Most such leaders did not necessarily seek British withdrawal from their territories as a reward for war-time support, but they certainly desired a larger slice of the political cake after the war.

Until the 1960s 'imperial defence' was an acknowledged term used as shorthand for the global military system, founded upon seapower, which provided for the security of Britain and the Empire. The system of imperial defence also guaranteed the freedom of the seas, a crucial element of the world order that Britain had created during the nineteenth century and that it had fought to defend in the First World War. The doctrine of imperial defence defined Britain's strategic world view, decided the way in which Britain approached the Second World War, and shaped the armed forces that it wielded. Imperial defence had for long been a recognized subject of political and public debate in Britain, a fact that should not be obscured by the attention lavished in the 1930s on the specific problem of how to defend Britain against Germany.

Imperial defence was based upon naval supremacy and the use of the British and Indian armies. This was just as much the case in 1939 as it had been in 1839. Many of the facts that had informed the theory of imperial defence had, however, changed over the course of the century, though in 1939 they were either insufficiently grasped or not easily adapted to. For example, the Royal Navy still classed battleships as the major units defining naval power and had done little to develop the use of aircraft carriers and the skills of naval aviation. Though awareness of the bomber's fatal power over land targets was widespread by 1939 ('the bomber will always get through', as Stanley Baldwin phrased it in 1932), at sea the spell of the battleship remained unbroken and British carrier aircraft were antiquated and few in number.

Pax Britannica had been based upon a virtual monopoly of naval might. Although in 1939 the Royal Navy was still the largest navy, it was certainly no longer the only one of any size, so naval hegemony – and with it the fundamentals of the classic formulation of imperial defence based on seapower – had vanished. Similarly the old precept that control of the North Sea and the English Channel secured global naval hegemony no longer held true, because nations beyond Europe now had sizeable navies. Non-European powers, notably Japan and America, had built up first-class navies, and Italy sat athwart a key imperial communication and trade route with a very respectable modern fleet. In the 1930s the grave threat to Britain in Europe and the Mediterranean posed by the dictators meant that the Far East could not be adequately reinforced. Therefore the Singapore strategy was fatally compromised. A fortress harbour without warships to operate from it was no real deterrent to the Japanese.

At the local level every colonial government was obliged to think about its role in a war and to plan for it. Every colony had a defence scheme, submitted to the Overseas Defence Committee in London, and was expected to maintain a local defence force and plan for air raid precautions and scorched earth denial schemes, should war ever come to the particular part of the world in which the colony was located. In July 1938 a memorandum dealing with the role of the Colonial Empire in imperial defence was circulated, dealing with subjects such as food supply in wartime, the control of shipping and wireless transmissions, civil defence measures in Malaya, defence policy in the Somaliland Protectorate, denial to the enemy of the oilfields of Sarawak and Brunei, and internal security in Tanganyika (where a sizeable German community existed). Despite such admirable preparations for war, defence schemes were no substitute for imperial military hardware capable of preventing the enemy from attacking in the first place, or of clearing them out later on, as many colonies were to find to their cost.

In 1939 Britain possessed a small professional army and had the use of the Indian Army. It had the world's largest navy, and an air force growing in strength in order to meet the threat of the Luftwaffe. The armed forces of the Dominions were small and firmly attached to British methods, equipment and strategic thinking; they were in practice still very much part of a British imperial military structure. Other than providing a measure of home defence, the armed forces of the Dominions were trained for deployment in support of imperial causes in places such as the Middle East. The main burden of defending the British Isles and every imperial territory belonged to the Senior Service, at least according to the doctrine of imperial defence current in 1939. It was an imperial navy like no other, maintaining fleets and squadrons all over the globe, along with all necessary port installations, shore bases, support units and ancillary vessels, from destroyer and submarine depot ships to boom-laying vessels and survey ships. The ships of the Royal Navy – river gunboats chugging up the inland waterways of China, vintage cruisers in the Indian Ocean, battleships repairing at Alexandria, submarines laying mines off the coast of Malaya, corvettes riding like corks atop mountainous swells on Atlantic convoy duty or ancient monitors skulking in Malta's Grand Harbour – bore names that, among other things, betrayed the navy's global heritage and association with Empire. There were 'Tribal' class destroyers (such as HMS *Afridi, Ashanti* and *Hakka*), 'Colony' class cruisers (such as HMS *Mauritius, Nigeria, Trinidad* and *Uganda*), and 'Ruler' class escort carriers (such as HMS *Khedive, Nabob, Rajah* and *Shah*). Many colonies and cities had ships named for them – HMS *Cairo, Calcutta, Cape Town, Colombo, Jamaica, Kandahar, Khartoum, Uganda* and dozens more providing a touch of colour alongside the *Cornwalls, Devonshires* and *Sheffields* of the fleet. Australian ships bore the names of the Dominion's cities, such as HMAS *Adelaide, Ballarat, Bendigo, Hobart, Perth* and *Sydney*.

The Royal Navy started the war with fifteen battleships and battlecruisers, six carriers, fifty-eight cruisers, one hundred destroyers, one hundred smaller escort vessels and thirty-eight submarines. By May 1945, and despite having lost 451 warships of all categories, the Royal Navy stood at fifteen battleships and battle-cruisers (five having been lost during the war, but five having been launched), seven fleet carriers, four light fleet carriers, forty-one escort carriers, sixty-two cruisers, 131 submarines, 846 destroyers, frigates and sloops (of 140 British destroyers lost during the war, forty-six had been lost in the Mediterranean), 729 minesweepers, over a thousand landing craft and minor war vessels, forty Royal Naval Air Stations supporting sixty-nine squadrons, and 150 self-accounting shore bases.

Based on ports in England and Scotland, the Home Fleet and Western Approaches Command (created in February 1941 to conduct the U-boat war with headquarters in Liverpool) were responsible for the defence of Britain and the Atlantic convoy routes.[31] They were also responsible for hunting the German commerce raiders, and the mighty battleships and battlecruisers that, if they evaded the watch of the navy and the RAF and escaped from their European ports, could wreak havoc with the convoys. Though with a far inferior surface fleet, the Germans used warships like the *Admiral Hipper* and *Graf Spee*, and disguised merchant raiders like *Atlantis* and *Thor*, to great effect. The giant battle-ship *Tirpitz*, sister of the *Bismarck*, could pin down considerable British forces just by sitting in her Norwegian fjord, simply because of the destruction she could bring to the Atlantic convoys if she were to cut loose (though her crew did not for a moment consider this an appropriate war role for their mighty weapon). In 1941 there were nearly 400 Royal Navy warships of all classes in the Atlantic. Over the course of the war the Allies lost 3000 merchant ships and 175 warships in this theatre. One other fleet operated in the theatre, the Reserve Fleet, brought rapidly to a full state of mobilization by its Commander-in-Chief, Admiral Sir Max Horton, as soon as war was declared. At the outbreak 12,000 reservists were called up and 133 Reserve Fleet warships were commissioned and provisioned.

The Mediterranean Fleet was based at Alexandria, following its removal from Malta during the Abyssinian crisis of 1935–36. The task of this fleet, second only in strength to the Home Fleet, was to protect the vital Suez Canal artery of Empire, and to keep the lid on the Italian fleet. A second large naval squadron, Force H, sent to the Mediterranean as a result of the fall of France and the loss of the French squadron's support, was based on Gibraltar. The African coast from West Africa to the Cape was important for shipping bound between East and West, and facilities were developed in the region, particularly at Freetown, for convoy assembly and escort. This region was the responsibility of South Atlantic Command. The Indian Ocean was patrolled by the Eastern Fleet, based on Ceylon and Kenya, with a remit stretching from the Red Sea to the wastes of the Southern Ocean, and west to east from the Swahili coast to the Bay of Bengal and the Malacca and Sunda Straits. In the Far East, British naval forces were negligible from the fall of Singapore until the end of 1944, when a powerful new force, the British Pacific Fleet, sailed for its Australian bases and its forward base at Manus.

After the First World War the British Army had demobilized rapidly and resumed its traditional imperial defence roles, so that by the 1930s the army was preparing for a war in defence of India, the navy was preparing for a war with Japan and the air force was preparing for a war against Germany. It was an army not primarily designed for a major European war, but for imperial defence and for helping to counter the Russian threat to India (where about a third of its strength was regularly stationed until the eve of the Second World War). It lagged behind the German army in departments other than size; its stock of tanks, for example, as well as its tank tactics, being notably inferior. In name alone, the Matilda was unlikely to be a match for the Tiger. Of course, this was in some ways unsurprising; unlike the Wehrmacht, the British Army had not been preparing for a war of European conquest. On the outbreak of war the Sherwood Foresters and their cavalry chargers embarked for Palestine. It might have been the Boer War. The Indian Army of about 200,000 men only began serious modernization in the 1930s, and in 1937 over 50,000 men were still committed to the North-West Frontier. Its role was Indian defence and the provision of troops for the Middle East and South-East Asia in the event of war. During the war the Indian Army grew to over two and a half million men. The 5th Indian Division fought the Italians in the Sudan, the Germans in Libya, the Iraqi army in Iraq and the Japanese in Burma, before occupying Malaya and disarming the Japanese garrison on Java. Australian and New Zealand troops served in the Pacific and the Middle East. South Africans fought in the Middle East and East Africa. Over the course of the war Britain and its Empire and Commonwealth mobilized 103 divisions or their equivalent. Only 47.6 per cent of them were raised in Britain. The Empire and Commonwealth also provided 39 per cent of the RAF's aircrew.[32]

During the war, army commands across the Empire coordinated the fighting and the logistics needed to sustain it on land. This required labour and supplies from the surrounding areas, as well as from Britain, America and elsewhere in the Empire, and the cooperation of civil authorities in the areas in which the army operated. The largest army commands were India Command and Middle East Command (MEC), with headquarters in Delhi and Cairo. There were other commands, such as East Africa Command, Far East Command, Persia and Iraq Command and South East Asia Command. Established in 1939, MEC was an overarching structure uniting the commands in Egypt, Palestine, Jordan and the Sudan. It was also responsible for Malta and Cyprus. It was then extended to cover forces in British East Africa and Somaliland, and any that might serve in Aden and the Persian Gulf, Iraq, Turkey and the Balkans. General Sir Archibald Wavell had the mixed blessing of serving in high command in the early stages of the war, when Britain was very much on the back foot, and of winning a number of smaller campaigns but generally losing the bigger ones. Wavell was Commander-in-Chief Middle East and then Commander-in-Chief India from mid-1941, briefly also taking on responsibility for South-East Asia and the East Indies as Commander-in-Chief American-British-Dutch-Australian Command (ABDA) as the region reeled from the first Japanese strikes. On leaving office as Commander-in-Chief India to become Viceroy of India in 1943, this truly imperial soldier recalled that:

> In just under four years ... I have directed some fourteen campaigns in the Western desert of North Africa, in British Somaliland, in Eritrea, in Italian Somaliland, in Abyssinia, in Greece, in Crete, in Iraq, in Syria, in Iran, in Malaya, in the Dutch East Indies, in Burma [and] in Arakan.[33]

The most visible contribution of the Empire to the air war was the participation of imperial pilots, particularly in the Battle of Britain. Many of 'the few' who helped preserve British independence in 1940 were from the Empire. Of the 2917 airmen who flew in Fighter Command between 10 July and the end of October 1940 there were 2334 Britons, 145 Poles, 126 New Zealanders, 98 Canadians, 88 Czechoslovaks, 33 Australians, 29 Belgians, 25 South Africans, 13 French, 11 American, 10 Irish, three Rhodesian and one each from Jamaica and Newfoundland.[34] It was very common for a Fighter Command squadron to be peppered with men from the Empire and Commonwealth and elsewhere. No. 1 Squadron, for example, was made up of Canadians, Americans, Australians, New Zealanders and Irishmen, as well as Britons, when it fought in France before Dunkirk. In the summer of 1944 the RAF had 487 squadrons, one hundred of them from the Dominions. Canadian bombers dropped one-eighth of Bomber Command's payload, and Canadian fighter pilots served in units such as No. 406 (Canadian)

Night Fighter Squadron. Overall, Canada provided one quarter of the RAF's pilots. In total, forty-seven Royal Canadian Air Force squadrons, twenty-three Royal Australian Air Force (RAAF) squadrons and twenty-eight South African Air Force squadrons served with the RAF.

In Britain imperial pilots learned their trade at the Empire Central Flying School at Hullavington in Wiltshire. One of the Empire and Commonwealth's major contributions to the war in the air was the British Empire Air Training Scheme (BEATS). This remarkable example of the kind of imperial outsourcing common during the war trained pilots and aircrew at specially-opened airbases in Canada, Australia, New Zealand, South Africa and Southern Rhodesia. All together the scheme produced nearly 170,000 personnel, of whom over 75,000 were pilots (Canada 116,417, Australia 23,262, New Zealand 3891, South Africa 16,857, Southern Rhodesia 8235). By the beginning of 1943 37 per cent of all Bomber Command pilots were from the Commonwealth, including an entire Canadian Air Group. By 1945 this figure had reached 46 per cent.

The RAF had been given priority in the rush to rearm in the 1930s, in both the provision of fighter aircraft and the development and installation of early-warning technology. Whilst adequate for contesting the issue with the enemy in the skies above Britain, however, the RAF was poorly represented given the scale of enemy activity and the quality of enemy aircraft it was soon to encounter around the world. There were RAF bases in Iraq, Egypt, Aden, India, Palestine, Singapore and elsewhere, but early in the war the squadrons there consisted of largely obsolete aircraft. In the inter-war period, the RAF had been seen in some quarters as a cheap way to police parts of the Empire, saving on the cost of army garrisons, and it was the senior service in places like Iraq and Aden and the surrounding regions. During the war, however, the demands of British home defence meant that there were precious few modern aircraft to go around, and that those that were available went mostly to build up the Western Desert Air Force, or to allies such as Greece, Romania, Russia and Turkey. The needs of the Dominion air forces were lower down the order. In some theatres obsolete aircraft were good enough to do the job – for example, RAF and South African Air Force aircraft were effective against the Italians in the East African campaign, against the Iraqi air force and against Vichy forces in Madagascar – but in others they were entirely inadequate, and the lack of preparation and of sufficient numbers of modern fighters and bombers was to cost dear in South-East Asia and the Dutch East Indies.

Britain's air forces were organized for home defence, on the one hand, and imperial defence and policing, on the other. In September 1939 the RAF's front-line strength stood at 1476 aircraft stationed at home and 435 stationed overseas. In that month, overseas distribution comprised RAF Middle East (formed around a group in Egypt and a wing in the Sudan), a squadron forming RAF Palestine and Transjordan, a squadron with British Forces Iraq, three squadrons with British Forces Aden, a squadron forming RAF Mediterranean on Malta, six squadrons and a squadron of the Indian Air Force forming Air Forces India, and nine squadrons forming RAF Far East.[35]

Operations behind enemy lines, conducted throughout the world by British organizations such as Special Operations Executive, the Chindits, the SAS, Military Intelligence 9 (MI9) – responsible for aiding Allied servicemen escape from enemy capture – and the Secret Intelligence Service (MI6), often used colonial territories as bases.[36] This was an important aspect of the Empire's provision of infrastructure during the war. Imperial territories provided Britain with a network of intelligence-gathering facilities to aid the work of the Government Code and Cipher School at Bletchley Park. Middle East Combined Bureau, for example, based at the former Flora and Fauna Museum at Heliopolis near Cairo, was connected directly to Hut Three at Bletchley. Japanese military and diplomatic codes were intercepted and broken in Australia, Bermuda, Egypt, Hong Kong, India, Malta, Mauritius, Palestine and Singapore.[37] The art of 'ungentlemanly warfare' in which SOE specialized was first taught by Britons who had developed such skills whilst policing the International Settlement in Shanghai, an area of informal British influence and control. SOE bases and training schools existed in Australia, Canada, Ceylon, Egypt, the Gold Coast, India, Malaya, South Africa and elsewhere.[38]

In 1945, there were street parties, bunting, speeches, march-pasts and dancing in the public squares throughout the Empire and Commonwealth, as there was in Britain. The Empire emerged from six years of conflict intact, all conquered territories regained and all enemies vanquished. Imperial Britain looked forward to a post-war world in which it would continue to shape world affairs, notwithstanding the rise of the two superpowers. But the moment of imperial triumph also marked a high-point of imperial exhaustion. Britain was never able to recover sufficiently from the war in order to play the role of imperial ringmaster or to withstand the ravages of nationalism, global economic shifts, new domestic demands, and the ideological struggles of the Cold War era. But in 1945 the end of Empire and the contraction of Britain were not on the agenda. Victory had been won, and the people of the British Empire and Commonwealth, all five hundred million of them, had played a central part in achieving it.

4

The Home Front

On 23 December 1941 eighty Japanese bombers and thirty fighters dropped the first bombs on Rangoon, the capital of Burma. They fell on women in the market places, cheroots between painted lips, behind their stalls of dried fish and betel nuts; upon worshippers on the marble way about the great Shwe Dagôn pagoda; upon coolies sweating beneath their burdens on the quays and in the Strand Road; upon British and Chinese merchants in their clubs or gracious bungalows – in a word upon people unprepared for war and in whom curiosity had ousted fear. It cost them dear. About 2000 were killed that day by fragmentation bombs. Forty-eight hours went by and then, as the Christian community was celebrating Christmas, the bombers came again in like strength and killed 5000 more.[1] In colonial cities ill-equipped with the kind of organizational infrastructure and air raid shelters common in British cities, inhabited by people with less knowledge about what to do during an air raid, and completely unprepared for there to be any enemy bombing in the first place, the results of enemy action could be devastating. Burma's second city, Mandalay, was similarly attacked by Japanese bombers as the colony was about to fall to the enemy. An air assault on 3 April 1942 was particularly devastating, as the city was defenceless and its fire-fighting apparatus had been lost in earlier bombing, so in a few hours three-fifths of the houses had been wiped out by high explosive bombs or fire and thousands of civilians had been killed.

The effects of the Second World War on the home front are well known. War brought a proliferation of different service uniforms to the streets, bars and clubs, rationing, blackouts, barrage balloons and anti-aircraft guns; the latter good for morale and of some use against enemy bombers and fighters. More useful, though as yet unproven, were radar installations and the protection afforded by modern aircraft like the Hurricane. To hinder enemy bombers, as well as the blackout, civilians were encouraged to join Air Raid Precaution (ARP) and other civil defence organizations. Society became uniformed – there were more foreign military personnel about than in peacetime, and civilians were encouraged to enrol in the Home Guard or to join the armed forces for local service and for service overseas. The production of goods and raw materials for export, and food to feed the home population, required the large-scale mobilization of the civilian population, as did construction of military facilities as enlarged garrisons and naval and air forces proliferated. The invasion of military personnel fuelled the demand for new barracks, bases and recreational facilities, and caused countless social flurries as overseas servicemen interacted with the home population. This build up of armed force was for home defence and because of the country's role as a springboard for Allied operations against neighbouring enemy territories. Enemy prisoners of war were accommodated in isolated camps and put to work. Ports were full of warships and merchant vessels, gathering for convoys or for naval operations to hunt enemy vessels and protect the convoys on which the island depended. Many families were affected as fathers, sons and brothers departed for distant war fronts. With more men in the forces, new opportunities were created for women in the workplace. Less visible than the civilian war work and the presence of the regular armed forces were the secret organizations born of the war, such as SOE and the intelligence-gathering installations associated with Bletchley Park. Fund-raising activities were good for morale and civilian focus, and the government was always exhorting people to buy war bonds and to 'dig for victory', as food was short and rationing stringent. This, of course, led to a thriving black market that the government struggled to control. Given the prospect of enemy bombing, civilians were evacuated from threatened areas. In terms of the general political mood, people knuckled down to the tasks of war and were resolved to endure its hardships, but many expected political change once it was over.

Although this might well be a familiar vignette of war-time Britain, it is in fact a description of war-time Ceylon. It could also stand as a general description of the scores of countries that, as British colonies or dependencies, had a war experience that paralleled that of Britain in many striking ways. The home front is a well-known aspect of the British war experience – almost a cultural presence – conjuring a host of images made familiar by television and radio documentaries, books and films. What is less well known is the extent to which the home front in Aden, Bengal, Cyprus or Palestine was similarly affected by the reach of a global conflict. Here, too, colourful posters adorned public walls, exhorting civilians to avoid gossip, to join the women's auxiliary forces or, in East Africa and elsewhere, to join the army and help 'Smash the Japs'. Here too rationing, bombing, invasion scares, black markets and the pulse of war were features of daily life.

The Second World War sent shock waves pulsing from imperial power centres throughout the Empire. On the home fronts of Empire no one was left untouched, be it by the call of the fife and drum, the trauma of invasion or bombing, the propaganda of colonial governments or the economic hardships of war. Events in one part of the world affected events in another over long distances, as if connected by a current. For example, the need of Middle East Command for military labour in 1941, as Rommel pressed towards Cairo, led directly to the recruitment of nearly 40,000 men from Bechuanaland, Basutoland and Swaziland. Later, the trying conditions encountered by Allied soldiers in Italy's Apennine mountains led to the recruitment of Basotho muleteers. All over the world improbable connections between requirements and resources were being forged by the demands of war, facilitated by the existence of a web of imperial networks.

Though the territories of the British Empire had been involved in world wars before, the Second World War was to demand a greater mobilization than ever, touching more lives than any previous conflict. Simple military measures, which in earlier days would have been the sole criterion of preparedness for war, had ceased to be sufficient. Now, on top of supplying labour for civilian and military war work, colonial governments had to take measures for passive air defence and general civil defence; for the control of the procurement, distribution and rationing of food and other essential commodities; for information dissemination through the media; for postal, cinema and publications censorship and propaganda; for internal security; for the accommodation of refugees and prisoners of war; and for the full development of all economic resources and the infrastructure needed to support its deployment. The rapid deterioration in the general supply situation had become noticeable in many colonies by 1941 and led to control and regulation strategies, including the extension of price controls to a wide range of commodities, rationing and bulk purchasing by government. Many parts of the Empire were called upon to produce war materials or to develop military facilities, and all were promised funds for post-war reconstruction and development. This led to significant changes in imperial financial arrangements, creating a system of sterling balances, credits set up in London to pay for imperial defence expenditure and the supply of strategic goods. Censorship was a new role for colonial governments, as was propaganda and information management and the gathering of all sorts of social and economic data. To begin with, all of this was done with a much reduced staff, as many colonial civil servants left to join the armed forces, though over the course of the war government bureaucracy and intrusions into the lives of its subjects increased massively. The demands of total war meant that even the colonial home front had to become more regimented and 'plugged in' to a global war effort and its multifarious economic, political and social currents. As in Britain, the tasks facing colonial governments because of the disruptions of war and its production demands led to an increase in the size of the state's apparatus, and an involvement in people's daily lives that was unprecedented. The colonies became firmly attached to metropolitan demands, and to the global organizational structures of London-based departments like the Ministry of Supply, the Ministry of War Transport (a May 1941 amalgamation of the Ministries of Transport and Shipping) and the Ministry of Food.

Total war affected all levels of social, economic and political life on the home front. The loss of imports caused by U-boat depredations and the shortage of merchant shipping led to rationing. This in turn contributed to inflation, profiteering and a thriving black market. Familiar foods became scarce or disappeared entirely, and ingenuity was required in preparing meals from unfamiliar food substitutes: in Mauritius, for example, Nutrition Demonstration Units toured the villages teaching Indians how to make bread, now that their staple foodstuffs had been cut off. This was because supplies of major imports, including Burmese rice, Madagascan meat and edible oils from the Agalega Islands, had been severed by enemy occupation in South-East Asia, Royal Navy blockade of Vichy Madagascar and a general lack of shipping. In parts of Africa, less popular crops like cassava and sweet potatoes had to stand in the place of more favoured staples like maize, and in many parts of the Empire wheat replaced rice.

The borderless privations of war's economic dislocations threatened to kill some colonial industries because their traditional markets were lost, and because shipping was not readily available because of restrictions and losses caused by enemy submarines and surface raiders. Thus bulk purchasing was embarked upon by the British government, at first to save industries that were faced with ruin by the dislocation of peace-time trade relations. This was, for example, the case for Gold Coast cocoa, West Indian sugar, Jamaican bananas and Palestinian citrus fruit. As the war progressed, however, such produce could find a ready market because almost any product was in demand in order to feed the insatiable appetite of full global mobilization. The war transformed the world economy from one of excess commodity supply to one of raw material shortage, and transformed the role of government in mediating the market and organizing production. East African cattle and grain, for example, were needed to feed the massive imperial armed forces based in the Middle East (with a ration strength of about a million by 1941). Australia went into resource deficit as it bore the brunt of the demands of American forces stationed in the region, to the extent that the government had to release men from the armed forces to serve in agriculture, as well as recruiting a Women's Land Army. Nigerian tin and Ceylonese rubber was needed to replace the output of Malaya following its conquest by the Japanese. Cypriot silk was needed for parachutes.

Many parts of the British Empire endured enemy bombing, and numerous territories were lost to enemy invasion and occupation. This represented a profound rupture in the fabric of Empire, and a failure on Britain's part to perform one of its fundamental tasks in the colonies; defence against external aggression. The threat of invasion was real for territories such as Malaya, Borneo, Hong Kong and Somaliland. For nearly two years Malta was a prime candidate for enemy invasion. If his strategic senses had served him better, Mussolini would have taken this strategic outcrop early in the war and saved Axis forces in the Western Desert enormous trouble in the battle for supply upon which the outcome in North Africa ultimately depended. Hitler might well have ordered a paratroop invasion of the island, had not the invasion of Crete proved so costly to his airborne forces. Aden, Cairo, Calcutta, Colombo, Darwin, George Town (Penang), Gibraltar, Haifa, Hong Kong, Kuala Lumpur, Malta, Mandalay, Nauru, Port Blair (Andaman Islands), Rangoon, Singapore, Townsville, Trincomalee and Vizagapatam (India) were all bombed by aircraft or shelled by enemy warships.

In Britain's lost Eastern Empire invasion led to years of harsh occupation by Japan. This, in turn, led both to the growth of significant guerrilla movements aimed at ejecting the occupiers, and to military and civil movements intended to support a nationalist cause in alliance with Japan. To the fore in such movements were nationalist leaders like Subhas Chandra Bose and Aung San. Occupation also meant that colonies remained active war theatres, due initially to behind-enemy-lines resistance, and then because of Allied bombing or reinvasion. Many resistance movements were assisted by British special forces, including Orde Wingate's Gideon Force in Abyssinia and his Chindits in Burma. Enemy occupation could lead to atrocities, and places like Singapore and the Andaman and Nicobar Islands in the Bay of Bengal were the scene of Japanese brutality in keeping with their vile record in China.

All territories of the Empire and Commonwealth were called upon to provide men for imperial fighting formations. The initial demand placed upon colonial manpower, however, and one that grew throughout the war, even when the military entered the labour market, was for non-military labour on the home front. This might take the form of a civil labour corps to assist in defensive preparations, such as the construction of airfields or improvement of port facilities, or to act as a rapid response unit in sectors of the economy requiring an injection of manpower, or for strike-breaking. But the main demand for labour on the home front was for agricultural and raw material sectors – plantations, farms, factories and mines. The pressing need was to produce more food, for domestic consumption and for export, and to increase the production of other commodities needed for the war effort. Thus chiefs used their traditional powers in Bechuanaland to get people – male and female – to contribute agricultural labour to the warlands scheme. This aimed to fill communal granaries with grain for use in times of shortage, thereby reducing the Protectorate's dependence upon imports from South Africa and Southern Rhodesia. Meanwhile, thousands of Bechuanaland's men were in the Middle East with the British Army, and thousands more were working in the mines of South Africa. In Tasmania men and women worked in war-related industries producing boats, mortar shells and sophisticated optical equipment, and also tilled the soil in order to feed the island – as well as to provide the ingredients for American and Indian Army ration packs. Whilst doing this, over 12 per cent of Tasmania's population of 247,000 served in the armed forces.

Most of this home front labour was voluntary, or was conscripted through traditional channels. In a few colonies, however, officially-sanctioned conscription was called for, though the Colonial Office required convincing evidence from the colonial government concerned before it would endorse the required legislation. Civil conscription affected Nigeria (100,000 people for tin mining on the Jos plateau), Northern Rhodesia (to provide wheat for local consumption), Southern Rhodesia (to work on European farms), Tanganyika (80,000 to work on the sisal plantations) and Kenya (for European farms). In the case of Tanganyika the British government was particularly wary of accusations of exploitation, but ultimately defended itself on the grounds of absolute necessity. As Harold Macmillan put it, every ton of food that was shipped from East Africa to the imperial forces in the Middle East saved a long haul around the Cape from Liverpool. Use was also made of prisoner-of-war labour, given the vast dispersal of captured enemy soldiers throughout the British Empire and Commonwealth.[2] Germans and Italians (the latter in particular) were sent to camps in Australia, Britain, Canada, Ceylon, Egypt, India, Kenya, Libya, South Africa and Uganda. In the Middle East local Arab labour was used in the Western Desert, and Indian labourers also went to the Middle East, alongside the tens of thousands of military labourers serving in the British Army's Royal Pioneer Corps and other service branches. Over 15,000 colonial subjects served at sea with the Merchant Navy, and about 5000 of the 30,000 merchant seamen who lost their lives during the war came from imperial territories. Particularly to the fore at sea were men recruited in eastern India and China, with West Africa also being strongly represented. Five hundred woodmen from British Honduras were recruited to work in the Scottish Highlands, one of the more bizarre permutations of the operation of the imperial labour market, and thousands of West Indians came to work in British industry, along with thousands more who made the sea voyage in order to join the RAF.

Labour was also required on an unprecedented scale for military work within many colonies. The home front in many parts of the Empire had to provide the labour that would enable the colony in question to become a base for Allied operations against the enemy, and war brought extensive building for war purposes throughout the colonies. This could lead to significant alterations in both the natural environment and the built landscape, as runways, railways, roads and all sorts of military buildings occupied virgin forest, agricultural lands or brown sites cleared for the purpose in urban areas; it also closed off behind barbed-wire areas of jungle, coast line or farm land previously used by the inhabitants.

Internationally, the Colonial Office embarked upon a subtle campaign to woo American opinion to a more favourable view of the British Empire.[3] In order to do this, it had to overcome the general ignorance of Americans on the subject and attempt to wean them from the idea that the colonial relationship was like that between a landlord and his peasant-worked private estate. The need to modernize colonial rule and its image helped tilt the balance in favour of colonial self-government becoming the generally accepted principle of British rule in the colonies. Men like Winston Churchill and Colonel Oliver Stanley, Colonial Secretary from November 1942 until the end of the war, were angered by the new era of external interference and international accountability that was being ushered in by the conditions of war. This was particularly true in the light of growing American imperialism and the sense that America, despite fine sentiments, was primarily interested in displacing Britain from imperial markets as opposed to furthering the cause of imperial freedom, whatever that might actually mean. Britons the world over found it particularly hard to stomach America's apparently effortless ability to remove the mote from its brother's eye whilst remaining blissfully unaware of the beam in its own, baulking particularly at American homilies on inter-racial relations in the imperial military structure when the racial divide in the American military was all too obvious to see.

In a profound reversal of historical flows, Britain ceased to be the Empire's creditor and became its debtor. The massive Indian war effort was undertaken on the understanding that Britain would pay for the use of the Indian Army beyond the subcontinent. Though at the outbreak of the war Britain froze all colonial and Indian sterling reserves held in London by declaring them non-convertible, India benefited financially from the war and the financial tables were dramatically turned. In 1939 India had owed Britain £350 million, but by 1945 Britain owed India £1200 million. Britain's debt to the Colonial Empire rose from £150 million to £454 million during the course of the war.

All colonies devoted financial reserves to Britain, in the form of interest-free loans or outright gifts, and through fund-raising events and war funds. Governments donated annual surpluses to the war effort, legislative assemblies voted interest-free loans, communities like the Mauritian sugar producers set voluntary profit taxes as a contribution to the war effort, and wealthy individuals and leaders like the Rajah of Sarawak sent money to swell the coffers in London ($2.5m on the Rajah's part by November 1941, the month before his domains were lost to the Japanese). Gymkhanas were held in Bechuanaland to raise funds for the Royal Navy's 'Sponsor-a-Destroyer' week, and many colonial charities raised money in support of war-related funds. Ever-popular was the 'Spitfire Fund', and schoolchildren in Mauritius were responsible for providing the first mobile canteen on the streets of London during the Blitz. 'Win the War' rallies were held in towns in Tasmania, and that distant Australian state's people contributed to numerous funds like the 'King George's Fund for Sailors' and the 'Relief for Air Raid Victims in Britain Fund'. Imperial charities like the Red Cross had branches in the colonies that passed the cap around diligently throughout the war, raising funds and packing boxes of medical and other supplies for imperial servicemen in prisoner-of-war camps around the world. Also easing the plight of the hundreds of thousands of people affected by enemy capture, be they the men and women themselves or their relatives, was an elaborate global postal system centred on the Postal Censorship Office in London.

The era of the balanced budget and financial autonomy for colonial governments ended with the war, as the metropole developed new ways of governing and using the Empire, and took full control of the colonies to serve the ends of British national economic autonomy in the harsh years of war and then of reconstruction. The war witnessed the inauguration of a remarkably centralized imperial economic system based on the pooling of sterling resources in London and their control by the British government. Britain was able to spend with no limit within the sterling area during the war, without exporting goods in compensation, and the Crown Colonies lent Britain the whole of their currency reserves.

In 1941 the Colonial Secretary, Lord Moyne, sent a circular to all colonial Governors urging the accumulation of sterling balances for future use and suggesting that they might make interest-free loans to the British government (to be returned after the war as development funds). Given the demands of war production, Britain was unable to provide all of the exports that the Empire traditionally absorbed. It was feared that as a result colonies would look to the dollar area and purchase goods in dollars or with gold. This would deplete the Empire's reserves and further threaten the capacity of sterling to remain an international currency. The colonies were therefore asked to limit import demands in order to conserve the sterling area's hard currency and ease Britain's balance of payments.[4]

As the prospect of war loomed in the late 1930s, regulations and guidelines on a range of matters were sent to Governors throughout the Empire. There were general guidelines for the control of imports into the colonies to save shipping and materials, for the encouragement of colonial exports to earn foreign exchange, for the control of exports to ensure that they did not reach the enemy, and for the maintenance of supplies within the Empire. On the outbreak of war each colony was issued with orders for the control of imports, currency exchange and shipping. Rationing and price controls were widely introduced, and bodies like the West African Control Board were set up for the controlled purchase and export of colonial products. Restrictions on trading with the enemy were enacted.

Colonies needed to build up food reserves, control prices and the cost of living, encourage saving to deflect inflation and limit the consumption of non-essentials. A few examples illustrate the kind of instructions sent from London to the colonies: the Governor of Northern Rhodesia was told that copper export licences could only be granted by the order of the Ministry of Supply; the Governor of Tanganyika was told that diamonds and copra ranked as essential war material for export to Britain only; the Governor of Zanzibar was permitted to grant export licences for cloves to any non-enemy country; and the Governor of Trinidad was instructed in October 1939 to deny oil fuel to Italian ships.[5]

The Empire produced many raw materials much in demand during the war, including rubber, tin, sisal, bauxite, oil, pyrethrum, oilseeds, copper, gold, pyrites and sea-island cotton. At the outbreak of the Second World War the British Empire and Commonwealth was responsible for producing a significant share of the world's total output of certain key raw materials: 15.6 per cent of the bauxite; 37.6 per cent of the chrome ore; 24.8 per cent of the coal; 29.8 per cent of the copra; 17 per cent of the cotton; 12.9 per cent of the iron; 98.9 per cent of the jute; 35.9 per cent of the lead ore; 36.1 per cent of the manganese; 87.9 per cent of the nickel ore; 42.5 per cent of the palm oil; 51.9 per cent of the rubber; 39.2 per cent of the tin ore; 25.2 per cent of the tungsten ore; 34.8 per cent of the vanadium ore; 45.7 per cent of the wool; and 29 per cent of the zinc ore.[6] Given the vast potential of this imperial treasure trove, the message from London was to maximize production, even if it damaged the longer-term capacity of the colony to supply.

Despite its considerable mineral wealth and its industrialized fringes, the main produce of the Colonial Empire was agricultural, and the war witnessed an intensification of agriculture in all colonies. To economize on shipping, colonial agriculture had to be diversified, on large estates as well as smallholdings, as 'Grow More Grain' and 'Dig for Victory' campaigns were mounted the world over. The overriding need, even ahead of a surplus for export, was to increase production for domestic consumption and aim for food self-sufficiency. This was a problem, for like Britain, many colonies were import-dependent. Given the widespread practice of subsistence agriculture in Africa, colonies there were in a better position to work towards food self-sufficiency than, for example, West Indian and Indian Ocean colonies. Even though primarily agricultural, most colonies could not feed themselves. Mauritius, for example, produced little else but sugar, which alone could not sustain its 400,000 people. Therefore sugar estate owners were obliged to turn over 28 per cent of their land to the production of food crops. In other colonies, like Barbados, the Seychelles and St Helena, landowners were obliged to turn a percentage of their land to food production. But hastily organized self-sufficiency drives rarely enabled a colony to stand alone without food imports. Before the war Colonial Office agricultural advisers had pointed out the danger of monocrop economies producing little or no food for domestic consumption, and the need therefore to build food reserves, especially in colonies likely to have to sustain themselves during a siege, such as Gibraltar, Hong Kong, Malaya and Malta.

The agricultural exporters of the Empire did not have to wait long, however, before the demands of a truly global war, leading to a general state of world food shortage, enabled their crops to find markets, even if the price paid was below normal levels. The British government came to acquire colonial crops through bulk purchasing schemes, which gave it a favourable price, ensured stable price levels and, in the early stages of the war, ensured that colonial producers were not ruined. It is often remarked that bulk purchasing paid the colonial producer less than the world market price, but normal trading conditions were hardly in force during the war. Certainly, one aim of bulk purchasing was to keep the price down for the home consumer, and this meant keeping the price paid to the producer down. It was generally believed that increasing the price to the producer would not lead to more production but to inflation, and it was argued that any difference would be spent later in the form of post-war development. Bulk purchasing also enabled crops to be bought at the right time for the seller, and for shipping to be timed to tie in with the arrival of the crops at coastal warehouses (rather than the alternative of crops delivered to the coast rotting in wharves for want of shipping). Given the loss of markets and the universal shipping difficulties, middlemen could make a killing, and this was another reason for government intervention. Bulk purchasing boards helped to regulate the imperial economy and attach Britain, and its markets, to sources of production.[7]

War rammed home the value of the Empire to Britain. It was to be a lesson not forgotten in Whitehall and Westminster as they looked towards the post-war years, unshakeable in their belief in victory, charged by a sense of righteous belligerence and a centuries old habit of winning. A keynote of British world policy from the mid-1940s until the mid-1950s was to be the extensive develop-ment of imperial resources to aid recovery from the financial and economic exhaustion brought by the war.[8] The British government's Drug Requirement Advisory Committee, for example, believed that the war had demonstrated Britain's reliance on drug imports, and that sources in the Empire should be iden-tified and exploited to make Britain self-sufficient in drugs and to prevent a repeat of war-time shortages. 'A strong and progressive industry will prove essential to the new NHS [National Health Service], assure against repetition of war short-ages, make a valuable contribution to the trade of the UK [and] offer useful opportunities to British and Empire farmers in the cultivation of vegetable drugs.'[9] In December 1939 the Colonial Secretary told the colonies of the desir-ability of maintaining a twelve-month supply of quinine. Much of it came from the Dutch East Indies, though this was lost to the Japanese in late 1941. The production of cinchona bark in Tanganyika was therefore stepped up, and a new scheme launched in Ceylon.

During the Second World War all territories of the British Empire witnessed civilian and military migrations on a massive scale. Millions of soldiers were shunted around the Empire in troop convoys, including the six million troops who passed through South Africa's main ports. Tens of thousands of captured imperial troops were also moved around as prisoner-of-war labour. Many parts of the Empire experienced the trials and opportunities presented by the arrival of service personnel in their midst. As well as the most basic need of finding accom-modation for thousands of people, the resulting social and ethnic mixture led to tensions and liaisons in almost equal measure, and to new economic opportuni-ties and new cultural inputs. Egypt teemed with imperial servicemen of many nationalities, as did India.

There were many other forms of human movement caused by the war. There was a general migration from the countryside to the towns across the world, places such as Halifax and Nairobi doubling their population during the course of the war and Freetown swarming with country cousins sucked in by the opportu-nities created by the development of the port. Tens of thousands of German and Italian prisoners of war were sent to Australia, Britain, Canada, Ceylon, India, Kenya, South Africa, Southern Rhodesia and other colonies, and Japanese soldiers were imprisoned in Australia. Jews escaping from Central Europe, refused entry by the British High Commissioner in Palestine, were sent to Mauritius as detainees, and refugee camps sprouted in places such as Southern Rhodesia and Uganda. The Axis offensive in the Balkans caused refugees to pour into Egypt. A great deal of movement was caused by people being evacuated from high risk areas by government authorities, or people fleeing of their own volition from areas likely to be invaded or bombed. European women and children were ordered to leave Hong Kong. Fifteen hundred women and children were evacuated from Baghdad when Britain went to war with the Iraqi government in April 1941, and hundreds more sought sanctuary in the city's British and American embassies. Fifty to 60 per cent of the Chinese inhabitants of Kuching in British Borneo migrated to remote rural areas rather than risk persecution from the Japanese occupying forces. Indians in Ceylon, fearing an invasion of the island, returned to their homeland, Ceylonese schoolboys were evacuated to the subcontinent too, and people in coastal towns like Colombo fled inland when Japanese aircraft raided the island, as did thousands more in Bombay, Rangoon and Vizagapatam when Japanese shells and bombs, or rumours of Japanese landings, hit the home front. Enemy bombing or shelling was a sure-fire way for the migratory trend from country to town to be momentarily bucked, as the dense streets emptied in exchange for the apparent safety of the jungles and the hills.

Closer to home, the evacuation of children in Britain involved not only urchins from the East End of London being deposited in villages throughout rural England, but also the shipment of thousands of children, including Elizabeth Taylor and the future Lord Lucan, from well-off families to distant homes in America, Australia and Canada. This was organized by the Children's Overseas Reception Board, which at one time was receiving 7000 applications a day from anxious parents fearing the devastation that enemy bombers might cause. This policy was brought to a standstill on 17 September 1940 when the *City of Benares* was sunk in mid-Atlantic, with the loss of eighty-four children.[10] As well as the well-known GI brides, 60,000 women emigrated to settle in Canada, having started relationships with Canadian soldiers based in Britain, many of them leaving before the end of the war.

After heavy bombing in June 1941, there were mass evacuations of between fifty and seventy thousand people from Alexandria and Port Said. The British Consul-General in Shanghai evacuated British citizens as the threat of Japanese invasion loomed, and evacuation plans were made by the New Zealand government for the cities of Wellington and Auckland, as they were by the Governor of Mauritius for his capital, Port Louis. In the West Indies thousands of islanders found work overseas, particularly in the agricultural industries of eastern America. Throughout the Empire tens of thousands of people were rounded up and moved because of their racial or national background, or interned or deported as 'enemy aliens' by anxious and reactionary governments. In parts of West and East Africa taken over by Britain from the Germans during the First World War (parts of Togoland, Southern Cameroon and Tanganyika) German colonists remained. Some were active Nazis, all looked suspicious and were therefore subjected to internment, often to the detriment of the local economy. Japanese-Canadians were moved away from the Pacific coast and were compelled to register with the government. They were also banned from serving in the armed forces and 4000 were repatriated to Japan. Moving in the same direction, the considerable

Japanese population of Malaya and Singapore left British South-East Asia in 1941 to return to their homeland before war broke out.

In all territories of the British Empire and Commonwealth government grew in size as it attempted to maximize the war effort of its people, calling for more government departments, more reports, surveys and statistics, more registers and legislative proclamations, and more intrusions into the everyday lives of ordinary people. From the 1940s onwards, welfare imperialism marked the colonial world as much as it marked the British home front, with its revolutionary new National Health Service, education innovations and town and country planning acts. A watered-down version of the New Jerusalem was fashioned for the colonies, to gild the sunlit uplands of the post-war world when peace would reign at last. But before that could happen, there was a world war to be won.

5

The Atlantic

It might be said that Britain's imperial war really began as soon as British soil ran out, so umbilically linked was Britain to its Empire and the material inter-dependencies wrought by its imperial heritage. For before troops were even deployed in close proximity to those of the enemy, British naval and coastal air forces were engaged in the waters off Britain's shores in the opening rounds of the grim struggle of the sea lanes that kept the British imperial world connected, supplied and secured. This battle was played out across the oceans of the world, a complex network of assembly ports, fleet bases, flying boat anchorages, air fields and sea lanes of communication, over which passed merchant ships and the escort forces that defended them. This battle was fought to keep open the approaches to the home islands that were crucial to Britain's survival as the world's greatest importing and exporting nation, and to ensure communications and supplies for the territories of the British Empire that depended, no less than Britain, on the sea for their sustenance and their defence. In the west, the security of the Atlantic bridge between Britain and the Americas was to prove crucial not just in the defence and sustenance of Britain, but to facilitate the massive military build up that enabled the British, Canadian and American allies to invade Nazi-occupied Western Europe in 1944. Like Egypt, India and Australia, Britain became one of the world's major *place d'armes*.

Keeping the sea lanes to Britain open was the fundamental reason for the Battle of the Atlantic. Both Britain and Germany had already tasted this deadly form of war in 1914–18, and sensibly the attempt to strangle Britain by severing its sea communications was the central plank of Germany's naval strategy in the Second World War. It was the unglamorous yet lethal war of the merchant sailor clinging to a life raft amidst mighty Atlantic rollers as depicted on the posters; the war of the convoy; the war of U-boat wolf packs and Allied depth charges, plucky corvettes, long-range Liberators, sonar technology and the intelligence intercep-tion associated with Bletchley Park and its German equivalent. Less often remembered, particularly in the early years, it was the war of the German commerce raiders, be they formidable pocket battleships like the *Graf Spee* or disguised and heavily armed merchant ships like *Atlantis, Komet, Orion* and *Pinguin,* all of which hunted far and wide in the North and South Atlantic terror-izing British merchantmen, laying waste fleets of Norwegian whalers and attacking neutral shipping wherever it was found.[1]

Right from the off in September 1939 Britain's gaze rested on the New World, the imperial frontier that since Elizabethan times had captured the attention of British politicians, thinkers, soldiers, traders and adventurers. Churchill in particular was aware of the war-winning power that America would bring as a full belligerent, and hooked his line accordingly. What was to become generalized as the Battle of the Atlantic was a testament to Britain's imperial endeavour in the North American continent over the centuries as well as to the looming productive power of the United States and the Dominion of Canada. It was to become the most important of a series of struggles at sea with the surface raiders and submarines of the German (and later the Italian and Japanese) enemy that took place around the world, as Britain sought to secure the imports it so desperately required in order to survive, and also to ensure the supply of foodstuffs, consumer goods, soldiers and war material to the colonies and overseas fighting fronts that in turn depended upon Britain. Whilst vast quantities of supplies of food and war material flowed from America and Canada, particularly under the Lend-Lease and Mutual Aid arrangements, supplies also went in the opposite direction, known to the British as Reciprocal Aid. From the early days of the war the Atlantic also became a path for tens of thousands of imperial troops sent to bolster the European front from Canada, and later still for American troops journeying to Britain to train and wait impatiently for the opening of the second front in Europe. In lesser numbers, though no less symbolic of an Empire at war, West Indians crossed the ocean to Britain and Europe as aircraftsmen, pilot officers, soldiers and workers, and the economies of their home colonies were deeply affected by the global struggle.

Much of Britain's imperial war was fought looking west, from Liverpool and the Western Approaches to the great New World ports of New York and Halifax, and to key landfalls in between like Iceland, the Azores and western Ireland, capable of harbouring precious escort vessels or aircraft to aid Britain and its allies in the war against the U-boat (and equally capable of harbouring enemy vessels and saboteurs). American and Canadian forces – even before the former joined the war – shared the Atlantic duties with the Royal Navy and RAF, as the Atlantic developed into one of the fiercest theatres of conflict from 1939 until May 1943 when Dönitz ordered the U-boats to leave the North Atlantic, thus conceding the battle. It had been a close-run thing, costing thousands of Allied and neutral ships, and even at the last the German threat was still potent. In March 1943, for instance, two British-bound convoys sailed from Halifax. Their seventy-seven merchantmen were attacked by twenty U-boats which, for the loss of a single one of their number, sent twenty-one ships to the bottom. The mighty 'HX' convoys were the singlemost important of the war, for on them rested the survival of Britain itself. The largest of them all, HX 300, consisted of 167 merchant vessels.

The Atlantic provided the dramatic backdrop for the first instalment of what was to become a familiar aspect of war-time communication and decision-making at the highest level: the globe-trotting summitry engaged in by the major Allied leaders. In August 1941 HMS *Prince of Wales*, Britain's newest battleship (shortly to become the first capital ship ever to be sunk by aircraft when attacked by Japanese bombers in the Gulf of Siam), transported a delighted Churchill to meet President Roosevelt across the dangerous Atlantic waters. The battleship made most of the journey without escort. By all accounts Churchill took to the venture like a schoolboy let loose for the summer holidays, spurred on by the whiff of danger and the sense of a historic moment in the making. The journey was made in great secrecy, the Prime Minister and his entourage of officials, Chiefs of Staff and newsmen travelling by rail from Marylebone Station to Scapa Flow, a remote Scottish naval base. There they were transferred to the *Prince of Wales* aboard the destroyer HMS *Oribi*, the battleship recently having returned from the shipyard after her duel with the *Bismarck*. On both the outward and homeward bound journeys Churchill entertained the wardroom each evening with a picture show, having brought with him a variety of films, from American comedies and westerns like *High Sierra* to stirring British historical drama like *Lady Hamilton* (tears in Churchill's eyes for this one), to cartoons and slapstick like Donald Duck's *Foxhunting* and Laurel and Hardy's *Saps at Sea*. Each day Churchill would wander about the ship and spend hours closeted with his Chiefs of Staff, or in bed with his papers, conducting the Empire's war effort from the high seas.[2]

The meeting in Placentia Bay in the British colony of Newfoundland was the first between the two great Allied war leaders, and set the tone for the war-time shuttle diplomacy that was to see Churchill and his Chiefs of Staff, together with the attendant flock of advisers and journalists, venture to such places as Bermuda, Cairo, Casablanca, Quebec, Tehran, Washington and Yalta for top-level discussions of grand strategy and its application. This kind of international summitry was a novel feature of the war, and was liable to place a great deal of mental and physical strain on the participants, especially given the long distances involved, often traversed in noisy and uncomfortable aircraft, and the ever-present danger of enemy action. Though Churchill believed it to be his first meeting with Roosevelt, the two had in fact briefly met in 1918. There was a great deal of ceremony aboard the battleship and the President's cruiser, culminating in a joint church service that filled the *Prince of Wales*'s deck with sailors and the strains of *Onward Christian Soldiers*. There was plenty of private talking between the two delegations, and a few lucky souls managed to get a run ashore in this strange land, also at war by virtue of its status as a British colony, though far removed from the fighting. British sailors noted how clean the American warships were, compared to the British vessel battered by two years of conflict. In particular, the meeting gave the world the Atlantic Charter, a document that with its promise to 'respect the right of all peoples to choose the form of government under which they will live' was to reverberate throughout the British Empire and would be cited ad infinitum by nationalists seeking a greater share in the direction of their countries destinies. This was a cat that Churchill was to rue letting out of the bag, for he had had the territories overrun by Germany in mind when framing it. The charter was greeted with some disappointment in Britain, and indeed among the company of *Prince of Wales*, who had hoped that the historic meeting in which they had played a part would be the drum-roll for an American declaration of war on the side of the British Empire. But, as Churchill said in an explanatory broadcast to the nation on 24 August 1941, 'the meeting was ... symbolic. That is its prime importance ... Would it be presumptuous of me to say that it symbol-izes ... the marshalling of the good forces of the world against the evil forces which are now so formidable and triumphant? ... This was a meeting which marks for ever in the pages of history the taking up of the English-speaking nations amid all this peril, tumult, and confusion, of the guidance of the fortunes of the broad toiling masses in all the continents'.[3] For Churchill, the meeting and the charter bound America more closely to Britain's cause, and moved America a step closer to joining the war as a full belligerent, a process that was completed four months later as American battleships burned at their moorings in Hawaii, and Germany joined its eastern ally and declared war on America.

Despite the attention lavished on Churchill's dramatic voyage across the Atlantic in 1941, to cement the growing alliance between Britain and America and reassure the world that Nazism and Fascism would not be allowed to triumph, he was pre-empted by a less well known visit to North America that took place in 1939 before war broke out. Largely forgotten in the wake of the global conflagra-tion that ensued, the King-Emperor George VI and his wife Queen Elizabeth made a very popular royal visit to Canada, and extended their stay in North America by visiting the Dominion's southern neighbour at the invitation of Pres-ident Roosevelt. During the visit the King was entertained and 'shown off' by the President, whom Churchill was not to clamp eyes upon until they stood facing each other beneath an awning on the deck of the American cruiser *Augusta* in Placentia Bay over two years later. The visit provides an excellent example of the utility of the imperial monarchy in aiding wider British diplomatic and public relations interests, and was important for President Roosevelt in his endeavours to secure greater American commitment to the British cause, should the expected war with Germany break out. In instigating the high-profile royal visit Roosevelt was seeking to counteract the isolationist tendencies widely found in middle America and Congress. Congress at the time was keen to amend the Neutrality Act to make it more effective in preventing American involvement with any belligerent nation should war come. The royal visit also enabled Britain to further its appeal to its Atlantic neighbour at a time when American support was viewed as invaluable in the emerging struggle in Europe, and to reaffirm the links between Britain and the most senior Dominion.[4]

Royal tours of the Empire and Commonwealth had become commonplace since the death of Queen Victoria, and were important for the iconography of Empire as well as its high-level diplomacy, strengthening the bonds between Britain and its far-flung territories and allies, and ensuring that reigning mon-archs were very much aware of Britain's overseas connections and responsibilities.

This was especially the case with George VI, who had gained a mass of global experience from tours and military service that equipped him well for his role as a war-time monarch. From childhood he had learned of his connections with the wider world. In the year of Queen Victoria's death the young Prince Albert, as he was then known, was left at home by his parents as they embarked upon a tour of Australia. Later, having gone through the Royal Naval College at Dartmouth, the future King joined the cruiser HMS *Cumberland* in 1912 for a voyage that took him to British West Indian islands such as Barbados, Bermuda, Jamaica and Trinidad, as well as to Canada and Newfoundland. In 1913 the Prince joined HMS *Collingwood*, flagship of the 1ˢᵗ Battle Squadron, and served in the Mediterranean before the outbreak of the First World War, visiting Malta and Egypt. The Prince saw active service in one of the ship's twelve-inch gun turrets at the Battle of Jutland in 1916.

After the war the Prince, now Duke of York, embarked upon a World Empire Tour, visiting Kenya, the Sudan and Uganda in 1924. In 1927 he was sent to open the Australian Federal Parliament, travelling on the battlecruiser HMS *Renown*, and the voyage was the cause of a general imperial tour that included visits to Fiji, Gibraltar, Jamaica, Malta, Mauritius and New Zealand, as well as visits to Australian states such as New South Wales, Queensland and Tasmania. The visit to Canada and America in 1939 was to be the beginning of a new world tour following his accession to the throne in 1937, though the war forced a postponement. (The tour resumed in 1947 when the Royal family visited South Africa, the High Commission Territories and Southern Rhodesia).

Despite the attempts of both the King and his First Minister to woo the western cornerstone of the Atlantic world that had been created by British imperial endeavour since the sixteenth century, it was from the Dominion of Canada that Britain drew its greatest real fighting aid in the early stages of the war, and in alliance with whom Britain sought to police the fast-emerging danger land of the Atlantic high seas. In 1939 Canada (population twelve million) was the senior Dominion, a remarkably autonomous part of the British Empire and Commonwealth, more advanced than the other Dominions in its political sophistication, and in its conduct of its own external affairs. It was the only Dominion using a non-sterling currency and was economically as bound to America as to Britain and the Empire. Reflecting its status as the senior Dominion, and the Atlantic orientation of so much of Britain's war policy, it was to Canada that the Royal Family were to be evacuated in the event of a successful German invasion of Britain. Canada's contribution to the Empire and Commonwealth's war effort in terms of industrial and agricultural products, military hardware and military and naval forces was to be quite staggering as the struggle unfolded, and Canadians were destined to serve all over the world, their nation emerging as one of the main Allied victor countries and a founder-member of the transatlantic alliance that created the North Atlantic Treaty Organization (NATO) in 1949.⁵

Canada and the other 'white' Dominions were the cornerstones of the British imperial world. As in Britain and Australia, the coming of war in 1939 was greeted with resignation in Canada. Its people remembered with pain the massed casualties of the First World War, and none of the blithe pugnacity of 1914 was to be detected amongst the same men, or their sons, a quarter of a century later. Defence of the British Empire was certainly not a prime motivation in causing Canada to enter the fight, though Canada's historic relationship with its distant imperial metropole and a world economy enabled it to see more clearly than its great southern neighbour that its interests – even though its soil was not seriously threatened – were intimately bound with those of Britain and the anti-Nazi powers.

Canada, in addition to its political, trade and foreign affairs autonomy, was also the most advanced territory of the British Empire and Commonwealth in terms of its industrial and economic development. It was so mature politically, in fact, that Canadian politicians had largely jettisoned imperial issues as topics of debate, unlike their peers in the 'white' Dominions club (particularly in Australia and South Africa, where struggling for and against the link with the 'mother' country was still the meat and drink of much political debate). This was largely because Canada's proximity to America had led it along a unique path. Though the imperial connection with Britain remained alive and strong for all the reasons it did in the other Dominions – cultural, historical, political, military and economic ties – Canada was different in that it was bordered for thousands of miles by an emerging superpower whose predominance on its own continent would not, realistically, be challenged by distant Britain, and against which Britain could not by the twentieth century, realistically, be expected to defend its Dominion. The proximity of America also meant that Canada had an alternative defence option that made it far less reliant on British seapower and the traditions of imperial defence, hence its avoidance of the trauma faced by Australia and New Zealand in early 1942 when it seemed that there was nothing to stop the Japanese invading. It had long-established economic and financial ties with America that made it less dependent on British investment and British import-export trade than were the other Dominions. Given its continental situation, Canada had taken advantage of the increased political autonomy that Dominions had begun to exercise in the twentieth century, recognized officially in the Balfour Declaration of 1926 and the Statute of Westminster of 1931. It had taken the lead in appointing overseas representatives and developing a government department for external affairs, moving away from the tradition of allowing Britain to supervise all foreign policy matters, and it had been the first Dominion to conclude, unilaterally and without official British participation, a treaty with a foreign power.

Canada nevertheless, and with reason, remained red on the map, and economically Britain continued to exercise significant imperial influence in Canada. Indeed, Canada had chosen continued British economic predominance to the looming alternative of American political dominance. In other ways, too, Canada remained subordinate to Britain, demonstrated in 1937 when the Privy Council in London ruled that Canada's equivalent of the American 'New Deal' was unconstitutional. Britain still remained Canada's major overseas economic partner and during the depression Britain had been vital to Canada (favoured particularly by the Ottawa agreements in 1932 that had seen the historic end of free trade as the Dominions sought shelter for their industries behind the walls of a new system of imperial preference). The war, and Britain's need for Canadian production, saved the country's economy and the government of Mackenzie King.[6] In 1939, despite its robust autonomy and an unequivocal stance of looking to Canada's interests ahead of those of Britain or the Empire, in common with all other territories of the Empire and Commonwealth Canada was orientated towards Britain in terms of economic and military relations. Its Prime Minister recognized that Britain was integral to the defence of Canadian soil, and the British government was at great pains before 1939 to be sure that, if war came, Canada and the other Dominions were on side and convinced that Britain had done all that it sensibly could to avoid war. More like an advanced industrialized nation state than a semi-colonial territory (whatever confusion might exist in the minds of Americans, many of whom had difficulty in understanding the more subtle forms of 'Empire' like the nexus between Britain and the Dominions), Canada operated throughout the war as a very large cog in the imperial war machine. A further reason compelling Canada's involvement in the war was the fact that it could act in some ways as a broker between Britain and America, and it was widely understood that if Canada had been reticent in its war participation, particularly in terms of production and the maintenance of the Atlantic bridge, Britain would almost certainly have bypassed it all together and dealt directly with America.

Of Canada's population of twelve million, one and a half million people served in the armed forces. Elements of the Canadian Army's 1st Division had arrived in Britain by Christmas 1939, and some saw service in France before Dunkirk, as did seven Canadian destroyers in the famous evacuation that ensued. A second division arrived in Britain in the summer of 1940. At that crucial juncture, when German invasion looked a distinct possibility as the Battle of Britain was contested in the skies above southern England, the Canadians represented the largest organized front-line force available for the defence of Britain should invasion come. Canadian soldiers fought in the Far East, the North Pacific, southern Europe and western Europe, providing an entire army for the Normandy landings (the date of which had been set by Roosevelt and Churchill at the Quebec conference in 1943). Canada ended the war with the world's third largest navy, having played a central role in the Battle of the Atlantic.[7] The Canadian contribution in the air was no less impressive, and an autonomous Canadian air group flew with Bomber Command from British bases.[8] In military matters, though Canadians might serve in British formations or alongside British servicemen (as when they landed together on Juno Beach in June 1944), there was never any doubt that the Canadian government and Canadian commanders were in charge of Canadian forces. Canada was much more assertive in its military relationship with Britain than were the antipodean Dominions. This did not always lead to successful deployments of Canadian forces, however, as political considerations queered the pitch. In his war diaries the Chief of the Imperial General Staff, General Sir Alan Brooke, regularly refers to uneasy meetings with the Canadian commander of forces stationed in Britain, as on 10 February 1943 when he recorded a 'harangue from Harry Crerar about the need to get some Canadians fighting soon for Imperial and political reasons'.[9] This understandable keenness to get the substantial forces built up by Canada into action was part of the reason why Canadians were selected for the disastrous Dieppe raid in 1942, and led in April 1943 to arrangements to replace the British 3rd Division with a Canadian division for the forthcoming attack on Sicily. Later in 1943 Brooke lamented that the Canadian government and military representatives had 'made more fuss than the whole of the rest of the Commonwealth concerning the employment of Dominion forces!' This was hardly surprising: the Canadians were building genuinely autonomous fighting formations on a vast scale, rather than units largely designed to operate alongside, and under the command of, larger British or American formations.

Canada was equally as abundant in other spheres essential to the prosecution of modern warfare. It accounted for one-seventh of the Empire and Commonwealth's war production. It made huge financial contributions to Britain on a scale exceeded only by America and, in proportion to size and wealth, exceeded by none. Overall, Canada gave Britain $4 billion worth of money and supplies. At the end of the war, when America made its famous loan to Britain of £3.75 billion, Canada loaned $1.25 billion, and in 1946 Canada cancelled Britain's war debt (including the $425 million owed for the running of the Canadian branch of the British Empire Air Training Scheme). Britain's dollar deficit in Canada was met by the repatriation of British securities and by Canadian acceptance of payment in sterling and in gold. When Canada's balance of dollars in London became very large in autumn 1941, it was converted to an interest-free loan of $700 million, and in January 1942 munitions and war supplies contributed as a gift amounted to one billion dollars. When British credit ran out in 1943, arrangements were made whereby Canada would donate its surplus production to the Allies through the Canadian Mutual Aid Board (by this method $1.25 billion went to Britain). Given this massive contribution to the war effort, it is no surprise that Canada's voice in Allied councils was significant, and the Dominion also provided a useful bridge between Britain and America before the latter entered the war.

For Canada the war demonstrated, as in so many parts of the world, that the old structures of imperial defence based on the British naval shield no longer applied with any certainty. Long before, it had been acknowledged that Britain could not provide a realistic defence of Canada against potential American aggression, though Canada still relied on the Royal Navy for protection from other threats. The Second World War was to see Canada do all it could to supplement the strength of the Royal Navy by developing its own navy, and was to bring an acknowledgement of America's role as the ultimate defender of Canadian territorial integrity as that nation's military formations at home and overseas came to dwarf that of every other nation bar Russia. As in the case of Australia and New Zealand in the Pacific, though imperial defence centred on Britain did not die, there was a turning to America that was a natural result of Britain's inability to deal with every single enemy in every single region at once. American defence guarantees were important when it looked as if Britain might succumb to Germany in 1940–41. The Ogdensburg Declaration of August 1940, issued by President Roosevelt and Prime Minister Mackenzie King, created a joint structure for the defence of the region. It permitted American troops to enter Canada's Maritime Provinces in the event of invasion. In these years of great uncertainty, deciding to embrace America – in Australia and New Zealand as well as Canada – was done in the full knowledge of the risk of American domination, and without a rejection of the imperial link. It was not the historic 'ending of an era' that it is sometimes presented as, but rather a prudent insurance and acknowledgement of the fact that Britain could not guarantee the defence of the free world alone. Far from the war sounding the death knell of the Commonwealth bonds, the war saw something of a revival of the Canadian link with Britain. The relationship between the two countries, shorn of the squabbles over power and consultation between London and Dominion capitals that had caused politicians to fret in previous decades, improved because of the war. This was especially true given Britain's obvious plight in the first years of the war, which led to a renewed sentimental attachment to the Old Country. There was also, of course, the need to continue to steer a Canadian course between Britain and America. Suspicion of American economic and military ambitions was widespread, leading, for example, to the Canadian government insisting on paying for all American installations constructed on Canadian soil. Even in turning to America, Canada had an imperial goal in mind, for, by allying with American power, that country was drawn further towards war on Britain's side, and American economic horsepower was better harnessed for imperial ends. In the early years of the war, before the machinery for swift direct links had been firmly established, Canadian politicians enjoyed playing the role of mediator between Britain and America.

Canada particularly welcomed American economic help. The suspension of sterling convertibility in 1939 meant that it was unable to use the surplus on its account with Britain to pay for its deficit with America. This meant that Canada ran short of dollars with which to buy war-related goods from America, whilst accumulating large though unconvertible sterling reserves. Roosevelt and Mackenzie King therefore concluded the Hyde Park Agreement in April 1941, which was to promote large-scale American purchases of Canadian war material and which 'effectively removed the border with respect to defence production'. American-made parts exported from Canada to Britain would also be charged to Britain's Lend-Lease account and then shipped to Canada. The agreement allowed Canada to wipe out its deficit with America. At the same time, Canada maintained its financial independence from America and was better able to finance exports to Britain and throw its full industrial weight behind the war effort. Inevitably, such economic arrangements accelerated Canada's advanced state of detachment from Britain, and locked it into a continental economic alliance with its giant neighbour.[10] On the trade front, what has been termed the Atlantic triangle – surplus trade with Britain permitting Canada to service its trade deficit with America – suffered greatly because of the war's effects on British financial and trading patterns. Canada attempted to prop up the British leg of the tripod by making gifts and loans to Britain, amounting to billions of dollars.

These military and economic agreements between Canada and America were viewed with gloomy suspicion by many in London. Some thought that they indicated unwarranted Canadian panic, given Britain's perilous position in the year following Dunkirk and the fall of France. Viewed from the Commonwealth point of view, the earmarking of Canadian uranium for America and the presence of Americans in Canada – constructing weather stations, airbases and roads in Alaska for Pacific defence – was cause for regret. By the end of the war Canada's relationship with Britain had been supplanted in numerous ways by a growing economic relationship with America, and a transformation in the defence arrangements of the continent given Britain's inability to provide adequately for Canadian defence. Politically, the relationship between Canada and America grew much closer, the Canadian government being treated by its American counterpart as a 'proper' government, somewhat in contrast to the metropole-colony relationship that still often pervaded Anglo-Canadian relations.

In becoming a belligerent it was important for Canada that its declaration of war was seen to be a Canadian, not an imperial decision, and the King was asked to declare war separately on behalf of the Dominion some days after the British declaration. Britain's declaration of war on 3 September, however, attracted far more attention than Canada's official response a week later. As in South Africa, Canada's European racial divide was a source of friction and political controversy, and required careful handling by the federal government. Mackenzie King's government held things together by pledging not to introduce conscription for overseas service, and to prosecute a war of limited liability.[11] The fall of France, however, changed things considerably, as the struggle was brought closer to home for the French-Canadian community. Nevertheless, the federal government was challenged by the Quebec premier Duplessis, who accused it of using the war to enhance central power and who played on French-Canadian fears concerning conscription. Meanwhile, English-Canadians in Ontario condemned the government for not prosecuting the war effort with sufficient vigour. A general election was called and Mackenzie King's Liberal Party was returned, to remain in power for the duration. It ensured that Quebec benefited from wartime economic opportunities, and promised social welfare reform as a means of staving off a return to the economic conditions of the 1930s. Even during the war years a start was made to the creation of a welfare state. Unemployment benefit was introduced in 1940, family allowances in 1944, veterans' benefit schemes were generous, provision of old-age pensions was improved, and there was huge investment in housing and housing subsidies. The government also started an export drive. As in Britain, big government had arrived, and over the course of the war the federal budget ballooned from $680 million to $5.1 billion. By 1950, $21 billion had been chalked up as war expenditure.

As in Australia, though conscription for home defence was sanctioned (in June 1940), pressure for wider conscription remained, particularly after Japan entered the fray. In 1942 Mackenzie King held a plebiscite to sanction his release from the promise that conscription for overseas service would not be adopted. This outraged many French-Canadians and the Prime Minister concluded that the issue was best left well alone. In 1944, however, the implementation of conscription for overseas service became a major issue again, as Canadian armies in Italy and France fell short of troops. The attempt to call up 60,000 men led to a political storm, though eventually 16,000 men were sent overseas and the protests died away.

On the home front, Canadian industry benefited from the deluge of war orders from Britain and Canada's military forces, and the manufacturing sector had almost doubled in size by 1945. Canada produced $9 billions worth of war-like stores. At its peak, its war industry employed 1.2 million people – over 13 per cent of Canada's population. Heavy industry experienced exponential growth. By 1943 Canada's rate of output of merchant vessels was only fractionally less than Britain's, and by the following year Canadian shipyards had built 410 merchant ships, 487 escort vessels and minesweepers, 254 naval tugs and 3302 landing craft. This from a shipbuilding industry that had been moribund in 1939. Among other ships, the Royal Navy gained from Canada twenty-five corvettes and frigates, sixty-two fleet minesweepers and many smaller craft. At its peak in 1943 Canadian dockyards were employing 126,000 people. In the air, Canadian factories manufactured 14,700 aircraft during the war. This total included thousands of training aircraft, Canada accounting for 22 per cent of Commonwealth output in this field. It also accounted for 4 per cent of the Commonwealth's output of service aircraft, including 1451 Hurricanes, 395 Lancaster bombers and 770 flying boats, as vital production was outsourced to the Empire. The Canadian branch of De Havilland, for example, built 1032 Mosquitoes, compared to 5200 built at its main factory in Britain and 212 built at its factory in Sydney. At its peak, the Canadian aircraft industry employed 116,000 people.

On dry land Canada's prolific automobile industry turned out 707,000 military vehicles and 45,710 armoured vehicles during the course of the war. By 1945, the Department of Munitions and Supplies had supervised a growth in the industry that led to the manufacture, in total, of 815,000 transport and combat vehicles. Small arms and munitions were also produced in great quantities. Seventy per cent of Canada's war production went to Britain and other allies, as gifts or as part of Canadian Mutual Aid, a scheme aimed at contributing effectively to the war effort whilst attaining full employment at home. In 1942 an outright gift of a billion pounds was made to Britain, largely to enable Britain to maintain the purchases of Canadian exports that had helped create the boom that Canada was experiencing. Full employment increased living standards, though savings rose due to the lack of consumer goods and government anti-inflationary measures were largely successful. Agricultural exports rose from $332 million in 1939 to $1.2 billion in 1944, over a third being sent to Britain.

Elsewhere on the home front, war with Japan brought measures to control the 23,000-strong Japanese-Canadian population. Fear of 'the yellow peril', and of its apparent advanced guard in Canada's midst, had grown with Japanese expansionism in the 1930s, and throughout the British Empire a general belief in the existence of 'fifth columns' stoked suspicion of any 'foreigners' or non-indigenous non-whites. Japan's striking early successes against the Allies in the Pacific, South-East Asia and the East Indies caused some panic in British Columbia, where most Japanese-Canadians lived. Defences on the Pacific coast were strengthened. A Special Committee of Orientals was created in 1940, and all Japanese-Canadians had to register with the government. They were banned from serving in the armed forces, and in January 1942 it was decided to move all men of military age inland. The property of Japanese-Canadians was confiscated, and the entire population moved. Those who resisted were interned. Nearly 4000 were voluntarily or involuntarily repatriated to Japan. Conversely, because of their instinctive opposition to the Japanese, Canada's Chinese community was viewed more sympathetically, and some use was made of Chinese Canadians for military and covert ends.[12] Like so many other parts of the Empire, Canada also became home to enemy prisoners of war, and there were 16,000 Germans in Canada by 1942.

As was the case throughout the Colonial Empire and in the other Dominions, Canada began the war in an unarmed state, reposing its trust in the historic shield of British seapower. Canada had extra reason to be relaxed in defence matters because America was so close at hand and was unlikely to stand idly by whilst another Great Power attacked in the north. Canadian defence formations were small and patterned very much on the British model. The Royal Canadian Navy (RCN) numbered 1900 men (3276 including the reserves) manning six destroyers and four minesweepers. The army numbered 4261, with a militia of 51,000. The Royal Canadian Air Force (RCAF) numbered 3000, but only thirty-seven of its 270 planes were combatworthy, and most of them were of obsolescent design. From little acorns mighty oaks grow, and Canada was to end the war, astonishingly, as one of the most powerful military nations on earth. The navy alone by 1945 consisted of 373 warships and 93,000 men, and its armies were prominent alongside British and American troops in liberating Western Europe.

The number of men and women enlisted by the three armed services over the course of the war tells its own story of mobilization and rapid expansion. The navy enlisted 106,552, the army 730,159, and the air force 249,662. The latter figure included the 17,000 members of the RCAF Women's Division. Of men between the ages of eighteen and forty-five, over 40 per cent served in the armed forces, 85 per cent of them volunteers. From Canada's population of 'Status Indians' at least 3000 volunteered.[13] 42,042 Canadians died during the war, and 54,414 were wounded. In addition to the fighting forces, Canada formed civil defence units in areas considered under threat, and by 1943 federal home defence forces had reached 225,000.

Canada was very quick to get troops trained and sent to Britain, a month or two before the antiopdean Dominions began sending the first echelons of their expeditionary forces to the Middle East. In September 1939 it was announced that two divisions would be raised for service overseas, and volunteers flocked to register. The first elements of the 1st Division had left for Britain by Christmas. Prior to its invasion by hundreds of thousands of American soldiers and airmen, Britain was to be 'softened up' by the arrival of tens of thousands of their North American neighbours, as well as a constellation of exiled European warriors and those from the other British Dominions. Canadians soldiers and airmen were the first of the North Americans to find their way, in their thousands, to airfields, camps and billets the length and breadth of Britain, where communities, settled and sedentary for a thousand years, were to find themselves exposed all of a sudden to the charms and the ways of foreigners, themselves usually very young and away from home for the first time in their lives. Here they were to have a novel impact on local economies, forging friendships, relationships and under-standings with local people and contributing to the kaleidoscope of war-time changes that were to alter Britain in so many ways.

Whilst seeing little action despite their early arrival on the scene, the plan was steadily to build the 1st Canadian Army, a process completed by the spring of 1943. It comprised two corps of three infantry and two armoured divisions, and a further two independent tank brigades. The fact that this Canadian Army spent so long in Britain without appearing to do much besides training led to pressure from the Canadian public as well as the military authorities. It was largely in order to get the Canadians into action that they partook in two unsuccessful and in many ways disastrous expeditions. One saw Canadian troops sent to Hong Kong shortly before the Japanese onslaught in the east. This unlikely commit-ment came about by chance. Major-General A. E. Grasett, himself a Canadian, handed over as Officer Commanding Troops Hong Kong to Major-General C. M. Maltby in July 1941, and returned to London by way of Canada. Whilst there, he told the Chief of the Canadian General Staff that the addition of a battalion or two would make the colony strong enough to withstand a prolonged Japanese attack. Itself seeking an opportunity usefully and actively to contribute forces overseas, and believing (mistakenly) that Britain had increased the secu-rity priority attached to the great eastern colony by revising its assessment of Hong Kong as an 'outpost', the Canadian government offered the services of its men. Therefore on 27 October 1941, a mere six weeks before the Japanese attack began, the 2000 men of the Royal Rifles of Canada and the Winnipeg Grenadiers, taken from garrison duties in Newfoundland and the West Indies, embarked for Hong Kong, where they were to sustain 40 per cent casualties before the year was out and the colony surrendered on Christmas Day.

The more famous gallant and disastrous deployment of Canadian forces occurred in August 1942, when nearly 5000 Canadians of the 2nd Division based in Sussex were chosen as the spearhead of a daring amphibious raid mounted against German-occupied France. Only 2211 of those Canadians made it back across the Channel from Dieppe to Britain, leaving behind them over a thousand dead and the rest captured as prisoners of war. Over one hundred aircraft were destroyed and another hundred damaged. Proportionately, these were the heaviest losses sustained in any Allied attack during the war. The raid was to provide a salient lesson in how *not* to mount an operation against the heavily-fortified defences of Germany's Western European empire, and loomed large in the thinking of the Allies as they contemplated the eventual invasion of occupied Europe that was central to the strategic planning of the British and Americans from 1942, the Americans in particular strongly believing that whatever victories might be achieved in other theatres, the key to defeating Germany was the invasion of France from Britain. The main body of men used to raid Dieppe were supposed to have been British paratroops, but pressure to get Canadians into action led to them being sent instead. Mountbatten's use of Canadian troops (as Chief of Combined Operations, Dieppe was his responsibility) earned him the ardent hatred of Lord Beaverbrook, the larger than life Canadian who owned the *Express* newspapers and held a string of prominent war-time political appointments (as Minister of Aircraft Production, Minister of Supply and Lend-Lease Administrator in America).

Canadian troops served in large numbers in the Mediterranean and southern European theatres. The 5th Armoured Division was sent to take part in the invasion of Sicily in the spring of 1943, and nearly 93,000 Canadians served as part of the Eighth Army in the Italian campaign. Again, political considerations played a part in this involvement, which some viewed as a waste of manpower, given that British troops were being sent in the other direction in order to begin the build up of the 21st Army Group in Britain in preparation for D-Day. The deployment of Canadian forces added a new imperial dimension to this most imperial of theatres. Alongside British units, Swazi pioneer companies, Bengal Sappers and Miners, the 5th Mahratta Light Infantry and the 2nd New Zealand Division, stood diverse Canadians regiments. These included armoured units such as the Royal Canadian Dragoons, Lord Strathcona's Horse, Princess Louise's New Brunswick Hussars and the Governor-General's Horse Guards, and infantry regiments including the Cape Breton Highlanders, the Loyal Edmonton Regiment, Princess Patricia's Canadian Light Infantry, the Saskatoon Light Infantry, the West Nova Scotia Regiment and the 48th Highlanders of Canada.

The least remembered Canadian deployment saw an infantry brigade take part alongside American troops in the attack on Kiska during the Aleutian campaign in the North Pacific. On 28–29 July 1943 the Japanese navy evacuated Kiska, and 34,000 American and Canadian troops landed to reclaim the island on 15 August. When it came to the invasion of German-occupied Europe in 1944, Canada was the only part of the Empire and Commonwealth to furnish forces on a significant and autonomous scale. The 1st Canadian Army was to the fore along with their British peers in hitting Juno Beach in Normandy on that fateful day in June when the western Allies began the final assault on Hitler's fortress Europe.

The Canadian contribution in the air to the Allied war effort was extremely impressive, and far larger than that of any of the other Dominions. The RCAF sent forty-eight squadrons and 98,000 men overseas, many serving with the RAF. After pressure from Ottawa, Canadian air force units were concentrated in separate Canadian groups, for example, the all-RCAF No. 6 Bomber Group. Eight Canadian bomber squadrons were based in Yorkshire, and Canadian aircraft dropped an impressive one-eighth of Bomber Command's total tonnage. For the Normandy landings, sixteen RCAF squadrons formed No. 83 Group to support the British-Canadian Second Army. Another major role for the RCAF was its convoy escort work in the Atlantic. By late 1943 the RCAF had increased to ten squadrons specializing in anti-submarine warfare, with another squadron stationed in Iceland and six squadrons for Coastal Command. RCAF units were using Gander airport in Newfoundland, a crucial Atlantic base, from 1939 (the Atlantic Ferry Organization, later Ferry Command, brought 2241 aircraft from North America to Britain via this route). By September 1943 the RCAF's Eastern Air Command had 165 aircraft organized in eleven maritime patrol squadrons, seven on the Canadian mainland and Prince Edward Island, four in Newfoundland.

Though their major contribution was to be over Europe and the Atlantic, Canadian aircrew and ground crew served in all major theatres of war. It was a Canadian in a Catalina flying-boat who spotted Admiral Nagumo's carrier fleet on its way to attack Ceylon in April 1942, and who managed to get off a warning message before being shot down. This pilot, Squadron Leader R. J. Birchall, had been posted to Ceylon along with the rest of RCAF No. 413 Squadron the previous month. He had not even unpacked his kit when he was shot down on this most important mission (which was singled out for individual praise by Churchill), presumed dead, though later found in a Japanese prisoner-of-war camp. At this time there were also nineteen Canadian Hurricane pilots in Ceylon. Canadian transport squadrons served in the Burma campaign and a Canadian fighter squadron and light bomber squadron supported American forces flying defensive patrols over the Alaska mainland, sent to the region in June 1942 after the Japanese had conquered two of the Aleutian islands. Over 17,000 RCAF personnel died during the war, 8200 of them whilst serving with Bomber Command in Britain. Of equal importance to the air war was Canada's leading role in the British

Empire Air Training Scheme, formed in 1940 at the suggestion of the Canadian and Australian high commissioners in London.[14] The great attraction of BEATS for the Canadian government was that it offered a way of visibly contributing to the war effort without sending significant numbers of men overseas and agitating political debate. It was good for national autonomy and good for employment in the form of orders for training aircraft and the huge base construction requirements. Between April 1940 and December 1941 fifty-one training schools were created. Over 116,000 air crew were trained during the war in Canada, and the Dominion funded the scheme as well as building the trainer aircraft flown by the fledgling pilots. During the course of the scheme's life, 48 per cent of the men trained were British, 25 per cent were Canadian and 25 per cent were from the other Dominions.

The Royal Canadian Navy's (RCN) star turn was its role in the Battle of the Atlantic, particularly its provision of mid-ocean escorts, a task that became the RCN's sole responsibility in 1944.[15] In February 1940 the Canadian government ordered sixty-four corvettes for convoy escort duties, the first of 122 to be built in Canada, as the RCN grew massively in size to become the world's third largest navy. Canada took responsibility for convoys in the Newfoundland region upon their leaving the great naval base and war-time convoy assembly port of Halifax in Nova Scotia, where the ships gathered in Bedford Basin. They were handed over to the Newfoundland Escort Force (NEF), then in turn handed over to the Iceland Escort Force, and finally handed over to the Royal Navy for the final stages of the voyage. The NEF (later the Mid-Ocean Escort Force) was a Canadian-led unit formed after the Admiralty requested the RCN to base warships at St John's to escort ships from Newfoundland to a point south of Iceland. The Canadian commander of this force reported to the Commander-in-Chief Western Approaches in Liverpool (where the headquarters of RAF Coastal Command were also established, facilitating the intimate air–navy cooperation that was to be so crucial in winning the Battle of the Atlantic). The NEF initially numbered seven Royal Navy destroyers, four sloops and four corvettes, and six RCN destroyers and seventeen corvettes. Initially all RCN destroyers serving in British home waters were withdrawn to join the NEF.

Indicating the growing significance of America's contribution to the Battle of the Atlantic, in October 1941 Canadian forces were removed from the direct control of the Commander-in-Chief Western Approaches and put under the 'coordinating supervision' of an American, though Canada and Britain continued to provide the lion's share of the forces of the Mid-Ocean Escort Force. By December 1941 there were eleven destroyers and forty-three corvettes of the RCN operating from Newfoundland. Even so, losses mounted. By July 1942 over forty ships had been sunk in the waters off Canada and Newfoundland, and between May and September 1943 U-boats managed to sink nineteen merchant vessels and two escort vessels in the Gulf of St Lawrence. This closed the Gulf for the rest of the war and an added burden was placed on Canada's railways, the port of Halifax and the navy. (The significance of Halifax was reflected in the rise in its population, from 70,000 in 1939 to 130,000 in 1945.)

By September 1942, with 188 warships and 16,000 men at sea, Canada was providing nearly half the surface escorts available for convoys from North America to Britain and Britain the other half, with America furnishing less than 5 per cent. From February 1942 Londonderry in Northern Ireland became the eastern terminus for Canadian warships escorting convoys to Britain, and thus became a familiar haunt for thousands of Canadian sailors (as part of Atlantic defence seventy-eight maritime patrol aircraft were stationed in Northern Ireland). The RCAF and RAF Coastal Command provided air cover save only for the North Atlantic 'gap', a point at which even the longest-range aircraft could not accompany the ships in the early years of the war.

With most of the transatlantic merchant sinkings occurring whilst the RCN was responsible for their safe passage, the decision was taken to withdraw Canadian ships for training on the safer Britain–Gibraltar route. The fact that the RCN was performing less successfully than the Royal Navy was due to a number of factors. Canadian ships were less technologically advanced and, having expanded so rapidly, the RCN was short on training. New anti-submarine technology (including ASDIC, improved radar, Leigh lights for spotting surfaced U-boats and forward-throwing depth charge platforms known as 'Hedgehogs'), the breaking of the new Enigma naval code and the closing of the air gap with the use of aircraft like the Very Long Range Liberators and B-17 Fortresses, began to turn the tide in the Battle of the Atlantic. In March 1943 the RCN returned to Atlantic waters in charge of a new North-West Atlantic Command. This was commanded from Halifax by Rear-Admiral Murray, the first RCN theatre commander in history. In the same month an American Army (Antisubmarine) Squadron was transferred from the Mediterranean to Newfoundland on Roosevelt's insistence. Before this, RAF Coastal Command Liberators had begun a shuttle service from Iceland to Newfoundland, and, all together, these measures succeeded in closing the air gap. As the submarine menace subsided from the spring of 1943, more RCN units were transferred to the eastern Atlantic.

In winning the Battle of the Atlantic, air power was as important as seapower. Shore-based aircraft sank over 40 per cent of all U-boats destroyed in the battle. Of the 326 U-boats sunk by shore-based aircraft, RAF Coastal Command destroyed 169 of them. Other improvements aided the campaign in the Atlantic, including the formation of a Joint Operations Headquarters by the RAF and the navy. It was also crucial that Coastal Command was able to keep some of the vital Very Long Range (VLR) Liberators out of the clutches of Air Chief Marshal Sir Arthur Harris's Bomber Command. By the end of 1942 there were fifty-two VLR aircraft with Coastal Command, and well over a hundred by mid-1943. Operating from Northern Ireland, Iceland and Canada, it was possible to organize continuous cover for every convoy. Technology, resources, bases and intra-Allied cooperation had all been vital in winning the Battle of the Atlantic. It was for many months touch and go, and the losses were huge. By the end of 1940, for instance, 1281 British, Allied and neutral ships had been sunk, half by U-boats. Only thirty-two U-boats had been sunk in this period, and Coastal Command had lost 323 aircraft.

Canadian naval forces served in theatres across the globe. RCN destroyers patrolled in the English Channel and took part in the Normandy landings, and Canadian Armed Merchant Cruisers served world wide. Canadian sailors manned British warships such as the cruisers HMS *Enterprise* and *Uganda*, and the RCN anti-aircraft cruiser *Prince Robert* was part of the British naval force responsible for retaking Hong Kong after the Japanese surrender. By 1944 the RCN commanded and provided most of the crew for two escort carriers, HMS *Nabob* and *Puncher*, and had grown to number nearly 400 ships. Canada's merchant fleet also expanded rapidly during the war, from less than forty ships in 1939. The government corporation Wartime Shipbuilding Limited built 410 ships, employing 126,000 people. Park Steamship Company Limited was also formed by the government to oversee the export of munitions and supplies.

Canadian intelligence facilities played an important role in Atlantic and imperial operations to monitor enemy signals traffic, forming the western branch of the imperial intelligence network that also encompassed major facilities in Britain (notably at Bletchley Park), Egypt, East Africa, Ceylon, India, Singapore and Australia. In 1942 the RCN's signal interception base and tracking room in Ottawa was given the task of monitoring U-boat signals in the Western Atlantic. Canadian intelligence services had other tasks, such as keeping the Japanese-Canadian population under surveillance. The External Affairs Department founded the Examination Unit based at Esquimalt, which monitored diplomatic and commercial traffic from Vichy legations in Canada, America and Indo-China. It also intercepted naval communications and monitored Abwehr establishments in South America. A senior Bletchley Park code-breaker was stationed in Ottawa and there was an intercept station in Nova Scotia. In western Canada, Japanese signals were intercepted in Victoria on Vancouver Island and further north on the British Columbia coast. The role of these stations was to extend the coverage to the vast region of the Alaskan peninsula and the Aleutian Islands, especially during the Japanese occupation of two of the Aleutians from mid-1942.

Canada was involved in other facets of the clandestine war against the enemies of the Empire and Commonwealth. The Canadian William Stephenson was the chief of British Security Coordination, a global intelligence network established by Churchill to challenge the spread of Nazism, with headquarters in New York and a base in Bermuda. Stephenson, knighted at the end of the war, was an important go-between for Churchill and Roosevelt during the war. Codenamed 'Intrepid', Stephenson also gave some training to a young aide to the chief of British Naval Intelligence, Ian Fleming, whose later James Bond novels were partly based on Stephenson and the 'secret agent' operation that he ran.[16] Fleming and a colleague from naval intelligence spent a few days in Hamilton, the capital of Bermuda, as they made their way to New York in May 1941. They were joined by Arthur Smith, the Assistant Colonial Secretary of Bermuda, as they travelled on to America. Their mission was ostensibly to examine security in American ports, but the real reason for the visit was to develop collaboration between the two countries on security matters.

Special Operations Executive established a North American base in September 1941 when a property was purchased near Oshawa on the north shore of Lake Ontario.[17] This became Special Training School (STS) 103, which prepared nearly 300 Canadians (and some Americans) to become SOE agents. A second North America base was established in Okanagan Valley, British Columbia, to train SOE agents for operations in the Far East. SOE in Canada recruited mostly from among the Dominion's French-Canadian community, though the Chinese-Canadian community furnished more volunteers. There was also recruitment from immigrants from Italy and eastern Europe, for SOE service in Italy and Yugoslavia. Canadian SOE agents also served in Borneo, Burma, Hungary, Malaya and Sarawak. Other Canadians served with MI9 (Military Intelligence 9), responsible for helping Allied prisoners of war and airmen shot down over enemy territory to escape. French-Canadians, like French-Mauritians, were particularly useful for SOE operations in occupied France, where an estimated total of 1800 SOE agents served between 1941 and 1945. Chinese-Canadians were particularly useful in the east, and service with SOE represented a dramatic shift for a community that until then had been barred from playing any role in the defence of their new country. Chinese people had come to Canada in the late nineteenth century to help build the Canadian Pacific Railway, and those who settled lived mainly in British Columbia. War service presented an opportunity to improve their status in their adopted country, as well as to help China against the hated Japanese.

Newfoundland was that strangest of imperial creatures, a lapsed Dominion.[18] It had enjoyed the privileges of Dominion status until 1934, but in that year, struggling with the effects of the depression, it ceased to be a Dominion and was taken under direct British rule. The ex-Dominion's constitutional status was put on hold for the duration of the war (in all parts of the Empire the London line was that constitutional issues would not be discussed until the cessation of hostilities). Canada was interested in Newfoundland's status as it hoped to absorb it as a new province of the federation, and America was also interested in the territory because of its strategic position. Newfoundland found a role in the war not only as the venue for the signing of the historic Atlantic Charter by Churchill and Roosevelt, but as a base of great strategic value for the defence of North America's eastern shores, as an operational headquarters in the Battle of the Atlantic, and as a key stop-off point in the Atlantic ferry route for aircraft flying from America and Canada to bases in Britain. It was extensively used as a base for warships escorting Atlantic convoys and as a base for aircraft patrolling the Atlantic. Canada spent a good deal of money preparing defences on the island, and the British had begun the construction of Gander airport before the war.

America gained an interest in Newfoundland when base rights were granted under the destroyers-for-bases agreement of September 1940, and American servicemen and construction workers soon began to arrive. From October 1941 American B17s were making anti-submarine sweeps of the north-west Atlantic from Gander airport. This war activity dramatically revived the territory's finances, leading to a large London-held surplus by the end of the war. Like so many other parts of the British Empire, the territory loaned millions to the British government. War-time investigations into the future of Newfoundland were conducted in Whitehall, though concern lingered that economic hardship might return to haunt the territory when the abnormal conditions of war came to an end. The British government was keen to divest itself of possible financial burdens, and this facilitated the discussions that were to see Newfoundland become the tenth Canadian province in 1949.

The British Empire to the west of the British Isles, concentrated in the Caribbean and the Dominion of Canada, also included numerous minor territories, peripheral to the general affairs of Empire, seldom mentioned in Parliament or the British press, but all in some way or another affected by the imperial war of 1939 to 1945. The Royal Navy had for long claimed the Atlantic as its backyard, and this, along with the actions of British explorers, settlers and whalers, had created a network of British islands in the North and South Atlantic. During the war the Royal Navy sought to counter, with its American and Canadian allies, the dire threat to Britain's imports posed by German U-boats and commerce raiders, many operating from Atlantic ports, and this required the extension of British and Allied bases into Atlantic territories other than those they claimed as their own.

In the upper reaches of the South Atlantic Ocean were the barren British revictualling stops, the outcrops of St Helena and Ascension Island. Ascension was part of the colony of St Helena and during the war was the site of an American air base established in 1942. Over 4000 men were employed building and manning an airstrip. On 15 June 1942, the first landing on Ascension by aircraft was achieved by a Swordfish on an anti-submarine reconnaissance mission flown from HMS *Archer*. Thereafter, Liberators, B-24s and B-52s were amongst the aircraft stationed there for anti-submarine patrols in the South Atlantic, and many aircraft making their way to the Gold Coast and the trans-African air route to the Western Desert Air Force broke their flight there. Britain also extended its military facilities in the region to the Azores, where bases were built to provide cover in the Battle of the Atlantic. Consistent pressure had been put on the Portuguese government to permit this in order to help in the war against the U-boats, because the islands were strategically located towards the middle of the North Atlantic. Further south was the British island of Tristan da Cunha, the site of a British radio and meteorological station from 1942.

In the North Atlantic Iceland was occupied by British and Canadian forces from July 1940 because its central position in the Atlantic made it an ideal spot for warships and aircraft engaged in convoy escort and anti-submarine patrolling. It was also important that these facilities be denied to the enemy. Therefore a Royal Navy shore base was established at Reykjavik, HMS *Baldur III*, and tin-helmeted Tommies swarmed over the island, manning anti-aircraft and coastal defence gun emplacements and a Bren gun carrier reaction force. As in other regions of dura-tion empire – new bits of the world taken over by British forces because of their strategic importance (like Persia) or because of their conquest by British arms (like Libya) – American forces later joined their British counterparts, taking over responsibility for Iceland in 1942, thus ending the 'British phase' of its Allied occu-pation (although Royal Navy and RAF units were to remain there until 1945 and 1946 respectively). A few weeks before the Atlantic meeting between Churchill and Roosevelt, in August 1941, American troops had landed in Iceland and America had decided to give naval escort to its convoys bound for Iceland. Churchill visited Iceland on his return from the meeting with Roosevelt in Newfoundland, being greeted by thousands of well-wishers in the capital, Reykjavik. There he addressed them from the balcony of the parliament building, promising a full return to independence as soon as the war was over. Victory in the Atlantic war in fact allowed this to take place earlier, and Iceland was re-established as an inde-pendent republic in 1944. The British and American occupation of Iceland, and the friendly and honourable manner in which the powers left the land when mili-tary necessity permitted, established future relations on a firm footing, and provided the foundation for Iceland's relations with NATO in the post-war years.[19]

Deep in the South Atlantic were the Falkland Islands and South Georgia. An infantry battalion was sent to the Falklands in 1942, for fear of German interven-tion aimed at stirring up the substantial German, Italian and Japanese communities in South America and attempting to snare the region's ultra right-wing regimes into the Axis camp. It was also important to garrison the Falklands given the territorial ambitions of Britain's enemy, Japan, and its rival claimant for the islands, Argentina. In December 1941 the British government believed that there was a chance of Japanese forces making a grab for the Falklands, which would then be handed to Argentina. The government's gaze rested upon Canada when it came to the matter of where to find the troops necessary to form a garrison. Canada, though looking for outlets for its troops, was not keen, having lost units transferred from West Indian garrison duties during the fall of Hong Kong. Britain was particularly keen to ensure that the Falklands were visibly defended because America was considering taking over Allied defensive responsi-bilities in the South Atlantic, and the British feared that it might ask Argentina to defend the islands, to which it had a long historic claim.[20] Throughout the war the Falkland Islands performed their role as a base for Royal Navy warships. In 1939 HMS *Ajax* visited and established a floatplane base on West Falkland. Three other cruisers followed shortly afterwards, bringing British reservists from Uruguay to help staff the Falkland Islands Defence Force. In the spring of 1940 two auxiliary minesweepers arrived to work in the area.

The Falkland Islands were Britain's gateway to its territorial holdings in Antarctica. Britain was the predominant power in Antarctica, and had in the 1920s aimed to make the entire area a splurge of 'pink ice' on the maps of the world.[21] With British attention directed to fighting fronts and imperilled sea routes the world over, however, Argentina seized its chance and sent expeditions to take over British bases in the Antarctic. In 1943 Argentina joined Australia, Britain, Chile, France, New Zealand and Norway in formally staking out claims in the region. Argentina's foray was not the only unwelcome interest, for in 1939 German hydroplanes had – in a modern version of the running-up-the-flag claims to islands and continents favoured by would-be colonizers in the eighteenth and nineteenth centuries – dropped five foot-long darts bearing the swastika across Queen Maud Land, one of the main segments into which Antarctica was loosely divided. Despite these unwelcome efforts on the part of rival powers, and despite being involved in a war of national survival, Britain showed its imperial pedigree and demonstrated the maturity of its strategic gaze by mounting more enduring and powerful operations itself.

In 1941 HMS *Queen of Bermuda* visited the old whaling station at Deception Island in the British South Shetland Islands (claimed in 1820) to destroy coal stocks and oil tanks, so that they could not be used by German warships. German raiders and submarines used islands in the region as hideouts and as rendezvous points for their supply ships (this was also the case in the remote French islands of the Southern Ocean, such as Kerguelen and Crozet, used by enemy raiders and submarines, and therefore visited by British warships and flying boats). HMS *Carnarvon Castle* visited in 1943 and removed Argentinean sovereignty markers. The main British effort came in 1944 with the mounting of Operation Tabarin. A hand-picked fourteen-man team led by Lieutenant James Marr, Royal Naval Volunteer Reserve, undertook the mission. Marr provides a good example of the use in wartime of people who had developed relevant skills through their own peace-time pursuits. One thinks of men like Wingate or Bagnold, known for their inter-war exploits in organizing irregular military forces or exploring deserts, and therefore plucked out by commanders looking for men to do specific war-related jobs. Marr was of this breed: a former Boy Scout, he had accompanied Shackleton on expeditions to Antarctica in the 1920s. He was therefore removed from his position aboard a minesweeper serving with the Eastern Fleet and given command of this latest Antarctic expedition.

The team arrived at the Falklands in January 1944. Soon afterwards their ships, HMS *William Scoresby* and HMS *Fitzroy*, entered the harbour of Deception Island through its narrow entrance, known as Neptune's Bellows (*Scoresby* was a 326-ton minesweeping trawler commandeered by the Admiralty in October 1939). There they found a deserted Norwegian whaling station, with enormous whale bones scattered on the shore. The Union Flag was hoisted, and Argentinean flags were painted out. Bases were established on Deception Island and on the Graham Land coast. Stamps were even issued by the Post Office, bearing an icy scene and the head of King George VI, as an important forward move in Britain's claims to sovereignty. Thus began many months of lonely occupation.

The reasons behind this extraordinary mission were varied, and to an extent are still shrouded in secrecy. Perhaps surprisingly, Churchill knew nothing of the mission. When he found out about it and made hurried enquiries, he was reassured by the Foreign Secretary that it was merely intended to assert sovereignty claims versus those of Argentina and Chile, and was not directed against America (which would no doubt have agitated Churchill). This intention was linked to wider war strategy, given Britain's concern about Argentina's neutrality and pro-Axis sympathies. There was also, of course, the reasonable intention of preventing enemy vessels using the region for shelter, replenishment or repair, though the mission was hardly equipped to take on surfaced U-boats or an armed merchant raider. On top of these reasonable explanations, it is also likely that the Colonial Office, masterminding the operation, had in mind the need to warn off America from interfering in the parts of Antarctica claimed by the British in the post-war years.[22] Those few experts in Whitehall who troubled themselves about policy in such a distant region were wary of the uncertainty of American intentions in the region, and therefore thought it prudent to assert Britain's prior claim and – most importantly – effective occupation. The first permanent bases in 'British Antarctic Territory' were established by Operation Tabarin, for purposes of scientific research but also to strengthen Britain's claims, and the presence that it established was the direct forerunner of today's British Antarctic Survey. A final reason posited, though as yet unsubstantiated, is that Britain was keen to establish bases in remote regions in order to persuade the Germans that their Enigma code system was still a secret, and that British intelligence was derived from its web of bases and forces dispersed about the globe, even on its very edges.

6

The Caribbean

The oldest overseas territories of the British Empire were to be found in the Caribbean and the Americas. In the days of the 'First British Empire', from the seventeenth century until the loss of the American colonies and the onset of the Revolutionary and Napoleonic Wars, Empire had been all about the Atlantic triangle, connecting Britain to the African slave coast and the plantation colonies of America and the Caribbean. This was the heartland of Britain overseas, and, until its decline in the nineteenth century, and the rise of new imperial holdings in the east, the Caribbean was the most valuable part of the Empire – even more lucrative than the thirteen colonies that became the United States of America. European global wars, in vogue from the early eighteenth century, regularly saw asset-stripping operations mounted against the Caribbean holdings of Britain's enemies, and much of the Empire had been gained through warfare and the energy of the large British settler community that had first come to settle the region in the days of the Pilgrim Fathers. Even after the loss of the thirteen colonies and the birth of the Unites States, Britain remained lodged on the American mainland (with its colonies of British Honduras and British Guiana), loyalists flocked to boost the British population in the Maritime Provinces of what in 1867 became the Canadian federation, and Britain remained the most significant imperial power in the islands of the West Indies. To this day the Caribbean remains the region with most external rulers, and most of Europe's remaining overseas possessions are located there.[1]

Britain's territorial spread in the Caribbean was extensive. The Lesser Antilles consisted of the Windward and Leeward Islands. The Windward Islands were Dominica (population 61,000), St Lucia (population 82,000), St Vincent (population 73,000), Barbados (population 221,000) and Grenada (population 85,000). The Leeward Islands included the British islands of Montserrat (population 13,000), the British Virgin Islands (population 7000), Antigua, Barbuda and Redonda (combined population of 45,000) and St Christopher (St Kitts), Nevis and Anguilla (combined population of 48,000). Jamaica (population 1,500,000) and Trinidad were much larger than all of the other British islands. Tobago (population together with Trinidad of 697,000) was a little north of Trinidad, the Caymans Islands north west of Jamaica (dependencies of Jamaica, population 8000). The Bahama Islands (population 70,000) were an extensive string to the north of Cuba and the Dominican Republic that also embraced the Turks and

Caicos Islands (dependencies of Jamaica, population 6000). Bermuda (population 39,000), not really a Caribbean island at all, was marooned in the Atlantic, hence its significance as a naval stronghold over the centuries. In Central America Britain held the colony of British Honduras (population 80,000), first settled by logwood cutters in 1638 and still prized for its mahogany forests and woodmen three hundred years later. Further south on the American mainland lay British Guiana (population 473,000).

It might have been expected that the West Indies, of all places, would remain remote from the war, thousands of miles from the main theatres of fighting and the enemy homelands, and secure in the knowledge that America – should the British naval shield fail – would not allow an enemy to establish itself in that great power's strategic backyard. But the region was not immune. In particular, German naval forces had a global reach, and the Atlantic from east to west and north to south was the ocean where their activities could do most fatally to damage the sea communications on which Britain's and its Empire's war effort depended. From the early days of the war the Caribbean was an active theatre. On 24 November 1940 the *Port Hobart* was sunk off Bermuda by the pocket battleship *Admiral Scheer*. In the previous month two sun-blackened and exhausted sailors were washed up in a lifeboat on the Bahamian island of Eleuthera. They had been on board the tramp steamer *Anglo-Saxon* transporting coal from Newport in Wales to South America, a typical jobbing ship of the British merchant marine engaged on a typical bread-and-butter imperial trading mission. On 21 August 1940 the *Anglo-Saxon* had been attacked and sunk by shells and machine-gun fire from the German liner SS *Weser*. Adrift for weeks, the sailors kept themselves alive with rainwater caught in a tarpaulin and the flying fish that landed inside their boat, until their providential arrival on the shores of Eleuthera, a minute British outcrop in the Caribbean, 3300 miles from where their ship had sunk. After America's entry into the war, enemy submarine activity in the region rocketed, and for many months merchant vessels were sunk with alarming frequency.

The Caribbean was involved in the global struggle on a number of levels beyond the infestation of its waters with enemy vessels threatening both British and American transatlantic and regional shipping. The Empire's need for manpower brought military and civilian recruitment to Bahamians, Hondurans and Jamaicans alike, and the transportation of many thousands of recruits overseas. British territories in the region produced valuable raw materials needed for the war effort. Export industries, like bananas, were also threatened by the disruption that the war brought to imperial trade and shipping. The Caribbean home front was affected by food shortages because of the loss of overseas sources of supply and by opportunities for work on military bases in the region and in America's agricultural industry; some West Indian colonies became involved in the war when a deal struck by Churchill and Roosevelt saw valuable escort vessels join the Royal Navy in return for the establishment of American military bases in the Caribbean; the West Indies contributed a million pounds to Britain for war purposes, three million in interest-free loans, £500,000 towards war charities and £500,000 for the purchase of aircraft; and, finally, the need to defend the region and America's eastern seaboard and to use Caribbean territories for training purposes increased the general level of Allied military activity in the islands of the West Indies.

War-time conditions and imperatives, as in other parts of the British world, brought increased American strategic and political involvement. As in South Asia, the Pacific, the Middle East and West Africa, the Caribbean was a region of traditional British imperial sway in which America became increasingly involved because of the war and the growth that it engendered in American political, military, and economic power, vis-à-vis Britain and vis-à-vis the region concerned. Thus, for example, although the British government wanted the West Indian colonies to import more British coal as a contribution to the war effort, boosting exports and saving precious dollars, the shipping situation was such that they came to rely increasingly on American coal. There simply weren't enough *Anglo-Saxons* to go round, and not enough British sailors to man them, so alternative sources of supply and transport had to be sought, and many British overseas markets were lost for good as a result.

Britain's Caribbean and North and Central American possessions were the only parts of the British Empire and Commonwealth not threatened by enemy invasion, even had Britain lost the war. The threat of air attack was not entirely absent, though the main threat came from German U-boats, which enjoyed notable success before proper defence measures were put in place (particularly before America adopted the convoy system in 1943). Britain made provisions for the region's defence and for the protection of merchant shipping from the outbreak of war in 1939. Long before becoming a belligerent, America was also involved in these measures, for example through the jointly-mounted Neutrality Patrol. The Caribbean islands were seen as flashpoints of espionage, economic warfare and submarine activity. There was a particular concern about Axis infiltration through the French territories in the region, French Guiana, Guadeloupe and Martinique, which remained attached to the Vichy government. The *ralliement* of Guadeloupe and Martinique to the Free French and Allied cause coincided, in the summer of 1943, with the culmination of the U-boat offensive in the Caribbean.

The Caribbean experienced a surprising degree of militarization during the war, as it gained strategic importance and was called upon to contribute to the imperial war effort. Around 20,000 West Indians served in British forces during the war in fighting units, air force roles and in formations like the Women's Auxiliary Air Force or the Auxiliary Territorial Service. War brought America to a greater pitch of strategic awareness and preparedness than ever before and this led to a 'friendly invasion', similar to that experienced in Britain, as supplies and personnel poured into Caribbean colonies as part of America's build up in the newly-designated Caribbean Sea Frontier (CSF) area.[2] For the Caribbean was, of course, a front line of American defence, and one that it was unlikely to ignore given the presence of German forces off of its very shores. Naturally America took primary responsibility for the defence of the Western Atlantic, and this led it to cast its military gaze far across the Caribbean. America's extension of its home defence provisions into the Caribbean, and Britain's pressing need to defend the transatlantic convoys, led to the famous destroyers-for-bases deal in September 1940 between Roosevelt and Churchill.[3] America had long harboured ambitions to secure new military bases in the Caribbean, and had eyed numerous British possessions as suitable sites for air strips and naval anchorages.

At the time of the First World War the American navy had identified several British, French and Dutch Caribbean islands that were desirable as part of a defensive outer rim in a future conflict. In June 1939 the British Ambassador in Washington heard of American proposals arising out of recent naval operations. If war broke out, America would wish to establish a patrol in the Western Atlantic, and would like bases to aid this deployment in places such as Bermuda, St Lucia and Trinidad. In May 1940 the British Ambassador to Washington, Lord Lothian, resurrected the idea. It was likely that America would soon approach the British government on the matter anyway. Lothian pressed London to earn some easy political capital by making a spontaneous offer. In August 1940 President Roosevelt offered fifty destroyers for base rights in the West Indies. The eventual agreement gave America the right to build naval and air bases in numerous British colonies on a ninety-nine year lease, in return for the transfer of the destroyers to the Royal Navy. Eight British territories were affected: Newfoundland; the Bahamas (naval bases on the islands of Mayaguana and Exuma); Jamaica (a naval base at Goat Island in Portland Bight, two miles off the mainland, and an air base at Fort Simonds); St Lucia (a naval air station on Gros islet for seaplanes and an army base at Vieux Fort); Antigua (naval and air bases); Bermuda; Trinidad (air bases, for example at Fort Read, and a naval base in the north-west peninsula); and British Guiana (a naval base on the Essequibo river and an air base at Atkinson's Field). The rights granted extended to airspace, territorial waters and jurisdiction over nationals. It was emphasized by the British government, mindful of the likely concerns of Members of Parliament, the Colonial Office, administrative staff on the ground and West Indian subjects, that sovereignty was not in question.

Quixotically, Hitler declared war on America after Japan's attack on Pearl Harbor in December 1941. In order to make good the declaration, German naval forces then began to attack American vessels wherever they could be found, concentrating particularly on the region off the east coast of America and in the Caribbean. The Battle for the Caribbean lasted from early 1942 until mid-1943. To fight it, America established the CSF with headquarters in America's major Caribbean colony, Puerto Rico, with a subordinate headquarters on the British island of Trinidad, where the submarine threat was particularly bad. At first, German submariners enjoyed such easy success in the region that the first months of the campaign were later referred to as the 'happy time'. This was before Allied convoy and air patrol organizations were properly established. There were two main areas of U-boat attack, one between Cape Hatteras in the American state of North Carolina and the St Lawrence River in Canada, and the other around the British island of Trinidad. A particular U-boat favourite were tankers carrying oil from the Caribbean and Venezuelan oilfields, easily visible at night against the bright lights of the undarkened American coastline.

The sea battle began in earnest on 13 January 1942 when Grand Admiral Karl Dönitz signalled the codeword 'Drumbeat'. Before the month was out five U-boats had sunk 330,000 tons of merchant shipping without loss. On 16 February 1942 five tankers were torpedoed, and the Anglo-Dutch oil refinery at Aruba was shelled. (Shell and Standard Oil had major interests in Aruba, and, like the Dutch territories in the East Indies, the island's defence was underwritten by Britain, as were other Dutch possessions in the region.) The battle was prolonged by America's slowness in adopting effective convoy tactics. America preferred its own system of surface and air patrols and hunting groups, which proved hopelessly unsuccessful. Merchant vessels moved along marked routes. In the first six months of that year, seventy-three American tankers had been sunk, a third of them off the eastern seaboard (in the same period sixty-eight British tankers had gone down in the Atlantic).[4] By November 1942 270 ships had been lost in the region and supplies of vital raw materials like bauxite and oil had been severely disrupted. In 1942–43 a 150-mile strip around Trinidad suffered the greatest losses registered anywhere during the war. The waters around Trinidad remained the most profitable for U-boats until the middle of 1943. This led the USAAF Anti-Submarine Command to base B-18s on Edinburgh Field, Trinidad, for eight months. U-boat supply submarines, known as milch cows, lurked off the north east coast of Bermuda, waiting to rearm and replenish their charges. Well over a million tons of shipping was lost off the eastern seaboard with almost as much again going to the bottom in the Caribbean and the Gulf of Mexico. The First Lord of the Admiralty, Admiral Sir Dudley Pound, was so concerned that he asked Churchill to intervene directly with Roosevelt. Convoy was eventually introduced, the sinkings stopped and the U-boats were withdrawn. The introduction of a convoy system greatly improved the situation for Allied merchant shipping. Vessels were escorted by warships when sailing on routes from Aruba, the Atlantic ports, Brazil, Curacao, Guantanamo, Guiana, Halifax, Panama, the Gulf of St Lawrence and Trinidad. New bases in the region, particularly those built by the Americans on British islands, together with aircraft carriers, provided air cover for the convoys, and the U-boat threat was weakened when some submarines were withdrawn by Admiral Raeder for operations in the North Atlantic.

American forces and organizations grew to meet the threat in a region where it assumed the responsibilities of senior Allied power. The USAAF established the Antilles Air Task Force, with bases in British Guiana, Antigua and elsewhere, B-18 medium bombers flying from British territory in support of convoys. In June 1943 Caribbean Defense Command numbered 111,000 personnel, many of them Puerto

Rican soldiers. Reflecting the decreasing threat to the region's security after that point, the number had fallen to 91,000 by December 1943, and stood at 67,500 on VE Day. By late 1944 Guantanamo, San Juan and Trinidad were the only naval stations with significant operational status.

Inevitably the unprecedented levels of joint Anglo-American involvement and cooperation in Caribbean affairs led to friction. The construction of American bases in so many Caribbean colonies was closely monitored in Whitehall, anxious to ensure that disagreements at the local level did not queer the pitch higher up the scale of Anglo-American cooperation. In October 1943 the Secretary of State for the Colonies asked the West Indian governors of colonies with American bases to report on their impact. It was generally agreed that some prosperity had been caused by the construction of the bases, though this dropped off with their completion. Relations at the higher levels were very good, and satisfactory relations were maintained between American forces and the general public. There were some complaints about Americans behaving as if they were in 'occupied territory', and after some resistance black American servicemen were withdrawn from the bases, rather as they were from the main population centres of Australia after protests from the Dominion's government. In terms of military cooperation, there were problems at a more senior level requiring personnel changes. In Trinidad, the southern hinge of the CSF, Governor Sir Hubert Young and Admiral Sir Michael Hodges, the Naval Officer-in-Charge, did not always enjoy cordial relations with their American counterparts. They were keen to assert British paramountcy in the local command system, which angered the Americans and led to pressure being brought to bear in London for their removal. Sir Bede Clifford was brought in from Mauritius to replace Young as Governor and smooth troubled waters. (A similar appointment was made in the Pacific, where Sir Philip Mitchell was sent as Governor of Fiji and High Commissioner for the Western Pacific with the express aim of damping down differences between British and American authorities in the region.)[5] Clifford was urbane, had served as Governor of the Bahamas before the war, had an American wife and knew the American President socially. In the spirit of reciprocity, the Americans picked a more amenable command team for Trinidad. To ensure no future doubts about the scheme of things, it was made clear that America would exercise paramountcy in command relations in Trinidad and throughout the CSF region and the Western Hemisphere. This, of course, was galling for colonials on the ground, but it was an unmistakable index of America's primacy on its own doorstep, and a harbinger of the greater American penetration of the British West Indies that was to come.

There was another security concern for the British Empire in the Americas, unrelated to the war. Guatemala had a long-standing claim to parts of the British Guianan territory the other side of the border. Amidst the elation of the collapse of Hitler's regime in May 1945 the Chief of the Imperial General Staff, Field Marshal Lord Alanbrooke, recorded that 'in the middle of the crumbling of Germany suddenly wild rumours appear that Guatemala is going to attack our colony of Honduras!' Caught forgivably unawares, Alanbrooke cast around for troops with which to meet this apparent threat, and was only able to come up with a Canadian battalion then based in Jamaica. Fortunately, it transpired that there had been a bad forest fire in Guatemala which could only be quelled through full mobilization of the army, and it was this that had put Honduran nerves on edge. Four months later, however, Guatemalan officially renewed its claim to the border territory.

Traditionally the Caribbean was a defence responsibility of the Royal Navy, though since the mid-nineteenth century Britain had acknowledged the fact that, by virtue of its size and proximity, America would grow to become the region's premier power. Despite this, Britain remained responsible for the security of its American and West Indian possessions. This meant the use of seapower, and the Royal Navy maintained naval stations for the South Atlantic and the West Indies, the latter based on the fortress colony of Bermuda.

The great distance of the West Indian colonies from the fighting fronts during the Second World War prevented the British armed forces from making as much use of local manpower as was generally the case in other parts of the Colonial Empire. Considerable use was still made of Caribbean manpower, however, one impetus for this being the fact that many people wanted the opportunity to join up. The Colonial Office consulted the War Office on how best to satisfy this demand, and announced the result in May 1942 with the decision to form a Caribbean Regiment. The regular army's West Indies Regiment had been disbanded in 1926, and on the outbreak of war in 1939 there was no full-time military formation in the West Indies, though part-time forces existed in every colony. The formation of the new regiment, however, was postponed. There were difficulties in equipping and transporting forces overseas, and the demands of essential production in the region, for example, of sugar and bauxite, needed a plentiful supply of manpower. Some West Indians were already working for the British war effort. The RAF had recruited thousands, and essential war work absorbed thousands more, some into unlikely sectors of the British domestic economy: 525 men from British Honduras, famed for its mahogany forests, formed a forestry unit for service under the Ministry of Supply in the Scottish Highlands. Taken all together, this was a significant migration, one that occurred before the arrival of the Empire *Windrush* in 1948 that started what is commonly regarded as the new era of movement from the post-war 'New Commonwealth' to the old country.[6] Many of these West Indians remained in Britain after the war, as did many of the other workers transported across the world by an Empire at war, including merchant seamen from Bengal and servicemen from the Dominions.

A new factor soon emerged to reverse the postponement of the formation of a West Indies regiment. Locally-recruited West Indian forces under the control of the War Office found a new role with the need to secure the American bases springing up in the region. This led to a re-examination of the formation of a West Indian unit for overseas service. In December 1943 it was decided to raise a West Indian battalion to go to the Mediterranean theatre as soon as possible. It was known as the 1ˢᵗ Battalion The Caribbean Regiment, and, after final training in America, it arrived in Italy in July 1944. It did not impress regional commanders and was sent for intensive training at Gaza in Palestine, and then on to Egypt (where it guarded prisoners of war, and had a falling out with South African troops). The battalion did not see any action. There had been resistance from army authorities in both India and Italy to the use of a West Indian regiment, and it was only on Colonial Office insistence that it be used in an active war theatre that it was dispatched to Italy at all.

Another locally-recruited West Indian military force was the Trinidad Naval Force, which rose in strength from 192 to 1201 men over the course of the war. In 1942, when the bauxite route from British and Dutch Guiana was exposed to severe U-boat attack, the force manned tugs and performed salvage and rescue operations along its length. Many West Indians also served in the Merchant Navy, recruitment for which was organized by the Ministry of War Transport. The West Indies provided more recruits for the RAF than any other part of the Colonial Empire when recruitment was opened later in the war. The recruits were assembled at a reception centre near Kingston, Jamaica, and transported to Britain for ground duties. Over 5500 journeyed to Britain, all but 900 of them from Jamaica. Unusual among territories of the colonial Empire, the Caribbean also provided RAF and RCAF aircrew. RAF numbers exceeded 300, of whom about one hundred were commissioned as officers. A scheme for training pilots was started in Trinidad in 1940, and the first batch of candidates was sent to Britain in early 1941. In Bermuda a Flying Training School was set up by private donors to train men for the RAF. In the Bahamas there was an Air Service Squadron set up on the suggestion of the Officer Commanding the RAF station at Nassau. At the end of the war it numbered over 300 tradesmen and skilled personnel. In addition to war work in Britain or military service in the British armed forces, many more West Indians went to work in America. An acute shortage of labour led to the recruitment of 10,000 Jamaicans and 4500 Bahamans, and in 1944 there were 24,000 workers from four British colonies in America. Over 50,000 West Indians went to work in the American agricultural and war industries over the course of the war.

So West Indians were intimately involved in the Allied war effort, at home and overseas. Throughout the Empire local leaders and British colonial officials emphasized why the fight, no matter how distant it appeared, was that of the people, be they in Fiji, Sarawak or Jamaica. Connie Macdonald from Kingston, Jamaica, recalled:

> I was given a decent Methodist upbringing ... It was the British influence. We didn't grow up with any Jamaican things – we grew up as British. [During the war] there was a mood of fear in Jamaica – they put the fear of God in us.

We were definitely positively told that the Germans wanted us because we were a stepping stone to the coast of America. So we were on our tenterhooks all the time ... So we damn well knew there was a war on. And that's why I joined up in the ATS and went into the British Military Hospital in Kingston.[7]

Billy Strachan, also from Jamaica, arrived in England in March 1940 to serve in the RAF. There he underwent twelve weeks of basic training before specializing as a wireless operator and air gunner. In 1941 he joined a Wellington bomber squadron flying missions over Germany. After completing his thirty missions, he opted to retrain as a pilot. At Cranwell, where he was sent for training, Strachan had his first batman: 'I was a little coloured boy from the Caribbean and instinctively I called him "Sir"'. 'No, Sir', he hastily corrected, 'It is I who call you "Sir".'[8] In such ways did the war accelerate shifts in perception and experience the world over.

Halifax and Bermuda were important naval bases in the western Atlantic region. Because of its location and harbour facilities, Trinidad also joined the ranks of the more significant ports around the world during the war, as it became – like Halifax, Freetown (Sierra Leone), Gibraltar and Galle (Ceylon) – a convoy assembly point. It was a gathering place in the western Atlantic for merchant ships and their escorts before the journey east was undertaken. Trinidad also ranked in the war-time Colonial Empire because it was one of the Empire's few significant producers of oil (the largest imperial producer in 1938), and it also produced cocoa and sugar. The oil was extracted by the British-owned Trinidad Oil Company (taken over by the Texas Company in 1956). As a result of this demand for its produce, the island's revenue increased by over 100 per cent during the war. Trinidad's oil was an important strategic resource. In December 1942, for example, Convoy TM1 carried 25 million gallons of fuel oil to North Africa for vehicles involved in Operation Torch. The establishment of American military bases was another visible effect of the war in Trinidad, and the superior attractions of working on the American bases, which attracted 30,000 workers, meant that labour shortages were experienced in other sectors of the economy.

Other British possessions in the Caribbean experienced a quickening demand for their produce because of the war. The main export of St Vincent and Montserrat was sea island cotton, and this substance was in demand from the Ministry of Supply for the manufacture of barrage balloons. St Vincent was also the world's main source of arrowroot, a tuber used in the manufacture of starch products. British Guiana was an important source of bauxite, a mineral containing alumina and used in the manufacture of aluminium. Illustrating intra-imperial trade links and resource interdependence, the Canadian aircraft industry relied upon bauxite from this source. The British Guianan bauxite industry underwent significant expansion, and the value of its sugar and timber output also increased. The rice industry encountered heightened demand because imports were no longer available from Burma, the Empire's rice bowl, or India, demonstrating the widespread effects of the war. Barbados was another colony where the war brought significant alterations in food demand and food produc-tion, achieved through a restructuring of the island's agricultural system that had until the war been based on sugar, accounting in 1937 for 97 per cent of all exports. The rotation of food crops alongside sugar cane became official policy, and 35 per cent of all arable land was devoted to food crops as much greater self-sufficiency became a priority for colonies around the world.

In a few territories of the British Empire the war period was notable for polit-ical advances as well as for its impact on the home front and for the recruitment of military personnel. Jamaica, which possessed a form of representative govern-ment dating back to 1662, was given a new constitution in November 1944 based on universal adult suffrage (introduced in Trinidad and Tobago the following year). This initiative was the most far-reaching constitutional development in the Empire during the war, and granted full internal self-government and a demo-cratically elected House of Representatives. Indicating the growth of the American factor in British colonial policy-making, this significant constitutional advance came more as a result of American pressure than pressure from Jamaican nation-alists. By the 1940s a political consciousness among middle-class Jamaicans was manifesting itself in political activity and a sense of cultural identity, though this was not characterized by expressions of intense nationalism, and a sense of loyalty to Britain persisted. This emerging political consciousness was not viewed as threatening by the Colonial Office, but rather as a current that might be chan-nelled positively given its compatibility with the idea of gradual constitutional progress within the Commonwealth.

Bermuda was one of the Empire's fortress colonies, historically a winter naval station for the British North Atlantic and West Indies squadrons of the Royal Navy and a centre of British seapower. By the 1940s some parts of the British Empire, particularly Caribbean islands, had become significant tourist destinations, and tourism in turn had become an important source of revenue. Bermuda was heavily dependent on the tourist industry, and thus was badly affected by the coming of war as tourists stayed at home. Despite gloomy economic predictions, however, new military and naval bases provided fresh sources of revenue, as Bermuda became an important air and naval base in the Atlantic war and a valuable British communications centre. Because the weather in the Newfoundland–Nova Scotia area was so poor, the Canadians, with British support, established a base in Bermuda as part of their convoy escort system, and sent an infantry company to help garrison the island at the request of the British government. Under the destroyers-for-bases agreement the Americans also established bases on the island. Bermuda was the site of a British Security Coordination outstation which inter-cepted mail, radio and telegraphic traffic sent from the western hemisphere to occupied Europe, headed by the British Canadian William Stephenson. From a population of 30,000 Bermuda sent men overseas to fight, as well as recruiting for a force for home defence. The Bermuda Volunteer Rifle Corps, a European formation predating the war, served in Europe as a company of the Royal

Lincolnshire Regiment. Members of the Bermuda Militia Infantry and Artillery served as the Bermuda Contingent of the 1st Caribbean Regiment sent to Italy in 1944. In April 1943 the island was also the venue for a secret conference of British and American officials to discuss the plight of Europe's Jews. Among the proposals considered was an approach to Hitler and the temporary abandonment of British restrictions on immigration into Palestine (maintained because unrestricted Jewish immigration inflamed Arab opinion). The only concrete result of the conference was the opening of a refugee centre in North Africa. In January 1942 Winston Churchill visited the island, and addressed its legislative assembly, upon his return journey from his meeting with President Roosevelt off Newfoundland.

The Bahama Islands were hardly ruled by Britain at all, even though they were resolutely red on the map and had been for over three centuries. The Bahamas' war history was colourful and chequered. Despite its infinitesimal significance in the global struggle, it was still deeply affected by world war and the ramifications of being part of an Empire under attack and struggling to fight back.[9] An entrenched House of Assembly, solely representative of the white social and mercantile elite (known as the Bay Street Boys, heirs of the pirates of yore), controlled tax-raising and was therefore able to thwart the policies of the British Governor and his administration. As far as they were concerned, a good Governor was one who confined his ardour to the golf course and the party circuit. Keeping the black masses poor and uneducated was an unspoken policy, and governors intent on visiting upon the island the more enlightened policies gaining currency in the Colonial Office were not at all welcome, as the Duke of Windsor was to discover. Nor were the elite particularly concerned to aid the war effort beyond their own self-interest: the House witnessed hysterical protests in May 1940 when the then Governor, Sir Henry Dundas, proposed to raise income tax as a contribution to the Empire's war effort. It was an island of idle rich, native poor, American tourists and cosmopolitan tax-evaders, and not a place where the government could do very much to improve the general welfare of the non-European population. Given these restraining conditions, and the traditional antipathy to imported colonial officials among the local whites, the Bahamas had a reputation as the worst posting in the British Empire. Inter-war farming schemes had largely failed and many men found work in America. This produced problems of absenteeism familiar in African migrant labour societies, and during Prohibition some of the colony's white elite had grown rich supplying illicit alcohol to Americans. Indeed the islands' economy had been saved in the inter-war years by illicit alcohol trading and by the growth in American tourism, as the colony became a playground for the American rich. Suspect financial dealings were a way of life in the Bahamas, and during the war the islands acted as a clearing house for Nazi currency coming from South America.

Into this troubled land of racial division, with its community of hard-drinking, beyond-the-law whites, stepped the Duke of Windsor and his Duchess, appointed Governor by the British government to get him away from Europe, out of harm's and temptation's way, and hopefully out of the headlines. It was not to be a happy war-time sojourn for the playboy prince of yesteryear. David Windsor felt isolated, feared assassination by the British secret service, became involved with the wrong type of people, talked rather too much of a peace settlement with Germany, worried about his finances and his estate in Canada, and became involved in very questionable business ventures. Whilst finding the governorship of this most awkward little colony frustrating, he hankered after a much bigger job, particularly favouring his appointment as ambassador to Washington following Lord Lothian's death (the post was filled by Lord Halifax), and leaning on people to secure him at least a role as a unique British ambassador-at-large in America. He was, of course, deluding himself, as no British government would want this accident-prone, somewhat limited man anywhere near high office, delicate negotiations or major British interests. Even when the Duke, after several years of hard and commendable work in the Bahamas, asked Churchill in person for a transfer (to something much more appropriate to his status was the *sotto voce* message), the best that the Prime Minister could come up with was the governorship of neighbouring Bermuda, hardly a glittering gubernatorial ascent. Whilst in the Bahamas the Duke of Windsor became an implacable enemy of the ruling white oligarchy, though something of a hero amongst the black population of the islands, who greeted the great grandson of Queen Victoria with something approaching messianic fervour upon his arrival, and appreciated his attempts to improve the employment prospects of the poverty-stricken Out Islanders, not least through employment on American military bases and in the Florida agricultural sector. White opposition to his appointment was somewhat mollified by the calculated knowledge that he would prove an incomparable draw for the American tourists, and a crowd of over 16,000 people heralded his arrival in August 1940.

It was not by any means the Duke of Windsor's first visit to the West Indies. Like his brother, King George VI, the Duke had devoted many months to touring the world on behalf of the British monarchy and government. In many ways the pioneer of royal world tours, as Prince of Wales he had got to know Britain's Caribbean positions in the years following the First World War (a war in which he had served with the Grenadier Guards in Egypt). He then embarked upon a series of lengthy imperial tours, conceived by Lloyd George's Cabinet as a means of expressing Britain's thanks to the Empire and Commonwealth for its support during the war. In 1919 he made an official tour of America, Canada and Newfoundland. This was followed in 1920 by a tour of Australia, New Zealand and the British Pacific islands, which included official visits to British West Indian possessions such as Antigua (capital of the Leeward Islands) Barbados, Bermuda, Grenada (capital of the Windward Islands), Trinidad and British Guiana in Central America.

Both the 1919 and the 1920 tours were made aboard the battlecruiser HMS *Renown*. The same warship conveyed the Prince of Wales on his next major imperial tour in 1921–22, during which he spent four months in India and a month in Japan. On the outward and homeward voyages he visited all the British possessions strung along the sea highway between Gibraltar and the Pacific. He inaugurated the new constitution at Malta and visited Aden, Brunei, Ceylon, Hong Kong, Malaya and Singapore. The young Prince was guest of the King of Egypt in Cairo and of the American government in the Philippines. During his long stay in India he traversed the subcontinent from sea to sea and from Madras to Afghanistan, and travelled through the heart of Burma and into the kingdom of Nepal. As well as inspecting units such as the Jodhpur Lancers and the 1/7 Rajputs, a feature of this tour was the unveiling of memorials – for example in Japan, Karachi and Singapore – to the First World War dead of the Empire and Commonwealth and its allies. In visiting limbless ex-servicemen in India, or meeting the relatives of Maltese soldiers killed during the First World War, the connection between Britain, Empire and war was strikingly underlined. His immense popularity with the people of the islands, as well as those of America and Canada when he visited those countries on private business amidst a swirl of media attention, bore witness to the affection in which he was held, much of it a direct result of his days of royal touring.

Given this pedigree of regal globetrotting, the Duke's appointment to the Bahamas for a five-year stint as Governor was a dramatic come down. The Duchess of Windsor made the best she could of this West Indian exile, and, like her husband, welcomed any chance to flee to the limelight and civilization of an American tour or visit. Given their status, the Duke and Duchess attracted massive attention wherever they went. Their part-tour, part-holiday to American in September 1941, including a visit to the Duchess's home town of Baltimore, received wide media attention. In Baltimore a crowd of 5000 gathered to greet them, and they toured the city's British relief societies. During their time away from the Bahamas they also visited their Canadian ranch, and the Duke presented wings to newly-qualified RCAF airmen. In the Bahamas the Duchess worked resolutely for the war effort as head of the local Red Cross, and when the Bahamas began to host large numbers of American and British servicemen she threw herself into their entertainment, as did other members of the white elite. The Imperial Order of the Daughters of Empire set up a canteen in the Masonic Building, and dances were held, for example at the Nassau Yacht Club. Some wealthy refugees made their way from Europe to the Bahamas, away from the war and its hardships. Most were upper middle-class Britons, including the rather over-zealously evacuated boys of Belmont School. The Duchess also did her bit for the poor inhabitants of the Out Islands through the Bahamas Assistance Fund. As the Duchess reminded the editor of *Picture Post* in August 1941, the Bahamas might be remote from the war, but the local branch of the British Red Cross had just raised nearly £2800 on Empire Flag Day, 80,000 garments had been sent to Britain, £26,000 had been raised for the RAF and £12,000 for the Citizens' War Relief Fund.

Unemployment stalked the Bahamas, and the single-most visible effect of Pearl Harbor was the death of the American tourist trade. This threatened new ruin, though the arrival of British and American forces and the construction of military bases in 1942 as part of the destroyers-for-bases deal shored up the colony's economy. War-time military employment proved to be the colony's economic salvation, though it also caused serious rioting that worried London. The Duke had thrown himself wholeheartedly into the planning for American and British bases in the island, to the benefit of many poor islanders, and as a contribution to the war effort. With America joining the fray, the Duke was transformed 'from mascot of a tourist playground to lord of a far-flung battle-line'.[10] The Duke, with very little cooperation from the House of Assembly, geared the islands for a greater participation in the imperial war effort. The local defence force was strengthened, controls were imposed on those entering and leaving the colony, measures were taken in conjunction with America to prevent U-boats from sheltering in the islands, and American naval forces based in Florida were detailed to provide cover for the Bahamas if needed. The Duke agreed to the immediate establishment of air and sea reconnaissance stations in New Providence, as well as a string of intelligence posts. President Roosevelt, on a holiday cruise in December 1940, had visited the Bahamas to meet the Duke and examine the proposed sites for American naval bases, engendering great hostility from the Foreign Office when told of this meeting by Lord Lothian. The British government was childishly sensitive to the 'damage' that this most awkward loose cannon could do to relations with America, and took pains to snub the Duke and Duchess, and to keep them away from important Americans on every possible occasion. This deeply upset the Duke. In spite of London's fears, the Americans were rather impressed by the Duke's ready and efficient cooperation.

British servicemen arrived in strength in the Bahamas, particularly members of the RAF training under the British Empire Air Training Scheme (BEATS). In April 1942 it was announced that a major RAF base would be built on New Providence under the Lend-Lease scheme, employing local labour in its construction and maintenance. The base was a result of the RAF's decision to outsource a great deal of its flight training to the Empire, especially to Canada, under BEATS. After Pearl Harbor it was decided to establish a new pattern of Operational Training Units (OTU) at key positions in the Atlantic. Their purpose was to train crews in a relatively safe location, whilst also offering useful cover in the all-important Convoy Escort System, oceanic reconnaissance and submarine-hunting. The OTU on New Providence was the third such base to be opened, and was located on Nassau's existing airport at Oakes Field. What was officially known as OTU 111, with an establishment of upwards of a thousand military personnel, gave the Bahamas an imperial military significance for the first time in its history. The submarine-hunting and convoy protection role of OTU 111 proved to be a great success. By April 1943, when the first batch of trainees returned to Britain, the base had a permanent establishment of eighty-four officers and 1300 other ranks, instructing almost 400 pupils. A year later the permanent establishment had risen to over 2000, with 750 pupils. The Commanding Officer was Group Captain Waite, renowned a few years later for his part in organizing the Berlin Airlift. Nassau was transformed from the ghost town that had so appalled the Duke and Duchess upon their arrival in 1940 to one humming with the bustle of thousands of British and American service personnel. The RAF development plan for the Bahamas military infrastructure also included an important new base for RAF Transport Command, as part of the Anglo-American infrastructure ferrying men and aircraft from America to Africa (for onward transit across the continent to the Middle East theatre) and to Britain itself. This role required the construction of a second base, ten miles outside Nassau, known as Windsor Field. The construction of both facilities was supervised by American forces employing two to three thousand unskilled and a thousand skilled local labourers. The Americans also built considerable facilities for their own forces.

The island's use as a staging post between America and Africa allowed some enterprising airmen to supplement their war pay in a manner that would not have disgraced the airmen of Joseph Heller's novel *Catch-22*: cut-price alcohol was flown to Ascension Island in mid-Atlantic or Recife in Brazil, where aircraft taking this circuitous route to Africa and thence to the fighting in the Western Desert stopped off to refuel, and sold on arrival, usually for American dollars. This money could be brought back to Nassau and exchanged for sterling, or could be taken on to Accra, site of the main airbase in the Gold Coast. Here diamonds could be purchased, for resale in Recife on the return journey.

In March 1942 the Cameron Highlanders arrived, followed by Canadian troops. The Highlanders had been occupying the Dutch oil island of Aruba, and the Canadians had escorted prisoners of war to be interned on the island. These troops were intended to defend Nassau and to guard Government House, which was also surrounded by electric fences. There were concerns in London, shared by Churchill, about the prospect of a royal kidnap attempt mounted by a U-boat raiding party. Enemy submarines were prowling the New Providence Channel, sometimes leaving smoke and oil trails on the surface of the water, and recently two ships had been sunk off the Bahamas by Italian submarines. In the light of this threat, extra security was needed, as the island's defences were rudimentary and the locally-recruited Bahamas Defence Force was considered unreliable.

Determined to ensure future employment for Bahamians, the Duke pressed the policy of allowing America to recruit agricultural workers in the islands. As usual, Whitehall was at first extremely dismissive of this plan, and the Colonial Office played its favourite game where anything to do with the Duke was concerned and constructed obstacles all along the way. The Duke's perseverance meant that in April 1943 he was able to announce on the radio that 2500 labourers had already departed for the annual bean crop in Florida. These men harvested beans and sugar cane, before special trains took them north to dig potatoes and cut vegetables in Virginia and North Carolina. Between 1943 and 1946 over 8000 Bahamians made the journey, priority being given to those volunteers from the particularly poverty-stricken Out Islands.

The extensive use of the Bahamas by British and American forces, and their employment of local labour, was an entry in the success side of the Duke of Windsor's ledger. These developments did, however, lead to trouble. Riots in Nassau between May and August 1942 were triggered by the wage grievances of locals working on the military projects. Under Lend-Lease arrangements projects undertaken by America in British territories were carried out by American contractors using local labour paid at local rates. The problem was that the Americans working on the same project were paid on a completely different scale, and the rumour got around that the Americans had been willing to offer greater remuneration to the local labourers, but had been prevented from doing so by the colonial government. Between 2000 and 3000 men downed tools and marched on the capital on 1 June 1942. The official report of the Commission of Enquiry into the riots was a victory for the Duke, as it lifted the lid on the island's poisonous racial relations and condemned the local white establishment and its attitudes, demanding rapid and sweeping reforms. The Duke was instrumental in settling the riots and initiating policies that would, at last and in the teeth of local white opposition, do something to improve the lot of the poverty-stricken mass of the population. The Nassau riots were significant beyond the islands, for they attracted Whitehall's attention and further convinced the Colonial Office – concerned in the 1930s about labour riots in the West Indies and in Mauritius – that significant and meaningful reform would be needed to secure the post-war colonial world.[11]

The imperial heyday of the Caribbean had lasted until the 1830s when sugar, slaves and the Atlantic economy ceased to beat at the heart of the Empire. By the 1930s fortunes had changed and the Caribbean had become an imperial poor relation. Riots and disturbances there during the depression were one of the major causes of the reappraisal of colonial rule undertaken by the Colonial Office during the war. This reappraisal led to a sea change in British imperial policy, symbolized by the Colonial Development and Welfare Acts of 1940 and 1945, which for the first time established the principle that the British government had a duty to provide funds to advance the social and economic wellbeing of its colonial charges (as it had recently begun to do for its subjects in Britain itself). This was motivated by altruism and the desire to better utilize colonial resources for the benefit of the British imperial economy. The Colonial Office was also mindful of the need to make 'shop windows' of colonies – particularly those on America's doorstep and therefore subject to easy scrutiny – as it undertook a sustained war-time propaganda and education effort to disarm American criticism of British 'imperialism'. There was also the need to ensure that enemy countries and dubious allies did not have ammunition to use against Britain in this most ideological of struggles.

Britain felt the need to respond to a growing American challenge for leadership in regions like the Caribbean in which Britain had hitherto enjoyed almost exclusive dominance. Even if rivalled, it had usually been by a weaker European power that lacked the dynamism and potential of America, and one that shared a similar ideology to Britain when it came to maintaining the status quo in the European colonial world. A measure of America's growing involvement in the affairs of the Caribbean – even in the British possessions themselves – was the creation in March 1942 of the Anglo-American Caribbean Commission (AACC).[12] This was a regional body set up to discuss issues of mutual concern and long-term policy, though one in which the British resolutely resisted American pressure, and which did not enjoy any executive authority vis-à-vis colonial governments. The Secretary of State for the Colonies was anxious to stress that the AACC was not an exercise in joint government, and that it had no executive authority. The AACC, however, allowed America a voice in decisions relating to development, political reform and trade. Not only was it symbolic of the foot in the door that the war gave America in many imperial regions, it was also a step in the direction of federation for the British West Indies. The prospect of a federation – historically the preferred British solution in regions of fragmented but contiguous 'red' on the map – was discussed by the Secretary of State for the Colonies and the West Indian governors in 1944 and 1945.[13] A common policy approach in the region had been adumbrated in 1940 with the creation of a Development and Welfare Organization with functions extending to all the British West Indian colonies (except Bermuda and the Bahamas), and in 1944 a British West Indian Central Labour Organization was established to regulate the flow of islanders going overseas to find war-time employment. The AACC also had its practical war-time uses where a regional approach was simply the most efficient utilization of resources. Thus the submarine onslaught in the Caribbean led the AACC to consider measures to ensure that famine did not visit the West Indies, given its dependence on imported foodstuffs.

South America is commonly viewed by imperial historians as one of the main areas of British 'informal empire' and, given Britain's extensive interests in the cone, and its offshore possessions, it rightly comes under consideration here. Britain, it is important to remember, was in 1939 the world's only genuinely *global* power, and therefore it naturally had interests far beyond the Empire and Commonwealth, large though these were. Since countries like Argentina, Brazil and Chile had gained independence from Spain and Portugal, in the early nineteenth century (with a large measure of British assistance), they had developed strong economic and even cultural links with Britain. In particular, Britain had been their major external trading partner. Ships of the merchant marine had carried South American produce overseas and British capital raised in the City of London had fuelled South American development. British investment had, for example, constructed the Argentine railway network, still British-owned at the time of the Second World War, and the utilities of burgeoning cities like Buenos Aires (Britain's links with Argentina were so strong that historians have termed it the 'sixth Dominion'). Though Britain's position in South America had been eroded by the natural rise to prominence of America, and the trade competition of other powers (notably Germany), until the First World War Britain had remained streets ahead in terms of investment. Even during the inter-war years links remained strong and British financial power considerable.

During the war Britain imposed controls on trade with South America, given its neutrality and the considerable Axis interests in the region (including a Nazi espionage network). The huge economic strain that the war placed upon Britain accelerated its decline in South America. On the one hand, Britain no longer had capital to invest; quite the reverse, it was selling overseas assets very rapidly. On the other hand, Britain was not able to supply its overseas markets to the same level as in peacetime because of shipping shortages and the reorientation of British industry towards the war effort. This, of course, opened the door to the only competitor in a position to take advantage, and here as elsewhere American economic power began to show more than ever before. By 1945, Britain took only 12 per cent of the region's exports and provided a mere 4 per cent of its imports.

As elsewhere, British policy-makers were convinced that America's aims in the region were not only to defeat enemy interests but also to undermine and supplant those of Britain and other allies. Argentina was an obstacle to American dominance, given its historic ties with Britain, its own ambitions to be a regional leader and the fact that it had some sympathy with the enemy cause. Britain was more tolerant of Argentina's neutral stance than was America. Argentina remained an important source of food for Britain – 40 per cent of Britain's meat came from Argentina – and was willing to accept blocked sterling balances in London in return (the £130 million held in London by 1946 was then used to buy out Britain's stake in the country's railway network and utilities). Argentina finally declared war on the Axis powers in March 1945. Before that, thousands of Argentineans had rallied to the British cause, reflecting the historic ties between the two countries. Over 4000 volunteers joined the British armed forces. Of these, 600 joined the RAF, many serving with No. 164 (Argentine-British) Squadron, which bore the sun of the Argentine national flag on its badge.[14] Brazil declared war on the Axis powers in February 1942, and this allowed Recife to become an important air staging base for American aircraft flying to the Middle East by way of Trinidad, Ascension Island and the Gold Coast, and meant that 25,000 Brazilians fought in the Italian campaign alongside Allied forces.[15]

As for military action, the naval Battle of the River Plate was fought off the coast of Uruguay. Three outgunned British cruisers, including the New Zealand ship Achilles, trapped the German pocket battleship Graf Spee in Montevideo, where it had gone to repair after a battle with the British warships. The local authorities insisted that, in terms of the laws of warfare and neutrality, the ship must leave within a set time. Believing that he faced a stronger British force than was in fact the case, the German captain decided to scuttle his ship.

So the Empire and Commonwealth to the west of the British Isles – from the mighty Dominion of Canada to barren rocks marooned in the mid-Atlantic and the tropical islands of the Caribbean – became part of a global war that required their resources, their manpower and their military basing facilities. In an imperial world that was so interlinked, where a splash in Europe could cause a significant ripple in the South Pacific, the defence of the Atlantic world was important for the defence of the Indian Ocean and Middle East, because of the sea routes that ran through the Atlantic and around the Cape of Good Hope. Just as important, the Atlantic had a narrow gateway, through the Straits of Gibraltar, that also led to the Middle East through the Mediterranean Sea, where the greatest of all the imperial battles of the Second World War was fought in a region stretching from Morocco and Gibraltar in the west to Persia in the east, and from the Sudan and Aden in the south to Austria in the north. As in the Atlantic, the British Mediterranean world was to be a scene of the utmost importance to the Empire at war and the survival of the Empire itself.

7

The Mediterranean

The Mediterranean and Middle East were sites of the greatest importance for the British imperial war effort, though if Mussolini had stayed out of the fray perhaps the Mediterranean would have been much more of a sideshow as Britain fought it out with Germany in the Atlantic and north Europe.[1] As it happened, the region formed the Empire's central front as it sought to achieve several objectives; to crush the Italian Empire; to retain naval supremacy in the 'inland ocean'; to prevent the Germans from capturing the vital Suez Canal; to clear the Red Sea of enemy bases and secure East Africa; and to counter any German thrust into the region through Turkey, Iraq or Iran, which would have jeopardized the Empire's main oil reserves and the security of India. It was from the Egyptian base camp, too, that Britain sought to uphold the independence of Greece, keep Turkey out of the Axis camp and threaten the Germans through the backdoor in the Balkans. As well as keeping the Germans out of the Middle East, what has been termed the British 'Mediterranean strategy' aimed at drawing German troops from the Western Front, knocking Italy out of the war and bolstering the region's friendly regimes.[2]

The Middle East and Mediterranean formed a massive theatre of diverse conflicts, most of them with roots in Britain's imperial past and imperial strategic predilections. Italy first brought war to the region with its invasions of Egypt and Greece, the independence of which had been guaranteed by Britain at the time of the Polish guarantee. Italy's egregious failure in both campaigns soon drew in a stiffening of German forces that prolonged the war in the region until 1943, represented most famously by the arrival of Britain's favourite wartime German general, Erwin Rommel, the 'Desert Fox', who so handsomely set about giving Eighth Army a succession of bloody noses when not escaping before its lumbering advances.[3] German success in prolonging war in the region also brought America into the theatre, with an entire army fighting in Sicily and Italy. General Dwight Eisenhower practised his role as supreme commander when he took charge of Allied forces invading French North-West Africa late in 1942, those forces themselves rehearsing a massive Allied amphibious attack eighteen months before the Normandy landings. The British and their imperial allies also fought extensive smaller campaigns in the Aegean, Crete, East Africa, Greece, Iraq, Iran and Syria, and the war at sea and in the air, a famous preserve of the colony of Malta, extended the vast fighting fronts over which Middle East Command, RAF Middle East and the Mediterranean Fleet presided.

Imperial communications, the movement of warships and troops, the defence of India and containment of Russia, and the lucrative trading business of the British imperial world, were all traditionally served by the Suez Canal, making the eastern Mediterranean a strategic nodal point without equal outside of home waters. As Ernest Bevin remarked in 1949, the Middle East was of 'cardinal importance, second only to the United Kingdom itself'. Even at the lowest point of Britain's fortunes in the Middle East in 1941–42, the War Cabinet did not consider abandoning the region, and was even prepared to denude Britain of soldiers and tanks for its defence. Signifying Britain's traditional imperial preoccupations, and the discounting in the 1920s and 1930s of a future European conflict involving a sizeable British force, Britain's main expeditionary strength was intended for intervention in the Middle East rather than Europe. Similarly, whilst RAF bases in the Far East and South Asia could whistle for modern aircraft, the Middle East was lavished with Spitfires and Hurricanes, even whilst the battle in the skies over Britain remained undecided.

By the twentieth century British predominance in the Middle East had become an article of faith. The Royal Navy had been a power in the region for nearly two centuries, attracted by the eastern Mediterranean terminus of the historic overland route to the riches of the East and by the need to support British diplomacy affecting the European balance of power. British warships had first appeared in the Mediterranean in 1620, attempting to curb the activities of Barbary pirates on the North African coast. Defence of the overland route to India also kept the British alert, and Napoleon's Egyptian expedition in 1799 brought an increased British commitment to the defence of its interests in the region. Throughout the nineteenth century a fundamental British policy had been Russian containment through support for the Ottoman Empire and the guardianship of the Dardanelles. This was the famous and never adequately answered 'Eastern Question'. Britain had played a role in fostering the ambitions of various states or would-be states in the region, and quashing the aspirations of others. In the early nineteenth century Greek independence had been fostered (leading, in part, to British attempts to defend it in the Second World War) and the expansionist aspirations of Egypt's Mehmet Ali quashed. The British fought in the Mediterranean against the Spanish and the French, establishing their naval power and gaining numerous island fortresses in the process. Wars with foreign powers, or wars between foreign powers that threatened to affect British interests, led to the acquisition of strategic footholds including Cyprus, Gibraltar, the Ionian Islands, Malta and Minorca. The completion of the Suez Canal made the region of paramount importance for Britain, and it became a central tenet of British policy that no other power should be allowed to dominate that strategic artery. As soon as the Suez Canal opened, in 1869, it rivalled the Cape route as the most important thoroughfare in the world for British merchant and naval vessels. It was, in Anthony Eden's words, 'the swing-door of the British Empire'.

Britain's determination to remain the supreme power in the region led to the invasion of Egypt in 1882 and the beginning of Britain's lengthy 'temporary occupation' (offering, in terms of the justifications for intervention and the expressed purpose of the forces that remained thereafter, a superb parallel with Iraq in the early twenty-first century). This intervention led to the birth of the Suez Canal military base that was to be so important in two world wars. The Royal Navy maintained a major base for the Mediterranean Fleet at Alexandria as well at Malta. From the late nineteenth century the newly-minted Great Powers of Italy and Germany arrived on the Mediterranean scene, jockeying for positions of imperial worth, or for the more subtle but more profitable benefits that might come from finding favour at the courts of the Sultan and the Shah. In the years leading up to the First World War German penetration of the region, in terms of propaganda, financial largesse (the proposed Berlin–Baghdad railway had British diplomats quivering) and diplomatic links, threatened to undermine Britain's position and appeared to offer regional leaders an attractive alternative to British overlordship. To add a new ingredient to this potent cocktail of strategic, diplomatic and economic reasons for viewing the Mediterranean as vital to British world power, oil was discovered and came increasingly to be depended upon. As First Lord of the Admiralty, Churchill supervised the transition of the Royal Navy from coal to oil in the years before the First World War. Though in 1938 the Middle East was only responsible for 5 per cent of the world's oil output, it was recognized as a region with great potential, and Britain had been chiefly responsible for developing it. Furthermore, in the Second World War Britain's entire war effort in the Middle East and Mediterranean region depended on oil from Iran and Iraq. If it was lost, in all probability the war in the region would be lost too, and possibly the war as a whole.

Triumph over the Central Powers in 1918 netted Britain the lion's share of the Ottoman Empire's former Middle Eastern provinces. Victory in the war rested at least in part, the British believed, on naval dominance of the Mediterranean, as had been the case in the Revolutionary and Napoleonic Wars, and Britain was therefore unlikely to relax its grip on the region in the two decades before the Second World War. Armed with Mandates from the new League of Nations, Britain carved out a new empire in Palestine, Transjordan and Iraq, and reinforced its position as the dominant power in this region cherished by imperial strategists. This dominance came at a price, however, and Britain found itself in the inter-war years having to manage Arab nationalism (stimulated by Italian and German propaganda), the rising ambitions of Fascist Italy (desirous of an African and Mediterranean Empire) and the claim for a Jewish homeland in Palestine given such encouragement by the Balfour Declaration of 1917. Italy was a particular problem, presenting Britain with the almost insoluble dilemma of a Great Power in a key region that believed that Britain's position fundamentally undermined its own. Mussolini was convinced that Italy could only be great if it possessed Egypt. Italian competition on the Egyptian–Libyan border was robust, the Italian community in Egypt was cultivated and Radio Bari broadcast pro-Italian propaganda in Arabic.

As Britain entered the Second World War its strategy in the region was the same as it had been at the outbreak of war in 1914: to safeguard imperial communications with India and the Far East; to keep open the Mediterranean, the Suez Canal and the Red Sea for British shipping; and to encourage and build up resistance in Turkey, Greece and the Balkans as defences against the invasion of the Middle East and ultimately India. Furthermore, if the enemy took Egypt, as it looked like doing for some time, the nightmare possibility of the Axis powers linking with Japan – itself eyeing Madagascar as a possible western target – could be glimpsed. This key region had to be mobilized to support a vast military and logistics establishment central to Britain's global war effort, without alienating public opinion in the Arab world. The stakes were almost impossibly high.

Though in 1939 British predominance in the Middle East and western Mediterranean was not for negotiation, the belligerence of Mussolini, and the impressive size and modernity of the Italian air force and navy (six battleships, nineteen cruisers, fifty-two destroyers and 113 submarines), was a cause for concern. This was doubly so because whilst preparing to contain Italy and protect the Suez Canal, Britain also had to be prepared to transfer units of the Mediterranean Fleet east against the Japanese. Once Britain was at war with Germany, this Mediterranean balancing act became even more difficult, for it was clear that, if Italy chose to commence hostilities, there was a strong possibility of Germany being dragged into the region. German penetration might also come about if Hitler chose to make war on Russia, because it could find itself in a position to attack the Middle East from the north.

Fortunately Britain was not alone in the Mediterranean but stood allied with the considerable power of France. The French Mediterranean squadron based on Toulon guarded the western end of the sea, and together with the British fleet in the eastern and central Mediterranean, held the Italian fleet in check. In North Africa and the Levant there were over a quarter of a million French and French colonial troops. This Armée d'Afrique provided a counterweight to the Italian army in Libya. Here, as in Europe and South-East Asia, the implications of French capitulation were not considered as a possibility, though they were to be almost catastrophic. France's surrender in June 1940 deprived Britain of its Mediterranean ally, and raised the unwelcome problem of how to deal with the French military presence in the region that was now in uneasy neutrality (leading to the imperial invasion of French Middle Eastern colonies, and the Royal Navy's attack on the French Mediterranean squadron at Oran). This meant that now Britain had to find even more naval resources to commit to the Mediterranean, and made the likelihood of a battlefleet being available for Singapore extremely remote. Vichy territories in the region remained hostile to Britain and friendly to Germany. In May 1941 the Vichy government promised to aid Germany in Africa and the Middle East, and granted German forces access to airfields in Syria and the port of Bizerta. Thus the fall of France transformed the strategic position in the Mediterranean. With the conclusion of the armistice, Italy's force of six battleships became the largest capital force in the Mediterranean and General Weygand's Armée d'Afrique expanded to 250,000. Marchese Rodolfo Graziani's army in Libya outnumbered the 63,000 troops of the Commander-in-Chief Middle East, General Sir Archibald Wavell, in Egypt and Palestine by nearly four to one, and in East Africa another, even larger Italian army was gathered under the Duke of Aosta. In the whole of Wavell's vast command, the number of troops fell short of 90,000, including 27,500 in Palestine – many of whom were horsed, ill-equipped and under-trained – and sundry units in the Sudan, Kenya and British Somaliland.

In spite of these odds, vast experience of imperial warfare had taught the British Army that it was not necessarily fatal to be outnumbered by an enemy.[4] In charge of the largest military command of its kind then in existence, Wavell was perhaps the most experienced *imperial* commander of the entire war. He was top dog in the Middle East at the time of Rommel's arrival in the Western Desert and also directed the campaigns in East Africa, Syria, Iran and Iraq, reigning in Cairo until Churchill's impatience saw him swap commands with the erstwhile Commander-in-Chief India, General Sir Claude Auchinleck.*

The overwhelming odds in Italy's favour following the fall of France were sufficient even for Mussolini to decide that the time was ripe for a declaration of war. If he failed to move now, Britain might be defeated by Germany alone, and Italy would be in a weaker position from which to claim a share of the region's imperial spoils.[5] So Mussolini launched his vast African armies against Britain's imperial borders in both the desert and East Africa, thus opening the see-saw struggle that was to take British imperial forces backwards and forwards across the deserts of the Maghreb for over two years. Mussolini, brimming with a confidence born of Germany's apparently imminent defeat of the RAF in the Battle of Britain, even had a white charger shipped out to Libya in anticipation of a triumphant entry into Cairo, clearly echoing the fantasized Fascist foundation myth of Mussolini's 1922 March on Rome. As an opening gambit, on 13 September 1940 Mussolini ordered an advance into Egypt. After advancing fifty miles

---

*   Wavell arrived in Delhi in time to take over the shattered rump of Far East Command in the aftermath of the defeat in Malaya, in addition to his Indian responsibilities. This saw him briefly command the American-British-Dutch-Australian Command based on Java, in which position he granted the General Officer Commanding Malaya, Lieutenant-General Arthur Percival, permission to surrender Singapore at his discretion. Wavell spent the rest of the war in India, responsible for the subcontinent's defence and mobilization as well as the campaign in Burma. From 1943 he became Viceroy of India upon Auchinleck's return to the subcontinent as Commander-in-Chief, a move that coincided with the creation of South East Asia Command to take over responsibility for the fighting fronts in Burma, India and Malaya.

Graziani's forces halted at Sidi Barrani and dug in, beginning what the British called the 'sitzkreig'.

The Middle East contained the greatest overseas concentration of British military and naval power, and the British forces facing the huge Italian colonial armies in Libya and Abyssinia were quickly built up as war in the region became increasingly likely. In the first seven months of 1941 convoys delivered 144,000 men from Britain, 60,000 from Australia and New Zealand, 23,000 from India and 12,000 from South Africa. The convoys from Australia were the first troop trips of the liners *Queen Elizabeth* and *Queen Mary*, which had been fitted out as troopships in Sydney. At the beginning of 1941 the ration strength of MEC was 336,000; in July 1942 the figure was 750,000, and it soon rose to over a million. As the Chief of the Imperial General Staff, General Sir Alan Brooke, had cause to note on more than one occasion, Churchill would grab for such statistics when he was in a bad mood and impatient with the apparent lack of military progress in the region. Why, he would ask, if there were 750,000 men on the strength, were only 100,000 taking the field against Rommel? An exasperated Brooke, Churchill's senior soldier for most of the war, wrote that he 'could not or chose not' to understand that MEC 'was a vast base for operations in various theatres besides the Western Desert'.*[6]

Early in the war the Middle East looked like one of the few regions in which British forces could expect success, and indeed the early performance of British imperial forces against the Italian army and navy was outstanding, leading by the spring of 1941 to the decimation of Italy's East African Empire and the battering of its forces in Libya. German intervention from February 1941, however, led to rapid reverses and the prolongation of the campaign in North Africa for two more years. What was particularly galling was that for Hitler the Middle East was a subsidiary theatre, whereas for Britain it was very much the main event in the first three years of the war. Hitler hoped to engage British imperial forces at low cost in the Middle East, and work with friendly governments in the region like those in Syria and Lebanon, bringing the Luftwaffe within range of the Suez Canal and the Iraqi oilfields and threatening Britain's position in the whole region. One result of the fall of France was that the governments of Syria and Lebanon aligned themselves with the Vichy regime, further threatening Britain's position in the eastern Mediterranean and inviting German involvement. Britain therefore faced the prospect of defeat in the desert, loss at sea, German penetration through the Caucasus, and a range of internal campaigns against German-leaning indigenous rulers hoping for German aid. All this whilst being at the end of the world's

---

*   Like most of his contemporaries in the armed forces, Brooke was an old hand at imperial soldiering, which augmented his capacity to direct the British Army's affairs during a global struggle. He had spent four year soldiering in Ireland before the First World War, and in 1914 he was serving in India, from where he brought the Secunderabad Cavalry Brigade to the Western Front.

longest supply route. Since the Mediterranean was closed to normal shipping from 1940–43, the precious cargoes of tanks, anti-aircraft guns, rations and soldiers had to arrive in Egypt via the Cape and the Red Sea ports.

Despite manifold setbacks, most noticeably when Tobruk fell to Rommel's forces in June 1942, the British ended up as resounding victors in the Mediterranean and Middle East, and its bases became the jump-off points for the Allied invasion of Sicily and Italy. Britain experienced a significant victory at the battle of Alamein, and ended the war as the premier Mediterranean power, armed to the teeth in the region and the possessor of a new military empire born of imperial campaigns in Italian East Africa, Libya, Syria and Iran. American influence in the region, however, was to grow by virtue of its role in Mediterranean fighting and supply, pointing the way to its eventual displacement of Britain as the prime external arbiter of Middle Eastern affairs.

This was all in a distant future, however, as Britain contemplated war in the region in 1939–40. In January 1940 the War Cabinet decided to establish base organizations in Egypt and Palestine, and to support the anticipated war effort in the Middle East. The region buzzed with activity as new camps, roads, pipelines, supply dumps, airfields and defences were constructed or enlarged. As Commander-in-Chief Middle East Command, General Wavell fully understood that the war could be lost or won in the Middle East and Mediterranean region, so he threw himself into converting Egypt into a suitable military base, expanding facilities far in excess of current requirements. Wavell was a man with a strong imperial pedigree, and valuable previous experience of the Middle East. Early in his career he had fought in the Anglo-Boer War and various frontier campaigns in India's North-West Frontier Province. During the First World War he fought in Flanders before getting his first experience of the theatre of operations that he was to dominate between 1939 and 1941, when he served under General Edmund Allenby in the Palestine campaign. This experience was reinforced in 1937–38 when he served as Officer Commanding Troops in Palestine and Transjordan. As was the case with Admiral Sir Andrew Cunningham, Britain was fortunate when war broke out to have in residence a commander with intimate knowledge of the region that was to become the main theatre of active engagement with the enemy. Wavell was given authority to accumulate stocks and develop a technical establishment to support nine divisions in Egypt and Palestine, after discussions with the Chiefs of Staff in the war's first winter. This initial requirement was raised to cater for the envisaged arrival of fourteen divisions by June 1941 and twenty-three by March 1942.

Major military bases were developed in the Tel-el-Kebir–Kassassin area of Egypt, including supply depots, ammunition depots, airfields and repair stations. From February 1940 Australian and New Zealand units began to arrive and needed accommodation and base support facilities. The port of Suez was developed to the utmost, as with the closure of the Mediterranean ships needed to unload here after the long trek around the Cape. The war thus brought extra burdens to ports in the Red Sea and eastern Mediterranean as Alexandria, Port Said and Suez became terminal points for convoy routes. They also had to handle the civilian imports of Egypt and the rest of the Middle East for onward tran- shipment. Egypt's transport infrastructure had to be improved because of the frequency with which enemy action closed the Suez Canal. In 1941, for instance, it was closed for a total of eighty-two days by forty-eight air raids. There was need therefore greatly to increase the capacity of the railways running from Suez to Ismailia, and to run a pipeline the length of the water way in order to pump oil from Suez to Port Said and the tankers of the Mediterranean Fleet. The caves of Tura, created by the quarrying of stone for the pyramids, were put to use as a giant workshop for RAF personnel repairing and overhauling aircraft. This was such an impressive, and necessary, feat of improvisation, given the distance at which aircraft were operating from their home base, that visiting senior officers were invariably taken on a tour of the RAF's cavernous maintenance facilities. Their work was vital, too: during the winter campaign of 1941, of 1000 damaged aircraft were recovered from the desert, 800 were sent back to fly again after being repaired in the caves. Elsewhere, a strategic railway was built to connect Palestine and Syria, should troops need to be moved rapidly from the Delta to counter a German invasion through Turkey.

To accomplish the tasks of infrastructural development a great deal of labour was needed. Some of this could be recruited locally, though much of it had to be imported. Because of Egypt's independence, Britain was not in a position to conscript local labour, and any effort to have done so would have resulted in major political unrest in a country where Britain already walked on eggshells. Therefore labour had to be imported, some of it civilian labour from India, some recruited in the Italian colony of Libya that Britain came to control,* some formed from the vast yield of Italian prisoners of war captured in 1940–41, and some of it conjured up in the form of British Army military-labour units recruited in the colonies. In this, as in all other major theatres of war, the Middle East saw an enormous build up of 'rear echelon' imperial military power. These were the soldiers of the Service – the non front-line fighting – branches of the British Army. The Middle East and Mediterranean campaigns of fighting formations like the Eighth Army were founded upon a shadow army of military workers, most notably in the form of the Royal Pioneer Corps (RPC) and its subsidiary branches such as the Auxiliary African Pioneer Corps.

In May 1940 a Directorate of Labour was established at Army GHQ Middle East, as fighting looked likely in the region given Mussolini's belligerent posture. With British units of the RPC already overcommitted in Britain and France, new sources of manpower were required, and British colonies were the natural recruiting grounds. Initially three companies from Palestine and Cyprus were formed, though their main strength – amounting to 4500 men – was lost during

---

* This was known as the Libyan Arab Force and came to employ about 15,000 people.

the Greece and Crete campaigns.[7] Thereafter, with fighting in the region esca-
lating following the arrival of German forces, tens of thousands more pioneers
were needed, and recruitment in 1941–42 shifted to all parts of British sub-Saharan
Africa and the Indian Ocean. Soon, a pioneer army of about 100,000 men was
keeping the Middle East and Mediterranean theatres active. These working
soldiers were crucial to the war effort in the Middle East, because, unlike the build
up of the military base in Bengal and Assam during the Burma campaign, the
region was short on civilian labour, due both to low population density (as in
Libya) and the politics of recruiting in territories officially neutral and unofficially
pro-Nazi (as in Egypt). Among their multifarious tasks, the colonial soldiers of
the RPC salvaged aircraft from the desert, dug tank traps, provided smokescreens
for infantry landings in Italy, built the Haifa – Tripoli military railway, manned
fire equipment, operated ports, guarded supply dumps, patrolled troubled civilian
areas, guarded prisoners, worked on army farms, constructed blast pens for
aircraft on Malta, bridged the River Po in Italy, built telegraph lines across Italy
and manned heavy anti-aircraft batteries defending Cairo.

War in the Middle East stretched from Iran in the east to Morocco in the west and
engulfed the waters of the inland sea and its annexes, including the Aegean and
the Adriatic. Access to ports dictated the supply fortunes of the opposing armies,
and in turn, air power was most usefully deployed when defending or attacking
supply convoys. Early in the Desert War the small imperial forces commanded by
Wavell enjoyed some remarkable successes against numerically superior Italian
forces, in tandem with the war against the massed Italian armies in East Africa.
From September 1940 until February 1941 the imperial Western Desert Force, also
known as the Army of the Nile (later the Eighth Army), pushed the Italians back
almost at will and captured huge numbers of prisoners, Australian troops, for
example, taking 45,000 at Bardia in December 1940. On 3 January 1941 the valuable port of Tobruk fell with the capture of 20,000 more Italians, and the
7th Armoured Division defeated the Italians at Benghazi. In the following month
at Beda Fomm, when Italian forces were caught between a desert hook and a
coastal thrust, 20,000 more went into the bag. In a period of six weeks Wavell's
forces had destroyed an army of nearly 250,000 men, taking 133,295 prisoners, 380
tanks and 845 guns. In ten weeks the British imperial forces had advanced over
700 miles at the cost of only 500 dead, driving the Italians from Sidi Barrani to
their final destruction at Beda Fomm.

The commander in the field, Major-General Richard O'Connor, was not
allowed to pursue the beaten Italians to their final redoubt at Tripoli (the Italians
last supply port), thus prolonging the desert war by permitting the rump of the
Italian army to be reinforced by German troops. Indicating the rapid swing in
Axis fortunes that the injection of German forces brought about, O'Connor was
promptly captured during the first thrust of the recently-arrived Rommel. The
reason for this failure to capitalize on the rout of the Italians was that imperial

forces in the desert had to be thinned in April 1941 when large numbers of troops, at London's insistence, had to go to the aid of Greece, recently invaded by Mussolini. Further weakening Western Desert Force, the 4th Indian Division was moved to East Africa to take part in the campaign against Italy's sub-Saharan African empire. The Greece campaign involved 58,000 Australian, British and New Zealand troops led by General Henry Maitland 'Jumbo' Wilson, and five RAF bomber squadrons (eighty aircraft in all). It was a political deployment as much as one born of sound strategic thinking. In Greece, and subsequently in Crete, imperial forces were squandered as German reinforcements took control of the region. Soon the Royal Navy, demonstrating the advantages conferred by seapower, evacuated 34,000 of these soldiers and diverted 16,000 for the defence of Crete, where forces were commanded by the British-born New Zealander Major-General Sir Bernard Freyberg. He was familiar with the region, having been decorated in the Gallipoli campaign a quarter of a century before. At the end of May, following the famous and costly German parachute invasion, these imperial forces also had to be evacuated, and the navy lost more precious ships. Crete cost 12,245 men lost as prisoners, vast quantities of equipment, 200 aircraft, three cruisers and six destroyers sunk, one battleship, one carrier, three cruisers and a destroyer severely damaged, and one battleship, four cruisers and six destroyers in need of considerable repair. In evacuating the army from Crete, 1828 seamen lost their lives.

At sea in 1941 the Royal Navy could still claim to be the master, having inflicted serious defeats on the Italian navy at Taranto and Cape Matapan. These reverses augmented Hitler's desire to see Axis prestige in the region restored, together with the need to get supplies across the sea from Italy to North Africa whilst blocking the British supply path to Alexandria, Western Desert ports and Malta. Whilst winning battles against the Italian navy, 1941 was a bad year for the Royal Navy in the Mediterranean in terms of losses. The aircraft carrier HMS *Ark Royal*, three battleships and Force K, a mixed force of cruisers and destroyers based on Malta, were either sunk or neutralized. HMS *Ark Royal*, ferrying aircraft to bolster Malta's air defences, was torpedoed in November by one of the twenty-five U-boats that Hitler had recently transferred from the Atlantic to the Mediterranean.

The arrival in February 1941 of the German Afrika Korps, led by General Erwin Rommel, marked a turning point in the Desert War, beginning the arduous struggle that was to see both forces advance and retreat along their supply lines.[8] Rommel began with a breathtaking attack in January 1941, bypassing the imperial garrison at Tobruk and taking Bardia, the British losing all of the new ground almost as quickly as it had been taken from the hapless Italians. A command shake up followed, Wavell swapping Middle East Command for India Command, Auchinleck travelling in the opposite direction. Auchinleck had come to prominence with the Indian Army. After finishing Sandhurst he joined the 62nd Punjab Regiment, and during the First World War had served in Aden, Egypt, Kurdistan and Mesopotamia. In 1929 he was appointed commanding officer of the 1st Battalion The Punjab Regiment, and in the following year served as a senior instructor at the Imperial Staff College at Quetta in Baluchistan. In 1933 he became commanding officer of the Peshawar Brigade, and distinguished himself in action against Afghan tribesmen on the North-West Frontier. Between 1936 and 1938 he was deputy chief of the Indian General Staff. In 1940 he commanded the British Expeditionary Force during its unsuccessful raid on Narvik, before taking over Southern Command in England.

'The Auk' began an offensive (Operation Crusader) in November 1941, and at the end of the year the Tobruk garrison was relieved.[9] Benghazi was retaken, and imperial forces took Sollum. Operation Crusader was the debut of the newly-formed Eighth Army, commanded in the field by Lieutenant-General Sir Alan Cunningham, recently mastermind of the victorious thrust against the Italians from Kenya in the East Africa campaign. (His brother was Commander-in-Chief Mediterranean Fleet.) He commanded 118,000 men, 455 tanks and was supported by 512 aircraft of Western Desert Air Force. His fighting force included a New Zealand, a South African and an Indian division, as well as British units such as the 7th Armoured Brigade. At the end of the operation it was believed that Rommel's force had been crippled, and the offensive appeared to have been a success. It was now the turn of the British to be fighting at the extreme limit of their supply line, however, and Rommel was to demonstrate his skill as a commander. He counter-attacked with astonishing speed, pushing the imperial forces back to Gazala–Bir Hacheim, achieving total surprise and chasing the Eighth Army from the battlefield in disarray.

After this, the two sides paused. A new Axis offensive opened on 26 May 1942, and within a month Tobruk had been captured. Troops from all over the Empire, and their families back at home, had all had the chance to familiarize themselves with the location and the Movietone footage of the port of Tobruk, which had withstood an Axis siege for months. In the Australian case, troops serving there earned the nickname 'the Rats of Tobruk', following a typical own goal from Lord Haw-Haw, who in a broadcast from Germany taunted the port's defenders for living like the notorious rodents. News of the fall of Tobruk left Churchill speechless when it reached him during a meeting with President Roosevelt at the White House in June 1942. An imperial garrison of 32,000 men was lost there (described by an Australian officer, Edward 'Weary' Dunlop, as 'that delightful seaside resort chiefly notable for dust, dive-bombers, derelict ships and death'). The garrison was commanded by the South African Major-General H. B. Klopper, and consisted of the 2nd South African Division, the 32nd Army Tank Brigade and numerous other troops who had been left behind in the desert and who had made their way to the stronghold. Churchill's response to news of the capitulation prompted Roosevelt's famous offer of help, and within two months Churchill's request had been delivered, 300 Sherman tanks and a hundred self-propelled guns being unloaded in Egyptian ports. It also compelled Churchill to send

50,000 fresh troops on a fast voyage in twenty-two transports from Glasgow to Suez. In the face of Rommel's sweep forward Auchinleck retreated to Alam Halfa near the railway junction at Alamein, a mere sixty miles from Cairo. A triumphant German entry followed by a victory parade was widely expected, and a pall of smoke hung over the ancient city as secret documents, including just about all of the records of SOE's Middle East mission, were burned in their thousands. The Mediterranean Fleet dispersed from Alexandria to Port Said, Haifa and Beirut, and plans were made to transfer the Egyptian government and its gold reserves to Khartoum. The first battle of Alamein, however, was a defensive success that halted the German advance, in the course of which two entire Italian divisions were removed from Rommel's order of battle.

This defensive victory, however, was not enough to satisfy Churchill. Yet another command shake up brought General Sir Bernard Montgomery to the head of Eighth Army, with General Sir Harold Alexander as the new Commander-in-Chief Middle East.* The sacked Auchinleck returned to India, replacing Wavell as Commander-in-Chief upon the latter's appointment to the viceroyalty, and remaining in post until Indian independence. Even Hitler thought that Churchill sacked British commanders in the Middle East with too fervent an abandon.[10] Biding his time despite coming immediately under the pressure from No. 10 Downing Street that had been a feature of the Desert War to date, Montgomery ensured that his forces, significantly superior in number to those of the Axis, were properly prepared for the meticulously planned battle that was to come. The second battle of Alamein was to go down in history as a major triumph of imperial arms, Britain's first 'big win' of the war, the cause for all the bells of all the churches in Britain to be rung in celebration (having hitherto been silent, to be rung only to warn of an invasion). Alamein, of course, was not an army victory alone. By October 1942 the RAF and FAA in the Middle East controlled ninety-six operational squadrons, including thirteen American, thirteen South African, five Australian, two Greek squadrons and one apiece from Canada, France, Rhodesia and Yugoslavia. When the massed guns of the British artillery opened up the second battle of Alamein, Eighth Army was supported by 1200 front-line aircraft in Egypt and Palestine and 300 more in Malta.

Following Alamein, the Eighth Army pursued the retreating Axis force, still skilfully led by Rommel. Unfortunately the battered remnants were not caught and killed quickly, despite ULTRA intelligence telling Montgomery of their

---

* Both Alexander and Montgomery had plenty of imperial pedigree. Alexander had commanded the Nowshera Brigade in India before the war. Having expertly supervised the British withdrawal from Dunkirk in 1940, in early 1942 Alexander was given responsibility for supervising the retreat from Burma. Montgomery had extensive pre-war experience of the Empire, having spent his childhood from the age of two in Tasmania, where his father was bishop. He returned to England at the age of fourteen and went to Sandhurst. After the First World War he served in Egypt, India and Palestine with the 1st Battalion The Royal Warwickshire Regiment, and as an instructor at the Imperial Staff College at Quetta in Baluchistan.

extreme weakness, and this allowed Rommel to retreat and regroup, keeping the North African campaign alive for months longer. By Christmas 1942 the Axis forces had been swept from Cyrenaica, and on the 25 December Sirte, the first town in Tripolitania, fell to imperial troops. The Anglo-American Operation Torch landings saw the Eighth Army join with the Anglo-American First Army to form the 18 Army Group. Massive naval forces were employed in these landings, mainly coming from the British merchant marine and the Royal Navy, though depending heavily on American-built landing ships and smaller craft. (Though its troops were not involved, Britain provided a great deal of shipping for the Franco-American invasion of Southern France in the following year.) Operation Torch in November 1942 was the first major Allied amphibious operation of the war. The Western Naval Task Force comprised 102 ships carrying 24,500 men direct from America to Casablanca. The Central Task Force brought 18,500 Americans to Oran, and the Eastern Naval Task Force brought 18,000 British and American troops to Algiers, supported by 650 ships. This was a striking lesson in the benefit of seapower, soon to be repeated when massive forces were transported to take Sicily, then to begin the conquest of Italy, and finally to open the battle for France in June 1944.

With the Axis finally eradicated from the African continent, the stage was set for the invasion of southern Europe, through Sicily and Italy in the east and southern France in the west. Imperial forces remained to the fore in this campaign, and imperial bases, including Egypt and Malta, were able to turn, finally and unequivocally, from defence to offence. On the surrender of Italy in September 1943 the Italian battle fleet put to sea from Spezia for Malta's Grand Harbour (save for the battleship *Roma*, caught by the Germans). This prompted Admiral Sir Andrew Cunningham's famous dispatch to the Admiralty: 'Be pleased to inform their Lordships that the Italian battle fleet now lies at anchor under the guns of the fortress of Malta.'

Egypt, along with India, was the headquarters of British power overseas. This ancient land was a base for army, navy and air force headquarters and all of their organizational infrastructure, a vast barrack for hundreds of thousands of imperial servicemen, a parking lot for thousands of fighting vehicles and aircraft, the major base for the warships of the Mediterranean Fleet, the home of the British Ambassador and Britain's political presence in the Middle East, the home of the Cabinet-ranking Resident Minister Middle East, and the home of numerous secret organizations integral to the British war effort, including Bletchley Park's Middle East Combined Bureau. Cairo was famous for its intrigue and, like other parts of the world where the British were not universally loved, there was plenty of activity by enemy spies and agents. At a crucial stage in the Desert War, the interruption of intelligence derived from the breaking of messages from America's Military Attaché in Cairo deprived Rommel of vital information. In May 1942 the German-sponsored Kondor Mission was broken up by Secret

Intelligence Middle East (like a stage farce, the Kondor Mission involved a belly dancer, her British lover, a Hungarian explorer, two Germans and a set of secret plans). The two German spies, Eppler and Sandstette, had been brought across the desert by the famous Hungarian explorer, Count Ladislas Almasy, but were eventually trapped and uncovered by Bletchley Park intelligence intercepts and their own rather incautious lifestyles.[11]

Clandestine organizations proliferated in the Cairo sunshine. Secret Intelligence Middle East had been formed in December 1939 and was responsible for security intelligence throughout the region. It was jointly run by MI5 and MI6 and operated through Field Security Sections in the army and MI6 Special Counter-Intelligence units. One of its main roles was to feed false information to the enemy. SOE's Middle East Mission was based in Cairo, and was responsible for operations in North Africa, the Middle East and the Balkans. It had a private navy based on Haifa (the 'Levant Fishing Patrol'), consisting mainly of inshore fishing vessels and fast motor-torpedo boats for deploying and collecting agents from occupied Europe. SOE operatives in Cyprus made plans in case the enemy occupied the island, communication and false rumour networks were established, as was a courier system, a wireless network and arms dumps. The island was used as a base for caique operations in the Dodecanese. In Palestine SOE built a stay-behind network in case of German invasion, with each cell connected by radio. A Special Training School (STS) 102, was established near Haifa, a monastery on Mount Carmel was requisitioned for secure accommodation, an old crusader camp near Athlit was used as a holding camp for undercover agents, and parachute courses were held near Nazareth. SOE's Malta base conducted missions in Italy, for example blowing up the railway at Punto de Stilo, and Yugoslavia, and trained agents during the Tunisian campaign. There was also a substantial SOE presence in Iraq (and a Secret Intelligence Service station in Baghdad), though it was criticized by Wavell for not having prevented Rashid Ali's coup in April 1941. There was also an SOE presence in Iran. Cairo was the home for the Combined Bureau Middle East, the major Bletchley Park outstation in the region. It was an army and RAF cryptanalytical centre in the suburb of Heliopolis, opened in late 1940 with an outstation in Nairobi. It was able to read Italian signals and, from March 1941, it handled the inward flow of ULTRA intelligence from Bletchley. From June 1941 it decrypted material coming from the German army in Turkey, and later the Balkans and North Africa. By mid-1942 there were four Special Liaison Units, responsible for controlling the dissemination of top secret Bletchley Park intelligence, in the Middle East, in Malta and Cairo and with the headquarters of Eighth Army and the Western Desert Air Force.

British experiments with special operations in the Second World War were unequalled by any other belligerent power, in terms of their size and the expectation placed upon them. Special operations were carried out in Europe, the Middle East and Asia throughout the war. Many of the men who rose to prominence during the Second World War as specialists in unconventional warfare had developed vital skills and perspectives through their pre-war experiences in the Empire and the wider world. The leaders of special forces were not slow to recognize the talents of men from different parts of the Empire and Commonwealth, and units like the Long Range Desert Group particularly favoured New Zealanders and Southern Rhodesians. Orde Wingate's career brought together many of these global strands, from trainer of Jewish irregulars in Palestine to desert explorer, from Abyssinian rebel leader to his most famous incarnation as creator and commander of the Chindits Long Range Penetration Force in Burma. During his time in the Middle East, he planned to get the Senussi people of Libya to revolt against their Italian overlords, and as a company commander in the Sudan Defence Force took part in a Royal Geographical Society expedition in search of the lost oasis of Zerzura on the Libyan–Egyptian border of the Western Desert. Fittingly, Wingate had been born in India, and his lifelong fascination with Oriental and Arabic studies led him to serve in the Sudan Defence Force between 1928 and 1933, before joining the Palestine Administration as an intelligence officer. In this role he organized Jewish resistance to Arab incursions against their settlements during the Arab Revolt. When war broke out he was summoned to North Africa by the new Commander-in-Chief Middle East, General Wavell, who had heard of his Palestine exploits when he had been the GOC Palestine and Transjordan in 1937–38. Wavell wanted him to lead a rebel campaign in Abyssinia against the Italians and to prepare the way for the return of Emperor Haile Selassie. In 1943, again called for by Wavell, Wingate found himself transported to the India–Burma theatre, where his Chindit Long Range Penetration Force soon commenced operations behind Japanese lines.

One of the most famous clandestine forces to emerge from the Desert War was the Long Range Desert Group (LRDG), formed in July 1940 to reconnoitre the Libyan Desert and infiltrate behind enemy lines.[12] The Group was known for favouring colonials because of their self-reliance, general levels of fitness and knowledge of vehicles (at the time it was uncommon for British soldiers to own vehicles). In the LRDG's early days 150 NCOs and men were picked from the New Zealand Divisional Cavalry Regiment and Machine-Gun Battalion. The LRDG provided invaluable intelligence, disrupted Axis lines of communication, destroyed precious Axis resources and considerably unnerved enemy troops, as small groups of heavily armed men travelled across the desert in open-topped trucks laden with equipment and supplies. An example of the Group's intelligence-gathering potential was its provision of accurate topographical information when the Egyptian Desert Survey was preparing maps of Cyrenaica for use during Eighth Army operations. The LRDG's final operation in North Africa was to navigate Major-General Sir Bernard Freyberg's New Zealand Corps as it outflanked the German Mareth Line in Tunisia in 1943, as the war in North Africa reached its climax. Thereafter the Group saw service in Italy and the Balkans. In the course of five years of war the LRDG conducted over 200 operations behind enemy lines.

Commando units also emerged from the war in the Middle East, as did the Special Air Service (SAS), formed by David Stirling in November 1941 to attack Axis airfields. Its first mission, in the following month, saw sixty-one Axis aircraft destroyed at two airfields. Special Boat Service (SBS) units operated from places such as Gibraltar (quartered aboard the submarine depot ship HMS *Maidstone*), specializing in clandestine coastal raids, reconnoitring and insertions. For example, in the run up to Operation Torch SBS teams secretly inserted American officers into French North-West Africa by submarine and canoe, including Eisenhower's second-in-command General Mark Clark. From Gibraltar SBS units conducted beach reconnaissance missions prior to the Torch landings. On the night of 8 November 1942 personnel from the SBS and the Combined Operations Pilotage Party provided navigational guidance for the landing craft bound for the beaches used by the British in the vicinity of Oran and Algiers. The Combined Operations Pilotage Party was an elite organization that provided vital information through surveying beaches before the major Allied amphibious landings of the war were launched.

Middle East Command (MEC) was the largest military command in the world. It was responsible for the British imperial war effort in countries and colonies across North Africa, the Mediterranean, East Africa, Arabia, the Middle East and the Balkans. At one time it found itself conducting nine separate military campaigns. MEC was responsible for the Eighth Army (Western Desert) and the Ninth Army (Palestine and Syria) and the Western Desert Air Force. The burden brought by a massive geographical spread was eased somewhat when a separate East Africa Command and a separate Persia and Iraq Command were formed. Before this, MEC's responsibilities had stretched eastward to meet the western limits of India Command's sphere. As the war in the Mediterranean and Middle East unfolded there was a massive build up of British and imperial forces in the region, with Egypt the hub and the spokes extending northwards into the Balkans, eastwards towards India, southwards towards Kenya and westwards towards Gibraltar. By November 1941 General Sir Claude Auchinleck, Commander-in-Chief Middle East, had 750,000 troops between Libya and Iraq, with over 14,000 in and around Cairo itself. With support troops, the ration strength of his army in July 1941 was one million, and this produced a huge demand for the region's produce and that of East Africa. The need to balance the huge military demand for food and other goods with that of a civilian population in the Middle East exceeding 100 million people led to the creation of an extensive imperial supply organization, the Middle East Supply Centre (MESC). The Middle East became unified on a strategic basis as never before, with MEC, MESC, a Cabinet Middle East Committee, a Cabinet-ranking Resident Minister stationed in Cairo, an Arab News Agency and a Near East Broadcasting Station.

The Mediterranean Fleet was a powerful force based primarily in the eastern Mediterranean, and traditionally second only to the Home Fleet in terms of strength. Malta and Alexandria were the fleet's main bases. During the war the Mediterranean Fleet faced the entire Italian fleet – large, modern and formidable – which enjoyed base facilities throughout the region, and on-paper superiority over the Mediterranean Fleet in heavy cruisers, submarines and destroyers. During the most crucial years in the Mediterranean the fleet was commanded by Admiral Sir Andrew Cunningham, widely regarded as Britain's finest sailor since Nelson, and one who knew the Mediterranean better than any other serving officer. Though renowned for his pugnacity, he was diplomatic enough in 1940 to persuade the French admiral commanding ships at Alexandria to immobilize his forces without bloodshed, and was regarded with great affection by those who served under him. Like the senior soldiers and airmen in the Middle Eastern theatre during the war, Cunningham had plenty of imperial experience to draw upon, much of it in the Mediterranean itself. He had entered the Royal Naval College at Dartmouth in 1897, where among his classmates were James Somerville, future war-time Commander-in-Chief of Force H in the western Mediterranean and then the Eastern Fleet, and Charles Little, future Commander-in-Chief of the China Station. Having expressed a preference for service on the Cape Station upon passing out, Cunningham found himself in South Africa when the Anglo-Boer War broke out in 1899. Thirsting for action, he managed to join a naval brigade operating mobile guns on land, and went as far north as Pretoria. In 1903 Cunningham began what was to be a long relationship with the Mediterranean when he was based there for six months aboard HMS *Implacable*. The experience of the Mediterranean that he was to accumulate was to serve him well in Britain's hour of need between 1940 and 1943.

During the First World War Cunningham served in the Dardanelles campaign, leaving the Adriatic, Crete, Greece, Malta and 'a multitude of lovely islands in the Aegean' as 'old friends' in 1917. This was to be a region of the bitterest naval conflict during his war-time command of the Mediterranean Fleet. From the summer of 1917 Cunningham assumed command of all destroyers based on Malta. In the inter-war years Cunningham added to his knowledge of Britain's overseas naval commands, particularly when appointed Flag Captain and Chief Staff Officer to the Commander-in-Chief, North America and West Indies Station, in 1925. In this appointment he worked at Admiralty House, Bermuda, when not aboard one of the squadron's light cruisers. The Station covered both east and west coasts of North America and the whole of the Caribbean, and, among other duties, Cunningham's work involved liaison with the Royal Canadian Navy.

Following a year long course at the Imperial Staff College in 1929, Cunningham was given command of the battleship HMS *Rodney*. He then returned to the Mediterranean in 1934 upon his appointment as Rear-Admiral Destroyers to the Mediterranean Fleet. From 1937 he commanded the Battle Cruiser Squadron in the Mediterranean, a position that made him second-in-command of the Mediterranean Fleet to Admiral Sir Dudley Pound, First Lord of the Admiralty for the first four years of the Second World War. When the war broke out

Cunningham was at the Admiralty in London serving as Deputy Chief of the Naval Staff. He was promptly replaced by Rear-Admiral Sir Tom Phillips, the man in command of HMS *Prince of Wales* and *Repulse* when they were sunk by the Japanese two years later, and Cunningham was dispatched to Alexandria, having been appointed Commander-in-Chief of the Mediterranean Fleet. His entire career to date had destined him for this job, in which he oversaw the defeat of the German and Italian naval threat in the region, before becoming the navy's senior officer in 1943 upon his appointment as First Sea Lord when Pound was forced into retirement through ill health. In the autumn of 1940, the strength of Cunningham's Mediterranean Fleet amounted to five battleships, two aircraft carriers, seventeen cruisers, twenty-eight destroyers, twenty-one submarines, four corvettes, five armed boarding vessels, nine escort trawlers, four whalers, two gunboats, seven minesweepers, a destroyer depot ship, a submarine depot ship, a hospital ship, a netlayer, a monitor, a repair ship and a supply ship.[13]

The RAF was well represented in the Mediterranean and Middle East on the outbreak of war, though it needed to expand significantly as the region became a major war theatre in which two powerful enemy air forces were to be faced. The Italian air force, the Regia Aeronautica, was an impressive and modern force, and from early 1941 the Luftwaffe entered the theatre. In June 1940 the RAF in the Middle East and Mediterranean region consisted of thirteen and a third squadrons in Egypt, one in Palestine, three in the Sudan, five and a half in Kenya, three and a half in Aden, one and a third in Iraq and one in Gibraltar. Focused specifically on the war in the desert and cooperation with the army, the Western Desert Air Force was formed in October 1940 with a strength of three Wellington, five Blenheim, three Hurricane, one Gladiator and three Lysander squadrons, and developed a successful method of providing tactical air support to the troops on the ground. Other RAF units concentrated on attacking enemy shipping, particularly the all important supply convoys from Italy to the ports of Axis North Africa. In 1941 Malta-based Wellington bombers attacked Tripoli over seventy times, and from June to October four Egyptian-based squadrons attacked Benghazi over one hundred times. In Iraq in April and May 1941 an RAF training school was largely responsible for crushing a German-aided rebellion. The RAF also made a crucial contribution in winning air superiority in the East Africa campaign.

The RAF's Western Desert Air Force (WDAF) became Britain's most powerful overseas air force in the first half of the war, enjoying significant support from the South African Air Force (SAAF), and from 1942 the United States Army Air Force (USAAF). WDAF was formed as a tactical arm to work with the imperial armies in the region. It was successful in developing a 'cab-rank' system whereby aircraft patrolled over ground positions waiting to be called upon to attack specific targets, and its methods were adopted as a model for 2nd Tactical Air Force formed to support the troops put ashore on D-Day. (3rd Tactical Air Force was formed in the India-Burma theatre). The Tactical Air Force, created in June 1943, replaced the Army Cooperation Command formed in 1940. By the middle of 1944 British imperial, American and allied air power in the Middle East and Mediterranean had been reorganized. Known as Mediterranean Allied Air Forces, it comprised the Mediterranean Allied Strategic Air Force and the Mediterranean Allied Tactical Air Force. This latter force was an umbrella for the Desert Air Force and 12th Tactical Air Command. There was then a Mediterranean Allied Coastal Air Force which included responsibility for air headquarters Malta. Middle East Command retained responsibility for air headquarters in Aden, East Africa, the Eastern Mediterranean, Iraq, the Levant and Persia, and a separate Balkan Air Force had been established.

In August 1941 the Middle East Air Force (excluding Malta) comprised forty-nine squadrons with a strength of 722 aircraft. The WDAF was created in October 1941 to contest Axis air power in North Africa. In the autumn of 1942 Air Chief Marshal Sir Arthur Tedder had at his disposal the equivalent of 104 squadrons (sixty-four RAF, seven FAA, sixteen SAAF, six RAAF, two RCAF, one Rhodesian, thirteen USAAF and two Greek). In October 1942 on the eve of the battle of Alamein, there were 846 aircraft, most of the latest design. There were subordinate air commands in Aden, East Africa, Iraq, Malta and the Sudan. Palestine and Trans-Jordan became Air Headquarters Levant in December 1941. By 1943, WDAF could muster ninety-six squadrons with 1500 aircraft, a formidable air armada that had by that time come through the trials of 1941–42, when huge German air fleets were transferred from the Eastern Front to join with their Italian allies in attempting to eradicate the threat posed by Malta and generally to contest the issue in the air. They failed. By 1943 the Allies had achieved air superiority.[14] This air superiority was crucial in winning the war in the region. As Rommel himself said: 'Anyone who has to fight, even with the most modern weapons, against an enemy in complete command of the air, fights like a savage against modern European troops, under the same handicaps and with the same chances of success.'[15]

As was the case with the army and the navy, the Empire and Commonwealth air formations in the Mediterranean and Middle East were commanded at the highest level by men of considerable overseas experience. Air Chief Marshal Sir Arthur Tedder had served as Air Officer Commanding Far East from 1936 and Air Officer Commanding Middle East from 1941, before returning to England in 1943 to become General Dwight Eisenhower's deputy for Supreme Commander Europe. Air Chief Marshal Sir Charles Portal had in 1934 been appointed Air Officer Commanding Aden, then an important base for the RAF in a region where it had been the senior service since Churchill's tenure as Secretary of State for War and Air in the early 1920s. Portal's inter-war service also took him to India, and he spent a year as an instructor at the Imperial Defence College. In March 1940 he took over Bomber Command, and for the rest of the war served as Chief of the Air Staff, the RAF representative on the Chiefs of Staff Committee. (Sir Dudley Pound and Sir Alan Brooke were the navy and army members.)

Senior operational commanders from the Dominions were particularly noticeable in the air force. Air Chief Marshal Sir Keith Park, a New Zealander, commanded an RAF Fighter Group during the Dunkirk evacuations and the Battle of Britain. He then served as senior staff officer to Air Chief Marshal Sir Hugh Dowding, Commander-in-Chief Fighter Command, before taking charge of 11 Fighter Group, responsible for the defence of South-East England. In January 1942 Park was appointed Air Officer Commanding Egypt, and shortly afterwards, because of his acknowledged talent and the island's desperate need, as Air Officer Commanding Malta. In January 1944 Park became Air Officer Commanding RAF Middle East, and in the following February was sent East to become Commander-in-Chief Air South-East Asia Command, responsible to Admiral Lord Louis Mountbatten for the prosecution of the air war against the Japanese forces in Burma and South-East Asia. Air Marshal Sir Arthur Coningham was an Australian raised in New Zealand. He served in the First World War in Samoa and Egypt, sailing for England to join the Royal Flying Corps upon being invalided out of the army. In the inter-war air force Coningham distinguished himself as a pilot in Britain, Egypt, Iraq and the Sudan, making the first east–west flight across Africa in 1925. He attracted Tedder's attention whilst commanding Fourth Group Bomber Command, and was subsequently ordered to Egypt, where Tedder was Air Officer Commanding Middle East. There he was given command of the Western Desert Air Force, which he led during the period of Allied victory until 1943 when he was recalled to Britain to take over the 2nd Tactical Air Force, which accompanied the Allied armies from Normandy to Berlin.

Egypt was the fount of British military power in the Middle East, defending the Suez Canal and an extensive network of bases and economic interests in British colonies or semi-colonies, and ready for use against any challengers in the region, from the west or from the east. It had been an imperial *place d'armes* for sixty years. Egypt and the waters of the eastern Mediterranean contained the greatest concentration of British military power beyond Britain itself. Egypt was home to the biggest military complex of its kind, the Suez Canal Base Area, with radar and wireless communications centres, a network of roads, railways, harbours and port installations, and hospitals, bakeries, sewage plants, ammunition dumps, airfields and a flying-boat station.[16] This imperial linchpin was the headquarters and entrepôt for the region's war effort, the centre of RAF power in the Middle East, the base that supplied armies as they fought across the desert, that dispatched warships to protect convoys as they fought along the Mediterranean corridor and to which servicemen flocked on leave. Egypt was also the last-chance saloon on which imperial troops fell back when it looked as if the game was finally up in the summer of 1942, as Rommel's arrival in Cairo was expected by the hour and fickle Egyptian politicians prepared to roll out the red carpet whilst remaining British personnel prepared to pile into their cars and head for the Canal and hope for evacuation. Also in retreat, it was to Egypt that evacuated troops repaired, delivered by the Royal Navy as the Greece and Crete campaigns proved costly failures, along with British civilians fleeing from Axis operations in Greece and the Balkans.

Cairo was an epicentre of the British imperial world.[17] It ranked alongside Delhi and Singapore as a centre of imperial government, administration and military power. It was home to all the most important institutions related to the war effort – MEC, Combined Bureau Middle East, SOE headquarters, Middle East Supply Centre (the economic and import-export regulator for twenty different states and colonies) and the British Embassy. It was also the temporary seat of the exiled governments of Greece and Yugoslavia. This great regional and imperial city was also home to the British Cabinet's Resident Minister Middle East. As in West Africa, North Africa and South-East Asia, there was enough at stake in the Middle East, and a sufficient profusion of military and civilian commanders and administrators competing for attention in Cairo, to warrant the appointment of a Cabinet Minister to smooth communications on the spot, between the Middle East and London and between British and American representatives. Oliver Lyttelton, President of the Board of Trade, arrived as Minister of State for the Middle East in July 1941, and immediately set up a War Council under his own chairmanship. (He was succeeded by Richard Casey, former Australian Minister in Washington in March 1942, then by Lord Moyne in January 1944, and by Sir Edward Grigg upon Moyne's assassination by Jewish terrorists that November.) The Resident Minister's principal task was to relieve the Commander-in-Chief MEC of extraneous responsibilities and settle promptly on the spot matters affecting several departments and authorities which had hitherto required reference to London, and to offer general political guidance.

During the war Cairo witnessed a massive growth in military and administrative personnel. It was an exciting war-time city, full of transient thousands on their way to or from dangerous war zones, subject to regular enemy bombing, set in a political atmosphere charged with the ever-present tension at the heart of Anglo-Egyptian relations and a security environment marked by the threat of enemy occupation. 'Cairo was one of the great assembly-points of British imperial power, where, in a setting suitably exotic, the imperial legions mingled in their staggering variety. Every kind of imperial uniform was to be spotted in Cairo, especially in the heady years between 1940 and 1943 when war was close at hand. There were kilts and turbans, tarbooshes, slouch hats and jodhpurs. There were Kenyan pioneers, Indian muleteers, Australian tank crews, English gunners, New Zealand fighter pilots and South African engineers.'[18]

Cairo's *de jure* status as a British military encampment led to a great deal of friction, as it also happened to be the capital of an independent nation. Anti-British feeling, especially in the army, remained strong in Egypt, and enemy agents and sympathizers were always active in seeking to undermine the British war effort. In May 1941 the former Chief of Staff of the Egyptian army, General Aziz Ali el Masri, attempted to escape the country and join the Germans. He had formed a secret anti-British organization within the Egyptian military establishment, and was in touch with German spies. Awash with British soldiers, Caireans of all classes resented aspects of the imperial presence. Egyptian army officers despised the patronizing attitude shown by the embassy towards their King, and ordinary Egyptians hated the predilection of British soldiers to play the 'tarboosh game' when on leave, driving around the city knocking the hats off the heads of its inhabitants. Gossip was rife and social life fast. European hostesses set up clubs for troops on leave, there were always officers lounging in wicker easy-chairs on the veranda of Shepherd's Hotel, and the nightclubs and brothels boomed.

Since 1922 Egypt had been an independent nation state but the British, relying on an alliance with the King (Khedive) and the nobility and on the 1936 Anglo-Egyptian Treaty, effectively held on to power in a number of crucial areas. Britain was responsible for defence, the militarized Canal zone, communications, the protection of foreign interests and the administration of the 'Anglo-Egyptian' Sudan. Britain's use of Egypt as the major base of its Middle Eastern war effort was legally founded upon an article in the 1936 treaty that committed the King to give all facility and assistance to Britain in the event of war, including the use of ports, airfields and means of communication. Effectively Egypt was under British occupation, and this was to have consequences after the war. Britain's overbearing use of Egypt as a military facility made its already unwelcome presence even more unpopular with elite Egyptians. The nationalists sharpened their rhetoric calling for a British withdrawal, and junior army officers, including Gamal Abdul Nasser and Anwar Sadat, dreamt of a future free of the British. Yet the British, despite their overwhelmingly powerful military presence, had to tread carefully and to try to retain as much political and public goodwill and acquiescence as possible. In order to prosecute the war effectively, they needed Egyptian cooperation, particularly in the provision of military labour, in day-to-day government and in the provision of military and communication facilities. Harnessing support was a delicate operation that sometimes necessitated press censorship: for example, news of the blitz in Britain was kept out of the public domain for fear it might create a bad impression and discourage Egyptian cooperation. Like other regimes in the Middle East, Egypt was not short of politicians and important people who had been wooed and impressed with German and Italian achievements and pronouncements over the years, and who were prepared to ally with their interests if it furthered the chance of ousting the British.

There was a good deal of support for the German cause in Egypt. At the outbreak of war the Egyptian Prime Minister Ali Mahir was pro-Axis, as was King Farouk, and Egypt did not declare war on Germany. (Farouk indeed was doing all he could covertly to aid the German war effort, leaking news of British plans for action against Iran to the Germans and the Shah, intelligence obtained from his father-in-law, the Egyptian minister in Tehran.) In June 1940, in the crisis-ridden aftermath of the fall of France, Sir Miles Lampson, the British Ambassador, forced the King to sack his Prime Minister. The opposition Wafd Party which was brought in to form a government – whilst as nationalist as every self-respecting Egyptian party had to be – wanted to cooperate with the British for the duration of the war, as the Egyptian political community faced similar dilemmas to their counterparts in the Indian National Congress. Even when Italian troops invaded Egyptian territory in September 1940, Egypt did not declare war. Air raids on Alexandria followed, and in June 1941 a single raid killed 650 of the city's people. Severe shortages led to rationing, a growing black market and mounting discontent. In January 1942, bakers' shops in Cairo were stormed by the hungry, and there were demonstrations in support of Rommel. Cairo was in the front line, and was to remain imperilled until victory at Alamein in November 1942.

Before that decisive victory, a further change of regime was to be demanded by the British. When Prime Minister Husayn Sirry resigned in February 1942, Lampson insisted that the Wafd Party be asked to form a government. King Farouk refused, so the Ambassador summoned his powers. British troops and armoured vehicles surrounded the Abdin Palace, and the King was presented with a choice – appoint a pro-British Wafd government or abdicate. An abdication instrument had been prepared by Sir Walter Monckton, who had done Edward VII the same favour in 1936. (Monckton was temporarily serving as the Cabinet's Resident Minister in Cairo.) Unlike Edward VII, at that moment reflecting on his fall from grace from the lonely confines of Government House in the Bahamas, Farouk decided to stay on his throne, and a pro-British government was duly installed. This was war imperialism in action, though in the long run it was to make the continuation of Britain's presence even more difficult. As with the rapid and uncompromising British suppression of the Quit India movement in August of the same year, the British showed their teeth in a manner that would not have been countenanced in peace-time because, whilst effective in the short term, such disagreeable actions eroded Britain's long-term capacity to remain in power, and recruited more people to the nationalist cause. But, in February 1942, with Rommel poised to attack in the desert and the ladies of Cairo warned by the Germans to be prepared to entertain their victorious troops any day soon, it was a question of immediate necessity. Long-term calculations about the future of Britain's presence went out of the window, as everyone focused on immediate survival.

Vast quantities of Egyptian labour were required during the war as Egypt became the main base from which Britain fought its way across the desert and into southern Europe and the Balkans. At the outbreak of war the General Officer Commanding British Troops Egypt, Lieutenant-General Sir Henry Maitland Wilson (better known as 'Jumbo' Wilson), was told to prepare plans for the invasion of Libya, should Italy enter hostilities.[19] In the first nine months of the war, before Italy came in, Wilson was very active in the minefield of Egyptian politics. The Egyptians, realizing that the Italians were sitting on the fence and biding their time, decided to follow suit. It therefore took all of Wilson's considerable diplomatic skills to get active Egyptian cooperation as the British tried to prepare their

Egyptian positions for war. Wilson took the opportunity afforded by Italy's reticence to prepare the army in Egypt for active operations in the desert, planning to take the offensive at the earliest opportunity. For example, he insisted on intensive all-arms training for the 7th Armoured Brigade and the 4th Indian Division then in Egypt, and he also encouraged the formation of Captain Ralph Bagnold's long-range Royal Tank Regiment patrols, which were to lead to the formation of the LRDG in June 1940.

Preparations mounted throughout Egypt. New workshops and ammunition and supply dumps were built around Tel-el-Kebir and Qassassin. At Qassassin a massive imperial transit camp rose out of the desert, capable of housing 26,000 men. The site, west of Ismailia, was chosen because it was conveniently located for the railway line and the Sweet-Water Canal. New roads, lines of communication and airfields had to be built, pipes laid to take Nile water into the desert, and water-purifying plants installed. Oil pipelines were laid across the country, and Egypt's transport infrastructure had to meet the demands placed upon it by the ever-growing military presence. The Egyptian State Railways, for example, were relied upon by the army. Given the great increase in freight, Egypt needed to tap Indian and South African sources of coal. The reduction of imports into the Middle East region because of the war, and the large-scale purchase of local supplies by the military, created acute shortages, particularly of coal, iron, steel and paper. The British Ambassador, Sir Miles Lampson, and Army GHQ pressed Whitehall to form a central supply organization for the region, eventually achieving their aim with the formation of the Middle East Supply Centre. Huge supply dumps in the desert, built and very often guarded by colonial soldiers of the Royal Pioneer Corps, were a vital part of the British imperial fight in the desert, as important to the men in the front line as air supply was to their contemporaries in the jungles of Burma. There was also a demand in Egypt for training schools, permanent bases, canteens and field hospitals. With Australia, Britain, Ceylon and India, Egypt was to be one of the most important bases of the Allied war effort, and every single person was affected by its transformation to a state of war readiness.

Egypt's lack of raw material resources, apart from food, compounded supply problems. On the outbreak of war GHQ Middle East put in orders for a variety of raw materials from the Far East, Australia and South and East Africa. The closure of the Mediterranean after the fall of France greatly exacerbated the problem of overseas supply. A journey of 3000 miles from Britain became a journey of 13,000 miles as ships made their way around the Cape, and Egypt's import capacity was reduced by 25 per cent. This disruption in shipping and supply also affected civilian supply and industries. In both 1940 and 1941 the cotton crop could not be exported, and on both occasions the British government stepped in to avoid the ruin of the industry by buying the entire crop. Here as elsewhere, it was the British government's policy of bulk purchase that spared a regional industry from disaster brought on by the war-time disruption of normal trade patterns. Legislation to reduce the acreage under cotton was of course unpopular, compounding civil disquiet and providing a good example of how war obliged the British to become involved in aspects of daily life and people's livelihoods where interference was inevitably resented. The reduced acreage for cotton allowed more land to be given over to cereal production (though, in this game of dietary snakes-and-ladders, a 60 per cent reduction in Egypt's cotton seed output made the Middle East deficient in fats and oils). The reduction in the cotton acreage allowed, however, for a 35 per cent rise in paddy rice, mostly used within the region, with much of the exported surplus going to Ceylon. Hoarding led to shortages of cheap cotton goods, flour, sugar and kerosene. The war financially enriched Egypt, mainly through the sums spent by Britain and its allies, and by the end of the war it was owed £300 million for supplies that it had provided. Local industries stimulated by the severence of normal import sources, however, found it hard to adapt to the resumption of normal trade. With the scaling down of the imperial war machine in Egypt over 300,000 people were put out of work.

A smaller imperial base than Egypt, the island of Malta was nevertheless of the utmost significance to the all-important battle of supply waged even when the armies facing each other in the desert were stood down, awaiting the next round in their struggle across North Africa.[20] The battle of supply was one in which the protagonists in the Western Desert depended absolutely on all manner of manpower and material requirements reaching them by sea. Malta's significance lay in the fact that it sat athwart the main Axis supply route from Italy to North Africa, and forces based on it could run amok amongst the convoys and hamper critically Rommel's ability to wage war. On the debit side however, Malta was a brief hop from major concentrations of Axis air power stationed in Italy and Sicily, yet a great distance from the nearest major British bases. Therefore a separate and costly campaign had to be waged to keep Malta itself supplied with aircraft for defensive and offensive purposes, and with vital food and commodities without which the military and civilian populations would be starved into surrender. This led to the famous battle of the Malta convoys, braving the narrow waters of the Mediterranean in which enemy surface vessels and submarines lay in wait, and above which Axis aircraft patrolled.

Malta's experience captured the paradox of imperial war. On the one hand, having pre-existing imperial bases ready for expansion and development in wartime was a boon. On the other hand, trying to cater for the defence of such bases against enemies determined to negate their strategic value was a nightmare. The outline of Malta's war history is widely known because it was in the front line for so long, holding out against the might of the Axis and living up to the favourite British self-image of plucky resistance against the odds. The appeal of Malta's struggle is also kept alive because the battle presents the history enthusiast with a war in miniature, in which the twists and turns of battle at the tactical,

operational and strategic levels are easy to discern. The Battle of Malta was a
Battle of Britain played out in the skies above a much smaller island. As was the
case in the Battle of Britain, Malta's battle was a war of survival against apparently
overwhelming odds, and against an official German invasion plan (Operation
Hercules). The price of failure was enemy occupation.

Despite the fact that twice Hitler switched fearsome air fleets to Sicily in order
to bomb Malta into submission, the island was never an abject underdog. In the
early stages of the Mediterranean war the battle in the air was fought against the
Italian air force, rarely as good in the air as it was on paper, though faced initially
with risible British forces based on the island. Then would have been the time for
Mussolini to bomb the island mercilessly and attempt to land troops for its
capture. As in his invasion of Egypt, however, measures were noisy but half-
hearted and overcautious. Even when the Germans arrived and Malta became the
most bombed place on earth, the British still had an ace up their sleeve in the
shape of mature and well-handled seapower. The Royal Navy and the Merchant
Navy – not without massive losses – were able to keep Malta supplied with aircraft
and essential commodities by virtue of the fact that the Italian and German naval
forces in the Mediterranean had not been able to win control from the British,
even though they came close to it. Still other factors contributed to Malta's
survival. The Germans shied away from using airborne forces against Malta after
the grim toll taken by the British imperial defenders of neighbouring Crete when
the paratroops descended in May 1941. Ultimately, confused Axis aims, and
Hitler's preoccupation with the Eastern Front, cost the Axis dear. In contrast,
British political and military leaders, from the Prime Minister and Chiefs of Staff
in London to the three Commanders-in-Chief in Egypt and the Governor and
service chiefs on Malta itself, were united and resolved.

Malta was traditionally the focal point of British naval power in the Mediterranean, the fleet base of first choice. Despite this, Malta's defences were
considered inadequate in the event of war, and in April 1939 the fleet's headquarters were moved to Alexandria. Malta's great strategic significance was purely an
accident of location. The Gibraltar to Alexandria sea route was crucial to the
fortunes of the British Empire. Lying between the two ends of the Mediterranean
Sea, Malta was Britain's only central outpost. Perhaps more importantly, the
island offered itself as an unsinkable aircraft carrier in a region of great importance because of the Axis need to supply its armies in Africa by sea from mainland
Europe. It was widely believed that the fate of the British imperial war effort
depended upon Malta, and some German planners saw the island as the key to the
conquest of Egypt, then Iran, and ultimately India. Malta was to play a pivotal and
heroic part in the Mediterranean war, and the failure of the Axis to conquer it,
silence its guns or destroy its airfields, was to prove costly.

Malta was also important in the new age of air power as a pit stop for aircraft
travelling from Britain to the Middle East (and beyond, following the Empire-
hopping air route to the Far East). There were air bases at Luqa, Takali and Hal

Far, and a flying boat base at Kalafrana. Before the war the RAF had argued that Malta should be abandoned if necessary, being unprepared to spare resources for overseas bases when its full concentration in the fight for resource allocation centred upon building up Bomber and Fighter Commands at home.[21] The Cabinet's Committee of Imperial Defence learned in 1934 that Malta was virtually defenceless. This sorry state softened British policy towards Italy at the time of the Abyssinian crisis, and the fleet was temporarily removed to the safer surroundings of Alexandria. In direct opposition to the recommendations of the RAF, the Admiralty argued that Malta should be reinforced and not abandoned, as it was a central Mediterranean base from which all units of the fleet could operate should Italy become an enemy. The fact that the Royal Navy eventually won the argument in Whitehall, and that reinforcements were spared for Malta, was to be crucial during the Mediterranean struggle that unfolded in the summer of 1940.[22]

Though Whitehall had been persuaded, getting resources committed and delivered was another matter. The recommended force levels for the defence of Malta were never met, and Malta had to fight hard for every light anti-aircraft gun, searchlight or bomb-proof shelter that it received. Perhaps more remarkable, however, is the fact that it got any at all, Britain finding resources for imperial defence even as its own survival appeared to teeter on the brink. In March 1940, only 108 of an authorized 1860 light anti-aircraft guns for *British* defence had actually been issued. In Malta a bombproof combined services headquarters was completed, protected storage for the oil reserve was built, and the Governor's proposal for the construction of deep shelters for the civilian population was given the go ahead. When Italy entered the war, however, although the island could boast thirty-four heavy and eight light anti-aircraft guns and twenty-four searchlights, it still had no fighter squadron. This was no surprise for an Empire caught unprepared for war. With the fall of France catastrophically altering defence appraisals across the world, thought was again given to abandoning the island. But that decision was not taken, and defences began gradually to be built up, and Malta fared well considering the global demand for imperial weaponry. Upon Italy's entry into the war Malta's complement of anti-aircraft guns was only just inferior to that of Alexandria, the home of the Mediterranean Fleet, and was superior to that of Singapore, the world's most expensive defended naval base. By July 1941 ninety-four heavy and ninety-six light anti-aircraft guns were in place and Royal Marine Artillery units manned the guns around Grand Harbour. As a further defensive measure, radar equipment was positioned on the Dingli Cliffs.

Malta's potential as a major thorn in the side of the Axis made it vulnerable to enemy attack, and this, together with the closure of the Mediterranean to normal shipping, made it a potential source of British weakness. It would require a costly effort on the part of the Royal Navy and the Merchant Navy to keep it in the fight and prevent it from being starved into submission. It was not easy to supply, given its position, and the proximity of Axis-held land and air bases. It was a thousand miles from Alexandria, the nearest British base, yet only sixty miles from land-based enemy aircraft stationed in Sicily. Almost inevitably, the Axis decided to bomb Malta to defeat, and nearly succeeded in doing so. An American pilot in the RAF said of Malta that he 'had never been to a place before or since that had such a visible atmosphere of doom, violence and toughness about it'.

As one of the Empire's fortress colonies since its acquisition in 1814, Malta by tradition was governed by military men. General Sir William Dobbie was in command at the start of the war, followed from May 1942 by Field Marshal Lord Gort, who had been Commander-in-Chief of the British Army in France before Dunkirk. Given Malta's great importance to the imperial war effort, Britain was fortunate that it did not suffer from the kind of political and civil agitation that afflicted Egypt, India and Iraq. But this relatively tranquil state of political affairs could not be taken for granted. Malta had enjoyed substantial self-government until 1933, when the Nationalist Party's conduct of affairs had evoked the anger of the British government, particularly its failure to prevent Italian intrigue and encroachment. In 1936 the island's constitution was revoked because of the increase in Italian influence. The attitude of the Maltese people following the entry of Italy into the war was enough to make the Colonial Office arrange for the resumption of self-government, however, because of their unparalleled loyalty and bravery under the most trying conditions (though people with strong Italian connections were interned, and forty-two people deported to the Sudan, including the former Chief Justice). For the people of Malta, more than most other civilian populations in parts of the Empire not actually occupied by the enemy, the war brought ever-present danger and hardship for two long years. The first air raids, as in so many other parts of the Empire, caused people to flee to the interior. An ARP organization was established, gas mask advice was published in the *Times of Malta* and underground shelters prepared for people to scramble to when the sirens sounded.

Malta was substantially garrisoned during the war against attack from naval or amphibious forces, and a third of the force consisted of Maltese troops. There were two main Maltese military units at the outbreak of war, the Royal Malta Artillery and the King's Own Malta Regiment, with a combined strength of 2300 men, a sizeable colonial contingent for a territory of Malta's size. The latter formation was a Territorial unit, and one company of the 2nd Battalion was made up of Boy Scouts. At the outbreak of war there were also four fully trained infantry battalions. By February 1941 the Malta Garrison included eight British infantry battalions in addition to those of the King's Own Malta Regiment, supported by two field batteries and a beach defence regiment of the Royal Artillery and a troop of the Royal Tank Regiment. Both Maltese formations were expanded at the end of 1942, and new units were created to support the work of other imperial arms stationed on the island. These included the Malta Service Corps and Malta Army Ordnance Corps. Eligible for the RAF on the same terms as British citizens, 1800 Maltese had enlisted by mid-1944, mainly for ground duties. Malta's chief military asset was to be its airfields, though, in a region where air supply was less developed than in the India-Burma theatre, the fabulous Grand Harbour at Valetta remained essential for keeping the island supplied and usable as a base for offensive air and naval operations.

Even at the worst point during the siege of Malta, the island never ceased to be a base of active naval operations against the enemy, although there were long periods when surface ships could not use the harbour. In October 1941, for example, Force K was specially created to operate from Malta. Consisting of two cruisers and two destroyers, its mission was to attack Italian convoys supplying Axis forces in North Africa and to attack Axis North African ports. It destroyed two convoys (mostly famously the *Duisberg* convoy) before a minefield off Tripoli crippled or sank three of its vessels after the first Battle of Sirte in December, leading to Force K's disbandment. In November 1941 Force K, together with the 10th Submarine Flotilla also based on Malta, had ensured that 77 per cent of Rommel's supplies were sunk before reaching Africa (greatly helping General Sir Claude Auchinleck's 'Crusader' offensive in the Western Desert). Force K was reconstituted in January 1943 after the siege of Malta had been lifted.

Malta's most prominent role during the war was as a base for the RAF, offensively and defensively. Scores of Spitfires and Hurricanes, most flown in from aircraft carriers, took part in the island's defence and harried enemy convoys. It was reconnaissance flights from Malta by long-range, American-built Glenn Martin Marylands, for example, that revealed the disposition of the Italian battle fleet at harbour in Taranto preceding the stunning raid by Swordfish torpedo-bombers. This sank three Italian battleships at their moorings, decisively shifting the balance of naval power in the eastern Mediterranean in the Royal Navy's favour at a crucial juncture. Later, Malta-based bombers raided Naples harbour, forcing the flagship *Vittorio Veneto* to retreat to Genoa, and immobilizing another battleship.

Given the premium placed upon the island's survival by the British government, and also the premium placed upon its neutralization by Hitler, it comes as a surprise that Malta's initial air defence depended upon a clutch of obsolete Gladiator biplanes discovered in crates at Kalafrana flying boat base by the island's Naval Officer-in-Charge. The first three in the air were aptly named *Faith*, *Hope* and *Charity*, though the myth that was built around them – and the level of the threat that they faced in the opening days of the war with Italy – has been exaggerated. Nevertheless, their achievements were significant. With their discovery began the charmed life of the Malta Fighter Flight. Despite its commitments elsewhere, the British government ensured that the island was reinforced, penny packets of Hurricanes being flown in, and eventually local air superiority was attained. The air ferry to Malta began on 2 August 1940 when twelve Hurricanes were flown off the veteran carrier HMS *Argus*. In the space of fifteen months 333 Hurricanes and 367 Spitfires had reached Malta by this route, Spitfires first appearing over the island in March 1942.

The build up of forces on Malta was a splendid example of imperial military housekeeping and of imperial awareness on the part of the British government and Chiefs of Staff. On 16 August 1940 the Malta Fighter Flight, with fifteen machines, became No. 261 Squadron. Glenn Martin Marylands arrived for photo reconnaissance, Malta being well positioned for gathering such intelligence. The Commander-in-Chief Mediterranean Fleet, Admiral Sir Andrew Cunningham, believed that the best way to attack Axis shipping was from Malta. He therefore did all that he could to base vessels there when the level of enemy activity permitted. For obvious reasons submarines were particularly valuable in this role. The 1st Submarine Flotilla was sent to the island to harass the Axis supply lines, and revived the Jolly Roger tradition, returning to port flying the skull-and-cross-bones if a kill had been made, the flags being embroidered by Maltese nuns. The flotilla's six British and three Greek submarines, based at Marsamxett Harbour, patrolled off Sicily and southern Greece as well as policing the supply routes from Italy to Africa. Famously, Lieutenant-Commander Wanklyn's HMS *Upholder* sunk the 18,000 ton troopship *Conte Rosso* with the loss of 1300 Axis soldiers.

The inward passage of troops and aircraft to Malta was constant during the struggle in the Mediterranean. Two thousand fresh troops arrived in September 1940, Wellington bombers in the following month. RAF Fighter Control was located in an underground complex of tunnels at Lascaris, built into the bastion overlooking Grand Harbour. The RAF commander, Air Vice-Marshal Hugh Pugh Lloyd, had a sleeping cubicle 160 steps underground near the exit to the cliff face overlooking Grand Harbour, and very close to the fighter control room.[23] Fleet Air Arm units also resided on the island, like No. 830 Squadron, flying Fairey Swordfish and concentrating their attention on Tripoli, the main Axis harbour in North Africa. Black Hurricanes of the Night Fighter Unit took to the skies, though for too long only exhausted Hurricanes were available from Britain. The RAF in Malta, as elsewhere, was a multi-national force including Americans, Australians, Britons, Canadians, New Zealanders, Rhodesians and South Africans.

Local air superiority allowed submarines, cruisers and bombers to use the island's base facilities, and for a time to wreak havoc on Axis supply routes between mainland Europe and the fighting fronts in North Africa. In June 1941, for example, 73 per cent of German shipping from Italy was sent to the bottom. In the same month, 143 Hurricanes arrived, and Malta-based Blenheims and Wellingtons regularly flew missions over Sicily. From January 1941 to May 1942 Malta-based submarines sank almost 400,000 tons of enemy shipping, and Malta-based aircraft accounted for 500,000 tons over the course of the war. Malta's value to the war effort in the region was incalculable. Though the Royal Navy in 1940–41 could not act decisively because of a lack of air power and submarines, Malta remained a great nuisance to the Axis and helped British convoys to traverse the perilous Mediterranean corridor. The Mediterranean Fleet's 15th Cruiser Squadron (under Vice-Admiral Philip Vian) escorted the convoys to Malta, and Force H then took over and shepherded them to Gibraltar and the Atlantic sea routes beyond.

This period of Malta ascendant brought the inevitable iron-fisted Axis response. Malta needed to be reduced as a naval base for British warships operating in the Mediterranean, and its dock infrastructure, valuable for repairing damaged ships, needed to be put out of action. But Malta's air facilities and aircraft were an equally important Axis target. Malta's effectiveness against Axis supply routes was intolerable. Rommel needed Malta out of the action so that supplies could arrive uninterrupted and the Afrika Korps and Italian forces could push on towards Alexandria and the Suez Canal. In order to achieve this, twenty-five German submarines were transferred from the Atlantic on Hitler's insistence and an air group was dispatched to Southern Italy and another to Sicily. Fliegerkorps X was transferred from Norway to solve the Maltese problem and seize the control of the central Mediterranean that had been lost by the Italians after Taranto. In November 1941 Field Marshal Albert Kesselring, commanding Luftflotte II in Russia, was appointed Commander-in-Chief South, and aircraft from Russia were sent to Sicily to form Fliegerkorps II. 'Smiling Albert' Kesselring soon had control of about 2000 front-line aircraft, and so began the period of mammoth air attacks on Malta.

In a six-day spell in January 1941, with the carrier HMS *Illustrious* in Grand Harbour attracting enemy bombers like bees to honey, there were five hundred air raids. There was some respite for Malta in the summer of 1941, when most of these aircraft were transferred to Poland for Operation Barbarossa and responsibility for the assault on Malta was returned to the less deadly hands of the Italians. It had not, however, all been one-way traffic; in April 1941 the commander of Fliegerkorps X reported to the Luftwaffe high command that he could not stand the rate of wastage over Malta for much longer. By the start of 1942 Malta had 112 heavy anti-aircraft and 118 light anti-aircraft guns and seventy-five Hurricanes. In early 1942, however, Hitler moved Luftflotte II to Sicily and Kesselring's command. In January 1942 there were 262 air raids on the island, and 263 the following month. Rommel's successful offensive in Libya meant that the Western Desert Air Force lost desert airfields that the Axis were then able to use to attack Malta. So the pendulum swung back in favour of the Axis forces. By February 1942 Axis shipping losses had dipped below 30 per cent, and supplies for the Axis forces in North Africa had begun to flow. The supply situation in Malta became desperate, both in terms of its fighting capacity and the survival of the servicemen and civilians living there. By April 1942 Malta's offensive capabilities had almost ceased to exist, the dry docks were put out of action and in that month the island was subject to twice as great a level of bombing as was endured by the whole of Britain that entire year. Shipping losses were unsustainable. Twenty-one Royal Navy vessels were sunk and thirteen damaged in Grand Harbour and its approaches in a six-week period centred on April 1942 alone. In March and April Malta received twice the tonnage of bombs that London had taken during the Blitz, and in May 1942 Kesselring, prematurely as it happened, reported to Berlin that Malta had been neutralized. Between January and July 1942 there was only one twenty-four hour period when no bombs fell on the beleaguered island. Fuel oil and petrol stocks were within weeks of running out and by August 1942 Malta was within a month of starvation, and its defenders had set a target date for surrender.

To counter the massive build up of Axis pressure on the island, its air defences needed to be continually augmented. The carrier USS *Wasp* was twice employed to fly aircraft in, the second time at Churchill's personal request, when it delivered forty-seven Spitfires. Churchill was determined not to let the island fall. By the time USS *Wasp* and the carrier HMS *Eagle* delivered another consignment of Spitfires in May 1942, 358 blast pens had been build on Malta's airfields to offer the aircraft some protection whilst on the ground, and twenty-seven miles of dispersal runways had been constructed. This infrastructural development was important. It was achieved by civilian labour, navy and air force personnel and up to 3000 soldiers labouring at any one time. In a model demonstration of inter-service cooperation, the RAF was able to count on the army to help fill runway craters, build aircraft pens, help bomb-up and refuel aircraft, drive lorries, control traffic and remove wrecked aircraft. This overcame the severe shortage of local labour. Many Maltese men had been conscripted into military formations and many others were working on the construction of shelters and repairing damaged housing. Work to expand the three existing air bases had started in June 1941. Of particular importance was the need to allow aircraft to disperse across the island in order to present the enemy bombers with a harder task. As new runways and interconnecting roads were built, the three compact Axis targets were replaced by something resembling a huge octopus with three nodal points, where aeroplanes were to be seen only when taking off and landing. Coupled with this, as many war-related activities as possible were put underground, even the repair of aircraft and motor transport. Takali and other heavily bombed Malta bases 'soon reverted to the caveman epoch'.[24] Deception measures also played a part, including the painting of hangar doors on rock faces and fake pilot-to-control wireless conversations when Malta had no aircraft to put in the sky.

The arrival of significant numbers of Spitfires proved to be the turning point in the battle for Malta. Their arrival from March 1942 was crucial. Other factors were important, such as the installation of smoke projectors to screen Grand Harbour and the dockyards from May 1942, and improved radar allowing enemy fighters to be intercepted north of the island from October 1942. In July 1942 Air Vice-Marshal Sir Keith Park, the New Zealand hero of the Battle of Britain, arrived to take over command of the RAF in Malta from Air Vice-Marshal Hugh Lloyd. Arriving after the worst of the Axis blitz had passed, Park brought with him more offensive fighter tactics and benefited by the work undertaken by his predecessor to improve Malta's physical infrastructure. Within two weeks of his arrival, daylight bombing over Malta had ceased. Park had sailed to Sierra Leone aboard the *Viceroy of India* in January 1942 before flying on to Cairo via the trans-African air route. He took up the position of Air Officer Commanding Egypt. At the same time another New Zealander, Air Vice-Marshal Arthur Coningham, was in command of the Western Desert Air Force. Like Montgomery and Mountbatten, Park had a flair for self-publicity and morale-boosting appearances. Upon arrival in Malta he was quick to flaunt his common touch and to talk of offence not defence. He issued his Fighter Interception Plan with a flourish. Often wearing an eye-catching white flying suit, he drove about the island in his red MG offering lifts to surprised pedestrians.

A renewed Axis blitz on Malta in October 1942 was brought about because Rommel, in the run up to the battle of Alamein, was receiving hardly any of the supplies sent from Europe. Rommel himself had postponed Operation Hercules in May 1942 when it looked as if he could move for the greater prize of Egypt and the Canal itself. He hoped then to knock the British out of Egypt, which would cause Malta to wither on the vine. This was a grave mistake, as from the autumn of 1942 60 per cent of all supplies at sea destined for Axis forces in North Africa were destroyed from Malta. The defenders responded in kind to the renewed enemy offensive; '82 in Four Days: Malta's Answer to Luftwaffe's New Bid' was the *Times of Malta*'s headline on 15 October. In the first week of October alone 114 Axis aircraft were shot down for the loss of twenty-seven Spitfires. (23 April 1942 recorded the one thousandth enemy aircraft to be shot down by RAF Malta since hostilities had commenced.) The imperial grip on Rommel's supply lines was tightening all the time. In the first seven months of 1942 eighty Axis ships were sunk; in the last five months of the year the figure shot up to 150.

Victory at Alamein and the subsequent Allied landings in North-West Africa completed the turning of the tide as far as Malta was concerned. By May 1943 Park had 16,000 air force personnel and civilians under his command; the army and navy many thousands more. The last air raid over Malta took place in July 1943. By the time the air battle over Malta had well and truly ended in mid-1943, the RAF had shot down or damaged nearly 2700 enemy aircraft for the loss of 707 aircraft destroyed and 735 damaged. In 20 June 1943 King George VI arrived aboard the cruiser HMS *Aurora* to visit the island on which he had bestowed the George Cross at the height of its suffering the previous year. Malta now became a forward offensive base for attacks on the Italian mainland, and the jump-off point for the invasion of Sicily. Further infrastructural development was needed for this new role, and in ten months 120 miles of fifteen-foot wide strips had been laid for runways and roads. By July 1943 there were 600 aircraft on the island. For Operation Husky, the invasion of Sicily, 4000 aircraft were employed as 160,000 men were landed in the first wave with 600 tanks, 14,000 military vehicles and nearly 2000 guns. These forces were transported by 2600 ships commanded by Admiral Sir Andrew Cunningham.

Malta's home front had been gravely affected by its involvement in the Mediterranean struggle. With a population of 270,000, Malta was the most

densely populated area of Europe. Its military role meant that the war had imme-
diacy for the island's people unmatched in most parts of the British Empire. With
the intensive bombing, the civilian population spent a lot of time underground,
in cellars or tunnels. Due to the failure of convoys to arrive, or to arrive intact,
health standards deteriorated, malnutrition spread and there was a typhoid
epidemic in the summer of 1942. Bombing alone caused nearly 1500 dead and
nearly 4000 wounded. By August 1942 10,000 houses had been destroyed.
Between August 1940 and August 1942 eighty-six supply ships were sent to the
island, thirty-one of them being sunk. Axis minefields around the island became
so thick that the 10th Submarine Flotilla based on Malta from January 1941, its
one remaining offensive weapon, had to be withdrawn. (By July 1942 the mines
had been cleared and the submarine flotilla returned.) All of this was happening,
of course, at a crucial time in the war in the Western Desert, when British
fortunes were at their lowest. Tobruk and its garrison had fallen in June 1942
and 'The Flap' was on in Cairo as the Eighth Army poured headlong back into
Egypt and waited for Rommel at Alamein. Many on Malta were despondent. On
his way to attend the Prime Minister at the Cairo conference in summer 1942,
the Chief of the Imperial General Staff, General Sir Alan Brooke, made sure to
visit the island and its Governor, Lord Gort, who was doing so much to lead the
people of Malta by his own stoical and cheerful example.* Since arriving from
the governorship of Gibraltar, Gort had thrown himself into ensuring that Malta
held out. He helped to secure the arrival of sixty Spitfires, and concentrated all
available firepower to destroy the Stuka divebombers attacking HMS *Welshman*
as she delivered a precious cargo. He also supervised the distribution of scarce
food and water supplies so that even at the height of the crisis 200,000 people
received rations each day. Brooke noticed that Gort was depressed, feeling that
he had been bundled into a sideshow and that the whole garrison might be
abandoned without the chance to give an account of itself. 'Depression increased
by the fact that he insists on living on the reduced standard of rations prevailing
on the island', noted a concerned Brooke. The CIGS was shocked by the destruction caused by enemy bombing, particularly when touring Valetta and the docks
on 2 August 1942, and was pained to see shoeless children rubbing their tummies.
'The destruction is inconceivable and reminds me of Ypres, Arras, Lens at their
worst during the last war. Travelled around Grand Harbour in admiral's barge
and looked at wrecks of last convoy', he recorded in his diary that evening.

Like so many imperial islands, including Britain itself, Malta was not self-
sufficient in food, and its limited cereal production had dwindled in the inter-war
years as vineyards took control and cheap cereals were obtained from Italy. With
food and other essentials having to be imported by sea, rationing became
essential. As in other colonies, all efforts were made to produce more food locally,

---

*   Gort had been CIGS himself between 1937 and 1939, and ended his war-time Mediterranean
     peregrination with a stint as High Commissioner in Palestine.

though not always successfully. An attempt to use human excrement as a fertilizer led to an outbreak of typhoid that killed ninety people. In February 1941 a Food Distribution Office was established to ensure even distribution and to discourage hoarding, and in April 1942 Maltese staples like pasta, rice and tomato sauce were rationed, as was sugar and bread. Victory Kitchens appeared amidst the rubble to offer a gruel-like soup to the hungry. The officially-approved daily ration allowed for 1100 calories per person and, at their peak in January 1943, there were two hundred Victory Kitchens feeding 175,000 people. As in Gibraltar, much life took place underground, in tunnels and shelters dug from the island's limestone interior. The Maltese relied on imported kerosene for cooking, heating and lighting (wood was scarce on the island and coal was expensive to import). The island's shortage of alcohol, however, made a happy outlet for the Alexandrian hooch industry, an example of war's stimulation of local industry and trade. Aside from food shortages, disease was a constant worry, and many people suffered from fleas.

What kept Malta alive and in the fight was the success of the Royal Navy and the Merchant Navy in fighting convoys through, often with great loss. This was testament to the British government's determination to do all that was possible to keep Malta out of Hitler's grasp. Military hardware, fuel, food and essentials like kerosene were the premium goods. When convoys could not be sent, submarines, or fast, forty-knot mine-laying cruisers like HMS *Manxman* and *Welshman*, would go it alone and deliver small but nevertheless precious cargoes. Submarines began what became known as the 'Magic Carpet Service' delivering more essential supplies. For example, in June 1941 HMS *Rorqual* delivered two tons of medical stores, sixty-two tons of aviation fuel and forty-five tons of kerosene from Alexandria. The February 1942 convoy was wiped out, alarming the War Cabinet in London. Another convoy was immediately sent, sailing from Alexandria on 20 March. On the way Vice-Admiral Vian's escorting cruiser squadron won the second Battle of Sirte, but very little of the cargo, and no fuel, got through to Malta. On 15 April 1942 the King announced the award of the George Cross to 'the island fortress of Malta'. Despite its desperate lack of food, fuel and ammunition, Kesselring was premature when on 10 May 1942 he declared the island neutralized and withdrew Luftwaffe units. A lull followed, and morale was boosted in Malta by the arrival of sixty-one Spitfires.

Problems in supplying Malta, aside from the presence of enemy vessels above and below the waves, were compounded by the Merchant Navy's dearth of fast tankers. The minimum speed at which a convoy could travel without being in mortal danger was sixteen knots. Even when heavily defended by Royal Navy warships, the convoys were still in peril, from air attack and from enemy submarines, surface vessels and minefields. Of the June 1942 convoy, only two out of seventeen vessels sailing from Haifa, Alexandria and Gibraltar arrived. Still too few vessels were arriving, and in that month the 'Vigorous' convoy had to turn back to Alexandria. The arrival of the famous 'Pedestal' convoy in August 1942 averted starvation, coming ten days before the Governor intended to surrender through lack of supplies. This epic convoy battle has come to typify the fight to supply Malta. The War Cabinet was determined to make one more attempt to save the island after the failure of 'Vigorous', and a fleet of fast merchant ships was assembled in Scotland by the Ministry of War Transport. Reflecting the importance attached to the convoy and the island's survival, two battleships and three carriers formed part of the escorting force, the first time that three carriers had been used together. One of them, HMS *Furious*, flew off thirty-eight fighters to join the defence of Malta on 11 August. The RAF commander, Air Vice-Marshal Sir Keith Park, had 136 fighter aircraft and thirty-eight bombers at his disposal, and a radar system to control fighter scrambles when attacks came in. In the 'Pedestal' convoy fourteen merchant ships were escorted by forty-four major warships, yet still only five of the merchantmen reached their destination. The 'Pedestal' convoy included the celebrated American Texaco tanker *Ohio* (or *OH 10* to its all-British crew), lying perilously low in the water as she entered Grand Harbour with a destroyer strapped to each side, but bearing 11,000 tons of precious fuel. The enemy made great efforts to meet the convoy, gathering E-boats, Stuka dive bombers, Junkers 88 bombers and major units of the Italian fleet. In fighting it through, the British lost the carrier HMS *Eagle*. The arrival of the 'Substance' and 'Style' convoys had boosted the Malta Garrison to a combat strength of over 22,000, and the anti-aircraft defence to 112 heavy and 118 light guns, with over 100 guns for beach defence.

Cyprus had been lopped off the Ottoman Empire in 1878 by a British Prime Minister anxious to check Russia's advance towards the Dardanelles following a Russo-Turkish war. Its main use during the Second World War was as a training and resting base for Allied troops, as a base for aircraft covering convoys in the eastern Mediterranean and for British military and naval operations in the Aegean.[25] Like every British territory, however great or small, it had a plan in case of enemy attack. The Officer Commanding Troops Cyprus had identified passes on the road from Nicosia to Kyrenia on the north coast as possible enemy landing places, and defensive measures had been taken in the light of this. Such preparation was entirely prudent: the German high command had developed plans to capture Cyprus, as it was seen as the key to the defence of Syria, and as a base offering facilities for commanding the eastern Mediterranean.

Cyprus supplied thousands of military personnel as part of the Colonial Empire's huge military contribution to the imperial world war. Before war broke out, it was decided to enlist Cypriots in the regular British Army and an infantry battalion was planned. This was abandoned in March 1939, however, and it was decided instead to raise units for the service branches of the British Army, including the Royal Army Service Corps (RASC) and the Royal Engineers. When war broke out five hundred Cypriots enlisted immediately in the Cypriot RASC and formed Mule Transport Companies. Five hundred Cypriots were sent to

France, the first colonial soldiers to take the field against the enemy, and were evacuated from Dunkirk on 29 May 1940. Cypriots, along with Palestinians, formed the main Royal Pioneer Corps (RPC) strength supporting the imperial forces in the Greece campaign. In the hasty withdrawal following its failure, however, a thousand Cypriot Pioneers were lost, mostly taken prisoner by the Germans.

In February 1940 the Governor accepted the proposal to form a Cyprus Regiment to include infantry, transport and pioneer units. In 1942 many Cypriot units were recalled to Cyprus to assist in the defence of the island. By the end of 1944 there were over 10,000 Cypriots in the army, 8500 in the Cyprus Regiment and the rest in the Cyprus Volunteer Force. This was a home guard formation, though 300 volunteers from it were accepted to serve with the Cyprus Regiment in Italy. In Italy five Cyprus Regiment Pack Transport Companies served with the Poles at Monte Cassino in May 1944, then in the fighting on the Gothic Line. Cypriots were also employed for ground duties with the RAF in Cyprus and elsewhere in the Middle East. Fleet Air Arm squadrons such as No. 829 were based on the island, and on 16 June 1941 Cyprus-based torpedo-bombers sank the large Vichy destroyer *Chevalier Paul*. In early 1943 HMS *Welshman* ferried 4000 troops from Syria to the island in six trips, as part of a plan to deceive Axis intelligence regarding the timing and location of the expected offensive against mainland Europe following the Allied victory in Africa.

Cyprus was threatened by the shipping and supply crisis that attended the war in the eastern Mediterranean. The Governor reported that, if there was a complete breakdown of shipping as a result of the Mediterranean war, the island could hold out for six to nine months with the enforcement of strict rationing. The Governor was instructed by the Colonial Office to introduce rationing, and was told that goods urgently required in Cyprus would be sent to Egypt to await onward shipping opportunities. Import shortages stimulated the local production of tobacco. All cereal requirements for Palestine and Cyprus were provided under the auspices of the Middle East Supply Centre. The war also disrupted the island's export trade as well as its imports, particularly as before the war Germany had taken 36 per cent of Cyprus's exports. A government campaign encouraged the local consumption of oranges. It was economic swings and roundabouts; the loss of the European market for cupreous ores brought the greater part of the mining industry to a standstill on the one hand, though military demands stimulated the production of potatoes and timber on the other. Military expenditure between 1941 and 1944 exceeded £14 million, nearly twice the expenditure of the Cyprus government in the same period. Military demand had, however, longer-term costs. The appetite for timber took its toll on the island's forests, and the Cyprus government was keen to take advantage of Colonial Development and Welfare Act money and was granted £400,000 towards afforestation and irrigation. The demand for natural silk for the manufacture of parachutes in Britain assisted the revival of an almost moribund industry, and the government assisted the wine and carob industries by purchases. Initial arrangements for price control left scope for profiteering. By an order in February 1941 additional profits allowed to importers over the pre-war level were reduced from 50 to 25 per cent. There was little public cooperation in the enforcement of price controls, and profiteering and hoarding were rife.

Gibraltar, like Malta and Bermuda, was a military colony. It had been taken for strategic reasons in 1704 during the War of the Spanish Succession and was traditionally governed by a soldier. It occupied a key position at the mouth of the Mediterranean, being well placed to provide naval cover in that sea as well as in the Atlantic Ocean. Its Atlantic face made it extremely useful as part of the convoy port system shepherding British, Allied and neutral vessels sailing from Europe to the East and back again. After the fall of France, it was the only part of continental Europe in Allied hands, and it was menaced by the threat of attack from enemy or Vichy territory, and by the dubious neutrality of Spain. The British government feared that a compliant Spain would allow German forces to approach the Rock, as Hitler wanted to capture it in order to close the western Mediterranean. Its location made it a natural target for Allied servicemen attempting to escape from enemy-occupied Europe, and it became a base for large garrison forces, RAF air power, a formidable Royal Navy squadron (Force H) and headquarters for General Dwight Eisenhower when he commanded the Allied invasion of French North Africa in November 1942.

Gibraltar was used extensively as an air base, being home, for example, to No. 544 Squadron which conducted photo reconnaissance missions over North-West Africa prior to the Allied landings (Operation Torch). From August 1940 RAF Group Gibraltar was placed under RAF Coastal Command, which was able to use the Rock to facilitate its coverage of Atlantic convoy routes. Work on a new runway started in 1941 for use by British aircraft in transit from Britain to Egypt, and American aircraft in transit from West Africa and Britain. Work was speeded up in 1942 so that Wellington bombers could land and refuel without having to stop on the beleaguered island of Malta as they journeyed to Egypt. This facility was to prove very useful for British and American aircraft as the desert fighting moved west towards Tunisia and Morocco. In preparation for Operation Torch large numbers of American aircraft were shipped to Gibraltar to be assembled. The Rock provided an essential base for six hundred Allied fighters covering the invasion of French North Africa, even though its solitary air strip, jutting precariously out into the Mediterranean, was exposed to Spanish guns and enemy aircraft. By the early hours of 8 November 1942 350 aircraft were crammed wing to wing around the runway. The runway had been made from rubble excavated from inside the Rock as the British dug a labyrinthine military town impervious to enemy bombs. The runway measured 1350 yards by November 1942 (being later extended to 1800 yards).

The main SOE headquarters in the region was located at the Villa Lourdes in

Gibraltar. From its Gibraltar base the ubiquitous SOE mounted an operation in advance of the Torch landings to remove a German ship-spotting device in the Straits of Gibraltar. Gibraltar had an important role as one of the main convoy assembly ports that dotted the sea lanes of the world, pens into which merchant ships were herded by the corvettes and destroyers responsible for their safe passage. It played an important role in passing Allied shipping along the Mediterranean as it headed east, and was used by ships plying the trade routes between Britain and America, and Britain, West Africa and the East via the Cape route. From early in the war Gibraltar was also a base for Royal Navy vessels engaged on anti-submarine and raider duties. The Rock guarded the western entrance to the Mediterranean, and was a base for British naval forces taking part in the Battle of the Atlantic. All in all, Gibraltar was an important strategic asset.

Gibraltar's strategic importance was greatly enhanced when the fall of France deprived Britain of the assistance of the French naval squadron in the western Mediterranean. This meant that the hard-pressed Admiralty had to find ships with which to provide a counterweight, leading to the creation of Force H in June 1940, commanded by Vice-Admiral Sir James Somerville (followed by the South African Rear-Admiral Neville Syfret).[26] Force H was a powerful squadron, and in peacetime would probably have been dignified with the title 'fleet'. In the autumn of 1940 its strength stood as two battleships, two aircraft carriers, seven cruisers, twenty-five destroyers, seven escort trawlers and four minesweeping trawlers. It was charged with ensuring that the French fleet did not fall to the enemy and that the Italian fleet did not escape the inland sea, and with the daily tasks of a navy at war like the search of neutral shipping and blockade of enemy territory. Force H was involved in the hunt for the *Bismarck* (an aircraft from its carrier, HMS *Ark Royal*, crippled *Bismarck*'s steering allowing British battleships to sink it) and in the Madagascar campaign, when units were sent to assist the Eastern Fleet in the Indian Ocean. It was regularly involved in the Battle of the Mediterranean, particularly in escorting Malta-bound convoys and handing them over to units of the Mediterranean Fleet at a midway point. It also attacked enemy shore targets, as on 9 February 1941 when it bombarded Genoa.

Force H's most noted role was the singularly unpleasant task of attacking units of the French navy anchored at Mers-el-Kebir on 3 July 1940, sinking or crippling three battleships and killing nearly 1300 French sailors. Though brutal, Churchill was determined to show the enemy and the great potential ally across the Atlantic that the fall of France had not diminished Britain's fighting spirit, and more importantly perhaps, to prevent the addition of France's considerable naval power to the Axis side. Before the British ships opened fire, the French were given the option of joining the British, sailing to French West Indian ports for demilitarization, or scuttling. Four days later Force H attacked the major French West African port of Dakar and damaged the battleship *Richelieu*. This raid on the Senegalese coast was inspired by the British government's desire to prevent the strategically valuable port from becoming a base for German submarines and to capture or destroy the powerful French battleship. Lending support was General Charles de Gaulle's desire to acquire a base on French territory for his nascent Free French movement.[27] Somerville's handling of Force H against German, Italian and Vichy forces impressed Churchill, and in October 1941 he was made a Knight Commander of the British Empire (to add to his existing knighthood, prompting his Mediterranean colleague, Andrew Cunningham, to send a saucy signal: 'Imagine! Twice a Knight at your age!'). Force H was disbanded in October 1943 when Allied victory in the region allowed a reshuffling of the naval pack (one beneficiary being the Eastern Fleet, gradually being built up in Ceylon prior to the creation of the British Pacific Fleet).

Gibraltar's convoy assembly and escort role attracted the attention of the Italian navy, and the Italian 10th Light Flotilla regularly attacked shipping in the region. Vichy bombers raided Gibraltar in retaliation for the attack on the French fleet at Mers-el-Kebir. Beneath the waves Italian human torpedoes entered Gibraltar Bay three times in 1940–41, nearly hit the battleship HMS *Barham* and succeeded in sinking three vessels. (On 19 December 1941 Italian frogmen succeeded in hitting the battleships HMS *Queen Elizabeth* and *Valiant* in Alexandria harbour.) From mid-1942 Italian frogmen launched from submarines or from Spain placed limpet charges on the hulls of merchant ships gathering in Gibraltar Bay for convoys, sinking several of them. Midget submarine attacks were also launched from the hulk of an old tanker, the *Olterra*, moored at Algeciras Bay opposite the Rock, the frogmen leaving undetected through a trapdoor. One British counter-measure was the firing of random depth charges into the harbour approaches. On 6 December 1941 this prevented an attack when the battleship HMS *Nelson* and the carriers *Furious* and *Formidable* were in harbour. Gibraltar, however, did not suffer the level of privation and the weight of air attack experienced by Malta, and members of the Mediterranean Fleet based at Alexandria disparagingly referred to the western Mediterranean as 'the Ladies' End'.

Before the war there was no local military force on the Rock, but the outbreak led to the creation of a small anti-aircraft unit called the Gibraltar Defence Force. This force expanded significantly as the war progressed, and in 1944 the Governor introduced conscription for eighteen to twenty-two year olds for heavy anti-aircraft gun training. The war had a marked affect on the civilian population. In the second half of 1940 nearly 17,000 men and women were evacuated from Gibraltar, first to Tangier and French Morocco, then to Britain, Jamaica and Madeira, another example of the mass migrations that affected the Empire at war. This left 4000 civilian males involved in essential war-related work. As this civilian exodus was taking place, in the other direction came about 20,000 British troops. A large programme of defence construction was carried out under the supervision of the Governor, Field Marshal Lord Gort. Massive excavation work inside the Rock created barracks, storerooms, magazines, power stations, headquarters, hospitals and offices. Like Malta, Gibraltar weathered the war as a troglodyte fortress. Military tunnels, increased from four miles to twenty-five miles, were intended to enable Gibraltar to withstand siege and attack by modern weapons. Even the racecourse was sacrificed to make an airfield. Work was conducted by Tunnelling Companies of the Royal Engineers and the Royal Canadian Engineers. On his visit to Gibraltar in August 1942, the Chief of the Imperial General Staff, General Sir Alan Brooke, wrote of the tunnelling work. 'Practically all stores, hospitals, distilleries, ammunition and accommodation for the garrison has been tunnelled out of the main rock. In addition a full-sized lorry road connecting the east and west sides of the Rock.'[28] On a return visit the following February, he was treated to a defensive fire demonstration after dinner. Driven to the top of the Rock, he had a magnificent view of the tracer bullets of machine-guns firing out to sea in a zone illuminated by searchlights, 'at the same time searchlights and anti-aircraft guns engag[ing] imaginary targets in the air'.

At the start of the war it was understood that Britain's Mediterranean colonies might well experience specific difficulties in maintaining food supplies. In the early stages there were problems in Gibraltar because part of the French fleet was stationed there and a number of vessels were deployed on contraband control, meaning more mouths to feed. As in other convoy assembly ports, like Freetown, there were also the food requirements of merchant ships awaiting convoy as well as the requirements of workers from Spain. In early 1940 an increase in merchant shipping in the port and an influx of civilian workers from Britain added to the problem. The solution came when London granted authority for an increase of up to 50 per cent in the food orders endorsed by the Governor.

Palestine had rapidly grown in strategic significance since its acquisition by Britain during the First World War. It was part of the land route from the Mediterranean to India, and of the land route piping Iraqi and Persian oil to the oilers of the Mediterranean Fleet. These land routes were considered vital should the Suez Canal be lost or closed. Palestine also became the main back-up to Britain's primary Middle Eastern possession, Egypt. It was the protective buffer of the Canal Zone, an indispensable geopolitical link in the Iraq route to India and the outlet for oil at Haifa.[29] If the Germans had succeeded in capturing Egypt, fighting would have continued from Palestine. The Mandate was home to units of the Middle East Reserve, and a training and assembly camp for British and imperial troops deployed to the region.

Even before the outbreak of war Palestine was a militarized colony. Political unrest, especially the 1936–39 Arab revolt, required an inflated British troop presence. On the outbreak of war there were eleven British infantry battalions in Palestine, two cavalry regiments and numerous auxiliary detachments. All but three of the battalions (part of the Middle East Reserve), were in Palestine on garrison duties. When Italy entered the war on Germany's side more troops were sent. Palestine was a base for troops in training or in transit. The Sherwood Foresters, for example, arrived in Palestine from Britain along with a thousand horses. These were soon to be scrapped as the regiment was mechanized, though long into 1941 the 1st Cavalry Division in Palestine remained largely horsed for want of motor vehicles. The Duchess of Ranfurly and her butler, Whitaker, followed her husband and his horses to Palestine in the early days of the war, being allowed to remain through the influence of friends in Cairo who wangled her a job as a headquarters secretary, enabling her to stay near her husband when most 'inessential' civilians were being evacuated (she was also spying on George Pollock, head of SIS in Cairo, for the Commander-in-Chief Archibald Wavell). Cairo was full of such women. Another was Freya Stark, who worked in Aden and Cairo for the Ministry of Information and as Lady Wavell's assistant.[30] The Australian 6th Division, bound for France in early 1940, stopped in Palestine for training and remained there when France fell, going on to become an integral part of the Western Desert Force. The 1st Battalion The Caribbean Regiment trained at Gaza in 1944. Palestine was also a launch pad for imperial troops engaged in regional offensives, particularly those in 1941 against Syria and Iraq. Palestine's strategic importance was heightened by the presence of a good naval anchorage at Haifa, which was also the terminus of the oil pipeline from the refineries of Abadan in Iran. Defensively, it was a territory that had to be well guarded because of the threat of German penetration of the Middle East from the north. Africans of the Royal Pioneer Corps spent much of 1941–42 constructing defences in Syria and Lebanon, and a military railway from Haifa to Tripoli.

Palestine was a powder keg of internal unrest because of the Arab–Jew dispute at the heart of the territory's affairs.[31] During and immediately after the war it was detonated by the effects of the Holocaust. Oppression in Europe caused tens of thousands of Jews to seek entry to Palestine as refugees, whilst Britain attempted to manage the influx so as not to turn Arab opinion violently against it. British policy since taking Palestine over after the First World War had been to maintain all British bases in the Middle East and to do what was possible to minimize Arab unrest that might threaten the security of those bases. The British had initially sponsored the notion of a 'homeland' for the Jews in Palestine because of genuine sympathy for their cause among senior figures, and because they seemed to represent a solid collaborative community in a notoriously unruly region where vital imperial interests were located.

The settlement that ended the Arab revolt in 1939 generally favoured the million-strong Arab community, and this led Jewish underground groups to take up arms against the British. Suppression of Arab political organizations during the revolt meant that during the war Arab political activity was severely limited. The 1939 White Paper reversed the policy of partition and instead planned a unitary state. The sale of land to Jews was heavily circumscribed, and Jewish immigration was restricted (there were about half a million in Palestine already). Though some powerful figures, including Churchill himself, were considered to be pro-Zionist, there was a strong pro-Arab tradition elsewhere, particularly in the Colonial Office. (The Foreign Office, a bastion of 'Arabists' itself, thought that the Colonial Office considered Jews to be 'enemies'.) To many in the British government, it seemed clear that, given the threat of war in the Middle East and the demand for Arab cooperation that war would entail, there was little choice regarding Palestine policy. As the Prime Minister, Neville Chamberlain, succinctly put it in April 1939, 'we are now compelled to consider the Palestine problem from the point of view of its effects upon the international situation. If we must offend one side, let us offend the Jews, rather than the Arabs'.

Of course, Britain naturally sought to work constructively with both sides in this intractable dispute. The Jewish community had always been valued, and the rising menace of Nazi Germany made their cooperation useful and easier to harness. The war altered things in Palestine because the issue of Jewish immigration became linked with the Holocaust, and any British attempts to stop people illegally entering Palestine, because they were nationals of another country, could be portrayed as morally wrong. Sophisticated Jewish politicians and propagandists also realized that Washington was the place to lobby as much as London, because American power in the Middle East and elsewhere was rising, and because key electoral districts in America were heavily populated by Jews.

The Jewish Agency was a quasi-government for Palestinian Jews set up under British auspices. It chose to cooperate in the British fight against Nazism, and organized the mobilization of Jewish agricultural and industrial resources. In September 1939 over 136,000 Jews registered their willingness to assist in the war effort. By 1943 63 per cent of the Jewish workforce was engaged in producing materials for British imperial forces. The Jewish Agency also pursued its own agenda, however, and acted as a *de facto* government-in-waiting. When unconfirmed reports of the Holocaust were validated, it began to lobby the Allies to do all that they could to end the suffering, leading to the inconclusive Bermuda conference of April 1943. Its agents in countries like Turkey helped thousands of Jewish refugees to get to Palestine, despite the fact that this conflicted with official British policy.

The Yishuv, the Jewish community in the Palestine mandate, mobilized itself for opposition to the British, and by late 1941 the Colonial Office and Foreign Office were alarmed by its growing radicalization and the proliferation of illegal organizations, as well as the start of the ultimately very successful Jewish propaganda drive in America. Jewish political leaders began to feel more than capable of defying the local British administration because of contact at the heart of government and with decision-making and opinion-forming circles in London, as well as their burgeoning links with America's Jewish lobby. There was also a disturbing willingness to turn to direct action, as in November 1944 when Britain's Resident Minister in the Middle East, Lord Moyne, was assassinated by the Stern Gang, a Zionist underground movement.

The Jewish Agency was the political master of the Haganah, a clandestine though semi-official Zionist paramilitary group. It was nearly destroyed by the British in 1940, but in 1941 it started forming special independent units sponsored by the British. In this field Orde Wingate gained expertise, training the Special Night Squads that helped turn the tide of Arab attacks against Jewish settlements. British-backed paramilitary units such as the Palmach were intended to defend the country and carry out acts of sabotage if it was invaded. Some were also used in intelligence gathering missions before the British imperial invasion of Syria, and in an abortive attempt to raid oil refineries in Tripoli. The Palmach was officially shut down when the German threat to Palestine passed, though not all units were disbanded or handed back their weapons. Whilst assisting the British, the Haganah also did all it could to aid Jewish refugees. The opportunity to hoard arms and form an intelligence-gathering organization was of great use after the war. As in Malaya, Britain had trained and armed a resistance movement that would turn against it in the post-war years; war-time expediency ran counter to established policy and the long-term interests of imperial survival. For example, in order to release seasoned British troops for combat, Churchill favoured reducing the British garrison in Palestine, in their stead recruiting locals for security duties. This went against War Office and Colonial Office policy of disarming the rival Palestinian communities.

Some British officials viewed Jewish immigration as a German ploy to undermine stability in the region and infiltrate spies. Churchill opposed the general trend of British Palestine policy, and American pressure encouraged change as well. When Churchill became Prime Minister in 1940 he told the Colonial Office to override restrictions on Jewish entry into Palestine, but the entry of Italy into the war saw them reintroduced. This policy of restricting access meant that many were turned away, sometimes with tragic consequences, as when in 1942 the *Struma* was torpedoed in the Black Sea after being denied permission to land its cargo of Romanian Jews at Haifa. The May 1942 Biltmore conference demanded a Jewish sovereign state, and increasingly Jewish propaganda was aimed at America. British policy was hamstrung; refugees seeking admittance to Palestine, usually after dangerous voyages on overcrowded boats from Central Europe, could not be let in wholesale because of the Arab reaction. Also, before the true extent and horror of the Holocaust was appreciated, these people were viewed as refugees, deserving help but not special treatment. Of course, to the Jews of Palestine they were brothers and sisters escaping persecution and returning to a nascent homeland that welcomed any additions to their numbers. A major strand of British policy was to get these 1940s 'boat people' transferred to other parts of the Empire that could offer the necessary facilities. After the war, they could choose to return to their newly-liberated mother countries. Berths were found in Australia, East Africa and Mauritius for some of the Jewish refugees. The Haganah and other Jewish organizations attempted to stop this process, sometimes with terrible results, as in November 1940 when it killed 250 Jews aboard the *Patria* docked at Haifa. The plan had been to sabotage the ship so that it could not deliver its human cargo to another imperial destination, but the explosive charge had been misjudged.

A more militant offshoot of the Haganah was Irgun Zvai Leumi, founded in

1937 to defend Jewish settlements against Arab attacks but increasingly hostile towards the British. From May 1939 the Irgun carried out attacks and sabotage against British targets in protest at British immigration policies. With the onset of war, however, it declared a truce and suspended anti-British activities. This resulted in the creation of the Stern Gang in 1940 by Abraham Stern, when he left Irgun in protest at this decision, and his organization continued hostilities against British forces. The Irgun resumed hostilities in December 1943, famously blowing up the British administrative headquarters at the King David Hotel in 1946 with the loss of ninety-one British lives. Menachem Begin, Prime Minister of Israel from 1977–83, led the Irgun after escaping from Poland and arriving in Palestine, and his organization became part of the Israeli Army when the state of Israel was born in 1948.

During the war tens of thousands of Palestinians served in various branches of the British Army. A mixed company of the Royal Pioneer Corps was the first to see action, sent to France in February 1940 on the heels of Cypriot Pioneers. In October 1940 the company became the nucleus of No. 51 (Middle East) Commando, which fought in the East African campaign. Altogether, 4000 Palestinians served in the RPC. They also served in Egypt and Greece, where over a thousand were captured in late 1941 during the British imperial withdrawal (leading to recruitment from the High Commission Territories in Southern Africa). As well as the RPC, in the early stages of the war Palestinians were recruited into the Royal Army Service Corps, Medical Corps, Ordnance Corps, Engineers and ancillary branches of the RAF. According to the Air Ministry 3000 men from Palestine, Cyprus and Malta were employed by the RAF in the Middle East during the war.

Palestine also provided combat units. In 1940 it was decided to recruit three separate Arab and Jewish infantry companies to be attached to the East Kent Regiment ('The Buffs'). This group of about 500 men then became the Palestine Regiment, intended for guard duty, though some saw service in the Syrian campaign. Total military enlistment at that date stood at 10,000 Jews and 4000 Arabs in the British armed forces. Many Jews had for some time fostered hopes of an autonomous Jewish Army. In August 1942 the Secretary of State for War announced to the House of Commons plans for a new Palestine Regiment of the British Army, to incorporate the existing Palestine Infantry Companies of The Buffs. This new regiment consisted of 1600 Jews and 1200 Arabs. In September 1944 it was finally decided to form a Jewish Brigade Group, after much pressure from the Jewish Agency. The British had dragged their heels on this matter as they were fully aware that to train and arm an exclusively Jewish formation to fight the Germans might be creating an anti-British force of the future. Nevertheless, with Churchill's support, the brigade was formed, with the infantry companies of the Palestine Regiment at its core. It came to number 5500 men, and a Jewish Canadian officer of twenty-five years experience, Brigadier Ernest Benjamin, was chosen to command it. The brigade served in Italy in the last weeks of the war, first tasting action in the Eighth Army's final assault in the region of Ravenna. Stationed deep in Europe when VE Day occurred, members of the brigade took part in the illegal immigration of Jews into Palestine, as well as committing indiscriminate acts of violence and murder against German civilians and servicemen. The Brigade was disbanded in 1946. All told, up to 30,000 Jews and 12,000 Arabs from Palestine served with British forces during the war.[32]

On the home front, Palestine was deeply engaged in the war, not least as a target for enemy bombers sent to attack Haifa and Tel Aviv. A third of its national output was absorbed by the military, the highest proportion of any country in the Middle East. Like many other parts of the Empire, Palestine served as a gathering point for enemy prisoners of war. There was, for example, a German prisoner camp at Gaza, known as Camp Mardi. Palestine's agriculture and industry were geared for war. There was some manufacturing capacity, and the Mandate produced water bottles, mess tins, stoves, pumps, electric cable, glass insulators, khaki drill uniforms, camouflage netting, tarpaulins, tents, crockery, razors, boots and nuts and bolts. It also supplied the armed forces with hundreds of tons of jam and marmalade. Despite this, the war jeopardized the future of the citrus industry, the Mandate's leading agricultural concern. With the Mediterranean route closed, there was a need to increase home production of foodstuffs to the greatest extent possible. Irrigation schemes were undertaken to bring new areas into cultivation. Palestine had never approached self-sufficiency in food, but Syria usually produced surpluses of grain, fruit and vegetables. Syrian imports ceased, however, with the fall of France. It was announced in the House of Commons in March 1942 that much had been done to increase production through propaganda and loans to farmers (£400,000 in eighteen months). These efforts, particularly to expand the production of vegetables, played an important part in meeting the requirements of the armed forces in the Middle East, and in the later years of the war Palestine was able to export to Egypt and Lebanon. Inflation and supply problems were augmented by the demands of the armed forces in Palestine for local produce.

As elsewhere in the Empire, the Palestine government feared a fall in revenue because of the war, but actually found that it was able to build up a substantial surplus. Increased recurrent expenditure, however, was a real concern. Palestine derived almost half of its income from customs duties and excise on tobacco, alcohol, matches, urban and rural property tax and postal charges. Local revenue was supplemented by substantial grants from the British government. As a result of the Arab revolt the British government removed the liability for a contribution to the maintenance of the military garrison and the excess on police and prisons. Under this arrangement the British government contributed £1.4 million in 1938–39, £1.9 million in 1939–40, and £2.92 million in 1940–41. This led to unexpected revenue buoyancy in the early years of the war, and Palestine's surplus balance rose to £4.4 million in 1941. The Treasury considered it absurd that the British taxpayer should be assisting Palestine to build up such a surplus while taxation was a great deal lower than in Britain itself. In response, income tax was introduced to Palestine in 1941.

Palestine provides a good example of the war's financial effects in the Empire. Restrictions on shipping after Italy's entry into the war led to a fall in customs revenue, but improved security conditions inside Palestine improved tax collections, and local revenue for 1940–41 exceeded £5 million. In 1943 defence and security were grouped under the same budgetary heading for the first time, and amounted in that year to over £5.2 million. This included £2 million for food subsidization, £1.5 million for cost of living allowances and £659,000 for civil defence and ARP measures. During 1943 currency in circulation increased by 39 per cent to £37 million (in 1937–38 there had been under £5 million in circulation). Bank deposits increased by 50 per cent to £54 million (between 1937–38 and 1944–45 bank deposits rose from £16 million to £69 million). Sterling balances were estimated at over £41 million in 1944–45. The value of imports rose from nearly £16 million to over £36 million, exports from nearly £6.5 million to over £15.6 million, and government revenue (including grants from Britain) from nearly £4.9 million to nearly £17.5 million. The Arab revolt and associated disturbances had greatly increased the cost of internal security, and hot on its heels came the need for expenditure arising out of the war. While total expenditure rose from £7 million in 1937–38 to £18 million in 1944–45, expenditure on security and war measures rose in the same period from £2 million to £12 million.

Trans-Jordan was another fruit of the dismemberment of the Ottoman Empire after the First World War, and was, like Palestine, a League of Nations Mandate administered by Britain. It was recognized as an independent state in 1928, but the British Resident retained important powers and the monarchy, established by the British, remained a buttress of British power. Trans-Jordan was, in fact, a model client-state. On the outbreak of war the Emir, Abdullah ibn Hussein, immediately pledged his full support for the British cause. Like all territories in the region, Trans-Jordan experienced the disturbance to peace-time economic and trading patterns that the war brought in its wake. It also became involved in the military side of the conflict. Trans-Jordan's capital, Amman, was bombed by Vichy aircraft, and its military forces supported British imperial campaigns. Trans-Jordan possessed two military formations. The British-raised Trans-Jordan Frontier Force (TJFF) rose to number 8000, while the Arab Legion, loyal to the Emir and commanded by a Briton, Brigadier Glubb Pasha, came to number 5000 and was placed at Britain's disposal for the duration of the war. (Making the most of resources to hand, SOE made Glubb responsible for organizing operations in Trans-Jordan in the event of an Axis occupation). The Legion was placed at Britain's disposal for the duration of the war. The TJFF had grown from the Gendarmerie established by Britain in Palestine at the end of the First World War. At the start of the Second World War it comprised three cavalry and two mechanized squadrons, and from 1941 came under War Office control (like other locally-raised forces throughout the Empire). With the reduction of the British garrison in Palestine brought about by the need to deploy seasoned British troops to active theatres, Britain was fortunate in having at its disposal local military formations that could step into the breach. From late 1940 the TJFF expanded. The 1st Cavalry (Horsed) Regiment was formed in January 1941, and the 1st Mechanized Regiment in the following month. A Line of Communications Squadron was raised to protect vulnerable points on the Haifa–Baghdad road, and ancillary services such as workshops, hospitals and a training depot were also developed.

In the Iraq campaign of April-May 1941 a relief force left Trans-Jordan to aid the beleaguered garrison at RAF Habbaniya, west of Baghdad. A TJFF squadron was supposed to go to the Iraq Petroleum Company's pumping station close to the border which was the assembly point for the invasion force. It refused to cross the border, however, which was within its rights, as the TJFF was not supposed to leave the country without a special proclamation from the High Commissioner. The formation did, however, take part in the Syrian campaign from June 1941. The imperial advance depended on the movement of supplies along the Haifa–Deraa – Damascus railway line, and it fell to the TJFF to secure bridges and viaducts. After the British conquest of Syria, unrest remained a problem for some time and a sizeable garrison was required to maintain law and order. So the TJFF spent several months in Syria, and later in the war was stationed on the Syrian–Turkish frontier to perform watch and ward duties. A further war involvement, though this time against a rather different enemy, came about in November 1943 when the Mechanized Regiment was sent to Bandar Abbas in the Persian Gulf to take part in the Anti-Locust Campaign.

The Arab Legion played a valuable part in imperial operations in Iraq and Syria. In Iraq the Legion's Desert Mechanized Force guided a mechanized British column five hundred miles through the desert to the Euphrates, and then led a detachment of the column northwards to cut the Mosul road before descending along the Tigris to Baghdad. In the Syrian campaign Arab Legion soldiers served as guides to a British column led across the desert to attack Palmyra, and then participated in the attack. To the regret of Emir Abdullah and Brigadier Glubb Pasha, the Legion was not required to take part in further campaigns. It was, however, required to carry out essential guard and internal security duties in Trans-Jordan, Palestine, Syria and Iraq, and continued patrolling the region.

Britain's war in the Mediterranean was extended deep into the Middle East by the need to protect vital oil resources from German attack, and to prevent local rulers from causing friction through intrigue and rebellion aimed at shaking off British control and courting the friendship of Germany. This extension of operations into the Middle East also brought British forces into overland contact with their Russian allies. British exertions in the region led to a number of remarkable military interventions in Iran, Iraq and Syria, as Britain sought to uphold its dominant position in the Middle Eastern lands between the shores of the eastern Mediterranean and the shores of the Persian Gulf.

8

Iraq, Iran and Syria

The demands of world war meant that in 1941 Britain added to its responsibilities in the Middle East by launching military campaigns effectively to annex Iraq, Iran and Syria. Iraq and Iran were independent states with a history of British influence and intervention, while Syria was a French League of Nations Mandate that had remained firm in the Vichy camp following the fall of France. These campaigns all bore witness to Britain's determination to maintain control of the region, and were testament to the extent of Britain's power and presence beyond the bounds of the formal British Empire. Campaigns in these countries also demonstrated the power of the German war machine. To cause the British to commit valuable resources to the defence of the region, so far from Germany and the main areas of Hitler's strategic interest, was a considerable achievement. For the British, war in the Mediterranean, should Italy become an enemy, had been foreseen. The fact that the war effort that was centred on Egypt spread so far eastwards, towards the boundaries of India itself, was a result of German economic and political penetration of the Middle East and of its early successes in the war against Russia.

Iraq was a former Ottoman province taken by the British during the First World War. It was a strategically important territory, and one in which Britain faced a German-backed indigenous uprising, the suppression of which required a full-scale military campaign.[1] This little-known campaign could have cost Britain the war in the Middle East if German assistance to the rebels had been more resolute and the British response less so. Its most striking feature was the heroic stand of the RAF's No. 4 Flying Training School at Habbaniya, sixty miles west of Baghdad. Using obsolete aircraft, its handful of experienced pilots and their students lifted a siege mounted by about 9000 Iraqi troops, crippled German aircraft sent to the country, and destroyed most Iraqi air assets before beginning the British fight back to Baghdad via Fallujah. By holding out and then going over to the offensive, the School bought crucial time for imperial relief forces from Palestine and India to concentrate and then deploy.

The British and Indian armies had fought in Iraq against the Turks during the First World War, winning ultimately though suffering a humiliating defeat at Kut in 1916. After the war Iraq became a British-administered League of Nations Mandate, though serious unrest in the country required the presence of over twenty infantry battalions. It was granted independence by the Anglo-Iraqi Treaty of Alliance and Mutual Support in 1930. The treaty's provisos, however, meant that Britain remained the main arbiter of the country's external and military affairs. Though British troops had left the country by 1937, the right remained to transit troops through Iraq should the British consider it necessary to do so, as Iraq was regarded as an important link in the land route from the Mediterranean to India, and a feature of the imperial oil network. Under the treaty Iraq was also obliged to give Britain use of all available facilities in the event of war. British advisers remained in the administration and the army, which was also supplied with British equipment under the terms of the treaty, and British airbases remained at Habbaniya near Baghdad and Shaiba near Basra. These airbases were important staging posts on the air route to India and the Far East. The overland route from Basra on the Persian Gulf, through Baghdad and on to Palestine, was also considered important by the British as an alternative to the Suez Canal and Red Sea for the reinforcement of Egypt should command of the seas falter (for example, if Italy successfully closed the Suez Canal in a future conflict).

Similar to the Anglo-Egyptian Treaty that afforded Britain extensive base rights, there were also economic and diplomatic concessions, including British stewardship of the Mosul and Kirkuk oilfields (a pipeline delivered oil from these areas to Haditha on the Euphrates, where it forked and carried oil to Haifa in Palestine and Tripoli in Syria). This continuing British involvement in Iraqi affairs, as in Egypt, was a source of much resentment, further stoked by the presence in Baghdad of the rabidly anti-British and anti-Jewish Mufti of Jerusalem, Haj Amin al-Husseini, exiled from Palestine in 1937. Together with German encouragement, much of it through Berlin's minister to Iraq, Dr Fritz Grobba, and the opportunities presented by the turmoil of war, this resentment led to a coup that ousted the pro-British Regent, Prince Abdullilah (ruling on behalf of the child Feisal II). His pro-Axis successor, Rashid Ali, supported by key elements in the army, thought the time propitious to rise up and throw the British out. The Germans, they believed, would be right beside them, with political support and the commitment of modern military equipment and troops. On 23 May 1941 Hitler himself called the Arab Freedom Movement 'our natural ally against England'. But by then Germany's tardy commitment of resources, and the professionalism and fighting spirit of British imperial forces, had had its effect, and the Iraqi usurper was about to flee the country before the British occupied his capital.

On the outbreak of war Iraq was ruled by the Regent and a government led by the pro-British Nuri as-Sa'id. The British government asked the Iraqi government to sever diplomatic relations with Germany, to intern all Germans and give all possible assistance to Britain under the terms of the treaty. Prime Minister Nuri as-Sa'id complied with the British requests and also introduced curfews, censorship, rationing and the power to rule by decree. Opponents thought these powers might be used against them, and tried to cultivate rival factions in the army whilst criticizing the government's pro-British stance. The Golden Square, a group of elite officers initially supportive of Nuri as-Sa'id, resented his Defence Minister's attempts to curb the power of the military, and in March 1940 as-Sa'id was replaced by Rashid Ali. He was closely linked to the Golden Square and, like its members, had pro-Axis sympathies. In January 1941 Rashid Ali and the Golden Square engineered a coup, and threatened the Regent with military action. On 2 April 1941 the Regent escaped, fleeing first to the American legation in Baghdad. He was then smuggled to RAF Habbaniya, from where he was flown to Basra where HMS *Cockchafer* was waiting to take him to Trans-Jordan. (*Cockchafer* was one of the ships of the China Station that had been transferred west on the outbreak of war with Germany.)

This rebellion could not be allowed to succeed, especially when the new Iraqi leader began receiving aid from Germany and initiated military action against the British bases. It was decided by the British government that pernicious Axis influence in Syria, Iraq and Iran had to be met head on and destroyed. If these countries fell to the German camp it would signal the destruction of British power in the Middle East and the loss of the oil on which its war effort depended. Iraq had experienced German commercial, political and ideological penetration before the war. The German Directorate of Propaganda espoused pan-Arabism, and German diplomats and military officials courted the Iraqi army. Germany promised military aid to rebels planning to move against the British, but it was not forthcoming in sufficient strength when Rashid Ali and his backers acted precipitately in April 1941. German aircraft were flown via Syria to his aid, and Vichy Syria also supplied war material. But this intervention was insufficient to enable Rashid Ali to defeat the British imperial forces. Here, as in most other theatres, British special forces had a role to play. British SIS and SOE agents, and even Palestinian Jews recruited by SOE from the Irgun, undertook sabotage missions. Fuel dumps were targeted and sixteen newly-arrived, American-built Northrop aircraft belonging to the Iraqi air force were destroyed on the ground, a telling blow in a campaign in which a more successful use of air power by the Iraqi leadership or its German supporters could have seen an entirely different outcome.

When Rashid Ali ordered his army to surround Britain's main air base at Habbaniya, London demanded action. The Commander-in-Chief Middle East, General Sir Archibald Wavell, said that his forces were too stretched to take any action to curb Rashid Ali, and that properly India Command should deal with a situation in a region of traditional Indian defence and foreign policy steward- ship. India Command was ready to take action. The willingness of the Commander-in-Chief India, General Sir Claude Auchinleck, to commit forces contrasted sharply with Wavell's stubborn reluctance. The contrast was not wasted on Churchill. Churchill's impatience with Wavell was unfair, because Wavell *was* very thinly stretched in the Mediterranean, North Africa and East Africa, and India Command had on the books a long-standing plan to send a division to the region for the protection of the Iraq and Iran oilfields. As early as January 1940 the War Office had ordered India Command to prepare a division for Basra, though this (the 5th Indian Division) was diverted for service in North Africa. In March 1940 representatives of MEC and India Command had met in Cairo to discuss plans for deployment to the region (Operation Sabine).

To address the situation in Iraq caused by Rashid Ali's aggression, forces from the Middle East would also be needed, and Wavell was therefore obliged to scrape the bottom of his manpower barrel. His reluctance can be explained by two factors: on the one hand, he frankly thought that he had bigger fish to fry, not least Rommel. On the other hand, he saw the region as one primarily of Indian responsibility. The Iran and Iraq region was of concern to both India Command and Middle East Command, though it was on the outer edge of the responsibilities of both and central to neither. Middle East Command had its eyes firmly fixed on the Western Desert. The situation with regards to Iraq was not aided by the fact that responsibility for it oscillated between these two giant imperial military structures. India Command was the more enthusiastic (its enthusiasm would surely have been tempered if the Iraq situation had erupted a year later, when the Japanese were rushing their forces through Burma). Wavell's reluctance to supply forces from MEC for a westward thrust towards Iraq marked his card with Churchill, whose strategic vision told him that a favourable resolution to the situation in Iraq was needed, and needed soon. Thus was Operation Sabine put into action in April 1941, and forces began to mass in western Indian ports for the sea journey to Basra.

The British Ambassador in Iraq, however, argued that, before landing forcibly at Basra, Britain should invoke its treaty rights to transit troops through Iraq. If rejected, Sir Kinahan Cornwallis suggested, Britain would have the legal right to intervene forcibly. Wavell and Lord Linlithgow, the Viceroy of India, agreed. On 16 April the ambassador informed Rashid Ali that the British intended to avail themselves of their treaty rights, and no objection was raised. On 17 April 1941 the lead brigade of 10th Indian Division, which had been destined for Malaya, landed at Basra. An advance party of headquarters staff from 20th Indian Brigade and 10th Indian Division had already been flown in by Douglas DC2 and Vickers Valentia aircraft of No. 31 (India) Squadron, based at Karachi. Two days later 400 troops of the 1st King's Own Royal Regiment were flown from Karachi to Shaiba, and then on to reinforce RAF Habbaniya, where ground defences were limited. Protected by the Australian sloop HMAS *Yarra* as they entered the Shatt-el-Arab, on 18 April troopships arrived at Basra and began disgorging elements of the 20th Indian Infantry Brigade, the 3rd Field Regiment Royal Artillery and the headquarters of the 10th Indian Division, commanded by Major-General W. A. K. Fraser (replaced by Brigadier William Slim on 19 May, Fraser moving to the post of military attaché in Tehran). On 21 April Rashid Ali asked that no more British forces follow, but the British government would give no such guarantee to a man who had usurped power in a coup. On 28–29 April the second troop convoy arrived at the head of the Gulf protected by HMS *Cockchafer, Falmouth* and HMAS *Yarra*.

The Indian Army was arriving in strength, and it was time for Rashid Ali to make an important decision.

The Iraqi leader decided on conflict, gambling on the ability of his own forces ability to check the British build up, at least until German aid arrived in strength. He ordered elements of the Iraqi army to invest RAF Habbaniya, and they left Baghdad on 29 April. The British Embassy in Baghdad was also surrounded. The embassy and its grounds became a refuge for 350 men, women and children, their communications with the outside world severed on 2 May when Iraqis entered the embassy and removed all wireless transmitters and receivers (though a hidden radio allowed embassy staff to listen to British, German and Iraqi broadcasts). A further 150 British people were sheltered by the American Legation, and 250 other civilians were moved to Habbaniya in a procession of cars, omnibuses and RAF lorries. (They were then evacuated on board two BOAC flying boats.)* At Habbaniya, thousands of Iraqi troops established positions on the plateau over-looking the air base, constructing defences and gun emplacements (the plateau rose to 150 feet at its highest). It was an unenviable situation for the British, particularly given Habbaniya's unsuitability for repelling large-scale infantry attack and artillery bombardment. Committed irrevocably to action, Iraqi diplomats engaged in intense negotiations with the Germans. Iraq severed diplomatic relations with Britain, resumed them with Germany and promised Germany the use of its air bases. All that remained was for German forces to make a meaningful contribution. In retaliation for this Iraqi move, British forces took over the airport, the docks and the power station in Basra.

The British base at Habbaniya was home to over a thousand RAF personnel and 1200 RAF Levies made up of British-officered Kurds, Arabs and Assyrian Christians. Earlier in the war, when Russia was allied to Germany, aircraft from Habbaniya had reconnoitred Russia as the British government was considering the practicalities of attacking oil wells and refineries in the Caucasus in conjunction with French forces operating from Syria. There were also eighteen RAF armoured cars at the base. Given this limited ground defensive capability, the arrival of the 400 men of The King's Own Royal Regiment was a most welcome addition. The numbers inside the camp were swelled by some 9000 civilian workers. This mixed bag of races made Habbaniya one of the more extraordinary outposts of Empire. Inside its eight mile long iron fence were hangars, two large repair shops and corrugated iron-roofed military buildings, a tall water tower, a power station, a gymnasium, a swimming pool, social clubs, and tree-lined roads with names like Piccadilly. There were also fifty-six tennis courts, riding stables, a polo ground-cum-racecourse, many vegetable plots, a large stock farm and a golf course, and it was sited close to Habbaniya Lake (covering an area of 100 square miles) on which BOAC flying boats bound for India and the Far East landed. The

* British Overseas Airways Corporation was the creation of a 1938 merger between Imperial Airways and British Airways.

airfield itself lay beyond the enclosed perimeter. Though Habbaniya was an RAF base, it had no operational units as it was a training facility, known as No. 4 Service Flying Training School (there was also a Communications Flight). The fact that it had not been sited or built with defence in mind was clearly demonstrated by the fact that the base was completely overlooked by a desert plateau.

Despite these impediments, the base was required to fight. Most of Habbaniya's pilots were unseasoned instructors, supported in this hour of need by aircrew drawn from amongst their pupils. Its aircraft were mostly obsolete: thirty-two Audaxes, eight Gordons, twenty-nine Oxfords, nine Gladiators, a solitary Blenheim and five Hart trainers. No. 244 (Bomber) Squadron was based at Shaiba (equipped with Vickers Vincent general-purpose biplanes), reinforced during the crisis by nine Wellington light bombers from Egypt. Seven Fairey Gordons were transferred from Habbaniya to Shaiba on 15–16 April to cover the arrival of the 5th Brigade from India. Throughout the conflict small but important RAF reinforcements arrived for service in Iraq. On 19 April, for example, six Gladiators arrived from Egypt; on 27 April No. 84 Squadron's Blenheims were moved to Aqir in Palestine; later, eight Wellingtons from No. 37 Squadron also arrived at Aqir, and four Blenheims from No. 203 Squadron were sent to Lydda. In Egypt an officer from No. 94 Squadron, in the process of re-equipping with Hurricanes, was ordered to collect five Gladiators from a maintenance unit and proceed to Habbaniya.

Though the struggle that followed Rashid Ali's decision to oppose British forces in his country was primarily an air and land affair, the naval component had valuable work to do, and it was, of course, the reality of British seapower that enabled the build up of forces in southern Iraq to take place at all. The Persian Gulf, a vital waterway long dominated by the Royal Navy, was policed by British, Australian and Indian naval vessels commanded by the Senior Naval Officer Persian Gulf, Commodore Cosmo Moray Graham. His immediate superior was the Commander-in-Chief of the East Indies Station based in Ceylon. At the time of the Iraqi rebellion, Moray Graham had under his command four small warships at Basra, but on 13 April 1941 the force was reinforced by the carrier HMS *Hermes* and the cruiser HMS *Emerald*, both of the East Indies Squadron. When attention switched to Iran a few months later, he was further reinforced by British and Indian sloops and an Australian armed merchant cruiser.

The Air Officer Commanding (AOC) RAF Habbaniya, Air Vice-Marshal H. G. Smart, had spent time preparing to improvise if his base was attacked, ensuring that his aircraft were able to carry the maximum possible bomb load if called in to action, even those not designed to carry bombs at all. Makeshift bomb-racks were cobbled together so that as many aircraft as possible could be bombed up, some dangerously overloaded in the process. Tests showed that the Audax, officially capable of carrying eight twenty-pound bombs, could take to the air with two 250-pound bombs. As reinforcement, a number of Wellington bombers were transferred from Egypt to Shaiba, though not as many as Air Chief

Marshal Sir Arthur Tedder, AOC Middle East, would have liked to have sent. The RAF in Iraq was left largely to rely on its own slender resources. Not only did it have the Habbaniya siege to contend with, it was known that the main body of the Iraqi army was still uncommitted, and that the Iraqi air force, with an operational strength of over seventy aircraft, was at large. On paper it was a stronger force than that fielded by the British, including twenty-five Nisrs (Pegasus-engined Audaxes), nine Gladiators, fifteen Breda Ba65 fighters, and fifteen Douglas-Northrop 8A-4 fighter-bombers.

On 1 May 1941, with the enemy massing outside his perimeter fence and no chance of quick relief by imperial land forces, Air Vice-Marshal Smart was given permission by the Foreign Office to act as he thought fit, and to do so decisively if he opted for conflict. This he duly did, deciding for a pre-emptive strike rather than the option of sitting it out and allowing the Iraqis the leisure to position their forces around his base. On 2 May all available aircraft from Habbaniya were flown over the Iraqi positions on the plateau overlooking the base, together with the Wellingtons from Shaiba. Smart's tactics were to mount continuous strafing and bombing missions with as many aircraft as possible. Forty-nine aircraft (including the Wellingtons) clustered and jockeyed over an area not much bigger than a minor golf course where the Iraqi ground forces were massed. On this first day of open hostilities Habbaniya-based aircraft flew 193 sorties. Twenty-two Iraqi aircraft at airfields near Baghdad were destroyed, though Iraqi shelling of RAF Habbaniya destroyed an equal number of British aircraft on the ground. Ten out of an available thirty-nine Habbaniya pilots were either dead or hospitalized after the first day of action. Nevertheless, the Iraqi positions around the base continued to be attacked, as did Iraqi airfields at Rashid and Baghdad. On the third day of the attack four Blenheim bombers from No. 203 Squadron arrived from Egypt. The wastage had been considerable, only four out of twenty-seven Oxfords, for example, remaining in service after the third day. On the ground, attacks were mounted by the King's Own and the RAF Levies against Habbaniya's besiegers. An Iraqi column bringing reinforcements from Baghdad suffered great destruction at the hands of the RAF as it approached from Fallujah. The column was attacked with low bombing and machine-gunning from forty aircraft. For two hours they bombed the long column of jammed vehicles, one pilot reporting a solid sheet of flame running for 250 yards.

Habbaniya's ground defences were augmented by two First World War field guns taken from outside the officers' mess and made ready for use. Suitable ammunition was flown in by DC2's of No. 31 (India) Squadron, and the Iraqi forces were led to believe that heavy guns were beginning to arrive from Basra, further diminishing their resolve as four and a half inch shells burst around them. On 6 May 1941, after further air strikes, the Iraqis withdrew from the plateau and the RAF armoured cars followed up, fighting a battle on the road leading to Fallujah. In the five days since Air Vice-Marshal Smart had grasped the nettle, 647 sorties had been flown and 3000 bombs dropped. The defenders of Habbaniya could now boast six howitzers, an eighteen-pounder gun, a tank, ten modern armoured cars, three pom-poms, thirty-four Bren guns and eleven Vickers machine guns.

Whilst Habbaniya toughed it out, MEC was assembling a force to march overland from Trans-Jordan to relieve the air base. This was the composite force that Wavell had managed to assemble from his overstretched resources. Habforce (Habbaniya Force), commanded by Major-General J. G. W. Clark, consisted of a mechanized brigade of the 1st Cavalry Division, a field regiment, a lorry-borne infantry battalion, 166 Field Ambulance and three mechanized squadrons of the Trans-Jordan Frontier Force (TJFF). Joined by 1500 men from the Arab Legion led by Major Glubb Pasha, Habforce amounted to nearly 6000 men. It was to march into Iraq from Trans-Jordan to try and lift the siege of Habbaniya before moving on to take Baghdad. Wavell doubted that this force would be of much use or whether it would arrive in time. The Chiefs of Staff, however, were adamant that all possible force should be used against the Iraqi army, in order to demonstrate resolve and forestall further and more resolute Axis intervention in the region. In the south of the country Indian forces were massing to defend the vital Basra region, and in preparation for a possible future intervention in Iran. On 8 May 1941 Wavell took operational control in southern Iraq as responsibility was transferred from India Command to MEC. He told the new local commander, Lieutenant-General Edward Quinan, that his task was to secure the Basra–Shaiba area and prepare a base to receive more troops. Quinan had arrived the day before to command what was to be known as Iraq Force. On that day the first German aircraft had touched down in Syria (base rights granted by the Vichy government) on its way to Iraq. On 5 May another troop convoy escorted by HMAS *Yarra* had docked at Basra, bringing the 21st Indian Brigade, as the build up in the region gathered pace.

To expedite the relief of Habbaniya, a flying column was detached from Habforce and sent on ahead. This column was known as Kingcol (King Column) after its commander Brigadier John 'Joe' Kingstone. It included the Household Cavalry Regiment, two companies and a carrier platoon of the Essex Yeomanry, units of the Arab Legion, a battery of the 60th Field Regiment, an anti-tank troop, a troop of the 2nd Cheshire Field Squadron Royal Engineers and ancillary services including a well-boring unit. In all, it comprised 2000 men and 500 vehicles. Kingstone's advance was harried by German aircraft, which also appeared over Habbaniya, as the Luftwaffe entered the fray. To the very considerable surprise of the British, Messerschmitt 110s were seen over Iraq, a worrying indication of Germany's growing military support for Rashid Ali.

On 12 May the Wellington bombers temporarily based at Shaiba were recalled to Egypt, leaving only the carrier HMS *Hermes* to project airpower in the southern region (though she was recalled to sea by the Commander-in-Chief East Indies Station on 19 May). Concerned about the build up of German forces entering Iraq via Syria, on 14 May London gave the RAF permission to attack German aircraft at Syrian airfields. Colonel Werner Junck had been appointed by Berlin to command the Luftwaffe in Iraq. This amounted during the crisis to two dozen fighters and bombers based primarily at Mosul, though it was intended that Fliegerkorps Irak would grow considerably. After appearing to have achieved victory single-handedly with the departure of the Iraqi army from Habbaniya, the RAF airmen were as unpleasantly surprised as were the men of Kingcol by the growing presence of modern German aircraft in the skies above Iraq. Heinkel 111 bombers and Messerschmitt 110s fighters attacked Habbaniya on 16 May, and sought to repel Kingcol by attacking the column in the desert. Habbaniya's strength was augmented on 17 May when four more Gladiators of No. 94 Squadron and six Blenheims of No. 84 Squadron arrived from the Mediterranean, and two days previously two long-range Hurricanes had arrived. One was lost on 17 May when British aircraft attacked the German base, destroying a Heinkel and a Messerschmitt. Two Gladiators were sent to reconnoitre Baghdad, and managed to destroy two more Messerschmitts just after they had taken off.

These successes against the limited German forces committed to Iraq were important, and on the ground the situation was moving in favour of the British. On 18 May Kingcol arrived at Habbaniya. There it planned to wait for the rest of Habforce, as the Iraqi army was believed to number 40,000 men, with considerable armour. Resistance, however, was crumbling in the face of defeat and limited German support. Arguably the most important thrust of the land campaign came when Kingcol and the ground forces at Habbaniya decided to try and capture the key bridge over the Euphrates at Fallujah. This was to be a joint attack with the RAF. On 19 May nearly sixty aircraft began the attack on Fallujah, which was eventually taken by the King's Own and the RAF Levies. The two imperial columns then began an advance towards Baghdad, taking out the garrison at Ramadi on the way.

Successful attacks were followed through to Baghdad, where the embassy was still cut off. The capital surrendered to imperial forces on 30 May and an armistice signed. On the previous day, realizing that the game was up, Rashid Ali and the German and Italian ministers had fled to Iran. Axis help had been far too little and far too late. In all, small arms and about thirty aircraft had been sent to Mosul. Of these, seven Heinkels, twelve Messerschmitts and two Junkers 52 transport aircraft were destroyed (a small number of Italian aircraft were also destroyed. On 23 May twelve Fiat CR42's had arrived). More importantly, Germany lost a great deal of prestige in the Arab world. At the conclusion of hostilities it was considered vital that British forces be seen in Kirkuk and Mosul, and so a Gurkha battalion was flown to the region, and units of the Household Cavalry set out from Habbaniya on 4 June 1941.

The majority of the Iraqis were not affected by this brief and geographically limited military interlude in their country. A call for jihad and government appeals for support in the media made little difference to the outcome. Many people failed to respond, or even helped the British, like the Shiite tribes of the south and the Kurds of the north. The collapse of government authority at the end of the campaign led to a brief period of violence against Jews in Baghdad, during which about 700 died. The military campaign had been a striking example of air warfare unsupported in the early stages by other arms. Thereafter, the campaign featured the close air support of infantry. The RAF flew 1600 sorties in total, dropping one hundred tons of bombs and firing about a quarter of a million rounds of ammunition. The Regent returned to Baghdad and in October 1941 a pro-British administration assumed power. On 17 January 1943 Iraq became the first independent Muslim state to declare war on the Axis.

Operations in Iraq were just the beginning of a busy period for British forces seeking to shore up their position in the Middle East. The next of the region's problem regimes on the British list was Vichy Syria, which after its conquest remained a part of Britain's war empire until 1946.[2] Military intervention in Syria had similar causes to the invasion of Iraq. The Vichy regime was a loose cannon that Churchill's government and the military authorities in the Middle East decided they could not tolerate. As in the case of Iraq, the momentum came from London, overcoming the reluctance of the regional commander, Wavell, who thought that his oversized command was already managing too many campaigns with too few troops. It was decided to occupy Syria and Lebanon once Iraq had been sorted out, particularly because the Syrian government was unable or unwilling to prevent the transit of German aircraft and military supplies through its territory. Furthermore, the Syrian government was itself providing military aid to Rashid Ali. ULTRA intelligence had revealed that the Axis planned to use Syria as a staging post for aiding Iraq, and it was reported that 2500 volunteers were leaving to join Rashid Ali's uprising against the British. On 15 May 1941 the British Consul in Beirut reported that three Messerschmitt 110s had landed at Rayak before leaving for Damascus, where there were fourteen German aircraft already. During the Iraq campaign German aircraft with Iraqi markings arrived in Syria and bombed British forces (Kingcol) as they entered the country. Syria, in short, was a provocative and obvious target, and the British were further prodded in the direction of intervention by the Free French, General de Gaulle always being keen to sponsor operations that might gain parts of the French Empire for the Free French cause.

As a result of all these factors, British imperial forces were turned against the 40,000 Vichy troops of the Army of the Levant, and the Syrian campaign opened in early June 1941. General de Gaulle had been keen on such a move for some time, though here as elsewhere was to be disappointed by the outcome (British, not Free French, control). For Operation Exporter Wavell scraped together an Indian infantry brigade, a Royal Marine commando, elements of the TJFF, a Free French contingent amounting to two brigades (including Legionnaires), the Cheshire Yeomanry with their horses, and two Australian brigades of the 7th Division (which were moved from Mersa Matruh, where they were replaced by the 5th South African Brigade, recently arrived from Kenya, and the Polish

Brigade). A number of imperial columns therefore converged upon Syria: the 10th Indian Division and Habforce advanced from Iraq along the route of the oil pipeline; the 6th British Division came from northern Palestine; and the 7th Australian Division (less a brigade still forming part of the garrison at Tobruk) advanced from Haifa, assisted by the Arab Legion, the TJFF and Free French units.

General 'Jumbo' Wilson, Officer Commanding Troops in Palestine and Trans-Jordan, was told to capture the airfield at Damascus, Beirut (the civil and military capital) and Rayak, before advancing to Palmyra, Homs and Tripoli. His land forces were supported on their Mediterranean flank by the 15th Cruiser Squadron, a landing ship and eight destroyers (including the cruiser HMNZS *Leander*). These in turn were covered by British fighters. The naval component was completed by two FAA squadrons, including a detachment of No. 815 FAA Squadron based on Cyprus. The FAA sank a French transport bringing reinforcements to Syria, and British aircraft were successful in searching sea lanes and attacking enemy shipping bound for Beirut. The RAF under Air Commodore L. O. Brown, Air Officer Commanding Palestine and Trans-Jordan, supplied two and a half squadrons of fighters, two of bombers (including No. 84 Squadron operating from Iraq) and a tactical reconnaissance flight (this force included No. 3 RAAF Squadron flying Tomahawks). Altogether, imperial ground forces could rely on a daily force of some eighty aircraft. As well as attacking shipping, the RAF also targeted railways, motor transport and grounded aircraft, a series of 140 sorties, for example, destroying thirty-six French aircraft and damaging over a hundred more. SOE attacked targets such as the Tripoli oil refinery (a failed attempt) and seized pumping stations along the pipeline connecting Syria and Palestine to Iraqi oilfields.

The Australians attacked objectives in Lebanon including Beirut, and the Indians and Free French were sent to capture Damascus, Homs and Aleppo. Imperial progress up the coastal strip towards Damascus was assisted by flanking naval action. The 10th Indian Division, Habforce (still in existence after its part in the Iraq campaign) and the Arab Legion, attacked Palmyrah and Aleppo. Most of the troops made slow progress, but, supported by naval gunfire, the 7th Australian Division broke through to Beirut from Haifa on 6–7 July and after a five day battle forced Dentz, the Vichy commanding officer, to sue for terms. Like the Iraqi campaign, the Syrian campaign was a dangerous venture. The French High Commissioner in the Levant had 25,000 regular and 20,000 local troops under his command, including Druse cavalry. Indicating their loyalty to Vichy, only 5700 of these troops opted to join the Free French on the conclusion of the campaign. The British conquest of Syria showed imperial awareness and resolve on the part of the British government at a time when Britain's enemies were in the ascendant. Victory in Syria shored up this vital region at a time when German influence was growing. It brought British forces into touch with Turkey, a neutral that the British government constantly wooed throughout the war, and gained valuable air and naval bases which deepened the defence of the Basra–Baghdad–Haifa route.

Needing to prepare Syria in case German troops came south from Russia, Wilson's force became known as the Ninth Army and he was charged with preparing a defensive plan for defending Syria from the north. The ubiquitous SOE played its part organizing a post-occupational sabotage network, as it had done in Iraq where it established cells in cities such as Baghdad, Karbala and Najaf. After the fall of Tobruk in June 1942, Wilson was further charged with providing plans for the defence of Palestine should Rommel attack across the Sinai. These attacks never came, though British military administration remained in place in Syria until that country's independence in 1946.

Astonishingly, Britain mounted a third major military campaign in the Middle East in 1941, this time invading Iran.[3] This campaign was the final act by which the area between the Mediterranean and the western frontier of India was cleared of Axis interference and intrigue. Iran had figured in British strategic policy for over a hundred years. Viewed as a crucial buffer against Russian expansion in Central Asia, the British and Indian governments were keen to sponsor a strong and British-influenced Iran, and the Persian Gulf remained a waterway that the British were determined to control. A small war was fought against Iran at the time of the Indian Mutiny, and, in an act of détente diplomacy in 1907, Britain and Russia deflated strategic tensions by agreeing to divide Iran into two informal spheres of influence, Russian in the north, British in the south. So Iran existed, in independence but with two Great Powers looking over the wall and ready to compromise that independence should circumstances so dictate. This they did in August 1941, when Iran found itself partitioned and occupied by British and Russian forces in order to forestall an enemy attack, to safeguard an important Allied supply route and to stamp out disruptive enemy intrigue.

Signalling the extent to which German links with Iran had been forged in the inter-war period, in 1936 the name of the country was changed from Persia to Iran, Iran means 'land of the Aryans'. This supposed ethnic link was one of Germany's bridges to political and cultural cooperation with the country. Economic links were extremely well developed. In 1929 Germany had become the most-favoured trading nation, a German directed the national bank, and in 1935 Hitler's economic minister visited Tehran. The Shah of Iran, Reza Khan Palavi, saw the Germans as a useful tool in his quest to retain his country's independence. This independence, and Iran's neutral stance in the war, was given due regard by senior British politicians, and the pros and cons of intervening forcibly in 1941 were strongly debated by British decision-makers. There were doves as well as hawks, Foreign Secretary Anthony Eden in the former camp, the Viceroy of India, Lord Linlithgow, in the latter. Churchill was positioned somewhere in between though leaning heavily, as ever, towards decisive action. Caution was urged by those who agonized about the damage that would be done to Britain's reputation if it invaded a neutral country (witness at the same time the reluctance to invade Siam, which would have better enabled Malaya Command to resist Japanese landings in December 1941). There was also concern to ensure that America supported and understood British actions, even if it was *sotto voce* support. To this end, Churchill had secured Roosevelt's general support for some sort of action against Iran when the two met off the Newfoundland coastline in August 1941, a matter of weeks before the joint Anglo-Russian invasion.

In convincing itself that decisive action against Iran was needed, the British government had some weighty opinion on its side. The two British generals controlling the vast Middle East–South Asia region, Auchinleck and Wavell, as well as the British General Staff and the American War Department, believed that Russian resistance to the ferocious German invasion would crumble within six weeks. This served to underline the need to prepare to defend Iran against enemy invasion from the north. On 22 July 1941 the commander of British forces in Iraq, Lieutenant-General Quinan, received orders to be ready to occupy the oilfields at Abadan and Naft-Shah, and the ports of Bandar-i-Shapur and Bushire. Continuing the inter-command exchanges that had hampered Britain's intervention in Iraq four months before, responsibility for the Iran–Iraq region had been returned to India Command on 18 June. Lieutenant-General Quinan thereafter answered directly to the Commander-in-Chief India. This was now Wavell, who had recently swapped jobs with Auchinleck. In contrast to his reluctance to intervene in Iraq and Syria whilst he was Commander-in-Chief Middle East, he was now – viewing events from Delhi – keen for bold action in Iran in order to prevent a disastrous German coup in the region.

As in Iraq, a German presence in Iran predated the war, and in mid-1941 the British estimated that there were between two and three thousand German nationals in residence, many occupying important positions in government services and on the railways. More arrived after the British overthrew Rashid Ali's regime in Iraq. Germany was a major trading partner, German ideological penetration was well developed and anti-Russian propaganda widespread. This German presence hindered the full use of Iran as a conduit for Lend-Lease supplies from Britain and America to Russia. It also gravely threatened Britain's control of Iran's vital oil resources. Iran was the Middle East's most important oil producer, and the Anglo-Iranian Oil Company's vast Abadan refinery represented one of the most valuable British overseas investments.

With German troops pushing eastwards through Russia, this central piece in Britain's Middle Eastern strategic jigsaw appeared to be threatened. After much deliberation, intervention finally came when the Iranian government rejected a joint Anglo-Russian ultimatum asking for the expulsion of Axis nationals and the closure of their legations and consulates. By the time that the ultimatum was presented to the Shah and his government the issue of expelling the Germans – over which the Iranian regime had temporized and sought to buy time – had become little more than a *casus belli*. Both the British and Russian governments had convinced themselves of the strategic wisdom of occupying Iran for the duration of the war, and, more importantly in terms of momentum, the requisite military forces had been positioned near to Iran's borders. Russia had 120,000 troops and a thousand tanks available, whilst Lieutenant General Quinan had 19,000 troops (8th and 10th Indian divisions), fifty light tanks, seven RAF squadrons and important naval assets poised for action in Iraq and the Gulf. With Tehran's refusal to comply with the wishes of the Allies (in one of the war's few theatres of joint Anglo-Russian military action), the invasion began, British forces in the south achieving considerable advantage through surprise. The Iranian forces that opposed the Allied invasion consisted of 67,000 men, with 200 vintage aircraft and naval forces amounting to seven sloops and gunboats.

The Senior Naval Officer Persian Gulf, Commodore Cosmo Moray Graham, had a number of naval units at his disposal. The sloop HMS *Shoreham* was a veteran of the Indian Ocean region and had played a significant role in driving the Italian navy from the Red Sea. HMS *Snapdragon* was one of the navy's new 'Flower' class corvettes, subsequently sunk off Benghazi in December 1942. HMAS *Yarra* was a 1080-ton sloop launched at the Cockatoo Dockyard, Sydney, in 1936. Her initial war service was in Australian waters, before transferring to the Gulf. Subsequently she served in the Mediterranean, before moving to Javanese waters in January 1942. Soon after the Battle of the Java Sea she was sunk after encountering a Japanese heavy cruiser squadron, with the loss of 138 of her 151-strong complement. HMS *Falmouth* was an old sloop, which in June 1940 had sunk an Italian submarine in the Persian Gulf, and in April 1941 had played a part in escorting Indian troop convoys from Karachi to Basra (as had *Yarra*). HMS *Cockchafer*, the ship on board which the Iraqi regent had fled his country in April 1941, was a Yangtse river gunboat transferred from the China Station to the East Indies Station early in the war.

For the naval side of the invasion of Iran (known as Operation Countenance), there were also a couple of tugs, the armed dhow *Naif* (manned by Australians) and the Royal Indian Navy's *Lawrence* and *Lilavati*. On 4 August this force was reinforced by the 12,000-ton armed merchant cruiser HMAS *Kanimbla*, intended specifically to provide berthing space for the landing party making the assault on Bandar-i-Shapur. The British flotilla's tasks were varied when zero hour came and the invasion of Iran got under way. The start of the British offensive on 25 August 1941 was signalled by HMS *Shoreham* when she opened up with her main armament on the Iranian sloop *Palang*. The ships under Commodore Moray Graham's command then had to assist British imperial landings at Abadan and Bandar-i-Shapur, attacking shore batteries, neutralizing enemy vessels and transporting soldiers. HMS *Falmouth*, for example, transported two platoons and a company headquarters of the 3/10 Baluchi Regiment detailed to subdue the Iranian naval base at Khorramshahr. Another task undertaken by the navy was the capture of eight German and Italian merchant vessels moored at Bandar-i-Shapur. The German ships (*Wiessenfels*, *Hohenfels*, *Marienfels*, *Sturmfels* and *Wildenfels*) were all of the Hansa Line, sister ships of the vessels interned at Goa and of the deadly German commerce raider *Atlantis*.

There were two main British advances on land, one to the ports and oilfields of the south west, the other to the oilfields on the western frontier near Khanaqin and then on to the Pai Tak Pass and the road through the mountains to Kermanshah. The occupation of the southern oilfield area, including the Abadan refinery, was carried out by the 8th Indian Division, transferred from Kirkuk to Basra in preparation, with essential support provided by Commodore Moray Graham's flotilla of British, Australian and Indian warships. In the north Major General William Slim's well-used 10th Indian Division arrived from Syria, and an Indian and a British armoured brigade advanced to Shahabad from the border town of Khanaqin. Slim, best known as the operational commander responsible for British victories over the Japanese in Burma later in the war, had prospered since nearly ruining his career in the attack on Gallabat during the East Africa campaign. Auchinleck chose Slim to act as Liuetenant General Quinan's chief of staff in Iraq. Within days of arrival one of Quinan's divisional commanding officers fell ill, and Slim was given command of 10th Indian Division.

The British advances into Iran were effectively supported by the RAF. Seven RAF squadrons supported the ground forces (four from Shaiba and three from Habbaniya). They bombed defended Iranian positions on the Pai Tak Pass, bombed aerodromes at Ahwaz (which severely curtailed the ability of the Iranian air force to fly), flew valuable reconnaissance missions and dropped propaganda leaflets on Iranian towns. On 28 August all resistance ceased, the government fell and the Shah abdicated. On 17 September British and Russian forces entered Tehran, marching down opposite sides of the street. Germans were expelled, and a Treaty of Alliance between the Allies and Iran was signed in Tehran in January 1942. The treaty committed the Allies to leave Iran six months after the end of the war, and gave the Allies the right to develop all means of communication across the country in the meantime. The occupation provided a taste of Cold War themes to come, for the Russians proved far less willing to stick to the terms of the treaty and leave after the war, bringing them into conflict with the American presence in the country that grew after the joint invasion.

With the invasion and occupation complete, Iran was fully opened up as a supply route delivering British and American aid to Russia. The political importance of this aid was as great as the value of the goods delivered, for it was one of the few tangible ways in which Britain and America could help Russia, given the delay in opening the second front for which Stalin constantly pressed. In August 1941 the British government ordered the United Kingdom Commercial Corporation (UKCC) to supply Russia through Iran. This enormous task, soon taken over by the army, required control of the Persian transport network as well as the procurement of food and manpower in great quantity. The Trans-Iranian Railway connecting the Persian Gulf to the Caspian Sea was much used, as were the roads and waterways, and over forty-one million tons of Lend-Lease aid – 23 per cent of the total aid delivered to Russia – arrived by this route.

After the occupation of Iran had been completed, British imperial forces began to develop the trans-Iranian supply route to Russia, and soon a new Persia and Iraq Command was formed to supervise them and finally end the oscillation of responsibility for the region between MEC and India Command. Given that Iran had no adequate harbour, it was supplied from Maqil in Iraq. A new railway was built, and supplies began to be transported by barge to Kut, then by rail to Khanaqin, and then by road through Iran. Work was undertaken to develop Iranian ports, including Ahwaz and Bandar-i-Shapur. The army formed an Inland Water Transport branch, which grew into the largest centrally-administered unit of Persia and Iraq Command, numbering 800 British officers and other ranks and 12,000 soldiers and civilians of Indian and other nationalities. Persia and Iraq Command also undertook the improvement of the Trans-Iranian Railway. In December 1942 British Railway Telegraph Companies and Indian Line of Communication Units worked to build a line from Ahwaz to Tehran, and a battalion of Frontier Force Rifles was sent to protect them from local saboteurs.

An important feature of the development of the Iranian supply route was the growing American involvement. American forces took over operation of the Iranian railway, ports and the bulk of the road haulage from the British in 1942–43, with British forces remaining responsible for inland waterways and lighterage, and for security and road haulage through Khanaqin. American personnel in Iran came to number 30,000, mainly logistical troops, organized under a Persian Gulf Command. By November 1942 the Americans had delivered 27,000 aircraft and 28,000 tanks to Russia via Persia, and 27,000 vehicles were involved in the movement of troops and freight. Because so much of Iran's transport infrastructure was devoted to supplying Russia, British and American personnel had to organize grain collection and distribution to feed the civilian population.

As well as the work undertaken to ensure that Iran was an effective conduit for aid to Russia, there were military dispositions to be made given the fact that the other main reason for invading Iran in the first place was in order to prepare to meet a possible German invasion from the north. Persian and Iraq Command was a short-lived imperial structure aimed at defending the Middle East from an anticipated German onslaught. The fact that the war moved on so quickly, particularly after the victory at Alamein and Russian success in blunting the German invasion after Stalingrad, meant that it was largely forgotten in accounts of the Second World War. But for a brief period it was one of the most important overseas commands in the eyes of the senior soldiers and politicians in London.

As has been seen, after the Iraq campaign in the spring of 1941 a new army command was established in southern Iraq, known as British Troops Iraq, which came under the overall control of India Command. In the first half of 1942 the British Cabinet and the Chiefs of Staff were extremely anxious about the security of Iran and Iraq. The region appeared to be in imminent danger of German invasion, from the west should Germany break through in the Western Desert, and from the north should they break through in the Caucasus. Despite this threat, both of the commands with responsibilities here, MEC and India Command, were preoccupied with affairs elsewhere. The loss of the oilfields and the refinery at Abadan would have made it very difficult indeed – and perhaps impossible – to carry on the war in the Middle East. As early as January 1942 Churchill suggested to Roosevelt that at least fifteen Allied divisions were needed to defend the oilfields of the Persian Gulf region.* At their meeting in London on 23 July 1942, the Chiefs of Staff discussed measures for the defence of the region, especially the Abadan oil field, should Russian resistance break. At the imperial summit in Cairo the following month, attended by the Chiefs of Staff, Churchill, Smuts and others, much thought was given to the security dilemma in the region. The British war effort simply could not continue without its oil. The Chief of the Imperial General Staff and the three Commanders-in-Chief in the Middle East all agreed on 4 August 1942 that the defence of Iran and Iraq ranked even higher than the defence of the Suez Canal, strategic pre-eminence indeed. As General Sir Alan Brooke added in a diary afternote:

> As all the motive power at sea, on land, and in the air throughout the Middle East, Indian Ocean, and India was entirely dependent on oil from Abadan, if we lost this supply it could not be made good from American sources owing to the shortage of tankers, and the continuing loss of these ships through submarines action. Therefore if we lost Persian oil we inevitably lost Egypt, command of the Indian Ocean, and endangered the whole Burma–India situation.[4]

It was therefore decided to separate the area from the distracted affairs of the Commanders-in-Chief in India and the Middle East, and give it its own Commander-in-Chief. Churchill had had to bamboozle the Cabinet by telegram on this issue, to which he devoted much thought. As the CIGS recorded on 6 August 1942 in Cairo:

> An elated PM suddenly burst into my room whilst I was practically naked. Then went round after breakfast, and he made me sit on the sofa whilst he walked up and down. First of all he said that he had decided to split MEC in two. A Near East taking up to the Canal, and a Middle East for Syria, Palestine, Iran and Iraq.[5]

The Cabinet telegraphed its agreement to this proposal two days later, though said that MEC should remain MEC, and the new command should be styled Iran–Iraq Command. In this great organizational shake-up General Sir Harold Alexander

---

* Naturally, here as elsewhere, the Americans and the British were both allies and rivals. A major source of rivalry was access to oil resources, the British having had a head start in the region given their historic presence, though the Americans were catching up fast. In March 1944 Churchill cabled Roosevelt, saying: 'Thank you very much for your assurances about no sheep's eyes at our oilfields in Persia and Iraq. Let me reciprocate by giving you the fullest assurance that we have no thought of trying to horn in upon your interests or property in Saudi Arabia'. David Reynolds. *In Command of History: Churchill Fighting and Writing the Second World War* (London, 2004), p. 414.

became Commander-in-Chief Middle East with General Sir Bernard Montgomery taking over the Eighth Army beneath him. General Sir Henry Maitland 'Jumbo' Wilson was given command of the new Persia and Iraq Command, being ordered to defend at all costs the oilfields and oil refineries of the region as the southern wing of the German armies swept towards Stalingrad and the Caucasus, and ensure the effective flow of aid to the Russian ally.

In this way a new command was created with its main task the defence of the region from northern attack. Though in the end war did not come to the region, it is a good example of imperial vision on a tight military budget. In the months before the battle of Alamein and the German reverses in Russia, it was considered 'more than probable' that the region would see enemy action. With the capacity of Russia to resist the German invasion still seriously doubted in London, the Chiefs of Staff were determined that if this happened the Germans should be made to fight every inch of the way for an area valued for its strategic access as well as its oil. It was not only a part of the Allied supply line to Russia and a vital oil reservoir. The area around Mosul was considered a potential sight for air bases from which to bomb the Caucasus. Basra was a potential source of reinforcements for the Middle East and a staging post on the air route to India and the Far East, as well as being the main port on the land route between the Persian Gulf and Egypt.

British oil interests had been established in Iran since early in the century. The Burmah Oil Company had formed Anglo-Persian Oil to exploit the Iranian oilfields, and a refinery had been erected in 1912. Oilfields in Mosul were also being developed. By the late 1930s the Persian oilfields were producing over ten million tons of crude oil a year, and from this the Abadan refinery could produce sufficient oil fuel to meet a year's war needs for the Royal Navy. From the Kirkuk oilfields in Iraq four million tons of crude were produced a year and piped to the eastern Mediterranean.[6] A refinery was constructed at Haifa in Palestine (completed in 1939), to which oil was piped from Iran. A second branch went to Tripoli in Syria. A pipeline from Suez to Port Said was completed in October 1941 alongside the Canal should it be shut to shipping, and a pipeline from Suez to Cairo was laid in 1943. In other defensive measures, splinter-proof walling was erected around tanks with a capacity of two million tons at Abadan, Aden, Alexandria, Apapa, Bahrain, Beirut, Cairo, Haifa, Mombasa, Port Said, Port Sudan, Ras Gharib, Suez, Takoradi (Gold Coast) and Tripoli (Syria). Like the Abadan facility, the Haifa refinery was intended primarily for Royal Navy supply, though its output of white products was to gain in importance when Romanian supplies were cut off by the Germans. Elsewhere, one million tons of crude a year was being produced in Bahrain, though Kuwait and Qatar had yet to commence production (these were all British client-states). Further afield, another important imperial oil source was Trinidad, which produced 2.2 million tons a year. The total of this Empire production was significant, though limited when compared to total world production of 280 million tons a year. But the imperial war effort

IRAN, IRAQ AND SYRIA 163

in the Middle East absolutely depended upon the region's output, and alternative supplies from the Americas would have been unavailable had the Germans taken Iran or Iraq. Abadan was also an important source of 100-octane aviation spirit for British and Russian consumption, called to increase its output given the loss of supplies from the Dutch East Indies following the Japanese invasion.

Even when the danger to the Iraq–Iran region from German aggression had subsided, its role as a major supply route linking Anglo-American Lend-Lease to Russia remained (it was not until early 1945 that the route to Russia through the Bosphorus and Dardanelles came back into use, marking the end of Iran's strategic significance). A great deal of effort went into enhancing the region's transport network. To do this, 'Paiforce' (as the army contingent in the region was known) first gave priority to port development. Basra had to be organized to receive and transport supplies for imperial troops already present, and for a future build up for general operations in the region. The new command also had to secure and develop all means of communication in Iraq, covering vast distances and utilizing river and rail transport, and develop port facilities (a British company ran the Basra Port Directorate already). There was an immense amount of infrastructural work to be undertaken, for example the installation of water pipelines. No. 1 Engineers Base Workshop Company came to number 1350 men – Iraqi, Madrassi, Punjabi and Sikh. Royal Electrical and Mechanical Engineers Base Workshops in the Maqil area came to employ 3300 men. Indian Posts and Telegraph Department units took six weeks to build a reliable speech and telegraph line from Basra to Baghdad following the line of the Euphrates. The Vehicle Assembly Unit at Rafadiya, near Shaiba, assembled 16,000 lorries for the long overland journey to the Russian front in northern Iran. Bulk oil vehicles were shipped to Iran, so that by the autumn of 1941 there were 110 tank cars on the railways, and this figure had risen to 400 by the spring of 1943. The number of tanker lorries rose over the same period from 260 to 500.

The next task was to develop communications between the Persian Gulf and the Caspian. This was a formidable additional burden on top of the administrative development to which India was already committed, undertaken in order to maintain forces in Iraq to meet a German invasion from the north. Persia and Iraq Command was responsible for protecting RAF installations (including RAF Habbaniya and RAF Maqil in the south, a stopover for transport aircraft destined for India); for protecting British subjects in Baghdad; for defending the Kirkuk oilfields and the Basra–Shaiba base area; and for securing the oil pipeline to Haifa. Another major task of the command was to develop in the Mosul area strength sufficient to meet a German force of up to five divisions invading via Turkey or from between the Black Sea and the Caspian through north-west Iran. There were never enough troops for static defence, so manoeuvrability was the key, and defences were prepared to provide for a mobile battlefront extending over a large area. There was an RAF station on the outskirts of Mosul, and defences were prepared – in one sector alone twenty-four miles of anti-tank ditches were cut through solid rock. From 1942 transport aircraft were landing at Basra laden with supplies bound for overland shipment to Russia.

Persia and Iraq Command was multinational in composition, consisting predominantly of men from the Indian subcontinent. In late 1942 forces in the region became known as the Tenth Army with headquarters in Baghdad under General 'Jumbo' Wilson. It was growing in size and becoming a real army, controlling three corps headquarters, seven infantry divisions, one armoured division, an independent armoured brigade and an independent motor brigade. With no prospect of operations until spring, Wilson concentrated in the last months of 1942 on planning the deployment of the Tenth Army to meet a German threat from Russia. The Russian counter-offensive in front of Stalingrad, however, changed everything. Persia and Iraq Command lost its operational importance virtually overnight. In January 1943 the in-demand Wilson was recalled to Cairo and told by Churchill that he wanted him to take over as the latest Commander-in-Chief Middle East (Alexander had been promoted to the crucial position of Eisenhower's deputy for the Torch landings). In the same month the Tenth Army was able to release the greater part of its fighting units for the campaign in North Africa. There remained, however, plenty of jobs for the army units that were left behind to perform. They supervised the arrival of Polish refugees, many of whom joined the army. These men were from among the tens of thousands of Poles taken prisoner by the Russians, and were brought out of Russia on board UKCC lorries returning from Lend-Lease delivery runs. All together, 115,000 Poles were evacuated from Russia in this fashion, and many of them went on to serve in Polish divisions fighting in other theatres. The human traffic in the region was immense, and between April and September 1943 700,000 British Empire troops passed through the transit camp at Baghdad.

One of the most profound effects of the Second World War in the Middle East was the creation of vast new markets for raw materials, food and consumer goods. A concomitant effect was the creation of numerous trade links among the states of the region, and between the region and the wider world. All of this had to be managed, and war-time commercial, supply and distribution organizations were an essential yet seldom acknowledged element of Britain's war effort in the vast region from Gibraltar to Iran. Organizations and structures are dull topics in many ways, but they were at the very heart of British operations, and eventual success, in the Second World War. Two striking examples were the United Kingdom Commercial Corporation (UKCC) and the Middle East Supply Centre (MESC). UKCC had been formed to stop Germany buying essential commodities on the open market by buying them first. This required painstaking work to build relationships with foreign governments and inevitably involved UKCC in the supply side as well. If Turkey was to be persuaded to stop selling chrome to Germany and start selling it to Britain instead, it would also require Britain to fulfil the other side of the economic relationship it had enjoyed with Germany, and buy Turkish exports of dried fruit, nuts and figs, and supply it with things it needed, even railway locomotives sorely needed elsewhere. This the UKCC managed to achieve, and it was a key factor in stimulating local production to meet local needs throughout the Middle East. Thus, for example, industry in Palestine was developed to supply Turkey with things such as tents, mess tins, water bottles, leather and army boots (popularly known as 'Churchills'). UKCC also went into the business of building regional surpluses of strategic materials and food, and of attempting to ensure that a shortage in Iraq was met from a surplus in Egypt, for example. When the Tenth Army moved into Iraq, UKCC was asked to organize local transport on their behalf, which it did from bases in Baghdad, Basra and Mosul. As the Eighth Army advanced through Libya, UKCC was called upon to be responsible for the import, storage and distribution of foodstuffs to the civil population. When Iran was developed as a Lend-Lease supply route to Russia, UKCC was handed the task of organizing the delivery of the goods. By October 1941 UKCC lorries were operating over three and a half million ton-kilometres a month. Soon, with use of 5000 lorries, that figure had risen to twenty-five million ton-kilometres a month.

Middle East Supply Centre was another major example of the regional governing structures created by the war, and a demonstrating of the sheer scale of the imperial war effort.[7] The history of the MESC also charts the rise of American influence in a region of erstwhile exclusive British dominance. World war dislocated peace-time trade and supply arrangements as well as creating entirely new demands for the movement of goods. With the sea lanes of the world threatened by the enemy's unrestricted warfare against Allied and neutral shipping, a global supply crisis had to be forestalled by carefully marshalling merchant marine resources and by the tireless efforts of Allied naval forces. A third vital strand in this effort to counter the threat posed by submarines and shipping shortages were strenuous efforts to cut dependence on imports on the home front, whether in Britain, Bermuda or Bahrain. The British sought to improve the allocation of shipping and to regulate more effectively the cargoes that ships carried. This demanded greater regional supply coordination and the Middle East, where colonial territories were considering ways to cut their shipping requirements from early in the war, provides an excellent example of a major initiative in this field.

Mirroring the geographical responsibility of its military counterpart, Middle East Command, MESC's territorial mandate was huge, making it a major force in supply and resource allocation for dependent territories of Britain, Italy and France and for independent countries and semi–independent countries. It covered Aden, British Somaliland, Cyprus, Cyrenaica, Egypt, Eritrea, Ethiopia, ex-Italian Somaliland, Iraq, Iran, Lebanon, Malta, Palestine, Saudi Arabia, the Sudan, Syria, Trans-Jordan, Tripolitania, Turkey, Yemen and the sheikdoms of the Persian Gulf. It therefore dealt with over twenty different governments or administrations and separate fiscal and monetary systems. MESC had to treat this region as a single unit, aggregating total requirements, allocating supplies as fairly as possible, reducing demands on shipping to the bare minimum, making the area as self-supporting as possible, and arranging for surpluses in one country to be sent to where there was a deficit.

In 1941 this massive regional supply organization came into existence at a time when the shipping crisis had reached a peak. The Ministry of War Transport was responsible for the creation of MESC, a regional system of economic planning with its own bureaucracy and technical staff serving under a Director-General, Sir Robert Jackson, enjoying the direct support of the Resident Minister in Cairo. By 1942 MESC was, bar Russia, the largest continuous area in the world with a central economic policy and administration. A number of factors propelled its creation. Supply problems leading to civilian unrest were part of the reason. In 1940 the reduction of Egyptian imports and purchases of local supplies by the British Army created acute shortages, particularly of coal, iron, steel and paper. The British Ambassador in Cairo, Sir Miles Lampson, and Army GHQ Middle East, pressed Whitehall to form a central supply organization. The task of reducing the region's imports whilst providing a massive military machine with all of its requirements had to be achieved without causing civilian shortages that might lead to unrest. Civilian unrest in a war zone was to be avoided at all costs, and Britain's longer-term interests in the Middle East were predicated upon Arab goodwill and acquiescence. The Resident Minister in Cairo, Oliver Lyttelton, was convinced of the need to overhaul and strengthen the existing supply organization in the Middle East, and it was following representations from him that the first proposals for a centralized supply of cereals for the Middle East came from London in August 1941. Forward planning, the licensing of imports, the stimula-tion of local production and the control of the collection and distribution of cereals were implemented across the region.

Other factors favoured the creation of such an organization. The region's climate, characterized in many places by very low rainfall, was a barrier to increased food production. Drought in 1941 was a major problem, and so the rationalization of imports and distribution was needed to prevent serious short-ages for the civilian and military populations. The British had to continue to manage and regulate a global economy founded on the Merchant Navy, even though there were hundreds of enemy vessels attempting to sink its ships. As else-where, regional and extra-regional trade links were diverse. For example, the Arabian Peninsula, Cyprus and Palestine depended upon Australian and Canadian wheat imports. When it became impossible to deliver these supplies it was up to MESC to move barley by rail and sea to Palestine and Cyprus. Similarly, Egypt required over 500,000 tons of Chilean fertilizer for its cereal production, and, on the other side of the ledger, Egyptian rice came to be the mainstay of Ceylon's food imports after its traditional Burmese source of supply had been lost to the enemy. (Egyptian rice was also used to feed Indian troops serving under MEC.)

MESC's main purpose was to cut imports to the Middle East to a minimum and to clear its ports, supply lines and communications infrastructure for military use. It developed and administered a programme of centralized overseas trade control and economic mobilization in a vast area, in order to reduce the use of shipping, to overcome the difficulties of regional distribution and to minimize civilian hardship. It was so successful that the British were keen to see it survive into the post-war period, and it influenced the establishment of the Arab League. Alongside the growth of American military forces in the Middle East from 1942, MESC was a platform for the growth of American influence in the Middle East. After America joined the Middle East War Council in May 1942, MESC became a model example of Allied war-time cooperation. America became an active participant in Middle East supplies when in April 1941 Roosevelt permitted American shipping to use the Red Sea and Gulf of Aden. After the Royal Navy had destroyed the Italian navy in the region, it was no longer considered a war zone in terms of the Neutrality Act.

MESC had to give military goods priority in the allocation of shipping space across the region, but to do this without disrupting the supply of essential civilian goods. It had to ensure that the region's 100 million people were fed and clothed. Therefore the management of staple foodstuffs became a major MESC task. It was also required to engineer a more efficient regional use of resources, and to cut imports from outside the region wherever possible. All of the region's territories needed imported manufactured goods and commodities such as coffee, hard fats, sugar and tea. MESC succeeded in reducing the region's imports of food and consumer and industrial goods by 72 per cent between the outbreak of war and its conclusion. Despite this reduction and the expansion of military shipments, the region's stability and prosperity were little affected. The Middle East even managed to produce munitions and other supplies for the war effort, including ammunition that would otherwise have taken weeks to arrive from Britain. MESC achieved this by mobilizing the workshops, factories and farms of the Middle East.

MESC pooled regional requests for essential imports, and encouraged the exchange of goods within the region where at all possible to save imports from outside. Ultimately it was hoped to promote a self-sufficient Middle Eastern economy. It also aimed to develop industrial facilities and direct them towards the needs of the armed forces, and to mobilize the entire region's transport system. In theory, it was an advisory body that depended upon the cooperation of the region's governments. Its success was founded on a large bureaucracy, however, and its trump card in getting regional governments on side was the fact that it controlled all Allied shipping in the region. Though a non-colonial state could in theory make independent import and export arrangements, and though in order to operate MESC had to gain the voluntary cooperation of such independent states, in practice requests for imports that bypassed MESC were unlikely to get the approval of the supply boards in London and Washington, or that of the controllers of shipping. The imperial armed forces led by example by ceasing to procure locally and instead going through MESC. In going about its business, MESC developed cooperative relationships between governments in the Middle East. It ensured that a country's imports were obtained from the nearest source, restricted the demand for civilian goods, assisted governments in controlling the distribution of imports, acted as a centre of exchange for information on agricultural and industrial production, and provided technical experts. Control of imports was exercised by the licensing of private traders and by the bulk purchase and pooling of imports through UKCC, launched in 1940 to buy up produce around the world.

The creation of MESC was necessitated by the transformation of the Middle East, Arabia, the Mediterranean and the Balkans into a major theatre of war, and the disruption that war brought to the global trading system that defined the British imperial world. By July 1941 the ration strength of the British Army and its labour force in the Middle East was one million. This meant one million aliens to feed, a complex task for the quartermasters and the bureaucrats who ensured that supplies of rice or bully beef actually reached the mouths of soldiers. Further to queer the pitch, the enforced use of the Cape route added ten weeks to the delivery time of supplies, and meant that ships, instead of entering Alexandria harbour, went to the Red Sea where port and rail facilities were limited. This therefore required a large-scale building programme and the conversion of locomotives from coal to oil, to transport supplies from Red Sea ports across the deserts to the main concentrations of armed forces further north.

The management of food and its distribution was a vital MESC role. The poor harvests that affected many parts of the Middle East prompted the fear of famine. In 1941 Turkey, Egypt, Iran and Syria – instead of having a surplus of over 100,000 tons of wheat to export to neighbouring countries as had been the case in 1940 – themselves needed imports of wheat and flour totalling 250,000 tons. MESC, therefore, faced formidable food supply problems in 1942. Internal shortages were compounded by the loss of supply from major imperial foods exporters, particularly India and Burma. India could not export because of famine, and Burma was lost to the Japanese. Given the loss of South Asian rice, the UKCC undertook to send supplies of wheat and millet from Ethiopia and maintain a reserve stock for Somaliland. Likewise India's inability to send supplies to Aden, and a succession of poor harvests in southern Arabia leading to famine conditions, meant that MESC had to find wheat and millet from Ethiopia as a substitute. For the same reasons MESC had to send supplies to the Gulf sheikdoms. When rice supplies from India ceased, MESC found barley and flour substitutes for Bahrain, Kuwait, Muscat, Saudi Arabia and the Trucial Coast. The enforced dietary change caused unrest and threatened political repercussions, and eventually rice supplies were obtained from Iraq. One measure to redress this import shortage was to authorize the Anglo-Persian Oil Company to bring grain back from Australia in its tankers.

The main reason for America's involvement in MESC was its growing significance as a provider of civilian and military exports. In October 1941 the UKCC mission in New York was asked to help in supplying essential goods by putting Middle East importers in contact with American suppliers and by finding space on ships controlled by the British Ministry of War Transport. Most countries in the region belonged to the sterling area or used the Bank of England. Before the war Britain had been the Middle East's principal supplier of manufactured goods, but American supplies became more important as the war adversely affected Britain's non-military manufacturing capacity. Despite the growth of America as a Middle East supplier and shipper, MESC remained a largely British-run organization. Britain continued to provide nine-tenths of MESC's personnel and to finance the operation, and British merchant vessels were the backbone of its import-export operations.

The work of MESC had some unusual permutations. For example, MESC encouraged the expansion of silk production in Lebanon, for purchase by the Ministry of Supply for the manufacture of parachutes. Anti-locust operations were also of great interest to the armed forces in the Middle East. From 1942 there were indications of an outbreak of desert locusts in East Africa, threatening the food and fodder supplies needed by both East Africa Command and MEC. Therefore the Middle East Anti-Locust Unit was formed and attached to MESC, and its campaign targeted breeding grounds began in 1943. Army GHQ Middle East was prevailed upon to provide two transport companies and two platoons from a tank transport company equipped with ten ton trucks. Thus 824 troops, together with 329 vehicles, found themselves detailed for anti-locust activities. In Iran the RAF was enlisted to dust locust swarms from the air. A thousand uniformed British soldiers, wearing Arab headgear, were sent into Saudi Arabia, where locusts were a valued dietary supplement among the desert-dwellers. Similar operations were also conducted in Abyssinia.

MESC faced many difficulties in going about its business. It had to work hard to win the trust of the region's independent governments. It was largely successful in doing so because it was seen to be standing up for the needs of the Middle East. MESC also had to overcome the backwardness of the systems of government that pertained in many Middle Eastern countries and which militated against a regional approach to supply (in many spheres of government British-administered territories were ahead of others in the region). To organize on a regional level MESC required information and administrative capacity that the Middle East lacked at the national level (for example, only Egypt and Palestine had any sort of central statistical service). The region's governments had inadequate civil services, poor communications and there was a general absence of support for the British cause in the war. There was no proper administration of the agricultural sector (Syria and Iraq, for example, did not even have Ministries of Agriculture), limiting MESC's ability to promote regional self-sufficiency. MESC was in a position to help governments that welcomed advice, providing, for example, a Director-General of Cereals in Iraq and a Coordinator of the Syrian Wheat Commission.

MESC was not in a position to dictate to independent and semi-independent Middle Eastern regimes, as this would have been politically counter-productive. Some governments were unprepared to impose the commodity and price controls that war demanded, leading to higher than usual rates of inflation in non-Empire territories (390 per cent in Iraq and 690 per cent in Iran). To try to overcome these difficulties without using coercive measures, a pool of technical experts was made freely available to the region's governments. With inflation getting out of hand in Iraq, British advisers were dispatched to improve the system of regulation and the control of commodity prices, resulting in the centralization of supply matters under a new Ministry of Supply.

Thus the Middle East was transformed by war on an epic scale, as it formed the backdrop for major battles and colourful minor campaigns, and served as a junction for numerous vital supply routes. Britain triumphed in the region and emerged in 1945, still, as the major external power in the Middle East, from Libya to Iran and north into Greece and Turkey. Victory, however, had come at a price. The pressure of war had increased discontent, and the Holocaust was soon to create an intolerable situation for Britain as it tried to manage its effects in Palestine whilst retaining Arab goodwill throughout the Middle East. The war had brought America into the region, and it did not go home when the battles had been won. A mere three years after the war, in fact, the British returned the Mandate for Palestine to the jurisdiction of the United Nations and the state of Israel was born, and America, through the Truman Doctrine, became the defender of Turkey and Greece, as Russia cast its shadow across the region more menacingly than ever before. Signifying the slow eclipse of Britain in the Middle East that followed the war, America's voice was strong in the decision-making that determined the fate of the former Italian colonies in the region, all, of course, conquered and occupied exclusively by British imperial troops.[8] In 1945, however, all of this lay in an unknown future. To the south, Britain also looked to decades of predominance in sub-Saharan Africa, a vast imperial region that had played an important role as a manpower reservoir and supply line for the fighting in the Middle East.

9

Sub-Saharan Africa

As the Second World War came to a close in 1945, the Colonial Office in London proudly summarized the contribution of British Africa to Allied victory. 'African soldiers', proclaimed an official memorandum, 'beat the Italians out of Somaliland and Abyssinia, defeating the best Blackshirt battalions and native levies the Italians sent against them. They defended British West Africa from attack from Vichy territory, helped take Madagascar, and went to the Middle East as Pioneers and to the Far East to fight Japan.' Beyond these martial triumphs, Africa had also played a very significant role as a supplier of raw materials and a manpower reservoir, and British colonies across the continent had been deeply engaged in helping to defeat the enemies of King George VI.

In sub-Saharan Africa (the African continent excluding the North African countries bordering the Mediterranean) Britain was the premier imperial power. Every region of the vast continent was home to British colonies and protectorates, and the Dominion of South Africa was the continent's solitary industrialized economy. During the Second World War British Africa provided hundreds of thousands of imperial soldiers, and Africa was one of the few regions in the world that produced raw material surpluses for export to parts of the world where deficit became the war-time norm. Because of this dual capacity sub-Saharan Africa found an important though usually overlooked role as a source of manpower, food and strategic raw materials for Britain and the fighting fronts. The continent was also the scene of numerous imperial campaigns and skirmishes, as well as the pivotal actions fought in North Africa from Cairo in the east to Tunis in the west. Finally, sea routes vital for the supply of fighting fronts traversed African territorial waters, and strategic overland highways delivered goods and aircraft to the Middle East theatre, by air from the Gold Coast to Egypt, by land from Kenya to Egypt, and by rail and road from South Africa, Southern Rhodesia and Northern Rhodesia to fighting fronts in Kenya and Abyssinia.[1]

Bringing British Africa to full war mobilization meant pulling out all the stops. This required the use of networks, political relationships and infrastructure – as well as a colonial culture – that had been generations in the making. It depended upon British civil and military officers working in partnership with their African counterparts, particularly the chiefly elite, who in turn passed the message on down the line and mobilized their people, be it to join the army, help build a runway, knit garments for soldiers or plant more crops for victory. Throughout

Africa imperial consuls worked with colonial governors and their young district officers, who in turn worked with African chiefs and kings, clerks and interpreters. These were men like Lord Swinton, an imperial consul sent to West Africa as Cabinet Minister responsible for overseeing all war-related activity in the region's four British colonies. In the east Sir Philip Mitchell began the war as Governor of Uganda, was recruited by General Wavell in Cairo to take over administrative responsibility for the captured Italian colonies, and ended the war as Governor of Kenya following a stint as Governor of Fiji and High Commissioner for the Western Pacific. Deep in Southern Africa, Charles Arden Clarke laboured as Resident Commissioner of Bechuanaland and later of Basutoland, working hard to mobilize the home front in support of the war effort whilst maintaining the morale of the 36,000 High Commission Territories men soldiering in the Middle East and Southern Europe. In turn, African chiefs and kings were crucial in mobilizing the continent for war. Rulers like the Kabaka of Buganda in Uganda, the Sultan of Sokoto in Northern Nigeria, the Ashantehene in the Gold Coast, King Sobhuza and the She-Elephant Queen Mother in Swaziland, and Chief Tshekedi Khama of the Bangwato tribe in Bechuanaland were all real leaders with real powers, and real allies in Britain's hour of need.

From early roots – gold and slave forts on the West African coast, an informal presence in Zanzibar and the East African hinterland, missionaries and prospectors in Central Africa, and naval and settler interests at the Cape – Britain's African possessions grew dramatically in the nineteenth century, working inland from coastal forts and bases as the dark continent yielded its secrets to European explorers and adventurers and a curious armchair public back at home. Though in parts of the continent its colonial holdings were outsized by the enormous African empire of France, Britain controlled by far the most valuable and populous territories, and further British expansion came as a result of the First World War which brought the acquisition of Tanganyika, South-West Africa, the Southern Cameroons and parts of Togoland.

The Union Flag was known in every part of the African continent. In West Africa there was the Gold Coast (population four million), the Gambia (277,000), Sierra Leone (population two million) and Nigeria (population 31 million, including the former German territory of Southern Cameroons). In North-East Africa was British Somaliland (population 640,000) and the Sudan (population ten million). In East Africa were the British possessions of Kenya (population six million), Uganda (population four million), Tanganyika (population eight million) and Zanzibar and Pemba (population 260,000). In Central Africa there was Nyasaland (population 2.5 million), Northern Rhodesia (population 2.1 million) and Southern Rhodesia (population 2.3 million), a Dominion in all but name given its political autonomy under white settler leadership and its status as a self-governing colony since 1923. In Southern Africa were the High Commission Territories of Bechuanaland (population 240,000), Basutoland (population 600,000) and Swaziland (population 200,000), charges of the Dominions Office because of their proximity to South Africa. South Africa, the continent's giant, was a self-governing Dominion. During the war Britain's African holdings grew as British military administrations were established in Abyssinia, Eritrea, Italian Somaliland, Libya and Madagascar following their capture from Italian and Vichy forces, lasting in the case of the Italian colonies for the best part of a decade.[2]

Africa was intimately involved in strategic, combat and supply equations of great importance during the Second World War. The Battle for Africa began when Italy seized the historic moment in 1940 when France had collapsed and Britain was on the brink of German invasion. Thus war came to Africa. Attacks were launched on British positions in Egypt, Kenya, Somaliland and the Sudan, beginning a war affecting most of north and east Africa that was to last for three years and become the main theatre of British–American land engagement with Axis forces until the invasion of Southern Europe in 1943. The outcome of the war had profound implications for Africa and its entire population. If the Allies had lost the war German colonial rule would have returned to Africa – probably in all of its most productive areas – and an increasingly Nazi-orientated South Africa would have become an even more vigorous vehicle for white expansion and domination north of the Transvaal.[3] Mussolini's dreams of imperial grandeur would have had ample opportunity for fulfilment in North and East Africa, and the white charger that he had had especially sent out in anticipation of a triumphal entry into Cairo at the head of a German-engined army would at least have had the chance to stretch its fetlocks. The fact that history took a different turn should not lead us to forget that Britain's African territories were genuinely menaced in the early years of the war when it was odds on a British collapse at home, never mind in the Western Desert. British forces in Africa were vastly inferior in number to the hundreds of thousands of troops maintained by Italy in Libya and Abyssinia, and greatly outnumbered by those maintained by France in North Africa. The ramifications of the fall of France reverberated across the broad belt of Africa from east to west. At a stroke British West Africa was surrounded by hostile territory, turning upsidedown all pre-war plans for the region's defence (which had been made in conjunction with the French) and jeopardizing the Cape sea route. Suddenly, West Africa Command became eager for the return of its front-line troops, then fighting in East Africa, and a Vichy invasion was expected by the day, whilst a German move on the Vichy port of Dakar was widely expected (as an ideal vantage point for extending the Battle of the Atlantic and countering British defensive measures).

In the east, plans for the defence of British Somaliland, should Italy enter the war, were torn up when French Somlaliland and its sizeable armed forces signalled their loyalty to Vichy and the British position became untenable. From late 1941 war with Japan threatened the British position in Africa and the Middle East, and the prospect of a Japanese–German link on Africa's eastern shores was viewed with grave alarm in London as well as in Pretoria, where the imperial strategist and statesman Jan Smuts kept watch on the Empire's position in Africa.

The fact that Japan never seized the moment by sending its carriers westwards to take Madagascar and assault African ports does not mean that the presence of Japanese vessels off the Tanganyikan coast was not keenly felt, or that South African's wasted their time fortifying their beaches in anticipation of a Japanese amphibious attack. From early 1940 until early 1942 the Empire's prospects looked bleak, and the fact that the high-water mark of Japanese power had been reached in 1942 was as unapparent to observers at the time as it is obvious to commentators now. With British seapower in the East crippled after the fall of Singapore, Japanese submarines sinking Allied and neutral shipping as far west as the Mozambique Channel, Axis agents operating from Portuguese East Africa and German raiders laying minefields off the Cape, the heralds of the enemy were treated for what they were – grim reminders of the reach of the enemy and the consequences that would follow an imperial defeat.

Africa and its coastal waters were of pivotal importance to the British imperial war effort. British Africa provided hundreds of thousands of soldiers, naval, armoured and air force units, produced food and raw materials on an unprecedented scale, and in South Africa was an important exporter of agricultural products, armaments, manufactured goods, minerals and precious metals. Africa provided land and sea supply routes connecting war theatres to the supplies upon which fighting depended. The continent was the scene of major battles – in North Africa and North West Africa where German, Italian and Vichy forces fought between 1940 and 1943 in the see-saw battles that flared from Sidi Barrani to Tobruk, Benghazi to Tripoli and Tunis to the Kasserine Pass. Another major campaign was fought in East Africa, where the imperial forces of Britain and Italy squared up to each other in 1940–41. The giant island of Madagascar off East Africa's coast was the scene of an amphibious imperial invasion intended to neutralize the island's Vichy administration and establish a strong Allied military presence, in order to pre-empt a Japanese strike across the Indian Ocean.

From the fall of France, and even before the arrival of Rommel and the Afrika Korps in February 1941, Britain was threatened by large hostile forces on the African continent. Italy maintained huge metropolitan and colonial forces in Libya and recently-conquered Abyssinia. The Vichy regime also controlled large African forces, as the French had traditionally made much greater martial use of their African subjects than had the British. Vichy ports, like Dakar, were a danger to British shipping travelling through the South Atlantic and around the Cape of Good Hope, and were potential bases for German submarines engaged in the Battle of the Atlantic. The grand natural harbour on the northern tip of Madagascar was also a menace whilst it remained in Vichy hands, and the British expected its employment as a base for Japanese forces, repeating what had for the British been a calamitous collusion in Indo-China. The Italian navy had a base at Massawa in Eritrea that threatened the security of Allied shipping in the Indian Ocean and Red Sea, and that had been conceived by Mussolini as a major threat to British security in the area of the vital Suez Canal artery.

1. Winston Churchill on board HMS *Prince of Wales*, August 1941. Four months later, on 10 December, *Prince of Wales* became the first battleship to be sunk by aircraft when attacked by Japanese bombers in the Gulf of Siam. (*IWM, H 12784*)

2. Canadian soldiers training on Hong Kong Island in December 1941. (*IWM, KF 189*)

3. HMCS *Uganda*, a cruiser transferred to the Royal Canadian Navy in 1944. By the end of the war the Canadians had the world's third largest navy. (*IWM, ABS 698*)

4. Flight Sergeant James Hyde, from Trinidad, a fighter pilot serving with No. 132 Spitfire Squadron, RAF, with 'Dingo', the squadron commander's pet dog, December 1943. (*IWM, CH 11978*)

5. West Indian volunteers, recently arrived in Britain, give a PT display watched by Colonel Oliver Stanley, Secretary of State for the Colonies, and Air Marshal Sir Arthur Barratt, July 1944. (*IWM, D 21131*)

6. Maltese women washing clothes in the ruins of their homes in Floriana, Malta, June 1942. (*IWM, GM 904*)

7. Members of the Gibraltar Defence Force man a 3.7 inch AA gun. (*IWM, GM 4392*)

8. Men of the King's African Rifles collecting surrendered arms at the Wolchefit Pass after the last Italians had ceased resistance in Abyssinia, 1941. (*IWM, E6064*)

9. New Zealand members of the Long Range Desert Group pause for tea in the Western Desert, March 1941. (*IWM, E 2307*)

10. Our Allies the Colonies. Royal West African Frontier Force poster. (*IWM, Poster Collection 8262*)

Africa was home to major imperial military and naval command structures. West Africa Command recruited 200,000 soldiers and supervised the transformation of the region into one capable of providing support for frontline theatres further east whilst defending itself from potential Vichy aggression. East Africa Command covered North East Africa, East Africa and British Central Africa. It was created in September 1941 to relieve pressure on the overstretched Middle East Command. Its headquarters were in Nairobi, and it was responsible for security, recruitment, military formations and military infrastructure in Abyssinia, British Somaliland, Eritrea, Italian Somaliland, Kenya, Northern Rhodesia, Nyasaland, Tanganyika, Uganda and Zanzibar. Its subsidiary Islands Area Command, with headquarters in Madagascar, was responsible for Madagascar, Mauritius, Réunion, Rodrigues and the Seychelles. South Africa was the base for Southern Command (or South Africa Command), which from October 1942 included Southern Rhodesia. After the Japanese raid on Ceylon in April 1942, the headquarters of the Eastern Fleet, responsible for guarding the sea lanes of the Indian Ocean and the eastern shores of Africa, was transferred to Kilindini near Mombasa in Kenya (along with the signals interception and code-breaking facility known as Far East Combined Bureau). The Royal Navy's South Atlantic Command was based on Freetown in Sierra Leone, an important port that became the region's main convoy assembly port. Extensive use was also made of bases in South Africa like Simonstown, Cape Town and Durban by both the Royal Navy and the South African Naval Force. RAF Coastal Command maintained a presence in West Africa for Atlantic operations, and squadrons of Catalina flying boats were stationed in South Africa to extend the range of searches for enemy vessels. East Africa was home to an RAF Group which took part in Indian Ocean patrols and searches in conjunction with the ships of the Eastern Fleet.

The continent was traversed by important supply routes. Across the entire breadth of the continent, from airfields in the Gold Coast to the fighting fronts in the Middle East, ran a military air route serviced by airstrips in Nigeria, Free French Chad and the Sudan. This important transcontinental supply route delivered over 7000 fighting aircraft to the Western Desert Air Force. 4800 of these aircraft were flown or shipped out from Britain, while the remainder travelled from America, with stop-offs in the Caribbean, Brazil and Ascension Island, one of the numerous examples of Allied cooperation and the growth of American influence and forces in regions of British dominance. (America had a toehold in the region already through its client state Liberia, where airfields and seaplane bases were developed, to which British forces had access.) Because of its significance as an air base, not just for aircraft travelling from Britain and America to the Middle East but also for American aircraft and personnel being flown to Britain in preparation for D-Day (eighteen days from Florida to Britain in a B-24 via Brazil, Ascension, Nigeria and Morocco), West Africa was created a separate Air Command. In East Africa the African Line of Communication (AFLOC) took supplies from Kenya to the Middle East, as East Africa became a major food supplier to the huge imperial military forces centred on Egypt and fanning out into the Western Desert, Greece, the Balkans, Syria and Iraq. Infantry battalions like the 1st Battalion The Northern Rhodesia Regiment were transported by road across British Africa to active fronts in North East Africa, and 13,000 South African-manufactured military vehicles travelled from their factories of origin to Kenya via Southern Rhodesia, Northern Rhodesia and Tanganyika between June 1940 and May 1941. Here as elsewhere the possession of Empire and its transport and organizational infrastructure gave the possessing power a head start in terms of supply lines and the extraction of resources.

Major Allied supply routes went around the African continent as well as across it. After the closure of the Mediterranean to the normal movements of merchant shipping in 1940, the Cape route assumed an importance unsurpassed since before the opening of the Suez Canal in 1869. Six million troops passed through South Africa's ports in transit during the war, and without control of the Cape Britain could not have maintained contact with the eastern Empire or the Middle East theatre of war. Ships sailed around the Cape bound for the Red Sea and Egypt carrying troops and all manner of supplies for armies and civilians alike. The fact that there was a war on did not for one moment mean that the trade upon which the British Empire lived could be abandoned for the duration. After the Italian naval presence at Massawa had been eradicated by the Royal Navy, President Roosevelt was able to declare the region a non-combat zone, thereby allowing American ships to join the battle to supply British imperial forces fighting out of the Middle East. The Cape route was also used by vessels destined for the Persian Gulf via the Mozambique Channel, where they deposited British and American Lend-Lease supplies for overland carriage to Russia. Merchant ships and troopships travelling these sea lanes were escorted in convoy by the Royal Navy. Vessels of the Home Fleet handed over to those of the South Atlantic Station at Freetown, which escorted the convoys around the Cape, after which the Eastern Fleet took over for the voyage across the Indian Ocean. Though threatened at sea by enemy bases, and the German, Italian and Japanese submarines and raiders that patrolled off Africa's coastline, British seapower held firm, meaning that Britain was at liberty to move forces from one point on Africa's coast to another, and to assure the security for most merchant ships making their way to and from Europe, the Middle East, South Asia and the Far East through African coastal waters. Enemy ports were blockaded and the forces in them flushed out and hunted down, so that British control of African coastal waters remained unbroken throughout the war.

As well as being the main source of military manpower provided by the Colonial Empire, African home fronts were mobilized to produce food for local consumption and to satisfy an ever-growing export demand for food and raw materials such as Congolese uranium, Nigerian tin and Northern Rhodesian copper. Almost any non-edible product could be consumed by the Allied war effort, and any edible product could find a market in a time of acute world food shortage. Labour – for the British Army and for the home front tasks associated with military preparation, export drives and domestic food production – became one of the main preoccupations of colonial governments the length and breadth of the continent. The impressive imperial mobilization of British Africa was achieved by manipulating labour supplies in a more intrusive way than ever before. Marshalling human resources meant that British colonial administrations leaned more heavily on their alliance with African chiefly elites, and this presented educated nationalists with opportunities to demand a greater measure of self-government after the war. The need to mobilize colonies could lead to unpopular measures such as labour conscription and to economic privations, and this could stir discontent. Throughout Africa chiefly elites were relied upon to provide labour for the army and in some cases for the European-owned farms and mines, and in many cases this was through compulsion. Mobilization was also achieved by novel colonial engagements with ordinary Africans – in the form of propaganda, information dissemination, public lectures, wireless broadcasts and political appeals and, in the case of the army, by offering wage rates and conditions that many found attractive, augmented by the appeal of a martial career. The army's success led in some regions to complaints from settler farmers, who could not afford to compete. As elsewhere in the world, even the most insignificant colonies and remote areas of Africa contributed to the war and experienced its effects: soldiers were recruited from the Okavango Delta, prices rose in Khartoum, and the tiny sliver of territory that was the Gambia recruited an infantry regiment that fought in Burma.

The war greatly enhanced Africa's value in the eyes of its colonial rulers. It was a revelation to imperial officials in London to behold Africa providing men and vital materials in abundance, as well as performing a strategic role that its size and geographical position alone dictated. This escalation in metropolitan interest in Africa meant that it became an integral feature of Britain's post-war planning, and a 'second colonial occupation' commenced in the later years of the war as a new breed of technocratic colonial official descended to increase Africa's productivity and minister to the welfare of its people.[4] Africa's dollar-earning potential, and the need to renovate imperialism and recast it in a more acceptable light for the consumption of both colonial subjects and domestic and American critics alike, meant that Africa shot up the British government's agenda. The new metropolitan awareness of Africa and the role that it could play in the war effort and Britain's post-war recovery meant that the administration of British Africa was transformed. The days of balanced budgets, laissez-faire governance and gubernatorial autonomy were passing rapidly. The shots were now to be called by Whitehall policy-makers and economic planners, with eyes fixed on the bigger regional and continental picture and the needs of Britain's national economy. Africa was also looked to as a source of a replacement army in the future, once India left the Empire. As elsewhere in the Empire, the need to mobilize colonies for war led to increasing state intervention in the lives of ordinary people, and the beginnings of the managerial state and planned economy that made great strides in Britain because of the depression, the total mobilization required by war and the concomitant need to promise the people so mobilized that the post-war world, be it in Birmingham, Bridgetown or Bathurst, would be a much better place. All manner of social and economic controls were improvised as the exigencies of world war obliged colonial regimes to fight for a grip on immature economies and polities suddenly laid open to powerful regional and global forces. With the loss of India imminent, a 'new imperialism' was unleashed upon what were seen as replacement jewels in the imperial crown, the seemingly priceless assets of South-East Asia and tropical Africa that sparkled brightly before the eyes of British Cabinet Ministers and senior mandarins struggling to fight Britain through the post-war peace.

But this was to look to the future. As soon as war broke out, British Africa was called upon to hike up the production of vital raw materials and food exports, as well as to feed domestic populations in a situation of ever-decreasing imports due to imperial and worldwide shortage and the many restrictions imposed by the global shortage of shipping. Africa was called upon to redouble its efforts when the loss of the resource-rich South-East Asian peninsula led imperial decision-makers to scour the Empire for alternatives, many of them being found to rest beneath African soil. Africa had an advantage over many other parts of the Empire in that a greater proportion of its people had some means of agricultural subsistence in the form of family lands or herds of cattle and small stock. This was in contrast to colonies in the Caribbean and Indian Ocean, where absolute reliance was placed upon imported foodstuffs and self-sufficiency proved impossible to attain in the short term. The demand for Africa's surplus food production as well as its raw materials meant that colonial governments had to walk a manpower tightrope as they tried to balance the demands of military recruitment with the demands of plantations and mines, whilst attempting to ensure that there was enough labour left to conduct the basic tasks of subsistence agriculture upon which people were told to rely as much as possible. Plantations in East Africa, the gold and diamond mines of South Africa and the copperbelt of Northern Rhodesia all demanded migrant labour in abundance. Back in Africa's rural areas, the need to clear land, plough, plant crops, weed, bird-scare and harvest meant that, in the absence of many of the able-bodied men, an increasing burden was placed upon women, children and the elderly. Though colonial governments might seek to channel labour, there was only so much that it could do to control its flow: Africans could vote with their feet. If they did not want to join the army, as was often the case in Nyasaland, they could slip across the border and sign up for work on the copperbelt; and if they did not want to work on a European farm, as was often the case in Kenya, they could move across the border into Uganda and attest for the army. In Bechuanaland, the administration banned South African mine recruitment companies from operating during the two main military recruitment drives, though Africans continued to wander over the border and attest for the mines. In East, Central and Southern Africa labour recruitment corporations like the Witwatersrand Native Labour Association, or private Southern Rhodesian tobacco or Kenya coffee farmers, might be prepared to co-operate with colonial governments for a while, but they had their own profits to consider and would go ahead with recruitment regardless if colonial policy did not conform to their wishes.

Meanwhile, African rural areas struggled on with fewer able-bodied men in the villages and at the cattle posts, the figure for absentees reaching 40 per cent in places like the Tati Native Reserve in Bechuanaland. Thus world war and global mobilization demonstrated its power to affect lives seemingly remote from battle fronts and the causes of conflict. Urbanization was accelerated by war as new opportunities sprang up in cities and ports, and civil labour conscription was implemented in colonies where settlers dominated the export industries or heavily influenced the government, or where the existence of vital products justified, in the eyes of the British government, almost any means to increase production. As in India, with backs to the wall in a global fight to the death, the British attitude was shaped by immediate necessity, even though this would obviously damage the fabric of colonial rule and store up troubles for the post-war future. War imperialism meant that Britain had to go against its colonial principles in an age in which outright despotism was no longer a favoured method of rule.

The demands placed upon African economies caused Africa to become more tightly meshed to the global economy, particularly after Allied losses in the East turned the spotlight on Africa as a source of replacement commodities. British South-East Asia had produced most of the world's tin and rubber, and its loss to the Japanese led to a massive demand for supplies of these essential commodities from West Africa. Similarly, sisal production in East Africa became hugely important for the American market, following the loss of supplies from the Philippines after the Japanese conquest. Africa also became an alternative source of commodities previously obtained from what were now enemy states. Thus British Africa was called upon to produce as much pyrethrum (flowers used for making insecticide) as possible, as Japan had been the world's leading pre-war supplier, and America had bought 85 per cent of the crop. In January 1941 the Belgian government-in-exile in London put the resources of the Congo at the disposal of the British government. Britain duly purchased the entire war-time output of the province of Katanga's copper mines. As well as copper, the Congo produced three quarters of the world's diamonds, was the largest producer of cobalt and radium, and supplied the uranium for the Manhattan Project experiments. In 1941 85 per cent of the Congo's exports were going to Britain, Southern Rhodesia, South Africa and America, as opposed to only 5 per cent in 1939, an extraordinary turnaround directly attributable to the world war.

If war revealed to Britain how valuable its African Empire was, it also served to emphasize to Africans how dependent they were upon the world market, a bitter lesson of the great depression. Many producers learned the hard way, as export markets were lost because former trading partners became enemies, or as acute shipping shortages limited the exports that could be removed from the continent's ports. Some industries faced collapse as others experienced booming demand for their produce. Africa's dependence upon imports was underlined as British production was geared towards war – meaning that the imperial centre was far less able to satisfy overseas demand for manufactured goods – and shipping shortages curtailed delivery of what few goods were available for export. Food imports were also reduced, leading, for example, to rice rationing in Zanzibar and maize rationing in Northern Rhodesia and the disappearance altogether of some crops, to be replaced by less popular foods such as manioc and sweet potatoes. Rationing was widespread throughout British Africa, and people queued for their tea and sugar allowance just as they did in Britain. The loss of markets for some commodities caused by the war's disruption of normal trading patterns led to government intervention to save industries from potential ruin. As something of a war-time trade pattern emerged, British demand for African produce grew, and it was in the Empire's interests better to coordinate the procurement, storage and export of commodities. Initial loss of markets, and British efforts to coordinate imperial trade, led to the establishment of production and supply councils, run by colonial administrators, settlers and merchants, as regional economic planning was forced by the war and carried over into the peace. Bulk-purchasing, using colonial businesses as intermediaries, was an effective way of connecting tropical products to Allied factories and Allied consumers. If it kept the price paid for African produce low, it meant that export markets continued to exist in a period of abnormal trade disruption.[5]

World war had many unusual imperial permutations. As already seen, in Arabia British forces embarked upon a campaign against locusts, and in Ceylon, Mauritius, the Maldives and elsewhere the Royal Navy took up the cudgels against mosquitoes. In East Africa there were similar enemies to be combated in the name of the imperial war effort. Ideal breeding conditions for desert locusts were to be found in the Turkana region in Kenya's North-West Frontier District where frequent downpours and warm sand made conditions perfect for the incubation of eggs. Given Kenya's important role as a supplier of foodstuffs for the armed forces in the Middle East, great efforts were made to destroy the insects before they reached maturity and left to devastate the agricultural areas. A large transport organization was set up to bring in poisonous bait, which was laid by East African Pioneer companies, who then dug trenches across the path of the marching hoppers.

Africa's most spectacular war contribution was the provision of over half a million soldiers for the British Army (presenting a favourable comparison with India's recruitment of about 2.5 million soldiers, given the relative population levels). The mobilization of Africa was all the more remarkable because of the fact that at the beginning of the war the enormous scale of Africa's potential contribution was not even glimpsed in Whitehall, by the Colonial Office or the War Office. Unlike India, Africa's imperial military infrastructure and tradition was extremely limited. In Whitehall's eyes Africa was to be a minor participant in a war that was expected to be more limited in every conceivable way. German intervention in Africa, and the fall of France and subsequent Vichy alignment of most French African colonies, was not predicted or planned for. It was also hoped that it would be possible to keep Italy out of a war even if Britain and Germany should come to blows, keeping the Mediterranean and North Africa from the front-line strategic agenda. The British government envisaged Africa playing a subsidiary war role. Its colonies would maximize domestic food production in order to relieve pressure on shipping, increase export production and embark upon a period of internal retrenchment in order to cut to the absolute minimum dependence upon scarce imports carried in scarce ships, and to cut dependence upon grants-in-aid from the British Treasury in those territories that received such disbursements. There would not be much call for African soldiers beyond the local employment of the small regular British Army regiments that Africa already sustained. These regular forces were small, and intended more for colo-nial policing and colonial campaigns than fighting European or Japanese troops in the context of a global war. It was, for instance, never seriously considered that African troops would be employed in large numbers in Asia. At the start of war the Royal West African Frontier Force (RWAFF) numbered 4400, the King's African Rifles (KAR) 2900, the Somali Camel Corps (SCC) 600, the Sudan Defence Force (SDF) 4500 and the Northern Rhodesia Regiment (NRR) 430.[6] There were also one or two other small military formations, such as the settlers only Kenya Regiment. From these small beginnings was to grow an African military strength totalling over half a million men.

Before the fall of France a major African military contribution to the war effort was not envisaged. In March 1940 the War Cabinet decided that the main military contribution of British Africa (excluding South Africa) should be the provision of an African division for possible service in Africa and the Middle East, joining other imperial units from formations such as the Indian Army and the Australian Imperial Force. Pre-war plans envisaged the dispatch of two West African brigades to reinforce East Africa should Italy enter the war. The recruitment of new combat units for service overseas was considered by the War Cabinet but rejected, and the idea of using Africans as Pioneer Corps labourers was also ruled out, for the time being at least. The need for large-scale African recruitment was not foreseen, and equipment shortages meant that it would be difficult to furnish new African fighting units with the necessary weapons, vehicles and kit.

The scale of the imperial war that unfolded, however, took everyone by surprise. As disasters befell the British Empire in the East, as the very independ-ence of Britain was threatened, and as reverses were experienced in Greece and Crete, African troops were needed in ever-increasing numbers as military workers and infantry soldiers for tasks in home regions, but more pressingly for tasks in the Middle East, Southern Europe and Asia. Tens of thousands of newly-recruited African troops were to confound earlier British assessments and be called to service far beyond Africa's borders. Before the end of the war the Burmese jungle would hear the voices of men from the Gambia, Somaliland and Northern Rhodesia, the Levant would witness men from the fringes of the Kalahari digging tank traps and constructing military railways, Basotho muleteers would support Allied infantry in Italy, and the flag of the Swazi nation would be paraded victoriously through the streets of Tunis, as world war caused a galaxy of the most unlikely connections to span the globe.

Existing military formations like the KAR and RWAFF were greatly expanded and fought in the East Africa campaign, in Madagascar and in Burma, as well as carrying out vital garrison duties in their home commands and in commands overseas. (For example, East African *askaris* were a mainstay of Fortress Diego, the force charged with the defence of the naval base in Madagascar.) In the Burma theatre alone 120,000 East and West African infantrymen served (including units drawn from Northern Rhodesia, Nyasaland, Somaliland and Southern Rhodesia). An example of expansion and far-flung deployment may be offered in the form of the 22 (East Africa) Infantry Brigade. Formed on 19 September 1939 as the 2nd (East Africa) Infantry Brigade (redesignated 22nd on 18 October 1940), it contained infantry battalions from the King's African Rifles formations in Kenya, Uganda, Tanganyika and Nyasaland, battalions from the Northern Rhodesia Regiment and the Rhodesian African Rifles (from Southern Rhodesia), and units of African field artillery and armoured cars from the South African Tank Corps. It served in East Africa, Italian Somaliland and Abyssinia, and in June 1942 the brigade sailed for Madagascar, where it remained for eighteen months. It then sailed for Ceylon, where it remained for five months, before ending its war service in Burma.

Perhaps most remarkable were the newly-created African units, such as the African Pioneer Corps of the British Army's Royal Pioneer Corps (RPC), that took tens of thousands of men from East, West and Southern African territories to the Middle East and Southern Europe, where they formed the backbone of the 100,000 strong logistics army that kept the supplies coming to the imperial troops of the Eighth Army.[7] The RPC was the military labour force of the British Army. As the Middle East became the main theatre of British Army operations, and after the loss of Pioneer companies recruited in Palestine and Cyprus during the Greek campaign, Africa was called upon by the Commander-in-Chief Middle East to satisfy an ever-increasing demand for military labourers and guards. Whilst some African soldiers fought the Japanese in Burma or blockaded Vichy French Somaliland, these 'rear echelon' soldiers transported petrol to armoured units in the Western Desert, salvaged damaged vehicles and aircraft, built-blast pens in Malta and airfields in Sicily, bridged rivers and created smoke screens to conceal Allied amphibious landings in Italy, dug tank traps in Lebanon, kept the peace between Jews and Arabs in Palestine, guarded supply dumps from Arab looters in Libya and worked with British heavy anti-aircraft regiments defending key

Mediterranean harbours. This colonial logistics army were in the 'service' arms of the British Army, including the RPC, Royal Army Service Corps (RASC), Royal Army Medical Corps (RAMC) and also the Royal Engineers, Royal Artillery and the Royal Corps of Signals. In the Middle East, alongside Pioneer soldiers from Britain's Indian Ocean and Mediterranean colonies, and Arab labour units recruited in Libya and Egypt, were 16,500 West Africans, 30,000 East Africans, and 36,000 Southern Africans (from the High Commission Territories). West Africa and East Africa recruited their own service branches, and East Africa even recruited its own Army Education Corps. These and other colonial soldiers performed unglamorous though absolutely essential 'static' tasks associated with warfare: garrison and police work, guarding and administering prisoners of war and providing a presence in newly-conquered regions where law and order needed to be maintained during a period of political and administrative flux. They were also frequently involved at the sharp end, swimming barrels of fuel ashore from burning vessels at Tobruk, carrying ammunition to Allied infantry and evacuating casualties at Cassino, being shelled by enemy artillery and being caught up in Rommel's breakthrough in the Western Desert in June 1942.

Though British Africa's main military contribution to the war was in the field of infantry and pioneer soldiers, its colonies also supported the Royal Navy and the RAF. Small local naval forces were recruited by the Royal Naval Volunteer Reserve in the Gambia, Kenya, Nigeria and Tanganyika. The Nigerian contingent numbered 700, and an estimated 3500 Nigerians served in the Royal Navy (and more West Africans in the Merchant Navy). Kenya's Naval Force rose from 109 to nearly 800 men during the course of the war, and performed minesweeping, patrol and escort duties off the East African coast. The force helped raid Italian positions during the East Africa campaign and transported imperial troops in coastal areas. During 1941 the greater part of the force worked on minesweepers and motor launches, helping to clear Kismayu and Mogadishu harbours and transporting troops to enemy ports. Seapower meant that such small-scale coastal moves could be made by British imperial forces; the Italians and Germans were denied such freedom because of British seapower in African waters, as in many other parts of the world. The RAF recruited thousands of West Africans for ground duties on the extensive air facilities developed in the region, and in East Africa a section of the all-white Kenya Regiment was converted into the Kenya Auxiliary Air Unit (KAAU). During the East Africa campaign the KAAU was employed on communications, reconnaissance and training tasks, and for anti-submarine patrols under the Royal Navy at Mombasa. A squadron of the Southern Rhodesian Air Force served in Kenya during the East Africa campaign, and Southern Rhodesia was a significant contributor to the British Empire Air Training Scheme, preparing over 8000 men for service in the RAF.

As in the First World War East Africa was a battlefield and a reservoir of manpower for imperial lines of communications and 'rear echelon' duties, and for infantry service in the region as well as overseas. East African waters were strategically important because of the sea route from the Cape to the Middle East via the Mozambique Channel, and because of the presence of British and enemy bases such as Diego Suarez, Massawa and Mombasa. Patrolling the Mozambique Channel, intercepting dhows breaking blockades mounted against Vichy and Italian territories, and maintaining control of the Red Sea, were all important tasks for the Royal Navy and locally-raised naval forces in East Africa. SOE and SIS agents operated in Portuguese East Africa, a notorious location for Axis spies. Malcolm Muggeridge spent some of the war working for MI6 in the Portuguese colony, attempting to prevent enemy agents acquiring intelligence about the movement of British shipping in the Mozambique Channel. In Lourenço Marques, Muggeridge shared accommodation with Huntingdon Harris, the head of America's Office of Strategic Services in the colony.[8] Because a full-blown campaign was fought in the region and a subsidiary one in Madagascar, territories like the Sudan and Kenya became concentration points for imperial troops from elsewhere in Africa as well as divisions from Britain and India.

War encouraged a regional approach to the management of resources in British East Africa. In 1940 an East African War Supply Board and an East African Economic Council were formed. East Africa was a participant in the Eastern Supply Group Council, a body comprising the eastern territories of the Empire and Commonwealth and dedicated to providing whatever aid it could to the imperial war effort, particularly in the Middle East. Harold Macmillan moved from the Ministry of Supply to the Colonial Office, and recalled the regional approach that the war fostered in areas like East Africa. (The up and coming Macmillan was himself to enjoy a sojourn in Africa when in late 1942 he was appointed as the Cabinet's Resident Minister in North Africa following the Anglo-American invasion.) The East African Governors' Conference covered Kenya, Uganda, Tanganyika, Zanzibar, Northern Rhodesia and Nyasaland, and conducted the affairs of the East African War Supply Board and East African Civil Supply Board. Among many other contributions to the war effort, East African factories produced clothing, mortar barrels, anti-tank mines and reconnaissance cars as part of the great outsourcing of war production from Britain to the territories of the Empire. East Africa was also an important source of food for military forces amassed in the Middle East. Efforts to satisfy the labour demands of army recruiters, European farmers keen to crank up export production and of domestic agriculture, meant that all of the region's colonies ran the risk of over-recruiting in one field at the expense of another, and the number of African men absent from their homes could contribute to famine conditions.

Military mobilization in East Africa was greater than in any other part of the continent, bar the Dominion of South Africa, reflecting among other things a proximity to major fighting theatres (notably the Middle East and Burma) not shared by West or Central Africa. Recent research shows that by the end of the war 323,483 men had served in East Africa's armed forces.[9] Of this number, 30 per cent were from Kenya, 27 per cent from Tanganyika, 24 per cent from Uganda, 10 per cent from Northern Rhodesia and other territories and 9 per cent from Nyasaland (which for military purposes was traditionally treated as a part of East Africa). The main use of this enormous African army was for fighting and rear echelon duties in East Africa and Madagascar (including the provision of garrisons for Madagascar, Mauritius, Réunion and the Seychelles), as rear echelon troops for the Middle East, and as combat and rear echelon troops for the war in Burma and the garrisoning of Ceylon. Of the total, 80,000 served in the Middle East and South Asia. Official casualty figures were 7301 dead, including 900 soldiers drowned when the troopship SS *Khedive Ismail* was sunk in 1943. The Kabaw Valley campaign in Burma cost 11 (East African) Division 1244 casualties. In one horrific episode in 1942, 202 soldiers of 1823 Pioneer Company surrendered on the fall of Tobruk and were murdered by their captors.

Front-line duties were performed by regular army units such as the King's African Rifles, the Royal West Africa Frontier Force and the Northern Rhodesia Regiment. The KAR rose from six battalions to forty-three, and also recruited six independent garrison companies and three division headquarters protection companies. Pioneer military labourers were recruited for tasks in East Africa and to support Middle East Command. East Africa recruited all of its own support troops: the East African Armoured Car Regiment, East African Army Education Corps, East African Army Service Corps, East African Artillery, East African Engineers, East African Medical Corps, East African Military Labour Service (EAMLS) and the field hospital units and coastal defence formations. To cater for this massive expansion the whites only Kenya Defence Force became the Kenya Regiment and acted as a training unit for new officers and NCOs. Initially, the formation of new infantry battalions was achieved in the traditional British way of the original battalions dividing to form 'daughter' battalions (this method was also adopted during the expansion of the Burma Rifles), though given the extent of the expansion, new battalions were raised that had no relation to the original KAR and no firm links to a specific territory.

About 230,000 East Africans were serving at the peak of the region's mobilization. East African troops were to the fore in the East Africa campaign and blockaded French Somaliland. 46,000 East Africans served in the Burma theatre, including units from Northern Rhodesia, Southern Rhodesia and Somaliland. East Africa had 90,000 men in the armed forces by the conclusion of the East Africa campaign, and 140,000 by September 1942. 31,000 East Africans served in the Middle East. By 1944 there were fifty-six East African Pioneer companies, six East African Army Service Corps general transport companies, the 5th Battalion NRR and 23rd Battalion KAR in North Africa and the Levant. The main East African contribution to the war in Burma was the provision of the 11th (East African) Division, which began deploying to Ceylon in March 1942. It consisted of fourteen KAR battalions, one from the Rhodesia African Rifles and two from the Northern Rhodesia Regiment.

This great expansion of East Africa's military structure meant that the dictums, doctrines and prejudices underpinning peace-time recruitment had to be revised, rejected or suspended in the name of military expediency. There were simply too few members of 'martial tribes' such as the Kamba and Nandi to go around. Increasingly, as the military came to demand skilled personnel, it was forced to turn to the populous though distrusted Kikuyu. There were attempts to reserve 'martial tribes' for front-line service, but the recruiting base had to be expanded. The number of Europeans permitted in East African forces was limited by the War Office, and this encouraged East Africa Command to form its own Education Corps and School of Education in order to train Africans as clerks, medical orderlies, signallers, teachers, censors, gunners, engineers and tradesmen. In the course of doing this the army became the third largest educational institution in the region. Much of this disturbed the white settlers of colonial Africa, who believed that education for 'natives' needed to be strictly controlled. Though they expressed their fervent support for the war effort, the fact is that for many settlers their support had conditions attached, usually linked to the profitability of their own farms or businesses, and their desire to ensure that the racial 'balance' of the colonial world – in other words, white domination – was not challenged. Thus settlers disliked the British Army, because it was a competitor for African labour often able to pay higher wages, because it provided Africans with exposure to novel situations and because 'enlightened' British soldiers often had views on racial equality that were incompatible with colonial social order.

The army naturally preferred volunteers as they made better soldiers. It paid wages that were attractive to Africans and irritating to the European settlers, who found it increasingly difficult to compete with the army's largesse and did everything they could to get the colonial government in Kenya to curb military recruitment. The army was able to avoid conscription for all but the least popular military unit, the EAMLS, which contained an estimated 10,000 conscripts in 1943. Its tasks included hard-graft jobs like stevedoring, routine non-combat ones like guarding prisoners of war and the more unpopular military tasks associated with hygiene and domestic services. Some men from the EAMLS transferred to the African Pioneer Corps. Reflecting the South Africa-like attitudes of Kenya's settlers and their power to influence government, it was guaranteed that they would not be used in Europe or mixed with other imperial units. (It wasn't just the settlers who pressed for assurances in this direction; many colonial officials and even African chiefs thought it was asking for trouble to allow Africans from one tribe or territory to serve alongside those from another. It might lead to all sorts of confusion, and, more to the point, one didn't want them comparing notes and developing any hare-brained notions of regional or continental solidarity.) In 1943 the Kenya government persuaded the Colonial Office that unrestricted military recruitment should be ended, citing disruption to food production as the main reason. The government estimated that an adequate stock of African food depended on 45 per cent of African males remaining in the reserves. The figure, however, had fallen to 35 per cent. But the 1943 ban on unrestricted military recruitment was really a demonstration of settler power in the Legislative Council, for the bottom line was that settlers depended on cheap African labour.

Some historians have suggested that East Africans did not join the army out of loyalty to the British, as many accounts written in the colonial period claim.[10] Men did not join to fight for 'King Georgi' (though authors writing closer to the war insist that many of them did) but enlisted because soldiering was the most lucrative form of unskilled labour available. The army also offered numerous attractive perquisites, possessed a measure of prestige enjoyed by few jobs in the civilian sector and entitled ex-servicemen to special treatment by the colonial government. The army was a route out of poverty for many men (as in South Africa, where many of the Union Defence Force's 80,000 Native Military Corps soldiers were recruited from the poor Northern Transvaal region). Of course, no general picture can adequately capture the diverse motives for joining up, for 'in an army of ten thousand, there are ten thousand reasons for fighting'.[11] Whilst there is no doubt that it was *not* the case that all Africans joined the forces with the same sense of loyalty or national duty common in Britain itself, fashionable accounts that de-emphasize anything approximating to 'loyalty' or a sense of duty are in danger of being as unbalanced as those of the colonial period that gave the impression that tens of thousands of Africans joined the army burning with the desire to help the King defeat Hitler.

Recruitment for the KAR in East and in Central Africa had to overcome suspicions where the KAR had a bad reputation. The memory of the dreaded Carrier Corps, a military labour and porterage unit recruited for the fighting in East Africa during the First World War, meant that the military had a sullied reputation amongst many people. It is a measure of how far colonial attitudes had progressed over the ensuing twenty years that the treatment received by Africans in the army in 1939–45 was incomparably better than in the previous world war. Throughout British Africa recruitment relied on the support of local chiefs, propaganda, the allure of military service and the financial rewards it could offer. As in Jamaica, it was also emphasized that African homes were at risk from German and Italian aggression and needed to be defended. Recruitment tours saw district commissioners, chiefs, army officers and smartly-turned out African servicemen visiting community gatherings. Films, the pipe and drums of stirring military music, and weapons displays added a jamboree atmosphere, as the Aldershot Tattoo was recreated in deepest Africa. Mobile Propaganda Units not only encouraged men to join up, they aimed to lift the war effort on the home front.[12] In 1942 East Africa Command created its own Mobile Propaganda Unit, which comprised twenty-eight hand-picked *askaris*. The unit's recruitment tours relied on the prestige of these model soldiers and live-fire displays, demonstrations of gymnastics, mine detection, unarmed combat and ceremonial drill to tempt people away from the villages and into the training camps and the wide world beyond.

As was the case with military units from elsewhere in the Empire that were sent to serve in distant theatres of war, serious efforts were made to keep East African soldiers in touch with their home communities, in order to make them more efficient and to limit the disruption to African life and colonial rule that could result, on the one hand, from their absence, and on the other, from their return. Newsletters reporting weather, crops, markets, community meetings and local gossip were published, and EAC published its own newspapers – *Habari Zetu* for troops in Abyssinia, *Heshima* and *Ulema* in South-East Asia, *Askari* and *Jambo* in East Africa and *Kwetu Kenya* in the Middle East and Islands Area Command. EAC also used radio to broadcast news to the Middle East.* Though some problems attended the service of East Africans in the army, these were quite unremarkable, particularly if one considers that most of the hundreds of thousands of men involved were recent, duration-only recruits, who not only performed their military tasks effectively but were then peacefully demobilized. Despite the attempts of successive historians to argue otherwise, it is now generally accepted that ex-servicemen did not form a powerful phalanx of would-be nationalists upon reinsertion into their home societies. On the whole they returned quietly to rural life. If they leaned in any political direction it was as likely to be towards conservative colonial and chiefly rule as towards nascent nationalism. As had been the case whilst on active service, upon their return home the disciplinary record of colonial troops compared favourably with other imperial units, including those from Britain. Whilst they were in the army there were concerns about venereal disease and sexual matters relating to African soldiers billeted in proximity to white women, these were mainly born of standard military concerns and the contemporary European attitudes to racial matters, blown out of proportion by the settlers. Living in daily contact with the Africans who surrounded them, they of course were full of concerns about the sanctity of white women and the need to keep Africans in their colonial place in an edifice of racial rule that depended absolutely upon separation in these most intimate matters.

As in other imperial armed forces, there were instances of discontent, for

---

*   News publications for imperial service personnel proliferated in all operational theatres during the war. Examples include the Australian *AIF News*, *Guinea Gold* and *Tobruk Truth*; the *Royal Air Force Journal, Middle East Edition*; the *Review* in East Africa Command (a fortnightly publication, more serious than *Jambo*); the *Ceylon Review: Ceylon's Weekly Journal for the Royal Navy, Army, RAF, Merchant Navy and Civil Defence Services*; *Contact* (for British servicemen in India and Ceylon); the *Phoenix* and *SEAC: The Service Newspaper of South-East Asia Command* for South-East Asia; the *Victory*, the India Command weekly newsletter; *Parade*, the Middle East theatre weekly; *Union Jack*, a British Army paper amalgamated with *Eighth Army News* and first published in Tunis; the *Neptune: For Merchant Seamen*; *Brand Flash*, published after the reinvasion of Malaya; the *Pacific Post*, the newspaper of the British Pacific Fleet; the *Canadian Press News*; the *Maple Leaf* for Canadian servicemen in Italy and France; the *New Zealand Times* for New Zealanders in Italy; *Springbok* for South African forces in the Middle East; and *Fauji Akhbar* for all Indian servicemen in Burma, Ceylon, India and Iran.

example over pay and leave, though this was never serious. 1821 Pioneer Company mutinied during the imperial retreat from Tobruk, and another unit refused to board ship for Ceylon. There was some desertion from the army and, in a very small number of cases, men maimed themselves in order to avoid recruitment. Such incidents, often used to demonstrate the reluctance of colonial soldiers to fight for a cause that was not their own, were of course no different to countless similar incidents affecting British forces, like the commandos who clung to the landing craft on D-Day, paralyzed by fear. The salient fact is that these hundreds of thousands of East Africans served successfully in the armed forces, contributing to the downfall of the Axis powers, and were then repatriated to their homes. As was the case elsewhere, efforts were made to maintain control of Africans once they joined the army. Their mail was censored, and a special Field Security Section had the task of keeping an eye on soldiers, and even infiltrating units. East African chiefs visited soldiers stationed overseas to assert their authority and to reaffirm the men's links with their home societies. Special 'intensive propaganda' was directed at new recruits in order to gain their loyalty; and, as the direct military threat to Kenya receded, the idea that the fight was for a cause and for principles was exploited, with emphasis placed upon Nazi racism. Naturally, soldiers were prevented from listening to Italian propaganda broadcasts, and promises were made of post-war reforms in order to contribute to military contentment and to show Africans that improvements would come about because of their loyal war service.

The major military struggle that took place in East Africa from the summer of 1940 until the summer of 1941 was a quintessentially imperial war. It was fought in its entirety across the territories of two European colonial powers by armies comprising large numbers of colonial troops, over terrain characterized by great distances and poor communications. On land and in the air the campaign rarely featured the latest military hardware. Elements of modern warfare, however, were to be found in the East Africa campaign, for it was distinguished in being the first land campaign in which the intelligence provided by Bletchley Park enabled British commanders to have intimate knowledge of enemy plans. To aid the prosecution of the campaign, the East African region was removed from the overstretched Middle East Command, and a new East Africa Command (EAC) was formed, to which all manner of troops from different parts of the Empire were called. EAC was responsible for operations in Abyssinia, British, French and Italian Somaliland, Kenya, Madagascar, Mauritius, Northern Rhodesia, Nyasaland, Rodrigues, South Africa, Southern Rhodesia, the Seychelles, Tanganyika and Zanzibar. British, Indian, Northern Rhodesian, South African, Southern Rhodesian and West African (all four colonies) troops were shipped in to support the infantry units drawn from the region's British territories – the KAR, the Somaliland Camel Corps and the Sudan Defence Force.

The East Africa campaign opened when Mussolini realized that his moment of destiny had come. France had recently been crushed and the Battle of Britain was about to commence, which would keep Britain desperately occupied close to home in the face of German invasion. In Africa the numbers of Italian men at arms dwarfed those of the British: there were 450,000 Italians and colonial troops in Italy's African Empire, compared to 88,500 British, Dominion and colonial troops in British Africa. This figure included Britain's African soldiers, numbering about 4500 in the Sudan, 9000 in Kenya, 3000 in Nigeria, 1500 in the Gold Coast and a thousand in Sierra Leone. It was most fortunate that, during the campaign against Italy in Libya and Abyssinia, the British had the use of two Indian divisions, and were supported by South African infantry, armour and air power. At the start of the East Africa campaign the Italians had 92,000 Italian troops and 250,000 Abyssinians under arms, as well as superiority in tanks. The British had 40,000 troops. The Italians could also claim air superiority over their rivals in East Africa (323 against 100 machines). Significantly, however, the British were able to reinforce their formations – not to the same numeric strength as the Italian forces, but with quality fighting units that made a difference. In contrast the Italians, cut off from reinforcements because of British control of the seas, were not so favoured. (Air supply from Libya was possible, but could never deliver significant numbers of troops and items of equipment.)

With the best odds he was ever likely to get, Mussolini took the offensive in the summer of 1940. On 10 June Italian forces entered the Sudan and seized Gallabat, Karoro, Kassala and Kurmak, all on or near the border. Moyale in Kenya was also taken, previously abandoned by the British, and from 5–19 August British Somaliland was invaded by 25,000 men and conquered. On 10 June 1940 a large Italian army entered Egypt from Libya, halting after sixty miles. This timid opening to the campaign against British Africa, however, marked the high-water mark of Italian achievement. Thereafter, the Italians suffered because of a defence-minded high command, the need to suppress Abyssinian resistance in an area only recently conquered, and a lack of relish for a fight that many Italians simply didn't believe in. They also suffered because of the successful exploitation of intelligence on the British side and the fighting qualities of imperial formations. In a very short period of time Mussolini was to suffer one of the most humiliating defeats inflicted by one European power on the forces of another in recent history.

As the Italians made their brash though tentative opening moves, British strength in the region was augmented, particularly by South African and Indian troops, the latter spared by the success of General Wavell's counter-offensive in the Western Desert against the Italians in December 1940, culminating in the victory at Sidi Barrani. One of the two Indian divisions, the 5th, was initially destined to guard the oilfields of Iran and Iraq, though sent to the Middle East for more useful employment in the Western Desert. Now a new fighting front beckoned. The 4th Indian Division was convoyed through the Nile Valley and the Red Sea and reassembled early in the new year. South Africa also committed significant forces to this region. British strategy was agreed at a conference in

Khartoum in August 1940, attended by Anthony Eden, General Smuts, the exiled Emperor Haile Selassie and Wavell as Commander-in-Chief Middle East. It was agreed to attack Gallabat and Kassala from the Sudan, to assess the possibilities of an attack from Kenya on Kismayu, and to channel more support to Haile Selassie's resistance movement. It was also at this conference that Major Orde Wingate was appointed as Selassie's military adviser, though nominally subordinate to Colonel D. A. Sandford, head of the British Military Mission to Abyssinia.

The British counter-offensive in East Africa began according to plan on 6 November 1940, when Brigadier William Slim's 10th Indian Infantry Brigade attacked Gallabat, a move designed to clear a route into Abyssinia. The attack went badly wrong, and could have ruined Slim's career (it didn't, and within the space of six months he was an acting major general commanding his own division in Iraq). Fortunately, other developments meant that the need to fight into Abyssinia was removed. In the same month the British position was greatly improved when Combined Bureau Middle East, the Bletchley Park outstation in Cairo, broke the Italian air force's cipher, adding to the information already derived following Bletchley Park's success against the Italian army's high-grade cipher. Therefore intelligence broken in Buckinghamshire, Cairo and its satellite in Nairobi meant that British commanders could read Italian plans and appreciations as soon as they were issued. Following British victories against Italian forces on the Libyan front in December 1940, a demoralized Duke of Aosta, Commander-in-Chief of Italian forces in East Africa, asked for permission to withdraw from the Sudanese border. With this information in hand, Major-General William Platt, Commander-in-Chief of the Sudan Defence Force, was able to pick his moment to strike.

Indian and Sudanese forces crossed into Eritrea and northern Abyssinia from their bases in the Sudan. The two Indian divisions (the 4th and 5th) headed for Gondar in the Amhara district. Their toughest fighting was in the region of Keren in Italian Somaliland, where Aosta had ordered the local commander to make a stand in ideal defensive country. It took until the end of March – a fifty-three day struggle – before Platt's forces entered Keren, and by the beginning of April they had reached Asmara. By gaining the heights at Keren the Italian nerve was broken. During the final stages of the battle imperial forces had fired over 100,000 shells, carried in a thousand trucks, a breathtaking logistical effort in a country presenting unique problems of distance and terrain. On 8 April 1941 the Eritrean port of Massawa surrendered after an attack by Indian and Free French troops (who had joined the British from Vichy French Somaliland). British imperial operations in this region had been greatly aided by the judicious use of air power, particularly in supplying troops besieging the Italian stronghold at Keren, ensuring that Italian air power was not used against imperial troops on the ground in any significant way and in bombing the Italian defensive positions. Without this local air superiority, the assault on Keren could not have been launched. Though most imperial aircraft in theatre were outmoded, the presence of a handful of Hurricane fighters of No. 1 Squadron South African Air Force provided a valuable cutting edge. The great superiority that they enjoyed over anything the Italians could put up against them had a telling effect. Long-range attacks against Italian forces, mounted for example from a captured airfield at Sabderat just inside Eritrea, were so demoralizing that the Italian air force withdrew from all of Eritrea. Whilst Hurricanes were in the forefront of the battle, it was mainly fought by slow-flying Lysanders, ancient Vincents and an assorted cellar of vintage aircraft flying over heavily defended areas across a sea of jagged mountains.[13] In this air war over Italian East Africa and the Red Sea, imperial forces based in Africa operated in cooperation with those under Air Vice-Marshal Reid in Aden.

In February 1941 a second front was opened from Kenya, with imperial forces from South Africa, East Africa and West Africa entering Italian Somaliland and southern Abyssinia. Here the commander of the thrust from the east, Lieutenant-General Sir Alan Cunningham, Commander-in-Chief Kenya, had 77,000 imperial troops at his disposal – 33,000 from East Africa, 9000 from West Africa, 27,000 from South Africa and 6000 Europeans serving with East and West African formations. Cunningham's troops were supported by six squadrons of the South African Air Force (SAAF). Moyale was recaptured on 18 February by an East African brigade and units of the 1st South African Division sent into the Galla–Sidamo province in the hope of stimulating an Abyssinian uprising, though this advance became bogged down. A second prong of Cunningham's attack, however, achieved rapid success. Two East African divisions were launched along the coast on 11 February. The Italians began to withdraw behind the River Juba in Abyssinia. Kismayu on the Somali coast was taken on 14 February, and Mogadishu followed on 25 February. Cunningham then moved on Harar in Abyssinia (sixty miles north of Mogadishu the Gold Coast Regiment liberated a prisoner-of-war camp which among its emaciated inmates included 194 Allied merchant seamen, survivors of the Indian Ocean spree of the disguised German commerce raider *Atlantis*, which had caused severe damage to British shipping). In March 1941 a third point of British attack was opened when an Indian force assembled in Aden was landed in British Somaliland to effect its reconquest and provide a shorter line of communication for imperial forces fighting in Abyssinia. Cunningham's troops had covered 1700 miles in eight weeks.

By 25 February 1941 most of Italian Somaliland had been taken. Addis Ababa, Abyssinia's capital, fell on 6 April and Emperor Haile Selassie was restored to the throne snatched from him by Mussolini in 1936. In returning Haile Selassie to his throne and subsequently sponsoring Abyssinia's independence, Britain made some restitution for its failure to defend Abyssinia from Italian aggression in the first place. Even after Selassie's return in May 1941, Abyssinia remained under British military administration until the following January. Yet to to be defeated were the Italian forces of General Gazzera in the south west of the country, amounting to 38,000 men and a growing number of fugitives. There were more Italian troops in the Galla–Sidamo province, and 41,000 under General Nasi in Gondar. Having by April 1941 secured the strategic objective of ridding the Red Sea of enemy forces and making it safe for Allied shipping (giving Roosevelt the necessary elbow room to permit American merchant ships to use this route), imperial units were withdrawn to other theatres, but a force left in Abyssinia that was considered sufficient to conclude the campaign and secure final and total Italian defeat. Of Major-General Platt's force, the two Indian divisions left for the Western Desert, most South African troops left General Cunningham's command in July 1941, and the 23rd Nigerian and 24th Gold Coast Brigades returned to West Africa to reinforce the defence of Freetown, which it was feared might be attacked by Vichy forces in retaliation for the British imperial invasion of Syria. Finishing off the Italians in Abyssinia was accomplished in two stages. Between April and July 1941 operations by Cunningham's forces in Gallo–Sidamo were supported by forces from the Sudan, and then in October and November operations against Gondar were concluded. Sporadic fighting and mopping up operations continued until November. The two main British forces then closed on the stronghold at Amba Alagi, where on 16 May 1941 the Italian Commander-in-Chief, the Duke of Aosta, finally surrendered.

For the loss of about 3000 imperial troops dead and wounded, 420,000 Italian troops had been killed, wounded or captured. East Africans had been to the fore in the fighting, and were used in the aftermath of victory to garrison conquered territory, to guard prisoners of war and to blockade Vichy French Somaliland. Soon after the conclusion of the East Africa campaign, East African and West African forces began their substantial contribution to the Burma campaign, rushed initially to Ceylon along with British troops to beef up the island's defences at a time when a Japanese assault was considered likely by the British Cabinet. In March 1942 the 11th (East African) Brigade sailed for Ceylon, and in the following month other East African units began preparing for operations in Madagascar.

Seapower had been a relatively low-key though valuable factor during the East Africa campaign, the Royal Navy going about its business and doing what traditionally it did best. Naval dominance permitted the British to land and evacuate forces at will from ports in the region including Aden, Berbera and Mogadishu. British seapower also meant that Italian land forces were cut off from supplies from home, forcing them to rely on the dangerous and unsatisfactory use of aircraft to bring supplies from Libya. With British imperial forces approaching the port of Massawa in Eritrea, the Italian warships stationed there left to raid Port Sudan. They were attacked from the air, however, and two of the six destroyers were scuttled and the other four sunk. After a joint Indian–Free French attack, Massawa, the Red Sea port that Mussolini had hoped would threaten the British position in the region, surrendered on 8 April 1941.

During the campaign in Abyssinia the British were allies of the deposed

Emperor, Haile Selassie. A group of his followers called the Patriots were trained and aided by a Special Operations Executive mission that planned to help him gain a secure area inside his kingdom from which to operate and establish contact with the anti-Italian resistance. Major Orde Wingate, later to achieve fame, notoriety and a lasting place in the annals of the Second World War through his behind enemy lines exploits in Burma (and the personal support afforded him by Churchill), cut his teeth in the East Africa campaign. His rise to prominence owed much to the fact that the Commander-in-Chief Middle East, General Wavell, remembered him from pre-war days. As General Officer Commanding in Palestine in 1937, Wingate had come to Wavell's attention whilst serving as an intelligence officer working against Arab terrorist groups. Wavell therefore called him to service in the Abyssinian campaign, where his task was to secure a stronghold for Emperor Haile Selassie in Gojjam province and to foment rebellion against the Italian regime. Wingate became Haile Selassie's military adviser and was responsible for training his special forces. His outfit, known as Gideon Force and comprising about 1600 men from the Frontier Battalion of the SDF, assorted British personnel and Abyssinian regulars and irregulars, succeeded in securing a stronghold in Gojjam and waged a guerrilla campaign against the Italians, greatly hampering Italian forces from the rear as they attempted to face the British invasion. Haile Selassie was restored to his throne on 5 May 1941. During its campaign Gideon Force captured seven mounted guns, fifty heavy and 120 light machine-guns, 300 horses, 700 Italian officials, 15,000 mules and vast quantities of equipment. The icing on the cake was the surrender of 8100 soldiers at Addis Derra on 20 May 1941.[14]

Taken together with the campaign against the Italians in North Africa, the East Africa campaign had ended Italy's claims to imperial status by the spring of 1941. This was a remarkable achievement of British imperial arms, even if it was subsequently overshadowed by the arrival of the Germans in Africa. Victory in East Africa was conclusive, though it left Britain with a lot of work to do, as Abyssinia, Eritrea, Italian Somilaland and Libya became new charges upon British resources. Hundreds of thousands of Italian soldiers and civilians had to be sent into internment or in some cases repatriated (the surrender of Addis Ababa alone yielded 40,000 Italian civilians, mostly old people, women and children, all in a state of panic on account of the reprisals they feared from the Abyssinians). Vast new territories had to be administered as the victor power was now legally responsible for them (Madagascar was added to the list in May 1942). Economies, currencies and supplies had to be managed, the peace kept, tax collected and railways and ports maintained or, in some cases, reopened as war gave way to peace.

It was to address these issues in Britain's burgeoning new African Empire that General Wavell, Commander-in-Chief Middle East, plucked Sir Philip Mitchell from the morass of the Nairobi government secretariat from which he had been coordinating East Africa's war effort. In June 1940 the Colonial Office had asked him to leave the governorship of Uganda to go to Nairobi as Deputy Chairman of the Governors' Conference, a body responsible for moving the British East African territories along the path of federation. More importantly, this organization had from before the war been preparing East Africa to liaise effectively with the armed forces for supplies and manpower, as it was correctly expected that the region would assume a major strategic importance should Italy ever go to war with Britain. All across the globe, mobilizing an Empire for war was a feat that required detailed planning. In East Africa as elsewhere, an executive organization had to be put in place, and key directing posts and financial responsibilities worked out between the War Office, the East African colonial governments and South African government, which as a major contributor to the military build up in the region had a powerful voice. Though Mitchell was a strong advocate of a properly federated East Africa and the creation of a High Commissioner to provide one overall head for the three contiguous British territories in the region, various factors prevented this from happening. As a next best thing to a central authority, therefore, an Economic Council was established. This set about making East Africa as effective a support as possible for the large military force building up in Kenya. Food and raw materials were in great demand, as was transport infrastructure. Mombasa and the other East African ports were worked hard, as was the Kenya and Uganda Railway, which performed notable feats of transportation as well as turning its workshops to the manufacture of ordnance, including mortars and land mines.

In the summer of 1940 Mitchell flew home to Nairobi from Delhi, where he had represented East Africa at the inaugural meeting of the Eastern Group Supply Council (a gathering of eastern colonies, India and the antipodean Dominions which sought ways to relieve Britain of the pressure of war-time manufacturing by themselves making military supplies to support the Middle East war theatre). His exhausting journey, which had also taken him to Ceylon, brought him home to Nairobi by way of Baghdad and Cairo. In the latter city Wavell invited him to dine at the Turf Club, and Mitchell found himself seated at the Commander-in-Chief's side as he was entertained by the Dominions generals Blamey, Freyberg and Duignan. Shortly after returning to Nairobi, Mitchell was asked to become Chief Political Officer to oversee the administration of the ex-Italian territories conquered by Wavell's forces. The Turf Club dinner had been an opportunity for Wavell to look over his man. Mitchell's organization, headquartered initially in Cairo but later in Nairobi, was an essay in diffused governance conducted on a manpower shoestring, a conjuring trick that British colonial officers were well practised in performing. It was a difficult task nonetheless, British district administrators having to get to grips with new indigenous peoples, limited resources, the Italian structure of colonial rule and manifold local rivalries. Their job was made more difficult by the fact that they were only caretakers, posted to Italian Somaliland or Eritrea only until higher authority had decided the ultimate fate of Italy's lost empire.

The fate of Italy's lost empire was to be a long time in the deciding. There were all sorts of proposals flying around, from British acquisition plain and simple, to the creation of a 'Greater Somalia' carved from the British, French and ex-Italian colonies, to international trusteeship under whatever body succeeded the League of Nations. The Colonial Office view differed from that of the Foreign Office, the British power centre in Cairo had its own strident views, and the War Office had its own plans pursued by the Chief Political Officer for Occupied Enemy Territories (Sir Philip Mitchell). Individual thinkers like Churchill also had their own pet schemes, South African voice was strong by virtue of its prominence in the fighting phase, and the Americans had developed, often divergent, opinions all of their own.[15] America's voice on the ultimate fate of the ex-Italian colonies was eventually as strong, if not stronger, than that of Britain. By the winter of 1941 there were already 3000 American civilian and military personnel in Eritrea working on Allied military projects. Final and binding decisions about the fate of these territories, however, would take a decade or so to be made, and until that time they remained British charges. There were many difficult decisions to be made: which aspects of Italian colonial practice to adopt, which to bin, which indigenous leaders to ally with, which development policies to adopt and so on. British rule in Italian Somaliland, and the effects of war on the three Somali colonies, also awakened a healthy sense of Somali nationalism.

An early British task was to repair and improve ex-Italian Somaliland's agricultural economy. By 1943 it was self-sufficient in primary foodstuffs, and cultivation was encouraged through capital loans and tractor fuel. There were still 8000 Italians in the territory who had to be cared for as they awaited repatriation. Normal trading patterns had to be re-established and law and order restored. It was decided to disband the Italian police force because it was found to suffer from indiscipline and unreliability. Law and order was a serious concern, as one of the tasks facing the new British administration was the disarming of the population after the region had been the scene of major fighting that had left thousands of weapons in civilian hands (most of them from defeated Italian forces). By 1943 there were over 3000 Somalis in the reformed, British-officered police force.[16] For many people in the former Italian colony, British military administration had a 'liberalizing effect' in terms of permitted social, economic and political activities.

Mitchell's position meant that he acted as British Plenipotentiary in negotiating an agreement with the Emperor of Abyssinia and conducted the preliminaries prior to his restoration. This did not take place until the end of January 1942, meaning that for nearly a year Mitchell and his officers governed Abyssinia, legislating by proclamation, subject to the Hague Convention, which dealt with the occupation of enemy territory.[17] Throughout his fiefdom Mitchell and his staff had to operate and control not only the administration and normal public services, including railways and harbours, but petrol and oil, power plants, hotels, banks and many other things. In Abyssinia, this included brothels, 'which appeared to be an indispensable part of the Italian government machine and caused us much embarrassment'. Handing over to Emperor Haile Selassie required numerous trips to London, flying via Khartoum, as Mitchell continued to build up his war-time air miles. His tally was about to grow, for soon after completing the transfer of power in Abyssinia, a telegram arrived from Lord Cranborne asking Mitchell if he would become High Commissioner of the Western Pacific and Governor of Fiji, a sensitive front-line region where relations between American, British, Australian and New Zealand civil and military officials required expert coordination. After visiting his wife at their orange farm near Grahamstown in South Africa, Mitchell duly flew off through Mombasa, Lagos, Liberia, Brazil, Trinidad and Puerto Rico, stopping off in Washington to have meetings with, amongst others, Lord Halifax, the British Ambassador, and General George Marshall, the US Army's Chief of Staff, before flying across America and the Pacific to take up residence in Government House, Suva. In 1944 the ever-mobile Mitchell was offered a return to Africa as Governor of Kenya, where he was to remain for over seven years.

In the early years of the war Kenya was preoccupied with military affairs. So long as Italian military power survived in East Africa the colony was within the zone of active hostilities. Kenya felt the impact of war more keenly than other territories in the region. It was in many ways the senior British territory of North and East Africa, its settler population was large and determined to profit from the opportunities thrown up by war. A central point for forces fighting in the region and moving north to the Middle East, it was home to East Africa Command and the region's major port (from April 1942 until September 1943 Mombasa was the headquarters of the British Eastern Fleet). Kenya was the region's main supplier of food exported to feed imperial military forces stationed in the Middle East (and the main conduit for the food exports of neighbouring territories as they were transported north).

Kenya was therefore deeply involved in the imperial war effort, although this did not mean that the carefree existence of its more elite settlers needed to change dramatically. In a case that caught the public imagination in Britain because of its whiff of adultery and royalty, and the fact that it seemed to confirm all of the 'Happy Valley' stereotypes that informed British views of the 'decadent' Kenya settlers, the Earl of Errol, who had 'rogered practically every girl in the colony', was murdered in 1940.[18] The finger of suspicion fell on Sir Jock Delves Broughton, who had recently migrated to Kenya with his beautiful young wife, with whom Errol, fourteenth in line to the throne, had been enjoying a very public affair. At the time Errol was a military aide on the Governor's staff, doing his bit for the war effort. With the Blitz, rationing and blackouts fast becoming the backdrop to daily life in Britain, it probably did people good to observe that sex, intrigue and the life of the exclusive Muthaiga Club was still the order of the day in the White Highlands.

The production and supply of food became a major theme in Kenya's war experience, and to a large extent offered the settler community a shot at economic salvation, as it finally made their agriculture viable. The colony's food exports helped feed the hundreds of thousands of imperial servicemen stationed in North Africa and the Middle East under the umbrella of Middle East Command. Its agricultural output was one reason for this, but just as important was its proximity to the fighting front – a relatively short sea journey from Mombasa to Suez and the other ports of the Red Sea. At a time when all efforts to save shipping and cut the time taken to deliver supplies were being made, it was inevitable that East African food exports would be in great demand.

The Mediterranean supply route was closed because of Italian and German air and naval activity until 1943; and, as Harold Macmillan put it, 'every shipment from Kenya to Egypt saved a long and hazardous voyage from Liverpool to Suez via the Cape'.[19] Therefore in 1941 the British Resident Minister in Cairo, Oliver Lyttelton, appealed to Kenya for more food for the imperial forces serving under Middle East Command, and the Kenyan government responded by doing what it could to increase production. It actively intervened to encourage the production of European maize, guaranteeing prices (lower prices were guaranteed for African-produced maize). Civil labour conscription was justified by the need to supply the Middle East, particularly because war had created so many employment opportunities for Kenyans (especially in the armed forces) that it became more difficult to find Africans willing to volunteer for low-paid agricultural work. Settler pressure on the government led to the conscription of Africans for 'essential' agricultural tasks. A report in December 1941 recommended the formation of an Essential Undertakings Board and District Labour Committees in Kenya, enacted by the Defence (African Labour for Essential Undertakings) Regulation. Thereby farms producing coffee, pyrethrum, rubber and certain foodstuffs were deemed to be 'essential' and therefore eligible for conscript labour. There was an estimated shortage of 22,000 agricultural labourers. By the end of 1942 the new regulation had put over 12,000 conscripts into the market – 5000 of them on sisal plantations and 3000 working on government services, including irrigation projects and the railways. In March 1944 the official figure for civilian labour conscription stood at over 14,000, rising to 18,000 by the end of the year. In 1944 conscript labour camps were established, causing concern in Whitehall where the labour policies of settler-dominated societies always caused a rash of hand-wringing of the 'it's not quite cricket but what on earth can we practically *do*?' variety. The food requirements of the imperial armed forces in the Middle East embraced meat as well as grain, and this led to a new demand for African-produced beasts. Slaughter cattle began pouring into Athi in Kenya from all parts of Africa, amounting to an estimated 80,000 head each year (mostly from Tanganyika). Cattle-rearing was more important in Africa than the other territories of the Colonial Empire, and the war brought expansion to all sides of the industry (meat, leather and dairy produce).

Illustrating the capacity of the Empire to transfer resources from supplier to consumer as war caused multifarious trade realignments, East African intra-regional trade grew, as Kenyan sugar, for example, was sent by road to the Sudan to save shipping space, and maize was especially grown in Uganda to help Kenya overcome periods of shortage. These efforts were never enough, however, to make up for the fact that the demands of military recruitment and food production for export left Kenya short of food for domestic consumption, requiring emergency imports and rationing. Kenya was normally an exporter of maize but in 1942–43 the colony had to import maize and wheat from Argentina and elsewhere. The cessation of rice imports from Burma, following its capture by the Japanese, further contributed to difficulties in feeding local labour. The food situation in Kenya approached famine conditions in some regions in 1943. Poor rains were one reason, but the situation was complicated by the presence of large armed forces in the colony, by the drain of men into the armed forces, and by the fact that many other Kenyans were working on settler farms and plantations and were therefore unable to produce their own crops. Among the Kamba this was known as the 'Famine of the Boots', because many people came to rely for sustenance upon the pay remittances of soldiers overseas. The commission appointed to investigate the serious shortages of 1943 concluded that, irrespective of poor rains, the situation was inevitable due to demand outstripping supply. Civil labour conscription was suspended in February 1943 because of the serious food situation, though it was resumed in June after representations from settler farmers engaged in 'essential production' agriculture.

Kenya walked the manpower tightrope during the war with a more dangerous gait than was usual in other British colonies, and nearly came unstuck. The diversion of civil labour to export crops coincided with crop failure. In the whole of East Africa, as the region's governors discussed at their conference in 1944, the nub of the problem was the requirement to feed employed labour – Africans away from their homes and away therefore from their own subsistence production as they worked on European farms, in government service or served in the army. The British Ministry of Food and Ministry of War Transport arranged imports where and when they could, though it was a close-run thing. At one point the Governor of Kenya complained to Whitehall that not enough manpower was being left for the colony's agricultural and military needs, and this had led to the manpower demands of the army being increasingly shifted to West Africa.

As far as the financial health of the Kenyan government went, the mass of war activity centred upon the colony was good for business. The colony's coffers were lined by local industry, increased customs revenue, good prices for exports (mostly sold to the British government) and the imposition of new taxes. It was the Europeans who were subject to tax increases, as a Personal Tax based on means as opposed to race came to replace the Non-Native Poll Tax. African direct taxation was not increased, an acknowledgement of the fact that for many Africans the war brought economic threats rather than opportunities. Though some benefited from the increased circulation of money brought about by the presence of large armed forces in the colony, there was no general rise in the price paid for African crops. There was also no general rise in wages but the cost of living increased. But the main threat to African wellbeing in Kenya remained food shortage.

The political power wielded by the Kenya settlers contributed to the precarious food situation. Their influence over the colonial government grew. A settler, Major F. W. Cavendish-Bentinck, for example, was appointed Minister for Agriculture, and settlers were able to use the imperial demand for food exports to further their own agricultural development and oblige the government to divert labour from domestic to export production. For the first time their farms were becoming universally profitable. To bring them properly under the plough mechanization proceeded apace and thousands of mainly Kikuyu 'squatters' were forced to leave the European-owned land that they had cultivated in the inter-war years. This migration contributed to overcrowding and overstocking in African reserves, and swelled the urban underclass of expanding towns like Nairobi and Mombasa. These areas would prove fertile recruitment grounds for the Mau Mau movement that was identified in the late 1940s and that dominated Kenya's political landscape in the 1950s, and which put the final nail in the coffin of the settlers' dream of being allowed to develop as a white self-governing territory along the lines of Southern Rhodesia. Not all Africans in Kenya, however, were threatened by war-induced change, and some African farmers were also able to cash in on war-time demand and to sell food crops to feed the increasing urban population. As occurred elsewhere in Africa, as Europeans came to monopolize the export market, Africans found a niche in the expanding internal market. As more and more Kenyans became employed in non-agricultural sectors of the economy, the demands of the internal food market grew and urbanization gathered pace. Nairobi's population rose by 50 per cent to 66,000, and Mombasa's doubled to 56,000. (Early in the war plans were made to evacuate Mombasa in the event of a successful Italian invasion.)

The Uganda Protectorate was mobilized for war in some depth, and presented its colonial government with a novel situation. The need to mobilize the territory's human and material resources efficiently meant that effectively *governing* Uganda, as opposed simply to *occupying* it, became an urgent task. As elsewhere in Africa, colonial governments were used to doing little more than holding the ring, and this had been the case in Uganda since British rule had followed the Uganda Railway inland from the Swahili coast nearly half a century before. When war began the task of mobilizing the Uganda Protectorate fell upon a British administrative establishment of a mere seventy-seven officers, and a police force built around a cadre of fifty-three Europeans.[20] As was common throughout Africa, Governor Sir Philip Mitchell faced a monumental task with skeletal resources.

What made this imbalance of greater concern was the fact that Uganda was one of numerous African colonies actually threatened by enemy action. This was because of the possibility of an Italian incursion from Abyssinia, though (unbeknownst at the time) the weakness of the Italian threat was to ensure that the protectorate's main military effort could be concentrated in support of the offensive operations of the King's African Rifles against the Italians, before moving on the fight the Vichy French and the Japanese. A further border concern after the German defeat of Belgium was the fate of the Belgian colonies of the Congo and Ruanda–Urundi, with which Uganda shared a wide-open land frontier. It was well within the bounds of possibility in the heady summer of 1940, when Germany was carrying all before it and Italy stood ready to pounce, that the surrender of the King of the Belgians could have resulted in the dispatch of a German military mission to the region. Given this situation, Mitchell broadcast to his people seeking to engender a sense of calm should there be an enemy raid on Ugandan territory:

> Do not be afraid. It is possible that you may see an Italian aeroplane or two over some part of Uganda. If you do, do not be frightened. Sit quietly in your banana groves, or under any trees, until it has gone away. It will do you no harm.[21]

Confronted by a threatening situation, rapid expansion of military forces and war-related civilian organizations was necessary. Compulsory civilian labour was not a high-profile issue as it was in Kenya. Early in the war a system of voluntary registration for Asians and Europeans was introduced, and in 1942 a Compulsory Service Ordinance was passed allowing the Governor to require any person to render war-related service. Africans were drafted, without conscription, for military service in the Uganda battalions of the KAR (starting with the 4th Battalion), as well as the service branches of the British Army. The British Army also took over the Uganda Territorial Regiment, which had been raised shortly before the war on the initiative of the colonial government to give urban Africans the chance of military training, and it became the 7th Battalion KAR. This battalion boasted several graduates from the territory's elite Makerere College, and a number of members of the Bugandan royal family (Uganda comprised the kingdoms of Buganda, Bunyoro, Ankole and Toro). Uganda's contribution to the KAR and other branches of the British military was substantial, amounting to 120,000 between September 1939 and October 1944. In October 1944 there were about 60,000 Ugandans serving in the armed forces, representing about 10 per cent of the adult male population in the relevant age group. This was judged to be the maximum withdrawal of men from the protectorate's rural economy that could be safely borne, as Uganda walked the tightrope of labour apportionment between domestic production, on the one hand, and export production and army service on the other. Some conscription took place, mainly to regulate the flow of recruits from different areas of the protectorate or to fill niche roles, as when a hundred Asians were conscripted into the technical branches of the KAR. In 1943 volunteers numbered 37,860, conscripts 14,527. Illustrating the world war's habit of forging the most unlikely ethnic and geographical connections, Ugandan soldiers saw service not only in Kenya, Abyssinia and Somaliland – at the time, a most unusual range of travel in itself – but also in Burma, Ceylon, Madagascar, North Africa and Palestine. The vast majority of uniformed Ugandans served in the KAR, but there was also a Uganda section of the Kenya Royal Navy Volunteer Reserve. For home defence the Uganda Defence Force was established as 'Dad's Army' went imperial (it was stood down in late 1943 when all conceivable threat to Uganda's territorial integrity had passed). As part of the civil defence effort, and to relieve military authorities of the need to find garrison troops for Uganda, a 300-strong Police Service Unit was also raised.

Many of the Europeans who enlisted in the forces served in the Uganda Platoon of the whites-only Kenya Regiment. About 150 of Uganda's 2000 Europeans joined up, and the colonial administration was seriously depleted as a result of secondments to the army. This came at a bad time. As colonial officials left the territory, the tasks for which the colonial administration was responsible began to increase dramatically and government grew bigger in the face of war-induced changes, including the need for rationing, emergency legislation, propaganda, censorship and military recruitment. Not only was the administration charged with maintaining normal services, but war added manifold extra duties, for example the operation of new services like the Supply, Transport, and Civil Defence Boards, an Information Office, an Industrial Committee, a Civil Intelligence Unit, and the organization and staffing of internment and refugee camps. Provision for prisoners of war and internees were required because Uganda was one of the many parts of the Empire called upon to accommodate displaced civilians and captured enemy soldiers. Camps were opened for 4000 Italian prisoners, 1200 Italian civilian internees and 7000 Polish refugees. The great increase in government agencies that accompanied the unprecedented new wave of administrative tasks had to be accomplished by a skeletal British administration that by October 1942 had lost a quarter of its manpower to the armed forces. Reflecting the situation in many other parts of the Colonial Empire, such a small administration could not achieve all of the targets set by the demands of total war, especially given the fact that it was operating with local societies where the habit of cooperating with large-scale state intervention was completely undeveloped. The fact that so much was achieved in these circumstances is remarkable.

As in all other parts of the British Colonial Empire, a key task of colonial officials in Uganda was the supervision of the country's drive for increased war production on the home front in order to supplement imperial resources and aid neighbouring colonies experiencing shortages. Uganda's main export was cotton, of which it was the Colonial Empire's largest producer. (Whilst attending the Eastern Group Supply Council meeting in Delhi in June 1940, Uganda's erstwhile Governor, Sir Philip Mitchell, arranged the sale of all East African cotton crops to the Bombay textile mills.) Uganda also produced coffee, pyrethrum, sisal, sugar, oilseeds (groundnuts, sesame and soya bean) and rubber (1000 tons per annum), all products able to find a ready market in wartime. Cotton, however, was

Uganda's economic mainstay, accounting for 80 per cent of its exports in 1939. Bulk purchasing was arranged through the Cotton Fund, which prevented the benefits of increased world prices carrying through to the producers (as an anti-inflation measure, according to the administration). Maize was grown to help redress the shortage in Kenya, 'even', in the words of the administration, 'at some hurt to our soil structure'.[22] As with the slaughter tapping of rubber plants officially sanctioned in Ceylon, many parts of the Empire were encouraged to produce to the maximum level with little regard for the medium- to long-term future of the crop in question. When famine hit Kenya in 1943 Uganda sent 11,000 tons of mixed African foodstuffs as a special contribution. Most of the protectorate's produce was marketed under control and sold or held under guarantee at the call of the British Ministry of Supply and Ministry of Food. Aside from its agricultural output, Uganda produced minerals including asbestos, mica, tantalite, tin and wolfram. A large phosphate deposit was developed near Tororo and used to supply Kenyan farmers with fertilizer. Timber for military railways was exported. Mechanical workshops were established by Uganda's Industrial Committee, along with projects for blanket-making, cotton-spinning and pottery, in order to save shipping by reducing import demands, as well as to provide useful training for Africans. A government salvage depot was also opened in order to save shipping space by reconditioning vehicles, and to make use of skilled internee labour. Uganda was a model microcosm of the Empire at war, mobilized on every front.

People all over East African gave money or goods to the British imperial war effort. By late 1943 over £770,000 had been donated by private individuals, including £7363 from the people of British Somaliland for the purchase of Spitfires (enough for one and a half at the going rate) and the Maasai of Kenya had contributed from their national bank in the form of 17,926 head of cattle. Thousands of Ugandans also contributed to the imperial war effort in the field of financial and material gifts to British charities and institutions. Shares were taken in the issuance of the East African War Loans, and there was a vigorous campaign to draw African savings into Post Office Savings Bank accounts (particularly those of servicemen). The Post Office Savings Bank, like the Red Cross and the Anglican Church, was one of those British institutions spread across the globe by virtue of Empire and productively utilized in a time of war. Attracting savings into bank accounts was seen as a means of avoiding inflation and preventing soldiers and their relatives from squandering their money. Moving money in the other direction, from the pockets of Africans to the war effort of the metropole, the Uganda War Fund was always making appeals for donations to buy warships or aircraft. In doing this the fund used occasions like Churchill's birthday to mount special money-raising drives, and in 1944 total contributions stood at around £250,000 (outright gifts or interest-free loans of surplus revenue over expenditure). The protectorate raised £83,000 to pay for the Uganda Squadron of the RAF, and the cruiser HMS *Uganda* was gifted inscribed silver bugles, a silk ensign, African drums, a coffee machine and a regular supply of Ugandan coffee. Certainly, no German, Italian or Japanese warship could boast the kind of exotic gifts and sponsors that were commonplace in the British fleet. It may not have been war-winning stuff on its own, but such gifts – coming from every one of the territories that made up the enormous British Empire and Commonwealth – were all contributions on the right side of the ledger, and striking illustrations of a global imperial heritage fusing with a global imperial war effort.

The former German colony of Tanganyika was a Mandate of the League of Nations, administered by the Colonial Office.[23] The war – particularly in the aftermath of British losses in South-East Asia – transformed Tanganyika into an economic asset of great value to both Britain and America; and, like the region's other British colonial territories, it experienced wide-ranging mobilization in order to provide recruits for the army and produce key raw materials for export. As in Kenya, the war was not a distant and irrelevant struggle even for rural Africans remote from its causes and from its major battlefields, but one which affected them indirectly (through rationing, inflation, military recruitment and propaganda) and also demanded their direct participation. In Tanganyika this was mainly in the form of conscription for both the KAR and for plantations producing sisal, a crop for which Tanganyika became the world's major supplier.

As elsewhere in British Africa, Tanganyika's new-found importance accelerated the process that saw the vital decisions affecting its future migrate from the governor and his senior staff in Dar-es-Salaam to the Secretary of State for the Colonies and senior staff of the Colonial Office in London. After the war, it was only to be expected that centralized control would continue. The war-time demand for Tanganyika's agricultural products led to large-scale labour recruitment, much of it by conscription. With this and a more interventionist style of government gaining ground, African discontent came to focus more on the colonial rulers than had been the case before, and the war stimulated a sense of territory-wide consciousness that was entirely novel. In other parts of Africa too, the quotidian presence of Europeans and the impact of colonial rule impinged on more lives than ever before because of the demands of war, and discontent began to escape the tribal structure and focus on the power rung above the chiefs – that of the British colonial administration itself. This process was compounded by the growth of government and its tasks caused by the war. With the need, for example, to control food and import distribution, and to find recruits for the plantations and the army, government became more bureaucratic and less personal in order to become more efficient. This war imperialism put a greater burden on the chiefs as intermediaries between the British colonial administration and the African people, and they became more authoritarian in order to implement government policies. Naturally, therefore, they became the focus for discontent and their legitimacy began to be questioned. It was a vicious circle for the British, as the overriding demands of war forced them to erode the basis of their rule. As in India and Egypt, the need to get the war effort into high gear led to pressures on the system of colonial rule that would tend towards breakdown in the post-war years.

Before the war non-Empire countries had been Tanganyika's principal source of imports, so Britain's imperial prohibition on trading with the enemy and on trading with non-sterling area countries meant a good deal of trade disruption. By 1942–43 its volume of imports had fallen by half of the pre-war level. Tanganyika had also relied on food imports, notably rice from Burma. At the beginning of the war export markets for major Tanganyikan products such as coffee, cotton, groundnuts and sisal collapsed, obliging the government to step in to support the industries concerned. The British government, for example, bought the sisal crop, the colonial government the cotton crop. Following this initial disruption, things settled down. Some crops, like cotton, stagnated, whilst others, including pyrethrum, tea and tobacco, became more profitable as war-time demand moved towards insatiability as war was exported from Europe into all corners of the globe. With the loss of all American and European colonies in the East, the demand for Tanganyika's sisal became limitless and its production soared to meet this demand, to such an extent that shortly after the war it was producing nearly half of the world's total crop. This, and demand for other 'war' crops, led the settlers who controlled the industry to demand labour conscripts and modern agricultural machinery. In February 1942 the governor asked London for special powers of conscription. Churchill overruled Colonial Office objections and conscription was introduced, on a scale unknown in all other parts of British colonial Africa bar Nigeria. By 1945 over 84,000 had been conscripted, mainly for sisal plantations but also for rubber, pyrethrum and essential foodstuffs. (Included in this number were replacements for those already recruited. So, for example, 8420 were conscripted in 1942, 22,820 in 1943 and 18,248 in 1944, many of them being replacements for released labourers.)

The scale of the Tanganyikan government's use of conscription was due almost entirely to the Allied demand for sisal, a hard fibre suitable for making rope and twine, first grown in Tanganyika in 1883. In peacetime East Africa's producers faced stiff market competition from the Philippines and the Dutch East Indies. To start with the war deprived East African producers of their market, particularly Tanganyika, as it had traditionally exported largely to Germany as a result of its historic links with that country. Further hurting the industry, among the 3000 German settlers interned in Tanganyika were many sisal planters, and large numbers of British planters and staff had joined the armed forces. In order to preserve an industry facing collapse, in 1941 the British Ministry of Supply undertook to purchase 100,000 tons of sisal (about the total of the pre-war annual crop). The following year the situation was transformed when the Philippines and the Dutch East Indies were conquered by the Japanese, though there were formidable obstacles to overcome before maximum production could be attained in Tanganyika. There was a shortage of African labour, and more plant and equipment was needed at a time when Britain was in a poor position to provide such material for export. Railway transport and port storage facilities needed improvement, and the world-wide shortage of shipping space presented a problem. America took a close interest in developments, however, and supplied equipment. Storage and shore facilities were improved, and, because of America's pressing need, the large-scale conscription of African labour was permitted.

In some regions where sisal was produced, land shortages and overstocking occurred. In 1943 there was a famine in the Central Province because of poor rains and low food reserves (conditions were so bad that some Tanganyikan soldiers gave up their leave to stay in the army rather than return to their homes). Shortages in the region were exacerbated by the need to feed the tens of thousands of Africans employed on the sisal estates. The situation was stabilized by the import of wheat from Australia, maize from Somaliland and manioc from Madagascar. Further exacerbating problems of domestic food supply, government encouraged the export of cattle and grain to feed the armies in the Middle East and North Africa. The planting of maize was encouraged above that of the hardier millet because of its export value. Settlers were given government support to plant more maize, given the demand for military food exports. The Northern Province Wheat Scheme was a government initiative to this end, using commandeered Maasai land.

Tanganyika's main military contribution to the imperial war effort was the provision of soldiers. The KAR traditionally recruited a Tanganyikan battalion, and as the KAR expanded to become a front-line imperial infantry unit Tanganyika's contribution increased accordingly. As in the field of civil labour, conscription for military purposes was more widely used in Tanganyika than in most other parts of British Africa. This was because volunteers were insufficient in number, and because conscription was regarded as the only means of regulating the inflow into different military units. Even volunteers were officially conscripted before final selection. Over 86,000 Tanganyikans served in the British forces during the war, and the Tanganyika Royal Naval Reserve exercised with the Royal Navy and units of the KAR using motor boats.

The need to mobilize Tanganyika's population for war required a propaganda drive to try and persuade people that what was asked of them was in a reasonable cause, and that defeat for Britain would directly and adversely affect them, however remote they might consider themselves from war, its causes and effects. Propaganda brought even remote communities in touch with events, for example through the official government newssheet *Habara Za Bita*. Conscription further disturbed still waters because it obliged, or tempted, many people to migrate across significant distances, taking them away from small rural communities often for the first time since birth and depositing them in towns, on plantations or in the army, amidst unfamiliar and ethnically-mixed people. Such dramatic alterations in personal circumstances forced hundreds of thousands of Africans across the continent to appraise the world around them anew and linked them to bigger issues, more diverse communities and wider geographical boundaries. For many, of course, this movement meant a new experience – urban life – as the population of Dar-es-Salaam doubled to 50,000 and as other towns grew equally rapidly. Discontent caused by the effects of war on the home front, and the officially-sponsored idea that it was a war of freedom against tyranny, increased criticism of the government. Though it cannot be said that such trends made post-war discontent inevitable, and though not all of Tanganyika's people were significantly affected, there can be no doubt that the overall depth of African war-time participation meant that things would never be quite the same again, and that few colonies would return to the hermetically-sealed colonial world that had characterized the inter-war period.

Though the fiction of joint Anglo-Egyptian rule was legally maintained in the form of the Condominium arrangement governing the Sudan, this vast country was in fact a British colony. It was ruled by the Foreign Office (as opposed to the Colonial Office) through a Governor-General and the Sudan Political Service (SPS), an administrative cadre that was, in the eyes of its members at least, as prestigious as the Indian Civil Service, the original breeding ground of the 'heaven's born' colonial administrator. Backing up the SPS in their task of ruling the Sudan was the Sudan Defence Force (SDF), founded in 1925 and headquartered in Khartoum. On the outbreak of war it numbered about 5000 men. Its five corps (later transformed into infantry battalions) were stationed in different parts of the Condominium; the Eastern Arab Corps in Kassala, the Western Arab Corps in Darfur, the Camel Corps at El Obeid in the Kordofan Province, the Equatorial Corps forming a garrison force in the Southern Sudan and a Northern Arab Corps (converted to artillery in 1941). Britain's search for soldiers to perform the many tasks associated with protracted conflict over vast regions led inevitably to the expansion of the SDF and the recruitment of Sudanese Pioneers for local service. This was particularly the case because the Sudan found itself used as an operational base during the East Africa campaign. Sudan was also a regional headquarters for imperial air power, supporting its own air group falling under the command of the Chief Air Officer Middle East. Towards the end of 1940 there were fifty aircraft as well as 9000 troops in the Sudan. 203 Group was formed in the Sudan in August 1940 to defend the vital strategic points of Atbara, Khartoum and Port Sudan, and to protect Red Sea shipping in conjunction with the RAF Group in Aden. (Between June and December 1940 the Aden and Sudan squadrons escorted fifty-four Red Sea convoys.) Sudan-bases squadrons carried out many raids against Italian targets, kept a close eye on the Italian ports of Assab and Massawa, and aided the Patriots fighting in Abyssinia. In April 1941 the local commander, Air Commodore Slatter, could muster No. 47 Squadron (Wellesleys), No. 237 (Rhodesian) Army Co-operation Squadron (Hardys, Lysanders and Gladiators), the Free French Bomber Flight and a few South African Air Force (SAAF) communications aircraft (joined in August 1941 by four more SAAF squadrons, following the conclusion of hostilities in the Galla–Sidamo province of Abyssinia).

The Sudan was vulnerable to enemy action when Italy entered the war, as it was bordered by the Italian colonies of Libya, Eritrea and Abyssinia. From June 1940 until imperial reinforcements arrived in September, only the SDF, the Sudan Police and local irregulars stood between the massive Italian forces in the region and the Sudanese capital of Khartoum. Meanwhile, the SDF, like other imperial units, underwent rapid expansion. European civilians and officials of the SPS who could be spared were recruited in order to boost the officer cadre. The most likely point of an Italian attack was in the north east, where the town of Kassala was strategically placed, linked by rail to the territory's only port, Port Sudan, and close to the junction of the White and Blue Niles. In September 1940 the Italians attacked Kassala with 8000 troops and eighteen tanks supported by strong air cover, and captured the town from two SDF motor machine-gun companies. When hostilities commenced the Commander (or *Kaid*) of the SDF, Major-General William Platt (Commander-in-Chief East Africa Command from September 1941), had under his command the SDF, three British infantry battalions (2500 British troops defending Khartoum, Port Sudan and Atbara) and seven obsolete bombers. This force was soon bolstered by the 4th and 5th Indian Divisions. By the time of his offensive against the Italians, Platt was supported in the air from the Sudan by three bomber squadrons, one Rhodesian army cooperation squadron, one South African fighter squadron and a flight of Gladiators transferred from Egypt. Slatter's air force was often called upon to support the Abyssinian Patriots, who greatly valued the sight and sound of friendly aircraft. The SDF took part in the imperial campaign in Eritrea and Abyssinia, and also provided a Frontier Battalion for Orde Wingate's Gideon Force that supported Haile Selassie's fighting return to his capital Addis Ababa, a campaign in which 13,000 camels, out of an initial force of 17,500, were lost, illustrating the nature of the war fought in the region. (Animals were important in numerous war theatres, including RAF elephants in Burma, army pigeons in France, mules in Italy and Burma, and cavalry horses in the Middle East.)

With the end of fighting in East Africa the SDF's role in offensive operations ended. There were still manifold military tasks to be undertaken, however, and as elsewhere it was colonial forces that were called upon to perform them, sparing front-line units from elsewhere in the Empire for combat duties. Throughout the Middle East, and in the vast, recently-conquered Italian territories, troops were needed to guard lines of communication, military depots and supply dumps. There was also the need for imperial troops to restore and maintain law and order in regions that had seen the collapse of civil government as a result of battle. In these capacities the SDF was heavily committed in Eritrea as well as in the Sudan, and was called upon to expand even further to provide a brigade for service in Libya (the brigade was later involved in a British deception plan in Cyrenaica, where it posed as the 12th Division). So the Sudan's role changed from military action to logistical support of the imperial war effort. This meant that the direct manifestations of war receded, whilst the indirect (and irritating) manifestations of war continued. Food shortages necessitated rationing, government intervention increased and the Sudan's trade was conducted under the aegis of the Middle East Supply Centre, which meant vexatious export restrictions and an excess profit tax on exports which was used to subsidize the price of necessities.

As elsewhere in Africa where British rule relied upon cooperation between traditional leaders and colonial officials, the demands of war strained the system of paternalistic government, though discontent was largely confined to the elites. War aims had to be explained to the people in order to win their support, and the majority of them remained acquiescent, not linked to the political agitation of their educated peers pursuing their ambition of greater participation in the government of their country or the return of effective Egyptian rule (absent since General Gordon was cut down by the Mahdi at Khartoum in 1885). Special efforts were needed to keep Sudan's intelligentsia on Britain's side.[24] As in every other part of the Empire, British rule depended upon a working alliance with indigenous political leaders. Many educated Sudanese worked as civil servants, and the Graduates' General Council drew most of its members from among the educated elite. The British had encouraged its formation, though reflecting the ambivalence with which colonial authorities viewed bodies like this and the Indian National Congress refused to recognize it as a political body. In April 1942 the Graduate's General Council demanded post-war self-determination. The British rejection of such demands meant that the Council was less prepared to cooperate, and turned towards Egypt as a source of release from British rule. The political situation was further complicated by the presence of powerful religious leaders. The son of the famous Mahdi who had presided over Gordon's picturesque death was leader of a sectarian organization called the Ansar. There was then the Khatmiya group, which sided with Britain against the Ansar, but which was pro-Egyptian and was therefore drawn closer to the Council as a result of its war-time stance. Playing the time-honoured colonial game of collaboration, the British reshuffled the pack and turned more towards the Ansar for cooperation, given its strident rejection of Egyptian overtures towards the Sudan. Egyptian nationalists, for their part, shrewdly wooed Sudanese nationalists seeking a British retreat or wholesale withdrawal by emphasizing that Egypt's claims to sovereignty over the Sudan were renounced. Thus the war stimulated Sudanese political participation and agitation whilst compelling it to play a role in the fighting.

British Somaliland was the only British African territory to be conquered by an enemy power during the Second World War. At the start of hostilities British forces in Somaliland were dwarfed by those in the neighbouring territories of Italian Somaliland and Abyssinia, and by those based in French Somaliland to the north (which declared for Vichy and as a result was blockaded on land and at sea by British imperial forces). Before the war it had been decided that, if Italy went to war with Britain, British Somaliland would be an easy conquest and so plans were made to evacuate the protectorate. This decision upset British officers serving with the Somaliland Camel Corps (SCC), as it meant the abrogation of Britain's treaty obligations to protect the Somali people and a concomitant loss of prestige. It also meant the disbandment of the SCC, as its troops could not be expected to leave their country when the other imperial units garrisoning the territory were evacuated. (As was the case with the indigenous elements of the Burma Army in 1942, the men of the SCC were told that they could return to their homes.)

In September 1939, however, the evacuation policy that had been adopted was reversed by the Commander-in-Chief Middle East, General Sir Archibald Wavell. But by then it was really too late to take effective measures to build up the protectorate's defences in order to cater for this policy about-turn, though piecemeal reinforcements amounting to over five infantry battalions were spared for yet another Middle East Command commitment. As well as the stationing within Somaliland of adequate military forces, the protectorate's successful defence was understood to rest on cooperation with French forces in neighbouring Djibouti. The fall of France, and subsequent adherence of Djibouti to the Vichy Republic, changed the strategic situation dramatically, and a fighting evacuation became the only realistic British option. As in the western Indian Ocean, the Gulf of Siam, the Mediterranean and West Africa, the fall of France had serious imperial ramifications.

As was widely expected, Mussolini grasped the opportunity presented by the defeat of France to invade Somaliland and at long last experienced the pleasure of conquering a British possession in the region of his dreamed of new Roman Empire. It was to be an evanescent experience for the imperial pretender. But before Mussolini's pretence was revealed to the world, before his forces were swatted aside by British imperial armies and before the rump of his living dreams were embalmed by German 'support' following Rommel's arrival in Africa, the Italian moment of victory came. When Italian forces crossed the border into British Somaliland on 4 August 1940 they were opposed by one British, two Indian, one King's African Rifles and one Northern Rhodesia Regiment battalions, the East African Light Battery and the SCC. At that juncture the SCC's strength amounted to fourteen British officers, 400 *askaris* and 150 reservists, organized into two camel companies, supported by a Nyasaland Rifle Company in Ford trucks (the SCC had been strengthened in October 1939 by the arrival of thirty-seven officers and NCOs from Southern Rhodesia). Finally, there was the quasi-military tribal police force, the Illalos, of about a thousand men. They were placed under district commissioners and stationed on military bases.

On 11 August 1940, one week after the Italians crossed the border, the officer commanding British forces in Somaliland, Major-General Godwin Austen, advised Wavell at GHQ Middle East that only a retreat to Berbera (British Somaliland's capital and only port) and evacuation could save his force from absolute defeat. Within a week the five battalions of troops had been successfully evacuated by the Royal and Royal Australian Navies, and the men of the SCC had been told to return to their homes (with their weapons). The decision to evacuate Somaliland upset Churchill so much that he cabled Wavell to protest at the small number of casualties and to request a court of inquiry. Wavell's response ended with the statement that 'a big butcher's bill was not necessarily evidence of good tactics', and this sent Churchill into a rage.[25] This acrimonious exchange began the souring of relations between the two men which led ultimately to Wavell's replacement by General Sir Claude Auchinleck.

Despite this, Italy's triumph was less firmly founded than the Japanese conquest of British colonies in South-East Asia and the Far East, and was to be challenged within the space of seven months. As in so many of the other 'sideshow' imperial campaigns of the war (Iraq, Iran, Madagascar and Syria among them) somehow the British regional commanders managed to come up with the forces to enable them to meet their far-flung commitments. Military improvisation continued to be an imperial art form, in this case transported by the ubiquitous ships of the Royal Navy. Forces for an invasion of British Somaliland were mustered in Kenya and Aden. The Italian navy, driven from the Red Sea by imperial air and seapower, could do nothing to prevent their voyage. On 16 March 1941 two battalions of Indian soldiers landed at Berbera, and British Somaliland was reconquered within a month.

Following the reconquest, Brigadier A. R. Chater, a former commanding officer of the SCC, was appointed Officer Commanding Troops Somaliland and Military Governor of the Somaliland Protectorate. The SCC was re-formed, most of the men who had been granted permission to return to their homes on the eve of the Italian conquest voluntarily reporting for duty when the British reappeared. They were needed, too, as the military tasks to be performed behind the front line in the war against the Italian forces in Abyssinia were legion. For a start, soldiers were needed to man the lines of communication that ran through British Somaliland to Harar in Abyssinia, as this became the main supply route for operations in that country. Soldiers were also needed to guard and administer the thousands of Italian prisoners of war that were 'passed back' by forward units in Abyssinia and Eritrea. For this particular role Brigadier Chater authorized the recruitment of two companies of Somali irregulars to form the Somali PW (prisoner of war) Guards, rising to four companies totalling 500 men.

Another military commitment behind the region's combat zones was the blockade of Vichy French Somaliland (in conjunction with the warships of the Eastern Fleet, which formed for this purpose the romantically-titled Red Sea Dhow Patrol). In March 1941 an attempt had been made to get French Somaliland to rally to the Free French cause, though this proved unsuccessful (although the Governor was willing to permit British forces to use the port of

Djibouti). Thus began the blockade of the French territory, the Vichy governor being told that it would continue until his territory swapped sides. In May 1941 the 26th (East African) Brigade arrived to take over responsibility for the blockade of the French territory. In September 1941 SAAF Junker 86s were sent to join the blockading forces. On the ground, the KAR proved too heavily equipped and therefore too static to effectively prevent Somali tribesmen running the blockade. So it was decided to deploy the more manoeuvrable Somali irregulars, and they were duly moved to the frontier area in December 1941. They proved so effective that their ranks were increased to six companies and in May 1942 they ceased to be irregulars and became a full army unit, formally designated the Somaliland Scouts in 1943. In June 1941 a small combined operation had eliminated the Italian garrison at Assab, and, together with victory over Italian forces inland, the Italian threat to the Red Sea was removed. Therefore Middle East Command, which had never been very keen on the blockade, gave it up in March 1942. The Vichy governor finally capitulated in December 1942.

Meanwhile the reconvened SCC was being converted into an armoured car regiment for service overseas. This did not prove a successful move, however, and in June 1944, shortly before the unit's departure for Rhodesia where it was to undergo training, many of its members mutinied at Burao. It is likely that a desire not to leave the country was a factor in causing the mutiny, as was the case for the 1st Battalion The Mauritius Regiment which had mutinied on Madagascar six months earlier.[26] A stated reason was the fear that Somali soldiers would be treated as African askaris, whom they looked down upon, and that they would not be treated correctly as Moslems in matters of diet and dress. As a result of this the SCC, after thirty years of valuable imperial service, was disbanded in September 1944. The Somaliland Scouts, however, continued to be a success, and a further use was found for Somali manpower when it was decided to incorporate a Somaliland battalion into each of the two KAR brigades being formed for service in Burma. Thus the 71st (Somaliland) KAR began forming in September 1942, and the 72nd in January 1943. In February 1944 the 71st KAR left for Burma as part of the 28th (East African) Brigade, where it saw action against the Japanese. The 72nd KAR was based in Kenya and supplied reinforcements for the 71st.

After an unpleasant interlude of fighting, followed by seven months of Italian rule, there was much work to be done in getting British Somaliland back on its feet. The Second World War was notable for British parliamentary promises of large-scale investment in the colonies, and in order to bid for a share colonial administrations needed surveys and reports in order to prepare development plans. British Somaliland was no exception (and the same applied to ex-Italian Somaliland too). Grazing and water resources were surveyed; measures to improve public health were embarked upon; educational provisions were increased; and radio and mobile cinema campaigns were launched to stimulate public awareness and support for the war effort. Berbera, the port and capital, had been badly damaged during the fighting, so it was decided to build a new government headquarters at Hargeisa. This was far inland. It put an end to decades of coastal administration and pointed in the direction of greater political unity within the territory.

Like East Africa, West Africa was a region whose contribution to the war effort was of much more than peripheral importance in British eyes, and it was itself affected by the war in many different ways. West Africa was an important manpower source, providing over 200,000 soldiers for the British Army. It was also an invaluable source of precious raw materials, and a key link in the supply route taking thousands of combat aircraft from Britain and America to the Middle East. Finally, it was an important base for merchant shipping making its way around the world, and for naval and air forces engaged in the Battle of the Atlantic. Like all imperial regions, West Africa was directly linked to other regions and theatres of war – to the Battle of the Atlantic, to the Middle East and East African theatres and to the war in Burma. West Africa was one of the Empire's most valuable sources of tin and rubber, required by Britain for its own industrial production and as a dollar-earning export to America. Its food exports were also vital to the imperial war effort. As Lord Swinton prepared to leave London to become Resident Minister West Africa, the Minister of Food, Lord Woolton, told him that the fat ration on the home front in Britain was the most important one to avoid cutting. 'It all depends what you can do in West Africa whether we can maintain it or not.'[27] So West Africa's traditional role as a supplier of palm oil, palm kernels and ground nuts was all-important. As a manpower reservoir West Africa's 200,000 soldiers catered for the defence of the region, particularly from Vichy attack (stationed in the Home Command were infantry units, garrison battalions, Pioneer Corps, reinforcements for overseas theatres and training centres), provided military labour at home and in the Middle East (where 16,500 West African Pioneers served), and furnished front-line combat troops for service in East Africa, India and Burma (two West African infantry divisions, totalling 73,000 men, fought in the Burma campaign). West Africans also served in the RAF and the Royal and Merchant Navies.

Before the war it was considered that the main role of the Royal West African Frontier Force, founded in the 1890s to provide a robust response to the encroachments and empire-building of the French, would be to reinforce East Africa should a general European war break out in which Britain was opposed by Italy. As with the Indian Army, imperial troops from West Africa had a designated role to play in reinforcing a distant theatre in the event of war. Thus the first RWAFF contingent to leave West Africa embarked for Kenya in June 1940 as tension between Britain and Italy mounted. HM Troopships *Lancashire*, *Devonshire* and *Dilwara* took the Nigerian brigade, and they joined the Gold Coast Brigade at sea off the West African coast for the voyage around the Cape (including stops at Cape Town and Durban, early eye-openers for the

African soldiers). In a successful union of African troops from opposite sides of the continent, the 23rd (Nigerian) Brigade joined 21st (East African) Brigade to form the 11th (African) Division, and the 24th (Gold Coast) Brigade joined the 22nd (East African) Brigade to form the 12th (African) Division. Like other imperial units drawn to East Africa in anticipation of war with Italy, West African troops underwent intensive training in bush and desert conditions along the Kenya–Italian Somaliland border. The first West African unit into battle was the 1st Gold Coast Regiment, in action at El Wak on the Kenya-Italian Somaliland border in December 1940 alongside South Africans troops. During the ensuing offensive against Italian Somaliland the capital, Mogadishu, was taken by the 23rd (Nigerian) Brigade at the end of February 1941. With its capture the 11th (East African) Division was able to use it as a port for their move inland to Harar in Abyssinia. At the same time Lieutenant-General Cunningham landed a force at Berbera in conjunction with the British commander in Aden, and it fell to the 3rd Nigerian Regiment to pursue the routed garrison during the reoccupation of British Somaliland. When the Abyssinian capital, Addis Ababa, was captured in April 1941, the 1st Nigerian Regiment provided the guard of honour for the return of the Emperor, Haile Selassie.

With the East Africa campaign coming to a triumphant end, and Italian forces in the region routed, there was some urgency to return West African troops to their Home Command because of the threat of attack from Vichy territory against important bases such as Freetown, a threat that (though an attack did not come to pass) was real enough at the time. The four British West African colonies were exposed to attack from the large Vichy forces over the border, being encircled by hostile forces yet with their prime fighting troops stationed overseas. This sense of threat was a driving force in West African military policy for nearly two years, only ended by victory at Alamein in October 1942 and the success of Allied operations in North-West Africa in the following month. After these turning-points, the Chiefs of Staff considered the threat of invasion to have passed. It was therefore safe, they believed, again to denude British West Africa of its front-line troops in order to supplement the large imperial army facing the Japanese in Burma. Therefore the 81st and 82nd West African Divisions began forming in March 1943, thus beginning the service of nearly 80,000 West African infantrymen in the Burma campaign, where they fought extensively in the Arakan (building the 'West African Way' into it). They became the first unit to be supplied entirely by air and provided a brigade for Major-General Orde Wingate's Long-Range Penetration Force (the Chindits) that fought behind enemy lines (known as 'Wingate's WAFFs'. The use of West Africans was initially posited by Delhi-based planners of India Command, desperate to avoid a first-class British brigade being broken up to support what they considered to be the crackpot schemes of the upstart Wingate).

West Africa was an important strategic junction for convoys traversing the Atlantic from east to west and west to east (not just those sailing from America and Canada, but also those bringing food from South America to Britain), and for those travelling through the South Atlantic on the Cape route to or from areas like Australasia, the Middle East, the Persian Gulf and South Asia. It was also the nodal point on a supply route that delivered aircraft from America and Britain to the Middle East war theatre, as well as a stop-off for many American pilots as they transported themselves and their aircraft to Britain to join the build up of American forces preparing for D-Day. This made it one of the main imperial regions in which American influence grew during the war. Sir John Shuckburgh, governor-designate of Nigeria on the eve of war though retained as Permanent Under-Secretary at the Colonial Office, wrote that:

> [The] territories are of vital importance for the sea communications of the United Nations from America to Britain and the Middle East, India and the Far East, and of air communications from Britain across Central Africa to the Middle East and India. The seaports of Freetown, Takoradi and Lagos, and airports of Bathurst, Lagos and elsewhere are now communications centres of major importance to the United Nations, and as such are the seats of considerable British forces. In addition to Bathurst and Lagos, [there are] important airports at Accra and Takoradi, of which the former in the latter stages became the main airport in West Africa.[28]

Unlike East and North Africa, West Africa was not the scene of major fighting, though it did witness some minor military engagements. British forces unsuccessfully raided Dakar in September 1940 in an attempt to establish Free French control and prevent the valuable Senegalese port from being used by German submarines (though the battleship *Richelieu* was damaged).[29] General de Gaulle had established his headquarters at nearby Duala in the French Cameroons, with another headquarters at Carlton Gardens in London.*

It was essential for Britain's capacity to fight in Asia and the Middle East that it maintained control of the sea lanes of the South Atlantic and the Cape of Good Hope. This meant protecting the convoy base at Freetown and ensuring that Dakar did not become available for use by Axis vessels. Here, as in North-East Africa and the Indian Ocean, the Royal Navy was charged with the task of blockading Vichy territory, and South Atlantic Command was ordered to stop all maritime traffic between French West Africa and the outside world. The navy was aided by RAF bombers and flying boats stationed throughout British West Africa. Other military activity in the region took a more irregular form. In one notable campaign, Long Range Desert Group units from Libya and Free French forces from Chad crossed the Fezzan desert to raid Italian positions with the intention

---

* The Dakar raid was the backdrop for the bloody run ashore of Evelyn Waugh's supremely barbaric brigadier, Ritchie-Hook, in the *Sword of Honour* trilogy. Ritchie-Hook was modelled on Lieutenant-General Sir Adrian Carton de Wiart, renowned for his fighting spirit and appointed as Churchill's personal representative to Chiang Kai-shek in October 1943. Waugh's regiment had taken part in the Dakar raid.

of preventing enemy interference with the Allied air route from the Gold Coast to Egypt. In another minor military engagement in the region an SOE team raided Fernando Po, a small Spanish island off Nigeria's south-east coast. The SOE team had been using a Brixham trawler to hunt for U-boat hideouts in the Gulf of Guinea. In January 1942 they employed two tugs to raid the Spanish island and towed off three Axis merchant ships from the port of Santa Isabel. These included the *Duchessa d'Aosta*, an Italian liner of 8000 tons carrying £200,000 worth of cargo. Further down the West African coast, off Gabon, a Royal Navy sloop forced the surrender of the only Vichy submarine in the region during fighting between Vichy and Free French forces in late 1940.

Though there was no major fighting, British West Africa did find itself surrounded by hostile territories as a result of the fall of France, a strategic reverse that had not been bargained for in pre-war plans for the region's role in a future war. The result was that the War Office took over responsibility for the region's defence from the Colonial Office in June 1940, and West Africa Command (WAC) was immediately established. General Sir George Giffard, later to command all Allied land forces in Mountbatten's South East Asia Command, was sent to form GHQ West Africa at Achimota College near Accra in the Gold Coast in July 1940. WAC was responsible for recruiting, training, accommodating, supplying and coordinating the 200,000 soldiers drawn from the region's four British colonies, and for supervising the thousands of British and American military personnel that came to be based in West Africa. Expansion of the RWAFF was rapid: by October 1941 42,000 troops had been recruited, a figure that had risen to 92,000 a year later. Unified RAF and Royal Navy commands were established at Freetown, the major port of Sierra Leone and main convoy assembly port for West Africa.

Whilst the war was causing depletion in the ranks of colonial administrations throughout British West Africa, as district officers joined the armed forces, other European communities were expanding. Thousands of white soldiers, sailors, airmen and technicians arrived for tours of duty in the 'white man's grave' of yesteryear, and were billeted throughout British West Africa. On the British side, there were many RAF personnel, as well as three infantry battalions, sent to help Giffard in his work of raising a new African army. Immigrants were also needed to recruit, train and lead the ever-expanding African armed forces. The military tasks facing WAC led to the arrival of hundreds of new army officers, all destined to lead African troops. Most were British, but there were also drafts from Southern Rhodesia and 400 from Poland, recruited from the units of the Polish army standing idle in Britain at a time when there was a general shortage of British officers, given the army's active commitments in the Middle East and Asia. There were plenty of African volunteers for the expanding RWAFF, though turning them from raw recruits into effective military units required not only officers and NCOs, but also training facilities and equipment. Equipment was difficult to come by, as West Africa naturally depended on Britain for such war material, of which there was little to spare given the huge demands for military exports to support the Empire's war efforts in other regions and the restrictions caused by the general shipping shortage. Self-sufficiency drives were the order of the day.

Therefore WAC endeavoured to supply as many of its needs as possible from local sources, no mean task given that almost all manufactured articles such as cloth, building materials and machinery were usually imported, as well as food-stuffs required by the European soldiers and civilians. Nevertheless great progress was made. Supplies of khaki drill cloth were obtained from the Belgian Congo, and in all four British West African colonies the army established industries to provide building materials, as well as farms for the cultivation of food (the army, for example, establishing large piggeries in the Gold Coast's Northern Territories). Market gardens were opened and even an indigenous biltong-manufacturing plant was created. Its produce became an integral part of army rations once a sceptical General Giffard had consumed a palatable stew made with the dried meat whilst dining at Lord Swinton's residence. In providing the infra-structure and supplies required to support the massive militarization of West Africa, an immense amount of work devolved upon the four colonial govern-ments and their public works departments as they were called upon to feed, accommodate and furnish the greatly expanded armed forces recruited in the region, and the thousands of British and American military immigrants. In raising an army of 200,000 men one of General Giffard's major headaches was providing accommodation for them all. In a tropical climate canvas was not good enough, given the rainfall, so hutted camps had to be built all over West Africa, demanding prodigious amounts of timber and also stimulating a local furniture-making industry that was one of the many military-induced success stories of the West African economy at war.

West Africa became the hub of a strategic highway that took nearly 8000 aircraft from Britain and America to the Middle East. This drew tens of thousands of Africans into the employment of the British and American armed forces, as West Africa went through something of an industrial transformation as it was prepared for a new strategic role. A great chain of airfields had to be constructed, and public works, harbours, hospitals, rails, roads, camps, water supplies and oil installations built and maintained. Air Ministry records show that between August 1940 and June 1943 over 4500 British aircraft (mainly Blenheims, Hurri-canes and Spitfires) were assembled at Takoradi, having been delivered in crates, and ferried to the Middle East war theatre. Between January 1942 and the end of the operation in October 1944 2200 aircraft arrived from America and virtually all were ferried on to the Middle East. Between January 1942 and October 1943 about 1000 American aircraft reached West Africa (including 630 Baltimores, 171 Dakotas and ninety-one Hudsons), of which all but one hundred went to the Middle East. Between October 1943 and October 1944 a further 1227 aircraft were delivered to West Africa (including 469 Baltimores, 312 Marauders and 161 Venturas), all but 208 going on to the Middle East. (198 Dakotas were sent to

India, where the Dakota was the mainstay of Allied air transport to China and the Fourteenth Army fighting in Burma.)

These developments centred on the Takoradi Air Route, from the Gold Coast to Egypt, that had been pioneered as a civil air route by the British aviation company Imperial Airways in 1936. Its strategic potential was noted at the time, and when Italy entered the war in 1940 and made the Mediterranean supply route hazardous, it was decided to use the trans-Africa route to reinforce the Western Desert Air Force, in addition to the only alternative – the much longer supply route around the Cape. On 14 July 1940 an RAF advance party was sent to Takoradi, and a month later the main party of 350 airmen arrived. At first, BOAC navigators and aircraft were used to plan the air route, though it wasn't long before aircraft destined for the Middle East began to arrive. Six crated Blenheim bombers were delivered on 5 September 1940, and thirty Hurricanes landed from HMS *Argus* on the following day. What was to be a massive trans-African supply effort had been commenced.

In all, forty airfields and flying boat bases and landing grounds were developed in British West Africa (thirty of them in Nigeria) as this remarkable essay in imperial improvisation, which later became one of the many examples of successful Anglo-American war cooperation, was developed with speed and skill, and with the vital aid of African cooperation. An assembly depot was established at Takoradi, the hub of the whole exercise. Aircraft coming from America had already journeyed via Brazil and a mid-Atlantic stop-off on Ascension Island, where the British had permitted the construction of an American air base. All along the African transcontinental route colonial governments, including the Free French administration of Chad, collaborated with the RAF in developing airfields. As in so many other theatres, the 'Allies' were not just British and American but included a galaxy of people from the territories of Empire whose cooperation was essential at so many junctures. Such cooperation would have been beyond the purchase of Britain and America if it had had to be forced.

An agreement between Britain and America in the summer of 1941 saw America assume increasing responsibility for ferrying the aircraft across the South Atlantic to West Africa, and then on to the Middle East. As in the case of Iceland and Persia, this was an example of America – in this case before itself entering hostilities – aiding the British war effort by putting bodies on the ground in non-combat zones in order to release British personnel for duties closer to the fighting. The main object of the agreement was to release RAF pilots and crews for combat duties, and the work was undertaken by Pan-American Airways and its subsidiary carrier 'African'. By the end of 1941 American companies were operating five services weekly between Takoradi in the west and Khartoum in the east, stopping in between at Accra, Lagos and Kano. At the end of 1942 full control of Accra airport was handed over to the American Army, and it remained in charge for two years. The American Army also operated a passenger and freight service between Liberia, Khartoum and Cairo, via Accra and Kano, and regular services flew from America to Brazil to Ascension to Liberia and on to Britain via Marrakech in Morocco. As a result of all of the greatly increased air traffic, Accra became one of the busiest airports in the world, just as neighbouring Freetown became one of the busiest ports. The organization of the air service saw the arrival of many American personnel, mainly to Nigeria and the Gold Coast. The headquarters of American Army Forces in Central Africa was established at Accra, and the commanding general also controlled the African–Middle East wing of American operations in the Middle East and India. In August 1943 there were about 8000 American personnel in British West Africa, including 5000 at Accra Air Base Camp and 1200 at Kano in Northern Nigeria.

The RAF recruited 10,000 West Africans for ground duties on its base installations in the Gold Coast, Nigeria, Sierra Leone and the Gambia in the first few years of the war. A mission was sent from Britain in 1942 to examine how to make further use of West Africans, resulting in the formation of the West African Air Corps in January 1944, which had grown to number 5000 by the end of the year. It was initially put under a commandant attached to Army GHQ Achimota to maintain close contact with the army and the Resident Minister, but eventually it was placed under RAF Headquarters West Africa, which was in Freetown. RAF training schools were established at Takoradi and Oshodi near Lagos. As well as being an important base for air operations in support of the Middle East theatre, West Africa became a base for RAF units protecting Atlantic convoys and hunting for U-boats. Thus RAF Coastal Command maintained forces in West Africa, including the long-range Sunderland flying boats of No. 95 Squadron based at Freetown. In June 1941 No. 200 Squadron arrived in West Africa with its Lockheed Hudsons for anti-submarine patrol duties in the Atlantic.

In West Africa labour conscription was less widely employed than in East Africa, reflecting historic differences between British West Africa and imperial territories in the rest of tropical Africa (centred on the absence of significant white settler communities). In November 1942 117 out of 800 men found sleeping rough in the Gambian capital Bathurst were conscripted after failing to produce evidence of employment. In Sierra Leone a few hundred men were conscripted into the Pioneer Corps, and in Nigeria not more than 350 were conscripted into the armed forces. In the Gold Coast 3500 men from the Northern Territory were compulsorily enlisted into the infantry and about a thousand drivers and tradesmen were conscripted prior to 1942 when recruitment for this branch reverted to a voluntary basis. A major exception to the general West African policy of limited conscription was the Nigerian tin-mining industry. After the loss of the world's biggest producer, Malaya, the British government was anxious to maximize production from any other imperial source that existed. To this end nearly 100,000 Nigerians were conscripted to work the tin mining fields of the Jos plateau in central Nigeria, though this was eventually stopped in 1944 because the British authorities had concluded that conscription was proving less efficient than alternative methods of recruiting labour.

As elsewhere in the Empire, war gave a fillip to plans for greater regional cooperation and centralization of authority, and to the provision of regional
administrative and economic services. This process also affected the scattered
West Indian islands and British possessions in East Africa. In West Africa debates
about greater regional cooperation among the four British colonies preceded the
war. In December 1936 the Colonial Secretary in London had raised the issue, and
during the war there was even discussion of the appointment of a Governor-
General of West Africa. Such political centralization did not come to pass, but a
regional approach to economic and supply problems was forced by the war. The
West African Supply Centre (WASC) was formed in 1941 after a meeting of representatives from the region's four colonial governments (similar in aims to the
Middle East Supply Centre founded in Cairo in the same year). It was to coordinate production and import policy for the whole region and ensure an adequate
pool of experience and resources. There was an Import Branch, Production
Branch, Shipping Branch, Distribution Branch, Information Branch and Military
Liaison Branch, an extraordinary though typical example of the extent and
capacity of imperial planning and action brought on by the demands of war. To
gain the support of the merchant community, without which official plans would
founder, the Association of West African Merchants appointed representatives to
WASC. Without the support of the region's merchants, particularly the United
Africa Company, mobilization would not have been possible to anything like the
extent achieved. The UAC put its whole organization at the disposal of the Resident Minister West Africa. In a vast region with a scattered population it was
impossible to organize a rationing system like that in place in Britain, so merchant
firms were very important in organizing distribution and preventing petty traders
from overcharging. In October 1941 WASC approached one of the other major
regional creations thrown up by the war, the Eastern Supply Group Council, with
a view to obtaining supplies from India.

In April 1942 the Chiefs of Staff concluded that the arrangements for coordination between the military and civilian authorities in West Africa were
unsatisfactory, and that a military governor-general should be appointed, similar
to the appointment of Admiral Geoffrey Layton as Commander-in-Chief Ceylon
with supreme civil as well as military power in the colony. (Layton was the first
supreme allied commander of the war, with absolute authority over all military
and civilian personnel in his area of command.) The War Cabinet did not sanction this and decided instead on the innovation of a Cabinet-ranking Resident
Minister for West Africa, a ploy tried though not properly tested in South-East
Asia (Duff Cooper arrived shortly before the Japanese invasion of Malaya), and
also applied to the Middle East (starting with Oliver Lyttelton) and North Africa
(Harold Macmillan). After the proposal had received Cabinet approval in May
1942, Lord Swinton duly arrived in July to establish his headquarters at Achimota
College, moving in with the headquarters of General Sir George Giffard's West
Africa Command. His office was to provide top level coordination of the region's

variegated war effort, liaising with the region's civilian and military commanders and communicating directly with London, cutting delays and overcoming difficulties among the various civil and military headquarters as they all sought to pull in a war-winning direction. He was also to oversee relations between the various British and American organizations in West Africa, all trying to win the war though all ploughing their own furrows. It was a development that signalled the great importance of West Africa to the British imperial war effort, and Lord Swinton, an experienced high-level minister who had served as Colonial Secretary and Air Minister before the war, had his work cut out for him. To achieve his mission one of Swinton's first moves was to establish a War Council consisting of the four governors and the three service chiefs.

British West Africa pioneered schemes for the purchase of the agricultural produce of industries that war-time trade dislocation threatened to kill off, schemes that connected valuable products to the British government as a bulk purchaser. Such schemes enabled the British government to procure agricultural products at low prices, and producers did not have an alternative export market. This process began with the creation of the West African Cocoa Purchase Scheme, an innovation intended to support the West African cocoa industry at a time when the normal operations of the world market would have ruined it (the government bought cocoa knowing that the lack of shipping meant that it would have to be destroyed). It later became the West African Cocoa Control Board. In peacetime British West Africa produced about half of the world's cocoa beans. War cut off some of cocoa's most important markets, and Britain's cocoa requirements on their own fell far short of total annual production. So, in the interest of the colonies concerned, the British government guaranteed to buy the total crop, undertaking the risk of loss on resale. Extra capacity for the 1939–40 crop was found in the American and Canadian markets, and the remainder was purchased and destroyed with a deficit of £200,000. The board was established to centralize purchase and disposal, and in 1942 it expanded to take on copra, groundnuts and palm produce, in its final guise becoming known as the West African Produce Control Board. This body arranged for the steady and consistent buying and pricing of the crops in question, selling to the British Ministry of Food. In the case of minerals, the board's main customers were the Ministry of Supply and the Ministry of Aircraft Production. In East Africa and other imperial regions, the war obliged closer cooperation among neighbouring territories in terms of supplies and also in terms of transport, through, for example, the Regional Shipping Control Centre based in Lagos.

Bulk-purchasing schemes are commonly held to have cheated African producers of the full 'free market' price that their produce would otherwise have commanded. To what extent a 'free market' can be said to have existed at a time when merchant shipping was being sent to the bottom by the warships and submarines of powerful industrial nations, and when many erstwhile export markets were enemy territory and therefore closed to exports, is open to question.

Furthermore, it should not be forgotten that the export of these crops would not have been possible in the first place without the British Merchant Navy. Finally, it might be argued that a lower than 'free market' price was a fair exchange for the fact that in the early years of the war much of the produce of such African export industries had lost its export markets and was saved from ruin by British bulk purchasing. Bulk purchasing was hardly a wicked act, though it was indeed a fruit of Britain's imperial history and the global connections that it had forged, in a world where the industrial nations generally had the upper hand in relations with non-industrial ones.

Nigeria was Britain's most populous tropical African territory.[30] Its educated elite was large, vocal and influential, though beyond the coastal towns it was traditional chiefs and Muslim emirs, like the Sultan of Sokoto, who ran the country in cooperation with the colonial administration. The educated elite was able to seek general political advances for Nigeria as a reward for backing the British war effort. In most cases, West Africa's politically active elite were well aware of the evils of Nazism and the dire consequences of British defeat. As early as January 1939 the influential newspaper the *West African Pilot* had denounced German attitudes towards Africans. Political leaders and articulate journalists, like Nnamdi Azikiwe (later the first Governor-General of independent Nigeria), publicized British propaganda statements that talked of a war of 'freedom' against 'tyranny', and documents like the Atlantic Charter with its promises of self-determination were widely commented upon and their application to Africa demanded. Though this stance of not opposing the war effort but demanding self-government exasperated colonial officials (in a radio broadcast Governor Sir Bernard Bourdillon said that 'you don't reward a man for failing to cut his own throat'), it proved effective, and Nigerian nationalists were able successfully to back the war effort whilst constitutionally approaching their desire for a greater share of the political cake when hostilities ceased.

Recruits came forward for the great expansion of the RWAFF, which relied for the bulk of its manpower on Nigeria. The country's role as a strategic base required thousands of local recruits to work on expanding and operating harbour, airfield, road and rail facilities. This in turn led to a greater movement of people from one part of the country to another than was normal. Managing the transformation of Nigeria from a peace-time to a war-time footing meant that the colonial administration had to undertake a greatly increased workload. In the early stages of the war it was ill-equipped to perform these manifold tasks. The administration shrank in size as the armed forces absorbed young district officers, and many of those who remained were disheartened by their distance from active war fronts.[31] Secretariat and district officers' duties piled up, and leave was more difficult to obtain. This led to demoralization in the ranks, as well as to the increasing Africanization of the administration at the lower levels.

The military and naval commanders in West Africa had to prepare to defend the region against hostile forces in neighbouring Vichy territory. The Governor of Nigeria wooed the Governors of French Chad and Cameroon towards the Allied camp by holding out the prospect of much-needed imports, and secret discussions were held to try and persuade the French territories to join Britain. There was, for example, a liaison between Governor Sir Bernard Bourdillon and Felix Eboué, the Governor of Chad, the latter wanting to know how Nigeria could supply and defend Chad if it declared its support for de Gaulle and the Free French cause. The stance taken by Chad was particularly important for the British because Italy's entry into the war had brought that barren land an unlikely strategic significance, as it was the only French sub-Saharan African territory bordering Italian territory and an essential link in the chain of the Anglo-American strategic highway ferrying aircraft from the Gold Coast to Egypt. Lord Swinton, Britain's Resident Minister in West Africa, was received in full state when he visited Eboué, its capital, and cordial relations were established between the two parties.

Nigeria was able to supply neighbouring colonies with food. In March 1941 the governor reported that the production of staple food crops was sufficient to ensure an adequate supply for civil and military requirements, and a surplus for export to Sierra Leone and the Gold Coast (especially for military use). The colonial administration tried to ensure that all of Nigeria's people took an active part in the war effort, including the children, and schools assisted in the rubber production drive by collecting wild rubber. Nigerian rubber output increased from 2573 tons in 1937 to 9564 tons in 1944. Nigeria's coal, cocoa, columbite, groundnuts, tantalite and vegetable and palm oils were also much in demand. Its coal industry had always produced enough coal to supply the Nigerian railways and other local enterprises, as well as coastal trade to the Gold Coast. It now had to up production in order to cut the need for West African imports from British coalfields. Nigerian coal was thus needed to supply all British and French West African territories, as well as the Belgian Congo. The major conscription issue in West Africa was the need for labour for the tin mines of the Jos plateau following the loss of Malaya. In 1943 and 1944 the average conscription was 16,000 to 20,000 people, and the total number of labourers conscripted throughout the war was 92,703. Eighty-five per cent completed the full sixteen-week period of service, and the last conscripts were sent home in April 1944. As in so many other cases of 'war imperialism' around the Empire, this was an unpopular move both with the people involved and the British authorities obliged to make it, forced by the overriding demand for total effort in order to secure victory.

In all other spheres in which Nigerians were required to support the imperial war effort, methods other than naked conscription were employed to try and win willing participation, and this better reflected the British approach to Empire that existed by the 1940s. To stimulate support for the war effort throughout Nigeria, Governor Sir Bernard Bourdillon made regular radio broadcasts, an Information Office was created, and government officials toured the country to discuss and explain war issues. Pamphlets were published in all vernacular languages, even reprinting extracts from *Mein Kampf* in order to highlight the nature of the enemy and Hitler's fundamental racism. Prayers were held in churches and mosques and fund-raising drives were as ubiquitous here as elsewhere in the Empire. The Nigeria Relief Fund, for example, raised £210,000, and there was also a Win the War Fund. Over the course of the war, Nigeria's revenue rose from £6,113,000 to £13,200,000. In the same period, reflecting the growth of government caused by the war in Britain and mirrored in all its colonies, government expenditure rose from £6,499,000 in 1939–40 to £10,693,000 in 1945–46.

It would be a mistake to think that in this part of Africa, or any other, the war was a distant factor with a limited presence in peoples lives, or an abstract concept that many were unable to grasp. Tangible effects were experienced by all – the disappearance of a common household commodity, the death of a son in action or employment on a military base – and tended to focus the mind. Culturally, too, the war became a presence in peoples lives, through official propaganda, the media and educational and work environments. 'Hitler' became a bogeyman figure, his name invoked in order to cajole naughty children. With palm kernel production in great demand for the war effort, the government of Nigeria launched a 'Crack for Victory' campaign (each nut had to be cracked open). Whilst on one of his regular tours of West Africa, the Resident Minister, Lord Swinton, visited a village school in eastern Nigeria, where the children had composed a 'cracking song'. In the region lived a reviled breed of lizard. In the song the lizard was called 'Hitler', and the song had a refrain about cracking him on the head and winning the war.

The focus on the war and events beyond Nigeria's borders heightened political awareness. Political opinion and demands for political advance were stirred by organizations such as the Youth Movement and the West African Students' Union, and by the media, particularly through African-controlled newspapers like Nnamdi Azikiwe's *West African Pilot*. The nationalists pressured the colonial government to make a statement on the political future of Nigeria. Azikiwe published a pamphlet entitled *The Atlantic Charter and British West Africa* in which he proposed independence within fifteen years. Azikiwe and a delegation presented this proposal to the British government in London in 1943, and in the following year the West African Students' Union extracted confirmation from Deputy Prime Minister Clement Attlee that the Atlantic Charter applied to everyone.[32] In August 1944 the National Council of Nigeria and the Cameroons was established to provide a formal and organized nationalist force, and it became one of Nigeria's three major political parties in the post-war period. Nationalists were able to capitalize on war-time discontent caused by inflation, the rise in the cost of living and measures such as the fixing of prices paid for Nigeria's export crops. Food became more expensive as the large military forces based in Nigeria vied for supplies, and more people left agriculture to work in war-related sectors of the economy. To stop traders hoarding and then selling at large profits, local control boards were established. In the Southern Cameroons, a former German territory taken by the British at the Peace of Versailles and subsequently administered as part of Nigeria, there was grave concern about the sizeable German community, which outnumbered British residents by three to one. A Nazi Party branch existed before the outbreak of hostilities, and the Ministry of Information did its best to counter German propaganda. As soon as war broke out B Company of 3rd Battalion The Nigeria Regiment (the Nigerian part of the RWAFF) and a mortar detachment were sent to Victoria, in the Cameroons, to prevent a hostile landing and to support the police in controlling German workers on the banana plantation at Tiko. Many of the Cameroonian German residents were interned on their plantations.[33]

The Gold Coast contributed 65,000 men to the 200,000-strong military contingent from the four West African colonies, raised money for the war effort and increased exports of its major commodities, bauxite, diamonds, manganese and rubber.[34] The colony's bauxite industry was particularly valued, as British aircraft production demanded the maximum aluminium output from imperial sources. There were two deposits in the Gold Coast. One had to be linked to a railhead sixty miles away and the other, atop a 2500-foot mountain ridge, had to be connected by road to the railway. There were many other examples of major feats of war-related infrastructural work requiring the sweat of thousands of African brows and the organizational skill of British military and civilian personnel. As in Nigeria, the colony's African leaders were important in driving forward the war effort and translating a sense of urgency to their people, and traditional figures like the Ashantehene, the king of the Ashante people, proved to be key allies in mobilizing the colony.

The Gold Coast was the headquarters of West Africa Command, based at Achimota College near the capital Accra, one of Africa's elite educational establishments. In 1942 the newly-appointed Resident Minister, Lord Swinton, also established his base at the college, in order to be as close as possible to the military command centre. Whilst these two major headquarters, with responsibilities across all of British West Africa, moved in, the life of the college continued as normal. The Gold Coast had some pressing war-time problems because of the fact that it was surrounded by potentially hostile French colonies after the establishment of the Vichy regime. The territory was left undefended because the Gold Coast Regiment, along with the main fighting units of the RWAFF drawn from the other three colonies, had been sent to fight in the East Africa campaign, necessitating rapid further recruitment. The airport at Takoradi, as has been seen, became the portal to a major Allied trans-African supply line, known officially as the West African Reinforcement Route, delivering combat aircraft to the Middle East, and in relation to this work the port became a centre of America's military build up in the region. Other air bases in the Gold Coast provided facilities for RAF squadrons focused on the war against the U-boats.

Though it might seem barely credible today, the Gold Coast was considered a very important strategic asset in the war, and a French invasion was, for two full years, a planned-against prospect. What eventually put an end to this threat once and for all was the Allied invasion of North Africa, which speeded Vichy's African demise. Until that time, however, all sorts of overt and covert manoeuvrings had to be made to defend Britain's position in the colony, not least the creation of credible land forces. An elaborate propaganda and espionage network was also built up in the Gold Coast which specialized in anything from rumour-mongering to sabotage and smuggling. SOE was prominent in the Gold Coast's secret war, working closely with General de Gaulle's Free French intelligence. SOE also found in the West African colony yet another exotic setting for the turf war with other British secret and military organizations which characterized and dogged Britain's management of such initiatives from Accra to Cairo to Singapore, mirroring, of course, the fierce rivalries back in London. SOE pulled off a significant coup through its Gold Coast endeavours, however, when in early 1942 it masterminded the 'defection' of a significant part of the Gyaman tribe from the Vichy colony of the Ivory Coast across the border into the Gold Coast. In this the people were led by their king. The people were settled in the Wenchi district, and the Allies derived considerable propaganda value on behalf of the Free French cause. For this reason, and for others, the Gold Coast figured prominently in the Free French cause. It served as a base for the creation of de Gaulle's African army, as it was the place where French officers and African soldiers unwilling to settle with Vichy gathered and regrouped. SOE in West Africa concentrated on subverting Vichy territory and countering German espionage. Bribes were offered to Vichy Governors and German ciphers stolen from the consulate in Liberia. The Vichy ship *Gazcon* was suborned, and a rubber company formed as a front for operations against diamond smuggling. These operations involved the construction of a ship and port observation network in cooperation with SIS. SOE networks in Angola built intelligence networks and attempted to seize Axis shipping. One of the networks, S organization, was a group of pro-British Portuguese with key positions in the railways, army and the post office, who monitored Axis activity throughout the colony.

The war experience of Sierra Leone and the Gambia mirrored those of the two larger British West African colonies in most ways. Military bases were located in both colonies – for example, flying boat bases on the River Gambia and the major port of Freetown in Sierra Leone. The latter in particular experienced an increase in its European population. Both territories were called upon to provide soldiers for overseas and local service, and were subject to the economic effects of war and the efforts of charities like the Sierra Leone Bomber Fund to raise money. Sierra Leone was also a major source of industrial diamonds and a source of iron ore. It was also able to achieve food self-sufficiency and a surplus for export. The Gambia traditionally provided a company for the RWAFF, though war-time expansion meant that more recruits were found in order to push the Gambian contribution up above the battalion level. Gambians were employed to construct new air bases. In particular, the British military authorities responsible for West Africa's defence saw the need to make provisions in Gambia in the face of possible French aggression, as it would in that event become the frontier of hostilities. Airfield construction in Gambia also anticipated American requirements for refuelling bombers destined for the war in North Africa during the Allied invasion in late 1942. They were therefore built to a length that enabled them to accommodate the heaviest type of aircraft. At the time, the Americans politely declined the offer, believing that refuelling facilities in Dakar would prove adequate. In the event, they were not, and the Gambian facilities were extensively used. President Roosevelt himself thanked the British authorities for their foresight and the use of their bases. On their way home from the Casablanca conference in January 1943, Roosevelt and Harry Hopkins spent a day in Gambia's capital, Bathurst, with Lord Swinton.

Sierra Leone's star turn in the war was undoubtedly its utility as a major cog in the wheel of imperial and Allied global shipping management. Freetown was the headquarters for the Royal Navy and RAF in West Africa (the army command remained in the Gold Coast), a necessary dual occupation because of the importance of the naval and air forces working together to protect shipping and hunt enemy submarines. The navy was under the Commander-in-Chief South Atlantic, the RAF under the Air Officer Commanding West Africa. To equip Freetown for its role as a convoy assembly port and major operational naval base, the Royal Navy built a 'young Devonport' which at its peak employed over 25,000 Africans on construction work, building electricity plants, hutted camps, oil installations, slipways, wireless stations and workshops. A complete new water system was put in place to bring water from the hills. Not surprisingly, this concentration of labour led to a significant growth of trade union activity among the swollen, and invaluable, workforce.[35] Skilled labour in particular was in short supply, and the environment was right for unionized action to be pursued successfully.

Freetown's importance came as a result of geography and German war strategy. The west coast of Africa was intimately bound up with the Battle of the Atlantic, and many merchant vessels were sunk off Freetown. Before the fall of France, Freetown had been the point from which ships homeward bound from the Cape and beyond had sailed in convoy. With the closure of the Mediterranean route and the diversion of shipping around the Cape, Freetown became one of the most important ports on the convoy route to the East, used for refuelling and for gathering merchant ships and their Royal Navy escorts. The closure of the Mediterranean and the introduction of a shuttle service between Britain and America meant that the great majority of ships called at Freetown. Freetown's importance was therefore a result of its strategic position and also its natural harbour, which could accommodate up to 150 ships. Upwards of fifty ships a day began to enter the port and it was common to see seventy or eighty ships gathered in the great natural harbour. The arrival of such a huge number of ships required a great deal of labour and supply work to victual and fuel them. In 1941 an average of 1700 tons of water was required each day to service ships in Freetown. In Freetown and other West African ports oil installations were also constructed on a large scale. In order to limit social problems, crew members and the passengers on board troopships were seldom allowed ashore when their ships docked at Freetown. Sick and wounded sailors were, however, landed for treatment, and substitutes recruited from among African seamen were added to the Merchant Navy Reserve Pool. Sierra Leone was allowed to order more food because of the population increase caused by the presence of British soldiers and the crews of British warships and merchant ships in harbour, particularly of those British dietary staples beer, potatoes and tinned food.

Ships leaving and bound for Freetown were frequently attacked by U-boats, whether travelling between north and south or east and west. For example, on 12 June 1940 the *Llanarth* set out unescorted from Freetown for Falmouth carrying a cargo of 7980 tons of wheat from Melbourne, and was sunk by U-130. On 27 November 1940 the *Newton Pine*, which had left Buenos Aires for Sierra Leone carrying 1134 tons of wheat and barley for British ports, survived a submarine attack en route. The southern limit of the U-boat war at sea until 1941 was Freetown, where the trade routes diverged to Europe or America. Solitary raiders operated in the South Atlantic and Indian Ocean in those years, though thereafter submarine warfare spread. To counter the enemy submarines that deliberately congregated off the coast of West Africa, British naval forces were built up to the greatest strength possible. Broken enemy intelligence became vital, and flying boats and land-based aircraft were employed to patrol shipping lanes, extending cover over convoys, and to hunt for enemy vessels. Espionage and counter-espionage also became a feature as enemy agents sought to garner information about shipping routes and expected arrival times, which could then be relayed to the predators submerged at sea.

British Central Africa does not appear to have been as dramatically affected by the Second World War as other parts of Africa, and it is even less often encountered in accounts of the British war effort than its East and West African neighbours. The region was land-locked and far from the fighting. It was also partially insulated from imperial currents because of the self-governing autonomy granted the settlers of Southern Rhodesia in 1923 and because of the British government's concern to ensure that the production of the Northern Rhodesian copperbelt was unaffected by the encroachment of other war-time demands. Central Africa's remoteness from the imperial war effort was more apparent than real, however, the product of historical narratives that have chosen to focus on local themes in the region's history, including the African struggle against settler political and economic domination and the protracted emergence of Zimbabwe. As in the case of South Africa, the region's war history has remained underdeveloped because of the preoccupation of historians with the lively and troubled internal history of the region. This has encouraged a parochialism avoided in some other parts of the former Empire.

During the Second World War Central African governments were as concerned as their peers in India or New Zealand or West Africa to contribute in every way possible to the Empire's struggle. To this end Central Africa contributed bountiful raw materials and 60,000 soldiers, and the war had notable effects on the home front. Half of the men recruited into the armed forces were from Nyasaland, which continued to fulfil its traditional colonial role as a labour reserve for the two Rhodesias and a recruitment ground for the King's African Rifles. So linked was the protectorate to the KAR that it was generally considered to be in the East African camp, forming part of East Africa Command's responsibilities as well as contributing to East African military formations. Well-established labour migration patterns took Africans from across Central and Southern Africa to work on the Northern Rhodesian copperbelt, Southern Rhodesian tobacco farms, South African mineral mines and even the Tanganyikan gold mines. The labour demands of these industries for migrant labour, familiar to hundreds of thousands of people from across Southern and Central Africa, grew during the war. Also continuing a longer-term trend, immigrants from Mozambique crossed the border into Nyasaland to take up the jobs vacated by those working in neighbouring territories.

Northern Rhodesia had its own infantry regiment, which was expanded and deployed in the campaigns in East Africa, Madagascar and Burma. Some Southern Rhodesian settlers enlisted in the British Army and the RAF (Southern Rhodesians flew in the Battle of Britain), and the self-governing colony also provided officers for the RWAFF and the SCC. Settlers officered the territory's African infantry formation, the Rhodesia African Rifles, which served under the East African Division in Burma.[36] The Southern Rhodesia Armoured Car Regiment served with the 6th (South African) Armoured Division in Italy. Southern Rhodesian squadrons flew in the East Africa campaign and there were four exclusively Southern Rhodesian squadrons formed by the RAF. So, whilst perhaps on a lesser scale than territories like Nigeria and Kenya because of geography and the established labour demands of already-developed and valuable industries, Central Africa's war role reflected that of other territories of the British Empire.

Southern Rhodesia's British settlers ardently desired Dominion status, and wasted no opportunity to demonstrate loyalty to Britain. To this end its population mobilized for overseas service alongside British and Dominion fighting units, the home front was mobilized for war-related fund-raising and production, and the African population was prevailed upon to enlist or labour for the cause. At the start of the war Southern Rhodesian forces had joined imperial forces in the Middle East, or West and East African forces, rather than throwing in their lot with South Africa. This was because of South Africa's wavering as to whether it wanted to join the war on Britain's side or not. Once this had been conclusively resolved, however, it made geographic sense for the two territories to pool their resources, so on 27 October 1942 Southern Rhodesia Forces became linked to South Africa Command. The most visible result of this was that the Southern Rhodesian Armoured Car Regiment, successful participants in the East Africa campaign, became part of the South African 6th Division. After a return to their home colony, broken by a deployment to the Northern Rhodesian copperbelt to quell unrest, in November 1942 the regiment assembled at Gwelo and became a part of the South African forces. It proceeded to Pietermaritzburg, where it was issued with new uniforms, and in January 1943 embarked from Durban for the Middle East. There it was to serve for the remainder of the war in North Africa and Italy as part of the Eighth Army and the American Fifth Army. Other Southern Rhodesians saw service with the RAF in Britain. No. 266 Squadron, re-equipped with Typhoons in 1942 whilst based at Harrowbeer in Devon, was a Rhodesian squadron, as was No. 237. No. 44 (Bomber) Squadron, based at Dunholme Lodge near Lincoln, was also primarily Rhodesian in composition. In October 1939 400 Rhodesians had been sent to West Africa Command to help its rapid expansion, and the 1st Battalion The Rhodesia African Rifles was sent to fight in Burma. The battalion took the Congo route to join East Africa Command in late 1943, before being shipped to Ceylon. There it underwent training before deploying in Burma as part of the 22nd East African Brigade. Southern Rhodesians, like their New Zealand counterparts, served with distinction in the Long Range Desert Group from its inception to its disbandment. A team of Southern Rhodesian military surveyors even found themselves dispatched from Colombo to survey the Cocos–Keeling Islands prior to their development as a strategic base in the southern Indian Ocean.

Despite all of this military activity, elements of the settler community believed that the colony was not doing as much as it should for the imperial war effort, and made disparaging comparisons with the First World War. In late 1942 the Chief Recruiting Officer, partly to counter these claims and their discussion in the media, revealed that 16,529 Southern Rhodesians were serving, or had served, in military units during the war to date. This figure included 7759 European men, 1009 European women, 209 Coloureds and Indians, and 7552 Africans. This total did not include the members of the British South Africa Police. Aiming particularly at those elements of settler society that had made the comparison with the First World War effort, it was pointed out that this meant that 52 per cent of the European male population between the ages of eighteen and forty had, or were, serving.

The colony was playing its part in other ways as well. Arguably its most notable contribution was the part it played in the British Empire Air Training Scheme (BEATS). In October 1939 Southern Rhodesia offered to train and maintain personnel for three fighter squadrons, three pairs of Flying Training Schools (extended to four), and an Observer School, as part of BEATS. By 1943 the headquarters of a Training Group, a Combined School, a Flying Instructors School, a Training Wing, a Central Maintenance Unit, two Aircraft Repair Depots, a Disposal Depot and a Central Flying School Group had come into existence, collectively known as the Rhodesian Air Training Group. By the end of 1944 over 8600 men had passed through its doors and into RAF units all over the world. The Rhodesian Air Askari Corps was formed to defend the airfields and lines of communication associated with this significant contribution to the Empire's war effort.

The colony also supported thousands of internees, as it became, along with many other territories of the Empire and Commonwealth, a holding ground for enemy prisoners of war or displaced civilian populations. The colony's five internment camps housed over 5000 people by the start of 1943, a figure that remained constant for the rest of the war. The camps were located at Fort Victoria, Gatooma, Salisbury, Tanganyika and Umvuma. Southern Rhodesia's efforts on behalf of the RAF and in accommodating internees came at a cost. The government recorded a steady rise in expenditure throughout the war, from £297,933 in 1939–40 to £5,334,701 in 1943–44. The colony also played a part in the imperial production drive associated with the Eastern Group Supply Council following its foundation in Delhi in 1940, and the home population contributed hundreds of thousands of pounds to the ubiquitous British and imperial charities, particularly the Air Raid Distress Fund, the Duke of Gloucester's Fund for Prisoners of War, King George's Fund for Sailors, the Help for Britain Fund and the Red Cross.

During the war settler farmers found tobacco an increasingly profitable crop, and the production of base metals and secondary industry overtook gold in the economy. The export of tobacco was worth between two and three million pounds per annum during the war. The creation of BEATS facilities in Southern Rhodesia contributed to a massive expansion of the domestic market, and the interruption of overseas imports was also good for the development of Southern Rhodesian industries. This all led to a rapid growth in secondary industry and the spread of prosperity amongst the white farmers. Factories in Bulawayo and Salisbury produced practice bombs for the use of the local RAF trainees. Chrome, asbestos and coal were produced for export. Mines at Shabani and Mashaba produced asbestos at a rate of over 1,500,000 tons per annum, and chrome was produced at 600,000 tons per annum. The production of Southern Rhodesia's major colliery at Wankie rose from 1,231,864 tons in 1939 to 1,992,678 in 1945, as it was called upon to supply the copper mines of the Congo and Northern Rhodesia. War-time tax increases kept the profits from this dramatic rise in output static until the final year of the war (tax increased from around five shillings and sixpence in the pound before the war to fifteen shillings and seven pence in the pound in 1944). Southern Rhodesian coal was used in Southern Rhodesia itself, on the Northern Rhodesian copperbelt and the Congo's copperbelt in Katanga province, by regional railways and for export. This increase in output was achieved entirely through the employment of more African labour.[37] Southern Rhodesia's developed industrial sector also produced items for soldiers overseas. For the Eastern Group Supply Council, it produced 460,000 pairs of military boots and 198,475 items of brassware.

Southern Rhodesia was not food self-sufficient and so needed to increase production, especially of maize, of which there was a general shortage in Africa during the war. This was made even more important by the arrival of over 13,000 new, mainly European, mouths to feed. District Food Production Committee's were established to encourage Africans to produce more for their own consumption. As in Kenya, the settlers needed cheap African labour in order to take advantage of the opportunities presented by the war, and so pressed the government to introduce conscription. Conscription was particularly desirable from the settler standpoint because settlers had to compete for labour from Northern Rhodesia and Nyasaland, people over whom they had no jurisdiction. Many Africans were able to choose not to work for settlers, as they were not dependent on wage labour and could in many cases subsist from the yield of their own lands and herds. A turning-point in government policy was the failure of the 1941–42 maize crop, which led to the passing of the Compulsory Native Labour Act in August 1942. From then on the Food Production Committees were able to conscript labour, and by the end of 1942 their labour gangs, together with BEATS operations, employed 15,000 Africans.[38] As a result, the production of maize rose steadily from 1,160,000 bags in 1942 to 1,673,000 in 1944, and the production of groundnuts also increased significantly.

Northern Rhodesia's military contribution to the war was impressive, although it has been largely written out of the country's history in favour of a focus on copper-mining and white-black labour relations. Northern Rhodesian soldiers served in Somaliland, Madagascar, the Middle East and Burma, and on the home front civil labour conscription was introduced on a limited scale in order to secure domestic food supplies. A separate Northern Rhodesia Regiment (NRR) had existed for decades, led on the outbreak of war by Lieutenant-Colonel W. A. Dimoline (later to be the land commander in the Madagascar operation), at which point its total strength amounted to 430 men. The regiment's motto was 'Different in Race, Equal in Fidelity', an interesting perspective on a gone-forever period of Africa's history. In the years to come it was to see significant expansion as this land-locked African territory dispersed battalions far and wide across the African continent and beyond. The regiment would logically have been a part of the King's African Rifles (as were the troops in neighbouring Nyasaland). This was not the case because until 1924 Northern Rhodesia had not been ruled as a British colony but as a colony of the British South Africa Company.

As soon as war broke out the NRR was used to reinforce KAR troops in Tanganyika, as there was a general concern about the activities of its German settler population. Suspect or enemy aliens were also a concern in Northern

Rhodesia itself, and 1160 were interned by the Northern Rhodesia Police. Intelligence reports about Nazi attempts to gain the output of the copper mines in the neighbouring Katanga Province of the Belgian Congo caused NRR and Northern Rhodesia Volunteer Force troops to be stationed along the border, and a guard was mounted on the Victoria Falls Bridge. Such deployments in an African backwater appear strange and incongruous when set against the more familiar history of the Second World War. But they were far from irrelevant at a time when no one knew what the war's outcome would be, when war was a global phenomenon, and when, from the standpoint of Britain and its colonies, defeat was a very real prospect with easily-discerned consequences. In Northern Rhodesia's case, defeat would have meant an enemy takeover. In the meantime it made crystal clear sense to make dispositions to deny the Germans access to the region's copper, one of the many vital commodities upon which industrialized warfare depended, and to secure a region susceptible to enemy penetration.

During the war Northern Rhodesia became something of a staging post for forces travelling overland to the fighting fronts in East Africa, and the South African Air Force established itself at the aerodrome in Lusaka. Thousands of military vehicles and pieces of equipment traversed Northern Rhodesia's roads as they made their way from Southern Rhodesian and South African factories to the fighting fronts in the north. The East Africa campaign relied upon a very large logistical 'tail' to sustain the fighting units, and the Northern Rhodesian railhead was the departure point for a huge amount of arms, men and equipment that then made its way by lorry to Kenya and beyond, another excellent example of the use of Africa as a strategic highway. Like so many other parts of the Empire, the Europeans stationed in Northern Rhodesia felt impossibly cut off from the action, despite the colony's war effort and the service of some of its 20,000 strong European community in the armed forces and the local volunteer force. They were subject to the feeling that they were 'missing out' – not in the line of active service, not being bombed alongside relatives and missing out on the spice that danger brought to life at a time of war. It was easy to feel sidelined and pointless in a part of the world that middle- and upper middle-class Britons had been bred to view as a remote and parochial outpost. Arriving in Northern Rhodesia as a district officer in 1943, having been granted permission to leave the army (such was the shortage in district administrations across Africa caused by the war), Cyril Greenall was leapt upon for information by the members of the territory's white community – in Lusaka, at the Gymkhana Club and everywhere else he went – poeple who felt cut off from British visitors and from first-hand accounts of news and conditions back at home.[39]

In 1936 the then Major-General George Giffard had been appointed Inspector-General of British African armed forces. Following his 1937 tour of inspection he recommended to the Army Council and the Colonial Office that the Northern Rhodesia Regiment be modelled more closely on the KAR.[40] This led to the replacement of the permanent British cadre that had until then officered the regiment by officers and NCOs on secondment from the British Army. In August 1939 the regiment was formally designated the 1st Battalion The Northern Rhodesia Regiment. Thereupon began a notable expansion that was to see the NRR's strength rise to eight battalions. In addition, Northern Rhodesia raised its own support units – an Army Service Corps, Field Ambulance and Local Defence Force. Some Northern Rhodesian units specialized in providing defence and security away from the front line. The 96th Independent Garrison Company, for instance, for some time provided the guard for GHQ East Africa Command in Nairobi. Duties at home in aid of the civil power, of course, did not cease just because there was a war on, and in 1940 D Company 2NRR found itself confronted by thousands of protesting copperbelt workers during a strike. The troops had occasion to open fire on the rioters after tear gas and rifle butts had proved ineffective, killing seventeen. The expansion of the NRR required the development of recruitment propaganda and the assembly of recruitment road shows to tour the rural areas in an effort to tempt men to the colours.

As a result of Northern Rhodesia's self-reliance in terms of support units, the NRR was able to transport the 1st Battalion NRR using its own lorries and drivers as it made the 2000-mile trip to Nairobi to take part in the defence of East Africa. The war movements of NRR battalions illustrate the contribution made by African forces to British imperial campaigns, particularly in performing the more mundane, though nevertheless essential, non-combat tasks. On its road journey north the 1st Battalion NRR halted in Tanganyika for intensive training. Upon arrival in Kenya in February 1940 it took part in large-scale exercises in the North-West Frontier District. On 11 May the battalion embarked at Mombasa for Somaliland to reinforce the protectorate's garrison following General Wavell's decision to defend rather than evacuate the territory. There the battalion joined the West Brigade blocking Italian progress through the five-mile gap in the Tug Argan Mountains. The West Brigade was a composite imperial unit that comprised the 1st NRR, the 1st East African Light Battery, the 3/15th Punjab Regiment, the 2nd KAR and the Machine-Gun Company of the Somaliland Camel Corps. It fought a defensive battle alongside men of the Black Watch, but it was inevitable that the Italian attack would succeed, so the garrison was evacuated in good order. The 1st NRR was transported by lighters towed by tugs to ships waiting off the port of Berbera on 17 August 1940, some going aboard HMS *Chantalla* and some aboard a British India ship which they shared with the Black Watch (Lord Louis Mountbatten was one of the naval commanders involved in this evacuation). The exhausted soldiers were taken across the Gulf of Aden to the British protectorate of Aden. The battalion sustained heavy casualties during the defence of and retreat from British Somaliland, losing 140 men killed, wounded and captured, and was awarded five African Distinguished Conduct Medals, two Military Crosses, one Military Medal and one British Empire Medal.

In October 1940 the battalion left Aden and was transported to Mombasa. On its return to Kenya the battalion joined the 21st (East African) Brigade for the forthcoming offensives against Italian Somaliland and Abyssinia. The brigade was deployed in the area of Lake Rudolf in Northern Kenya (Lake Turkana today) as part of a deception plan aimed at preventing the Italians from transferring large numbers of troops into Jubaland, where the main British imperial advance was to be launched. The battalion later took part in a battle with Italian forces at Soroppa at the end of March 1941, and 'A' company was present at the triumphal entry of British imperial forces into Addis Ababa. The rest of the battalion was employed at the time in the Lake Rudolf area, attempting to maintain order as local tribes like the Turkana caused civil disorder, many armed with looted Italian weapons. A year later the 1st NRR sailed for Ceylon, still as part of the 21st (East African) Brigade. It later moved to Assam and took part in the 11th (East African) Division's advance down the Kabaw valley and on to the Chindwin river at the end of 1944, ending an extremely effective and valuable contribution to imperial military campaigns both in Africa and Asia.

Whilst the 1st NRR represented Northern Rhodesia in South Asia, the 2nd, 3rd and 4th Battalions had been formed into the 27th (Northern Rhodesia) Brigade, and took part in the Madagascar campaign. The 3rd Battalion was later sent to Burma to form part of the 22nd (East African) Brigade, alongside the 1st Battalion KAR and the 1st Rhodesia African Rifles. The 2nd Battalion was sent to Somaliland for garrison duties and the 4th Battalion joined the 31st (East African) Brigade and was also sent to Somaliland. The 5th Battalion NRR served in Somaliland and Palestine, the 6th in Somaliland, the 7th in Madagascar and the 8th in Abyssinia, all on garrison and internal security duties.

On the Northern Rhodesian home front the war had numerous manifestations, most obviously the recruitment of Air Raid Precaution personnel and the conscription of Europeans for the armed forces. A refugee camp for 4000 Poles was opened at the disused Bwana Mkubwa mine, and 1500 Italian prisoners of war arrived from the Middle East. Police reported a rise in break-ins and the theft of domestic items, as war-time shortage made mundane things like blankets and pots and pans harder to obtain than in peacetime. Northern Rhodesia experienced acute food shortages in late 1941 as a result of crop failure, and Governor Sir John Maybin reported that maize reserves were nearly exhausted. The British government in London, keen to ensure that nothing disrupted the colony's copper production, stepped in to scour Africa for possible sources of supply. Emergency imports were sought from neighbouring territories, but none were available. It was then that the British Ministry of Food agreed to release stocks from elsewhere in Africa if an exportable surplus could be found. Nigeria was, however, not in a position to help, there was no surplus in South Africa, and the entire crop of the Belgian Congo had already been bought by the governments of Northern and Southern Rhodesia but would not be available until the spring of 1942. In view of the urgent need, the Ministry of Food therefore agreed to release 10,000 tons in the Middle East already purchased from South Africa. To avoid repetition the following year, local production had to be increased. It was difficult to obtain the necessary labour, however, and, as the need to prepare the land in time for the planting season was urgent, the Colonial Secretary in London sanctioned labour conscription for up to two months. A scheme came into operation in February 1942 and 730 men were conscripted into a labour corps. In May 1944 an extra 600 men were recruited for farm work, and in 1945 a further thousand. Another example of the intrusiveness of war on the African home front, where all necessary official measures were taken to avoid any kind of instability, was the banning of the Watch Tower Society and the confiscation of its literature. There was a long history of antagonism in the colony between the administration and this African religious movement inspired by the teachings of the Watchtower Bible and Tract Society of Pennsylvania (the parent organization of the Jehovah's Witnesses), because it was by nature underground, unofficial and non-European, and therefore an easy target for accusations of sedition.

The expansion of the copper industry was Northern Rhodesia's most valuable contribution to the British imperial war effort, the copper being bought by the British government through bulk purchase agreements. Expansion of the copper industry meant that the colonial government's revenue in 1944 was three times greater than it had been a decade earlier, and output peaked in 1943 at 250,000 tons. By 1945 Northern Rhodesia was established as one of the world's major copper producers, accounting for about one eighth of the non-communist world's production. There were valuable spin-offs from copper-mining, including the development of underground mines at Broken Hill yielding rich new supplies of lead, vanadium (metal used in the manufacture of armoured plate) and zinc. Northern Rhodesia also produced cobalt and mica. The expansion of these industries kept the labour migrant market buoyant, and by 1943 there were 33,000 Africans working on the copperbelt, many from Nyasaland. War-time demands accelerated the trend away from circular rural-urban labour migration and towards a settled urban population, a trend that was to have significant effects in the post-war world. Some rural areas gained from the expansion of mining, especially the maize-growing areas along the railway line in the southern and central provinces, because new urban populations needed to be fed as war caused the internal market to expand.

The Nyasaland Protectorate achieved practical self-sufficiency in essential food-stuffs, and the war did not bring the 'extremes of severe poverty or embarrassing opulence experienced in some colonies'.[41] The demand for its main crops, tea and tobacco, was buoyant, and other exports like cotton were stimulated. In the five decades since the imposition of colonial rule in Central Africa, Nyasaland had developed as a supplier of labour to the more export-orientated, settler-developed economies of its neighbours, and many people from the protectorate were at any time to be found working on farms in Southern Rhodesia, on the copperbelt in Northern Rhodesia or in the mines of South Africa. In addition to the 103,000 people from Nyasaland working on the copperbelt in Northern Rhodesia, the KAR recruited 28,000 men from the Protectorate. As elsewhere in Africa, therefore, the government of Nyasaland was forced to walk the manpower tightrope in order to balance the needs of domestic agriculture with the demand of labour and military recruiters across the border and overseas. This led to acrimonious exchanges with the government of Southern Rhodesia, as the Nyasaland government wanted to suspend migration to that colony in order to meet its other manpower commitments. Unlike the other British colonies in East and Central Africa, there was no recruitment of military or civilian labour units in Nyasaland during the war. In 1939 the governor had promised the people that there would be no new Carrier Corps, the First World War military labour unit of ill repute, and this promise was adhered to. Despite recruitment problems for the KAR, Nyasaland did not resort to conscription. The South Africa and Southern Rhodesian governments exerted pressure to prevent compulsion, and officials agreed that, given the ease of crossing the border and finding work in those neighbouring countries, it would be futile anyway.

Military service was less popular in Nyasaland than in Kenya, partly because the recruiters had to compete with the familiar pull of migrant labour. By October 1940 Nyasaland had filled only 60 per cent of its KAR quota. The governor therefore imposed a temporary ban on labour migration, suspending the issue of identity certificates needed for work in Southern Rhodesia. This kind of control had to be used sparingly, however, and in 1942 labour recruitment companies and settlers threatened to employ Nyasa workers legally or not, forcing the East African governors conference to lower Nyasaland's KAR enlistment quota from 14,000 to 11,000 for the 1942 recruitment drive. These problems of labour migration and army quotas were familiar in Southern Africa too, where three British protectorates were brought to war alongside, and sometimes in spite of, the war effort of their overbearing neighbour, the Dominion of South Africa.

The four Southern African territories of the Empire and Commonwealth supported the British war effort vigorously. This harnessed the energy of an industrial powerhouse fielding sophisticated fighting forces, along with the impressive contributions of three poor rural territories which, among other things, furnished the British Army with tens of thousands of soldiers recruited by their traditional kings and chiefs for service with the Eighth Army. In rural Southern Africa, as in many other parts of the Empire and Commonwealth, vast distances, both physical and mental, were bridged to bring people untouched by the modern world into contact with new forms of global connection. As Mmatsheko Pilane of Mochudi village in eastern Botswana said of her husband when he left for the Middle East in 1941:

> When he left he said: 'My wife, remain with God. We are going to help with the war and we will be using bullets, and some of the bullets might kill us.' He was

going to fight Hitler, but I didn't know whether Hitler was a place or a country. I believe the Bakgatla were going to help Queen Victoria [confused with Queen Elizabeth] who was protecting us. The chiefs know what she helped the country with but the people didn't know anything. The chiefs couldn't tell us the secret between them and the Queen.[42]

Whilst her husband spent four years with the British Army in Egypt, Italy, Libya, Palestine and Syria, Mmatsheko Pilane remained in Mochudi. There, she was affected by the manifestations of war on the home front, as well as being connected to the war by the anxiety and manifold trials associated with wartime separation. She learned to use air mail letter cards in order to keep in touch with her husband. She joined the African Women's War Workers, a territory-wide network of women who knitted balaclavas, socks and gloves for the soldiers overseas. Along with the rest of her people, she was asked by the chief of the Bakgatla tribe to help cultivate 'war lands' in order to establish a communal grain reserve, given the food shortages that the war had caused. She was obliged to resist the advances of numerous other men who preyed on the wives and girlfriends of absent soldiers, attracted by their solitude as well as their army pay remittances. Even here, on the fringes of the Kalahari Desert, the Empire's war was the people's war.

In the annals of British imperial history the High Commission Territories – Basutoland, Swaziland and the Bechuanaland Protectorate – attract far less attention than almost any other area of British colonial endeavour on the African continent.[43] South Africa, whilst attracting plenty of historical attention – often for the wrong reasons – has a far less developed war history than any of the other Dominions, though the history of its fighting formations and industrial contribution is well covered.[44] The lack of adequate general coverage of South Africa's war effort, embracing the political, social, economic and military aspects, is due in part to the attention lavished on other aspects of its troubled history and the magnetic pull of the Anglo-Boer War of 1899–1902 as a research topic. Furthermore, many Afrikaners participated in the Second World War reluctantly, meaning that the country's war role was not so easily integrated into a celebratory version of South African history in the post-war years. Another cause of the relatively undeveloped state of South Africa's Second World War historiography is that only recently has the war effort of non-Europeans begun to receive the attention that it merits. This relative lack of historical literature firmly integrating the Second World War into the country's history has contributed to a sense that South Africa's war effort was more half-hearted than that of the other Dominions. The evidence, however, does little to support this conclusion.

The British Parliament created the Union of South Africa in 1910, a result of British victory in the Anglo-Boer War and fulfilment of the long-held British wish to unite the four settler territories of South Africa. The act brought together the Cape Colony, Natal and the former Boer republics of the Transvaal and the Orange Free State. South Africa became a Dominion in which a white minority, split between those of British and those of Dutch descent, ruled over a much larger population of Africans, Indians, Malays and people of mixed race. Opposition to participation in the war, however, did not come from the country's indigenous African inhabitants. The Dutch-speaking community (or Afrikaners, who after three hundred years of continuous settlement would have argued that they qualified for indigenous status by any standard) had historically resisted British encroachment and built a nationalist tradition centred on anti-British sentiment, a nationalism fully blooded in the tragedy of the Anglo-Boer War. South Africa was brought into the Second World War in the teeth of fierce resistance from Afrikaners who wanted no part in Britain's war. Many of them admired Germany, a country with which South Africa had enjoyed close links for half a century. Germany's racial and anti-communist stance was also widely admired. From the 1930s a significant Nazi-style movement flourished in South Africa, and there was more vociferous opposition to participation in the war than in any other Dominion, as there had been in the First World War, when a Boer rebellion greeted South Africa's entry into the conflict.[45]

Given the level of opposition to the war effort from within the Afrikaner community, and the need of the South African government to avoid aggravating the problem, the extent of South Africa's war effort was remarkable. South Africa underwent an industrial transformation and became a major supplier of arms and goods to Britain and other parts of the Empire, particularly as a producer of armaments, personal military kit and tinned and preserved foodstuffs, as well as its traditional agricultural and mineral exports. (South Africa's role as an arms exporter was particularly useful to Britain before American and Canadian production came fully on line in 1941.)[46] Its manufacturing industry developed rapidly as Britain fell away as a source of imported goods, necessitating South African import-substitution. Whilst contributing supplies to other parts of the Empire, South Africa was able to become fully self-sufficient, feeding and equipping the substantial infantry, armoured and air forces that it sent overseas to participate in the campaigns in East Africa, North Africa, Italy and Madagascar. The Dominion's location on the vital Cape sea route also ensured that it played an important strategic role in the war at sea, one which the Germans tried hard to diminish.[47]

In the 1930s South African participation in the event of war with Germany was considered crucial by the British government as it sought to ensure that a united Commonwealth front was maintained. South Africa was certainly a part of that Empire and Commonwealth, even if some Afrikaners wished that it was not. Like its sister Dominions, South Africa was dependent on Britain for defence and import and export markets, and it was culturally linked by the presence of a sizeable community of British stock and the home of millions of pounds worth of British assets. Britain's interests in South Africa were represented by a High Commissioner (the most senior African appointment in the British gubernatorial world). An important British naval base was maintained at Simonstown, imperial shipping routes called at other South African ports, notably Cape Town and Durban, and a British Military Mission oversaw military cooperation between the two Commonwealth partners. South Africa was home, however, to a large and politically powerful white community antipathetic to most things British and, as luck would have it, supportive of most things German (especially if they involved doing down the British). The Afrikaner problem in imperial affairs was as well known to the British as the Irish problem, and many South Africans applauded the stubborn neutrality of Ireland, a reluctant Dominion, during the war.

South Africa, with a population of fourteen million, was a regional power of growing significance, economically invaluable to the Empire and occupying a key strategic position. In the years immediately before the outbreak of war, however, the British government and Chiefs of Staff began to plan on the assumption that South Africa might stand aside in the event of war with Germany. During these last years of peace the National Party, anti-British and pro-republican, was gaining popular support (it came to power in 1948), and the Broederbond (Association of Brothers), a society of Afrikaners dedicated to uniting Afrikanerdom and freeing South Africa from the British, was extremely active. In 1938 another powerful organization championing Afrikaner unity had been formed in the aftermath of the successful celebrations of the Voortrekker centenary, called the Ossewa Brandwag (Oxwagon Sentinels). There were even suggestions that the German-born Defence Minister, Oswald Pirow, encouraged neutrality and kept the Union Defence Force (UDF) short of money and equipment to further the chances of South Africa remaining neutral in the event of war.

Given this situation, a sigh of enormous relief was audible in Westminster three days after hostilities commenced when a vote in the South African Parliament took the Dominion to war on Britain's side by a margin of eighty votes to sixty-seven (the vote was in favour of Jan Christian Smuts's amendment to Prime Minister J. M. B. Hertzog's neutrality motion). Hertzog resigned, and Smuts was asked to form a government. This delighted the British, for Smuts was an old friend and a member of the Imperial War Cabinet formed by Lloyd George in 1917 to prosecute the First World War. He was a respected imperial statesman and confidant of Churchill. He was the leader of moderate South African opinion, and argued that, despite the Briton-Boer antipathy of the past, even South Africa's Afrikaner community could, and indeed should, work within an imperial framework. This 'loyalty' did not come free, however, and Smuts immediately sought political benefits by reawakening South Africa's historic claim to the High Commission Territories, targeting Swaziland as a potential early gain. African leaders in the High Commission Territories resisted vigorously, and the British government ruled out discussion of the issue until after the war (it was partly because of this reactivated South African claim to their territory that the chiefs of the High Commission Territories were so keen to send men to war in order to make it more difficult for the British government to countenance transfer). Because South Africa went to war divided, conscription was from a political point of view considered too inflammatory to be used as a mobilization technique, and everything possible was done to isolate South Africa, and particularly its white population, from the economic privations of war in order to maintain domestic stability. Precautions were taken to avoid a repeat of the 1914 rebellion of Afrikaners opposed to participation in an imperial war. The government gathered the powers necessary to allow for internment without trial, and all firearms had to be surrendered.

South Africa went to war disarmed, a situation similar to that which prevailed in the other Dominions and territories of the British Empire and Commonwealth. In 1939 the Union Defence Force consisted of nearly 5500 men supported by a part-time Active Citizen Force of nearly 13,500. There was no capacity to defend ports and coastal cities, and there were no ocean-going naval vessels and only forty operational aircraft. Initially, therefore, only a very limited military role for South Africa was envisaged, concentrating on local defence and a small capability for operations elsewhere in Africa in support of British forces. (As in the First World War, South African governments relished the opportunity to pursue the Dominion's 'manifest destiny' in other parts of the continent.) South Africa's military capacities grew rapidly as the war unfolded and the extent of its contribution was revised upwards, as Britain stared defeat in the face and Smuts worried about the implications for South Africa's status if Axis forces triumphed in North and East Africa. A further burst of war-like preparation greeted the irruption of the Japanese menace into the Indian Ocean and the threat posed by enemy naval forces to South African ports and coastal waters.

The resulting expansion saw the UDF and its ancillary non-European corps grow to number 345,000 volunteer soldiers, and regiments like the Imperial Light Horse, Cape Town Rifles, Transvaal Scottish, Duke of Edinburgh's Own Rifles and Natal Carbineers saw service in East Africa, Madagascar, the Middle East and Southern Europe. Many South Africans served in the RAF. The forty aircraft that the South African Air Force (SAAF) could muster in 1939 had soared to 394 by the following year, and by 1945 the Dominion had twenty-eight active squadrons and its air power had played an important role in imperial campaigns in East Africa, Madagascar and the Middle East, particularly important at a time when the RAF's resources were stretched to breaking point. In all, 44,569 South Africans served in the SAAF. Further augmenting imperial air power, South Africa played a role second only to Canada in the British Empire Air Training Scheme (BEATS), preparing over 33,500 airmen for active service in the RAF and other Dominion air forces at facilities such as No. 23 Air Training School at Waterkloof, Pretoria, and No. 24 Bombing, Gunnery and Navigation School at Moffat. At sea, from virtual non-existence in 1939, the South African navy grew into an impressive local force with seventy-eight vessels, capable of performing escort, minesweeping and reconnaissance tasks in home waters. The South African Naval Force (SANF) contributed vessels to the Mediterranean Fleet, and took delivery from the Royal

Navy of the frigates HMSAS *Good Hope, Natal* and *Transvaal* in return for its provision of men for service aboard British warships. Over 9400 men served in the SANF.

The rapid expansion of the UDF required robust propaganda and publicity campaigns to tempt new recruits, particularly from the Afrikaner community, where it was widely argued that service in a surrogate British army in a British war was a betrayal of Afrikaner heritage. Some Dutch Reformed Church ministers even refused to allow soldiers in uniform to attend services. Therefore recruitment propaganda was designed to appeal to both English- and Afrikaans-speaking communities and the sense of 'armed patriotism' that informed South Africa's frontiersman identity, in order to call people to defend a threatened imperial as well as national citizenship.[48] Propaganda was sophisticated, employing print, posters and the South African Broadcasting Corporation. Recruitment centres were opened in all large towns, and the country was toured by military road shows and even a war train. Recruitment from among South Africa's white population was a great success, and 190,000 from an eligible adult male population of 570,000 joined up. This cut a hefty chunk out of the white labour force, providing new opportunities for non-Europeans in the factories as well as on the farms and in the mines.

The South African armed forces also recruited actively from among the country's non-European population, and successfully mobilized over 120,000 volunteers. A Directorate of Non-European Army Services was established to supervise the large-scale mobilization of Africans, Indian and Coloureds for military purposes.[49] The general South African policy was not to arm non-Europeans (though there were some exceptions) but to use them in support roles, within South Africa and overseas. Three separate non-European corps were formed in 1940 – the Cape Corps, the Indian and Malay Corps and the Native Labour Corps (which became the Native Military Corps – NMC). Some non-Europeans served alongside white troops, particularly when white units were 'diluted' by non-whites in order to release white troops for other duties without seriously diminishing the operational effectiveness of the unit in question. Thus for example, the 6th South African Brigade in June 1941 numbered 1072 non-Europeans in its total strength of 3783. Despite the general policy of keeping non-Europeans unarmed (because of the common settler fear that training subject peoples for violence would increase the likelihood of armed uprisings), 2000 men of the Cape Corps were given small-arms training and deployed as garrison troops and guards in South Africa and North Africa. By the end of 1943 the Cape Corps and the NMC had a combined strength of 92,000, 37 per cent of the men serving in the UDF. There were also 15,000–23,000 Africans working as casual labourers at military bases throughout the country.

As elsewhere in the Empire, motives for non-Europeans joining the armed forces varied. For some, poverty was a compelling reason to seek the relatively high wages and favourable conditions offered by military service, which also bore a certain measure of prestige. Many NMC recruits came from the particularly impoverished Northern Transvaal region. As in previous imperial conflicts (the Anglo-Boer War and the First World War), many Africans thought that supporting the war effort would further the chances of attaining political advancement, and volunteers were not difficult to find (hundreds of Africans crossed the border from Bechuanaland, Basutoland and Swaziland to join the NMC before those territories had formed their own military units). Some non-Europeans recognized the greater evil of Nazism, and hoped that in a war situation the South African government might be more prepared to compromise on its racial policies. For many others, recruitment road shows and displays proved irresistible, or the army's promise of good food and clothing.

South African forces would have taken to the field later if it had not been for the parlous state of Britain's war effort in 1940, and Smuts's fear that Axis success in North and East Africa would lead to a push south, and bring closer the possibility of bombing from Axis bases. In an early manifestation of its role as a major regional power, South African leaders had for decades considered East Africa as their own backyard, in the affairs of which the Union's voice needed to be heard. The smaller settler communities of Southern Rhodesia, Northern Rhodesia and Kenya viewed South Africa as a sympathetic uncle compared to Britain's disapproving parent, and South Africa was never shy of encouraging such communion and extending its own interests and perspectives. It was, in short, a regional power with interests far beyond its own borders. Whilst, on the one hand, there might be a great deal of admiration of the ways and aims of Nazi Germany, South African politicians were not looking for an aggressive new imperial power in Africa with which it might clash. Therefore South Africa was more than willing to devote forces to the East Africa campaign. South Africans then went on to form a major element in the Commonwealth fighting formations of the Eighth Army. The conquest of Abyssinia relied to a great extent on South African bush, desert and mountain proficiencies, supported by the ascendancy in the air of SAAF aircraft. The 1st (South African) Division was ready for deployment by July 1940, and was sent to Kenya to join other imperial units for the Abyssinian campaign. By December 1940 it was fighting alongside the Gold Coast Brigade and the Nigerian Brigade at the battle of El Wak. In March 1941 the division was moved to the Middle East, where it was joined in the desert by the 2nd (South African) Division in October 1941. For the campaigns in North African from June 1941, South Africa deployed two divisions and an air wing. In September 1941 there were 60,000 South African troops in Egypt (including 15,000 blacks). Disaster befell the 1st Division at Sidi Rezegh in November 1941 when Rommel captured over 3000 men of the 5th South African Brigade. Fresh disasters awaited South African forces, for at the fall of Tobruk in June 1942 two thirds of the 2nd Division were captured and over 10,700 South Africans went into captivity as part of the 33,000-strong garrison. In contrast the 7th (South African) Division landed at Diego Suarez to participate in the victorious and relatively bloodless

Madagascar campaign five days after Tobruk's capitulation. From February 1943 the 6th (South African) Armoured Division was raised. It landed at Taranto in April 1944 for service in the Italian campaign.

The South African Army became a key element of the Eighth Army's Order of Battle and won a reputation as glowing as that of its peer formations from Australia, Canada, India and New Zealand. In the East Africa and Madagascar campaigns South Africa provided the largest white contingent. South Africa's air force, engineering expertise and transport facilities were much relied upon by other imperial units in these theatres. In Kenya at the start of the East Africa campaign the East African brigades of the KAR were bereft of logistical support and their motor transport companies were without vehicles. The air arm consisted of four flights of the Kenya Auxiliary Air Force and a Rhodesian squadron equipped with outdated Hart light bombers. The injection of South African units transformed the logistical situation and beefed up the region's air cover. In May 1940 three SAAF squadrons arrived in Kenya with thirteen Junkers medium bombers, twenty-four Hartebeest close-support bombers, six Hurricane fighters, six Fury fighters and a Fairey Battle light bomber. Similarly, the South African Anti-Aircraft Brigade provided the only anti-aircraft cover available to defend the vital port of Mombasa, through which all imperial forces taking part in the campaign entered the theatre. In June 1940 the first in a series of convoys that were to deliver 13,000 South African manufactured vehicles to Kenya within the space of a year left Broken Hill in Northern Rhodesia. South Africa equipped thirty-three of its own and twenty-five East African motor transport companies, and it was South Africa's achievement to provide East Africa Command with the wheels for its campaign against the Italian forces. As well as this, and in addition to providing over a third of the infantry brigades taking part in the East Africa campaign, South Africa provided artillery units and its engineers played a major role in building roads and airfields in the region. Other South African skills were employed for specific tasks, notably expertise in underground work derived from its mining industry. A railway line from Egypt to Palestine terminated at Acre, and a line from Turkey terminated at Tripoli. The one hundred mile gap in between had to be closed to provide a continuous military supply line, and in November 1941 South Africa was asked to establish a specialist mining unit for the purpose. This gave birth to the 61st Tunnelling Company, Mines Engineering Brigade, South African Engineering Corps. Its 715 men tunnelled through the mountains of Syria, and then dug irrigation tunnels that brought 8000 acres of arable land into use along the coastal strip between Tyre and Saida.

For Britain the Cape of Good Hope had been a first-class strategic point since the Revolutionary and Napoleonic Wars, during the course of which it was occupied and eventually taken from its prostrate Dutch rulers because of its value as a base for revictualling and attacking shipping travelling between East and West. Thereupon the Cape became an unsurpassed strategic asset for Britain and the system of global trade, communications and rule that it developed. Warships, troopships and merchantmen going about the business of the British imperial world plied the Cape route. The Cape never lost its importance for shipping in war and peace, even with the opening of the Suez Canal, and it was clear that in times of war it would be called upon more and more as the Mediterranean–Suez route was threatened by enemy action. The Cape route, and South Africa's numerous ports, therefore played an important role in the Second World War in sustaining the contact between East and West without which Britain could not have supplied its forces in the Middle East, carried Lend-Lease goods to Russia via the Persian Gulf, or done anything to support imperial forces facing the Japanese in Asia and the Pacific. This was especially true during the three-year period in which the Mediterranean was closed to merchant shipping because of the threat of the Italian fleet, German U-boats and land-based Axis bombers. The Royal Navy had a naval base of its own at Simonstown, and South Africa's other ports, notably Cape Town and Durban, became assembly points for convoys and bases for the operations in South African waters of the Royal Navy and South Africa's own growing naval force as they escorted merchant ships, hunted enemy vessels, searched for mines and patrolled the Dominion's exposed coastlines. (Convoys were organized, for example, for ships proceeding from Durban to Mombasa, Madagascar, Mauritius and the Seychelles.) In 1942 Durban became the head-quarters and assembly point for the British imperial task force formed to invade Vichy Madagascar. South Africa, along with Ceylon, became an important repair and maintenance facility for warships and merchant vessels, repairing over 13,000 ships in its yards during the war (a particularly valuable role following the loss of Singapore). As in so many other cases, the infrastructure of Empire proved its worth during a time of global conflict.

When in January 1941 the Commander-in-Chief of the Mediterranean Fleet suspended convoys through the Mediterranean, the Cape became the main supply route for operations in the Middle East, Far East and Europe, and remained so for three years. Use of the Cape route added forty days to the average voyage from Britain to the Suez Canal, but without the Cape, and the seapower to guard and use the sea routes that linked it to the other major staging posts on the mariner's map of the world, there would have been no connection at all. The increase in traffic around the Cape was instant. Ocean-going merchant vessels calling at Cape Town and Durban increased from 2971 in 1939–40 to 4523 in 1942–43. When the Mediterranean was reopened to regular convoy traffic in 1943, the figure dropped to 2030 in 1943–44. The point is underlined more dramatically by figures recording the visit of naval vessels to Durban, a rise from fifteen in 1938 to 222 in 1943. Cape Town recorded a similar increase from ten in 1938–39 to 306 in 1942–43 (these figures do not include naval vessels visiting Simonstown). Over four hundred troop convoys carrying six million soldiers went through South African ports over the course of the war, many of them the 'WS' ('Winston's Specials') convoys that shunted British servicemen between Britain, the Middle East, South Asia and South-East Asia.

246   THE BRITISH EMPIRE AND THE SECOND WORLD WAR

The Germans recognized the significance of the Cape route and, together with Japanese forces, brought active hostilities to South African waters. The Germans, however, had difficulty operating in maritime zones far from their bases, making submarine warfare in the South Atlantic and Indian Ocean more difficult than it was in the North Atlantic. Similarly, without bases in the region, it was not possible to use the combination of naval and air power that so disrupted Allied shipping in the Mediterranean. But this was no reason for not trying, particularly as the success of the German war effort in the Western Desert and Southern Europe would be greatly enhanced by disruption of the 'WS' convoys that supplied the British imperial forces in the Middle East via the Cape. The Germans used surface raiders in the South Atlantic and Indian Ocean, and later sent U-boat packs to the region, both types of vessels being sustained by elusive supply ships that could skulk in the desolate Southern Ocean and meet up with their charges on a prearranged date in a prearranged quadrant. For the British imperial naval forces, it was like hunting for a needle in a haystack, though the hunt was prosecuted remorselessly, by destroyers and cruisers of the Eastern Fleet and South Atlantic Command, and by long-range flying boats that extended the patrol range of the ships to the most desolate banks and islands in the Atlantic and Indian Oceans. Squadrons of Catalina flying boats came to be based in South Africa to extend the search range of the hunters. These welcome additions to British–South African forces protecting convoys and hunting enemy vessels arrived from RAF squadrons in Britain, Ceylon and East Africa in February and March 1942, and were based at Durban, Port Elizabeth and St Lucia.

Germany's U-boat offensive in the Indian Ocean began in 1942, and a total of thirty-two U-boats operated in South African waters, as did a small number of Italian submarines (most of Italy's substantial submarine fleet concentrated on operations in the Mediterranean). South African waters, and such ports as Durban and Lourenço Marques in Portuguese East Africa, were threatened by (among others) the four U-boats of the Seahound group (which sank twenty ships totalling 122,716 tons) and the five U-boats of the Monsoon group. The Eisbär group sank fourteen ships off of the Cape during its first attack between 7–10 October 1942. A weakness in British shipping defence in this region was the absence of a regular convoy system. Due to a dearth of escort vessels, lack of sufficient escort and anti-submarine vessels bedevilled the Eastern Fleet (based on Ceylon and Kenya) and the South Atlantic Station (based on Freetown and South Africa). Between October and December 1942 only the most important ships in Cape waters were escorted, and all losses occurred among ships independently routed. Given the lack of corvettes, trawlers or destroyers to escort merchant vessels, the principal defence measures were air patrols and evasive routing. The Commander-in-Chief South Atlantic Station (whose responsibilities extended to include the Royal Navy's Africa Station) cited the handicaps faced by the naval forces in South Africa that were attempting to protect the merchantmen: insufficient warning, limited air cover, and the fact that his only available escorts were destroyers on loan from the Eastern Fleet (never exceeding six in number) and an average of five corvettes. In December 1942 the destroyers of the Eastern Fleet were recalled and only six corvettes and a single anti-submarine trawler remained in South Africa. A lull in submarine activity for two months from December 1942, however, gave the South Atlantic Station time to overhaul the Cape region's anti-submarine defences. On Christmas Eve four Royal Navy escort trawlers arrived, the vanguard of a group of eighteen which had been loaned to America earlier in 1942 when German U-boats had begun to enjoy great success in sinking unescorted merchant vessels off the east coast.

Japan's entry into the war and its run of stunning victories against the Allied powers in the East recharged the naval importance of South Africa, exposed it to a new and deadlier threat, and accelerated the development of South Africa's own naval resources. These were designed to work in tandem with the Royal Navy and relieve it of some of its responsibilities in the Dominion's own territorial waters. Japanese submarines joined those of the Axis in operating in the region, particularly favouring the Mozambique Channel as a hunting ground and using the aircraft carried by their larger I-boats to survey the coastline and ports of South Africa. Given Japan's successes since entering the war, a major thrust west-wards by the Imperial Japanese Navy was a distinct possibility foreseen by political and military leaders in South Africa and Britain. There was also the prospect of the Vichy governor of Madagascar permitting the Japanese to use the island's bases, as had happened in French Indo-China. The threat of Japanese invasion was taken seriously, and barbed wire and crocodiles' teeth defences appeared on South African beaches. The government even planned to arm Africans, should landings take place. Port defences were augmented by the installation of radar and anti-aircraft guns.

The threat posed to South Africa's home security by Japanese expansion caused people to look outwards, and some South Africans began to realize that their country was an Indian Ocean power as well as an African one. Smuts realized that a Japanese occupation of Madagascar would threaten South Africa with attack and cause Durban to become a major base for British operations. He therefore encouraged Churchill to invade the Vichy island as soon as possible. South African forces subsequently played a central role in the imperial invasion of Madagascar in May 1942 (the man in charge of the naval component of Operation Ironclad was himself a South African, Rear-Admiral Neville Syfret, commander of the Gibraltar-based Force H which provided most of the invasion fleet's firepower). The Japanese defeat at Midway the following month, together with the manifold strategic priorities keeping Japanese forces busy much further east, meant that the threat to South Africa subsided almost as quickly as it had arisen, though this was far from clear, even to those with access to the best intelligence, at the time.

The coastal waters of South Africa, and the wider bounds of the western Indian Ocean and South Atlantic, were active fronts in the war at sea, and many men lost their lives. On 22 July 1943, for example, the *Cornish City*, loaded with 9600 tons of coal, joined convoy DN53 bound from Durban to Aden. The convoy of four merchant vessels was escorted by two armed trawlers of the SANF, though they were unable to prevent the *Cornish City* from being attacked and sunk by a U-boat. The survivors were picked from the water by the destroyer HMS *Denizen* and taken to Port Louis in Mauritius. Within a thousand mile radius of the South African coast Axis raiders captured or sank twenty Allied ships amounting to 125,000 tons, and U-boats captured or sank 133 merchant ships amounting to 750,000 tons. Of these ships 117 were sailing independently and fifteen in convoy. The Dutch submarine depot ship *Colombia* was also sunk and the destroyer depot ship HMS *Hecla* seriously damaged. *Hecla* was a new ship, launched on Clyde-bank in March 1940. After service in Iceland, she was on her way around the Cape in order to join the Eastern Fleet in April 1942, a matter of days after the raids on Ceylon that had sunk many of its ships. The German minelayer *Doggerbank* had recently laid eighty mines off Cape Agulhas (the southernmost point of South Africa), and it was one of these that *Hecla* struck, exploding beneath her huge workshop and storeroom. Twenty-four men were killed and 112 wounded. She was taken in tow by the cruiser HMS *Gambia* and, with the SANF minesweepers *Southern Barrier* and *Terje* going on ahead, taken to Simonstown to be laid up in dry dock. Here she remained until September 1942, when she became operational again. It was only a matter of two months, however, before the unfortunate *Hecla* was sunk by a German U-boat off North Africa during Operation Torch. 279 of the 847 men on board perished. In November 1942 the *Nova Scotia* was sunk by a submarine near Durban, with a hundred South African troops and 800 Italian prisoners of war on board. 750 men, including 91 South Africans, were killed, and over one hundred bodies were washed up on the beach at Durban. For their part, South African forces attempted to seek and destroy enemy vessels in South African waters, as when a SAAF Junkers bomber disabled the German liner *Watussi* off the South African coast in late 1941.

Despite their successes in South African waters, however, the U-boat command decided in August 1943 that their operations in South Atlantic waters did not pay high enough returns. In eleven months 102 ships had been sunk off the South African coast for the loss of only two submarines, but even this return was considered uneconomic. Local anti-submarine measures were improving, and the success of Allied operations in North Africa had reopened the Mediterranean and lessened the strategic significance of the Cape route. Italian naval power in the Indian Ocean had also been erased, forces were increasingly available to escort convoys on the route connecting Durban, Mombasa, Aden, Bombay and Colombo, and strong air and sea patrols covered focal areas. Finally, U-boats were being more successfully hunted by British forces, with new hunter-killer groups formed in the Indian Ocean, as were their supply ships. Of the ten 740-ton submarines of the Monsoon group dispatched to the Indian Ocean in mid-1943, only five reached the region. Still, U-boats remained a menace.

When the *Dahomian* was sunk in South African waters late in the war, Cape Town–Durban convoys were immediately reintroduced, and the 3rd and 4th Escort Groups withdrawn from the Mozambique Channel to cover them. Though the submarine sinkings in South African waters did not account for a large share of the world's total, the strategic significance of the Cape meant that the menace was serious. For over three years the Cape route was the only link between the eastern and the western territories of the British Empire and the crucial highway for troops and equipment moving to the war fronts in the Middle East and Burma.

The South African Naval Service had been founded in 1922, though it was given little chance to grow in the inter-war climate of disarmament and economic depression. In 1939 its strength stood at a mere five officers and ratings. Larger and more active was the British Royal Naval Volunteer Reserve (South Africa) – (RNVR-SA) – based at Simonstown under Admiralty command. The South African government permitted the RNVR-SA to recruit South Africans for both shore and sea service. At the start of the war about two hundred South African volunteers were used to crew numerous British Armed Merchant Cruisers (AMC) and Defensively Equipped Merchant Ships (DEMS), and others were recruited for shore duties, including work with the Examination Service and Port War Signals stations that were an essential element in a port's ability to identify vessels entering port and communicate with them. The personnel of these organizations would report their findings to the vessels sent to examine newly-arrived ships, and to the coastal batteries cautiously tracking their approach. (Similar arrangements were in place at many other ports of the Empire and Commonwealth, including Hobart in Tasmania and Port Louis in Mauritius.)

Smuts was anxious to relieve the burden on the Royal Navy in South African waters as much as possible, and to develop South Africa's capacity to play more of a role in policing its waters and defending its ports. A retired British admiral was therefore given the task of forming a new force, the Seaward Defence Force (SDF), established in November 1940 (known to the wags as the 'Seaweed Defence Force'). Recruitment for the new force was undertaken and some men from the RNVR-SA were transferred to form its core. They served aboard requisitioned and converted fishing trawlers and whalers which were used for minesweeping, anti-submarine work and escort duties. After the 1939–40 whaling season, for example, the whaling fleet was taken over by the government for military purposes, and by the end of 1939 fifteen minesweepers were available. By the end of 1941 the SDF numbered 1232 men aboard twenty-four minesweepers and eight anti-submarine vessels.

The SDF relieved the Royal Navy of much of the responsibility for shore-based work and minesweeping and anti-submarine patrols in South African waters. It also maintained a base at Walvis Bay in South African-controlled South-West Africa (ships bound for the east – for India, Australia and the Middle East – assembled here). South African anti-submarine ships also accompanied small convoys sailing to the Seychelles, Mauritius and Madagascar. The converted whalers of the SDF were better than the coal-burning trawlers of the Royal Navy for escort work. In May 1940 the SDF began a major sweep of a minefield off Cape Agulhas laid by the German raider *Atlantis*, and in November 1940 it was requested by the Royal Navy to supply anti-submarine vessels for the Mediterranean Fleet. This took the 22nd Anti-Submarine Group (four converted whalers) to Alexandria in early 1941, where they immediately began sweeping the coastline and escorting convoys in the Tobruk area (where one was lost in February). The Admiralty then requested eight SDF minesweepers, which became the 166th and 167th Minesweeping Flotillas, working primarily off the Libyan coast. The SDF also supported the Royal Navy in operations, such as Kedgeree and Bellringer, to intercept Vichy convoys, and the captured vessels were taken to South African ports as prizes. In August 1942 the Admiralty approved the amalgamation of the SDF and the RNVR-SA to form the South African Naval Force (SANF). Thus, as in so many other parts of the Empire, the war had created something – in this case a South African Navy – out of virtually nothing.

Larger ships were added to the SANF's minesweepers, trawlers, and corvettes as the war progressed. In return for providing 3600 recruits for the Royal Navy, South Africa was permanently loaned three Loch class anti-submarine frigates (HMSAS *Good Hope, Natal* and *Transvaal*). As was the case with the other Dominions, as well as manning their own vessels, many South Africans served aboard Royal Navy vessels all over the world. About 120 South Africans died whilst serving with the Royal Navy, going down with HMS *Barham, Cornwall, Dorsetshire, Gloucester, Hecla, Hermes, Hollyhock* and *Neptune*. By the end of the war the SANF numbered over 8000 officers and ratings, of which nearly 3000 were on secondment in the Royal Navy.

The South African home front was deeply affected by the war. Visible manifestations were manifold – uniforms on the streets, warships in the harbours and gun emplacements on the coastline. There was also the presence of tens of thousands of Italian prisoners of war, as the hundreds of thousands captured in the early campaigns of the African war were dispersed and put to work in Britain and the Dominions. Women were recruited into military units such as the Women's Auxiliary Naval Service (numbering nearly 300), and others went to the Middle East for clerical employment. Over 65,000 served in the South African Women's Auxiliary Service, and thousands more in the Military Nursing Service. There was strong support on the home front for political movements with extreme right-wing and anti-war leanings. The Ossewa Brandwag (OB) had been established in 1938 to defend Afrikaner culture, and became a Nazi-supporting and paramilitary organizations that rejected participation in another British war.[50] It numbered 300–400,000 by the outbreak of war. Nazi-style uniforms, paramilitary formations and association with firearms and rifle clubs featured strongly in the OB's structure. With such widespread support it was a potential threat to the

Smuts's government, especially as it undertook acts of sabotage and aided German internees to escape (this particularly was a role performed by an elite organization within the OB called the Stormjaers). Cutting telegraph wires, interfering with railway lines and destroying post offices were means of drawing forces away from the war effort in order to guard strategic positions across the country. The police were even implicated in some acts of sabotage. The German Abwehr (the Wehrmacht's intelligence organization) attempted to aid the OB to foster an uprising through the use of agents and wireless equipment, and in early 1940 the Germans made an attempt to use National Party leaders to secure South Africa's withdrawal from the war. As a reward, in the event of victory, Germany would permit the Union to take the three High Commission Territories and Southern Rhodesia. In June 1942 the Nationalist Party leader and post-war Prime Minister, Dr Daniel Malan, publicly asked the Germans and Italians what they would plan to do with South Africa if it switched to a policy of neutrality. War-related intelligence was transmitted from South Africa to the German Consul-General in Lourenço Marques in Portuguese East Africa. Through reading his telegraphs, the British knew that the Italian Consul in Lourenço Marques was also helping gather intelligence and maintaining contact with well-placed people in Pretoria. Some agents were interned, as were about 2000 of the OB's members. The OB was adept, however, at getting internees released and then funnelling them to neutral Portuguese East Africa. The organization's appeal waned significantly in the last years of the war as Germany's chances of success diminished perceptibly. Thus it was a European nationalist movement that posed the main internal threat to South Africa's war effort. African discontent was not a major threat to the war effort, although rumours of Japanese invasion in 1942 prompted some interest in millenarian movements promising freedom from white rule. In 1943–44 the communists organized mass protests against the pass-laws that restricted African movement from the reserves to the towns, and in 1944 one of the first major bus boycotts was launched in Alexandria township north of Johannesburg. The African National Congress revived in the late 1930s though it did not notably enter the political arena for a decade. White concerns about the mass movement of Africans to urban areas, accelerated by the Dominion's war effort, were harnessed for electoral purposes by the Nationalist Party and used to criticize Smuts's 'dangerous' liberality.

The presence of anti-war elements in South Africa and of enemy agents in the region led SOE to take an interest in South Africa. An SOE organization had been established in Portuguese East Africa in early 1942, to counter enemy agents collecting intelligence on British shipping movements and communicating by radio link with Berlin, to counter the German threat to the Rand, and to break a diamond-smuggling ring. Germany saw South Africa as the best target for destabilization within the Empire and Commonwealth. From 1939 Smuts ensured that money was available to build an intelligence capability for the UDF, creating a Directorate of Intelligence responsible to the General Staff in December 1939, in part because he feared the tried and tested German method of conquest from within, operating with sympathetic elements in the security services and government (where there were many OB sympathizers), causing unrest in the mines and courting South Africa's burgeoning right-wing political organizations. Britain welcomed South Africa's connection to the imperial intelligence network and sent MI5 and MI6 agents to the British Military Mission in Pretoria in 1941.

On the industrial home front, South Africa was one of the Empire's power houses, experiencing industrial transformation and growing economic prosperity. Gold and diamonds were more in demand than ever, and there were chromium, nickel, tungsten and vanadium reserves to be exploited. South Africa possessed specialized engineering skills because of the mining industry, a sophisticated transport infrastructure, and an industrial base that supported large corporations like ESCOM (coal and electricity) and ISCOR (Iron and Steel Corporation). Industrial growth was impressive. Coal exports rose from about 950,000 tons in 1940 to 4,200,000 tons in 1945. The Union's industrial output doubled during the course of the war, with expansion in the mining, steel, textiles, chemical and armament industries to the fore. As in Australia, in 1942 manufacturing industry overtook mining and agriculture's contribution to gross national product, though gold production continued to drive the economy. For use by its own armed forces and for export South Africa produced six million infantry blankets, twelve million pairs of boots and shoes and 6000 armoured cars. Companies like African Explosives and Industries Ltd produced 500,000 twenty five-pounder heavy shells, 500,000 anti-tank land mines, twelve million rounds of small-arms ammunition, 11,000 three-inch mortar shells, five million grenades, two million steel helmets, barges, aircraft, tyres and cables. South Africa also produced motor launches for the SANF and Royal Navy, some of which saw service with South East Asia Command.

In order to achieve this massive industrial and manufacturing leap forward, an Industrial Development Corporation was established, as was a Central Organization for Technical Training. In 1941–42 the industrial workforce rose from 124,000 to an astonishing 413,000. This deepened South Africa's dependence on African labour from colonies further north, as local Africans moved into better-paid factory work in the towns. The black labour force in new industries expanded by 74 per cent and the white labour force by 21 per cent. This led to a growth in the Dominion's consumer market, and to the expansion of the cities at the heart of mining and industrial endeavour. Given this massive expansion and the concomitant movement of people, white control of African urbanization decreased, pass-laws were relaxed to meet the need for workers, and 'illegal' squatter towns developed on the outskirts of major cities. The government was so concerned about strikes on the part of this new and growing black labour force that the price of key foodstuffs was pegged. The expansion of the consumer market made further demands on South African industry, as did the expansion of its industrial base, because manufactured imports from Britain were declining given British industry's concentration on war production. South Africa was one of the main founder-members of the Eastern Group Supply Council (EGSC), created to relieve Britain of some of the burden of maintaining the fighting front in the Middle East. The Delhi meeting in 1940 that created the EGSC represented a historic departure for South Africa, as it was asked to turn its industry to the supply not just of its own forces but those of its Commonwealth allies. As a sacrifice for the general good, it was agreed that South Africa would receive raw material supplies only after the needs of India and Australia, both closer to the fighting fronts, had been satisfied.

South African food production greatly increased during the war, particularly for export to Britain. 28,000 tons of tinned fruit and 25,000 tons of jam arrived on British tables from South Africa's food processing industry. Meat production increased as the demand for essential foodstuffs became insatiable. This meant that the Union dropped its protective weight restrictions on imported cattle, which had a regional knock-on effect by allowing the cattle industry of neighbouring territories like Bechuanaland to experience something of a boom. Apart from meat, other parts of the cattle industry benefited from war-time demand. Britain ceased to require raw hides from South Africa, so the Dominion started to produce its own finished products in the form of leather equipment items and military boots (many of which found their way to Russia via the Persian Gulf). South Africa's textile industry turned out uniforms, clothing and blankets, and overall South African factories produced 34,250,000 pieces of personal equipment.

South Africa benefited economically from the war, and many of its people prospered because of industrial expansion. Britain sought to make its sterling area connection with South Africa more profitable through a series of war-time and post-war bargains in which British willingness to purchase the Dominion's agricultural goods and provide capital goods to the gold-mining industry were used as bargaining counters. As a result Smuts's government agreed to increase the amount of gold available to Britain. Over the course of the war South Africa's gold reserves increased by £150 million, its overseas debts were reduced by over £70 million and its sterling balances grew by £30 million.[51]

The strength of Afrikaner nationalist opposition to participation in the imperial war effort, it has been suggested, probably reduced South Africa's capacity to free itself from economic dependence on Britain. Generally people in South Africa did not undergo the level of economic hardship experienced in Britain and other parts of the Empire, particularly the Dominion's white population. Domestic consumption in South Africa was less restricted than in almost any other part of the Empire. This was because Smuts was unwilling to impose greater austerity or higher levels of taxation and further incite opposition to the war effort and his government. Therefore levels of exchange reserves, domestic savings and even industrial production were smaller than they might have been, had the electorate been more committed to the war.[52] For its part, Britain was prepared to go to great lengths to keep South Africa in the war. It guaranteed to buy almost all of its primary products, so there was no need for the Dominion to start expanding its domestic market in order to compensate for the loss of export markets.

In another respect the war demonstrated Britain's continuing power to shape South African affairs. The diamond industry that had first made Cecil Rhodes rich in the late nineteenth century was still booming at the time of the Second World War. The British government in the 1930s was well aware of the importance of industrial diamonds in a period of rapid rearmament, and the Food (Defence Plans) Department and the Foreign Office studied ways of denying iron ore and other minerals to Germany in the event of war. The results of these investigations were passed on to the Board of Trade, which considered controlling the diamond market through London long before the war. Britain's need for industrial diamonds was relatively small, though it was believed that Germany had been stockpiling through barter trade agreements with South Africa. The Board of Trade set up a Diamond Export Committee in October 1939, focusing on ways of denying industrial and near-industrial stock to Germany. Britain also exerted pressure on South Africa to cut down on independent diamond exports to America, as well as making moves to curtail the growth of a diamond-cutting industry in Palestine based on imported South African diamonds cut by the Mandate's burgeoning refugee community. London fought hard and successfully to retain its status as the diamond capital of the world, which was worth £1.5 million to the Treasury in peacetime and £4–5 million per annum in wartime. During the war South Africa lost influence over the Central Selling Organization, and the British government utilized the Diamond Corporation and its Trading Company to exercise control over supply and distribution for strategic and economic ends. British insistence on the continued location of central selling in London ended Sir Ernest Oppenheimer's plan for moving the wholesale market to America. (Oppenheimer was the founder of the Anglo-American Corporation and had a controlling interest in De Beers Consolidated Mines. By 1940 he controlled the lion's share of the world's diamond market as well as controlling much of the South African gold industry, and had connections with seven of the companies mining in the Northern Rhodesian copperbelt.)[53]

The High Commission Territories of Bechuanaland (population 241,000), Basutoland (population 600,000) and Swaziland (population 200,000) were British protectorates in Southern Africa. They had come under British rule, by and large, at the request of African rulers anxious in the late nineteenth century to avoid incorporation into settler-dominated South Africa, already weakened by the inroads made in the region by European settlers, traders and missionaries and the unrest caused by internal African wars and migrations. Their history was overshadowed by the proximity of South Africa and its continued desire to incorporate them. Right up until the 1950s this was an option that successive British governments never firmly ruled out. With transfer from British to Union rule remaining a live political issue, it remained a cause of grave concern for the

African leaders of the protectorates, who had no desire whatsoever to become a part of their giant neighbour and face the prospect of land loss and diminished political and economic autonomy that had befallen the numerous African king-doms that *had* been taken over by the South African settler state. The notion of the British crown agreeing to protect these polities from South African settlers upon their own request therefore became embedded in the political relationship between the British and the African chiefs that still pertained at the time of the Second World War. The symbolism of the 'protecting' Queen Victoria remained so strong, indeed, that many men went to war in *her* name in 1941–42 – not King George VI's – when army mobilization came to the three protectorates. Unlike many other parts of British Africa, therefore, the High Commission Territories were not territories of British conquest and subjugation, and the British made sure that this fact – that they were there largely upon request and for the good of the African populations as defined by their leaders – was never forgotten. When it came to army recruitment in the Second World War, district commissioners and chiefs presented it as a duty, in return for the favour done by the British Queen, to go and fight now that she needed help against Hitler.[54]

The fact that the High Commission Territories were intimately tied up with British–South African relations meant that British policy towards them was always formulated with an eye focused firmly on the fraught diplomatic relations between Britain and its awkward Dominion. South Africa had numerous ways at its disposal of threatening the territories, and thus British policy. As the region's economic giant, South Africa employed tens of thousands of the protectorates' people in its mining and agricultural sectors, and controlled the transport infra-structure on which imports and exports reached and left the territories. (Basutoland, indeed, was entirely surrounded by South African territory.) South Africa's policies, for example the weight restrictions imposed on cattle entering the South African beef market which discriminated against the generally under-weight cattle from Bechuanaland (thus severely hampering the development of the single industry that the British believed offered the protectorate a viable export industry), could provide a significant factor in British calculations. As soon as Smuts took South Africa to war on Britain's side, he began a renewed attempt to have the High Commission Territories transferred as a reward. Resisting this, and morally binding Britain to stand by its commitment never to transfer the territories unless their people and the British Parliament agreed, became a major war aim of the protectorates' traditional rulers. This situation meant that Britain also had to be careful when raising and training soldiers in the High Commission Territories, the South Africans taking exception to the prospect of trained 'black armies' existing near their borders. Despite pressure, however, the British insisted that the High Commission Territories soldiers would be armed when deployed overseas, and not left carrying sticks and knobkerries as was the norm for South Africa's black military formations.

Traditional rule in the High Commission Territories took various forms. In

Basutoland there was a Paramount Chief (or King), his Basutoland National Congress and lesser chiefs in the districts. In Swaziland there was also a Paramount Chief, a Queen Mother, a council and lesser chiefs. In Bechuanaland there were eight 'independent' chiefs ruling the eight main tribal groups and the eight reserves into which the territory was divided, and they all convened annually as the African Advisory Council to consult the colonial government in Mafeking. The desire of the traditional rulers of the three High Commission Territories *never* to become part of South Africa and endure the segregation and dispossession that had marked the history of African societies in that settler-dominated state meant that they had good reason for supporting, as visibly as possible, the British imperial war effort. Here were to be found African rulers positively falling over themselves to get men into British uniforms and shipped off to war fronts, with very definite political goals in mind, quite apart from whatever loyalty to the imperial connection they felt.

As elsewhere in tropical Africa, British rule in the High Commission Territories rested firmly upon an alliance with these traditional rulers, who were far more than puppets of the British and were possessed of real power vis-à-vis their people and enough power to influence and alter British policy. Indigenous colonial rulers like the chiefs and kings of the High Commission Territories were perfectly capable of supporting an imperial cause whilst resisting or seeking to amend the policies of the local colonial government. Chief Tshekedi Khama of the Bangwato tribe had made a career terrorizing the local British administration in Bechuanaland, always quick to contest its policies and enlist his considerable knowledge of British legal precedents, his contacts in the House of Commons and his gifted Johannesburg lawyer. Likewise King Sobhuza II of Swaziland was an absolute ruler in the eyes of his people and one not to be bossed around by the British. The nature of the relationship was captured by Colonel Herbert Johnson, the man sent to recruit soldiers in Swaziland and subsequently given the solemn task of keeping King Sobhuza's 3600 men together whilst they were in the Middle East and of being responsible for their safety. As Colonel Johnson wrote to his superiors 'the political relationship between the Swazi Nation and the [British] Administration is such that not a single company could have been raised by the Administration [itself]'.[55] Cooperation, therefore, was the key in mobilizing their territories for war. As the Ashantehene in the Gold Coast supported the war effort of the British and encouraged his people to participate, so too did the traditional rulers of Basutoland, Bechuanaland and Swaziland. They were quick to offer, and were even more quickly offered the opportunity to offer, their support for the British war effort when news of the expiry of Neville Chamberlain's ultimatum to Hitler filtered through to district offices across the continent in the first week of September 1939.

Given the history of the coming of British rule to the High Commission Territories, war service was portrayed as a duty of the people to help the monarch, for by making the territories British Queen Victoria had extended her protection to the people and prevented their subjugation by Afrikaners and unscrupulous representatives of imperial penetration like Cecil Rhodes and his British South Africa Company. So the story went, and the colonial government and the African chiefs stuck firmly to it. There were other reasons for supporting the British war effort. Some chiefs were, for personal reasons, anxious to court the goodwill of the British. Chief Kgari Sechele of the Bakwena, Bechuanaland's most senior tribe, joined the army himself and became a regimental sergeant major, keen to support the British and win the respect of a tribe that had not entirely accepted his rule. Chief Molefi Pilane of the Bakgatla tribe, on the other hand, joined the army at least partly to impress the British, who had only recently restored him to the throne after deposing him in 1937.

In late August district commissioners in the eight tribal capitals of the Bechuanaland Protectorate were told to warn their chiefs that hostilities with Germany were likely, and telegrams informed them of the actual outbreak in the following month. An emergency meeting was convened at the Bechuanaland administration's central headquarters at the Imperial Reserve in Mafeking on 7 September 1939. As elsewhere in the African Empire, though with perhaps more meaning, loyalty to the King was expressed by the chiefs at this meeting convened by the Resident Commissioner, Charles Arden Clarke. (The High Commission Territories were headed by resident commissioners as opposed to governors. This reflected the fact that the British High Commissioner to South Africa was the constitutional governor of the three territories, responsible for them to Whitehall and administering them through the three resident commissioners.) The chiefs were told that because of the war, and in order to begin making a contribution to the war effort as soon as possible, development programmes would have to be cut as a way of relieving the imperial treasury of financial burdens. They were also told that more responsibility would devolve upon them as war inevitably took men away from the district administration and into the armed forces (46 per cent of the skeletal Bechuanaland administration had left to fight by 1940, along with 10 per cent of the protectorate's white population). The chiefs were told that, for the time being at least, their role in the Empire's war effort would be a subsidiary though nevertheless important one, in which the High Commission Territories must strive to increase agricultural output, establish and build tribal grain reserves, and continue to supply migrant labourers for the South African mines. This was hardly a glamorous vision of war-time participation, but in the root-and-branch global war effort that was to be demanded it was vital nonetheless.

The Bechuanaland administration's initial response to the war was to station two mobile police columns, complete with Lewis guns, at Maun in the north and Gaberones in the south, to respond to any attempted sabotage, particularly from German settlers in the region. Measures were taken to protect the railway line between Mafeking and Bulawayo, a strategic asset of great importance to the war effort, as it connected South Africa by rail to the Northern Rhodesia railhead from which lorries, troops and supplies would soon proceed overland to the fighting front in East Africa. A proclamation from the High Commissioner gave the resident commissioners of the three territories all necessary emergency powers to deal with the problems that war might stimulate: powers of censorship, control of the means of communication and civilian movements, powers to prevent subversive propaganda and for passive defence measures. Bechuanaland was divided into defence areas, Europeans formed a small defence force, and weapons ancient and new were begged and borrowed in order to drill them. In line with other colonial administrations around the world, the Resident Commissioner had a defence scheme on file (a copy also lodged in Whitehall), and even plans for a 'scorched earth' policy in the unlikely event of an enemy invasion. In 1939–41, however, the appearance of enemy forces in places like Bechuanaland was not as far-fetched as it might now appear. Had Germany defeated Britain and the Empire become the centre of continued British resistance, individual colonies would have had to have faced the inevitable enemy attempt to begin effectively subordinating the spoils of their victory. Alternatively, a situation similar to that which afflicted the French Empire could have transpired, whereby some Britons sought to continue the war against Germany using the resources of the Empire, whilst others sought a peace settlement and accommodation with the victors. As has been seen, South African nationalists were offered the High Commission Territories by the Germans, if they pulled out of the Empire's war effort.

As was the case in other parts of the Empire, the impact of the war was unevenly felt between the years 1939 and 1945. Many in the former High Commission Territories today associate 1941 with the start of the war, as the years 1939–1941 were relatively quiet and the effects of war were more indirect; the three territories contributed to the imperial war effort through their labour, some rationing and inflation was experienced, and fund-raising drives were held for imperial and war-related charities. But the one million, mainly rural, people of the High Commission Territories lacked a more concrete connection with this apparently distant conflict. Before the unexpected demand for High Commission Territories military labour came in 1941 from General Sir Archibald Wavell, Commander-in-Chief Middle East, it was considered unlikely that the High Commission Territories would be much affected by the war, even though some of the chiefs in the territories continued to press the British administration to allow them to send men to serve. The High Commission Territories endured the depletion of the administrative cadre in the same way as everywhere else, and knew from pre-war Colonial Office circulars how best they could contribute to the war effort: step up domestic food production in order to build a reserve and thereby cut import requirements. Having no important export crops, their labourers should continue to migrate to the South African mines and their cattle should continue to be driven to the Johannesburg meat market; and they should do all that they could to cut their financial dependence upon Treasury grants-in-aid, which in the case of Bechuanaland was running at £65,000 per annum.

Other factors meant that the war did not have the dramatic effect on the home front that was experienced elsewhere in the Colonial Empire. There were no urban areas where unrest might foment, no significant settler community on whom African grievances might come to focus, and not even the vaguest of nationalist groups worthy of the name. There were no major industries or ports to be stimulated by the demands of war-time labour and construction. Power was firmly in the hands of the traditional African elites, and on any matter concerning the war they cooperated wholeheartedly with the British. This, together with the absence of educated elites observing world events from outward-looking cities or ports, reporting them in newspapers and perhaps asking for greater political freedom in exchange for support during the war, meant that the momentous events occurring in Europe, the Middle East and Asia did not penetrate directly beyond the Drakensberg Mountains, and petered out in the Kalahari sands.

This is not to say that the High Commission Territories home fronts were not significantly marked by the war, however, and their war experience altered dramatically in 1941 when they became recruiting grounds for the British Army. What brought the war more directly to the lives of all the people of Bechuanaland, Basutoland and Swaziland was Wavell's call for soldiers from all corners of the African Empire and beyond. In 1941 there was a pressing need for military labour to support the fighting fronts in the one place in the world where the British Army, together with its imperial allies the Australian Imperial Force, the New Zealand Expeditionary Force, the Union Defence Force and the Indian Army, was directly engaging the enemy on a large scale. Following the fall of France Britain's major overseas military effort had come to focus on the Middle East, and it was to this theatre that the High Commission Territories soldiers were to travel. A Directorate of Labour had been established under GHQ Middle East in May 1940 to supervise Middle East Command's military labour requirements. Two Palestinian and one Cypriot Pioneer companies had been recruited, and over 10,000 civilians were employed by the army. The Greece and Crete campaigns in the spring of 1941 cost the Pioneer Corps over 4500 men, however, so with fighting in the region intensifying and reaching new areas, MEC desperately needed a new labour force, and this is where the High Commission Territories entered the equation. With the escalation of the Middle Eastern battlefronts following the arrival of German forces in spring 1941, and the growing need for operations in the Balkans, Iraq and the Levant, the need for rear echelon soldiers to perform a galaxy of crucial military jobs was great. Hence Wavell's appeal for High Commission Territories African pioneers, and the sound of the fife and drum in distant Butha-Buthe, Kanye, Mbabane, Maseru, Mochudi and Molepolole.

The British officials in Bechuanaland set about achieving their war goals, on the home and recruitment fronts, with the help of their allies, the African chiefs. By cutting development projects and tightening belts all round, by 1941–42 the Bechuanaland administration had balanced its budget and cut its dependence on a British grant-in-aid for the first time since 1926–27. By 1944–45, the administration had managed to accumulate a surplus of over £210,000. As in every other corner of the Empire, appeals and funds were set up. In Basutoland enough money was raised by the Spitfire Fund to kit out a whole squadron, whilst Bechuanaland raised the money (£10,400) to pay for two of the aircraft, and photos and a plaque were duly dispatched from the Air Ministry to thank the people of the protectorate for purchasing 'Bechuana' and 'Kalahari'. With a much larger population, Basutoland was able to afford to purchase more of the aircraft, and the Basutoland Spitfire Squadron was funded by a £100,000 gift from the Basutoland National Congress. The Basutoland squadron had some pedigree, as during the First World War No. 72 Squadron had been created following the gift of twenty-four Sopwith Camels from the people of Basutoland. In the Second World War No. 72 Squadron again flew Basutoland aircraft, and seventeen out of a total of seventy named aircraft that flew with the squadron came from the Southern African protectorate. War Funds raised money for Britain, and charities collected donations and held fund-raising events (a Sponsor-a-Destroyer Week was even held in Bechuanaland, though only a tiny fraction of the population had ever seen the sea).

African leaders, however, wanted to do more for the war effort from early in the war. *The Times* reported that 'Basuto Offer Army to Britain'. The chief of Bechuanaland's most populous tribe offered to pay for and equip a force of a thousand men to then be placed at the disposal of the British Army. This desire to participate did not extend to sending men to join South Africa's Union Defence Force's Native Military Corps, because the chiefs and kings of the three High Commission Territories had no desire for their war effort to be subsumed within that of their overbearing neighbour. It was a measure of how badly the war was going for Britain in 1941 and 1942 that it decided to recruit soldiers from these territories, in which no military formation existed on which to build. The need of the Middle East for military labour led all three territories to begin the process of recruiting men for the African Pioneer Corps (APC). Pioneer Corps Headquarters consisting of a core of British soldiers were sent out from Britain to organize the recruitment and training process that was to see over 10,000 Batswana, 3600 Swazi and 22,000 Basuto recruited into the British Army and dispatched from Durban to the Middle East. (Of these, Basutoland lost 1216 soldiers, 633 going down with the troopship SS *Erinpura* en route to Malta in May 1943, Bechuanaland lost nearly 400 and Swaziland 122. Disease was the main cause of death.) A further 3200 Bechuanaland and Basutoland men served in the Union's NMC. In each protectorate a military camp was hastily constructed by the Public Works Departments: in Basutoland, Walker's Camp emerged near the capital Maseru; in Swaziland the former Agricultural Show Ground at Bremersdorp was converted; as in Bechuanaland was the Imperial Cold Storage Warehouse at Lobatsi. These camps became the centre for the initial training of High Commission Territories recruits, supervised by British officers and NCOs who were usually rather surprised by the Southern African postings.

In raising APC companies in the High Commission Territories forced recruitment, as elsewhere in Africa, was simply not an option. Military units raised at the point of the rifle or the sjambok would have been of no use to the British Army, and such recruitment techniques would have flown in the face of the training, outlook and inclination of British colonial civil servants as well as official British government policy. Even at a time of war, the 1940s were not the 1890s, and attitudes towards race, and what constituted acceptable behaviour in the colonial world, had progressed significantly. That did not mean, however, that all recruits were smiling volunteers. The British were able neatly to sidestep some of the issues surrounding compulsory enlistment by turning a partially-sighted eye as their chiefly allies cajoled and coaxed men to the attestation points, and by arguing that, if African societies traditionally compelled people to work in times of war, who were the British to interfere? Inveterate respecters of tradition as the British were, they could also soundly argue that African societies were indeed threatened by German and Italian aggression. If the British lost, Germans or South Africans would end up ruling them. In the High Commission Territories, without chiefly cooperation the British could not have used African military labour. Chiefs were permitted to exact compulsory labour dues that were considered to bear the force of legitimate tribal tradition and therefore to be distinct from forced labour. Abuse in the application of tribal tradition, however, was to be countered wherever it was detected by British district officers.

In practice many of the recruits were willing to join the army, for cash, for adventure, because of peer pressure – the usual motives for young men joining up – though few could have known quite what they were letting themselves in for. The chiefs and kings of the High Commission Territories began their recruitment by calling out age regiments, traditional units of men initiated in age groups at regular intervals and circumcised, inducted in the traditions of the tribe and their duties as grown men to the tribe, including military service when necessary. In Basutoland and Swaziland recruitment was carried out by the order of the Paramount Chiefs. Paramount Chief Sobhuza II sent war messengers to all Swazi chiefs and charged them with the responsibility of furnishing men and accounting for absentees. Recruitment was encouraged during tours by chiefs, district commissioners, resident commissioners and Africans already in the army. Using fit, healthy, uniformed African soldiers from the same district was an alluring technique, as was the use of military bands, such as the leopard skin-clad Bechuanaland Drum and Bugle Band, parades, drill and firearms demonstrations. As Sergeant E. Mohapeloa from Basutoland expressed it in 1943, 'many of our young men were spirited away by the deadly rhythm of that band, and before they knew it they found themselves in the army'.[56] Whilst volunteerism and acquiescence were by no means uncommon, there is no doubt that many Africans went to war from the High Commission Territories because their chiefs and village headmen told them to. These were, after all, societies in which age brought authority and demanded obedience. Some men decided to hide. In one notable case in Basotuland there was a mass desertion of recruits from the Butha-Buthe district.

Robert Kgasa captures the tone of recruitment in Bechuanaland in recalling a meeting in the tribal court of the Bangwaketse people at their capital, Kanye:

> At a recruiting meeting Chief Bathoen said: 'Hey look. I'm doing this because His Majesty is at war with Germany and they're going to beat the whole world. And what are we doing about it? We should have our young men join the army.' It wasn't forced on people. But some were scared and ran away. They said, 'We are going to die'. Those who understood, like me, we are volunteering. Some were forced to go: 'Your own [age] regiment has left. Why are you here? You must go!'

Miriam Pilane recalled a similar meeting in Mochudi, capital of the Bakgatla tribe:

> We were so frightened to hear that our husbands were going to war ... We had no slight idea what the war was about, the thing is, we only heard that Queen Victoria [confused with Queen Elizabeth] has asked for help, so they are going to fight for the Queen. We then know that this involves us, if the Germans are fighting the Queen, as we were her people. We were under her, and she helped us against our enemies and with other things, so we had to help her. We didn't know how long they were going to take at war. Even if we were afraid we just encouraged them to go in the name of God, we will also pray for them whilst gone, so that they can help the Queen as she helped us.[57]

Once recruited the men were presented to British attestation officers in order to be officially signed up, following a medical inspection, and were then transported in trucks and by rail to the military camps, where basic training could get under way as thousands of Africans were initiated into the rites of the British Army, from square bashing to uncomfortable boots, from kit inspection to bawling sergeant majors and foul language. In the High Commission Territories, as in so many other parts of the world over the course of the previous three centuries, the British were to show considerable expertise in producing fine soldiers from non-European material.

Before leaving home many High Commission Territories soldiers underwent traditional doctoring ceremonies. In parts of Bechuanaland this involved slaughtering a fierce black bull. The Swazi Prince Dabede, sent to join the army by Sobhuza as his personal royal representative, was given a ritual baton containing the King's magical power. It seems fair to say that most of the 1941 recruits were either volunteers or acquiescent followers of chiefly direction. The 1942 call naturally met with less enthusiasm – the genuine volunteers had already gone to war and there were fewer men around. One historian labels the 1941 recruitment drive in Swaziland as 'the triumph of tradition', and 1942 as 'the time of coercion'.[58] There was some discouragement to counter the official support for army recruitment. French Canadian Roman Catholic priests in Basutoland inveighed against military service, as did Afrikaner farmers in Swaziland, anxious to safeguard their labour force. The South African government, inevitably, expressed concerns about 'black armies' on its borders, and was particularly unhappy about the British decision to train High Commission Territories soldiers to use rifles, and, what's more, to actually issue the weapons once they arrived in the Middle East. But the British would not bow to pressure on this point, reinforced by the fact that the African chiefs and kings were adamant that their men were to be weapons-trained and wielding, no matter that their primary role was in the sphere of non-martial military tasks. It was a sensible decision, for the High Commission Territories soldiers were called upon to perform numerous duties, including guarding supply dumps, providing garrison forces and peacekeeping in Palestine which required more than knobkerries, bows and arrows. In recruiting for the army there was competition from the traditional mass employer of the Southern African region, the mineral mines. In order to recruit successfully, whilst catering for the labour needs of domestic agriculture and the South African mines, the administrations of the High Commission Territories had to regulate the flow of men. When the 1942 army draft was being raised, a ban was put upon mine recruitment, though many men found it a simple matter to cross the border into South Africa and attest at a 'bolt hole'.

From Durban the troopships carried the High Commission Territories soldiers to Port Suez, from where they were transported by rail and road to the Pioneer Corps Base Depot. This was a huge military camp in the desert near the sight of the Battle of Tel-el-Kebir in 1882, at which a British force had defeated the Egyptian army. Qassassin camp was capable of accommodating 26,000 soldiers. It was a base for acclimatization, training, rest and recreation and dispersal. The pioneer companies, each consisting of about 350 soldiers, were dispersed throughout the region in labour groups (one group usually comprising six companies) that nearby army commanders could draw upon when necessary. Thus, for example, the Eighth Army in the Western Desert was supported by 62 Group at Tobruk, 59 Group at Fort Capuzzo, 44 Group at Bardira, 55 Group at Sollum, 58 Group at Mischiefa and 73 Group at Mersa Matruh.

The tasks undertaken by the pioneer soldiers of the High Commission Territories, and from those other colonies, were legion. One of the Pioneer Corp's early tasks was the construction of fortifications in Lebanon in anticipation of a German thrust from the Caucasus directed at Britain's Middle Eastern heartland. The Lebanon and anti-Lebanon mountains were fortified, tank traps dug and a military railway laid between Haifa and Tripoli. Some pioneer companies spent months in Syria, Palestine and the Delta with the Ninth Army preparing for a German thrust from the north, and others worked for the Eighth Army in North Africa and, following victories and advances, in Malta, Sicily, Italy and Yugoslavia. In the desert the supply issue was paramount for both the Eighth Army and the Afrika Korps. High Commission Territories troops worked the ports and carried supplies. They camouflaged military installations, constructed dummy tanks, took part in movement deception measures, built and guarded supply dumps, transported supplies to combat units in the field, operated as stevedores running ports like Tripoli and Tobruk, provided smokescreen cover for infantry landing on the Italian beaches, manned army forage farms, guarded prisoners of war, formed specialist fire-fighting and salvage units, acted as security forces in volatile places like Egypt and Palestine, trained as clerks, craftsmen, drivers, medical orderlies, map-makers, firemen and military policemen, built roads, telegraph lines, bailey bridges, tank traps, aircraft blast pens, railways and airfields and joined fighting units like heavy anti-aircraft regiments and mountain regiments of the Royal Artillery. Basotho muleteers, especially recruited because of their skill in working with the beasts in their mountainous homeland, carried ammunition and supplies to imperial soldiers fighting in the Italian mountains and on the return journey evacuated the wounded to casualty clearing stations. In April 1943 Batswana gunners took part in an artillery barrage during the battle to cross the River Po in Italy:

> One battery provided line of burst to guide the heavy bombers, the other battery advanced in close support of two famous British infantry divisions firing altogether 16,114 rounds and continuing until the Po was crossed. This meant constant overnight moves, shifting the guns to new positions, plenty of firing and lots of hard work with very little sleep. But the enthusiastic Batswana seemed to enjoy it all, and they never tired.[59]

High Commission Territories soldiers were extremely proud of their war role, as recorded in a letter from Company Sergeant Major Kosolo to Chief Tshekedi Khama in August 1944:

> We have made a name for ourselves among the Italians, Poles, Americans and Indians here and these people are always expressing their admiration of our work ... They all say that after the war they will come to Southern Africa but I don't know if coming to Southern Africa will give them strength and endurance like ours ... Chief, the important thing in my mind is that most of the Bechuanaland soldiers now realize why they came here. We have asked that some men be returned home as they were old but Chief these men refuse, saying: 'We have come here to serve our country (to die for our country). We have not come to an ordinary job '... Truly we have fought – we have captured Rome, the capital of Italy, and Florence, and little remains before we have taken the whole of Italy.'[60]

A condition of recruitment in Swaziland was that all of the men were kept together and not mixed with other units. This was a specific request made by Paramount Chief Sobhuza II, and one taken seriously by the man to whom he made it, Colonel Herbert Johnson, the officer responsible for recruiting and training in Swaziland. After a brief division of the 3600 strong force, which had Johnson, Sobhuza and in turn the Dominions Office badgering the military authorities in the Middle East to stick to their side of the deal, they were united and served for the remainder of the war as a single unit, known as the Swazi

Enclave. It had its own newspaper, provosts, field punishment centre, hospital and leave camps, and spent five months operating the docks in Tripoli and five months at Bône in Algeria. In the victory parade through Tripoli in May 1942 the Swazi military band bore the Swazi flag and the Swazi royal colours, made especially by the She-Elephant the Queen Mother and her royal ladies. One Swazi company was trained as a smokescreen unit and took part in the Allied landings at Salerno in September 1943. It created a fourteen thousand foot long smoke-screen to protect the landing of elements of the 46th Division. Another part of the company served with 201 Guards Brigade at the same time portering arms and ammunition to the front line. Units from this 1991 (Swaziland) Company later had the distinction of being the first troops into conquered Rome behind the infantry in June 1944.

Colonial and chiefly control and order were extended into the army. Senior African royals and even chiefs served as company or regimental sergeant majors and district commissioners were seconded to the army to serve as roaming welfare officers attached to the Adjutant-General's branch. Chiefs from home, as well as the resident commissioners, occasionally made tours amongst their men. The head of the Adjutant-General's branch specializing in the welfare of High Commission Territories soldiers, for example, was the Government Secretary of Basutoland, Colonel D. W. How. Colonial officials in the army were also able to keep an eye on matters and ensure that the army met its commitments to the men and their welfare. Colonel How was described by the High Commissioner in South Africa as his 'eyes and ears' in the Middle East. The collective action of the colonial governments prevented the army from using High Commission Territories soldiers in the Far East (though a Basotho company did end up in India by mistake), after battle had been joined by the Colonial Office and the War Office over the issue. The colonial officials' argument was that the men had joined up to fight Hitler, before the Japanese war had started, and that it would be a serious breach of faith if they were shunted to the war in Burma once things had quietened down in the Middle East. All three of the territories also sent their own missionaries to the Middle East to minister to the religious needs of those men who professed a faith. For example, the Reverend Arthur Sandilands, a London Missionary Society minister from Bechuanaland, became Deputy Chaplain-General MEC. Chiefs also saw the war as an opportunity to regain some control of people who worked in the South African mines, for long considered an unruly element beyond tribal authority. Chief Tshekedi Khama asked to be allowed to visit the Rand to berate Bangwato there for not returning to the protectorate, and joining the army. Tshekedi believed that chiefly visits to troops overseas and the insertion of senior men into the army as sergeants, company sergeant majors and regimental sergeant majors, meant there was a much greater opportunity to maintain traditional control over men in the army than over men working in South Africa, the major employer of High Commission Territories migrant labour. Similarly using 'loyal' support of the imperial war effort as a smokescreen for advancing more parochial ends, chiefs could use army recruitment as an officially-backed method of extending their control among sub-tribes – immigrant communities living under their authority – considered to be insufficiently subservient to their rule. Tshekedi Khama pursued his long-standing tussle with the Kalanga immigrant community by trying to oblige them to increase recruitment; and when a train exploded at Foley Bridge in central Bechuanaland in 1940 he ordered the Bakhurutshe people of Madinare to provide labour gangs. Chief Bathoen also used recruitment to exert his authority over sub-tribes like the Bakgatla of Moshupa.

It was very important to keep the men in touch with life on the home front, and they were anxious to keep an eye on their personal affairs at home. There was a great drive to get men to write to their families, and to get those families to write back (not easy given relatively low levels of literacy). Many men sent photographs of themselves home, as well as the ubiquitous airmail letter cards. A special Setswana supplement was published for the Bechuanaland soldiers and inserted in the South African NMC's newspaper *Indlovu/Tlou,* and the *Swazi Gazette* was published for the men of the Swazi enclave. Soldiers were particularly anxious to remain in touch with home affairs. On the home front missionaries could perform a useful function by disseminating war news and helping people to write and read letters, and the Education Department began producing a newsletter early in the war. *Indlovu* was distributed throughout the country. Another war-time innovation was the foundation of the Protectorate's first ever national newspaper, *Naledi ya Batswana* ('Star of the Batswana'). Film of High Commission Territories troops in the Middle East was shown on the home front during recruitment drives. All of these developments, together with the more extensive use of radio broadcasts, represented a war-induced communications explosion that linked people to new thoughts and new regions. Radio sets were installed in public places and regular broadcasts began in Setswana on 1 October 1942, beginning a regular war bulletin service. The English translation of part of that historic broadcast gives a flavour of the kind of news relayed to rural Africans on the eve of the Battle of Alamein, and its conversion into language that would be immediately understood by the listeners:

> The government gives its greetings to the chiefs, headmen and the Batswana tribesmen ... here is some news about the war. In the far north of Africa our army and that of the Germans stand facing and watching each other, and each is ready to make a pounce whenever the opportunity occurs. The British found thirty aircraft and destroyed them as one destroys guinea fowl sleeping in a tree ... Some of the bombs the British are dropping on German factories weigh as much as forty bags of mealies ... To drop them our aircraft had to fly further than from Mafeking to Bulawayo and back. We continue to receive good news from our men with the African Pioneer Corps ... They want their relatives to write to them and tell them home news.[61]

War was felt on the home front in numerous ways. Church services were held to pray for peace and for loved one's serving in distant lands encountered by most people only as biblical place-names. In Bechuanaland the African Poll Tax was raised by three shillings per male, income tax was introduced for the first time and the administration benefited from rising customs and excise revenue from the railway line that passed through the territory. By 1945 the War Fund had raised over £45,000 for the war effort, collected voluntarily, though it is clear that some of the chiefs obliged people to contribute. In 1941 Africans ceased contributing to the War Fund when the African War Levy was introduced. This raised £92,000 by 1945. Over £60,000 was given to Britain in the form of gifts and interest-free loans, much of it coming from special tribal donations by chiefs 'on behalf of' their people. It also funded the Bechuanaland Soldiers' Benefit Fund, which made small grants to returning soldiers. By 1945 there was over £240,000 of soldiers' deferred pay in Post Office Savings Bank accounts.

Shortages of certain foodstuffs, queuing for tea and sugar, and rationing became commonplace, and profiteering by traders was a constant source of work for the overstretched administrations, depleted, as elsewhere in Africa, by the coming of war. The Gifts and Comforts Fund raised money to provide troops with items like footballs, cigarettes and magazines. The Women's War Workers organization involved women from all over Bechuanaland knitting mittens and scarves for their men overseas, amounting to over 30,000 items. These were particularly welcome to Batswana troops experiencing the bitter depths of a Syrian winter for the first time. In that protectorate a countrywide effort was made, using traditional chiefly prerogatives, to get people to contribute labour to the preparation, tending and harvesting of warlands, the produce of which would be stored in communal granaries for use in times of shortage. It was (forlornly) hoped that, if the warlands scheme was a success, not only local needs but the needs of 'the armies of the north' could also be supplied. As in other parts of the Empire, like Britain, Ceylon and Mauritius, the war led to unsuccessful but commendable efforts to become self-sufficient. The idea behind the warlands was to use traditional chiefly powers to call for communal labour to build tribal reserves of grain, to be disbursed in times of need. With the war calling for a cut in imports of staple foodstuffs, Bechuanaland would try to maximize its own production. The scheme was only a partial success, and hopes to provide a surplus over domestic needs, to add to the pool of available food for export to armies overseas or needy colonies, were never realized. Cattle exports rose, and South Africa dropped its prohibitive weight restrictions that in times of less demand had protected South African farmers from competition from less well-developed cattle from over the border. Cattle smuggling continued, as farmers were anxious to avoid the war-time Cattle Export Levy. Official figures record that 215,000 head of cattle were exported during the war, as well as small stock and 2,500,000 pounds of butter.

At the end of the war it took many months for all of the High Commission Territories soldiers to be repatriated, and this relied upon elaborate planning by the local colonial administrations and the military authorities in the Middle East that had begun almost as soon as the first troops had disembarked at Suez in 1941. During the war, like its counterparts across the Empire, the Bechuanaland administration appointed committees to examine the protectorate's post-war needs in the light of the promise from London of hundreds of thousands of pounds worth of Colonial Development and Welfare Act money. With some relish, the administration looked at ways of improving the basics in life, like access to water, and hoped to be able to develop to such an extent that Bechuanaland ceased to be so dependent on South Africa and migrant labour remittances. Even in the land of the Kalahari Desert the New Jerusalem promised to the people of Britain as their post-war legacy cast its reflection, pale but unmistakable nevertheless, as the outposts of the Empire sought to manage the transition from peace to war, to reabsorb thousands of men whose perspectives had been transformed by what they had seen and what they had done and to preserve the Empire in a complex and more uncertain new world.

10

The Indian Ocean

The Chief of the Imperial General Staff, General Sir Alan Brooke, realized in April 1942 that Britain's global war effort was at risk of being snapped in two, should the Japanese strike westwards across the Indian Ocean and the Germans' successfully drive through Egypt to the Suez Canal and the oilfields beyond. He recorded in his diary that at the time:

> We were hanging by our eye-lids! Australia and India were threatened by the Japanese, we had temporarily lost control of the Indian Ocean, the Germans were threatening Iran and our oil, Auchinleck was in precarious straits in the desert, and the submarine sinkings were heavy.[1]

Given the stark assessment of the Empire's fortunes offered by the Empire's most senior soldier, the panic that gripped the poor inhabitants of the island of Rodrigues when the cable link across the Indian Ocean was broken as a result of Japanese shelling was not entirely misplaced:

> At Oyster Bay [in Rodrigues] was heard a humming that was the sound of people praying aloud, even those who had never prayed before, that they would be saved from the Japanese. Rosaries were cut into pieces and shared with neighbours.[2]

The break in the imperial cable link was caused by a Japanese attack on the cable and wireless station on the Cocos Islands in March 1942, a tiny speck of British territory over a thousand miles south south west of Singapore. Illustrating the extraordinary reach of Britain's imperial war, by the latter stages of the conflict this scrap of British territory was jam-packed with British servicemen eavesdropping on enemy signals and flying sorties over Japanese-occupied Malaya to drop bombs and, when victory came, to drop supplies to Allied prisoners of war. Similarly Rodrigues, located off Mauritius in the western Indian Ocean, sent men to fight in the Middle East and was garrisoned by troops guarding the island's own cable and wireless station from possible enemy attack. Similar build-ups of men, materials and military infrastructure occurred on other seemingly insignificant Indian Ocean islands, such as Diego Garcia in the Chagos Archipelago and Addu Atoll in the Maldives. Larger islands in the region, such as Madagascar, Mauritius and the Seychelles, also acted as imperial bases, whilst on the Indian Ocean's rim, East Africa, Arabia, South Asia, South-East Asia and the Dutch East Indies were all deeply involved in the ebb and flow of the fighting.[3]

The oceans of the world were as much a part of the imperial structure as were the islands and continents painted imperial red on the map. Since the Revolutionary and Napoleonic Wars the Indian Ocean had been a 'British Lake', though Britain's pre-eminence in the region was to face its sternest challenge during the Second World War, particularly from the mighty Imperial Japanese Navy after it had made short work of Allied battleships at Pearl Harbor and in the Gulf of Siam in December 1941.[4] The Indian Ocean is rarely presented as a theatre of conflict in accounts of the Second World War, though its availability to British shipping was absolutely essential to the imperial war effort in Africa, Burma, the Middle East and South-East Asia. This was because, in war as in peace, it was the Indian Ocean that contained the sea routes that kept the trading and security interests of the Empire connected. It was an imperial Clapham Junction, and its sea lanes were used to convey hundreds of thousands of imperial soldiers and all manner of warlike supplies, together with trade cargoes, to Europe, the Middle East, the Russian front, the Burma front, South-East Asia and the Australasian Dominions. Without control of the Indian Ocean's sea lanes, the British Empire and Commonwealth simply could not have existed, and the imperial war of 1939–45 could not have been fought. In keeping these vital shipping lanes open during the war, and in maintaining supplies of food and essential goods to colonies and fighting formations in the region, Britain relied on the ships of the hard-pressed Eastern Fleet (known as the East Indies Fleet before December 1941 and again after November 1944).* Though the Indian Ocean is a neglected theatre of war now, it was not at the time, and the term 'Indian Ocean Area' was commonly used by those plotting the global movements of the British merchant marine, as well as the headquarters staff of Admiral Lord Louis Mountbatten's South East Asia Command.[5] Freetown was its gateway as it stretched around the Cape and on to the Middle East, South Asia and Australasia.† Upon the security of this huge imperial region hung the fate of the Empire's war effort in all imperial theatres of operation, along with the wellbeing of millions of imperial subjects dependent on the import and export trade of the imperial economy.

Churchill considered that 'the most dangerous moment of the war, and the one which caused him the greatest alarm, was when the news was received that the Japanese fleet was heading for Ceylon and the naval base there'.[6] How could this small island have attained such strategic significance? It all came down to

---

*   The Eastern Fleet comprised the ships of the China Station and the East Indies Station, and new ones sent out from Britain. The former commanders of the two stations, Vice-Admiral Sir Geoffrey Layton and Vice-Admiral G. S. Arbuthnot, remained in the East. Layton, who took over the rump of Force Z and command of the entire Eastern Fleet on Sir Tom Phillips's death, became Commander-in-Chief Ceylon. Arbuthnot remained on the East Indies Station, with his flag at Trincomalee, and retained responsibility for the defence of the Station's shore bases and trade protection on the East Indies Station.

†   This definition of the Indian Ocean included its 'annexes' – the Arabian Sea, the Bay of Bengal, the Persian Gulf and the Red Sea.

communications and logistics. Ceylon, after the loss of Singapore, was the only naval base capable of significantly shaping the war in the Indian Ocean, on which depended the sea routes that allowed military forces to be deployed and sustained in crucial fighting theatres like the Middle East and South Asia, and the sea routes keeping the Australasian Dominions, and their troops, in touch with the wider imperial war effort. In those vital months following the entry of Japan into the war and the rapid succession of Allied defeats, this was perhaps *the* Allied centre of gravity in a moment of crippling weakness. A Japanese occupation of Ceylon and naval rampage across the western Indian Ocean could well have brought down the Raj, severed the Persian Gulf route to the only theatre where the Allied powers were in overland contact with one another, cut Britain's access to its oil supplies, and broken British supply lines to Egypt.[7] The stakes couldn't have been higher.

Most of the territory that framed the Indian Ocean was either British or British-dominated. Thus the Union Flag flew from the Swahili coast to the coast of Arabia and the sheikhdoms of the Persian Gulf, across the Indian subcontinent to the east coast of Burma, down the thin protrusion of the Malay peninsula and on to the west coast of Australia. The British retained a strong strategic interest in the Dutch East Indies and Britain was the predominant power amidst the desolate islands of the Southern Ocean and the pack ice of the Antarctic. Set amidst the waters of the Indian Ocean, framed by British-dominated land, were British islands and atolls. Aden and the island of Perim guarded the entry to the Red Sea and the Arabian Sea. There were the Seychelles and the Amirantes Islands, and the colony of Mauritius from which an Indian Ocean sub-empire was administered, including the Aldabra Islands, the Agalega Islands, Rodrigues and the Chagos archipelago. Off of the Arabian coast were the British islands of Kuria Muria, Socotra and Masira. Further east lay Ceylon, the Laccadive Islands, the Maldives and the Andaman and Nicobar Islands. Towards Western Australia were the Cocos–Keeling Islands and Christmas Island. Most of these islands were to find a role in the Second World War as air or naval bases, whilst others were important because of their communication installations and their provision of troops. Britain's control of the islands of the Indian Ocean was extended during the war as enemy territories joined Britain's war empire. Madagascar was subjected to an imperial invasion in order to pre-empt a similar Japanese move, and Britain also took over the French Comoros Islands, located in the Mozambique Channel, and toppled the Vichy regime of Réunion.

During the Second World War the Indian Ocean remained 'a British Lake', though this was largely a result of victories won elsewhere and the gradual decline in the fortunes of German forces in the west – their failure to knock Britain out in the Middle East and push the Russians back far enough to make an attack through Iran a realistic prospect – and of Japanese forces in the East, particularly after their naval wings had been clipped at the Battle of Midway. As well as the threat of the Imperial Japanese Navy, the Indian Ocean was the scene of German

U-boat and surface raider activity, and also played host to Italian and Vichy forces. To counter this, the Indian Ocean became home to substantial British forces, in particular the Royal Navy's Eastern Fleet and maritime units of the RAF which were charged with the task of defending convoys and patrolling the sea lanes of the Indian Ocean as the British set about holding on in a theatre where they had reigned supreme since the days of Nelson.[8] As well as granting it the use of the sea lanes, Britain's control of the Indian Ocean enabled it to neutralize Italian and Vichy power on its western rim, to defeat the challenge of German and Japanese submarines and raiders, and to mount military campaigns in Iran and Iraq.

During the crucial period of the war in 1941–42, when defeat or victory for Britain hung very much in the balance, and when the Mediterranean was closed to shipping, the route around the Cape and north through the Mozambique Channel became the most important sea route in the world along with that connecting Britain with Canada and America.[9] Passage across the Indian Ocean was also vital for all manner of supplies being sent to build up British and Allied strength in India ready for the major offensives in the Burma–China theatre from 1944, as well as for the ferrying of troops and supplies to and from Australia and New Zealand. Despite the gravity of the tasks, Britain's position in the Indian Ocean was maintained on a shoestring as other theatres took precedence when it came to the apportionment of scarce military resources. In the end, victory was only assured by Japan's initial neglect of the strategic possibilities in the Indian Ocean, then by its growing post-Midway weakness.

The importance of the Indian Ocean's sea routes to the survival of the Empire and Commonwealth during the Second World War cannot be overestimated. In the first year of the war 274,402 imperial servicemen moved through the waters of the East Indies Station. By March 1941, the number had risen to 643,198.[10] The first troop convoy to sail around the Cape – the start of the 'WS' or 'Winston's Specials' – was in June 1940. 'WS' convoys thereafter sailed on average once a month for the next three years, carrying troops principally for Egypt, India and the Far East. Between August and December 1940 50,000 sailed from Australasia and India, and 77,000 from Britain. As an illustration of these impressive trans-oceanic troop trains, WS10 sailed from Britain on 2 August 1941 and consisted of twelve troopships, which stopped at Freetown, Cape Town, Durban, Mombasa, Aden, Suez, Bombay, Colombo and Singapore.

All manner of peace-time and war-time supplies plied the same sea lanes in addition to troopships. Ships carried ammunition, barley, coal, chrome ore, diesel, kerosene, military vehicles, mules, petrol, railway materials, salt, sugar and tinned meat. In October 1940 the ships of the East Indies Station escorted 127 merchant vessels and troopships north to the Red Sea, and 106 travelling south. By the end of February 1942 Britain had sent forty-nine tankers to the Indian Ocean, more than 12 per cent of Britain's total tanker tonnage working in the British oil supply programmes in the West when Japan entered the war in

December 1941. There was a call for more tankers in the Indian Ocean as imperial losses mounted, large oil stocks being lost, for example, on the surrender of Singapore, and oil stocks and future supplies being lost when Burma was evacuated by British forces and occupied by the enemy. Burmese oil, carried in small tankers across the Bay of Bengal, had supplied much of India's needs, and these now had to be replaced from Iran in ocean tankers sailing to Karachi and Bombay. Trade in the Indian Ocean began to assume a new war-time pattern, contacts with the outside world being almost entirely conducted by means of the military cargo ships.

Britain's position in the Indian Ocean was threatened by enemy activity on its land borders (in East Africa, the East Indies, the Middle East, South Asia and South-East Asia), and by enemy surface vessels and submarines, starting with German raiders, joined later by German, Italian and Japanese submarines. In early 1942 Germany's greatest interest in the Japanese war effort was its capacity to launch telling strikes across the Indian Ocean, a point repeatedly made to Tokyo by the Japanese Ambassador in Berlin, Baron Oshima. The German U-boat Commander-in-Chief, Grand Admiral Karl Dönitz, was confident that British overstretch made the vastness of the Indian Ocean a profitable haunt for U-boats. As bases the Axis had at their disposal the captured strongholds of Penang, Sabang, Singapore and a new base at Sourabaya in eastern Java. At least 385 British, Allied and neutral vessels were sunk in the Indian Ocean during the war, amounting to 1,787,870 tons of shipping.

The Red Sea was menaced by Italian naval power based on Massawa in Eritrea, which Mussolini wanted to develop into a naval base capable of having a decisive strategic impact in the region of the Suez Canal. The Red Sea and its ports were invaluable to Britain during the war, because of the lengthy closure of the Mediterranean and the frequent need to close the Suez Canal because of enemy bombing and minelaying raids. When the Canal was shut, the Red Sea ports became the disembarkation point for troops and supplies en route to the Western Desert and beyond. British imperial forces fought a campaign in East Africa to neutralize the Italian threat in the region, and the Eastern Fleet in the Indian Ocean dealt with the naval forces maintained in Italian ports. The Arabian Sea was one of the most popular venues for enemy submarine activity, for the waters off Aden were traversed by important sea lanes for vessels bound to and from Indian ports, and from the Red Sea and the Persian Gulf. Sailings in this region escalated in 1943 with the reopening of the Mediterranean–Suez Canal sea route, and U-boat attention escalated commensurately. The Indian Ocean was also of great importance because it gave on to the Persian Gulf, from where oil was shipped in tankers and from where the invasions of Iran and Iraq were mounted. The Gulf was also the second most important pathway for Allied aid going to Russia. The Bay of Bengal played an important part in the Burma campaign, and was raided by a Japanese carrier force in early 1942.

Elsewhere in the Indian Ocean region Vichy territories in the western Indian

Ocean were considered a menace by Churchill and the South African Prime Minister Jan Smuts, fearing their use by the enemy. The inter-war years had seen the French pour money into the naval base at Diego Suarez in Madagascar, although, as the British were themselves to discover at Singapore, a great base without its own great fleet presented a tempting hostage to fortune and did little to project power. The Mozambique Channel was an important shipping route for traffic destined for the Middle East or the Persian Gulf, and was the site of French bases and of German and Japanese submarine campaigns. British intelligence agents tried to prevent enemy agents from gathering intelligence in Portuguese East Africa and Madagascar concerning the movement of British shipping in the Mozambique Channel. Enemy naval intelligence assigned officers in both territories to monitor British fleet traffic through the ports of Cape Town, Durban, East London and Port Elizabeth. The relative ease and low cost of victory in the Malayan campaign encouraged Japan to look even further westwards, and Tokyo's eyes rested briefly on Madagascar, egged on by the Germans. Further to the south the waters around the Cape became a hunting ground for enemy submarines and mine-layers, and the Royal Navy, the RAF and the South African Naval Force had to develop methods to defend Allied shipping at this nodal point on the global communications map.

The Indian Ocean was home to many different branches of the British armed forces, and colonial governments throughout the region put their services at the disposal of the military. The most important formation was the Eastern Fleet, a powerful naval force that was an amalgam of the China Station and the East Indies Station, commanded briefly by Admiral Sir Tom Phillips before he went down with HMS *Prince of Wales*, then commanded throughout its most important years by Admiral Sir James Somerville.[11] Somerville was familiar with the region, having been Commander-in-Chief of the East Indies Station from July 1938, though illness had seen him recalled to Britain in early 1939, where tuberculosis was diagnosed. He was promptly knighted and placed on the retired list, though the outbreak of war saw his active career dramatically extended. He was called to command Force H in the Mediterranean, where he impressed Churchill so much that at the end of December 1941 he was charged with the task of replacing Phillips in the desperately exposed, yet still vital, East of Suez theatre following the loss of HMS *Prince of Wales* and *Repulse*. For much of his time in eastern waters, Somerville's was to be the most awkward and frustrating of naval tasks, that of keeping a 'fleet in being', exerting its influence by virtue of its existence rather than its offensive actions at a time when Japanese naval power was too great to be squarely confronted.

As well as a mix of surface vessels, aircraft and submarines, the Eastern Fleet maintained shore bases and facilities, including Royal Naval Air Stations, throughout the Indian Ocean region. There were well-developed fleet bases in Kenya, Madagascar, the Maldives, Mauritius and the Seychelles. There were seven Eastern Fleet shore base and depot ships in India, and about a dozen elsewhere in the region. Overall headquarters were at the shore base HMS *Lanka* in Colombo, with HMS *Highflyer* the shore base at Trincomalee, commissioned in April 1942. (By 1944 there were 2000 officers and ratings accommodated in the grounds of Admiralty House at Trincomalee.) Other shore bases in the region included HMS *Euphrates* (Persian Gulf), HMS *Ironclad* (Madagascar), HMS *Jufair* (Bahrain), HMS *Maraga* (Addu Atoll in the Maldives), HMS *Oman* (Kuwait), HMS *Sambur* (Mauritius), HMS *Sangdragon* (Seychelles), HMS *Sheba* (Aden) and HMS *Tana* (Kilindini).[12]

By virtue of its longstanding connection with the region the Royal Navy had a well-prepared base infrastructure in the Indian Ocean, available for use and further development during the Second World War. The Eastern Fleet's work across the Indian Ocean required a good deal of infrastructural support, from anti-aircraft guns to protect its bases, torpedo booms and mined harbour approaches, port war signals organizations to identify and inspect incoming vessels, and the heavy guns with which to fire upon them if they proved unfriendly. A network of radio receivers and transmitters was also extended across the ocean to connect British and Allied vessels and to detect the transmissions of hostile ships. Along with the RAF, the navy's Fleet Air Arm (FAA) also required air stations and anchorages for fighters, bombers, meteorological aircraft and the all-important long-range reconnaissance flying boats. There were major facilities at Colombo, Mombasa and Trincomalee, a new defended fleet base in the Maldives (the secret 'Port T' on Addu Atoll), and smaller facilities for naval vessels at Port Victoria in the Seychelles, Port Louis and Grand Bay in Mauritius, Aden and, from its capture in May 1942, Diego Suarez in Madagascar. The Seychelles were a focal point for monitoring and protecting shipping passing to and from the Cape, Ceylon, East Africa and the Far East, and to the west of the islands traffic between the Cape and the Red Sea converged. The Seychelles were also a connecting point on the cable lines between Aden, Ceylon, Mauritius and Zanzibar. There were naval and air bases on the Indian coast and in the Persian Gulf, and facilities at places like Diego Garcia in the Chagos archipelago.

The RAF in the Indian Ocean was organized in groups, which controlled squadrons and squadron detachments parcelled out across the vast expanse of water between Africa and South-East Asia. RAF Group headquarters were bases in Aden, Ceylon, East Africa and India. On the Indian Ocean rim, there were RAF bases at places such as Karachi and RAF Khormaksar and RAF Sheikh Othman in Aden. There was also an Imperial Airways and RAF staging post at Sharjah in the Trucial Oman state, particularly useful for aircraft being flown from Europe to South-East Asia and Australia by way of the Middle East and South Asia. Numerous islands in the Indian Ocean had air strips and flying boat anchorages for the use of aircraft on operations, and towards the end of the war new bases were opened in places such as the Cocos Islands for the use of fighters and bombers projecting recrudescent British air power against enemy-occupied South-East Asia.

The British Army maintained garrisons in the Indian Ocean region and there were numerous locally-recruited colonial military formations. There were, for example, the Aden Protectorate Levies, recruited to support RAF establishments in the colony and protectorate and its offshore islands. Another good example is provided by Mauritius, where there was a permanent British Army garrison under the Officer Commanding Troops Mauritius, supported by the locally-recruited Mauritius Territorial Force and various garrison artillery formations. Mauritius was also the source of about 6000 soldiers, who joined the British Army for service on other Indian Ocean islands and in the Middle East, and similar units were also recruited in the Seychelles. Ceylon became a major concentration point for soldiers, sailors and airmen given its pivotal role in the region, and the army was strongly represented by brigades sent to protect the island as well as those on their way to or from the fighting fronts in Burma. The army's largest groupings in the Indian Ocean region existed on the ocean's rim. India Command, and from its creation in 1943, South East Asia Command (SEAC), disposed of massive strength, and had numerous Indian Ocean responsibilities. SEAC controlled all air, sea and land forces in the region from 1943, including those operating against the occupied Dutch East Indies, and earlier in the war India Command had deployed troops in the Persian Gulf at important places like Bahrain and Kuwait, and had sent elements of the Ceylon Garrison Artillery to defend the Seychelles. In the Iran–Iraq area Persia and Iraq Command controlled the Tenth Army. East Africa Command had forces dispersed throughout British East Africa, ex-Italian East Africa and out into the Indian Ocean, where its reach was extended through its subsidiary Islands Area Command, responsible for the defence of Madagascar, Mauritius, Rodrigues and the Seychelles. This defence was provided by battalions from King's African Rifles and Northern Rhodesia Regiment, garrison artillery companies from Hong Kong, Singapore and India and newly-formed units like the Mauritius Regiment and the Seychelles Defence Force.

At the start of the war with Germany in September 1939 the Admiralty shuffled its naval pack, transferring vessels from one imperial fleet to another as challenges arose and were met. The Royal Navy's China Station, for instance, began transferring ships to other theatres, particularly the Indian Ocean and Mediterranean. The China Station became virtually an Indian Ocean force, a fact that was recognized when Admiral Sir Percy Noble, Commander-in-Chief China Station, moved his flag to Singapore, and shortly afterwards the East Indies Station and China Station were unified under one command and became the Eastern Fleet. The resources of both fleets combined to patrol the vital convoy routes of the Indian Ocean. The cruisers HMS *Emerald* and *Enterprise* of the East Indies Station, for example, together with the China Station's cruisers HMS *Danae*, *Dauntless* and *Durban*, spent a great deal of time in the early months of the war patrolling the trade routes searching for raiders or waiting to intercept blockade-runners. The carrier HMS *Eagle* and the heavy cruisers HMS *Dorsetshire* and *Cornwall* were formed into a raider-hunting group in the Bay of Bengal when war broke out, the Admiralty being particularly concerned to have effective modern units in the Aden–Singapore–Simonstown triangle. Soon the China Station's submarines were also heading west, as were sloops, much needed, for example, to escort coastal convoys in the North Sea. With virtually no riverine trade in China to be protected anymore, and given that the river gunboats were such a great source of irritation to the Japanese, it was decided to transfer many of them to the East Indies Station. At Singapore they could be converted into minesweepers or anti-submarine vessels. They were also to prove valuable in the Persian Gulf area of the East Indies Station's responsibilities. Thus HMS *Aphis, Cockchafer, Cricket, Gnat, Ladybird* and *Scarab* served in the Mediterranean and Persian Gulf. Many of these ships, however, were transferred east only to be lost when the Japanese took Singapore, including HMS *Dragonfly, Grasshopper* and *Scorpion*.

Surface raiders were the first enemy vessels to challenge British hegemony in the Indian Ocean region.[13] German naval strategy in the Second World War depended upon disrupting British shipping routes. Submarines were joined in this endeavour by commerce raiders, which were either dedicated warships or converted and disguised merchant vessels bearing heavy armaments. They sailed under false names, added fake superstructure to alter their appearance and concealed their battle ensigns until the last moment when approaching a victim at sea. Their task was to hunt British shipping on the high seas, usually operating alone and refuelling and replenishing stores and ammunition from supply vessels lurking in remote waters. Raiders were also used to lay minefields, for example in the approaches to Indian ports and in the region of the Cape of Good Hope. Hunting surface raiders and protecting convoys from their attentions tied down precious British naval resources. At the start of the Second World War Britain lacked enough escort vessels to give all of the Empire's convoys proper cover, and the offensive potential of larger warships could be nullified if the destroyers that were used to provide their screen were removed for escort duties. This was a dilemma regularly faced by the Eastern Fleet. The lack of escorts led to the phenomenon of the Armed Merchant Cruiser (AMC), merchant vessels fitted with guns and carrying Royal Navy personnel to operate them, as well as the conversion of trawlers and whalers for escort or minesweeping duties.

In total the Germans deployed nine 'auxiliary cruisers', as the raiders were known, seven dispatched from European waters in 1940. There success lay not so much in their sinkings and captures (though this averaged fifteen ships per vessel) but in the sheer disruption that they caused. In comparison with the mighty German battleships *Bismarck* and *Tirpitz*, it might be argued, these vessels were incomparably more cost effective and more likely to sink enemy merchantmen. The nine 'auxiliary cruisers' were converted merchant vessels like the notorious *Atlantis* and *Pinguin*, and they were joined in their commerce raiding role by dedicated warships like the pocket battleship *Graf Spee* which during its Indian Ocean raid sank the *Africa Shell* in the Mozambique Channel, before sailing for

South America and destruction off Montevideo in the morale-boosting Battle of the River Plate (captured in the 1956 film *Battle of the River Plate*, starring some of the original cruisers). Illustrating the capacity of a solitary German raider to tie down British naval resources, *Graf Spee*'s cruise in the Indian Ocean in October 1939 saw the formation of several hunting groups in both the Indian Ocean and the South Atlantic. The pocket battleship *Admiral Scheer* also made an Indian Ocean commerce raid in early 1941, operating successfully off Madagascar and the northern Indian Ocean, where she sank the *Canadian Cruiser*. Numerous units of the Eastern Fleet were near at hand, and were ordered to intercept her. The cruiser HMS *Enterprise* was at Brava, the cruiser HMS *Ceres* at Mogadishu and the carrier HMS *Hermes* and the destroyers *Capetown* and *Kandahar* at Mombasa. The cruiser HMS *Emerald* was accompanying convoy WS5BX bound for Suez, and the cruiser HMS *Hawkins* was escorting the convoy WS5B steaming towards the Persian Gulf. Also nearby was the cruiser HMS *Glasgow*. Though an aircraft launched from *Glasgow* sighted her, the *Admiral Scheer* escaped the closing net and left the Indian Ocean unharmed, to the Royal Navy's frustration.

The commerce raider *Kormoran* operated in the Indian Ocean for many months, though with little success. In June 1941 she entered the Bay of Bengal to mine the approaches to Madras. The Commander-in-Chief of the East Indies Squadron took steps to catch her. On 1 July 1941 Force T (the aircraft carrier HMS *Hermes* and the cruiser *Enterprise*) left Trincomalee to search between Ceylon and Sumatra, and the cruiser HMAS *Australia* was sent to search around the Kerguelen and Crozet Islands deep in the Southern Ocean. Force T visited the Seychelles, again finding no trace. The failure of these ships to find *Kormoran* was to lead to one of the Royal Australian Navy's worst war-time disasters when on 19 November 1941 *Kormoran* engaged HMAS *Sydney* 200 miles off the coast of Western Australia. Luring the more heavily gunned cruiser close before opening fire, *Kormoran* was eventually abandoned and blew up, 315 crew members reaching safety in Australia. *Sydney*, though, was lost with all hands, and no trace of her was ever found.

A particular menace in the Indian Ocean was the raider *Pinguin*, the former Hansa Line ship *Kandelfels*. The *Pinguin* sunk 136,000 tons of Allied and neutral shipping in the space of a year. The Commander-in-Chief East Indies Station received reports of a German raider in the north west of the Indian Ocean in April 1941. At the time, Force T (*Hermes* and *Enterprise*) was in the Persian Gulf supporting imperial troops suppressing Rashid Ali's uprising in Iraq, and it had escorted two convoys of Indian troops sent from Karachi to Basra to take part in the campaign. (Before being recalled from the Gulf, *Hermes*'s aircraft conducted strikes against Iraqi targets near An Nasiriya, Amara, Samawa and Al Qurna.) Therefore the cruisers HMS *Cornwall* and *Hawkins* and the carrier HMS *Eagle* were ordered up from Mombasa to join the hunt. *Pinguin*, masquerading as a freighter, rendezvoused with a tanker at the entrance to the Persian Gulf. On 8 May 1941 a signal from her was intercepted on board *Cornwall* 500 miles south.

She launched her Walrus seaplane, which spotted the German vessel and brought the heavy cruiser to a position from where it could engage. A shell exploded among the mines that *Pinguin* was to lay at Karachi, and she sank.

The raider *Atlantis*, the former Hansa Line ship *Goldenfals*, sank sixteen vessels in the Indian Ocean between April 1940 and 11 November 1941. In December 1940 *Atlantis* had run aground whilst resting at Kerguelen Island, deep in the southern ocean, so repaired there until the following month. For such reasons did the warships and the flying boats of the Royal Navy and RAF vigilantly mount lonely patrols and quadrant searches in even these, some of the most remote waters on earth. The *Atlantis* had had a successful career sinking merchant vessels, mostly those of the British merchant marine going about the business of keeping imperial trade flowing. In May 1940, for example, the *King City* left Cardiff for Singapore carrying 5000 tons of Welsh coal. After breaking her journey at Cape Town, she encountered the *Atlantis* 180 miles north of Rodrigues and was sent to the bottom. MV *Automedon* was a 7500-ton Blue Funnel liner bound for Penang when she was closed by the *Atlantis* in the Java Straits on 11 November 1940. The German raider was flying a Dutch ensign and some of the crew visible on deck were disguised as women. Captain Bernhard Rögge's ship crippled the unsuspecting *Automedon* with broadsides from its 5.9-inch guns fired at point blank range. Among other things, the *Automedon* was carrying aircraft, cars and textiles from Britain to the Far East. The crew did not have time to destroy the ship's secret papers, and the German boarding party reaped a rich reward. They found maritime codebooks, shipping route charts and the courier mail for British Headquarters Singapore, including a secret War Cabinet and Chiefs of Staff report on the whole Far East situation destined for the Commander-in-Chief Far East, Air Chief Marshal Sir Robert Brooke-Popham. Rögge decided that these papers needed to reach Berlin without delay. Therefore the *Ole Jacob*, a Norwegian ship taken by *Atlantis* the previous day as it travelled from Singapore bound for Suez, was dispatched to Japan with the papers, which reached Germany on 30 December. In Japan the *Ole Jacob*'s 10,000 tons of aviation fuel was exchanged for 11,000 tons of diesel fuel and an aircraft. The papers were significant in deciding Japan to take the plunge and go to war, given their revelations about the weakness of Britain's position in the East, of which the Japanese had not been aware. In recognition of the value of his haul, Rögge was later presented with a samurai sword by the Japanese Emperor.[14] *Atlantis* was sunk on 21 November 1941 by the cruiser *Devonshire* whilst refuelling U-126 500 miles south of St Helena.

Hunting for these raiders was a major drain on the resources of the East Indies Station, involving a great deal of unrewarded patrolling. On 18 August 1940, for example, the cruiser HMS *Capetown* was sent from Colombo to search for a reported raider in the area of the Andoman and Nicobar Islands. Nine days later, another old six–inch cruiser, HMS *Colombo*, was ordered from Mombasa to Mauritius. On 11 September 1940 the Commander-in-Chief East Indies created Force V consisting of the cruisers HMS *Neptune* and *Capetown* and AMC *Arawa* and *Westralia*, and charged it specifically with anti-raider duties. The force was soon reinforced by another old six-inch cruiser, HMS *Ceres*, and the cruiser HMS *Dauntless* transferred from the China Station (*Westralia* left for convoy duties). On 7 September HMS *Neptune* left Simonstown to probe the uninhabited southern islands for enemy vessels. Force V did not find any enemy raiders, though by its mere existence it vindicated the German commerce raiding strategy. Other raiders, such as *Komet* and *Orion*, also cruised in the Indian Ocean, though the raider threat faded out in 1943 as they were all hunted down and destroyed. The *Michael*, the last of the raiders, operated in the Indian Ocean in June 1943. British detection techniques were improving, and the increase in naval and air forces in the region made it increasingly difficult for raiders to operate successfully. German supply ships were being sunk, and even the most remote, unvisited and uninhabited islands were being patrolled by British forces. ULTRA intelligence was, unbeknown to the Germans, becoming an important aid, and new technology like Leigh Lights, radar and improved depth charges came into service.

In addition to hunting enemy auxiliary cruisers, British forces also targeted Axis merchant vessels in the Indian Ocean. In one of those minor epics of the war, four Axis merchant ships interned in the neutral Portuguese harbour of Goa on India's west coast were attacked in March 1943 by superannuated members of the Calcutta Light Horse and the Calcutta Scottish. These were Indian Auxiliary Force units that had not seen active service since the Anglo-Boer War, and were more used to rounds in the club bar than rounds on the firing-range. Their escapade was the brainchild of SOE's India Mission, which had been charged by London with the destruction of a secret wireless transmitter aboard the German ship *Ehrenfels*, which was relaying intelligence on the movement of Allied ships leaving Indian ports to U-boats that would surface in the Indian Ocean at a prearranged time in order to receive messages. *Ehrenfels* was a Hansa Line sister ship of the raiders *Pinguin* and *Atlantis*. The intelligence was gathered by the Axis spy network in India before being transmitted to the waiting U-boat captains, momentarily surfaced somewhere in the moonlit Indian Ocean. SOE India was ordered to put a stop to the transmissions, which were leading to the loss of merchant ships. It was considered essential that the mission be absolutely clandestine and unofficial, for the Government of India and the British government could not risk the political ramifications that would attend a breach of Portuguese neutrality. This was why the Calcutta Light Horse was chosen by SOE as the unlikely and therefore unsuspected instrument of destruction, making a roundabout trip from east to west India by rail and ship. The superannuated Calcutta Light Horse heroes mounted a train to Calcutta, from where they boarded the 1912 hopper barge *Phoebe* for a round-India trip to Goa, where their targets lay at anchor. The mission ended in complete success with the destruction of the *Ehrenfels* and five other German and Italian ships.[15]

Throughout the Second World War the Indian Ocean was a theatre of sustained activity for Japanese and German (and to a lesser extent, Italian) submarines, potentially a far greater threat than that posed by the surface raiders. Enemy submarine packs patrolled the Indian Ocean from the Malacca Strait to the Mozambique Channel, and from the southern islands to the Persian Gulf. Submarines sent from European ports relied on rendezvous with supply boats or supply submarines known as 'milch cows', though Japanese and German submarines did have access to port facilities at Penang, Sabang and Singapore, all valuable bases captured from the Allied powers.[16] By the end of the war fifty-seven German U-boats had operated in the Indian Ocean, and most British Indian Ocean islands and rim territories had been surveyed by the aircraft carried aboard the large Japanese I-boats.

The ships of the East Indies Station gave continuous support to the land operations of imperial forces in East Africa in early 1941. Enemy ships flushed out of East African ports by land operations were intercepted, troops were ferried along the African coast or transported to and from ports like Berbera and Aden, and a special Red Sea Dhow Patrol was constituted to counter contraband smuggling in the region. For the Italian naval forces caught up in the East Africa campaign the prospects were bleak: imperial land forces were pressing at their rear; the Suez Canal was controlled by the British; and if an effort were to be made to break out and head for home around the Cape, the gauntlet of the Royal Navy had to be run. Despite the odds, many Italian vessels tried to do just this. The fruit-carrying ships *Ramb I* and *Ramb II*, which had been converted to armed cruisers with the addition of four 4.7-inch guns apiece, were ordered to break out from Massawa, Italy's main Red Sea port, and make for Japan along with the colonial dispatch ship *Eritrea*. *Ramb II* and *Eritrea* successfully accomplished this challenging mission, docking at Kobe, whilst *Ramb I* was sunk by the cruiser HMNZS *Leander* off the Maldives on 27 February 1941. The ships that reached Japan were supposed to operate as raiders in the Pacific, though the Japanese never permitted them to interfere in that theatre.

The four Italian submarines remaining in East African ports (*Archimede, Ferraris, Guglielmotti* and *Perla*) also needed to be got away, with the British closing in on victory in the East Africa campaign and planning their attack on Massawa. The first of the submarines left on 1 March 1941. Operation Supply was mounted against the submarines by British forces, using Mauritius as a base. In March 1941 HMS *City of Manchester*, HMNZS *Leander* and HMAS *Canberra* set out to find the submarines, which, it was feared, might make a 'death or glory' attack on British bases or convoys in the Red Sea. The submarines successfully evaded their hunters, however, and arrived in Bordeaux after rounding the Cape. Three Italian cargo ships attempted to break out from Massawa and reach Rio de Janeiro, two evading British patrols in Assab Bay and completing the journey. Five other Italian ships made for the French harbour of Diego Suarez, two of them evading capture. Massawa was occupied by British tanks and troops on 8 April 1941. Even then the Italian navy did not give up the fight, scuttling cargo vessels in the harbour and destroying port installations. A motor torpedo boat successfully targeted the cruiser HMS *Capetown*, which had to be towed to Port Sudan for a year-long repair job.

The Royal Navy had enjoyed a measure of success against its Italian counterpart in the Indian Ocean soon after Italy had declared war in June 1940. On the outbreak of war the submarines *Galileo Galilei* and *Toricelli* were patrolling off Djibouti in French Somaliland, where the *Galilei* sank the Norwegian tanker *James Stove*. British naval and air activity forced the submarines to leave their patrolling duties and take evasive measures. *Galilei* successfully evaded the British patrol in the Perim Strait on 23 June, intent on making for the Eritrean port of Massawa. On this stage of the journey, however, she was sighted by the sloop HMS *Shoreham*, and the hunt was on, the Italian submarine soon finding herself pursued by three destroyers and two gunboats, as the Commander-in-Chief East Indies Station concentrated the destroyers HMS *Kandahar*, *Khartoum* and *Kingston* along with HMS *Shoreham* and the anti-submarine trawler HMS *Moonstone*.* Gloster Gladiators of No. 94 Squadron from RAF Sheikh Othman near Aden were joined by Blenheims and Vickers Vincents of No. 8 Squadron from RAF Khormaksar in Aden to assist the surface units. The Italian submarine put up a magnificent fight against daunting odds. Not only did she hit *Shoreham*, which put into Aden for repairs, but she damaged *Khartoum* so much that she had to be declared a total loss. Eventually the Italian submarine was captured and a prize crew put aboard to take her to Aden. In recognition of the gallantry of his crew, the commander was treated as the guest of honour at a dinner given by the British naval commander in Aden. On the same day that *Galilei* was giving the Royal Navy a bloody nose, *Toricelli* was sunk by the destroyers HMS *Kandahar* and *Kingston*, aided by *Shoreham*. During the action, however, the destroyer HMS *Khartoum* exploded and sank off Perim Island. On the same day the Italian submarine *Galvani* sank the Royal Indian Navy sloop *Pathan*, though she was then herself sunk on the following day off the Gulf of Oman by the sloop HMS *Falmouth*. Thus by the conclusion of the month in which Italy entered the war her submarine forces in the Red Sea area had been decimated.[17]

Italy's Red Sea destroyer force shared the fate of its submarines. In October 1940 the British convoy BN7 was attacked by Italian destroyers based at Massawa.

---

* HMS *Shoreham* was a 1105-ton sloop of the East Indies Station, stationed in the Persian Gulf on the outbreak of war, when her responsibilities were extended to the Red Sea. *Shoreham* took part in the occupation of the Gulf port of Abadan during the Iranian campaign in August 1941. On 24 August 1941 Rajputana and Kumaon Rifles embarked in motor-boats from Basra for the fifty miles journey to Abadan where, at zero hour, the guns of HMS *Shoreham* opened up on a Persian sloop, reducing it to a blazing wreck, signalling the start of the attack. Following service in the Gulf, *Shoreham* worked as an anti-aircraft ship at Suez before rejoining the Eastern Fleet at Colombo as an anti-submarine escort in June 1942. After a refit in Bombay she served at Alexandria and in the Levant before taking part in the invasion of Sicily, finally returning to the Eastern Fleet in September 1943.

The convoy's Eastern Fleet escort force, which included the cruiser HMNZ *Leander* and the destroyer HMS *Kimberley*, drove the Italian ship *Nullo* ashore with gunfire, where she was destroyed the following day by RAF Blenheim bombers. Other Italian destroyers were flushed out by land operations during the East Africa campaign and sunk. This was not before the three largest Italian destroyers (*Leone, Pantera* and *Tigre*) attempted a daring attack on Suez, through enemy-invested narrow waters. The Luftwaffe agreed to help by bombing the Canal at the same time, though this operation had to be cancelled. The destroyers set off on 31 March 1941 regardless. One promptly grounded itself on the islets off Massawa and was so severely damaged that it was sunk by gunfire from its two sister ships, which, as daylight was approaching, returned to port. The three smaller destroyers (*Battisti, Manin,* and *Sauro*) had planned to make an attack on Port Sudan, which the two remaining large destroyers now decided to join. They departed on 2 April 1941, secure in the knowledge that success was almost impossible. British air reconnaissance removed the element of surprise, and thirty miles from Port Sudan a sustained air attack developed, aircraft flying from Port Sudan itself and the carrier HMS *Eagle*. *Pantera* and *Tigre* were able to make it to the Arabian coast and scuttle. The other two ships, *Manin* and *Sauro*, continued to fight until both were sunk by shore-based Swordfish from *Eagle*. Thus the Italian naval presence in the Red Sea, a crucial waterway that Mussolini had hoped to dominate, came to a gallant if pointless end.

These naval victories, even less heralded than the victories on land against Italian forces in East Africa in 1940–41, signalled the utter destruction of the Italian Empire in Africa, and, among other things, were testament to British superiority at sea and in the air. They did not, however, entirely end Italian naval operations in the Indian Ocean region. At the end of 1942 five specially modified submarines were sent out from Europe, three of them modified to carry 150 tons of cargo to trade with Japan. Three reached Japan in the spring of 1943, and were moored there at the time of the Italian surrender to the Allies. The *Da Vinci* had a 120-day cruise in the Indian Ocean, in which she sank nearly 60,000 tons of shipping before being sunk near the Azores on her homeward journey. The *Cagni* made a record-breaking 137-day cruise, and was ninety days into her second Indian Ocean tour when the Italian surrender occurred, upon which she surprised the port of Durban by surfacing to surrender on 21 September 1943.

The Indian Ocean remained dangerous for merchant shipping throughout 1943, as illustrated by the fate of the *Fort Mumford*, which on 18 March left Colombo bound for the Mediterranean via Aden, carrying a cargo of military supplies that included crated fighter aircraft on deck and some landing craft below, destined for use in the imminent Allied invasion of Sicily. The ship was a real war-time imperial creation. Built in Canada for the British Ministry of War Transport, her maiden voyage had taken her from Montreal to Vancouver via the Panama Canal and on to Lyttelton in New Zealand. She then sailed for Ceylon. On 20 March, ninety miles off Suheli Par, the southernmost of the Laccadive

Islands, she was sunk by the Japanese submarine I-127. The sole survivor was picked up by an Indian dhow sailing from Malabar to Mikindani in Tanganyika.

From the middle of 1943, as British naval forces were gaining in strength in the Indian Ocean, the Japanese requested that the German U-boats operating off south-eastern Africa be transferred to the Arabian Sea. This was because Britain was building up large forces in India and Ceylon for the offensive in Burma (ships could now sail via the Mediterranean and therefore traverse the Arabian Sea, rather than being obliged to go around the Cape). Dönitz decided to wait until after the next monsoon, when he thought that the arrival of a new force of U-boats in the northern Indian Ocean – the Monsoon group – would have a telling effect. Only five of the ten U-boats sent out from Europe reached their destination, however, to take up their positions in September 1943. The remainder were destroyed by the Royal Navy en route. Eastern Fleet headquarters, which had returned to Colombo on 4 September after a sojourn in Mombasa following the Japanese raid on Ceylon in April 1942, was aware that four or five submarines were moving north from Madagascar, and recent Japanese sinkings in the Arabian Sea meant that there was no chance of a surprise German blow. Enemy submarines were concentrating on shipping in the Arabian Sea as it had become much busier since the reopening of the Suez Canal. Convoys were introduced on routes from Durban to Mombasa, Aden, Bombay and Colombo, and strong air and sea patrols covered focal areas. Nevertheless, submarine attacks continued into 1944, demanding increased convoy protection, which demobilized the Eastern Fleet by depriving its battleships of the destroyer screens essential for their use in offensive operations.

Developments after the reopening of the Mediterranean required a general rethink of British operational strategy, given the redeployment of enemy submarine forces. Much more British shipping returned to the Red Sea–Arabian Sea area as it journeyed from the Suez Canal to eastern destinations and back in the other direction. An added attraction in the region was the Gulf of Oman, giving onto the Straits of Hormuz and the Gulf itself. Submarines that had been hunting in the Mozambique Channel and off the Cape switched their attention to the northern Indian Ocean. To meet the expected new challenges in this region Britain reinforced naval and air assets. No. 621 Squadron, flying Wellington bombers, and twelve Catalina flying boats from Nos. 295 and 265 Squadrons were moved from East Africa to bases covering the Gulf of Aden. Mauritius and Tulear in southern Madagascar were reinforced with flying boats as well. From November 1943 it was decided that Aden's operational area would be extended to cover the Persian Gulf, working closely in the region with No. 222 Group, South East Asia Command. This brought a unification of operational command which was vital if effective protection was to be provided for shipping dispersed over such a wide area.

In 1944 the Indian Ocean became less attractive as an area for U-boats operations with the sinking of their much-hunted supply ships *Brake* and *Charlotte*

Schleimann through the combined efforts of Eastern Fleet destroyers and cruisers, RAF flying boats and ULTRA intelligence. *Charlotte Schleimann,* a 7747-ton support ship, was run to ground in January 1944. A plan drawn up by Admiral Sir James Somerville, Commander-in-Chief Eastern Fleet since the end of March 1942, saw warships concentrate on Mauritius for the operation against the supply ship. HMS *Kenya, Newcastle* and *Suffolk* arrived from Ceylon, *Canton* and *Nepal* from Durban, and the escort carriers *Bann* and *Battler* from the Arabian Sea. Catalinas were flown from East Africa to Mauritian bases, and fuel oil had already arrived courtesy of the Royal Fleet Auxiliary *Olynthus.*

In March 1944 intercepted intelligence told Somerville that German submarines hunting British merchant vessels in the Arabian Sea would soon need refuelling. In that month *Brake,* the other German supply ship, rendezvoused with U-188, U-532 and U-168, and Eastern Fleet headquarters learned of this concentration. Mauritius was again used as the operational base. A force code-named CS4 gathered in the island's ports, consisting of the escort carrier HMS *Battler,* the cruisers *Suffolk* and *Newcastle,* the destroyers *Quadrant* and *Roebuck,* and seven Catalina flying boats from Nos 259 and 265 Squadrons. The force sailed from Mauritius on 6 March 1944, with *Battler's* aircraft making long reconnaissance sweeps ahead of the task force in spite of appalling weather. On 12 March one of *Battler's* aircraft spotted a tanker and two submarines. One of them, U-188, had just finished refuelling after having recently sunk the SS *Fort Buckingham* and SS *Fort La Maune* in the Arabian Sea. HMS *Roebuck* was homed in by an aircraft from *Battler* dropping messages on board, giving range and bearing. The destroyer spotted *Brake* at thirteen miles and opened fire, sinking her in half an hour. The two U-boats were attacked by *Battler's* aircraft, one being severely damaged, though U-188 escaped unscathed. After this, in the period from May to August 1944, the U-boats found the Indian Ocean further diminished as a rewarding hunting ground as the Eastern Fleet became better equipped as well as better trained. Shipping zones were constantly patrolled by aircraft, Diego Garcia and Addu Atoll now played their part as mid-ocean air bases, and a hunter-killer group was formed by the Eastern Fleet consisting of nine frigates and sloops and the escort carriers HMS *Begum* and *Shah.* The hunt for the supply boats demonstrated the use of imperial territories as operational bases that was a feature of the imperial war effort. It also demonstrated the importance attached to the destruction of submarines and their supply vessels in the Indian Ocean. Allied merchant ships simply had to be protected, and doing this occupied the efforts of large numbers of valuable naval and air assets. In the Indian Ocean, as in the Atlantic, the availability or non-availability of escort vessels was crucial in determining whether ships were protected or not, whether enemy vessels could be run to ground and destroyed or not, and whether capital units like battleships could raid enemy targets or not.

The need to juggle destroyers and escort vessels could prove costly. On the whole the British were both skilled and lucky when it came to protecting their troop-carrying ships during the Second World War. In February 1944, however, the SS *Khedive Ismail*, part of the five-ship troop convoy KR8 sailing from Mombasa to Colombo, was sunk by the Japanese submarine I-27 (which had earlier sunk the *Fort Mumford*). This cost the lives of 1134 people, most of them members of 301st Field Regiment, East African Artillery, on their way to join the 11th East African Division. The ship's 1511 passengers included, in addition to the 996 officers and men of the 301st Field Regiment, 271 Royal Navy personnel, 178 crew members, fifty-three nurses and nine members of the Women's Transport Service.[18] The submarine was sunk by the destroyers HMS *Petard* and *Paladin*, sent from Colombo to escort the convoy on the final leg of its voyage. After ramming the submarine, HMS *Paladin* made for the secret naval base Port T at Addu Atoll in the Maldives, within sight of which the *Khedive Ismail* had been sunk. There she was repaired by the repair ship HMS *Lucia* (damaged in the Japanese raid on Trincomalee in April 1942). After this, still damaged but seaworthy, *Paladin* went out again to look for survivors, as did a salvage ship.

An investigation into the sinking, ordered by Admiral Somerville, blamed the lack of adequate escorts for the tragedy (the Eastern Fleet had only twenty destroyers at the time). While the *Khedive Ismail* was at sea, Eastern Fleet escort forces and RAF aircraft from Ceylon were busy covering the movement across the Indian Ocean of a giant floating dock that was to be installed at Trincomalee. (In August 1944 the dock sank with the battleship HMS *Valiant* inside, causing damage requiring nearly two years of repairs back in Britain. The dock remained on the bottom for another twenty-five years. The First Sea Lord, Admiral Sir Andrew Cunningham, was so angry that he ensured that uncompromising disciplinary measures were taken.) Furthermore, operations in support of the army in Burma were scheduled to take place soon, which would require destroyer cover. Major warships in Ceylon, including HMS *Illustrious* and *Renown*, were due in the Pacific at some point in the near future, and therefore needed their destroyer escorts to hand. Fortunately other troop movements were achieved without loss, a remarkable record.

The escort afforded major convoys crossing the Indian Ocean often appeared sparse. In January 1943 the Australian 9th Division massed in the Gulf of Suez awaiting transit home. The 'Monsters' – the world's largest ocean liners converted to use as troopships (*Aquitania, Ile de France, Nieuw Amsterdam* and *Queen Mary*) – all called at Suez to collect their quota (along with the AMC *Queen of Bermuda*). They were escorted clear of the Gulf of Aden by Mediterranean Fleet destroyers, and handed over to a solitary cruiser, HMS *Devonshire*, which escorted them through the Indian Ocean. Though submarines remained a threat into 1944, and convoy protection remained a priority duty of the Eastern Fleet, the balance was swinging in the Allies' favour. The shift in fortunes in the war at sea was indicated by the fact that the sinking of a mere eight ships in the Indian Ocean in August 1943 made it the most dangerous area for shipping in the world. The Mediterranean had by that time been cleared, the Battle of the Atlantic won and

Japan's naval power in the Pacific seriously compromised. The returns for enemy submarines were getting lower and lower. In January 1944 nine Japanese submarines based at Penang sunk only two ships, though as late as March 1944 there were fourteen German and Japanese submarines in the Indian Ocean. Behind such encouraging figures, however, the war at sea and the dangers involved remained very real for those involved in the perennial tasks of fetching and carrying on which the Empire's survival depended. On 1 September 1944 the *Troilus* was homeward bound from Colombo, carrying coconut oil, tea and copra for the Ministry of Food. She was routed to sail independently via Suez, but halfway between Colombo and Aden she was torpedoed. The frigates HMS *Taff* and *Nadder* were sent to search for survivors.

Destroyer escort was essential when the capital ships of the Eastern Fleet were called into offensive action, as when they supported the army in Burma with coastal bombardments. Convoy escort duties made the Eastern Fleet less potent as an offensive force, however, because it grounded the capital ships. Fortunately the Japanese fleet based on Singapore, which in late 1943 and early 1944 could muster eight battleships, three carriers and eighteen cruisers, did not take advantage of the immobility of the Eastern Fleet's battleships. Faced with this concentration of enemy forces, Somerville even considered a tactical withdrawal to the Maldives, though the Admiralty thought this would be bad for morale. It was discovered that the Japanese were undertaking a docking programme at Singapore now that their main base at Truk in the Pacific was within range of American bombers, rather than massing for strikes to the west. The only Indian Ocean activity by Japanese surface ships was that of the heavy cruisers *Chikuma* and *Tone*, which sank the British ship *Behar* between Australia and Mauritius on 1 March 1944 as they searched for merchant vessels to capture at a time when Japanese merchant losses were mounting dangerously. Seventy of *Behar*'s crew were put to death, though fifteen were picked up and taken to Batavia. As a result of this attack, Admiral Somerville made a sweep along the Australia–India trade route, sailing from Ceylon on 21 March 1944, meeting the aircraft carrier USS *Saratoga* en route, which was being loaned to the Eastern Fleet because of the Japanese build up of forces at Singapore, as was the Free French battleship *Richelieu*.

The Eastern Fleet and the British Pacific Fleet that it gave birth to in August 1944 are overlooked features of the global dispersal of British forces during the Second World War. These naval forces have been dubbed the 'Forgotten Fleet', operating in support of the 'Forgotten Army' (in the skies, inevitably, flew the 'Forgotten Air Force').[19] The Eastern Fleet deserves greater acknowledgement, for as the Mediterranean Fleet fought bravely to overcome the combined strength of the Italian navy and Hitler's U-boats, the Eastern Fleet fought doggedly to ensure that the Indian Ocean remained a 'British Lake' across which the Empire's vital convoys could pass without molestation by the forces of Germany, Italy and Japan. It then transformed its main strength into the British Pacific Fleet, the most powerful

British fleet in history. Using Australian bases, this fleet faced the kamikazes in the closing stages of the Pacific war and heralded the huge British air, sea and land build up in the East that had been promised as soon as the European war had ended, though it was never fully deployed because the bombing of Hiroshima and Nagasaki brought the eastern war to an earlier-than-expected end.

The idea of creating a 'proper' Far Eastern fleet at Singapore, rather than simply promising that a fleet would be sent if needed, had been considered before the outbreak of war. The idea revolved around a plan to send out the five vintage 'Royal Sovereign' (usually referred to as the 'R') class battleships. In 1939 the Foreign Office examined this idea, arguing that Britain was facing a real potential enemy in the East and that concentrating all capital units in European and Mediterranean waters, therefore, was a questionable policy. If, as proposed, the 'R' class ships were soon to be scrapped, they might just as well be sent east. Waiting for an emergency to develop in the Far East before dispatching the capital ships was recognized as a very risky strategy. The Admiralty considered this proposal in spring 1939, though it decided that a Far East battlefleet could not at that stage be completed. (One of the reasons cited was that the new battleships, the five 'King George V' class vessels, would not start to complete until early 1941.) Therefore the original plan remained in place: to send a fleet to Singapore if and when Japan threatened war. Until then, British maritime interests East of Suez would be looked after by the ships of the China Station and the East Indies Station.

Before the entry of Japan into the war, in December 1941, the British position in the Indian Ocean was worrying but not critical, because the East Indies Station fleet was equal to the challenge presented by German and Italian submarines and raiders. But after Pearl Harbor the main strategic challenge to Britain's position in the Indian Ocean was posed by the Imperial Japanese Navy. The long-standing promise to send British capital ships to Singapore was fulfilled on 3 December with the arrival of Force Z, HMS *Prince of Wales* and *Repulse* and their destroyer escort. The size of the force was disappointing though, and the aircraft carrier that was supposed to accompany it, HMS *Indomitable*, had run aground on 3 November 1941 in Kingston Harbour, Jamaica, after a refit in America. But confidence was high, apart from amongst those select few who had an inkling of the type, size and quality of the forces that Japan might unleash against them.[20]

The arrival of these ships and their diminutive commander, Admiral Sir Tom Phillips, heralded the creation of the new Eastern Fleet, which superseded the East Indies Station and the China Station commands. Admiralty instructions to Phillips on 2 December 1941 told him of their Lordships' decision to replace the Commander-in-Chief China, previously the senior naval commander in the east, with a new appointment styled Commander-in-Chief Eastern Fleet. Phillips arrived in Singapore by air from Colombo at the end of November 1941, and his two capital ships arrived three days later. Vice-Admiral Sir Geoffrey Layton remained in temporary command of the shore establishments and the

China Station, of which he had become Commander-in-Chief in September 1940. On 8 December, the Admiralty ordered that the China Station be merged with the Eastern Fleet and all naval forces in the Far East then came under Phillips's command. On that day Phillips's fleet consisted of the two capital ships, the cruisers HMS *Danae, Dragon* and *Durban,* four destroyers (the two at Hong Kong were on their way to Singapore), three gunboats (at Hong Kong; a fourth, HMS *Petrel,* was sunk by Japanese forces at Shanghai on the same day), two armed merchant cruisers, and a cruiser and six destroyers refitting or under repair. Based at Ceylon were the battleship HMS *Revenge* and the cruiser *Exeter,* with the cruiser *Enterprise* and the carrier *Hermes* refitting. On the Australia Station were two New Zealand and five Australian cruisers.

On 9 December 1941 disaster struck this newly-created, though unbalanced and untested, Eastern Fleet, when in the Gulf of Siam the two capital ships, hunting for reported Japanese transports heading for Malaya, were wiped out by Japanese bombers based in Indo-China, the first battleships ever to be destroyed by aircraft. Phillips went to the bottom with his flagship, *Prince of Wales,* the pride of the fleet, which had so recently transported Churchill across the Atlantic to confer with Roosevelt off Newfoundland. Following the sinkings of *Prince of Wales* and *Repulse,* and the subsequent Allied defeat in the Battle of the Java Sea and the surrender of Singapore, the Eastern Fleet – now based on Ceylon – was Britain's only naval presence East of Suez, and was faced by what temporarily was the most powerful navy in the world. With Phillips's loss command of the Eastern Fleet defaulted to Vice-Admiral Sir Geoffrey Layton, who transferred his flag to Ceylon after the formation of American-British-Dutch-Australian (ABDA) Command, the short-lived Allied command headed by General Wavell, formed to regroup Allied forces in the East in the wake of Anglo-American reverses. The removal of the Eastern Fleet to Ceylon, a tactical withdrawal from waters in which the Royal Navy could no longer contest the issue with the ascendant Imperial Japanese Navy, meant that Ceylon became the only major British naval base between the Cape of Good Hope and Australia. In March 1942 the pugnacious Admiral Sir James Somerville, the former commander of Force H in the western Mediterranean, arrived to take over the Eastern Fleet, and Admiral Layton was made Commander-in-Chief Ceylon.

The loss of *Prince of Wales* and *Repulse* demonstrated the gap between British expectations and the reality of the Japanese threat. It revealed, in a sudden and violent manner, the vast disparity between British naval capabilities in eastern waters and those of the new enemy. The capital ships sent east were too few, *Prince of Wales* was inexperienced and *Repulse* was superannuated. They also lacked the air cover that was to become essential to successful operations in the Second World War, as the battleship ceased to be the ultimate arbiter of military might. Just as significantly, British appraisal of Japanese forces, capacities and intentions failed them badly. Churchill had fought hard for the dispatch of Force Z because he thought that their presence would greatly boost the morale of the Australasian Dominions and force caution upon the Japanese by their very presence. Churchill was wildly out of touch, but then so was just about everybody else at the time. The Admiralty Naval Staff's plan was less spectacular, though, after *Prince of Wales* and *Repulse* were sunk, it was this that was adopted. The Admiralty intended gradually to build up naval forces based on Ceylon until a point was reached at which operations against the Japanese further east could be undertaken. Admiral of the Fleet Sir Dudley Pound told Churchill that by April 1942 he could build a force around the battleships HMS *Nelson, Rodney* and *Renown* operating from Ceylon with the carriers HMS *Hermes* and *Ark Royal* and supporting cruisers and destroyers, while the four surviving 'R' class battleships (the fifth, *Royal Oak*, had been sunk by a U-boat in Scapa Flow shortly after the start of the war) would be available for covering troop convoys in the Indian Ocean. Churchill, however, wanted bolder action than this, and he wanted it now. Distinct from Churchill's bombastic plan, the Admiralty emphasized that its plan was intended first and foremost to ensure the protection of trade in and across the Indian Ocean, not, as in the case of Churchill's, to try and teach the Japanese a good lesson by sending a couple of battleships to Far Eastern waters.

The responsibility for sending an understrength force to Singapore, however, does not rest exclusively with Churchill. The popular historical view of a domineering Churchill getting his way over and above Admiralty objections must be tempered with an alternative explanation that reverses the roles. At the crux of this interpretation is the role that Admiralty planners expected America to play if war with Japan broke out. Meetings before the outbreak of the Japanese war had seen the Americans insist that Britain made efforts to defend the Malay barrier, whilst American forces would assume responsibility for the Atlantic. A fleet, including the 'R' class battleships and at least one newer capital unit, should gather on Singapore then operate even further east, using Manila, in the American Philippines, as a forward base. Under the arrangements discussed with the Americans, the American Asiatic Fleet would operate from Singapore. This prospect of American support entered the calculations of those planning naval operations from Singapore when Japan went to war, though the expected American help did not arrive in those crucial days following 8 December 1941, given the turmoil in American naval circles caused by the attack on Pearl Harbor. Given all of these pre-war ruminations, when in September 1941 the Secretary of State for Foreign Affairs, Anthony Eden, and the Australian Prime Minister, John Curtin, called for a strong reaction to Japanese aggression, Churchill agreed that sending a couple of ships, including one of the most modern, would be a prudent gesture. The Admiralty was unenthusiastic and had its eyes fixed firmly on a force built around six capital ships operating from Manila.

At two Cabinet Defence Committee meetings in October 1941, Churchill argued for the value of sending one or two fast modern battleships as a deterrent measure. Whilst this force alone would be unable to take on the main strength of the Imperial Japanese Navy, it could – like the *Tirpitz* in European waters – tie down many Japanese units, and cause trouble for Japanese strategists by appearing at different vulnerable points in the Far East, a veritable Pimpernel. The First Lord of the Admiralty, Sir Dudley Pound, favoured retaining all of the 'King George V' class battleships in Home waters given the threat of the *Tirpitz* breaking out and bringing death and disruption to Britain's vital transatlantic supply route. But the Admiralty's real objections were that it wanted to send a larger force of slower but heavy-gunned battleships to the Far East as a signal to the Americans that Britain meant real fighting business when it came to defending its Far Eastern Empire. This could not be fully explained to Churchill, as the Admiralty was playing a game of its own. The 'R's would be sent out, and whatever their faults born of old age, with American forces diverting the bulk of Japanese attention to other waters these ships would be sufficient in a defensive role, to protect convoy routes and to demonstrate to the Americans that there was blood, metal and bone behind the alliance in the East.

At the Defence Committee's second October meeting, Churchill said that the Cabinet was willing to take the risk of the *Tirpitz* breaking out, and that the American Navy was taking a more active role in the Atlantic. He repeated his belief that a fast, modern capital ship in the Far East would have a stirring effect, on Britain's friends and foes alike. The First Sea Lord repeated that he preferred to keep all 'King George V' battleships in Home waters and that a solitary fast ship sent east would hardly be a significant deterrent. What also troubled Admiral Pound was that such a small force would inevitably mean that Britain's commitment was to the Indian Ocean, whereas the Admiralty was working for a much more forward policy based on cooperating with the Americans in the Far East. This meant defending the Philippines, operating from Manila, and allowing American forces to deal with the Japanese in the Pacific. The Admiralty nearly got its way, though the disaster of 10 December 1941, when the advanced guard of this new fleet, HMS *Prince of Wales* and *Repulse*, was sunk, changed everything. The four 'R' class battleships, still on their way east, thus became the nucleus of an Eastern Fleet with an entirely different mission: holding on in the Indian Ocean and protecting the vital convoy routes.

So when Churchill's unrealistic 'deterrence' hopes, and the Admiralty's clever Anglo-American eastern strategic plans, went down with the two capital ships in the Gulf of Siam, it was the less spectacular but absolutely essential role of convoy protection in the Indian Ocean that became the main task of the Eastern Fleet. It performed this role from the dark days of early 1942 until 1944, when its increased strength, and the weakening of Japanese naval power, enabled it to also take more offensive action against Japanese forces and Japanese-occupied territories. But in the gloomy days after the sinking of *Prince of Wales* and *Repulse*, when taking the offensive against Japan was a long way off, retreat was the order of the day. By March 1942 the British government realized that it was in the Indian Ocean that maritime power would have to be reconstructed, with Ceylon as the main base of a fleet kept in being and building for future offensive operations. For the time

292   THE BRITISH EMPIRE AND THE SECOND WORLD WAR

being, it had to be accepted that the Royal Navy in the waters east of Ceylon was a spent force that must await a return to the Far East as and when the general war situation allowed. Meanwhile, there were convoys of troops and supplies crossing the vital sea routes of the Indian Ocean that needed protection if the Empire were to survive.

Until the hoped for victories that would enable the white ensign to return to the waters of the Far East and its bases in Singapore and Hong Kong, the Eastern Fleet's primary task was to patrol the world's third largest ocean and protect the convoys that crossed it. Admiral Somerville at naval headquarters Colombo had subordinate officers at naval shore bases in Aden, Addu Atoll, Bahrain, Bombay, Calcutta, Cochin, East Africa, Hormuz, India, Kuwait, Mauritius, the Persian Gulf, the Seychelles and Shatt-el-Arab. The Eastern Fleet's tasks were many. Its bread-and-butter was escort duties to protect convoys crossing the Indian Ocean – the vital role on which the Middle Eastern and South Asian war theatres depended. The fleet attempted to sink enemy warships when they entered the Indian Ocean, supported the army in the Burma campaign, the East Africa campaign and the Persian Gulf, and raided Japanese targets in occupied territory. The fleet was responsible for hunting and killing enemy submarines and raiders, and blockading Vichy and Italian ports in the region. It sought to intercept enemy convoys such as those seeking to connect Vichy France with its loyal colonies in Africa, the Indian Ocean and South-East Asia, and to disrupt the submarine traffic in technology and industrial raw materials between Japan and Germany. It supported Allied special forces fighting behind enemy lines in South-East Asia and the Dutch East Indies. In the crucial period following Pearl Harbor and the raid on Ceylon in April 1942, arguably the Eastern Fleet's most important duty was to evade being destroyed by the Imperial Japanese Navy whilst trying to deny the enemy the free use of this vast ocean.

In 1943–44 the Eastern Fleet grew in size and power, and from 1944 it was able to undertake more offensive operations whilst continuing to carry out its essential defensive tasks. The fleet attacked Japanese bases, harried Japanese shipping attempting to supply the Imperial Japanese Army in Burma and the Andaman Islands, and mined the approaches to Japanese-occupied harbours like Penang and important seaways like the Malacca Strait. The fleet's minelaying and minesweeping role became more important. The Eastern Fleet's submarines played an important role in inserting behind-the-lines forces in Japanese-occupied or influenced territory like Malaya, Sumatra and Thailand, and aircraft of the Fleet Air Arm joined the RAF in patrolling the Indian Ocean and defending Ceylon. Another major role of the Eastern Fleet was to support army operations in the Indian Ocean region. It provided, for example, air cover and troopship escorts for the British invasion of Iraq in April 1941. It supported the land operations of the East Africa campaign in 1940–41, contributed ships to the Madagascar campaign in May 1942, and operated in the Bay of Bengal during the Burma campaign, covering the Arakan offensives and the amphibious assault on

Rangoon. It also played a key transport and covering role in the amphibious assault on Malaya in September 1945.

At the high-water mark of Japanese power in 1941–42 the Eastern Fleet was powerful, but not nearly powerful enough to contest the issue with the Imperial Japanese Navy. The Eastern Fleet was one of the largest British fleets to assemble since the Napoleonic Wars, and a powerful weapon, the loss of which would have been catastrophic for the imperial war effort. The War Cabinet hastily reinforced the fleet following the loss of Singapore, so that by the end of March 1942 Admiral Somerville had five battleships, two fleet carriers (*Indomitable* and *Formidable*), the vintage carrier HMS *Hermes*, seven cruisers, sixteen destroyers and seven submarines (two of the cruisers and two of the submarines were Dutch). This fleet was simply no match, however, for the five carriers and four modern battleships that formed the core of Admiral Nagumo's fleet which had raided Pearl Harbor. Four of Somerville's five battleships were of First World War vintage (the 'R' class vessels HMS *Ramillies, Resolution, Revenge* and *Royal Sovereign*), slow, and lacking armoured decks and therefore easy pickings for Japanese carrier-borne aircraft. The 'R' class had been designed for short-range work in home waters, consequently requiring frequent refuelling stops when operating over much greater distances in the Indian Ocean. The fifth battleships, HMS *Warspite*, was actually pre-First World War, though she had been extensively modernized. The Eastern Fleet lacked fleet training, sufficient firepower, modern aircraft and adequate harbour protection at Trincomalee and Colombo. The Japanese fleet that confronted it from December 1941 was temporarily the most powerful navy in the world, superior on every count to the Eastern Fleet. Given their several handicaps, the 'R' class battleships needed to be kept well away from possible engagements with the Japanese, leaving only the modernized HMS *Warspite* to operate with the fleet's two main carriers. This meant that anything like a fleet action against the Japanese would have been a disaster, and the fleet's priority in the period of Japan's greatest strength was therefore to keep itself 'in being' and to attempt to perform its crucial convoy escort and policing duties in the Indian Ocean. In the war against Japan, therefore, the Eastern Fleet's role was to act as a deterrent barring the approaches to the Indian Ocean, a holding operation before victories in other theatres of naval conflict allowed the fleet to be strengthened sufficiently for it to take the offensive.

In April 1942 Admiral Nagumo's carrier force raided Ceylon, attempting to repeat Pearl Harbor against the Eastern Fleet and secure Japan's western perimeters after its four months of conquest and expansion. Though he failed to destroy the main units of the fleet, the raids cost over a thousand British and Ceylonese lives, two cruisers, a carrier, two destroyers, twenty-three merchantmen, a number of smaller vessels and over thirty fighter aircraft. Following the raids Admiral Somerville withdrew the 'R' class battleships to Mombasa in East Africa, partially abandoning the eastern Indian Ocean to concentrate on the defence of the western area and its vital supply route to the Middle East and Persian Gulf.

Somerville did not entirely abandon the eastern Indian Ocean, however, and continued to use the secret base at Addu Atoll in the Maldives (a British protectorate since 1887), and the ports of Ceylon, though Somerville's headquarters were removed from Colombo to Mombasa, the latest in a line of retreats that had already seen British naval power pull back from Hong Kong and Singapore. In the period before the waning of Japan's naval star, the Eastern Fleet's main purpose was to *deter* the Japanese from striking across the Indian Ocean. It was a game of bluff in which, as Somerville put it, he had 'to lie low in one sense but be pretty active in another – keep the old tarts [the 'R' class battleships] out of the picture and roar about with the others'. As he wrote in his diary, 'air cover [is] quite inadequate to dispute this Command'. As in all other theatres of the Second World War, air power was proved to be a crucial variable.

The Japanese threat to Ceylon and the Indian Ocean reached its height in April 1942 with the raids on Colombo and Trincomalee, when the carriers that had devastated the American Pacific Fleet sought to extend the favour to the British Eastern Fleet. The Chief of the Imperial General Staff, General Sir Alan Brooke, arrived for his daily meeting with the Chiefs of Staff in London on the morning of 6 April 1942, and 'discovered that most of the Japanese fleet appears to be in the Indian Ocean with our Eastern Fleet retiring westwards. Up to the present no sign of transports [meaning an army invasion force]. I don't like the situation much as we are very weak in the Indian Ocean'. Slightly more cheering was the news of the air defence that had greeted the Japanese carrier-borne aircraft when they had attacked Colombo, Ceylon's capital, the day before: 'At any rate the air action over Ceylon was successful yesterday and we downed 27 Japs!'[21]

The Japanese were also keen to attack Ceylon because the British fleet posed a threat to Japanese shipping in the Bay of Bengal. A successful attack would secure shipping bound for newly-captured Rangoon and impress Indians across the subcontinent with Japanese power at a time when Anglo-Indian relations were in the doldrums, and Sir Stafford Cripps had just embarked upon his famous mission to offer India independence after the war in return for support during the conflict. In what was to be the Japanese navy's only major offensive westward, Nagumo hoped to catch the Eastern Fleet in harbour and to destroy what remained of British sea power East of Suez, as he had caught the Americans – also on a Sunday – the previous December. At the beginning of April Nagumo steamed towards Ceylon with the First Air Fleet's five fleet carriers and the 3rd Battle Squadron's four battleships, escorted by three cruisers, eleven destroyers and seven submarines, having left the Celebes on 28 March, passing south of Sumatra and entering the Indian Ocean on 3 April. Somerville had only arrived in Ceylon (on board the carrier HMS *Formidable*) on 24 March to take command of the Eastern Fleet, and the four 'R' class battleships and six of the destroyers did not arrive to rendezvous with the fleet until the very end of March. Somerville's two main carriers carried far fewer, and far less modern, aircraft than Nagumo's (each Japanese ship carried about sixty machines). HMS *Warspite* had recently been repaired in America after suffering damage off Crete. So the Eastern Fleet was not only inferior, it was completely unprepared.

The imminent Japanese attack on Ceylon was reported on 28 March 1942 when Far East Combined Bureau, the island's Bletchley Park outstation, intercepted a Japanese signal spelling out the name of the target: KO-RO-N-BO. As a result of this information Somerville put to sea from Addu Atoll, the Eastern Fleet's secret base in the Maldives, with his most modern ships, expecting to encounter the Japanese fleet on 1 April 1942.[22] He sailed to meet the rest of his fleet which had left Ceylon on 31 March. Somerville hoped to launch a night attack against Nagumo's fleet, realizing that this was the only realistic chance that his inferior fleet had of scoring a hit on the enemy force. Even in doing this, many were to think afterwards, Somerville was taking an unacceptable risk that might have seen the main strength of the Royal Navy East of Suez destroyed in a fleet action. Somerville's cast-iron duty – driven home by the First Sea Lord Admiral Sir Dudley Pound – was to keep the fleet 'in being'. The fleet was divided into Force A, HMS *Warspite*, the two modern carriers *Indomitable* (twenty-four Albacores, twelve Fulmars, nine Hurricanes) and *Formidable* (twenty-one Albacores, twelve Martlets), four large cruisers (*Cornwall, Dorsetshire, Emerald* and *Enterprise*), and six destroyers; and Force B, a supporting force consisting of the four vintage battleships, the similarly-aged light carrier *Hermes* (twelve Swordfish), two light cruisers (*Caledon* and *Dragon*), a Dutch cruiser and eight destroyers (one Australian, one Dutch).

Having failed to locate Nagumo's force after three days and two nights of searching, Somerville's ships returned to Addu Atoll to replenish and refuel, and it was decided to allow normal shipping movements to be resumed. There was nothing to indicate an imminent Japanese attack, and the chances of detection by Japanese submarine were increasing. HMS *Hermes* and her destroyer escort HMAS *Vampire* were sent to Trincomalee to prepare for participation in the forthcoming Operation Ironclad (the carrier was to have her boilers cleaned first), the invasion of Madagascar, an appointment that they were not destined to keep. The heavy cruiser HMS *Cornwall* sailed for Colombo to escort a convoy. Her sister ship *Dorsetshire* was sent to Colombo to resume a major refit. Sending these ships back to Ceylon indicated the fact that Somerville believed the codebreakers had got it wrong (another problem was that no one appreciated the great range of the Japanese aircraft, so it was thought that the Japanese fleet would have to approach very close to Ceylon to launch an effective attack). Whilst at Addu Atoll with Forces A and B on 4 April, however, Somerville heard that a large enemy force steering for Ceylon had been sighted by a Ceylon-based Catalina flying boat 350 miles south east of the island. The aircraft was flown by a Canadian, Squadron-Leader R. J. Birchall, who had arrived in Ceylon three days previously and had not even had time to unpack his kit. After getting off his all-important radio message Birchall was shot down, presumed dead, though discovered later in a Japanese prisoner-of-war camp.

Given Birchall's sighting, it was clear that the original intelligence concerning Japanese intentions had been correct. Vice-Admiral Sir Geoffrey Arbuthnot ordered all shipping in harbour to disperse, as tightly-packed ships would have little chance against air attack in Ceylon's ill-defended harbours. Forty-eight ships left Colombo, though twenty-one merchantmen and eight Fleet Auxiliaries were still in harbour at the time of the raid. HMS *Dorsetshire* and *Cornwall* were ordered to put to sea without delay and return to Somerville, and HMAS *Vampire* and *Hermes* were ordered to clear Trincomalee as soon as they had finished refuelling. Somerville's ships at Addu Atoll were immediately dispatched, but were too late to prevent the attack on Ceylon on 5 April. The order had also been given to clear India's eastern harbours, for whilst Nagumo attacked Ceylon, Vice-Admiral Ozawa Jisaburo led Malaya Force – a light carrier, six cruisers and four destroyers – into the Bay of Bengal to attack shipping off the east coast of India. There he destroyed twenty-three merchant ships (112,000 tons) and bombarded the towns of Cocanda and Vizagapatam. His force played havoc amongst the unescorted and unprotected merchantmen which had been sent south from Calcutta and other eastern ports to avoid being attacked in harbour. Japanese submarines torpedoed a further 32,000 tons of Allied shipping off the west coast of India. British shipping along both coasts of India was therefore brought to a standstill. Shore bombardment from the Japanese ships, the sinking of so many merchantmen close to the Indian coastline, and the arrival of corpses and survivors on many different beaches caused much alarm. When on 6 April bombs were dropped on Cocanda and Vizagapatam – the first to fall on Indian soil – alarm became panic. This spread to Madras, where an exodus began after an air raid warning on 7 April. The Governor advised people to leave if they could, and the government secretariat withdrew inland. The Indian Army's Southern Command ordered 19th Division to concentrate to defend Madras from attack, and the civil and military authorities began to immobilize the port and dislocate the railways. Having been driven ignominiously from South-East Asia and fleeing from Burma, the very foundations of the Raj were shaking.

At just before 8 o'clock, on the morning of 5 April 1942, Ceylon became the latest British imperial outpost to be visited by Japanese fighter-bombers. Thunder clouds hung over Colombo and intermittent showers of heavy rain fell, accompanied by strong gusts of wind. But the defenders were alert, radar picked up the attackers, and Vice-Admiral Layton's precautions meant that damage to shipping and port installations was comparatively light. Meanwhile Somerville steamed towards Ceylon, and Layton reported a force between Ceylon and the Maldives, fearing for the security of Addu Atoll. Whilst Eastern Fleet aircraft searched all day for the Japanese ships, which had withdrawn to the south east, aircraft from Nagumo's carriers combed to the south and the east for Somerville's ships. The raid on Colombo harbour damaged installations, as half of the attacking force targeted infrastructure – learning from the omission at Pearl Harbor – and the other half targeted ships, sinking the destroyer HMS *Tenedos*, AMC *Hector* and the submarine depot ship HMS *Lucia*. At the time of the raid *Lucia*, preparing to load torpedoes onto the submarine HMS *Trusty* moored alongside, was hit by a bomb that went right through her deck and out through the bottom of the ship without exploding. As an eyewitness in Colombo recounted, 'you've never seen anything like it. An absolute shambles – planes on fire, ships on fire, buildings on fire, the guns crashing away at some high bombers which had broken out of the cloud in perfect formation, just like a Hendon Air Show'. By 8.35 all enemy aircraft had left the scene, and half an hour later fourteen Blenheim bombers took off to try and attack the Japanese fleet. Japanese aircraft refuelled aboard their carriers, before fifty-three bombers took off to follow up the report of a reconnaissance aircraft, successfully locating and sinking the heavy cruisers HMS *Cornwall* and *Dorsetshire* in a textbook demonstration of air power at sea.

In the face of the 300 or so carrier-borne planes that the Japanese fleet had at its disposal for the raid on Ceylon, the Air Officer Commanding 222 Group Ceylon, Air Vice-Marshal J. H. D'Albiac, had just fifty serviceable Hurricanes, fourteen Blenheims, six Catalinas and a few squadrons of Fulmars. The Order of Battle on 31 March 1942 consisted of Nos 30 and 258 (Hurricane) Squadrons at Ratmalana, No. 261 (Hurricane) Squadron and No. 273 (Fulmar) Squadrons at China Bay, No. 11 (Blenheim) Squadron at the Racecourse, and detachments of No. 205 and No. 413 Canadian (Catalinas) at Koggala. No. 261 Squadron had served in India in 1940 with Gladiator biplanes, and had become famous for providing the handful of aircraft that formed Malta's only air capability when Italy entered the war. The FAA had ashore Nos 803 and 806 (Fulmar) Squadrons at China Bay, as well as No. 788 Squadron (Swordfish and Albacore). During the raid on Colombo thirty-six Hurricanes and six Fulmars opposed a force of 130 Japanese planes that included thirty-six Zero fighters. Anything up to nineteen Japanese fighters and bombers were shot down for the loss of fifteen Hurricanes (of Nos 258 and 30 Squadrons), two Catalinas and four FAA Fulmars. Also on that day six FAA Swordfish (No. 78 Squadron), bound from China Bay for Ratmalana in the south in preparation for a torpedo attack on Nagumo's fleet, were shot down. No. 258 Squadron had been reformed with Hurricanes after service in Malaya with Brewster Buffaloes. In Ceylon it started life at Ratmalana but then moved to the Racecourse and was housed in well-appointed bungalows in the Cinnamon Gardens district of Colombo. The squadron was a typical imperial mixture: the commanding officer, Squadron-Leader P. C. Fletcher, was Rhodesian, and his pilots were from America, Argentina, Australia, Britain, Canada, New Zealand and South Africa.

On 8 April shore-based reconnaissance aircraft resighted Nagumo's fleet 400 miles east of Ceylon, and Trincomalee was once again cleared of shipping. (Trincomalee harboured warships, and in the surrounding jungle there were about fifty oil tanks, built from 1922 as part of the Royal Navy's move from coal to oil.) China Bay radar detected the attacking aircraft, though again not much could be done to deter them. Seventeen Hurricanes and eight Fulmars got airborne, eight of the former and three of the latter being shot down. Twenty-four kills were claimed by the British; although this number is certainly too high, the Japanese themselves admitted to higher losses than during the Colombo raid. Most of the shipping in the harbour had been ordered to sea, though the monitor HMS *Erebus* was immobilized, as was the merchant ship *Sagaing*, which was holding a military cargo that included four aircraft and, allegedly, lots of whisky. *Erebus* was one of the few monitors that had avoided the breakers' yard and survived to serve in the Second World War. Built during the First World War and unique to the Royal Navy, monitors mounted one or two fifteen-inch guns, and their sole purpose was coastal bombardment or the defence of friendly coastal areas from attacking warships. On the day of the raid on Trincomalee nine Blenheims attacked the Japanese fleet, concentrating on Nagumo's flagship, the giant carrier *Akagi*. They were unsuccessful and only four returned to Ceylon. The major losses of the day were the aircraft carrier HMS *Hermes*, the Australian destroyer HMAS *Vampire* and the newly-arrived 'Flower' class corvette HMS *Hollyhock*, all caught at sea and sunk after dispersing from Ceylon's harbours. Agonizingly, the fighters that were ordered the mere sixty miles from their bases in Ceylon to the position of the carrier *Hermes* failed to get the message. She was to be the first aircraft carrier ever sunk by the aircraft of another carrier, just as in the previous December HMS *Prince of Wales* and *Repulse* had gained the distinction of being the first battleships ever sunk from the air (by land-based aircraft from Indo-Chinese bases).

An examination of one of the British ships sunk in the raids on Ceylon, too insignificant to warrant a mention in most accounts, provides an insight into the operations of Eastern Fleet vessels based on the island. HMS *Tenedos* was an 'S' class destroyer launched in 1919. In December 1941 she had formed part of Admiral Sir Tom Phillips's Force Z based on Singapore, the main units of which were HMS *Prince of Wales* and *Repulse*. On 5 December 1941 *Tenedos* and HMAS *Vampire* escorted the battlecruiser *Repulse* on her visit to Darwin in Australia to show the flag to the poorly-defended Dominion. On the fateful day of 9 December, when the battleship and battlecruiser were sunk, *Tenedos* left Singapore with the two ships on their final voyage. At 18.25 *Tenedos* was forced to turn back to Singapore to refuel, though she was spotted by Japanese aircraft and attacked, straddled by bombs but not hit. *Tenedos* next escaped from the Battle of the Java Sea, when the naval forces of General Sir Archibald Wavell's hastily-arranged ABDA Command were heavily defeated, leaving the Indian Ocean undefended.

After surviving these naval disasters *Tenedos* joined ABDA Command's Western Striking Force, along with the cruisers HMS *Danae*, *Dragon* and HMAS *Hobart*, and the destroyer HMS *Scout*. The force's main duty was to patrol the Sunda Strait separating Sumatra from Java, attempting to intercept Japanese invasion forces. Between 18 February and 8 March 1942, *Tenedos* took part in an operation involving ten ships, in which 2600 people were evacuated from Padang on the west coast of Sumatra as the Dutch East Indies fell to the advancing Japanese. Between them *Tenedos* and *Scout* ferried 1800 people to the waiting cruisers. (Many Europeans from the Dutch East Indies were evacuated to Australia.)

Tenedos's luck ran out when Japanese aircraft raided Colombo on Easter Sunday 1942. An eye witness recorded the destruction of the destroyer:

> When the raid occurred we were completing the refit of the Destroyer HMS *Tenedos* which was lying at the end of our jetty. A stick of bombs fell, some on the jetty and the remainder on the stern of the destroyer setting off the after magazine and torpedo warheads. The resulting explosion was of considerable force and forty feet of our very solid reinforced concrete jetty disappeared entirely and the destroyer was sunk. Parts of the destroyer actually fell in our works machine shop area some 150 yards from the jetty.[23]

The explosion was particularly severe because her depth-charges detonated. This damaged the neighbouring merchantman *Benledi*, also hit by a bomb, as she was unloading motor vehicles and bombs. Moored near *Tenedos* was AMC *Hector*, which was also sunk. It was in the process of being decommissioned from military duties, having spent two and a half years escorting convoys from the Middle East, India and Australia, serving on the East Indies and South-West Pacific stations, playing a part in rounding up German raiders, and on her last voyage, bringing the Hurricane pilots to Ceylon who successfully engaged the Japanese over Colombo on 5 April.

As a result of the raid on Colombo the Admiralty suggested that the 'R' class battleships might be withdrawn to East Africa. It was clear that none of Somerville's ships could withstand the level of attack that had been visited upon *Cornwall* and *Dorsetshire*, and the slow, outgunned vintage ships were considered more of a liability than an asset in an area dotted with Japanese carriers and modern battleships. Based in Kenya, however, these ships could usefully protect the vital reinforcement and supply route to the Middle East and Persian Gulf, as well as work on collective training. Thus Force B left for African shores at 2 o'clock in the morning of 9 April 1942. After the Japanese raids Somerville also moved the Eastern Fleet's headquarters from Colombo to Kilindini, near Mombasa, as he realized that to remain based in Ceylon was to court destruction. Until September 1943 the older battleships were stationed in East Africa and the newer one's operated from Addu Atoll. Until the waning of Japan's star, the Eastern Fleet's purpose was to continue to protect convoys and deter Japanese operations in the Indian Ocean whilst keeping itself in being. As Somerville reported to the Admiralty, he could 'only create diversions and false scents, since I am now the poor fox'. Fortunately Somerville's bluff was never called, as the Japanese failed to mount any further major operations in the Indian Ocean.

The two raids on Ceylon had resulted in considerable British losses, but the main units of the Eastern Fleet had not been destroyed. The Japanese losses had been insignificant, but they had not achieved victory. The Japanese pilots who attacked Ceylon were surprised on three accounts: first, the harbours had not contained the Eastern Fleet, to be decimated like the American Pacific Fleet at Pearl Harbor; secondly, the Japanese bombers had encountered accurate and heavy fire from anti-aircraft guns; and, finally, they had also come under fire from modern fighters for the first time in their brief history of conquest. The first substantial loss of Japanese aircraft in the face of modern fighters manned by experienced pilots had broken the spell of invincibility that they had enjoyed over the last four months. But this was hardly a major setback for the Japanese, and the Eastern Fleet had been lucky to get away with some not inconsiderable losses, as opposed to total destruction. In the space of four days the British had lost two heavy cruisers, a light carrier, two destroyers, a corvette, an armed merchant cruiser and twenty-three merchant ships sunk, two naval vessels damaged and at least twenty-seven aircraft destroyed. Installations had been damaged, and nearly one hundred civilians killed. Nearly a thousand servicemen had perished, the majority on board the cruisers and the carrier.

The Eastern Fleet was now on the back foot in the Indian Ocean. Morale among the Ceylonese population suffered a major setback, though the stout defence of the island was cause for some elation amongst the Europeans and the service personnel. After disasters against the Japanese elsewhere, they could be forgiven for seeing this as something of a success, not unlike the sentiments elicited by the evacuation from Dunkirk. Despite the further whittling down of the operational strength of the Eastern Fleet, the raid on Ceylon can be counted as a failure for the Japanese in a number of respects, especially as it was the first and last time that they attacked in the Indian Ocean. Nagumo failed even to locate the bulk of the Eastern Fleet, his radar not picking it up. On the other hand, however, at inconsequential expense, Nagumo had ensured that there would be no British counter-attacks in the region of the Malay barrier for two years, and had secured the south-western flank of the Greater East Asian Co-Prosperity Sphere.

When British fortunes improved the Eastern Fleet was able to return to its Ceylon headquarters in September 1943. The turn in the fortunes of the Eastern Fleet in 1943 was founded upon twin factors: the improving naval and military situation facing Britain and its allies around the world; and the relative decline in the fortunes of Japan. But 1943, though less dangerous than 1942, was a frustrating year for the Eastern Fleet: it was not strong enough to take the offensive, and had to content itself with its unglamorous but essential policing role in the Indian Ocean. The war in the Atlantic and the Mediterranean and the watch on the Channel ports meant that other theatres had priority for scant naval resources. The Eastern Fleet was denied ships newly-launched or newly-released from other theatres, or stripped of major ships required more urgently elsewhere, for example losing its main carriers, HMS *Indomitable* and *Formidable*, to the battle to supply Malta in 1943 and the Anglo-American invasion of French North Africa. Most of the transfers were out of the Indian Ocean. During 1943 no less than forty-eight ships were transferred from the Eastern Fleet to the Mediterranean. The carrier HMS *Illustrious* left for a refit, the battleships HMS *Warspite* and *Valiant* were transferred, as was the modern cruiser HMS *Mauritius*.

One of the main obstacles barring British amphibious operations in Malaya was the lack of landing craft, a class of vessel over which the Americans had some-thing of a stranglehold because they were responsible for manufacturing most of them. Given that the Supreme Allied Commander South East Asia, Admiral Lord Louis Mountbatten, plumped for an amphibious assault as his major plan of attack (Operation Zipper), the lack of landing craft was a problem. At one point the landing craft that he had managed to get together were taken from him as the Allied high command prioritized the Normandy landings in 1944. All of this meant that the Eastern Fleet was consistently under strength in 1943, struggling to conduct its convoy and patrol duties and unable to take proper offensive action. The fleet had been so reduced by November 1943 that it could only with difficulty act even as a trade protection force. It consisted of the 'R' class battle-ship HMS *Ramillies* ('The Ram'), the escort carrier *Battler*, seven cruisers, eleven destroyers, the 4th Submarine Flotilla, two AMC, thirteen escort vessels and some landing craft. With the destroyers engaged on escort duties, the submarines were the only force that could be employed offensively.

As the Japanese threat in the Indian Ocean diminished and the tide of war shifted in the Allies' favour elsewhere, the fleet's fortunes began to change as well. Pressure on British naval resources eased because of victories in other war theatres – the crippling of *Gneisenau*, the sinking of *Tirpitz*, Allied victory in the Mediter-ranean, triumph in the Battle of the Atlantic and the continuing success of the Americans and Australians in the Pacific. This meant that more ships could be spared for British operations east of Suez, and this meant the strengthening of the Eastern Fleet better to carry out its manifold duties and to prepare for a British re-entry into the Pacific and the reinvasion of all Allied occupied territory under SEAC. There were more battleships, more destroyers and, as they slipped out of American shipyards, more escort carriers. The battleships HMS *Queen Elizabeth*, *Renown* and *Valiant*, the carrier *Illustrious*, the carrier/repair ship *Unicorn* and seven destroyers were ordered to the Indian Ocean in January 1944. In a move symbolizing the eastward swing of British naval power, the Admiralty chose to call this the 1st Battle Squadron, a title which for years had been held by the main Royal Navy force in the Mediterranean. By the end of March there were enough submarines in Ceylon to form a second flotilla (the 8th). In July 1944 the fleet carriers HMS *Illustrious* and *Indomitable* arrived in Ceylon.

Reinforced, the Eastern Fleet was able to take proper offensive fleet action against Japanese land forces and installations for the first time. Its tasks were to continue to deny the use of the Indian Ocean to the enemy, to cut the supply lines of the Japanese army in Burma and the Andaman and Nicobar Islands, and to provide diversionary attacks against Japanese positions in the region with the aim of drawing off forces from the Pacific. It bombarded military positions on the

Andaman and Nicobar Islands and oil installations in Sumatra, attacked Japanese shipping and aided the land forces fighting in Burma (for example, shore bombardments during the third Arakan offensive from December 1944). The Eastern Fleet cleared Japanese minefields and carried out major sweeps of shipping routes used by vessels supplying Japanese land forces. It also laid minefields to disrupt Japanese shipping, usually with submarines based on Ceylon. From July 1945 the Eastern Fleet turned its attention to minesweeping areas soon to be invaded, particularly as part of SEAC's assault on Malaya. By August 1945 there were over thirty minesweepers on the strength.

The Eastern Fleet attacked Japanese surface vessels when they presented themselves, though after the Ceylon raid there were few incursions by Japanese warships into the Indian Ocean. The submarine HMS *Tallyho* sunk the light cruiser *Kuma* in January 1944 and the former Italian U-boat U-It 23 the following month. In January 1944 the submarine HMS *Templar* badly damaged the cruiser *Kitagami* near Penang. The heavy cruiser *Haguro*, the last major Japanese warship sunk during the war, was attacked in the Malacca Strait by the five ships of the Eastern Fleet's 26th Destroyer Flotilla, after attacks from the escort carrier HMS *Emperor*, on 16 May 1945, working on intelligence derived from the broken Japanese naval code JN 25 intercepted by Far East Combined Bureau in Ceylon. Sixteen ships left Ceylon on 8 May 1945 after news of *Haguro*'s presence in the region was revealed by intelligence intercepts and confirmed visually by two British submarines patrolling in the Malacca Strait. The British force comprised the battleships *Queen Elizabeth* and *Richelieu* (Free French), the cruisers *Cumberland*, *Royalist* and *Tromp* (Dutch), the escort carriers *Emperor*, *Hunter*, *Khedive* and *Shah* and eight destroyers. The ships remaining at Trincomalee, the cruiser HMS *Nigeria* and three destroyers, were sent to join them. Intelligence later led to the torpedoing of *Haguro*'s sister ship the *Ashigara* by the submarine HMS *Trenchant* in the Bangka Strait south of Singapore on 8 June 1945. (*Trenchant* was one of the British submarines based on Fremantle). The *Haguro* and *Ashigara* had been sent to evacuate Japanese forces after the fall of Rangoon, and were the last two large Japanese warships in the area. The operation against them reflected growing British naval power and waning Japanese naval power as the Pacific war took its toll. After their sinking, the 10th Area Fleet based at Singapore was left with a solitary destroyer, the appropriately-named *Kamikaze*.

By March 1944 the Eastern Fleet consisted of three battleships, the carrier HMS *Illustrious* and the fleet maintenance carrier HMS *Unicorn*, twelve modern cruisers, three flotillas of destroyers, seventy anti-submarine ships, numerous submarines and the American carrier USS *Saratoga* and her destroyer screen. Major raids in April and July 1944 saw the Eastern Fleet attack oil and harbour installations at Sabang off the northern tip of Sumatra (a big favourite of Churchill's – the Chief of the Imperial General Staff, General Sir Alan Brooke, often had to put the Prime Minister off the idea of a major amphibious assault here). These raids were mounted in cooperation with American forces in the Pacific, which had requested such moves, aimed at drawing as many Japanese vessels away from the theatre as possible whilst MacArthur attacked Hollandia. Sabang was selected by Somerville as it commanded the entrance to the Malacca Strait and contained valuable Japanese installations, including a radar station, dockyard and airfield. Thirty Japanese aircraft were destroyed on the ground. The April 1944 raid (Operation Cockpit) involved carriers, battleships, cruisers and destroyers and was covered by RAF reconnaissance flights. The increase in the fleet's destroyer strength enabled it to protect the main units of the fleet whilst simultaneously escorting convoys. In May 1944 the Eastern Fleet attacked Sourabaya, the main Japanese base in Java, as the USS *Saratoga* returned to the Pacific and the Eastern Fleet sailed from Ceylon to Exmouth Bay in Western Australia. The bombing of the dry dock severely hampered the Japanese ship repair programme, 35,000 tons of shipping was sunk and the destruction of oil installations curtailed the supply available to the Japanese army in Burma.

On 27 October 1944 Liberators of South East Asia Command's Strategic Air Force attacked and mined the approaches to Penang, the main enemy submarine base in the region, used by both Japanese and German vessels. The attack persuaded the Germans to withdraw their submarines to Batavia. Another offensive task of the Eastern Fleet was severing the lines of communication and supply for the Japanese forces in Burma. With air superiority achieved by the British and American air forces flying from India and Ceylon, this was of grave significance for the beleaguered Burma Area Army. From February 1945 anti-shipping sweeps in the Andaman Sea aimed to prevent the evacuation or relief of Japanese land forces. Attacks were mounted against the Andaman and Nicobar Island garrisons as well as their supplies. In March 1945, for example, four Eastern Fleet destroyers and two groups of RAF Liberators attacked a Japanese convoy sailing from Singapore to Port Blair in South Andaman. The work of the 'Dido' class cruiser HMS *Phoebe*, launched in 1939, illustrates the range of the Eastern Fleet's offensive operations at this time. Transferred from the Mediterranean Fleet to the Eastern Fleet in May 1944, she took part in strikes against the Andamans, Sabang and the Nicobar Islands, and in January 1945 switched to supporting amphibious operations in Burma and was subsequently in action against Akyab, Ramree Island, Cheduba Island and Rangoon. From 16 May 1945 she and several Royal Indian Navy sloops patrolled between Mergui and Port Blair, hoping to intercept Japanese warships or transports.

Ceylon's role as a submarine base began early in the war with the arrival of the depot ship HMS *Lucia* (damaged in the raid on Trincomalee).[24] She had been captured from the Germans in the West Indies in 1914 and converted to a submarine depot ship. On the outbreak of war in 1939, she was brought out of retirement at Bombay, recommissioned, and sent to Ceylon to sustain the newly-formed 8th Submarine Flotilla based at Colombo (created partly to counter the threat posed in the region by the German pocket battleship *Graf Spee*). The flotilla's submarines patrolled to the Maldives and to the Seychelles in search of German vessels. These submarines and all others in eastern waters were moved in March 1940 as tension mounted in the Mediterranean, so that when Japan entered the war there was only one British submarine east of Suez. In 1941 Dutch submarines escaping from the Dutch East Indies went to Ceylon, where they came under Eastern Fleet command. More British submarines arrived as well. HMS *Adamant* arrived as a depot ship, and what was known as the 4th Submarine Flotilla was moved from Colombo to Trincomalee. In March 1944 a second depot ship, HMS *Maidstone*, arrived and the force was split to form a second flotilla. With the arrival of the depot ship HMS *Wolfe* in August 1944, *Maidstone* sailed with her flotilla of ten submarines for Fremantle, Australia, to operate under the Americans in the South China Sea. These Ceylon-based submarines were transferred to Australia as tasks in the Indian Ocean region decreased, and it was thought that there were too many submarines for the limited number of targets off the coasts of Burma, Malaya and Sumatra. Nevertheless, in September 1944 twenty-six submarines remained based on Ceylon. Ceylon's submarines laid 490 mines and patrolled off enemy coastlines in an extensive minelaying campaign from the spring of 1944, concentrating on the Malacca Strait and the Thai and Burmese coasts. The aim was to force Japanese shipping away from the coast and into deeper water where it could be attacked. Submarine patrols from Trincomalee were extended to the Malacca Strait, the western coast of Burma and both coasts of Sumatra.

In August 1944 Admiral Somerville relinquished command of the Eastern Fleet and was replaced by Admiral Sir Bruce Fraser. (Somerville had been having problems with Mountbatten, and was also in demand as a heavyweight naval figure to represent the Admiralty in Washington.) In that month battleship and carrier attacks were made on Padang in Sumatra (where a cement works supplying pillboxes and tank traps to Japanese forces was targeted), and in the following month operations were mounted against targets in Sumatra and the Andamans for training purposes and photo reconnaissance. In October 1944 there were further offensive operations, partly as a diversionary exercise at the time of the American assault on Leyte in the Philippines. On 22 November 1944 the Eastern Fleet was split in two and ceased to exist. The more powerful element became the British Pacific Fleet (BPF) under Fraser, who hoisted his flag in the new battleship HMS *Howe*, which had arrived at Trincomalee in August to replace *Valiant*, damaged when the floating dock at Trincomalee was sunk. On 2 December 1944 Fraser and the BPF advanced guard left Ceylon for Australian bases to re-establish the Royal Navy's claims in Far Eastern waters and ensure a British role in the final defeat of Japan. Palembang was attacked on the way, as it was again when Vice-Admiral Vian left Ceylon for Australia in January 1945 with the rest of the BPF. The not insignificant force that remained became the re-formed East Indies Fleet commanded by Admiral Sir Arthur Power. Its task was to work exclusively with SEAC. It amounted to over seventy vessels and gained in strength so that by

August 1945 it comprised 263 vessels of all types, including two battleships, sixteen escort carriers, thirteen cruisers and forty-three destroyers.

The reconstituted East Indies Fleet continued to have an important role to play in the Indian Ocean and in support of the Fourteenth Army's campaign in Burma. Ramree Island was assaulted by HMS *Queen Elizabeth, Phoebe,* two destroyers, a British sloop and an RIN sloop, covered in the air by Thunderbolts, Mitchells and eighty-five Liberators. An amphibious operation to capture Rangoon was launched on 27 April 1945, when two naval forces left Trincomalee to give protection to the convoys during their voyage to the mouth of the Rangoon River, and to intercept Japanese forces attempting to leave. The fleet was central to the success of Operation Zipper, the assult on occupied Malaya. Thus the unheralded East Indies Station ended the war as part of the victorious British command that retook South-East Asia's British, Dutch and French colonies from the enemy. It had secured Britain's vital naval interests in the Indian Ocean region since Pearl Harbor and the loss of HMS *Prince of Wales* and *Repulse* had thrown Allied strategy into untold confusion, and laid bare the eastern approaches to India and the Middle East. It also gave birth to the fleet charged with Britain's naval renaissance in the Pacific. Throughout the war, the Royal Navy was dependent upon the islands of the Indian Ocean in order to secure the sea routes, and important fighting fronts on land – such as the Middle East and Burma – garnered important support from the territories of Britain's Indian Ocean island empire.

11

The Islands of the Indian Ocean

All British territories in the Indian Ocean felt the impact of the war to a surprising degree, particularly the island of Ceylon. Yet the war experience of the Indian Ocean islands has not been integrated into the history of the British war effort, mirroring their general exclusion from the history of British imperialism. Despite this, British troops sweated out lengthy tours of duty on peripheral military bases in places such as Diego Garcia and Mauritius, and specks of territory like Addu Atoll in the Maldives and the Cocos Islands were developed as strategic bases in order better to prosecute the war against Japan. Madagascar was invaded by British forces in a dry run for the much larger amphibious assaults that were to come in North Africa and Normandy, the Andaman and Nicobar Islands were subject to years of Japanese occupation, Aden remained a centre of British air power throughout the war, and even Zanzibar in the western Indian Ocean was affected by the economic effects of global conflict.

In early 1942 Ceylon, a tear-drop off the southern pinnacle of the Indian subcontinent, became one of the most vital strategic colonies in the Empire. As Churchill told the House of Commons on 23 April: 'After [the] virtual annihilation of British, Dutch, and United States light forces in Javanese waters and the loss of Singapore, Java and Sumatra, we naturally consider Ceylon as a key point we have to hold.'[1] Ceylon's role was that of an imperial base camp, a similar role in the Indian Ocean to that performed by Egypt in the Middle East – a base for military forces but also a conduit giving access to nearby theatres of operations. It was the home base of the Eastern Fleet and many RAF squadrons, a base for British and imperial soldiers built up as a garrison force and in transit to or from the fighting in Burma, and from summer 1943 the home of Mountbatten's South East Asia Command responsible for prosecuting the war in Burma, China, South-East Asia and the Dutch East Indies. Ceylon also became an important intelligence-gathering outpost of Bletchley Park and a regional headquarters for Special Operations Executive.

Aside from the military aspect of Ceylon's war effort, its civilian government was called upon to mobilize the home front for war. The Governor, Sir Andrew Caldecott, and his Ceylonese Board of Ministers pumped manpower and raw material resources into the imperial war effort. Ceylon recruited tens of thousands of men for home defence and military labour at home and overseas, attempted to become self-sufficient in foodstuffs and produced essential commodities such as rubber and tea (Ceylon's entire crop went by contract to the Board of Trade in London.) Even organizations in the private sector could make a major contribution to a colony's war effort. A Colombo-based civil engineering firm, Walker Sons and Company, that in peacetime specialized in providing machinery for the tea and rubber industries, turned the hands of its 3600 workers to naval and military tasks, and during the course of the war repaired or refitted a staggering 167 major warships, 322 minor warships and 1932 merchant vessels. Among the vessels repaired or refitted were the aircraft carrier HMS *Eagle* and the cruisers HMS *Cornwall, Cumberland, Devonshire, Gloucester, Kent, Liverpool* and *Manchester.* Work was also undertaken to install kite gear on sixty merchant ships and the liners *Queen Elizabeth* and *Queen Mary* as part of their conversion to troopships. This work involved fitting a miniature crow's nest at the top of the ship's main mast with gear to control the running out and drawing in of the cable attached to the kite. The purpose of the kite was to make dive-bombers avoid coming low over the ship because of the risk of being caught in the trailing cable, and so being deflected from picking a suitable run in. The company also made dummy Hurricanes, dummy Bofors anti-aircraft guns, and dummy radar towers for the deception of Japanese aerial reconnaissance, and 39,000 pieces of furniture for the burgeoning military complex built up on the island as Allied service personnel poured in, not least the 10,000 who accompanied Mountbatten and SEAC headquarters when it was transferred from Delhi.[2]

Ceylon experienced a war of two halves, the second half commencing with Japan's attacks upon British and American forces in December 1941. Before this the war was distant and its effects apparent but not alarming. The Europeans of Ceylon were confident, fighting fronts were far away, Singapore and Trincomalee were considered mighty naval bases, British prestige still stood high, and the Japanese would be no match when confronted with the discipline and traditions of British troops, whatever they had achieved in China. As a schoolboy Gerard Robinson felt sorry for the Japanese as he watched the modern battleship HMS *Prince of Wales* dock alongside *Repulse* at Colombo on 28 November 1941. Two weeks later both ships were at the bottom of the Gulf of Siam. After this tragedy of British seapower and the American defeat at Pearl Harbor, Japan's menace to South Asia was clear for all to see and Ceylon entered the front line, with a Japanese army forcing Burma Corps to retreat into India, and the carriers of Admiral Nagumo at liberty to strike far and wide against their much-diminished enemies.

Given the grave situation facing the island, as Japan digested its startling conquests in early 1942, Ceylon became an armed camp. Churchill and the Chiefs of Staff determined that it could not be allowed to fall and therefore stuffed it with troops and diverted precious cargoes of aircraft to fly from its newly-completed air strips. In January 1942 Nagumo's formidable force supported the landings on Rabaul in New Guinea, and on 19 February attacked Darwin in Australia, before extinguishing Allied naval resistance in the region at the Battle of the Java Sea. Nagumo was now free to turn his marauding carriers westwards to destroy all British naval forces in the Indian Ocean. This meant attacking Ceylon, where the Japanese expected to find the Eastern Fleet, believed to be even stronger than the American Pacific Fleet. Though Japanese generals opposed the navy's plan to invade and occupy Ceylon for logistical reasons, the navy continued to believe that, with the example of a crushing naval victory, the army would be forced to change its mind.

In the eighteenth century Trincomalee was coveted by the Royal Navy because it was ideally positioned for the defence of both coasts of India, at a time when the global struggle with France was at its height. Nelson considered it the finest harbour in the world. The island of Ceylon (population eight million in the 1940s) was annexed by the British in 1806 after it had been seized from the Dutch during the Revolutionary and Napoleonic Wars. For a century and a half Ceylon had been a junction and gathering point for the shipping that in a very real sense kept the eastern and western territories of the British Empire together, illustrated by the fact that in the 1930s Colombo received a greater annual tonnage of shipping than all of the harbours of British India combined. This meant that Ceylon became one of the major convoy assembly ports that marshalled British merchant ships across the war-torn oceans of the world, along with the likes of Freetown, Gibraltar, Halifax and Trinidad. Ceylon was part of the traditional imperial defence and communications network that provided Britain with a chain of bases athwart the major strategic highways of the world. The Royal Navy had used Ceylon as a base since the eighteenth century, and though its primacy fluctuated as other bases were established in eastern waters (for example Singapore and Hong Kong), or new naval squadrons created (for example the China Station), it never waned to the point of insignificance, and as the Second World War was to show, developments elsewhere (notably the loss of Singapore and eradication of British naval forces in the Far East) could cause its significance dramatically to increase.

Churchill discoursed at length on the defence of the island and the strategic situation in the Indian Ocean when announcing the fall of Singapore to the House of Commons in secret session. Defeats for all of the Allies in the Pacific, South-East Asia and the East Indies meant that the Indian Ocean was now exposed to Japanese attack and inescapably in the front line. The threat to Ceylon led to the installation of radar, barrage balloons and heavy and light anti-aircraft guns to defend the harbours. It also led to a build up of aircraft and British forces on the island, and the execution of the Admiralty's plan to gather a strong force of battleships and carriers based on the island as and when the situation in other theatres allowed. Though they had little hope of resisting a determined Japanese attack, it was hoped in the crucial months of early 1942 that these forces would be a sufficient deterrent, as the army force alone rose towards two divisions. In this the British War Cabinet and the Chiefs of Staff demonstrated an imperial awareness. In the House of Commons Churchill described the need to defend Ceylon now that it was in the front line:

> This cannot be done without adequate shore-based aircraft and ample anti-aircraft artillery. Our resources were limited and there are, as I have said, many clamant calls upon them. However, casting aside a great many other needs, we did manage to give considerable measure of protection to Colombo and Trinco-malee, and also to place in Ceylon military forces sufficient to require a substantial invading army to overcome them.[3]

The seriousness of the situation facing Ceylon led to the subordination of the island's civilian government to military command, with the appointment of Admiral Sir Geoffrey Layton as Commander-in-Chief Ceylon. Churchill and the Chiefs of Staff considered it imperative that Ceylon be held in the face of the expected Japanese assault, and did not want a repeat of the Malayan campaign when lack of a unified command had disastrously hampered efforts to defend the peninsula. This was the first time that a unified command structure had been applied to an operational theatre. Layton was subordinate to the Commander-in-Chief India in military matters, and to the Secretary of State for the Colonies in civilian matters. Subordinate to Layton was the civilian Governor of Ceylon, Sir Andrew Caldecott, who set about directing Ceylon's resources towards the war effort. Layton immediately began preparing the island for a Japanese attack and established a War Council in March 1942. In breaking the news of his subordination to the military commander, the Secretary of State for the Colonies, Lord Cranborne, told Governor Caldecott that Ceylon and its dependencies were to be designated a 'military area' under a Commander-in-Chief Ceylon, given the island's position as a vital communications link and base for the concentration of forces and the real menace posed to the island by the Imperial Japanese Navy.[4] Layton was given almost dictatorial powers, as Ceylon's defence was considered so vitally important by the Cabinet and the Chiefs of Staff in London ('Do not ask permission to do things. Do them and report afterwards what you have done'). Layton was profoundly shocked by the state of lethargy and ineffectiveness in Ceylon. There were go-slow strikes in Colombo on a regular basis, so that some-times as many as fifty valuable ships were lying exposed in the outer anchorage waiting to discharge their cargoes. No. 222 Group RAF had only one obsolete Vildebeeste torpedo-bomber squadron on the island at the turn of the year, and a detachment of No. 205 (flying boat) Squadron. There was no radar, the fire-fighting arrangements were rudimentary, and there were no gas masks. Efforts were immediately taken in hand to increase rubber exports, civil defence was reorganized, an improved air raid system implemented in Colombo, and an air strip on the racecourse completed (which the Japanese knew nothing about).

Apart from its crucial role as a naval base, Ceylon was home to several important war-time organizations. It was a forward base in the war against Japan conducted by the British, Indian and African troops of General Sir William Slim's Fourteenth Army in Burma. In 1944 Ceylon became home to SEAC, the Allied command responsible for the Burma–China–South-East Asia theatre and for the reoccupation of Burma, Malaya, Singapore, the Andaman and Nicobar Islands and Dutch Sumatra (French Indo-China was later added to the command's responsibilities). SEAC had been formed in October 1943 to improve the direction of the ramshackle Allied war effort in the region and to draw Japanese forces away from the Pacific to the Burma–China theatre. In April 1944 its headquarters were transferred from New Delhi to the Royal Botanic Gardens, Peradeniya, a few miles from Kandy. Mountbatten himself, almost inevitably, took up residence in the King's Pavilion. There was kept a thirty-member band, a golf course and a Cadillac complete with outriders and sirens.

Mountbatten had a great deal of pre-war experience of the Empire and the wider world. In the early 1920s he had accompanied the Prince of Wales on his imperial tours aboard the battlecruiser HMS *Renown*, having managed to get himself appointed as flag-lieutenant to the Prince's naval chief of staff. Mountbatten learned a great deal about the Empire during the trip (and developed a fascination with India that was to be more fully indulged when he was appointed Britain's last viceroy in 1947). After touring the world with the Prince of Wales, Mountbatten served in the Dardanelles aboard the battlecruiser HMS *Revenge*, part of the International Fleet monitoring the dispute between Greece and Turkey in the early 1920s. He then served on the battleship HMS *Warspite* as part of the Mediterranean Fleet, and in 1933 was given his first command, the new destroyer HMS *Daring*, which he promptly took to Singapore to be handed over to the China Station in exchange for the elderly destroyer HMS *Wishart*. Mountbatten returned to the Mediterranean for the first years of the war as commander of the Mediterranean Fleet's 5th Destroyer Flotilla, before a meteoric elevation saw him join the Chiefs of Staff Committee following his appointment as Chief of Combined Operations. In 1943 he was chosen to fill the new post of Supreme Allied Commander South East Asia, and it was he who insisted on the Command's headquarters being moved from Delhi to Kandy.

Ceylon was 500 miles further away than Delhi from the battlefield in Burma. Mountbatten's decision to move, however, reflected his desire to adopt a maritime strategy in defeating the Japanese in Burma and Malaya, rather than pursuing the Japanese overland. It was also hoped that the move would enable the command to escape the stifling immobility that seemed to afflict India Command's headquarters. It was also made because Mountbatten believed that Europeans worked better in a cool climate like that found in Kandy. Despite Mountbatten's preference for amphibious operations in getting to grips with the Japanese in Burma and Malaya, it turned out to be the Burmese jungle where the major defeats of Japan were to take place at the hands of the Fourteenth Army. With over a million men, 700,000 of them Indian, it was the largest army operating as a single unit in the world. The planned amphibious assault that was to take the British back into Malaya (Operation Zipper) was delayed because of the withdrawal of the command's landing craft for use in the Normandy landings, and the atom bombs ended the war before it could be properly launched.

Several months before SEAC had even been established, the Chiefs of Staff recommended that the new Supreme Commander's headquarters should be away from India and probably in Ceylon. Mountbatten wanted to leave Delhi as soon as possible, so that his fledgling command could exercise its independence away from the social and political atmosphere of a large capital. Admiral Somerville, Commander-in-Chief of the Eastern Fleet, encouraged the move because it brought SEAC closer to his own base, and because he loathed wartime Delhi. The move was opposed by the Americans and was viewed with some scepticism by the Commander-in-Chief India, General Sir Claude Auchinleck, and by the regional air commander. But Mountbatten would hear nothing of their objections.

SEAC's headquarters gained something of a reputation for luxury and high living, and for being grossly overstaffed. Mountbatten had calculated that 4100 people would be required, but the figure rose to near 10,000. This apparent extravagance was frowned upon by the Chiefs of Staff in London, as well as raising eyebrows locally. Mountbatten also came under fire for having an unreliable airstrip carved out of the mountains nineteen miles from Kandy, and having a little-used caravan built by workshops in Colombo. His biographer, however, makes the point that all of this came with the Mountbatten phenomenon – 'Mountbattens do not come on the cheap' – 'and though it irritated some it encouraged many others. Kandy was an efficient headquarters, but it was also an expertly contrived theatrical entertainment'.[5]

The arrival of SEAC led to a massive demand for local civilian labour, particularly for the construction of airfields. Ceylon was being prepared as the bridgehead of invasions in Malaya, Sumatra and Burma. Superbly illustrating the impact that participation in a world war could have on a domestic economy and society, these labour demands eradicated the unemployment problems that had characterized Ceylon's inter-war years. By 1945 83,500 civilians were employed on military bases and in their construction, and unemployment was down to a thousand, four per cent of the 1939 level. SEAC and its network of bases led to heavy military expenditure, having an invigorating economic effect. At its peak in 1944 expenditure was estimated at 435 million rupees (approximately £32.5 million), up from 264 million rupees (approximately £19.7 million) in 1943.

Ceylon was also a major base for SOE personnel operating in Burma, Malay and Sumatra.[6] SOE's operations in France are well known, though it also maintained major headquarters and conducted operations in the Middle East, South-East Asia and the Far East, from bases in China, India, Ceylon, Egypt and Australia, as well as innumerable smaller operations in places like West Africa and Mauritius. In September 1942 Christopher Hudson flew to Ceylon to organize an SOE branch for the India Mission based in Delhi. There he found Innes Tremlett already having begun preparations. The main headquarters at Kandy was established in a purpose-built compound, a training facility was accommodated in a beachside mansion at Mount Lavinia (the home of a former Governor, Sir Edward Barnes), and holding camps were constructed at Horana near Kandy (for men destined for Burma), and on an island in China Bay. In January 1944 three bungalows were acquired in Ceylon for the use of SOE men destined for Malaya. SOE's fourth main training establishment in the region, an Advanced Operations School, was located on an island near Trincomalee, and SOE stores and ammunition supplies were maintained. A bungalow buried deep in a tea plantation at Yawalatene was also acquired. SOE operatives were inserted behind enemy lines by aircraft or submarine (British and Dutch submarines based on Ceylon specialized in this).

From March 1944 the SOE presence in South-East Asia became known as Force 136, and it was run from Meerut and Kandy. Force 136 was divided into Burma, Siam, Malaya, French Indo-China and Anglo-Dutch subsections, and was also responsible for Force 137 in Australia. In December 1944 Ceylon became the main SOE base in the region, when Colin Mackenzie, Head of Mission India, followed Mountbatten and moved his headquarters to Kandy, which meant that Ceylon had been transformed strategically from a relative backwater, a mere operations sub-branch of the India Mission, into Force 136's main base. Its operations in surrounding Japanese-occupied British, French and Dutch territory were manifold, and the arrival in October 1944 of General Blaizot and French troops to establish the Free French Military Mission to the Far East bore witness to Ceylon's growth as the behind-enemy-lines capital of the east. The first operation launched from Ceylon was Operation Bunkum, a reconnaissance of the Andaman Islands, in which agents were inserted by submarine and maintained wireless contact with Calcutta. A great deal of work was done to support armed resistance in Siam. For example, a group of Siamese students from England were sent to Ceylon, from where they boarded the submarine HMS *Tactician* and were taken to a rendezvous off the coast of Siam. By August 1945 Force 136 had armed several thousand Siamese. Ceylon was also used to train agents for Mountbatten's assault on the island of Phuket off the Siamese coast. Force 136s Ceylon-based Anglo-Dutch subsection focused its attention on Sumatra. RAF Special Duties squadrons, usually flying long-range Liberators, were used to parachute agents and supplies into occupied territory, and most sorties were flown from Ceylon bases. Freddie Spencer Chapman's Force 136 team in occupied Malaya was in contact with headquarters in Ceylon, as will be seen. Air supplies from Ceylon supported the 3500 Malayans trained to harass the Japanese when the British mounted their amphibious assault late in the war. Liberators of No. 357 Squadron from Minneriya in Ceylon, for example, flew 249 sorties in June and July 1945 in support of forces in Malaya. Ceylon was a base for other clandestine organizations. The Secret Intelligence Service (MI6), under the guise of the

Inter-Services Liaison Department (ISLD), mounted missions in occupied territory, for example transferring agents to Penang Island aboard HMS *Tactician*. As
in most others parts of the world, no love was lost between SOE and MI6. The
American equivalent of SOE, the Office of Strategic Services (OSS), was granted
permission by Mountbatten to establish itself in Ceylon and to open training
camps in Galle, Clodagh and Trincomalee, with headquarters at Kandy and a
supply depot at Colombo.

Ceylon did not begin the war with a large RAF presence. In 1941 there was only
one Vildebeeste torpedo-bomber squadron (biplanes known as 'flying coffins'),
and elements of a solitary Catalina flying boat squadron. A squadron of Sunderland flying boats was sent for anti-submarine work. These forces were augmented
significantly, for the immediate defence of the island given the threat of a Japanese
carrier attack in early 1942, to strengthen the island's role as a base for Indian
Ocean operations, and for its use as an air base for offensive operations against
Japanese forces in the Burma theatre and Japanese-occupied territories
throughout South-East Asia. The island sprouted air strips. A new air base was
built on the Colombo Racecourse in the suburb of Cinnamon Gardens, for which
even the Chief Justice had to have his house pulled down to make way for the
runway. Ceylon's other main air bases were the Ratmalana civil airport, a base at
China Bay and a flying boat base at Koggala lagoon. New bases were built at
Kankesanturai, Negombo (Katunayake), Minneriya and Vavuniya. In September
1941 Ceylon became home to an RAF Group Headquarters (No. 222).

Catalina and Sunderland flying boats were indispensable in the vastness of the
Indian Ocean, extending reconnaissance cover far wider than that achievable by
warships alone and presenting a grave threat to enemy submarines and supply
ships.[7] Flying boat squadrons were based in Arabia, Ceylon, East Africa and India.
For specific operations or whilst on patrol they used anchorages in Indian Ocean
islands like the Comoros, Diego Garcia, the Maldives and Mauritius. Catalinas
even started a regular air service between Ceylon and Australia, a non-stop flight
of 2650 miles. With the fall of Singapore, Ceylon became a stop on the BOAC
service between Britain and Australia.

Before the Japanese raids on Ceylon, the island's air forces were bolstered by
the arrival of ground crew and pilots that had managed to escape after the RAF's
defeats in Malaya, Sumatra and Java.[8] For example, though badly mauled in those
campaigns, No. 258 Squadron was re-formed in Ceylon on 30 March 1942, just in
time for its Hurricanes to meet the Japanese planes that raided Colombo six days
later. It scrambled fourteen Hurricanes, nine being shot down with the loss of five
pilots. Many other men from the Sumatra and Java campaign also made it to
Ceylon, denying the Japanese prison guards their prey; on 23 February 1942 many
left on board the P&O ship *Orcades*, and the grossly overcrowded tramp steamer
Kota Gede made it to the island with 2500 men rescued from Java.

As the British government identified the defence of Ceylon against Japanese attack as a primary aim in the spring of 1942, its air defences were augmented. General Auchinleck sent thirty Hurricanes, twenty medium bombers and a squadron of torpedo-bombers from Middle East Command. In early March 1942 the Eastern Fleet's aircraft carrier HMS *Indomitable* flew off two squadrons of Hurricanes (Nos 30 and 261), brought from North Africa and initially earmarked for Java. Eight Hurricanes had arrived on 23 February after being assembled in Karachi, and on 28 February a Blenheim bomber squadron (No. 11) arrived from the Middle East to be based at the Racecourse Airstrip (the squadron had fought in the Iraq campaign a year before). There were two FAA squadrons of Fulmars (Nos 803 and 806), one of Swordfish (No. 788) at China Bay, and a composite squadron (No. 273, flying mainly Vildebeest), also at China Bay. HMS *Hermes* flew off her squadron of Swordfish (No. 814) to reinforce China Bay on the eve of the raid. Catalina reinforcements were brought in from Gibraltar and Britain. Despite the advantages of radar and ULTRA intelligence, the arrival of the Japanese bombers and fighters on 5 April 1942 took the British aircraft by surprise. As one browned off British pilot put it, 'it was a carbon copy of what 258 and other squadrons had more or less become accustomed to in Singapore, Sumatra and Java – insufficient early warning and an enemy force outnumbering the defenders eight or more to one'.[9]

By February 1944 Ceylon could boast three Hurricane night fighter squadrons, two Beaufort torpedo bomber squadrons, one Beaufort night fighter squadron, a Liberator long-range reconnaissance squadron and three Catalina squadrons. Spitfires were beginning to arrive, and in April 1944 the aircraft transports HMS *Athene* and *Engadine* and the escort carriers HMS *Begum* and *Atheling* arrived with four squadrons of bombers and four squadrons of fighters. By early 1945 air control of the Bay of Bengal and the Indian Ocean had been regained. Ships could now sail without escort, save for troopships. Whilst anti-submarine operations remained a central task for general reconnaissance aircraft operating from East Africa, Aden and Ceylon, the diminishing Japanese threat led to a new emphasis on tasks such as minelaying and photo reconnaissance over areas including the Andamans, Malaya and Sumatra. The Liberators of No. 160 Squadron, flying from Minneriya in Ceylon, specialized in aerial mining. On 26 March 1945 eight of its Liberators made the 3460-mile round trip to Singapore, the first RAF aircraft to fly over the great city since February 1942.

Later in the war the air situation was transformed, as India and Ceylon became home to about 3000 British and American aircraft, most coming under SEAC and some under separate American command and dedicated to supplying China over 'the Hump'. Bombers, reconnaissance aircraft and fighters came to enjoy almost total air superiority as Japanese aircraft numbers in the region plummeted. Ceylon became a major base for aircraft conducting bombing missions over Burma and Malaya, for behind-enemy-lines support and, after the Japanese surrender, for transport and supply missions to liberated prisoner-of-war camps. As soon as the war ended, aircraft from India, Burma, Ceylon and the Cocos

Islands mounted Operation Mastiff, dropping food, medical supplies and wireless sets to prisoner-of-war camps. Released prisoners in places like Malaya were then evacuated by air to Ceylon.

Ceylon was a stop-off for troops crossing from Australasia to the Middle East and Europe, and a rest, training and acclimatization base for those destined to fight the Japanese in Burma. Units in Ceylon included the 16th and 17th Australian Brigades of the 6th Division, encamped near Colombo whilst awaiting transit home as they returned from the Middle East in 1942. In withdrawing Australian forces from the Middle East for home defence, Prime Minister John Curtin consented to Churchill's request that two of the five brigades be retained in Ceylon as a garrison force at a crucial moment, where they remained until August 1942. Troops were rushed to Ceylon from other parts of the Empire in March 1942 as a Japanese attack was anticipated, so that by the end of March the garrison was equivalent to two divisions. 5000 East African troops were also in Ceylon by September 1942, as well as the 34th Indian Division. The 16th British Infantry Brigade disembarked on 14 March 1942. The 11th East African Division's headquarters moved to Ceylon in 1942, where the 21st East African Brigade arrived on 21 March 1942. Later in the war troops of the King's African Rifles (including battalions from Northern Rhodesia) spent months in Ceylon undergoing jungle training in preparation for the 11th East African Division's Kabaw Valley campaign in Burma.

In the crucial early months of 1942 General Sir Archibald Wavell, recently transferred from Middle East Command to become Commander-in-Chief India, argued with Churchill and the Chiefs of Staff over the maintenance of front-line British troops in Ceylon, particularly the 16th Infantry Brigade sent to strengthen the garrison. The Chiefs of Staff explained that, following the loss of Singapore, the Eastern Fleet would have to be built up to defend the vital communications in the region, and for this it was essential that Ceylon be kept safe as its main base. A successful Japanese bid for Ceylon might have cut off British communications and supplies from the East, posed a grave menace to the Royal Navy in the Red Sea and Persian Gulf, and raised the nightmarish possibility that Axis and Japanese forces could meet at Suez, thus snapping the British Empire in two. Wavell argued for India's priority, but the Chiefs of Staff were adamant and would not allow him to remove the 16th Brigade from Ceylon, ordering an East African brigade there as well. With the loss of Rangoon and the evacuation of the Andaman Islands between 8 and 12 March, and their subsequent occupation by the Japanese, Ceylon and the coast of India were placed under even greater threat. London's resolve on this matter reflected Churchill's belief that Admiral Nagumo's raid on Ceylon was the prelude to a full-scale invasion.

Quite apart from the tens of thousands of British and Empire troops based in Ceylon or passing through its ports, the colony recruited soldiers of its own. Its overall locally-raised military strength rose from 3500 in 1939 to 26,000 in 1945.

Ceylonese troops in British uniform served as part of local defence formations to counter the threat of invasion, as garrison troops for other Indian Ocean islands, and as support soldiers for British and imperial fighting units in the Middle East and Southern Europe. From 1941 the War Office and Admiralty took command of locally-raised military and naval units in the colonies, and began to meet their costs.

Of the 26,000 Ceylonese enrolled in military formations 16,000 came under the aegis of the Ceylon Defence Force (CDF), which had numbered 2300 in 1938. The CDF was rapidly expanded after Japan entered the war and an attack on Ceylon seemed likely. It included the Ceylon Light Infantry (five battalions), the Ceylon Garrison Artillery, medical detachments, an anti-aircraft regiment, coastal artillery, signallers, the Ceylon Engineers, pioneers and service corps personnel. A contingent of the Ceylon Garrison Artillery was the first Ceylonese unit to leave the island when it was sent to the Seychelles in April 1941 to defend potential landing places with rifles and Bren guns. Port Victoria was defended from Pointe Conan by two elderly six-inch guns recently installed after their removal from HMS *Gnat*. Another artillery contingent was sent to the Cocos–Keeling Islands to protect the cable and wireless station, and a detachment of the Ceylon Light Infantry escorted enemy prisoners of war to the Middle East. A separate unit, the Ceylon Royal Artillery, came to number 1488 by 1943 and was stationed at Trincomalee.

Another locally-recruited military outfit was the Ceylon Railways Engineering Corps that operated an armoured train equipped with First World War machine guns between Colombo and Mount Lavinia. The corps was formed by the militarization of railway personnel and the arrival from India of an Anglo-Indian Railway Personnel detachment. There was also a military role for the employees of the excise department, organizing a coast-watching system to report shipping movements. The all-European Ceylon Planters' Rifle Corps (CPRC) was formed in 1938 by an amalgamation of the Ceylon Rifle Corps and the Ceylon Mounted Rifles, first raised in 1892. It did not survive the war, however, as this 'Dad's Army, colonial style' was unable to maintain its strength due to the demands of essential war industries. Most of its men came from the coconut, tea and rubber planting communities, but in May 1942 its strength was down to 350 because of drafts sent to India and the Middle East, and because some of its strength had not been called up because of the needs of the tea and rubber industries. Before its disbandment, the CPRC sent several fifty-man contingents for officer training at Dehra Dun in India. Earlier in the war the CPRC had been assigned guard duties at vulnerable civilian installations, after pressure had been put on the government to give the corps something constructive to do.

Of Ceylon's total military mobilization of 26,000, approximately 6800 served in the British Army, as opposed to locally-raised units like the CDF and Ceylon Planters' Rifle Corps. They served in the Royal Army Service Corps, the Royal Artillery, the Royal Engineers and the Royal Pioneer Corps. Some served in

Ceylon, but 4500 served overseas, mainly in the Royal Pioneer Corps providing military labour and clerical support for the Eighth Army, seeing service in the Middle East, Sicily, Greece, Italy and France. According to standard British racial categorization, Ceylonese troops were preferred in light motor transport or clerical work 'because of their high standard of education and poor physique', just as Africans were preferred for demanding physical work.

Ceylonese soldiers provided valuable if undramatic assistance to the British Empire's war effort. Only one outbreak of insubordination was recorded, when on 8–9 May 1942 fifteen Ceylon Garrison Artillery soldiers, prompted by pro-Japanese and anti-European sentiment, mutinied and tried to take over their gun battery on Horsburgh Island in the Cocos–Keeling Islands. The instigator was a Bombardier Gratien Fernando. The mutiny failed, but one loyal soldier was killed and a British officer wounded, and seven of the mutineers were sentenced to death. Three were eventually executed, the only soldiers of the Empire and Commonwealth to have met their end in this way.[10]

Another way in which colonies quietly but usefully supplemented the Empire's war-making capacity was in maintaining local naval forces. The largest colonial naval contingents outside of the Dominions were in Ceylon, Hong Kong, Malaya, Kenya and Trinidad. Founded in 1937 by the Volunteer Naval Defence Force Ordinance No. 1, the Ceylon Naval Volunteer Force (CNVF) led by Commander W. G. Beauchamp rose from 150 officers and ratings in 1939 to over 1200 in 1945.[11] Its primary object in wartime was to keep Colombo Harbour open, and to provide adequate protection for merchant shipping, thus reducing the tasks of the Royal Navy. At the start of the war the force cut its teeth manning the Port Commission tugs *Samson* and *Goliath*. During the war its activities were extended and it acquired the armed trawler *Overdale Wyke*, collected from Port Said and used for minesweeping and escort duties. Anti-submarine and mine-sweeping patrols were extended to Trincomalee, and the force undertook escort duties between Colombo and Cochin, Madras, Trincomalee, Addu Atoll, Male and Diego Garcia. It also checked out suspicious vessels in local ports and at Addu Atoll, manned the Port War Signal Station at Trincomalee, provided personnel for the Coding Office at Colombo, serviced thousands of military vehicles destined for Burma, provided Mountbatten's SEAC headquarters with stewards, serviced the lighthouses in the region, manned boom defences and controlled minefields. The force then acquired the *Balta*, *Hoxa*, *Okapi*, *Semla* and *Sambhur* – all trawlers and Arctic whalers – and the tug *Barnet*. It also manned several motor fishing vessels and other auxiliary vessels. Two hundred and forty-eight victims of Japanese air attacks were fished out of the waters between Ceylon and the Maldives by the force. The force provided support in the Burma region, and was even called upon to accept the surrender of the Italian destroyer *Eritrea*, and escort her to port with a prize crew on board. In 1943 the Royal Navy assumed responsibility for the CNVF, and it became the Ceylon Royal Naval Volunteer Reserve. Its base was commissioned as HMS *Gamunu* (a base with 1500 personnel by the end of the war). In early 1944 a Royal Navy Aircraft Ceylonese Training Establishment was created to train Ceylonese for work at the navy's air stations, thus releasing FAA personnel for service aboard the Eastern Fleet's carriers. Some Ceylonese men served with regular British units, drawn mainly from among the European community. Jack Thornhill, born in Kandy, joined the Royal Navy. He ended up serving in his home region, sent initially as a junior gunnery officer aboard the cruiser HMS *Glasgow* to perform convoy duties. In the latter stages of the war he served aboard the escort carrier HMS *Hunter* in the Indian Ocean, based at Trincomalee. Thornhill flew a Seafire aircraft, a specially developed Spitfire with strengthened undercarriage and folding wings, flying patrols as far afield as enemy occupied Singapore. The carrier's main role was to support amphibious army or marines operations. Thornhill shot down three enemy Zeros in the Malacca Strait.

The connectedness of disparate and scattered territories was a hallmark of the British imperial world, for modern Empire had the capacity to reach people all over the globe. The war had many ramifications on the home front in Ceylon. For example, weapons training for Ceylonese soldiers brought a novel element to crime on the island – armed gang robbery – necessitating the formation of a police Gang Robbery Unit. The shortage in the supply of manufactured goods and the non-availability of spare parts – experienced throughout the colonial world because of shipping shortages and Britain's inability to provide normal exports as its industry was devoted to war production – meant that Ceylon's rail network was run down and much of the rolling stock became dangerous and unusable. In Ceylon, as elsewhere, the war deeply affected home society. War led to the mass movement of people as refugees, evacuees, soldiers and labourers. The movement of people is one of the enduring themes of the Empire's history during the war, and in Ceylon there were numerous permutations. One was internal migration. The threat of Japanese bombing and invasion caused panic, particularly amongst the people of coastal towns that were likely targets. Stories of Japanese brutality towards civilian populations had travelled from China and Singapore, and many people fled Colombo and other coastal towns on the strength of this and the fact that from late 1941 an attack on Ceylon seemed inevitable. This internal migration led to a steep rise in rent demands in inland towns. Other people decided to stay, but when Japanese bombs started to fall they also fled. On the day of the Colombo raid Gerard Robinson cycled to Galle Face Green to see a Hurricane that had been shot down, and found himself travelling against a 'stampede' of people heading for the hills. This flight to the hills dramatically affected the work force of Walker Sons and Company, repairing naval vessels in Colombo harbour. As a result of the raid, most of the company's employees fled – of 3600 on the books at the time of the raid, only 123 turned up for work on the following Monday, and it took six weeks to reach 700 and a full year to reach 2000 employees. For two months after the raid Colombo and other coastal towns were deserted.

Then there was out-migration. Young European administrators, merchants and planters departed for the forces, thereby creating job opportunities for non-Europeans. Many Indian businessmen, money-lenders and traders returned to India fearing a Japanese invasion of Ceylon, as did thousands of other Indians, contributing to general panic as they poured into the Madras presidency. The wives of many Europeans left the island, mostly destined for that common bolt-hole for Europeans fleeing war zones, South Africa. Finally, there was in-migration. The island began to teem with European troops (called 'white ants' by the locals) and those of other races. Australian and New Zealand troops en route for the Middle East or returning home stopped off at Ceylon, others arrived from Britain and Africa to join the build up of forces intended to drive the Japanese out of Burma, and those already fighting the Japanese visited Ceylon for rest and relaxation. There were African, Australian, British and Indian troops, and the thousands who accompanied Mountbatten's headquarters. Italian prisoners of war also arrived to be interned at Trincomalee, as did young European women serving in the women's branches of the army, navy and air force. Another significant movement of people was the immigration of thousands of Indian workers, like the 20,000 required by the Minister of Agriculture in 1943 to increase rubber production, and the 3000 requested by the Commander-in-Chief Ceylon in January 1943 for aerodrome construction (the subject of Indians in Ceylon caused acrimonious clashes between Indian and Ceylonese political leaders over the status and political representation of these migrants).[12]

The escalation in the number of European troops on the island had social effects. Rodney Ferdinands recalls that, until the servicemen arrived, Kandy was a sleepy little town. 'If the British troops woke up Kandy, the Americans took it by the throat and shook it.' He also recalls that Burgher girls were suddenly much in demand as clerical assistants. With thousands of soldiers seeking a date, 'the world of the Burgher girl became much more cosmopolitan and exciting', and new forms of employment were opened to women for the first time. The presence of African soldiers also had interesting effects. A censored letter, sent by an army driver to his home in the kingdom of Buganda in Uganda, recorded that 'we are having enjoyment with white ladies. We pay seven and a half rupees to have a go with them'. In October 1943 the General Officer Commanding in Ceylon told the War Office in London that sexual assaults by Africans were causing a political backlash in the State Council. It is likely that – as elsewhere – the thought, as much as the fact, of Africans engaging in consensual or forced sex with members of other races triggered an avalanche of racial concern, almost certainly far greater than the issue warranted.

Estate-owners and other members of the European community played host to visiting European soldiers, and, like their counterparts throughout the Empire, 'did their bit' for the war. A Service Welfare Organization Committee was formed. Fund-raising was a common method of raising money for the war effort whilst sustaining community morale and focus. The *Times of Ceylon* organized a 'Send a Plane' Fund and there were collections for manifold funds like the Spitfire

Fund and the Gloucester and Local Sailors' Fund. Warships in Colombo harbour put out the bunting and turned on the lights for propaganda and morale purposes, to the accompaniment of the Royal Marines band. An outdoor fair called 'London Calling' was held at the Racecourse, and there was a floating extravaganza on Colombo harbour called 'Harbour Lights', with two Royal Navy cruisers dressed overall entertaining visitors and a Royal Marines band providing musical accompaniment. Even bastions of European colonial society had to make sacrifices for the war, as tennis courts were turned into vegetable gardens and the Colombo Cricket Club was requisitioned by the RAF.

For some people in Ceylon the war was a boon, as the huge military presence on the island meant that the market was almost inexhaustible. New money in the colony gave the Ceylonese Board of Ministers funds with which to pursue social welfare policies. An Essential Services Labour Corps was formed so that defence and military work would not be hindered by strikes or labour shortages. Government sought to cushion the ill effects of inflationary pressures – discontent among white collar and urban workers – by raising wages and salaries, though these increases did not keep pace with inflation. From 1942 a special war allowance based on the cost of living index was paid. The cost of living index rose by 100 per cent and the active money supply rose by 69 per cent between 1942 and 1945. Inflation led to some social discontent arising from an increased money supply, partly caused by massive defence expenditure on the island from 1943. Government resorted to a policy of controlling prices and rationing essential consumer goods, and from mid 1943 it went a stage further by freezing the prices of several important food items and subsidizing others. Importing and distributing rice, wheat flour and sugar was taken over by the state in order to make price control and rationing more effective. Like most other colonies, and Britain itself, the war brought bigger government to Ceylon. The state became more intrusive (for example, all able-bodied men were listed on a register of manpower), new reports on social and economic issues flew off the press, and new government departments were created and others expanded. Because of the demand for Ceylon's major export products, the island became an important dollar-earning territory of the Sterling Area. Ceylon ended the war with sterling balances of 1260 million rupees (approximately £94 million).

War meant that almost any raw materials or foodstuffs that a colony produced could find a ready market, and maximum production was encouraged by the Colonial Office. Britain's possession of Empire meant that it was able to control resources across the globe, and Ceylon, like other imperial territories, had bulk purchase agreements with Britain for exports in demand, notably tea and rubber. Naturally this led to some tensions between Ceylon as producer, on the one hand, and Treasury and supply departments in Britain as purchasers and distributors, on the other, requiring the Colonial Office to act as intermediary. Whilst bulk purchase arrangements prevented prices from reaching their free market level – as also did the lack of shipping – they helped to limit inflation.

Ceylon's raw materials were very important for the Allies after the loss of Malaya, particularly its output of that essential war commodity, rubber. The island produced 60 per cent of Allied rubber, and by 1944 practically all tyres and inner tubes used by American forces in the South Pacific were manufactured in Australia with Ceylonese rubber. Given the Allies desperate need, Ceylon's rubber restriction scheme was abandoned and producers were encouraged to increase output to the maximum by 'slaughter tapping' (harvesting rubber to a point at which the life of the plant was threatened). Tea was traditionally one of the island's major export crops, and it produced roughly one-fourth of the world's supply. During the war the British Ministry of Supply contracted to buy Ceylon's tea, and under the system of intra-imperial food exchange much of it was exported to Iraq, one of the few countries in the Middle East where tea was drunk more than coffee, and also to Aden.

Ceylon exported copra (the dried kernel of the coconut), and during the war became the Empire's most important source of graphite, a commodity which had previously been sold mainly to Japan. Minor products, like coir fibre (made from the outer husk of the coconut, and used, among other things, for making door-mats) and kapok (a cotton-like substance found surrounding the seeds of tropical trees, used for stuffing cushions as well as the Mae West lifejackets worn by RAF pilots), benefited from Ministry of Supply demand as it sought to provide emergency bedding in Britain in the aftermath of air raids. Finally, Ceylon developed a cinchona bark scheme in answer to the Colonial Secretary's request in December 1939 for increased production of quinine throughout the Empire (the major source had been the Dutch East Indies, lost to the Japanese in early 1942).

Lines of regional and trans-regional food interdependence criss-crossed the British Empire. Ceylon depended heavily on imported food, as did other islands of the Empire, and as indeed did Britain itself. There were optimistic plans in Ceylon to grow more food, given the likely dearth of exportable surpluses elsewhere, the breakdown of peace-time trade routes, the shortage of shipping and submarine depredations. The food production drive featured propaganda and an Emergency School Production campaign involving 5000 schools. Investment in peasant colonization schemes in dry zones was increased, and the range of free services offered by government to agricultural colonists was expanded. Guaranteed prices were paid to cultivators, free artificial manure and seeds were offered and grants of Crown Land were made available on easy terms. There were also government farms producing food. Traditional agriculture was stimulated by incentives for food production, like the 1942 Internal Purchase Scheme which offered guaranteed prices for rice set above the world market price. The State Council tried to build food reserves and hoped to make Ceylon permanently independent of imports.

Despite these hopes, Ceylon did not manage to become self-sufficient, an unrealistic short-term goal given the traditional scale of the island's reliance upon imports. In fact, rice shortages became severe enough to affect the morale of the island's work force. Burma, the source of 70 to 80 per cent of its rice imports, fell to the Japanese in 1942, and this served to underline heavily Ceylon's dependence on imports. On 20 October 1942 Ceylon's rice stocks were down to 23,000 tons, no more than a fortnight's supply. The island turned to India as a substitute, but, like many parts of the Middle East, Ceylon was denied exports because of the subcontinent's own grave food situation in the year of the Bengal famine. Ceylon then turned for help to the Middle East Supply Centre, which itself was facing a general crisis of cereal supplies in the Red Sea area, augmented by the failure of rains in Yemen and the Aden Protectorate. But Ceylon's urgent demands were met, largely by Egyptian exports, and it became dependent on Middle Eastern rice supplies until the end of the war. The movement of Egyptian rice to fill the gap left by the loss of Burma became a major operation in Allied food strategy. The United Kingdom Commercial Corporation undertook to buy as much of Egypt's surplus crop as possible. Out of the first 75,000 tons bought in 1943, 31,000 tons went to Ceylon, 24,000 tons to the army (mainly for Indian troops serving with the Eighth Army), and the 20,000 ton balance was held in reserve. Given that there was expected to be a shortfall in the purchase of the next 75,000 tons, MESC put in a strong plea for Ceylon to be cut off. But London overruled this, given the seriousness of the position in Ceylon.[13]

In the years 1934–38, Ceylon's average annual production had been 180,000 tons of milled rice, and its average import 529,000 tons, equalling an annual rice quota of 709,000 tons. The war dramatically cut the import figure, and by the end of the war the figure for domestic production had been halved.

Ceylon (thousand tons of milled rice)

Year	Production	Imports	Total
1942	184	263	447
1943	179	141	320
1944	158	114	272
1945	98	182	280

Ceylon also had to look for a new source of imported sugar, when in December 1941 its normal supplier, Java, was lost to the Japanese. The Ceylon government applied to the Ministry of Food in London for the release of Mauritian sugar.

Ceylon was constitutionally the most advanced territory in the Colonial Empire, having enjoyed universal suffrage since 1931. Ceylon, Jamaica and Malta were the colonies that made the most conspicuous progress towards self-government during the war (though the Colonial Office turned down a State Council request for Sir Stafford Cripps to visit Ceylon when he visited India). On the outbreak of war Ceylon already enjoyed a significant level of self-government, particularly in financial matters, and the war was to lead to major advances towards independence. The Board of Ministers, with the encouragement of the Colonial Office, became a quasi-Cabinet. Unusual in the British Colonial Empire, indigenous people held senior positions in the political and governmental structure, and this practice continued during the war. An astute move was the appointment of a future Governor-General, Oliver Goonetilleke, to the important position of Civil Defence Commissioner, and the leading politician and future Prime Minister, D. S. Senanayake, was given a prominent role in negotiating food supplies.

Whitehall wanted to postpone serious consideration of constitutional advance for the duration of the war, though it was obliged to change its mind in the case of Ceylon and take the issue up in 1944. This was a result of pressure from senior British military and civilian officials in Ceylon *in favour* of a significant advance towards full self-government. In a nutshell, this was because of the remarkable cooperation demonstrated by top Ceylonese politicians in helping the British prosecute the war from Ceylon. The Ceylonese leaders saw that collaboration augmented their bargaining position, and the Board of Ministers took every opportunity to emphasize the importance of the island's contribution to the war effort and to press Britain for reform towards Dominion status (*not* outright independence outside of the Commonwealth, an important fact as far as Whitehall was concerned). Ceylon's war-time role as a major source of raw materials and as a strategic base worked to the advantage of the island's nationalists.

The war saw the emergence of a genuine political partnership between the Board of Ministers and the Governor. In absolute contrast to India and Burma, the political leadership of Ceylon wholeheartedly backed the war effort, not baulking at Britain's declaration of war on behalf of the island in September 1939 and offering active support for the war effort thereafter. Even the subordination of civilian to military government with the appointment of Layton as Commander-in-Chief Ceylon in March 1942 was accepted with grace. This built British confidence in the Ceylonese leaders, and garnered the support of Layton, Governor Sir Andrew Caldecott (replaced by Sir Henry Moore in October 1944) and later the Supreme Allied Commander South East Asia, Admiral Lord Louis Mountbatten. These powerful advocates petitioned the Colonial Office for constitutional advancement. As a result of this pressure, London was persuaded in 1944 to agree to the appointment of a commission to examine a new constitutional scheme. The Soulbury Commission duly arrived in Ceylon in December 1944, and Ceylon was set on course for independence after the war. The cooperation between British and Ceylonese leaders meant that there were no painful political rifts as a result of the war.

The moderate movement that pressured Britain for political advancement was far more significant in winning it than the island's more radical elements. From 1939 the anti-war propaganda of the Marxist Lanka Sama Samajist Party (LSSP) alarmed the Colonial Office in London. The LSSP had encouraged strikes, rattling the planter community and causing it to call for an end to all political activity.

Such a marginal party could be ignored in the 'phoney war' phase, but with the fall of France the party was declared illegal and its leaders arrested. With the LSSP banned the Communists came more to the fore, especially among the working class of Colombo and its periphery, though they were not inclined to encourage strikes. Inflation increased working-class and white-collar discontent, though major strike activity was curbed by the lack of encouragement from political parties and the Defence Regulations and Avoidance of Strikes and Lockouts Act.

Mauritius (population 400,000) became an island in uniform as over 5000 men were dispatched to the Middle East as members of the British Army's Royal Pioneer Corps, and 2500 more were recruited into the Mauritius Defence Force (a Home Guard formation).[14] An ARP organization and military ambulance service were established, the Fire Service was overhauled and air raid shelters were prepared. When Japan entered the war and Singapore was lost, a Japanese attack or invasion of Mauritius became a realistic prospect. Mauritius was a colony with plenty of military and strategic pedigree. It had once been the capital of French power in the east and the base from which corsairs pursued British merchantmen as they plied their trade between India and Europe. It had been captured from the French in 1810 by a force of nearly 10,000 Indian Army soldiers, and had since then been a British naval base well placed on the Cape to Ceylon route. It was, in the words of the colony's own modest motto, the star and key of the Indian Ocean.

Given this history there was already a British garrison on the island, and naval activity in Mauritius grew throughout the war, as it was used as a base for operations in the Indian Ocean. Flying boat bases were developed and an aerodrome constructed, and the Admiralty maintained fuel and ammunition stockpiles on the island. The locally-raised professional military force, known as the Mauritius Territorial Force, expanded until it comprised two battalions. Renamed the Mauritius Regiment in 1943, the 1st Battalion was sent overseas to form part of the garrison around the naval base at Diego Suarez in Madagascar, and for much of the war a King's African Rifles battalion garrisoned Mauritius for fear of an enemy raid. A home guard formation, the Mauritius Defence Force, came to number over 2000 men. There was also a Coastal Defence Force patrolling the gaps in the reef surrounding Mauritius in thirty-foot motor vessels. Over a thousand women served in the Auxiliary Territorial Service, some in Egypt, 4500 Mauritian men served in the Royal Pioneer Corps in the Middle East and over 8000 men were conscripted into the Civilian Labour Corps, as the colonial government took the necessary powers to control the allocation of labour for war purposes. Mauritian forces were also used to garrison the island's Indian Ocean dependencies, guarding, for example, the cable and wireless station on Rodrigues, and providing forces to defend the naval base on Diego Garcia. New communications links were created by the conflict. From being an island that in 1939 had never seen an aircraft, by 1942 Mauritius boasted numerous RAF and Fleet Air Arm facilities, including a Royal Naval Air Station, and by 1944 a regular air service linked it with Madagascar and South Africa. The island was also part of the navy's wireless network across the Indian Ocean. Considerable defensive work had to be carried out to prepare the island better to withstand an attack better, including the installation of anti-aircraft guns, torpedo booms in the main ports and minefields in the approaches.

As well as acting as a base for military operations in the region, notably the naval and air operations to sink German supply ships and submarines, Mauritius was also used as a gathering point for warships blockading Vichy territory and attempting to intercept Vichy blockade-runners travelling between Indo-China, Madagascar and Europe. Operation Kedgeree in August 1941 and Operation Bell-ringer in October 1941, for example, were aimed at Vichy convoys and made use of Mauritian facilities. The latter consisted of a convoy from Tamatave, Madagascar, bound for France and escorted by a Vichy sloop. The British naval forces took 40,000 tons of shipping and ended the formal challenge to the Royal Navy blockade of Vichy trade with Madagascar. Prize crews were put aboard the captured vessels that were then sent to Mauritius.

Mauritius was also a base for covert operations against neighbouring Vichy territories. SOE broadcast propaganda from a secret wireless station in a sugar-cane field, and mounted operations in Madagascar and Réunion. In the case of Réunion SOE agents were inserted from Mauritius, and operations were conducted along with a Free French destroyer to force the island's staunch Vichy governor and his garrison to surrender. In a further contribution to the work of SOE, the island's elite Franco-Mauritian community provided a significant number of French-speaking SOE operatives for active service in occupied France. Some sections of the Franco-Mauritian population, however, were regarded with suspicion by the British colonial government because it was believed that their affinity to Vichy France, and sense of outrage over British attacks on Vichy French territory and forces (such as the invasion of Syria and the destruction of the French naval squadron at Mers-el-Kebir), made them a subversive threat. There were even tales of such disaffected French sympathizers signalling with their head-lights to enemy submarines off the Mauritian coast. Given the threat of Japanese attack or invasion, considered real enough in the early months of 1942, SOE organized stay-behind teams to harry Japanese occupiers and supply British forces with intelligence, and plans were made for a scorched earth policy to be activated when attack appeared imminent. The bells of all the island's Catholic and Anglican churches fell silent in January 1942, to be used only in the event of a Japanese attack, and the Labour Department prepared a plan for the evacuation of the capital, Port Louis. A network of prostitutes was organized in Port Louis to garner information from Japanese soldiers should the latter ever find themselves at leisure on the island.

The Mauritian home front was deeply affected by the war, particularly because of the island's abject dependence on food imports, from far afield and from neighbouring countries like Madagascar, from where fresh meat had been obtained before enmity between Britain and Vichy severed it as a source of supply, and the Mauritian dependency of the Agalega Islands, from where oil foods had been shipped. Given the need, as in Britain, to start digging for victory in an effort to attain food self-sufficiency, the government obliged the island's sugar planters to devote 27 per cent of their land to food crops. Vital supplies of Burmese rice were cut off, and an effort was made by touring nutritional demonstration units to educate the majority Indian population in the preparation of new types of food, including bread. Fund-raising schemes saw Mauritius donate hundreds of thousands of pounds to the war effort, buying a Spitfire squadron and providing the first mobile canteens to appear on the streets of London during the Blitz in 1940. Two thousand Jewish detainees, denied entry into Palestine after escaping from Nazi-occupied territories in Europe, arrived in Mauritius in 1940 for the duration of the war, where they remained interned in the central prison at Beau Bassin. Many marriages were contracted with haste as thousands of Mauritian servicemen prepared for overseas deployment, partly because of the soldiers' remittances that the women might then have access to (they were known as 'Madames Pioneres').

One of the more remarkable aspects of Mauritius's war effort was its contribution to the secret war of signals interception associated with Bletchley Park. The head of the Labour Department, Edward Twining (later Sir Edward Twining, Governor of Tanganyika, later Lord Twining of Godalming and Tanganyika) was charged with the task of running the government's Censorship Department and conducting its propaganda campaign through the newspapers and the radio. Twining had seventeen newspapers and forty-nine cinemas to censor, and propaganda aplenty to beam to Mauritians and the inhabitants of neighbouring Vichy territories. He was also able to intercept all cable traffic bound for the Vichy territories (by law, Cable & Wireless, the main provider company, had to allow the British government access to all its cable traffic). Twining also set up a wireless and cable interception facility that came to employ over 300 people, providing a valuable addition to the work of Far East Combined Bureau, the region's main Bletchley Park outstation engaged in the work of intercepting Japanese military and diplomatic codes, and those of the region's Vichy regimes. The Wireless Interception Centre on Mauritius came to rely on experts sent out from Britain, including academics from Hull University, the wives of colonial officials and the daughters of wealthy Franco-Mauritian families. Initially the work was centred on the cable traffic that passed through Mauritius (neighbouring French territory, for example, relied on British cables in the region), though it increasingly came to play a role in intercepting and deciphering French and Japanese diplomatic, commercial and military wireless traffic. As elsewhere in the Empire, government became more interventionist as a result of world war. It introduced rationing, and took steps to regiment the labour force, for example creating a Manpower Board and a national register. As in Britain, the war also witnessed a flurry of official government reports into all aspects of the colony's social and economic life, as the promise of a post-war New Jerusalem, applied in the Empire as at home (even if in a dilute form) through the vaunted Colonial Development and Welfare Acts, required surveys, information and statistics so that government could bid successfully for funds.

Like so many other peripatetic Britons required to travel all over the world on the errands of a global Empire at war, Twining notched up an impressive travelling record. During the war he left Mauritius frequently and visited Burma, Ceylon, the Congo, the Dutch East Indies, Egypt, Greece, Iraq, Iran, Madagascar, Mozambique, Nigeria, Palestine, Singapore, South Africa, the Sudan, Tanganyika, Thailand and Uganda. He travelled by road, by rail, by flying boat, by transport aircraft, by battleship, by cruiser and by steamer. As he aptly put it in a letter to his wife on 26 November 1941, 'sick to death of this continual travelling! 20,000 miles in eight weeks!'

British interests in Bombay had been particularly keen to explore the Chagos Archipelago since the mid-eighteenth century, when Diego Garcia had first been visited. The islands were formally claimed by a British force from Bombay in 1786 in order to establish a victualling station, to which end several ship loads of soil were landed from India. This move did not prevent the French from contesting the claim until the Treaty of Paris in 1814 ceded most of France's Indian Ocean portfolio to the victorious British, and once and for all silenced its claims in disputed regions. During the Second World War Diego Garcia began its career as a military base, albeit in a modest fashion. Diego Garcia today is part of the British colony of British Indian Ocean Territory, and it is home, under lease, to one of the most important American military bases in the world. During the Second World War the atoll became part of Britain's impressive Indian Ocean defence system. In May 1940 the Admiralty designated a convoy route (XC) from the Chagos Archipelago through the Maldives to Ceylon, and this route was used throughout the war. A reverse convoy route, Colombo–Maldives–Chagos (CX), was set up in April 1943. Diego Garcia was ideally placed to defend the convoy route at this mid-ocean point. In March 1941 RAFA (RAF Association Ship) *Anne* arrived from Singapore with huts, an Air Ministry World Department officer and coolies deployed to establish a seaplane outpost. From then on Diego Garcia became a base for flying boats that throughout the war provided a valuable reconnaissance capability. Thought was also given to the island's defence in the event of an enemy raid. A brace of six-inch naval guns were installed at Eclipse Point (site of the seaplane base) in February 1942, and a small body of troops moved in to operate the guns and provide small arms defence. Two platoons of Indian Garrison Troops guarded the RAF camp. The island was reconnoitred by the Japanese submarine I-16, though never attacked. Placed in charge was Captain J. Alan Thompson of the Royal Marines, whose experiences on Diego Garcia left such an impression that he subsequently published three novels about his war-time experiences there. Diego Garcia was a frequent stop-off for vessels traversing the Indian Ocean, and a base at which rescued seamen would be deposited after their ships had been sunk. Unremarkable, though providing important imperial service-station facilities, Diego Garcia could also be used as a base for ship repairs, as was the case for HMIS *Bengal* after her encounter with a Japanese cruiser.

Keeping Britain's burgeoning Indian Ocean defence network supplied was a specialist task requiring dedicated services. The Australian Oriental Line operated two 4500-ton passenger-cargo ships, *Taiping* and *Changte*. Both were chartered by the Admiralty as Victualling Stores Issuing Ships. Each vessel carried enough food to feed 20,000 men for six months, including over 5000 gallons of Bundaberg rum for the Royal Navy's daily tot. *Taiping*'s service started in September 1942 when she left Sydney for Trincomalee. One of her first tasks was to victual the Eastern Fleet at Addu Atoll, a task which involved replenishing about forty ships. Beyond its work of supplying the navy afloat, *Taiping* had to keep the various British bases topped up with stores. This involved regular visits to Addu Atoll, Diego Garcia, the Seychelles and the Persian Gulf. On most missions the supply ships were accompanied by the tanker *Appleleaf*, the water tanker *Singu* and an ammunition ship, frequently escorted by Australian corvettes. Also fulfilling a passenger role, the ships carried British and Indian Army personnel for garrison duties, and occasionally livestock for Muslims serving in the Indian Army. For her part, *Changte* worked on a supply shuttle service to Mombasa, Aden, the Red Sea and Persian Gulf ports.

An extraordinary imperial utilization of a speck of Indian Ocean territory came with the development of Addu Atoll as a fleet and air force base during the war.[15] Before the war the Admiralty had begun to prepare Addu as a secret base at which ships could refuel and resupply and be safe from submarines. Known as Port T, the base infrastructure that was developed on the islands and atolls of the Maldives was planned in absolute secrecy as a vital link in the convoy route across the Indian Ocean. By the end of 1939 the Admiralty had begun to withdraw ships from the China Station for European and Home waters and for convoy protection duties in the Indian Ocean. In December 1939 the Air Ministry decided to examine the possibility of laying down stocks of fuel on various Indian Ocean islands to enable the flying boats from Trincomalee to move at short notice to the Seychelles, Mauritius and the Cape of Good Hope, enabling them to provide air cover for the Admiralty's convoy protection programme. In early 1940 the first flying boat mooring and refuelling facilities had been established at Malé Atoll in the Maldives; in this the Sultan of the Maldives had proved himself to be extremely cooperative. In addition to the flying boat facilities at Malé emergency stores for the Far East were also built up.

Even before the Air Ministry established the Maldives refuelling depot at Malé, the Admiralty had been considering how best to counter the threat to Allied shipping in the Indian Ocean if Japan entered the war. If the main Indian Ocean ports were blockaded, some safe haven would be needed between South Africa and the Far East, well away from mainland Africa and India, and capable of being defended. The Maldives had been frequently charted and recognized as potentially of strategic value since the nineteenth century. The most southerly atolls had the added attraction of being so remote as to be immune from land-based air power. With this in mind, Lieutenant Colonel W. B. F. Lukis of the Royal Marines was put in command of a reconnaissance party consisting of Fleet Air Arm, Royal Artillery, Royal Engineers and Royal Navy personnel. The party sailed from Ceylon in the strictest secrecy aboard HMS *Glasgow*. Landing on the island of Hitaddu (Addu), the party was met by the Sultan's nephew, Abdullah Afif Didi. This was the opening shot in the escalation of facilities at Addu Atoll, referred to in all communications as Port T.

What the navy wanted was a defended fleet anchorage that could be used if Singapore was lost and British forces had to fall back into the Indian Ocean. From the air force point of view, the Maldives could be developed for the use of land-based aircraft as well as flying boats. Shipping putting into Ceylon was increasing dramatically as the war progressed. By March 1941 Colombo alone was dealing with well over 200 ships per month, and the need for improved air cover in the Indian Ocean was becoming urgent. Given these compelling reasons, it was decided in London that large-scale defences should be constructed on Addu Atoll in order for it to be fully utilized as a naval and air base. Two Mobile Naval Base Defence Organization (MNBDO) units were transferred from the Mediterranean, one known as Force 'Piledriver' and the other as Force 'Shortcut', together amounting to over a thousand men. The two units left the Mediterranean aboard two ships on 20 September 1941, escorted to Addu Atoll by the Eastern Fleet cruiser HMS *Cornwall*. Permission was sought from the Sultan (some time after the work had actually commenced) for this additional defence work, and was granted.

There was plenty of work to be done. The lagoons had to be properly surveyed if they were to harbour the various classes of warships, and at one point the Eastern Fleet cruiser HMS *Mauritius* spent time at Addu Atoll doing harbour trials in the lagoons. Gun emplacements needed to be constructed to defend the base from the air and the sea, and link roads cleared. The gun batteries then had to be linked by telephone and submarine cable. Underwater defences had to be installed, along with controlled minefields, booms and indicator loops at the entrances of the main lagoon. All of the new construction and the presence of hundreds of white troops created a strange new world for the Adduans. At first, Matador lorries driven up the beaches caused villagers to flee. Palm trees were torn down, land was built over, local labour was required, and cigarettes and beer – religious taboos – entered the islands' exchange networks. The opportunities and disruptions caused reflected those experienced by Pacific islanders at the same time. Fishing, trading and cultivating were disrupted by, among other things, islanders having to work for the military whenever required and by the presence of a growing number of troops. For the soldiers themselves, the working conditions were extremely trying because of the climate, malaria, remoteness, poor mail service from Britain via India and Ceylon, and the nature of the work which included stevedoring, digging and constructing all manner of military facilities. There was also the fear that the Japanese would see Addu Atoll as a fit target for a repeat of Pearl Harbor. Conditions placed such a strain on Port T's medical staff that HM Hospital Ship *Vita* was sent out for a month. On 26 November 1941 Force 'Shortcut' left for work on other Indian Ocean islands, becoming a highly mobile force working on various Indian Ocean islands until late March 1942, when it was disbanded.

By December 1941 the MNBDO troops had made great progress. They had cleared sites, filled in swamps, built roads, installed and tested coastal artillery and generally established a military tented garrison. The atoll had been converted into a defended base with the Gan Channel, the main entrance to the harbour, defended by a minefield controlled from a hut on the island of Wilingili. Submerged indicator loops spanned the channel so that if any metallic object passed over them its presence would be indicated on a screen. This was monitored by sailors, who could detonate the channel mines. The Admiralty was informed that Port T was now in operation as a defended port. With the completion of this project the Admiralty decided to increase Port T's role to that of a main fleet base, with maximum facilities for the maintenance of an entire fleet (the main lagoon was large and deep enough to accommodate even the largest class of warships). Indian troops were sent to replace MNBDO troops as soon as the initial stages of construction work had been completed on Boxing Day 1941. An advanced party of 642 Indians arrived at the end of December. One of the tasks associated with Port T's increased status was to develop a proper aerodrome so that the Fleet Air Arm could operate permanently in the area. This required the dispatch of a new survey team, which eventually decided that Gan Island was suitable (after the war the RAF took over this facility and RAF Gan remained operational until 1975). The main Addu Atoll shore station was named HMS *Haitan* after Port T's base ship. Each shore station was linked by telephone, and the garrison rose to number over 4000 men by the end of 1942.

By early 1942 all of the basics were in place at Addu Atoll, including store ships, tankers, hospital ships and searchlights. The Ceylon raid of April 1942 led the Admiralty temporarily to scale down developments at Port T, so as not to attract Japanese attention and offer the enemy, in the event of a successful attack, ready-made facilities. This lull did not last long and in June 1942 the Admiralty and the Commander-in-Chief Eastern Fleet agreed to restart the development work. The Royal Marine Engineers 'Q' Company arrived on HMS *Chitral* on 19 August 1942 to lay the aerodrome runways, a force consisting of 720 men providing expertise in every aspect of engineering and construction. Work on Gan aerodrome and its three runways necessitated the evacuation of all the villagers, a further example of the disruption brought to people hardly touched by the Western world until the war. Throughout the Maldives, defence establishment camouflage and deception measures were taken to protect the new facilities; searchlights and observation towers, for example, being made to look like native structures, and tents being hidden among the palm trees. On 8 February 1943 the cruiser HMS *Gambia*'s Walrus seaplane became the first aircraft ever to land on Gan. The following day a convoy containing thousands of Australian troops en route from Aden to Fremantle, on board the luxury liners *Aquitania, Ile de France, Nieue Amsterdam, Queen of Bermuda* and *Queen Mary*, together with their escorts, broke their journey at Addu Atoll. Whenever vessels approached the port it became an established precaution to dispatch from Gan aerodrome a navy Sea Otter, flown by an Australian, for submarine detection.

Another major feature of Addu Atoll's rise to military prominence in the Indian Ocean was the installation of radar and wireless facilities. By July 1943 ground clearance programmes were virtually complete, a fighter control office was operational, navigation beacons had been erected on Maruda and Gan, and the searchlight and anti-aircraft gun emplacements completed on Wilingili. A chain overseas low tower (radar) had been erected by December, standing 180 feet high and manned by ratings from the Royal New Zealand Navy. The 7000-ton tanker *British Loyalty* arrived at Addu Atoll in October 1943, where she was to remain anchored in the lagoon to serve as a storage hulk and refuelling station for Allied shipping in the Indian Ocean. *British Loyalty* had already been sunk by a Japanese submarine at Diego Suarez in Madagascar in May 1942, though subsequently raised from the shallows a few months later. Although lightning is never supposed to strike in the same place twice, on 9 March 1944 *British Loyalty* was torpedoed at anchor by U-183, which managed to aim and fire through the Gan Channel that gave access to the main lagoon. Several thousands gallons of crude oil escaped from the ship and spread over the water and the shore, though for years after the vessel remained usable as a storage facility.

Increased military activity meant more disruption for the islanders. Traffic congestion problems became acute because so many vehicles had been brought to the islands, requiring the issue of licences and the employment of motorcycle police on traffic control duties. New wells were bored in order to relieve the base of its dependence on fresh water shipped from Ceylon. Food shortages affected both islanders and troops, for whom rationing was introduced. Some of the islanders were better off than those in other parts of the Maldives, because their diets were supplemented by the military. The Maldives suffered because general stores in India and Ceylon, and the effects of the loss of rice from the Far East, had dramatically increased the price of imported food. Rice, a staple, was not grown anywhere in the Maldives. The government authorities responsible for the Maldives handed over to the military full control for introducing and controlling rationing and the distribution of food throughout the Maldives. Control was exercised by headquarters staff in Ceylon, with distribution by ships and flying boats. In an effort to become more self-sufficient in the Maldives, troops were allocated to farm duties and several hundred goats, chickens and rabbits were imported from Ceylon, a worthy though unsuccessful scheme. In other spheres of activity, sports pitches were laid and in April 1943 the 'Empire Cinema' was opened.

As is often the case with military bases rapidly expanded to meet a certain eventuality, when that eventuality did not arise, Addu Atoll's significance waned accordingly. From mid-1943 it was very unlikely that Port T would be needed as a major fleet hideout or a main servicing base. It retained, however, its importance in other areas. It remained an important link in the imperial chain between Africa and the Far East, valued for its refuelling and servicing facilities in sheltered waters. It was also from 1943 a communications link important for shipping in the Indian Ocean. The base ship *Haitan* acted as the communications centre for all signals traffic with the outside world, maintaining a constant radio link with Colombo and transmitting messages for visiting ships which where thus able to maintain radio silence. It also mounted a continuous listening watch for distress signals, and London shipping messages were received each day and retransmitted.

As a major naval base, however, it was decided in early 1944 that Addu Atoll had served its purpose and had now become obsolescent. Port T's function was therefore redefined as an occasional fleet base and a temporary base for flying boats. Its communications value remained though. With the departure of HMS *Haitan*, Plan 'R' was implemented. This was a multi-site shore-based naval communications station with wireless transmitters and towers housing the chain overseas low equipment, the transponder radar unit and the RDF equipment (other Indian Ocean islands like Mauritius were also part of the chain). On 1 February 1944 the base was commissioned as a RNAS shore establishment named HMS *Maraga*. There were plans for the construction of ten wireless transmitter and receiver towers of between 80 and 110 feet. The transponder radar unit and chain overseas low installations did not function for long, however, as there was no longer a need for an air raid intelligence service across the Indian Ocean. Despite Addu Atoll's diminished status, in July 1944 there were still 1349 Indian troops and a hundred British troops on station (and an Indian general hospital with 400 beds). Slowly parts of the base were dismantled or decommissioned. Four of the eight Bofors anti-aircraft guns and the coastal defence searchlights were removed. Nine of the gun emplacements on Gan and Wilingili, comprising one four-inch and eight twelve-pounders, were also declared redundant and the guns dispatched to the Far East. Six–inch batteries on Midu and Hitaddu were abandoned but not removed. As the military slowly withdrew, leaving things behind them, the indigenous village communities made use of everything that was left – cordage, corrugated iron, forty-gallon drums, non-ferrous metals, reparable tools and discarded tentage all found welcome homes. In March 1945 the shore base HMS *Maraga* was closed, and the Addu Atoll facilities were redesignated as a refuelling facility and RAF observation centre. Though the RAF was to remain for a further thirty years, the Admiralty classed the base as non-operational from October 1945. Over £180,000 and three years of hard labour had been invested on the island since 1940.

Zanzibar provides a good illustration of the impact of world war upon local trade. Lying off the Swahili coast, the islands of Zanzibar and Pemba had for long been at the heart of a western Indian Ocean regional economy that connected peoples and goods from Africa, Arabia and India.[16] Dhows, monsoon winds, cloves and mangrove poles were integral to Zanzibar's history, as was a British presence that had grown over the course of the nineteenth century from informal advice, given to the Sultan by a Government of India resident, to the establishment of a British protectorate in 1890. Zanzibar (population, including Pemba, 260,000) was touched in many ways by the Second World War. The severing of commercial links with countries that became enemy territory, coupled with the dearth of merchant shipping, created serious food shortages. Like Britain, Mauritius, Ceylon and many other parts of the Empire, Zanzibar was dependent on food imports, and it was one of the many territories that had depended on rice from Burma.

The need to bring more land under cultivation in order to produce more food contributed to soil erosion, which in turn contributed to the silting up of the Chake Chake creak on Pemba and the encroachment of mangroves into the creak's channel, making it impassable. The colonial government and the Zanzibar Naval Volunteer Force made plans for the defence of the wireless station at Chake Chake, and carefully monitored the arrival of immigrants. War-time conditions led to a renaissance of the dhow trade. For decades the colonial government had tried to replace dhows with modern steamers, though the chronic lack of such vessels in the Second World War allowed the dhows to claw back some of the lost ground. Before the war dhows had dominated private shipping between Pemba and Zanzibar, but the carriage of the valuable clove exports was reserved for steamers, as was the carriage of government supplies. But with the general war-time shortage of shipping, as more steamers were requisitioned for war service and as the Royal Navy requisitioned one of the Zanzibar government's steamers (the *Al-Hathera*) for minesweeping duties, the government had no choice but to turn increasingly to dhows. In 1942 the Clove Growers' Association, a bastion of the steamer service, was forced to do so as well. Dhows therefore carried the cloves from Pemba to Zanzibar and then filled in for the steamers by transporting them overseas, to India, for example, where over a fifth of Zanzibar's cloves were consumed. Even the mail to Pemba was sometimes delivered by dhows, as well as government employees.

Imperial trade networks here as elsewhere were severely disrupted by war-time shipping shortages. In December 1939, for example, neighbouring Tanganyika was allocated 19,400 tons of cargo space for goods destined for Britain. At the time, however, there were 70,000 tons of goods awaiting shipping to Britain. As well as ocean-going shipping there was also a dearth of coastal shipping, essential to trade links between the African mainland and offshore islands such as Zanzibar. The war-time shortage of fuel meant that lorries that might otherwise have stepped into the breach and delivered goods to coastal ports were laid up. All of this was a severe headache for the colonial authorities in the region, but good news for the dhow owners. They were kept so busy that demand exceeded their capacity to carry, and dhows from Arabia sailed south to take advantage of the employment bonanza brought on by the war. The trade routes between Arabia and Africa that had characterized the western Indian Ocean world in the nineteenth century had declined dramatically in the twentieth. But here was a last hurrah. In March 1941, for example, the district officer in Rufiji reported that the mangrove season was going poorly because the Arab dhows on which it depended were too busy shipping food between Lindi, Mombasa and Zanzibar. Food shortages in Arabia made the northward run highly profitable for local dhow owners, as well encouraging more Arabian dhows to visit. War-time food regulations and shortages also created a black market, and many dhows illegally shipped Mozambiquan sugar to Arabia. Clove-exporting firms bought new dhows to cope with the demand, encouraged by the belief that these traditional sail vessels were less likely to attract the attention of enemy submarines. By 1944 nearly a quarter of Zanzibar's exports were being carried by dhow, representing over half a million pounds-worth of trade.

War saw colonial officials leave Zanzibar to join the forces, and this led to a decrease in colonial record-keeping as new duties fell on the narrowed shoulders of the administration. In one area, however, record-keeping kept up with the pace. Surveillance of ocean-going dhows was conducted with enthusiasm and records were meticulously kept. Above all else, this indicated the colonial government's wariness of these vessels in wartime. The detailed reports of dhow arrivals, their previous ports of call, destinations, owners, cargoes and crew were circulated to the Economic Control Board, appointed to regulate the protectorate's imports and exports during the war, and the Military Security Officer. Whilst the government had been forced into a new reliance on dhows, those hardy legacies of the nineteenth-century era of slaves, sail and spices, it was wary of them by tradition. It was thought that dhows could be used to transport infiltrators or saboteurs from enemy territory such as Italian Somaliland, or from neutral territory hosting enemy agents, such as Portuguese East Africa. In 1940 concern about the number of enemy nationals living in Tanganyika (a former German colony) led the government of Zanzibar to pass a regulation that forbade the movement of ships after dark within three miles of the coast of Pemba or Unguja.

Thousands of miles away from Zanzibar, on the other side of the Indian Ocean, lay the British possessions of Christmas Island and the Cocos Islands. Christmas Island, south of the western tip of Java, had been annexed in 1888 and from 1900 formed part of the Settlement of Singapore. During the war it was occupied by the

Japanese. The Cocos Islands were coral atolls located further west, 1040 mile south south west of Singapore and strategically placed near Japanese-occupied Java and halfway between Ceylon and Australia. Despite the presence of a cable station on one of the islands, Direction Island – part of the trans-Indian Ocean cable route linking Africa and the Middle East with Australia – the Japanese had never taken the islands, though they regularly reconnoitred them. The cable and wireless station, guarded by a small force of imperial troops, continued relaying traffic throughout the war, though there was a brief interruption in communications with Australia when the islands were shelled on 3 March 1942. To lessen enemy attention the flying boat anchorage was not used, and the islands were removed from official maps. Initially a garrison was provided by troops from Ceylon, though fifteen of them mutinied in May 1942. They were replaced by a King's African Rifles platoon, manning six–inch guns covering the main anchorage on Horsburg Island. All of the local inhabitants lived on Home Island.

Corporal Fred Roles was serving with 357 Wireless Unit (part of the 'Y' Service listening to enemy wireless transmissions) in Ceylon in early 1944 when he found himself dispatched to the Cocos Islands. There he worked alongside the civilians running the cable and wireless station, and Royal Navy wireless operators. His unit installed new antennae by getting local boys to climb coconut trees and conceal them, given the need to deceive Japanese reconnaissance flights into thinking that Direction Island was uninhabited. The unit's task was to listen to transmissions made by enemy shipping, particularly submarines that surfaced at night to receive and transmit signals, and to enemy air traffic, and to report their findings to headquarters in Colombo. There were also Australian meteorologists on the island, and Catalinas flew over most nights travelling from Perth to Colombo. Direction Island was bombed on one occasion, and a petty officer killed. In August 1944 Royal Marines with anti-aircraft guns arrived.

The Cocos Islands found a significant new war role later in the war as British thoughts turned resolutely towards reconquering territory lost to the Japanese. John Behague of No. 99 (Liberator) Squadron left India on the troopship *Dilwarra* with no idea as to his destination. Some days later he was ordered to disembark, scrambling down netting and into a landing barge, before being conveyed to the shore of West Island. There he and his comrades slept rough until tents arrived, and those early days were dominated by the hazards of falling coconuts, land crabs, giant poisonous centipedes, a perilous reef, and weapons training with Sten guns. Behague spent his time on the Cocos Islands on wireless duties by day and in producing the Cocos forces newssheet, *Atoll*, by night, using news pirated from Reuters transmissions. It was, indeed, a strange way and a strange place in which to spend a war.

There was, however, a strategic point to this. Behague was deployed as part of a new force created to make offensive use of the Cocos Islands. With British impe-rial forces in India and Burma on the offensive, and plans for the reinvasion of South-East Asia and the Dutch East Indies in the air, the Chiefs of Staff in London decided to investigate the practicability of building a staging post between Ceylon and Australia for aircraft that might need to be moved between South-East Asia Command and the south-west Pacific. The Supreme Allied Commander-in-Chief SEAC, Admiral Lord Louis Mountbatten, realized that such a base might also be valuable for photo reconnaissance, minelaying by aircraft in waterways and ports frequented by Japanese vessels and bombing operations over enemy-occupied territory. Therefore he enthusiastically supported the project. A sizeable force ultimately numbering 6500 (mainly RAF) personnel, including construction workers and an army contingent, was built up. Two all-weather air strips were cleared on West Island (bulldozing coconut trees and thereby damaging liveli-hoods), featuring 2000-yard pierced steel planking runways. As in Burma, specially-recruited RAF elephants were employed to haul aircraft back on to the steel surface of the runway if they skidded off and landed in the mud. In April 1945 Spitfires of No. 136 Squadron arrived to provide air defence for the island's main units, RAF Liberators, the first of which touched down on 28 May 1945. By the end of July two Liberator squadrons had arrived to provide air support for the planned invasion of Malaya. From then on the aircraft based on the Cocos Islands stood ready to attacking enemy radar installations, railways, airfields and shipping prior to Operation Zipper (the amphibious invasion of Malaya). Also using Cocos Island runways, RAF Mosquitos flew photo reconnaissance missions over Sumatra and Malaya. In August 1945 Nos 99 and 356 Liberator Squadrons based on the Cocos Islands were placed at the disposal of Force 136 operating behind enemy lines in Malaya and Thailand, and in August and September 756 sorties were made from Ceylon and the Cocos Islands. Nos 99 and 356 Squadrons flew to Singapore on 28 August 1945 as part of Operation Zipper. Following Japan's surrender these squadrons began working on Operation Birdcage, the delivery of relief to Allied prisoners of war and internees in Malaya.

The Andaman and Nicobar Islands in the Bay of Bengal were British possessions governed from India. Though the Chiefs of Staff in London had discussed the defence of these islands on 25 February 1942, they were abandoned by their British garrison when Rangoon fell to the Japanese the following month. In March a party was flown to Nancowry in the Nicobar Islands charged with the demolition of installations and supplies, as well as the evacuation of personnel. Fuel stocks were torched, bombs dumped into the sea and huts smashed and burned. The Japanese swiftly occupied these islands, attracted by their useful strategic position in the Bay of Bengal close to important shipping routes and the coasts of India and Burma. For a long time an attack on the Andamans aimed at reoccupation was under consideration by Churchill and the Chiefs of Staff, particularly because the Americans and the Chinese were keen for a British forward move in the Indian Ocean. (Chiang Kai-shek at one point made the commitment of Chinese troops to a joint American-British-Chinese campaign in northern Burma condi-tional upon the appearance in the Bay of Bengal of a force of three or four Allied battleships and six carriers, of which there was no chance whatsoever.) From its formation in 1943 Mountbatten's SEAC was naturally eager to oblige with any kind of plans for operations in their region if this meant moving up the queue for resources, especially the all-important landing craft, without which the major amphibious attacks could not take place. Plans were made for an attack on the Andaman Islands by SEAC, but they came to nothing. On 13 December 1943 the Chief of the Imperial General Staff, General Sir Alan Brooke, recorded in his diary that he was delighted to have discovered that President Roosevelt had agreed to the British cancelling the proposed Andaman Islands attack. His reason for relief was the desire to keep all available landing craft in the Mediterranean, rather than dissipating these particularly precious craft by supporting operations in too many theatres at once. So Mountbatten's plan for an amphibious fleet assault on the Andamans, known as Operation Buccaneer, was stillborn and Allied conferences in Cairo and Tehran finally ended the plan to invade the islands. (Stalin's insistence on the opening of a second front in Europe at the Tehran conference was a further nail in the coffin of the SEAC plan.) Churchill had persuaded Roosevelt that Buccaneer should be abandoned and all landing craft returned. On 9 December 1943 Churchill informed Mountbatten that the operation was off, adding, in a communication that struck Mountbatten as most unfair, that 'everyone here has been unpleasantly affected by your request to use 50,000 British and Imperial troops ... against 5000 Japanese'. Sporadic British attacks on the islands continued, as they had since the Japanese occupation began. In April 1942, for example, a Hudson reconnaissance aircraft from Akyab reported nine Japanese flying boats moored in Port Blair harbour. Attacks went in and destroyed them, greatly reducing the scale of Japanese aerial reconnaissance in the Bay of Bengal.

Japan was still in occupation of the islands at the end of the war. From 1944, however, with its position strengthening by the month, the Eastern Fleet began to mount sustained attacks on the Andaman and Nicobar Islands, and was responsible for ensuring that the Japanese garrison did not receive supplies and was not evacuated. In March 1945, for example, Force 70 – the Eastern Fleet destroyers HMS *Rapid*, *Saumarez* and *Volage* – were attacked in Stewart Sound, Great Andaman, and in the same month a Japanese convoy from Singapore to Port Blair was attacked by an Eastern Fleet–RAF force consisting of four destroyers and two groups of Liberator bombers. Hellcat strikes were made on the Nicobar Islands, and photo reconnaissance Mosquitos from Ceylon surveyed the islands. Japanese atrocities included the transportation of 300 'useless mouths' to uninhabited Havelock Island, where all but eleven perished. The islands were given over to the administration of Subha Chandra Bose's Indian National Army at the end of 1943.

Aden (population 900,000, split between a coastal colony and a hinterland protectorate), once a prosperous port connected to the frankincense trade, was taken by 700 British and Indian troops in 1839 as a strategic outpost at the joint of the Red Sea and Indian Ocean, well positioned to guard British sea routes to India, to suppress piracy in the region, and to serve as a coaling station for shipping bound for or sailing from India. Aden was an Indian dependency until 1937, and the Government of India maintained small forces there, though in the inter-war years its defence was taken over by the RAF as air power became the preferred and cheapest method of projecting British power in its Middle Eastern domains.[17] Thus Aden, like Iraq and Trans-Jordan, became an Air Command in 1927. With the end of Indian rule in 1937, Aden became a crown colony, encompassing Kuria Muria and Perim islands. RAF Khormaksar became the main RAF base and head-quarters, and air strips sprouted across Aden. In order to guard the new RAF installations the Aden Protectorate Levies (APL) was formed in 1928, a typical imperial use of local manpower. On the outbreak of war the APL numbered 600, and Aden was reinforced from India by a battalion of the 5th Mahratta Light Infantry. The APL, under RAF command, expanded to more than double its orig-inal size and was used for guard duties in Aden, in Sharjah on the Trucial Oman coast, and in the offshore British islands of Socotra and Masira. A base at Salaya in Oman was used by the Royal Navy. Masira, measuring forty miles by ten miles and about fifteen miles off the coast of Oman, had in the 1930s become one of a number of unmanned staging posts between the RAF bases in Iraq and Aden. The war led to a major expansion of activities on Masira. Anti-submarine flying boats and land-based aircraft were based on the island together with high-speed rescue launches. The island also continued to serve as a BOAC facility and military staging post to the Far East. During the war there were over a thousand service personnel on station, and the RAF built a military railway.

There were a few Italian bombing raids over Aden early in the war, and the colony and its excellent port served as a base during the East Africa campaign; the garrison of British Somaliland was evacuated to Aden, and during its reconquest Indian Army units were transported from Aden to Berbera. Aden then provided the base for the subsequent advance into Eritrea and Abyssinia, and Aden-based RAF squadrons attacked Italian forces in East Africa and the Red Sea. Aden-based air power was a key piece in the jigsaw of Indian Ocean convoy protection and offensive operations against enemy surface and subsurface vessels throughout the war. Another major role for Aden was its utility as a convoy assembly port for shipping in a region that contained some of the Empire's busiest shipping lanes, heavily used once the Mediterranean–Suez sea route was reopened in 1943. East of Aden lay the four sultanates of Wahidi, Qa'iti, Kathiri and Mahra, known as the Eastern Aden Protectorate. In January 1940 the Hadhrami Bedouin Legion was formed, and by 1944 there were over 300 regulars and a hundred reservists. The APL grew to a total strength of 1800 in 1945. In addition, an Aden Pioneer Corps of 2000 was raised and placed under Air Ministry control to support the APL.

In June 1940 the Governor of Aden suggested buying the whole of neigh-bouring Yemen's crop of millet, from which Italian East Africa had previously drawn supplies. Of this, part could be consumed in Aden and British Somaliland,

and the rest be at the disposal of the British government. This was approved by London. The war years brought a fourfold increase in the government of Aden's expenditure, and its revenue benefited not only from the imposition of additional tax but also from the activities of the port and the circulation of money by the imperial armed forces frequently passing through or garrisoning the territory. In spring 1944, after three years without rain, people in the inland Hadramaut region faced famine conditions (people in this region were losing £600,000 per year through losses on property owned in Malaya and Java). The British government voted £300,000 for relief, and food, milk and medical supplies were sent to the port of Mukalla for distribution. There was no method, however, of taking the food inland to the 15,000 affected people. RAF Headquarters Middle East therefore formed a Famine Relief Flight and on 29 April 1944 six Wellingtons based at Riyan began to fly between there and a landing strip at Qatn. During May a total of eight and a quarter tons of milk and nearly 413 tons of grain was delivered. Efforts established a four-month ration of grain, and prevented famine.

A small defence force was raised in the Seychelles (population 37,000) after the outbreak of war and placed under War Office control, and two companies (totalling nearly 1000 men) – one of Pioneers and the other an Artisan Works Company – were sent to the Middle East, where they and Indian Ocean Pioneers from Mauritius and Rodrigues joined tens of thousands of others recruited from Cyprus, Palestine and the Empire's African colonies in forming a rear echelon military labour force to support the fighting formations of the Eighth Army. All together over 1500 Seychellois served in the forces. In December 1942 HQ Troops Seychelles was responsible for the 27th Coast Battery Hong Kong and Singapore Royal Artillery, the 3rd Indian Garrison Company and the Diego Garcia Garrison Company. It also commanded the Seychelles Defence Force which consisted of a transport unit, Royal Engineers unit, a rifle and machine gun unit and a coast-watching unit. The scattered Seychelles were difficult to supply, given their remoteness, and in anticipation of war the colonial government advanced money at low interest to traders in order that they might build food reserves. In a bid to develop local production and relieve the unemployment arising from the depression of the market for copra and guano caused by the absence of shipping, the government arranged to employ 500 workers on Crown Land to produce food.

The giant French island of Madagascar was a source of anxiety for the British War Cabinet because of the fear of enemy occupation, or enemy use of the island as a base at the invitation of the Vichy government (as had happened disastrously in South-East Asia when Indo-Chinese bases were granted the Japanese by the Vichy government and then used to attack Malaya).[18] In Diego Suarez, at the island's northern tip, Madagascar boasted a fine natural harbour ideally suited as a major naval base, capable of taking the entire Japanese fleet. Japanese submarine offensives in the Mozambique Channel, the stretch of water separating

Madagascar from the African mainland and used as a major shipping route, were common from the summer of 1942. On 14 March 1942 Grand-Admiral Raeder told Hitler that the Japanese were eyeing Madagascar for bases after occupying Ceylon. In the following month Vice-Admiral Nomuwa, the Japanese Naval Attaché in Berlin, and Admiral Fricke, the Chief of Staff at the German naval high command, discussed the commitment of Japanese forces to the western Indian Ocean.

At the same time, the Chiefs of Staff in London were discussing Madagascar with the Prime Minister, and in this instance the British were to show themselves ahead of the Axis game. On 24 April 1942 plans for a British assault on the island were considered. Churchill was all for it, though the Chief of the Imperial General Staff, Sir Alan Brooke, was of the opinion that the Japanese would not make a move to occupy the island. In fact, Brooke feared that an attack on the island might persuade the Vichy government to give German forces the run of important bases like Dakar and Bizerta, and the use of French warships. It might also lead to the retaliatory bombing of Gibraltar. Whilst these discussions were in motion, SOE was busy in Madagascar, running agents from its regional headquarters in neighbouring Mauritius. A Franco-Mauritian agent, Percy Meyer, and his wife regularly relayed intelligence by wireless, and in February 1942 even made an attempt to bribe the French naval commander to give up his post.

Following their conquest of South-East Asia, the Philippines and the Dutch East Indies a dramatic move westwards across the Indian Ocean from the buoyant Japanese would not have been a surprise. Intelligence reports suggested that Japanese warships were already visiting Diego Suarez (they were discovered to be Vichy ships after the British government had requested reconnaissance missions from the South African Air Force). Even though there reports proved to be unfounded, it was known for sure that Japanese submarines were operating in South African coastal waters and the Mozambique Channel. The South African Prime Minister, Jan Smuts, was particularly concerned by the possibility of a Japanese strike, which would threaten African territories, disrupt sea routes around Africa to the Middle East and Far East, and present the prospect of the Japanese linking hands with Axis forces in North Africa. The prospect of Japanese forces in Madagascar brought home to South Africans the reality of the threat of invasion. Startled to find themselves threatened from this quarter, South Africans realized that their country was in fact an Indian Ocean power. Smuts, a friend and counsellor for whom Churchill had all the time in the world, urged a pre-emptive strike. For obvious reasons he appreciated the island's strategic value, but, looking further into the possible future, he recognized that nearby Durban might have to become a principal fleet base for the Royal Navy should Japan came to dominate the Bay of Bengal or successfully attack Ceylon. It is instructive to note that in 1942 the main German interest in the Japanese war effort was the prospect of major operations in the Indian Ocean region, and Berlin strongly encouraged Tokyo to seize Madagascar.

The fall of Singapore made a pre-emptive strike against Madagascar worth-while, and the passage of a British troop convoy destined for Ceylon provided the opportunity, reminiscent of an earlier reallocation of imperial fighting resources when a troop convoy destined for the Second Opium War in China was stopped at Cape Town and redirected to India to take part in the suppression of the Mutiny of 1857. As in so many other parts of the world, in mounting the invasion of Madagascar the British benefited from having established bases in the region, where the locals were friendly and the infrastructure well-established. Land forces were sent out from Britain to join with South African forces, to be under the overall command of Major-General R. G. Sturges of the Royal Marines. The major naval component was to be provided by the Gibraltar-based Force H and came under Rear-Admiral E. N. Syfret. The land and sea commanders had their first chance to discuss the operation in Freetown as the troopships and warships steamed south. Syfret's fleet, supplemented by units of the Eastern Fleet, comprised the battleship HMS *Ramillies*, the aircraft carriers HMS *Illustrious* and *Indomitable*, the cruisers HMS *Devonshire* and *Hermione*, eleven destroyers, six corvettes, six minesweepers, five assault ships (including a relatively new innova-tion, a Landing Ship Tanks), three troopships, six stores and mother transport ships, one hospital ship and an oiler. They were opposed by about 8000 Vichy troops, five submarines and about thirty aircraft (two French submarines were sunk by joint sea and air attacks on 7–8 May).

The commanders conferred with General Smuts when their ships docked at Cape Town. The imperial invasion force then assembled at Durban, the expedi-tion's advanced base, late in April 1942. On the ground British troops joined with South Africans, and later East African and Northern Rhodesian battalions played a major role. As soon as Diego Suarez had been secured, the British troops origi-nally bound for Ceylon were required to continue their journey east. The initial target was the north of the island and the major naval facilities at Diego Suarez itself, and the attack here went in successfully. The Vichy administration of Mada-gascar, however, refused to capitulate. There was stiff resistance in the north, and imperial forces had to push southwards and mount further amphibious landings to force surrender and capture the other main ports including Majunga and Tamatave, in order fully to prevent all enemy use of the island (for the Tamatave landing on 18 September 1942 the transports and landing craft were escorted by three cruisers, a battleship, a carrier and numerous destroyers and minesweepers). The French governor and his garrison finally surrendered in November 1943. British and imperial losses on the ground had been low, though on 30 May 1942, exploiting a weak point in the British line of communications, remote both from air patrol and anti-submarine vessels, a Japanese midget submarine attack was launched against British shipping in the Grand Harbour at Diego Suarez. For the loss of two midget submarines, the Japanese badly damaged HMS *Ramillies* and sank the oiler *British Loyalty* (the Royal Navy's sole outright loss during the campaign was the corvette HMS *Auricula*, sunk by mines). The South African

Air Force supplied reconnaissance aircraft and thirty-five bombers to supplement the machines of the Fleet Air Arm during the campaign. Once the campaign in the north was over, more front-line troops were moved out, and less experienced infantry units called in to form the garrison at Fortress Diego (including the 1st Battalion The Mauritius Regiment, which mutinied in Madagascar in late 1943 and was subsequently disbanded).

Thus Madagascar became another part of Britain's war empire. Most of the island, after a period under British military administration, was handed over to a Free French administration, though Britain retained control of 'Fortress Diego' in the north. The British took other French territory in the region too. In June 1942 it was decided to occupy Mayotte, Pamanzi and Dzaoudzi in the French Comoros Islands in the Mozambique Channel. The airfields at Mayotte were considered a threat to Allied shipping in the channel, and made a useful addition to the British network of flying boat bases in the region.

RAF units were distributed throughout the Indian Ocean region and played an important part, alongside the ships of the Eastern Fleet, in protecting convoys, hunting for enemy vessels, extending the reconnaissance range of the naval forces in the region, defending territories like Ceylon from enemy attack and taking the offensive against the enemy in Japanese-occupied territory. As has been seen, the face of the mounting Japanese threat in 1941 Ceylon's air defences had been steadily augmented. The Fleet Air Arm had a few squadrons of Fulmars on the island, and Hurricanes, Blenheims and Swordfish were flown in from the Middle East and India or flown off of the Eastern Fleet's carriers. Some RAF aircraft escaped to Ceylon after the defeats in Malaya and Sumatra. The RAF, again like the navy, also had a role in intelligence-gathering (through photo reconnaissance) and in inserting agents behind enemy lines. There were major RAF bases and group headquarters in India, Aden, East Africa and Ceylon. Aircraft from these areas, along with those of the Fleet Air Arm, relied on an extensive network of airstrips and flying boat anchorages in the British colonies scattered throughout the Indian Ocean region. There were RAF airfields, Royal Naval Air Stations and flying boat anchorages in the the Andaman Islands, the Cocos Islands, the Comoros Islands, Diego Garcia, Kenya, Madagascar, the Maldives, Mauritius, the Seychelles, Socotra and Somaliland. Mauritius, for example, had an air base (today's international airport) built during the war, was used by RAF Catalina flying boats on anti-raider operations and also by Spitfires specializing in the gathering of meteorological intelligence. There were also bases in South Africa, and from early in 1942 Catalina flying boats arrived in order to extend protection of shipping in South African waters.

An important role for aircraft in the Indian Ocean was survivor rescue, and the knowledge that the RAF routinely searched for survivors was an inestimable comfort to the men of the merchant marine. These men had not only to deal with the prospect of death through drowning or starvation at sea, but the knowledge that both Japanese and German forces were known to have perpetrated atrocities in the Indian Ocean, even beyond the common machine-gunning of survivors in the water. Hundreds of survivors were rescued by the efforts of RAF aircraft and Royal Navy warships. In February 1944, for example, Nos 205 and 413 Squadrons from Koggala in Ceylon flew 800 miles to search for survivors of the SS *Fort Buckingham*, sunk near the Laccadive Islands by U-188. On 29 June 1944 a Japanese submarine sunk the Pacific and Oriental liner *Nellore*, and three days later the American ship SS *Jean Nicolet*. In an operation lasting fourteen days, thirty-four sorties were flown by Catalinas based on Diego Garcia and Liberators and Sunderlands from Addu Atoll in the Maldives. As a result, 234 of *Nellore*'s complement of 341 were rescued, and those from the American ship who had not been bayoneted or shot by the Japanese. The Liberty ship *Jean Nicolet* had sailed from San Pedro, California, stopping at Fremantle in May before sailing for Colombo and Calcutta. Her cargo included heavy machinery, trucks, steel plates, landing barges and steel mooring pontoons (the latter two items clearly destined for Mountbatten's planned amphibious assault on Malaya). About 900 miles south of Ceylon she was hit by two torpedoes from the Japanese submarine I-8. After the crew had abandoned ship successfully, the submarine surfaced and the men were ordered to leave the life-rafts and swim towards it. As they climbed aboard, men were knocked unconscious and pushed over the side, or had their hands tied before being bayoneted and pushed over, after their valuables had been removed. Others were tied in a crouching position with rope or wire and beaten. Others were forces to run the gauntlet on the after deck through two lines of Japanese sailors wielding bayonets. When an aircraft was reported and the diving bell rung, about thirty men were left tied on the deck. The aircraft was a British Liberator answering the *Jean Nicolet*'s distress signal. On 4 July HMS *Hoxa* arrived to rescue the survivors, twenty-three out of a crew of one hundred, who were taken to Addu Atoll.

Ceylon-based aircraft supported Force 136 operations in occupied Malaya. Three thousand five hundred men had been trained to harass the Japanese during the planned British invasion of Malaya, and these men were airlifted into their zones of operations. Specifically for this type of operation, No. 160 Squadron was converted from minelaying to become a Special Duties Squadron. Many bombing sorties were flown over Malaya from bases in Ceylon, supplemented by RAF Liberators from the Cocos Islands. When the Japanese surrendered, aircraft from Burma, Ceylon, the Cocos Islands and India commenced Operation Mastiff, dropping food, medicine and radios to all prisoner-of-war camps in Japanese-held South-East Asia and the Dutch East Indies. Later still, many of the inmates of the prisons were air evacuated to Ceylon and to freedom.

Fortunately for the British, after the raid on Ceylon in April 1942 Japanese aircraft never again entered the Indian Ocean in strength. In July 1943 the Air Officer Commanding 222 Group Ceylon, Air Vice-Marshal Lees, was given operational control of all general reconnaissance aircraft in the Indian Ocean theatre (excluding Bengal) from East Africa and Aden as far as the Japanese perimeter in the east. Improvements were made in controlling aircraft operating from the many bases in the region, especially needed as the submarine offensive in the Indian Ocean gathered pace. Though cooperating with the Eastern Fleet, distances and inadequate communications meant that regional air officers-in-charge had to retain operational control. A significant improvement in terms of central control and coordination came in May 1944 when new staff joined No. 222 Group Headquarters Ceylon to supervise the operations of all reconnaissance formations in the Indian Ocean. This led to the creation of Indian Ocean General Reconnaissance Operations, a unified control centre for all RAF reconnaissance units in the Indian Ocean region that applied knowledge and skills gained in the Battle of the Atlantic.

Flying boats and land-based reconnaissance aircraft in the Indian Ocean were, like the navy, dedicated to protecting the shipping lanes, the main ones being those in the Persian Gulf, the Gulf of Aden and the approaches to Bombay and Ceylon. No. 191 Squadron provides an example. Disbanded in 1919, the squadron was reformed in May 1943 at Korangi Creek, near Karachi, as a general reconnaissance squadron equipped with Catalina flying boats. Until the end of the year, the squadron patrolled the Arabian Sea and Persian Gulf, sending detachments to bases in Bahrain and elsewhere to extend its cover. In 1944 the squadron's activities were concentrated off the east coast of India and its machines were based in Addu Atoll, southern India and Ceylon. The squadron was disbanded in June 1945 due to a lack of enemy naval activity in the region.

Between January and July 1944 general reconnaissance squadrons flew 3696 sorties over the Indian Ocean, as the build up of forces in India gathered pace. At the end of a long supply route, safe shipping lanes were essential to SEAC. The submarine threat that had for long been the Ceylon-based 222 Group's reason for being had passed by the end of 1944, though its Catalinas and Liberators kept patrolling Indian Ocean shipping routes until May 1945. The air group also had increasing opportunities for attacking Japanese targets. For example, the Japanese were increasingly dependent on coaster-size ships for supplying their forces in Burma, given the disruption to communications inland wrought by the Fourteenth Army and the RAF and American air forces supporting it. So from February 1945 222 Group mounted attacks off the Arakan coast using Liberators of No. 203 Squadron, operating from Kankesanterai in the north of Ceylon. On 26 March 1945 six Liberators joined forces with the Royal Navy to destroy an enemy convoy trying to reach the Andaman Islands. Liberators of No. 160 Squadron, flying from Minneriya, were used to drop mines in the approaches to key Japanese ports. On 26 March 1945 eight Liberators of No. 160 Squadron made the 3460 mile round trip from Ceylon to Singapore, the first RAF aircraft to fly over the island stronghold since its capitulation in February 1942. A great deal of effort was directed at intercepting the wooden coastal vessels – ferries, coasters, junks and sampans – that the Japanese had taken to using for supply and communication purposes as their ocean-going vessels were destroyed and not replaced. The liabilities of far-flung conquest could not be met by a decimated Japanese merchant marine after the Imperial Japanese Navy's loss of control of the seas. Some of these vessels crept along the Chinese coast and entered the Indian Ocean through the Malacca Strait, where British submarines were often waiting for them. Such vessels were prey to British flying boats and Liberators further north in the Bay of Bengal, as well as the fighter aircraft which scoured the coasts and the creeks. Light coastal forces of the Royal Navy and Royal Indian Navy also lay in wait for these vessels. Sawmills on the Andaman Islands, ordered to produce more wooden coastal vessels, were targeted by British carriers. As the noose tightened about the neck of Japanese supply and communications, whole armies and garrisons were left marooned in the furthermost reaches of Japan's high tide of imperial conquest.

Based throughout the Indian Ocean, Catalina and Sunderland flying boats played a vital role patrolling the region and greatly extending the search capacity of the Eastern Fleet, as did land-based bombers in Aden, India and Ceylon. Among the land-based bomber aircraft in the Indian Ocean were three Liberator, three Wellington, one Bisley and two Beaufort squadrons, based mainly in Ceylon, India and Aden. On the flying boat strength were a Sunderland and nine Catalina squadrons, based mainly in Ceylon, India and East Africa. American aircraft made an appearance in Ceylon in August 1944, when forty-five B-29 Superfortresses of the 30th U.S. Army Air Corps, operating from China Bay, bombed oil installations at Palembang in Sumatra.

The Indian Ocean was the scene of important intelligence-gathering facilities connected to the global hub at Bletchley Park in Buckinghamshire. It was also a theatre of war in which ULTRA intelligence was used to locate and destroy enemy forces, being particularly useful in the search, across vast distances, for German U-boats and their supply vessels. Initially, the main intelligence-gathering facilities were based in Hong Kong and Singapore, and complemented other facilities in the eastern Empire such as Wireless Experimental Centre (WEC) and its outstations in India, and Far East Combined Bureau based in Cairo.[19]

The main Royal Navy code-breaking establishment in the Far East was forced by Japanese warmongering to move first from Hong Kong to Singapore, then to Colombo and then swiftly on to Mombasa. Far East Combined Bureau (FECB) then had been established as an inter-service intelligence facility at Hong Kong in the mid-1930s. Its radio intelligence facilities included radio fingerprinting, direction-finding stations, a 'Y' service station and a naval and military cryptanalysis section. In August 1939 it moved to Singapore and the army and RAF sections returned to their respective services. Some army and RAF codebreakers were sent to WEC in Delhi, India's Bletchley Park outstation, and the navy codebreakers were sent to Ceylon, to be established in Pembroke College, an Indian boys' school near Colombo. The codebreakers arrived here on 14 January 1942.

British codebreakers made a significant contribution to breaking Japanese codes, alongside their American allies. It helped, for example, to break the Japanese JN 25 cipher, and this led to effective interceptions of Japanese forces, some of them in the Indian Ocean. The heavy cruiser *Haguro* was a victim of British intelligence-gathering:

> The sinking of the *Haguro*, and the contributions played by [HMS] *Anderson* [the code-breaking unit] in providing intelligence on the Japanese navy's movements and intentions during the attacks on the Philippines, Okinawa, and Rangoon, led to a congratulatory telegram from Bletchley Park and a morale-boosting visit to the station from Mountbatten himself, during which the Supreme Allied Commander South East Asia told the Royal Navy codebreakers they were worth 'ten divisions'.

Indian Ocean colonies like Ceylon, Kenya and Mauritius provided bases for intelligence-gathering facilities responsible for intercepting and breaking Japanese military, naval, and diplomatic codes. Neighbouring India was part of an imperial signals intelligence network which stretched from Britain to the Far East. Over a thousand people worked at WEC in Delhi, and by mid-1944 WEC was intercepting clearly some 2000 Japanese signals a day. Ceylon was also an important link in this Bletchley Park chain, as home of the FECB.

When Ceylon was raided in April 1942, the unit moved with Admiral Somerville's Eastern Fleet headquarters to Kenya, to take over an Indian boys' school a mile outside of Mombasa, which became the shore base HMS *Alidina*. The civilian wireless operators had been left behind in Colombo with two codebreakers to attempt to keep continuity on the JN 25 operation, and they were able to make a major contribution by decrypting Japanese JN 25 messages revealing Japanese movements in the Pacific before the Battle of the Coral Sea. Along with Allied codebreaking bases in Melbourne and Hawaii, Colombo also correctly identified Midway as a major Japanese target from as early as 7 March 1942, over two months before this defining naval engagement. The main body of Ceylon's code-breaking outfit returned to Colombo in September 1943 with the Eastern Fleet, to be established as the shore base HMS *Anderson*.

> The intercept station and codebreaking operation had to be set up on the only available site at the Anderson Golf Course, just six miles from the Colombo [naval] HQ ... This was hardly an ideal site for intercepting radio traffic, stuck between the railway line and a main road, directly under the flight path of aircraft flying into the Racecourse Aerodrome and far too close to a 33,000-volt high-tension electricity supply.

Here the unit carried on the work of intercepting and breaking Japanese signals. The main receiving room held about one hundred receiver bays, and radio communications between all the main Japanese bases in South-East Asia were monitored at *Anderson*. Many young female service personnel arrived in Ceylon as members of the Women's Royal Naval Service (WRNS), to perform the manifold tasks associated with intercepting and breaking codes. Most were accommodated in Wrenneries like the one in Galle Road, Colpetty, Colombo. From late 1943 the Colombo codebreakers experienced major improvements in results because of improved reception, a dramatic increase in staff and equipment, and the promise of direct access to American intercepted code recoveries. This was as part of the BRUSA (British-USA) Agreement reached between Bletchley Park and the American army in 1943, and by June 1944 Colombo was linked to Hawaii and Melbourne code-breakers. Intelligence breaks were not all in the one direction, though over the course of the war Allied intelligence interception and cooperation was light years ahead of that of the Axis powers. In May 1942 the Australian steamer *Nankin* was captured by the German auxiliary cruiser *Thor* off Western Australia. It was carrying mail for Ceylon, including top secret summaries of the combined operations intelligence centre in Wellington. It referred to ULTRA intelligence, though, very luckily, the material was not passed to the Japanese (who would have seen that their naval cipher had been broken). This intelligence lapse could have had catastrophic consequences, and was kept secret by British governments for decades after the war. Ceylon's intelligence-gathering reach was extended by ships at sea. For example, enemy signals in and around Sumatra and Java were monitored by vessels taking part in offensive operations east and south east of Ceylon, an enormous tract of water which was particularly hard to cover through normal intercept arrangements.

Germany and Japan failed to wrest control of the Indian Ocean from the imperial power that had for a century and a half policed, controlled and supervised this most central of global highways. Even the Ceylon raid of 1942 was a strategic failure for the Japanese, for the Imperial Japanese Navy failed to detect the Eastern Fleet, let alone destroy it, and failed to prevent massive convoys crossing the ocean to keep alive the battlefronts of the Middle East and South Asia. It is easy to understand why Indian Ocean operations were the main German interest in the Japanese war effort in 1942, and why German pressure on Japan to act decisively in the region increased after defeat at El Alamein in October 1942. But by then the Japanese high-water mark had been reached, and the Indian Ocean had become 'a sea too far'. As for their efforts to challenge British mastery of the Indian Ocean, both Germany and Japan recognized its great significance – particularly the high commands of their respective navies – but were never able to overcome jealousies and translate their awareness into effective cooperative action. The Indian Ocean was one of the great might-have-beens for the Axis, and their failure to work together here was just another sign of how inferior their alliance was to that forged by Britain, the Commonwealth, America and Russia.

British capacity in the region, and its fringes, must surely also have had something to do with the imperial strategic vision that centuries of empire-building had bequeathed the British people. Even when faced with the prospect of Japanese ascendancy in the Indian Ocean and possible defeat in the Middle East, the British succeeded in acting and thinking imperially, sending scarce resources, often in minute quantities, to protect tiny islands or to at least give the show of doing so: flying in penny-packets of Hurricanes and obsolete biplanes to defend Ceylon against the might of Nagumo's carriers; sending destroyers to the most remote islands of the Southern Ocean to hunt for German submarines or supply ships; constructing dummy wooden guns, fighters and radar installations on Ceylon to fool Japanese aerial reconnaissance; installing a brace of ex-naval 6-inch guns at Port Victoria in the Seychelles, manned by Ceylon Garrison Artillery troops; deploying an East African infantry battalion to beef up the defences of Mauritius in case of Japanese invasion; moving 4000 marine defence experts from the Mediterranean to Addu Atoll to construct a new fleet base; and sending Mauritian part-time soldiers to garrison Rodrigues and its cable and wireless station. Luck and skill, and hard-won victories here and in other regions, meant that at the end of the war the Indian Ocean was still a 'British Lake', and sea lines of communication still kept the Empire in touch.

12

India and Burma

Though it is often a poor relation in accounts of Britain and the Second World War – a distant fourth behind the North African, West European and Italian campaigns – Burma was the scene of the most comprehensive defeat suffered by the Japanese army, achieved by the million-plus men of the Burmese, Indian, African and British Fourteenth Army led by General Sir William Slim, which formed from 1943 the main land force of Admiral Lord Louis Mountbatten's South East Asia Command. The Burma campaign was also the British Empire's front line in the war against Japan, following the early Japanese conquest of the Malay peninsula and the Empire's inability to contribute large-scale land, sea and air forces in the decisive years of the Pacific war. Victory in Burma was founded upon the rock of the British Raj, particularly the supply infrastructure developed in its eastern border regions, and also proved to be the swansong of that quintessential imperial creation, the Indian Army.[1] Fighting on the other side, and symbolizing the severe imperial headaches faced by Britain in this region, an Indian National Army of up to 60,000 men and women fought alongside the Japanese in the name of Indian freedom. Many of these men were recruited from the tens of thousands of Indian soldiers taken into captivity by the Japanese at the fall of Singapore.

The Burma campaign was noteworthy for the controversial achievements of behind-enemy-lines forces like the Chindits, led by Orde Wingate, and of Naga tribesmen loyal to the British. What the Americans called the China–Burma–India theatre was also noted for the air delivery by American forces of 650,000 tons of supplies to their Chinese allies, as well as unprecedented British and American efforts to keep large-scale ground forces supplied entirely by air. Given the scale of the fighting in the region – retreat, occupation, reconquest – the people of Burma were ravaged by the fighting that took place around them, whilst India became, like Australia, Egypt and Britain itself, one of the Allies most important military bases for the prosecution of the war.

Popular memory of the Burma campaign has been so peripheral that the victorious British–Indian army has for long been known as the 'Forgotten Army'. It might be pointed out, however, that the soldiers on the ground at the time did not feel woefully forgotten, a point well made by George MacDonald Fraser in his elegiac memoir of a private soldier's experience in Burma, *Quartered Safe Out Here*. According to him, the British soldiers of the Fourteenth Army understood full well that the media gaze was fixed on theatres nearer to home, but that the people who mattered – their loved ones back in Carlisle or Glasgow – never forgot them. The fighting in this theatre brought together a truly imperial army, as was also the case in the Western Desert. In the India–Burma theatre Canadian pilots, Gurkha *naiks*, British infantrymen, Karen irregulars, Sikh tank drivers and American Dakota ground crew rubbed shoulders with the men of units such as the 2nd Company King George V's Own Bengal Sappers and Miners, the 3rd (Naga Hills) Battalion The Assam Rifles, the Mandalay Battalion The Burma Frontier Force, the 72nd (Somali Scouts) Battalion The King's African Rifles and the Gold Coast Regiment of the Royal West African Frontier Force. Macdonald Fraser writes that:

> Fourteenth Army's various divisions had rather exotic badges which were worn with considerable pride out of the line, but not in action. The oldest was the Black Cat of the 17th Indian Division ... but equally well-known was the Cross Keys emblem of the 2nd British Division ... There were two Dagger divisions, the 19th Indian (downthrust) and the 20th Indian (upthrust); the Spider was worn by 81st West African Division, and crossed assegais by the 82nd West African. Probably not even the legions of Rome embraced as many nationalities as Fourteenth Army.[2]

Whilst facing east and standing firm against the high tide of Japan's westward expansion, amassing the forces that would be led to victory by General Slim, India also looked after its traditional imperial security duties, guarding the North-West Frontier against German encroachment, making Iraq a backyard of the Indian Army, contributing key divisions to the fighting in the Western Desert, and becoming a vital component in the imperial production line supplying food and equipment to civilians and soldiers throughout the Empire. This last role – that of gigantic military base – was vital to British fortunes. In undertaking it, the presence of General Sir Archibald Wavell (Field Marshal from January 1943) as Commander-in-Chief was fortunate, for he had already gained valuable experience whilst turning Egypt into an imperial base camp whilst Commander-in-Chief Middle East between 1939 and 1941. As Commander-in-Chief India, Wavell had to cater for the needs of internal security as well as the army overseas, and the massive demand for military labour within India itself. As in Egypt in the first two years of conflict, his task was to create a nationwide network of airfields, roads, railways, stockpiles and all the installations from which an effective offensive could be launched. To accomplish this, eight million Indians were employed on defence tasks and at least six million were drawn into war industries and the expanding railways.

India was the jewel in the imperial crown and one of the Empire's main engines of war. Burma was an inconsequential imperial sideshow that was to become the setting of the British Empire's biggest battle with the Japanese, resulting in over 150,000 Japanese dead. The Empire's land forces were supported by nearly 150,000 airmen from Britain and India, the Royal Navy's Eastern Fleet based on Ceylon, Chinese divisions under Chiang Kai-shek and tens of thousands of American airmen. India, with a population of over 350 million, was the second pillar of the British Empire after Britain itself. Reflecting this, there were plans to make India the seat of imperial government should Britain be overrun by Germany, though even there they might not have been safe, for German war plans were advanced enough to envisage a descent upon India following victory in Russia.

Thus one of India's traditional defence preoccupations, the security of its northern borderlands, also came in to play during the Second World War, as the Raj also faced a novel and unexpected threat from the east. Following Japan's successful conquest of Malaya and Burma, India had to be defended against a new enemy, who planned to enter India with the aid of a popular revolt and end British rule on the subcontinent. With Japan in occupation of its eastern borderland, India had to be developed as the major offensive base for the imperial war effort against Japan. American efforts to supply the forces of Chiang Kai-shek in southern China meant that American manpower and money entered yet another formerly exclusive imperial reserve as a result of the strange permutations of global conflict. As well as being the jump-off point for the reconquest of Burma, India, along with Ceylon, was to be the base for the repossession of Britain's South-East Asian colonies, and those of its European allies, France and Holland.

Long before the Japananese threat materialized, and long afterwards as well, India was a major supplier of troops and military resources for the fighting in East Africa, the Western Desert and even Italy. India was also charged with building and supplying a major new army command formed to prevent Iran and Iraq from falling without a fight to a German thrust through the Caucasus. India was a major contributor to the massive garrison of Malaya and Singapore that marched into Japanese captivity in February 1942 and provided the infantry shield in Borneo. Finally, it should not be forgotten that India itself was invaded, and that the pivotal battles of the Burma campaign were fought amidst the ruins of two rather inconsequential Indian settlements in Assam Province, the names of which will forever burn bright in the annals of British military history, Kohima and Imphal.

For well over a century India had been a sub-imperial powerhouse pursuing Anglo-Indian interests and projecting military power around the world, in Central Asia, South-East Asia, the Indian Ocean, the Persian Gulf, Eastern Africa, the Red Sea and the Middle East. The Second World War was to see this tradition continued. India was the Empire's greatest reservoir of military manpower, and during the war provided millions of imperial soldiers and adapted its agricultural and industrial sectors to war conditions, whilst at the same time experiencing unprecedented levels of political and social turmoil, and the horrors of famine. Like Egypt, it provided the British with a reservoir of supplies and labour in the rear of a major fighting front, a resource not enjoyed by the Axis or Japanese forces, which instead fought at the end of long and vulnerable supply lines with (particularly in the German case) no real grip on major sea lines of communication. India's status as a major imperial producer was symbolized by its leading role in the formation of the Eastern Group Supply Council in 1940, a collection of eastern colonies and Dominions aiming to supply the Middle East war theatre to the greatest extent possible in order to relieve Britain's economic burden. As so many other territories were to prove, established Empire gave the British something of an advantage when it came to mobilizing resources. The infrastructure, be it transportation, administrative, political or conceptual, was in place, though the Second World War was to require unprecedented speed in its further development. In achieving this momentum, particularly in bringing India fully to bear on the imperial war effort, the British applied extreme short-term pressure to the Raj and fundamentally altered the peace-time norms on which their rule had been founded. In driving Indian society hard for the war effort, and in visiting the multiple traumas of modern warfare and occupation upon Burma by failing to defend it successfully, the prospect of a return to humdrum peace-time imperial rule in the post-war years was greatly diminished.

India's role as the major base of the British war against Japan had not been foreseen.[3] All pre-war plans for a general war – indeed, all the history and the traditions of imperial defence – had envisaged India's main military role as being the security of the North-West Frontier Province first and foremost, with a subsidiary contribution to the Middle East theatre (both the Western Desert and Iraq were earmarked as spheres of major Indian westward deployment in the event of a general war). The first two years of the conflict, when only Italy and Germany were the King's enemies, were devoted to performing these tasks. When the Empire's fortunes plumbed new depths with the growing hostility of Japan, however, India was also called upon to provide over 60,000 troops for the defence of Malaya, as well as small forces for the defence of Hong Kong and British Borneo. The fall of Borneo, Burma, Malaya, Sarawak and Singapore in the grim winter of 1941–42 were unexpected disasters that made more urgent the need for India to switch its defensive attentions and resources from the west to the east in defiance of generations of Indian military tradition.

Following the early and sweeping success of Japanese arms against the Allies, the Chiefs of Staff in London acknowledged that India Command had to be greatly strengthened for the defence of India and Ceylon and the eventual reconquest of Burma and Malaya. It was a matter of faith in London that it would be an imperial disaster if the soldiers of another power, at best America and at the worst China, were to be responsible for liberating the colonies that Britain had so ignominiously lost in 1941–42. By May 1942 most of Burma was in Japanese hands after the gruelling retreat of Burmacorps, which fell back time and again until it eventually entered India, defeated – in the eyes of many ignorant starched uniforms in Delhi disgraced – but not destroyed, and still a coherent force. From its rump would emerge the army that would eventually crush the Japanese in India and Burma. In the dark days of early 1942, however, with Japan carrying all before it in every theatre, it was the air force in particular that needed strengthening, given the fact that air power, the importance of which was barely glimpsed before the war, was to be the key to victory in this theatre as in all others. But of course the build up had to be gradual because of Britain's vital commitments elsewhere. The massive air force that was eventually assembled in India was dependent on seapower for its existence and its supplies (though some aircraft came overland from the Middle East via Aden and Karachi). The ability of the Eastern Fleet and maritime aircraft of the RAF to keep the convoys crossing the Indian Ocean was crucial in this undertaking, and the Imperial Japanese Navy would have reaped rich rewards if it had followed up its raids on Ceylon in April 1942 and had ensured the absolute destruction of British naval forces east of Suez. For by 1944, when it was too late for the Japanese to do anything about it, the commanders of the three services in India, Ceylon and Burma disposed of over a million soldiers, the carriers and battleships of the Eastern Fleet, and an air force of nearly 4000 aircraft, and had won back control of the Bay of Bengal. What is more, with breathtaking organizational skill, the Government of India and the armed forces had overseen an extraordinary development of India's transport and supply infrastructure, on the back of millions of Indian labourers, developments which were essential in order to launch this force effectively against the Japanese army in Burma and reconquer Allied possessions in South-East Asia and the Dutch East Indies.

In India one encounters the paradox of Britain's imperial war. Although India was a superb base from which to prosecute the war in Burma, if it had not have been for distant imperial gains that had never had much to do with the will of British governments or their electors, Britain would not have been required to maintain a vast force fighting in this distant region at all, or to place the strain of total war upon the people of the subcontinent. Burma had been gained by the rulers of the Raj, and until as late as 1937 was a mere province of India. Similarly, in the inter-war years of disarmament and collective security, a realistic and up to date view of the defence requirements of Burma had been entirely lacking. Burma and eastern India, it was thought, would never be threatened. Singapore wrapped up imperial security in the East, and strategic thinking relating to Burma stopped precisely there.

In 1939–45 the Indian Army was required to defend India itself, for the first time, from the invasion plans of a major industrial and military power. Only the attack was to come from the east, not from the north, as a century of watchful-ness and derring-do in the North-West Frontier Province and the Afghan no man's land beyond had led the Indian Army, institutionally, to expect. It was hard for the Indian Army and imperial defence policy-makers to recalibrate their plans. As late as 1942 an Indian Field Company (Madras Sappers and Miners) was stationed in the North-West Frontier Province carrying out experiments to find a satisfactory way of blowing up the road through the Khyber Pass should the Germans determine to come south through the Caucasus and Afghanistan into India. This might seem far-fetched with the wisdom of hindsight to hand, but in the first half of 1942 the Germans and the Japanese looked as if they could do almost anything they wanted, and Britain found itself struggling to keep its imperial head above water in the Indian Ocean, to defend the critically valuable Iranian and Iraqi oilfields and to prevent Rommel from entering Cairo. Indeed, the Germans did in fact plan to challenge British India from the north, had their armies continued to roll back the Russian frontier, so the Indian Army's northward gaze was as necessary in the 1940s as it had been in the 1840s. Then, of course, the enemy had been Russia, as the two great powers engaged in a lengthy cold war centred on Central Asia. Even in the 1930s the writer John Masters and his Gurkha regiment, along with about 50,000 other troops of the Indian Army, were still patrolling in Pathan country.[4]

India supplied so much material for the imperial war effort, and the Indian Army was used in so many overseas theatres of war, that by 1945 Britain owed India £1.3 billion. In 1939 Britain had agreed to pay for the Indian armed forces if they were not engaged in operations related specifically to India's own defence, so Britain lost the free use of its eastern military wing. The traditional view that India helped save Britain's bacon in the Second World War with its provision of fighting forces, however, is only one perspective on the situation. Turning on its head the usual Indian defence equation – that the Indian Army was a massive imperial benefit to Britain – it might be suggested that in fact Britain subsidized Indian defence in this period. In 1940–41 Britain paid £40 million towards Indian defence, and India paid £49 million. A year later, Britain was paying £150 million, and India £71 million. In 1942–43, Britain's bill had soared to £270 million. In 1942 with the Japanese pressing against the frontiers of Bengal and threatening Calcutta, this was defence at bargain prices.[5] Whatever the debate about the rights and wrongs of Britain's presence in India in the first place, the fact was that, as things stood in 1942, India was there for the taking in a global struggle that would have ended with a wholesale imperial repartition of the world if Britain and its allies had been defeated. The Japanese, it can be said with a degree of confidence, would not in the long run have been viewed as an improvement on the British when it came to imperial rule, whatever their promises of independence, Asian brotherhood and freedom. A victorious Japan, whilst initially preoccupied with the successful economic and political integration of its planned-for imperial conquests – the Philippines, the East Indies and Malaya – would have soon gotten round to putting the shackles more effectively on Burma and India – its windfall imperial gains borne of British collapse and the speedy success of Japanese arms in sweeping westwards.

The British, though shocked at suddenly finding India in the front line, were aware of the possibilities for further imperial loss and disaster and wasted no time in readying the defences. Preparing eastern India to operate as the launch-pad of a major military thrust against the Japanese required the employment of millions of Indians, especially given the fact that India Command had never contemplated an attack from the east. Roads, railways, airstrips and all manner of military and communication installations had to be developed in Bengal and Assam. In December 1941, for example, the Commander-in-Chief India, General Wavell, arranged for the Assam Public Works Department to widen the Imphal road and extend it to Tamu on the Burma frontier. This employed about 50,000 people until completion in April 1942. Major supply depots were built at Benares, and Dimapur became the main supply depot for the all-important Assam region, the main rail, road and river communications axis for all imperial forces in the region. Here the local tea planters' association helped with the recruitment of labour in a most important way, an example of pre-existing infrastructure being turned to effective military account given the grave and pressing war situation. In early 1942 the government asked the Association to provide labour for the development of infrastructure, in this case 25,000 men for the Manipur road and 75,000 for the road from Ledo into Burma (Imphal was the capital of the state of Manipur). It was the mammoth supply dump at Dimapur that the Japanese were determined to capture when they attacked from Burma into India in 1944, sparking the crucial battles of Kohima and Imphal which finally gave the Allies the ascendancy against the Japanese in the China–Burma–India theatre.

As in all other territories of the British Empire and Commonwealth, war-time conditions offered major new employment opportunities, and Indian women entered social and professional services that had been entirely closed to them before. A Women's Royal Naval Service was formed, as was a Women's Auxiliary Corps (India), started in April 1942 and with 10,000 members by 1944. One million Indians alone were engaged in the construction of airfields, emblematic of the significance that air power was to play in this theatre, be it in knocking Japanese reconnaissance aircraft out of the sky, attacking ground positions in support of Fourteenth Army with Spitfires from Calcutta, sending tons of supplies to the Chinese in Dakota transport aircraft from bases in northern Assam, or in supplying columns of Chindits operating far behind enemy lines with Liberators flying from bases in Bengal and Ceylon.

To cater for the massive growth in the strength of the Indian Army and the tens of thousands of British, American and African servicemen arriving from overseas, new military camps were needed all over the country. Two hundred airfields were cleared, extensive new railways, pipelines and roads were laid, air defences and radar installed, and 130 new hospitals built. Ports had to be expanded and Bombay, Calcutta, Cochin, Madras and Vizagapatam were all extensively developed. The Government of India ordered fifty-two Portal cranes, twenty-one rail mounted cranes, 103 mobile cranes, 497 harbour craft and 114 fork-lift trucks. As in Canada, Ceylon, Hong Kong and South Africa, Indian ports also offered facilities for shipbuilding and ship repairs as the Empire shared the burden that otherwise would have had to have been shouldered by distant British shipyards alone. The weight of this development was in the east, as Assam and Bengal became base areas for the major offensive against the Japanese Empire from

Burma to the Dutch East Indies. In January 1944, for example, the lines of communication in Assam were maintaining 450,000 men (including 100,000 Americans and Chinese) and 15,000 animals.

Handling the delivery of fuel was a Herculean task in itself. For example, between mid-1944 and mid-1945 oil consumption by the armed forces in India and Ceylon was almost twice its 1943 level. Calcutta was the main oil port for Bengal, as well as the locus of much of the Raj's military activity, and there were also major fuel facilities at Budge-Budge. Chittagong was developed as a tanker port for oil deliveries. Pipelines were laid to deliver oil to the other main locus of India's war against Japan in north-east Assam. In 1943 American forces began a project to build 850 barges, each with a capacity of 100–150 tons, to move aviation spirit up river, as India's inland waterways were developed in an effort to answer the questions constantly posed by supply. Ports on the rivers were connected by road to the airfields of Assam, the fortress province from which China was supplied and the Japanese army repelled.

The military build up in the east of India caused a demand for fuel requiring major infrastructure development in the west, as India's western ports became central to the import of goods either no longer available from eastern sources, or unable to use eastern ports because of their proximity to the enemy. With the Bay of Bengal dominated by the Japanese, more of the supply burden was placed on western Indian ports and cross-country rail and road networks. The handling capacity of western ports, and the railways leading from them across India to the east, therefore required huge investments of capital and labour. For example, the loss of Burma as a source of oil meant that more oil was coming from Iran and Iraq, and being offloaded in the west to be transported overland.

Quite apart from the labour demands imposed by this need to criss-cross India with new roads and railways connecting new military camps, supply depots and air bases, an exponential growth in the output of Indian industry was demanded by the war. India used its existing manufacturing capacity to produce war-related materials, and as in 1914–18 this, together with the loss of imports, led to a leap forward in industrialization. There was a subcontinent-wide expansion in local manufacturing and repair work of all kinds, for example in railway workshops and in the improvement of harbour facilities. Though the war called on Indian agriculture to produce as never before, it simultaneously encouraged greater urbanization. India's contribution to the imperial and Allied war effort in terms of materials should not be underestimated, though it is understandable that its massive provision of fighting men has become the most memorable aspect of India's war. By 1943, India was producing more goods for war supply than Australia, New Zealand and South Africa combined, putting it in the top three imperial production centres along with Canada and Britain. Between 1941 and 1946 India provided £286.4 million worth of materials for the British, and £130 million for the Americans, mainly in the form of textiles, clothing and ordnance. War encouraged industrial expansion, in the arms industry, textiles and leather.

The steel, chemicals, paper and paint industries boomed. Limits to the extent of Indian industrial expansion were set, however, by certain factors. The general shortage of capital goods experienced throughout the Empire and the shortage of skilled workers was one such brake, the official policy of restricting the manufacture of non-essential consumer goods in the interests of the war effort another.

As a major supplier of war materials, India was at the centre of a supply initiative in the early years of the war that demonstrated the potential of the Empire and Commonwealth to shoulder the burden of world war, relieving Britain of the pressure entailed by its position as the Empire's major source of industrial and manufactured goods. This was the creation of Eastern Group Supply Council (EGSC) in Delhi in 1940, a fine example of imperial outsourcing. It was also an excellent example of the use of imperial infrastructure – from factories to transport networks to political connections to shared ethos and direction – to help prosecute the war. On the one hand, the British government was keen to see the eastern territories of the Empire cut their dependence on Britain for supplies to the greatest extent possible. On the other hand, with Egypt and the Middle East becoming an operational base second in importance only to Britain itself, the fact that the region was separated from Britain by 11,000 miles of dangerous ocean following the closure of the Mediterranean immeasurably increased the value of any 'local' supplies drawn from closer imperial territories. In short, if India or Australia could supply the armies fighting out of the Egyptian stronghold with guns, boots or butter, so much the better. Thus the stage was set for Viceroy Lord Linlithgow's initiative to try and coordinate the supply of all war-like materials produced in the Eastern Empire for the greater imperial good.[6]

Linlithgow's ideal was to form a more or less self-supporting eastern zone of the Empire based primarily on cooperation between India and Australia. In October 1940 Linlithgow organized a conference in Delhi attended by representatives from Australia, Ceylon, East Africa, New Zealand, Palestine, Shanghai and South Africa. The meeting of top colonial officials and Whitehall civil servants was chaired by Sir Zaffrullah Khan. Britain was represented by a Ministry of Supply Mission, illustrating the autonomy of the Raj and the fact that this was an Indian show. A Central Provision Office was established in Delhi, and the general idea was that all imperial territories in the region would produce what they produced best; these goods would then be allocated centrally according to the demands of the various war theatres. Thus New Zealand led the field in the supply of broadcast receivers, accumulators, electric cable and electrodes. Hong Kong was the largest supplier of mess tins and webbing equipment. Palestine was a good source of electric cable and razor blades. It was an excellent idea, but its chances of anything more than qualified success suffered a severe setback with Japan's victorious entry into the war in late 1941. Even before Japan's declaration of war, it had proved impossible to supply the lion's share of the Middle East theatre's needs from EGSC territories alone, underlining the fact that, whatever the industrial potential of places such as Australia and India, it was still very much Britain that was the hub of the Empire's manufacturing and industrial base. War against Japan demanded all eastern territories of the Empire to refocus their attention away from the Middle East and helping Britain, to the Far East and helping themselves. As the need for Indian military expansion hit the ceiling, it became clear that India would be hard-pressed to supply itself and prepare for the defensive battles to come, never mind supplying imperial forces fighting thousands of miles away in places like Libya and Greece. An abrupt about-turn was executed, as India's gaze came to rest uneasily on the East. Equally, Japanese hostility focused Australian attention on its own undefended backyard, and thoughts of supplying the Middle East via the EGSC faded as Japanese bombers cast their shadows over Australia's coastal towns. Finally, Japan's conquest spree meant that many of the territories that had formed part of the pool contributing to the efforts of the EGSC – including Burma, Hong Kong and Malaya – were lost to the enemy.

As in Britain and all other parts of the Empire, bigger government and unprecedented state intervention in social and economic affairs became the war-time norm in India. The government became involved in new activities, from ARP and civil defence, to food procurement and distribution. Fund-raising drives were all the rage, and by mid-1943 over £6.5 million had been contributed to the Viceroy's War Purposes Fund. Though Britain was to pay for much of the Indian war effort in terms of things like soldiers' wages and construction bills, the money was not readily available and so internal sources of capital had to be found. This required tax increases, loans and an expanded money supply. The Indian home front was profoundly affected by the war, in many of the ways familiar to Britain and other parts of the Empire. There were price controls and inflation, and increased purchasing power for many though fewer consumer goods to be bought. There were food shortages and rationing, and even starvation on a massive scale. The Bengal famine of 1943 killed over three million people, caused by harvest failures, the loss of the Burmese rice supply (Burma supplied about 15 per cent of India's rice in 1940), transport problems caused by the war, and the failure of government to organize distribution across regional boundaries and to divert shipping space.[7] In requisitioning grain to fight the famine, the government angered wealthy peasant farmers, just the type of collaborators on whom British rule relied. India was a major imperial food exporter, and colonies like Mauritius consumed Indian foodstuffs but had their access severely restricted because of the desperate food situation on the subcontinent itself. A disaster similar to the 1943 Bengal famine was feared in the following year as India's wheat crop failed. Wheat supplies were reduced and millet and barley substitutes distributed, but still a deficiency of 484,000 tons of wheat was predicted. Because of the world shortage of shipping, London could only muster 50,000 tons of Australian wheat. The Commanders-in-Chief of India Command and South East Asia Command, Wavell and Mountbatten, were alive to the situation, and in March 1944 offered to forego one tenth of their military imports, thus releasing twenty-five ships to carry 200,000 tons of wheat to India.

Another impact of war on the home front was the arrival of a portion of the 500,000 Italian prisoners of war harvested during the East and North Africa campaigns. Before leaving his post as Commander-in-Chief Middle East, General Wavell had been anxious to get as many Italians out of Egypt as possible, and India was one of the many parts of the Empire that answered the call. In March 1941 the Government of India had agreed to accept 68,000, and by November 46,000 had arrived. Officers, including most of the Italian general staff, were billeted in camps around Dehra Dun, with another camp for officers at Yol in the Punjab. Other ranks were accommodated in Bangalore, Bhopal and Ramgarh. Tens of thousands more went to camps in Australia, Britain, Canada, Central Africa, Ceylon, East Africa and South Africa, and Germans too formed part of this pan-imperial diaspora of enemy soldiers, encamped in the Middle East, Britain and Canada. In India some Italian prisoners joined the Italian Auxiliary Pioneer Corps and undertook projects such as road-building. Attempts were made by the Political Warfare Executive and SOE to find recruits for a Free Italy movement from amongst the thousands of captured men, based on the Mazzini Society, an anti-fascist organization founded in New York.[8] By December 1942 there was also a camp of over 2000 Japanese internees at Purana Quila near Delhi.

From the British point of view, there was a downside to India's utility as a *place d'armes* and source of war supplies. This was the fact that India was the Empire's political powder keg. As Indian resources and bases became more desperately important to Britain as a Japanese army approached from the east, the political situation became ever more volatile. The fact that India was so politically challenging for imperial policy-makers reflected its status as the largest and most advanced non-white colonial territory and its mature indigenous political structures. Indians had been involved in their own governance – as politicians and civil servants as well as traditional rulers – for decades, and as a reward for loyal participation in the First World War India had been elevated to the waiting room outside the door of the 'white' Dominions club. A sophisticated political elite had emerged in India long before any other non-white imperial dependency, and in the twentieth century the steady political progress being made by the Indian National Congress (INC, founded in 1885) and the Muslim League (founded in 1906) was given a boost by the style of mass politicking that Gandhi brought to the scene, with civil disobedience and 'traditional' protest through marches, fasting and boycotts, to the fore. Constitutional methods of obtaining reform alternated with civil disobedience. Responding to nationalist demands, the 1935 Government of India Act passed by the British Parliament sought to satisfy Indian demands for a substantial share in power-sharing at the provincial level, whilst reserving Britain's dominant role at the centre.[9]

To many Indian nationalists the war presented an unmissable opportunity to put extra pressure on Britain to devolve more power more quickly, because of the massive strain that the imperial system endured given its three-fronted struggle in the east and the west. Their efforts to forward their demands, and the intransigence with which they were met, destined India to become the scene of the greatest war-time challenge to imperial control, right at the time when the Japanese had overrun the British position in South-East Asia and were nearing the eastern gates of the Raj. In that crucial period, when all that mattered to Britain was holding India to the Empire as it performed its vital role as an imperial base and troop factory, acquiescence was all-important. This led to an offer of immediate independence upon the cessation of hostilities, and to old-style colonial repression when the offer was turned down and the 'Quit India' movement launched, the greatest rebellion to arise in India since the Mutiny of 1857.

Despite this turmoil, the Indian Army and security forces, and the heavily-Indianized Indian Civil Service, held true, and the administrative integrity of the Raj survived its greatest ever trial. In fact, imperial strength was overwhelmingly in evidence, despite the common emphasis on imperial weakness, as India was grasped firmly by British political and military structures and its resources were harnessed for British ends a mere two years before India became the world's largest democratic nation state. In holding it all together, however, there is no doubt that Britain pushed India to the limits, and the Raj began to fracture, compounding pre-war factors that made a British withdrawal from India appear less unpalatable and less damaging to Britain's continued imperial status. By 1945 one of the fundamentals upon which Britain justified its rule around the world – the maintenance of law and order – could no longer be guaranteed as Indians fought Indians in many parts of the subcontinent and civil disobedience affected other parts. Thus one of Britain's biggest reasons for remaining in India was seriously undermined.

This difficult internal state of affairs coupled with Britain's political and economic exhaustion meant that Indian independence could not be denied without the unacceptable and pointless deployment of tens of thousands of British troops. War-time nationalists, however, were pushing at a door that was already ajar, irrespective of the diehard rhetoric of politicians and viceroys like Churchill and Linlithgow. Other powerful figures, from Attlee to Amery to Wavell and Mountbatten, had less innate resistance to Indian independence, and did not see it as threatening a lethal blow to Britain's continued status as a global military and imperial power of the first rank. India's role in imperial trade had been declining long before the war anyway, and the war left Britain, not India, the major debtor in the relationship. Even the old economic arguments for maintaining the Raj, therefore, had been largely consigned to history by the 1940s. Finally, the war had led Britain to mention the previously unmentionable. India had been told that after the war it would be free to become an independent nation state, within or without the Commonwealth, and Attlee's Labour government had no intention whatever of reneging upon this promise (although the uncompromisingly imperial Foreign Secretary, Ernest Bevin, wanted Britain to remain for another fifteen years). So Indian independence after the war was hardly something to marvel at, for Britain was simply delivering on a war-time promise.

India had traditionally been at the heart of imperial defence. It was the reason for the existence of much of the rest of the Empire (the African colonial acquisitions of the late nineteenth century were memorably described as 'a vast footnote to the Indian Empire'), the centre of a web of sea routes that required patrols and garrisons, an expansionist power in its own right, and the barracks for a huge army that Britain hurled around the world, whether eastwards to occupy Java against Napoleon or westwards to intimidate the Russians in the Mediterranean or to discipline the Emperor of Abyssinia.[10] From December 1941, India faced a possible Axis thrust from the west and a Japanese thrust from the east. Both London and Washington acknowledged that the loss of India to the Japanese would be disastrous for the Allied global war effort. To meet its variegated defence responsibilities, it was not to airpower or seapower that India looked, but to the rock of the Indian Army, the force that had for centuries made Britain a major land power in the east.

To service war theatres in Burma, North Africa, the Middle East and South-East Asia the Indian Army grew from about 200,000 men in 1939 (excluding the 83,000 soldiers of the Princely States), to about 900,000 by the end of 1941, reaching a peak of about 2,600,000 in 1945. All of this was achieved without recourse to conscription; unlike in Africa, there could be no hint of compulsion even if channelled through indigenous political leaders. Reaching its greatest ever level of militarization, the number of British troops stationed in India also rose steeply, from 43,000 in 1939 to 240,000 in 1945. Over the course of the war the Indian Army sustained 24,500 killed, 6000 wounded, 12,000 missing and 80,000 taken prisoner. Of the 900,000 Indians under arms at the end of 1941 a third were in Iraq, the Western Desert and Malaya. 150,000 were in the North-West Frontier Province, on watch and ward duties, and 300,000 were undergoing training. Recruits were being taken up at the rate of 50,000 a month, and training camps were being opened all over India. As had been the case since the early nineteenth century, the Indian Army was supplemented by soldiers from the independent kingdom of Nepal. On the eve of the Second World War the Brigade of Gurkhas comprised twenty battalions. The outbreak of war with Germany led to the immediate offer of further assistance from the Nepalese Prime Minister, who even promised to send eight of his country's own battalions to bolster the defences of India. Within months of the fall of France the Brigade of Gurkhas had risen to forty-five battalions, and the Nepalese offer of help had been accepted. During the war Gurkhas soldiered in every theatre of conflict, and a total of 250,000 men from Nepal saw service.[11]

Indian soldiers saw service all over the world. Nearly half of the 130,000 troops lost in the Malayan Campaign were Indian. The 4th and 5th Indian Divisions were sent to the Middle East, where they became a mainstay of the Eighth Army following participation, via the Sudan, in the defeat of Italian forces in East Africa. India's traditional supervision of British affairs in the Persian Gulf region meant that when Iran and Iraq were occupied, Indian troops were to the fore. General William Slim's 10th Indian Division, for example, after advancing on Baghdad from Basra in the Iraq campaign, then took part in the invasion of Vichy Syria before crossing into Iran in August 1941. The newly-formed Persia and Iraq Command was subordinate to India Command and consisted mainly of Indian Army troops. Indian animal transport companies served in France before Dunkirk, and Indian infantrymen attacked the seemingly impregnable mountain-top position at Monte Cassino in Italy as the Eighth Army inched its way up the Italian mainland.

At the outbreak of war the Indian Army was a dated force, more than a match for anyone in a conventional colonial setting but no match for the modernity represented by the Wehrmacht. Modernization started perilously late, and the committee appointed to examine the matter in 1938 was shocked at how far the Indian Army (like the British Army) had deteriorated as a fighting force since the First World War. The army's transport and signalling were outmoded, it lacked mortars and anti-tank guns, and its cavalry regiments were still mounted. India was home to a complex military command structure centred on Delhi, which disposed of forces spread over a massive area. India Command's responsibilities included Burma, though Far East Command (FEC) in Singapore assumed this role in 1940. This was an ill-advised transfer. India Command knew Burma well, whereas the fledgling FEC had its plate full dealing with the prospect of a Japanese attack on Malaya and had little time for this distant province. When FEC and its short-lived American-British-Dutch-Australian Command successor collapsed in February 1942, Burma returned to India Command. Delhi was awash with military, civilian, and ancillary base and headquarters facilities. The Commander-in-Chief India was in charge of all three services and sat on the Viceroy's Council. He presided over a Defence Department, renamed the War Department in July 1942. After assuming the post following his removal by Churchill from Middle East Command, General Sir Archibald Wavell altered the command structure in the light of the Japanese threat to India. Regional commands were created, Central Command supervising the North-West, South and Eastern Armies (in December 1942 the Eastern Army became Fourteenth Army).

In a further adjustment to the region's command structure, in October 1943 a new joint Allied supreme command was created, South East Asia Command (SEAC) under Admiral Lord Louis Mountbatten. This was to oversee the Allied war effort in the India–Burma–China theatre and to plan for the reconquest of Malaya (Operation Zipper). The operational responsibilities of GHQ Delhi, and air force headquarters, were transferred to SEAC, and in 1944 SEAC headquarters moved from Delhi to Kandy in Ceylon. In November 1943 Mountbatten was formally given responsibility for defending India in the east by the Viceroy in Council, thereby reducing India Command's defensive responsibilities to the guarding of the North-West Frontier. India Command was further reduced when it was relieved of operational responsibilities in the Iran–Iraq region when a separate Persia and Iraq Command was formed in 1942. Thus shorn of responsibility for policy and operations in the Middle East and Burma–South-East Asia, India Command could concentrate on expanding and maintaining India's war effort whilst keeping a lid on civil unrest.

India became the base for a major Allied air offensive as the Americans sought to supply the Chinese and aid the British imperial war effort in Burma, and as the British developed a strategy based on air supply in a theatre where overland transit presented significant difficulties (notably an abject lack of roads and lots of mountains). On the outbreak of war in 1939 India was dangerously deficient in air cover, possessing seven vintage squadrons, and the demands of the European and Middle East theatres for the output of factories producing the latest types of aircraft meant that India was somewhere down the pecking order beneath Malaya. The situation had not improved much when Wavell flew to India to take up his new command in the summer of 1941. Touching down at Jodhpur, he saw a squadron of obsolescent Audax army cooperation aircraft masquerading as fighters. (Tiger Moths were requisitioned from flying clubs for No. 2 (Indian) Elementary Training School at Jodhpur.) There were no modern aircraft anywhere in his new command. This situation was compounded by the fact that the RAF was very much the poor relation in Indian service politics. India Command was first and foremost an army command, and the RAF was therefore subordinate, unlike in Aden and Iraq where the RAF was the senior service.

The dramatic imperial losses in Malaya and Burma, and the threat of an attack on Ceylon, meant that all possible was done to shift military hardware eastwards. The build up of forces included more warships for the Eastern Fleet, more British and African troops for defensive duties in India and Ceylon, and as many aircraft as could be spared. In March 1942 plans were afoot for the construction of 215 new airfields in order to accommodate the ambitious scale of forces anticipated. Ceylon was reinforced from the Middle East and India itself, and the air build up in India continued – in March 1942 forty Hurricanes, forty Blenheims and ten Wellingtons from Middle East Command were sent to India Command, and fifty-seven crated Hurricanes arrived for assembly at the RAF depot in Karachi. The forces of the Empire were on the move, at sea, on land and in the air. The build up of air power is demonstrated by RAF strength in India at different stages of the war. The India–Burma theatre represented one of the RAF's biggest overseas commitments, testament to the scale of the war in the region and the central role played by air power in prosecuting it. In September 1941 there were 11,600 RAF personnel in India and Burma, representing 2 per cent of the RAF's total strength.

In September 1943 the figure was 80,000 (9 per cent of the RAF), in September 1944 93,000 (over 10 per cent) and in May 1945 there were 122,000 RAF personnel in theatre (13 per cent of the RAF's total strength). This was an extraordinary feat of arms and an often overlooked triumph of RAF organizational and operational skill. By the latter stages of the war total air superiority had been won back from the Japanese. The memory of enemy bombers over Calcutta was fading fast; entire imperial divisions were being shifted and supplied by Allied Transport Command; and it was an RAF Spitfire that flew low over George MacDonald Fraser's Nine Section, part of the 17th Indian Division, and performed a victory roll to announce Victory in Europe as the company lined up for an advance on a Japanese-held village ('Ev ye told Tojo, like?', and 'Get the boogers out 'ere!' were the immediate thoughts of Fraser's Cumbrian colleagues). By that time the Allied Strategic Air Force's Combat Cargo Task Force, consisting of seventeen squadrons of transport aircraft, was supplying 356,000 men of the Fourteenth Army in the field. Air power in India had come a long way since the sight of ancient Audaxes had troubled Wavell on his arrival in India as Commander-in-Chief.

Fighters and bombers were central to this growing air strength, though reconnaissance aircraft were just as important, particularly in protecting the all-important sea lanes. American-built Catalina flying boats were indispensable to the war effort in the Indian Ocean region, and by mid-1943 there were six squadrons (including a Canadian squadron) patrolling from the Andaman Islands to the Arabian Sea from bases in Ceylon, Karachi and Madras. Hudson general reconnaissance aircraft flying from bases like Dum Dum near Calcutta covered the Bay of Bengal, attacking Japanese forces when the chance presented itself, in April 1942, for example, destroying thirteen Japanese flying boats at anchor in Port Blair in the recently-occupied Andaman Islands. By November 1943 India Command had 2820 aircraft on the books, rising from 426 in April 1942 (of the 2820, 672 were front-line aircraft). The 10th United States Army Air Force (USAAF) had eighteen squadrons based in India. At the height of Fourteenth Army's struggle with the Japanese 15th Army, the RAF had nearly 130,000 men in India, with 3700 aircraft. As in other theatres, inter-service cooperation was well developed by the end of the war. The American air force presence was nearly as large as that of the RAF, a massive footprint in a part of the British Empire unused, before the war, to the sights and sounds of America. By November 1943 140 new airfields had been completed in India, sixty-four with all-weather runways and seventy-one with fair-weather runways. The number had risen to 275 a mere four months later. At one point over one million men were engaged on airfield construction and the facilities needed to accompany them, and aviation fuel was being transported from Britain's major oil refinery at Abadan in Iran. To protect this new infrastructure air defence measures were required. A comprehensive India and Ceylon wireless telegraphy and signals project was undertaken, and units of the RAF Regiment deployed to defend air assets throughout India (the RAF Regiment was formed during the war to provide

11. Men from a mule company of the Royal Indian Army Service Corps on guard duty in England, July 1942. (*IWM, H 21632*)

12. Members of the South African Royal Naval Volunteer Reserve on one of the 16 inch guns of HMS *Nelson*, July 1941. (*IWM, A 4606*)

13. Australian sailors row towards their ship, the cruiser HMAS *Perth*, in the Mediterranean, August 1941. *Perth* was sunk by the Japanese off Java on 1 March 1942. (*IWM, AUS 533*)

14. A tender conveys aircrew to a Short Sunderland Mark III flying boat, Addu Atoll, Maldive Islands, July 1944. (*IWM, CF 620*)

15. HMS *Templar* arrives at the depot ship at Colombo, Ceylon, after a successful patrol in Far Eastern waters, February 1944. (*IWM, A 22500*)

16. Australian troops among the ruins of a Crusader castle at Sidon, Lebanon, July 1941. (*IWM, AUS 533*)

17. Australian nursing sisters at a general hospital, New Guinea, December 1943. (*IWM, AUS 1702*)

18. Indian soldiers mingle with men of the 81st West African Division, in India for jungle training. The first African colonial troops to fight outside Africa, the 81st Division went to Burma in December 1943. (*IWM, IND 2864*)

19. The Battle of Imphal-Kohima, July 1944. British 3 inch mortar detachments support the 19th Indian Division's advance along the Mawchi Road, Burma. (*IWM, IND 4723*)

20. Men of the Royal Garwhal Rifles search captured Japanese soldiers at Kuala Lumpur, Malaya, 1945. (*IWM, IND 4858*)

21. A Matilda tank of 'B' Squadron, 2/4th Australian Armoured Regiment during mopping-up operations on Bougainville in the Solomon Islands, May 1945. (*IWM, HU 69099*)

22. The ship's company of HMS *Anson*, in Sydney Harbour, climb the superstructure to get a bird's eye view of VJ-Day celebrations, 1945. (*IWM, ABS 517*)

ground defence for deployed assets). By the end of 1942, fifty-two radar sets were operational in India and Ceylon, wireless observer units operated across India, and 'Y' Service facilities listened to enemy radio transmissions.

India's own fledgling air force also expanded during the war. Over 47,000 Indian non-combatant and civilian workers assisted the RAF and Royal Indian Air Force (RIAF).[12] Established in 1933, the Indian Air Force grew rapidly as a result of the war, rising from 1600 to 28,500 men.* The RIAF operated alongside the RAF in the retreat from Burma and played a significant role in its reconquest, flying in fighter, tactical reconnaissance and ground attack roles. Over 16,000 sorties were flown by the RIAF during the war, amounting to over 24,000 operational flying hours. Losses were high: nearly 700 personnel were killed and a further 231 died in the field. The RIAF was built around nine operational squadrons – three fighter reconnaissance, two ground attack, two light bombers and two fighters (including Hurricane, Spitfire and Vengeance squadrons). Its personnel also serviced RAF and USAAF bases in India. Europeans were not allowed to hold commissions in the RIAF. Over 1300 women from India and Ceylon served in the Women's Auxiliary Air Force. Though the RIAF shared the Indian Army's no conscription policy, the same could not be said for the local elephant population, recruited to tow aircraft throughout India and Burma, and even shipped overseas to distant airfields like that on the Cocos Islands.[13]

On 2 March 1942 Air Marshal Sir Richard Peirse arrived to take command of all air forces in India and Ceylon. The squadrons operating in his theatre were distributed in different groups throughout the region. The Order of Battle in September 1942 amounted to eight (mainly bomber) squadrons under No. 221 Group at Calcutta (which had been based at Rangoon before the loss of Burma); seven (mainly fighter) squadrons under No. 224 Group also at Calcutta; a squadron of Catalina flying boats under No. 225 Group at Bangalore; nine mixed squadrons under No. 222 Group in Ceylon; and four squadrons of the Indian Air Force under No. 223 Group at Peshawar. By June 1943, the squadron figures had risen. No. 221 Group had seventeen squadrons; No. 224 Group had nine squadrons; No. 225 Group had ten squadrons; No. 222 Group remained on nine squadrons; and No. 223 Group had seven squadrons. In addition to these groups, there was No. 227 (Training) Group at Lahore, responsible for all air training, and No. 226 (Maintenance) Group at Karachi. Up until 1942 the RAF Depot at Karachi had met the needs of the small force kept in north-west India, but it now needed to expand, as it was to act as a transit point for aircraft travelling from the Middle East to eastern India and beyond, as well as being the main supply and maintenance base.

Air power was essential to Allied operations in the India–Burma theatre and to the imperial triumph over the Japanese. For their part, the Japanese were slow to grasp the significance of Allied command of the air and what it would enable their

* The 'Royal' was added later in the war in recognition of the force's contribution to the Allied war effort.

enemies to achieve, even when their forces were entirely surrounded. Just as the Japanese had enjoyed air superiority when they first advanced into Burma, the Allies by 1944 enjoyed even greater superiority themselves. Just one example will illustrate the nature of such support. In a week of intensive fighting leading to the capture of Kangaw on 30 January 1945, 900 sorties were flown by RAF Thunderbolt fighter-bombers (the American-manufactured P-47s), dropping 750 tons of bombs and 17,000 gallons of napalm, used for the first time in Burma in early 1945. Vital to the campaign, American factories churned out transport aircraft in their hundreds and the RAF shifted more fighters eastwards as things improved elsewhere. Supply and artillery support for forces fighting in Assam and Burma came to depend on the skies. Aid to China went by air, Chindits behind enemy lines in Burma or Force 136 agents and their local allies in Burma and Malaya were supplied by air, as were liberated prisoner of war camps after the Japanese surrender. With silk for parachutes scarce, the Indian jute industry was called into play, manufacturing simple canopies that became known as 'parajutes'. Air power also allowed Fourteenth Army to build an enviable record in casualty evacuation, an extraordinary 130,000 wounded troops being whisked away from the battlefield by aircraft. During the Battle of Imphal 120,000 British and Indian troops were supplied entirely by air for three months, an entire division was flown into theatre at a crucial moment, and 50,000 administrative personnel and ten thousand sick were flown out. Also flown in were the 861 tons needed per day to provision the army (this was up to 1800 tons per day by April 1945). In March 1944 350 aircraft of the American Air Transport Command were operating over 'the Hump', five hundred miles from north-eastern Assam over the mountains to Kunming in China. From July 1942, when this supply highway opened, to the end of the war, six hundred aircraft and one thousand crewmen were lost, and 650,000 tons of aid delivered to Chiang Kai-shek.

India's ports and coastal waters featured on the Royal Navy's global map and in the Admiralty's division of imperial naval forces, even though India was not host to one of the major British overseas fleets. India was renowned for its land, not its maritime power by the middle of the twentieth century. India's naval defence was the responsibility of the East Indies Station (the Eastern Fleet from early 1942 to late 1944), and by the outbreak of war the Raj had its own fledgling navy as well. There were numerous Royal Navy shore bases on India's coast, and some ports, like Vizagapatam, were important naval bases. The administration of India's naval shore establishments was supported by the Women's Royal Indian Naval Service, formed in 1944 and led by the Director of Women's Auxiliary Corps (India), the Countess of Carlisle, and her Deputy Chief Commander, Ranga Rao.

The main role of the Royal Navy in Indian waters was to protect the convoys on which the build up of forces in India depended. In patrolling the coast and the trade routes leading to and from India the Royal Navy was helped by shore-based aircraft of the RAF and the Fleet Air Arm. Fortunately the Japanese did not devote any significant attention to maritime attacks on India, though in April 1942 a raiding force in the Bay of Bengal sank over twenty ships and bombarded eastern ports, whilst a submarine force sank vessels off the west coast. Such attacks were damaging to morale and severely disrupted normal working practices as people fled and took weeks or even months to return. Thus when Calcutta was bombed in December 1942, though the damage and casualties were light, an exodus of over one and a half million civilians disrupted public services for months. A similar pattern emerged when Bombay was evacuated by the regional government, leading to an exodus of the port's citizens.

The naval burden in India, as was the case in places such as Ceylon, Kenya, South Africa, Tasmania and Trinidad, was shared by locally-raised forces operating mainly in coastal waters. The old Indian Navy, inherited by the Government of India from the East India Company in 1858, had been disbanded in 1863 and its duties assumed by the Royal Navy. In the mid-1930s, however, an Indian navy was reborn with the creation of the Royal Indian Navy (RIN). It strength rose during the war from 1700 officers and ratings to 30,000, manning ten sloops, three frigates, four corvettes, twenty-one minesweepers and other vessels, including a landing craft wing of forty-one boats. The RIN's main role was to recruit, train and administer. It was also given patrol, escort and minesweeping duties in Indian coastal waters. In March 1943 Admiral Sir John Godfrey was moved from his post as Director of Naval Intelligence to become Flag Officer Commanding RIN. His force was independent of Admiral Sir James Somerville's Eastern Fleet, though he liaised closely with him. The RIN acted as a feeder force for the Royal Navy, for when RIN warships had commissioned and completed trials, they were allocated to the operational control of the Royal Navy. In this way some Indian warships came to serve beyond Indian coastal waters, some undertaking convoy work in the Mediterranean and Atlantic. In the Mediterranean the sloops *Sutlej* and *Jumna* played a part in the invasion of Sicily. In the Indian Ocean the minesweeper HMIS *Bengal*, together with a Dutch tanker, destroyed the 10,400-ton six-inch gunned Japanese cruiser *Hokoku Maru* on 11 November 1942. One shot from *Bengal*'s solitary twelve-pounder caused the cruiser to explode, and a second Japanese cruiser left the scene. India was also home to numerous small, irregular naval forces, like the Sundarabans Flotilla formed for reconnaissance and defence purposes in the Ganges delta, consisting of four companies each operating twenty armed motor launches.

Thousands of Indians also served at sea in the British Merchant Navy, continuing the long-standing tradition of 'Lascars' in British ships. Eastern Bengal in particular was a nursery of seamen for Britain's huge merchant fleet. Here, in today's Bangladesh, families endured the same anguish known to families in Britain who had sent men to sea with the Merchant Navy. In particular, places like Chittagong, Noakhali and Sondip were renowned for sending men to sea, and in the heartland of the Sylhet region there was even an area known as the Seamen's Zone. To support these men when their ships docked in Britain there was an established network of people from that part of the world who had settled there, often running boarding houses and eating establishments in places such as Birkenhead (Liverpool), Canning Town (London) and Greenock (Glasgow). This was part of the fascinating non-white underbelly of British society that was well established by the 1940s, featuring the London sojourns of indigenous rulers and their families, associations for West African students, clubs for West Indian servicemen, rest hostels for Mauritians run by well-to-do expatriates, and the manifold exchanges between British universities and elite colleges throughout the Empire.[14]

A well-documented facet of India's war effort is the recruitment and deployment of Indian forces fighting for the Japanese and Germans *against* British and Indian forces. Though numerically small and militarily inconsequential, these forces have attracted deserved attention because, depending on the point of view, they can be seen as a part of India's struggle for independence against the British, or as traitors and opportunists keen to avoid internment in the wake of imperial defeats throughout South-East Asia. It would be ludicrous to suggest that the Indian National Army (INA) would ever have grown to the strength that it did if Britain had not been defeated in Malaya and thousands of Indian soldiers taken captive. Equally, the Burma National Army would probably have never got off of the ground if it had not been for the fact that Burma was conquered by the Japanese. Nevertheless, these organizations were also a barometer registering the dissatisfaction or indifference that many people in these countries felt towards the established system of British rule that the Japanese so rudely interrupted.[15]

Though it is the case that many Indians and Burmese in military units on Japan's side had genuine nationalist hopes, many were quick to swap back to the Raj's side when it was clear that their Japanese sponsors were going to lose the war. In the eyes of many Britons at the time, of course, they were traitors, pure and simple. Some of the men joined the Japanese-sponsored forces simply in order to get back to Indian Army lines as quickly as possible. Others, who may have been committed to the cause of joining Japan's bid to topple the Raj, began to consider switching sides as it became clear that Japan's vaunted doctrine of Asian harmony and equality was to a large extent imperialist hot air with a menacing brutality and racism thrown in for good measure.

Whether one sees the soldiers of the Japanese-Indian army as glorious freedom fighters, traitors, or victims of war, such men are needed in the foundation myths of new nations, and whilst their role and significance should not be overplayed, nor should it be overlooked. Their potential significance in undermining British rule in India by the fact of their existence, as opposed to their fighting potential, certainly worried the British enough to ensure that a steady stream of propaganda and media censorship surrounded their activities. Some of the movements that attempted to put Indian men into combat against the Allies (not that the Japanese were ever keen on them having much other than menial military roles) had

pre-war roots, and so were not just the *ad hoc* creation of dramatic turns in imperial military fortune. Subhas Chandra Bose was not a war-time opportunist, but a
nationalist leader of great stature who had been decades in the making before he
was transferred from a German to a Japanese submarine south of Mauritius on
his way to take up the leadership of the Indian Independence League (IIL). The
IIL had been established outside of India before the war, and worked to undermine the morale of Indian troops fighting in Malaya. After its Malayan victory
Japan permitted the IIL to operate as the only legal political organization in the
colony. Working among Malaya's sizeable Indian community, it was a significant
organization in the eyes of thousands of Indians. For many Indians, Bose is as
important a figure as Nehru or Gandhi in the struggle for Indian freedom, firm in
his belief that only armed struggle would remove the British from his homeland.
In some ways he was right, though it was to be global war that hastened British
departure from the subcontinent, as opposed to internal Indian rebellion.

Earlier in the war, and thousands of miles from India, the Indian Legion was
founded by Bose with recruits from the 4500 Indians captured by the Germans in
the Western Desert in 1941. He arrived in Germany in April 1943 and presented
the German government with a plan for the creation of the Legion. The soldiers
were formed into three battalions of a thousand men each, officered by Germans.
After Bose left for Singapore later in 1943, these units disintegrated because the
men only wanted to fight the British, whereas the Germans wanted to deploy
them against the Russians, the idea being that they would fight their way to India
with German forces via Russia. The Indian soldiers were eventually absorbed into
the German army and served in France. Meanwhile the globe-trotting Bose travelled east to ply his trade in a theatre rich with promise. The Japanese were keen
to court him, they had scores of thousands of Indian prisoners of war among
whom he could recruit, and they were standing undefeated at the gates of India.
In Malaya, Bose would assume the leadership of a much larger force, the Indian
National Army.

The lion's share of the INA was recruited from amongst the 60,000 Indian
soldiers captured by the Japanese in the Malayan campaign. Statistics vary. Some
claim that up to two thirds of the captured Indian soldiers joined the INA, others
that it never exceeded 43,000, over half of these being recruited from among the
civilian population of Malaya. In December 1942 Pritam Singh, the then INA
leader, had been arrested by the Japanese and the INA virtually disbanded. It
was given a new lease of life under Bose, who assumed command upon arriving
in Singapore in July 1943. There he was given a rousing reception at a mass
rally, attended by Japanese Prime Minister Tojo Hideki himself. Bose wanted the
INA to play a significant role in the Burma campaign, believing that its visible
deployment could lead to mass Indian revolt against the British. This fitted well
with the thinking of the general commanding Japanese forces in Burma, who
hoped that his 'March on Delhi' would prompt massive civil unrest and, together
with his victories in the field, topple the Raj. The Japanese did not share Bose's

optimism about the INA's military efficacy, however, and usually deployed it in penny-packets or employed its personnel as guides, interpreters and propaganda agents. The problem regarding the successful integration, training, equipping and use of the INA was threefold. First, on the whole Japanese officers were not interested in the Indian cause and did not see Indians as anything other than as racial inferiors among whom the Japanese walked as kings. Secondly, the INA was regarded at best as a peripheral ally of no military value by the vast majority of Japanese officers, bar the handful of enthusiasts who championed its cause. Finally, the INA began to come into its own at a time when Japan was beginning to lose the war, and this situation could never provide the appropriate setting for the successful growth of the INA. The only large INA contingent involved in the fighting, the 8000 men engaged in the battle for Imphal, was badly trained and equipped, and suffered from poor morale. Over 2500 of them surrendered. The 3000 men of the 1st Division surrendered tamely near Pyu as the British advanced towards Rangoon, as did the 5000 strong garrison of Rangoon itself.

The INA had other roles besides fighting, and was not as flaccid an organization as its military record alone would suggest. It was in fact only the military wing of a larger political organization, the Azad Hind League, which concentrated on recruiting civilians from Indian overseas communities in South-East Asia. The Azad Hind League was one of those heady experiments in indigenous political organization that could only have existed in wartime, and that made the reimposition of colonial rule at the end of the war, amongst people who had experienced politicization on a new level, extremely difficult. In July 1944 the Azad Hind League had 200,000 members in seventy-two branches in the region. The Singapore branch had 60,000 members, Kuala Lumpur's 30,000 and Penang's 20,000. Bose's re-formed INA recruited women, most famously into the Rani of Jhansi Regiment led by Lakshmi Swaminathan, a Madras-born doctor (the Rani of Jhansi was the most famous female leader during the Indian Mutiny of 1857). The use of radio in a war marked by its inventive and widespread use of visual and wireless propaganda was a speciality of the INA. At its Penang camp recruits received training in radio, Morse code and wireless operations. The INA was responsible for propaganda broadcasts to Indians throughout Asia, Bose himself speaking on the radio from Berlin and Rangoon. Broadcasts from Japanese-occupied South-East Asia were regularly picked up in India, and the Government of India's Counter-Propaganda Directorate had its hands full in trying to diminish their impact. Other underground organizations attracted the attention of the Raj's police and intelligence agencies, such as the Malayan Association, which distributed propaganda from Japanese-occupied South-East Asia in western India. Radio stations were also set up on the India–Burma border, and a special INA station targeted soldiers in the Indian Army and aimed at encouraging disloyalty in the ranks.[16]

To further the cause of a free India, and to boost the standing of the INA and its Japanese sponsors, a provisional government of Azad Hind was formed in October 1943 with Bose as the leader in waiting, duly recognized by Germany, Japan and seven pro-Axis nations. This government-in-exile promptly declared war on Britain and America. The Japanese thrust into India in 1944 that led to the decisive battles of Kohima and Imphal was based on the hope that the Indian population would rise up against the British and aid them in their task of crippling British military power and Britain's capacity to govern India. Conquest of the subcontinent was not envisaged; the aim was to strengthen the Japanese position in Burma, itself only an outworking of Japan's original imperial wish-list. To help facilitate this, units of the INA were to the fore in the attacks on Kohima and Imphal, for it was thought that, if INA soldiers appeared in Assam, risings might occur and spread throughout India. The Japanese, and for that matter the INA, almost certainly overestimated the strength of likely risings and underestimated the capacity of the regarrisoned Raj to suppress internal unrest. In the end it was academic anyway, as the Fourteenth Army held and defeated the Japanese attack. From then onwards it was the turn of the Japanese to retreat, their ambitions for India lost in the fortunes of war and the men of the INA scrambling to return to British-Indian lines or to melt back into the subcontinent.

Intelligence and propaganda were important elements in the war in the East, and India was home to major intelligence-gathering facilities, and to a host of smaller ones. It was also dotted with links in the imperial signals network which stretched from Britain to the Far East. The major Bletchley Park outstation was Wireless Experimental Centre (WEC) Delhi, which occupied the buildings of Ramjas College, formerly part of Delhi University. This was the main Indian Army interception station and was at the forefront of efforts to break Japanese army codes. Among its thousand personnel were members of the British Army, the RAF and the Indian Army, as well as West African servicemen and Indian civilian wireless operators. WEC had two major outposts of its own, Western Wireless Signal Centre at Bangalore and Eastern Wireless Signal Station near Calcutta. By 1944 WEC was intercepting 2000 Japanese signals a day. Also based in Delhi was an American unit called US8, a large facility working on Japanese army and air traffic (so large, in fact, that one American officer used a scooter to get around the building). The central British intelligence-gathering facilities were connected to many mobile or temporary facilities in outlying districts, often travelling alongside the fighting forces. These were known as Special Wireless Units. At Cox's Bazaar in Bengal, for example, RAF 367 Wireless Unit could overhear conversations from aircraft over 1200 miles away in Sumatra. At Abbottabad near Rawalpindi in the North-West Frontier Province was the Indian Special Wireless Depot, opened in the inter-war period to intercept Afghan, Russian and Iranian signals, though capable of casting its web far wider as it was to do during the war. For example, in September 1942 it revealed Japanese plans for an attack on Milne Bay in New Guinea, where their forces were heavily defeated by the Australian troops that, thanks to this intelligence, were in position waiting for them.

There were many other war-related offices and outposts scattered throughout India. For example, there was a Combined Services Detailed Interrogation Centre in the Red Fort in Delhi for interrogating Japanese prisoners of war, which became South-East Asia Translation and Interrogation Centre when it moved to Singapore to deal with the enormous number of prisoners of war yielded by the surrender of Japan. There were military facilities like the RAF Air Landing School at Chaklala, the Parachute School in Delhi, the Ordnance Training Centre at Jubbulpore, the wireless training centre at Meerut, the Demolition School at Poona and four military hospitals at Secunderabad. Relics from previous wars could be given a lick of paint and pressed into service again, as was the case with an old Boer War prisoner-of-war camp in Ceylon, redesignated a rest centre for imperial servicemen in this latest conflict.

Clandestine organizations operating in the field were also important in furnishing intelligence. In the American set up, the Office of Strategic Services (OSS) controlled all clandestine groups while the Office of War Information dealt with propaganda. For the same functions and in the same area the British had ten organizations, five of them concerned with sabotage, training guerrillas and gathering intelligence. There was the Inter-Service Liaison Department (the Indian version of MI6); Force 136 (the Indian branch of SOE) specializing in subversion, the preparation of resistance movements and sabotage by secret agents and raiding parties from bases established in occupied territory; GSI (Z), or Z Force, responsible for internal security in India and the collection of information by patrols deep inside enemy territory; Small Operations Group; and V Force, which sustained fighting patrols gathering intelligence close behind main enemy positions. In addition, the Burma Intelligence Corps provided guides and interpreters for these outfits. The profusion of British organizations, as in the Far East, West Africa, the Middle East and Europe led to problems. The Inter-Service Liaison Department, for example, was ultra-secretive and totally unwilling to cooperate with other services engaged in the same kind of work. In London there was no central control, and lots of different departmental fingers were in the pie: the Colonial Office, the Foreign Office, the India Office, the three service ministries and the Ministry of Economic Warfare. To compound difficulties, before the war the Commanders-in-Chief India Command and Far East Command, and the Governors of Malaya and Burma, did little to help new and shadowy organizations like SOE. Despite these difficulties, India became an established base for SOE operations, sharing the base role with Ceylon as operations were mounted throughout Japanese-occupied and influenced territory in South Asia and South-East Asia. India also made some unlikely contributions to SOE's operations in other theatres. Noor Inayat Khan, a direct descendant of Tipu Sultan of Mysore, was living in France before war broke out. Fluent in both English and French, she worked in the Women's Auxiliary Air Force as a wireless operator before joining SOE in February 1943. She was sent to France five months later as a radio operator for an SOE cell ('Prosper'), though was soon betrayed to the Gestapo and arrested. Refusing to provide any information, and attempting twice to escape, she was sent to Dachau where she was executed in September 1944. In 1949 she was posthumously awarded the George Cross.

The British authorities had to work hard to counter Japan's propaganda offensive against India, aimed at emphasizing Asian brotherhood and the ripeness of the time to rise up against the white colonial masters. Japanese and INA propaganda directed against the Indian Army also had to be countered, and in doing this, British propagandists emphasized that Japanese culture was anti-Hindu, that their attitude towards women was backward, and that their track record as a colonial power was frightening. In order to counter the effects of Subhas Chandra Bose, the INA was kept out of the public domain as much as possible through effective media censorship. The British used intensive and effective radio propaganda, particularly to counter Bose's regular radio broadcasts from Germany and later from South-East Asia and Burma. Controlling the media gave the British an obvious advantage in policing the information received by the Indian population. One of the tasks of SOE's India Mission was to write items of propaganda camouflaged as news, and place them with Indian newspapers and radio programmes.

Behind-enemy-lines operations were a mainstay of the Burma war and the campaigns to stir resistance in Japanese-occupied territories like Malaya and Thailand. The exploits of the Chindits demonstrated that the Japanese were not invincible jungle fighters, as sizeable imperial forces being sustained for months at a time behind the Japanese front line. The Chindits will forever be associated with Orde Wingate, the man who had organized the behind-the-lines Gideon Force appointed to fight a guerrilla war to aid Haile Selassie's return to his throne in Abyssinia. He was brought to India by General Wavell, who was well aware of his peculiar talents. Wingate was given powerful backing by Wavell and Churchill as he developed an organization capable of inserting columns of men into the rear of the Japanese army to disrupt communications and gather detailed intelligence. Whilst in the field they were supplied entirely by air drops, flown by RAF aircraft based in India and Ceylon. Earlier in the war Wingate had worked at the Bush Warfare School at Maymyo north east of Mandalay, where he met Major Mike Calvert, the Chindits' most celebrated leader, who had arrived after training Australian and New Zealand Independent Companies in SOE techniques in the Australian state of Victoria.

Wingate, a complex figure who elicited admiration, suspicion and loathing in almost equal measure, has had a similar affect on subsequent historians. Wingate had formed the Long Range Penetration Force in July 1942, and their first mission, whilst not achieving a great deal strategically, pointed the way towards the potential of such operations against the Japanese. Wingate's 77th Brigade of 3000 men left for Burma in February 1943 and remained behind enemy lines for four months (2182 of the men returning). This operation was a boost for British morale, deflated by the apparent superiority of the Japanese in fighting in jungle conditions, and was turned into a great propaganda success at a time when there was little good news coming out of the Burma theatre.[17]

Wingate's operations sufficiently impressed Churchill for him (and his wife) to be whisked off at a moment's notice to the Anglo-American Quebec Conference in August 1943. This and his rapid promotion – major to major-general in less than eighteen months – did little to endear Wingate to officers in India Command, many of whom displayed an inevitable suspicion of anything marked 'new' or 'special'. 'Ordinary' British infantry soldiers had their own reasons for thinking that the Chindits were given undue prominence, believing that there wasn't much they did or could do that conventional infantrymen couldn't do just as well. But the prospect of a hardy and elusive guerrilla army behind Japanese lines had an understandable appeal for politicians tired of defeat or ineffective advances against Japanese troops. The Americans were keen on Wingate's ideas too, eager to endorse anything that distracted Japanese forces and contributed to the American priority of reopening the land route to China. The Commander-in-Chief India, whatever his earlier backing of Wingate, was furious, because the British government ordered the breaking up of the crack British 70th Division in order to form the first Chindit formations. Powerful backing from London, however, symbolized by Wingate's direct access to Churchill should he encounter any obstacles, meant that his star was in the ascendant, and that a large-scale Chindit operation involving 20,000 men was to be mounted. This came about when Operation Thursday was launched in March 1944, the biggest behind-the-lines operation of the Second World War, and also the longest involving so many men. Wingate had six brigades, known as Special Force (or the 3rd Indian Infantry Division for deception purposes). Special Force consisted of the 3rd West African Brigade, 14th, 16th and 23rd British Infantry Brigades, 7th and 11th Indian Infantry Brigades, and supporting units like Dahforce (Kachin Levies), the 2nd Battalion The Burma Rifles, two artillery regiments, logistics and commando engineers. It even had its own air force in the form of No. 1 Air Commando USAAF. The most successful Chindit operation supported the American advance down the Hukawng valley into Burma. They established airstrips and strongholds named after British cities, streets and areas of London, and cut the Mandalay–Myitkyina railway. Following Wingate's death in an air crash on 24 March 1944, however, the Chindits ceased fighting in the role for which they had been developed. Shorn of the clout Wingate had wielded at high command levels, the Chindits fell under the Anglophobic command of General Joe Stilwell, who chose to employ them as conventional infantry.

The Chindits were by no means the only behind-enemy-lines forces deployed in the Burma theatre. Before the fall of Mandalay, Governor Sir Reginald Dorman-Smith had sent one of his experienced Frontier Service officers, Henry Stevenson, to coordinate guerrilla units in the hills. They became known as the Chin and

Kachin Levies. On the borders of China, Chin, Karen and Shan people fought a long guerrilla war against the Japanese who were invading their sacred lands in the company of the hated Burmans. In April 1942 the Commander-in-Chief India, General Wavell, ordered the creation of a guerrilla organization to attack enemy lines of communication, should the Japanese invade Assam from Burma. This was as the remnants of Burmacorps approached India, pursued by the advancing Japanese. So was born V-Force, built around platoons from the Assam Rifles augmented by about a thousand hill tribesmen. The Assam Rifles consisted of five military police battalions maintained by the Assam provincial government, made up of Gurkhas commanded by British officers seconded from the Indian Army. As Japan did not follow up its early victories and penetrate far into Assam, the role of V-Force changed to intelligence-gathering and the maintenance of a line of outposts ahead of the main British units facing the enemy.

V-Force famously employed the services of a remarkable English woman, Ursula Graham Bower.[18] Before the war she had lived in Nagaland as an ethnographer and had come to know its people and their customs intimately. Nagaland was a particularly remote area of the India–Burma borderlands, with its administrative capital at Kohima. As Bower put it, 'a barrier lay between us and the outside world'. War came even to such remote regions, however, in this case with the advance of the Japanese in the spring of 1942. Bower promptly joined the Women's Auxiliary Corps (India). Though even the attack on Pearl Harbor seemed like a remote and irrelevant incident in Nagaland, war was drawing near, manifest first by the appearance of a growing stream of refugees as people fled to India in the wake of the Japanese northward advance. Bower was a woman of intense energy and recruited a team of Zemi Nagas to serve on the roads helping refugees. In March 1942 she was ordered to Lumding Junction to run a refugee canteen. Here, illustrating how war could break down political, racial and social barriers the world over, Bower teamed up with an Indian nationalist organization and set about 'dealing with thousands of uprooted and demoralized human beings', up to 2000 a day calling at the canteen on their journey to India. The people, both those passing through as well as those living in the surrounding area, were extremely frightened. It was not a war of their making or understanding, and, whilst they heard tales of the brutality of the Japanese, they also heard rumours that the British were planning to abandon them to their fate.

In August 1942 Colonel Rawdon of V-Force visited Bower and asked her to form a watch and ward network in Nagaland, recuiting hill tribesmen for service as intelligence-gathering scouts. Thus Bower began the recruitment of the North Cachar Watch and Ward. Two months later her progress was checked upon by a visit from Colonel Critchley, who had been Wingate's adjutant in Abyssinia. With a credit facility at the Haflong Treasury to defray any costs, Bower pressed ahead with the recruitment of the Zemi and Kukis. Their tasks were to watch paths and roads through the forests, to bring in any strangers for questioning and inspection, and to look out for parachutists. Bower needed to build up trust with the 150 or so people that she had recruited, for they were with her entirely of their own volition. Important in building this trust was the issuing of red blankets as a sort of uniform, as well as the distribution of weapons, money, wireless equipment and medical supplies. In command of the region's V-Force units was Assam Zone headquarters at Imphal (V-Force's main headquarters was at Comilla). Former tea planters, forestry officials and timber company staff joined V-Force. There was also a platoon of Nepalese State Troops. Other units included the Lushai Brigade, formed in March 1944 to hold the Lushai Hills and harass the Japanese in the Chin Hills. It consisted of a battalion each of Assam Rifles, Biharis, Jats and Punjabis, the Lushai Scouts, two V-Force groups and the Western Chin Levies.

Another behind-the-lines outfit to operate in India was the ubiquitous and global SOE. SOE's India Mission carried out numerous operations from bases in India and Ceylon, and was particularly useful in establishing and training anti-Japanese groups in places like Malaya and Thailand, arming them and coordinating sabotage operations against the enemy, or open warfare when Allied forces moved in for the reconquest. They also had a role to play in propaganda and counter-intelligence in India itself, and mounted operations like that sent to destroy German and Italian vessels harboured in Goa. India Mission also took over the Government of India's Directorate of Military Intelligence. SOE headquarters were established forty miles north of Delhi at Meerut in a bungalow at the Cavalry Lines. There was also a small office in Delhi and a sub-branch in Calcutta. From March 1944 SOE's India Mission became Force 136, and subordinate to it was Force 137, the Australian branch of SOE. Agents were managed through a front organization, the School for Eastern Interpreters, based in a Bombay house owned by Mohammed Ali Jinnah, leader of the Muslim League.

India Mission ran operations in Burma, China, the Dutch East Indies, French Indo-China, India, Malaya and Thailand. The country sections of Groups A (Burma, French Indo-China and Thailand) and C (China) remained based in India with operational bases in the countries concerned. For example, SOE maintained a camp and an airfield at Lashio in Burma which proved a useful staging-post on the way to Chunking, Chiang Kai-shek's capital. An SOE Special Training School (STS) was established near Chunking in March 1942. SOE organized networks of stay-behind groups early in the war to harass the enemy and supply intelligence, should a region be conquered by the Japanese. In India Mission's region only Burma and Indo-China could be reached overland, but sometimes hostile local populations made this a risky entry route. So RAF Special Duties squadrons and submarines were used for most behind-enemy-lines insertions (a lot of these operations were coordinated and deployed from Ceylon). In Malaya, command disagreements had prevented SOE from properly organizing stay-behind teams before the Japanese conquest, but in both India and Burma a network was organized to harry the enemy, conduct sabotage and maintain contact with British military authorities.

The author Peter Fleming (brother of Ian) had been sent to Cairo by SOE in early 1941 to raise a 'Garibaldi Legion' from among the mass of Italian prisoners of war captured in Libya and East Africa, before being sent by the Commander-in-Chief Middle East, Wavell, to 'blow things up' in Greece. Wavell was soon thereafter transferred to India as Commander-in-Chief, and in early 1942 was also given the dubious honour of commanding ABDA Command, the Allied rump based in Java. From there Wavell sent the War Office an urgent appeal for staff officers familiar with the East. He specifically asked for Fleming, who had travelled extensively in the region before the war. On 17 February 1942 Fleming duly boarded the carrier HMS *Formidable* at Glasgow, and spent the journey from Britain to West Africa getting to know a fellow passenger, Admiral Sir James Somerville, himself travelling east to take over as Commander-in-Chief Eastern Fleet. It was a necessarily slow journey. Fleming disembarked at Freetown, and then flew across Africa to Cairo with stops in Liberia, the Gold Coast and the Sudan. He then flew on via Sharjah in the Persian Gulf, Karachi and Gwalior, before finally reaching Delhi. By the time that Fleming arrived, ABDA Command had fallen with defeat at Singapore, so he linked up with Wavell in Delhi, where he established his headquarters. Fleming's job was to conduct deception measures against the Japanese: deliberately crashed cars, lost dispatch cases and intelligence reports and private correspondence meant for London were all intended to put the Japanese on a false scent and deceive them as to British intentions, plans and strengths. Fleming was also responsible for running a network of spies and informers. In preparing for his job Fleming travelled to Burma to meet Orde Wingate and General Sir Harold Alexander, at the time supervising the retreat of Burmacorps. He also travelled to China and to Afghanistan, a neutral country awash with spies and secret agents. In March 1944 Fleming's outfit was taken over by SEAC and renamed D Division, which in the following year became Force 456.

The Japanese were in control of the whole of Burma by early 1942, apart from the northern hills where the Karens commanded the jungle. Only native Burmese were likely to welcome a British return, so they made natural allies for SOE, which put several groups through Special Training Schools. Hill tribesmen were recruited, and by the time of the British retreat to India there were 1500 Karens in the forests to cover the withdrawal, as well as numerous Chins, Kachins and Shans. Later in the war SOE also armed the Burmese Anti-Fascist Organization (AFO) – formerly the Japanese-allied Burma National Army (BNA) – which killed many Japanese soldiers. Railway lines were cut, bridges sabotaged, roads mined and convoys ambushed. Force 136 had been trying to establish contact with the AFO since late 1943, after learning that it was prepared to rise against the Japanese. On 1 January 1945 a wireless message told Force 136 that 8000 BNA soldiers were ready to switch sides. The leader of the BNA, Aung San, met General Sir William Slim in May 1945. Not everyone was impressed, and the Governor of Burma, Sir Reginald Dorman-Smith, was particularly angry that these erstwhile enemies should so soon be welcomed as allies. As always, the military politics of winning wars differed markedly from the politics of civilian rule.

In the last months of the war SOE in Burma was responsible for preventing Japanese personnel from crossing the border into Thailand. Jacques Taschereau was a French-Canadian who had served with SOE in occupied France. In March 1945 he went to SOE's Eastern Warfare School in Canada to learn about jungle survival and local languages and customs, and was then parachuted into Burma along with seven other Canadians. As part of SOE's Operation Character Taschereau linked up with Karen guerrillas and ambushed Japanese troops attempting to reach Thailand across the mountains. Paul-Emile Thibeault and Joseph Fornier from New Brunswick lived with the Karen in Burma, the former instructing them in the use of explosives, the latter providing a wireless link with SOE's Burma Section in Calcutta.

Even during the long absence of the British and Indian armies from Burma, SOE personnel and their indigenous accomplices continued to act against the Japanese occupiers, and towards the end of the war as many wireless operatives as could be spared were sent in. In northern Burma Force 136 had established a headquarters in the Kachin Hills in 1943. There they helped raise a force of 2000 Kachin Levies for service with Detachment 101 of the Office of Strategic Services, the American SOE equivalent. (India and Ceylon played home to regional OSS headquarters. Group 404 was based in Ceylon, 303 in New Delhi and 505 in Calcutta. Indeed, SOE experienced some difficulties because both Slim and Stilwell had a high regard for OSS operations in the area.) Such special forces and operations were important in weakening Japanese positions just at the point of Anglo-Indian attack. In March 1945, for example, 10,000 Karen levies led by British officers played a part in preventing the Japanese from reinforcing Toungoo, killing many thousands of them. General Slim belatedly recognized SOE's contribution, which involved tying down an estimated 50,000 Japanese troops in the Karen Hills alone. Two major operations were launched to assist Fourteenth Army's advance when imperial soldiers returned in force to Burma, and SOE's India Mission claimed that one of these, Operation Nation, killed 3381 Japanese troops and wounded 201. As in Palestine and Malaya, the work of stimulating indigenous resistance could unite bedfellows unlikely to remain on good terms once the war was won. For example, to the consternation of the Government of India's Special Branch, 150 Communists were selected for post-occupational sabotage work and put through a special training course at Kohima. In the immediate post-war years it would be the anti-Japanese and anti-fascist fighters in Malaya and Burma who presented the British with their sternest test as colonial rule was reasserted.

It is impossible to discuss the war in India without at least outlining the seismic political events that unfolded as a result of its involvement in the Second World War and the longer-term trend that had seen an educated Indian elite seek political concessions from the rulers of the Raj since the late nineteenth century. India, the non-white Empire's most politically sophisticated territory, was the centre of the most serious resistance to the British war effort found anywhere in the Empire, though even this, it might be argued, was of limited significance to the imperial war effort, the Japanese war effort or the cause of Indian independence.

Though underwritten by the police and the army, British rule in India had always relied on the collaboration of Indian leaders, be they princes or politicians. Force alone was never a practicable basis for rule. The war, however, reduced the number of Indian leaders willing to act as collaborators. Therefore British rule came increasingly to depend on public acquiescence, the loyalty of British and Indian members of the Indian Civil Service (ICS) – the subcontinent's governing bureaucracy – and the unwavering loyalty of the police and the Indian Army. Fortunately, the police and the army remained loyal. So too did the ICS, though it suffered significant demoralization and weariness, and in 1943 the new Viceroy, General Wavell, feared that it was reaching breaking point. With British recruitment having dried up and many members departing for the armed forces, the ICS was understaffed at its moment of greatest trial, and the British had to tread carefully to ensure that it did nothing to make the Indian members of the ICS have cause to alter their allegiance.

Before the war, provisions for Indian involvement in government at the provincial level, introduced by the 1935 Government of India Act, were working with some success. The 1935 act, rather than part of a phased British withdrawal, had been designed to detach elite Indians from the more extreme side of the Indian National Congress (INC), and to harness them instead to supporting the continuance of the Raj. The war hijacked this cooperation between the Government of India and the subcontinent's premier nationalist organization, however, and led the British to rely more heavily on the Muslim community, the mainstay of Indian Army recruitment, in the process making the prospect of a separate Pakistan a concrete reality. It also led to a more crude deployment of imperial power in the form of bayonets on the streets, as Britain struggled desperately to keep control in India as it simultaneously struggled to contain the threat of Japan on the eastern border.

One of the reasons for the breakdown in cooperation between the British and the leadership of the INC was the outmoded way in which India was taken to war, which inflamed nationalist opinion. Without even the pretence of consultation, Viceroy Lord Linlithgow coolly announced that India was at war because Britain was at war. The INC protested and withdrew from cooperation in the provincial governments, eight of eleven of which it had controlled since the 1937 elections. The INC's decision was intended not just to register protest at the manner of India's entry into the war, but also to boost INC unity and refocus attention on the movement's aims, which had slackened off since power-sharing with the British had come about in the provinces, and dramatically to demonstrate the fact that the government paid far too little heed to an organization of such stature. The resignations were not supposed to signal a long-term withdrawal from the machinery of government, but the INC fully intended to make hay while the sun of British tribulation shone so brightly from the east. The effectiveness of the INC, however, was lessened by divisions within its ranks between moderates wanting to help Britain in return for major political concessions and those favouring neutrality and non-violent protest.

For his part, Churchill thought that the INC was attempting to profit from Britain's war-time difficulties. Given his ultimate supremacy in deciding Britain's India policy, the die was cast for a trial of strength between the Raj and its indigenous pretenders. The conservative Viceroy busied himself with a Revolutionary Movements Ordinance to deal decisively with unrest, while the more progressive Secretary of State in London, Leopold Amery, argued for a concession on the Indian right to frame a constitution, proposing full Dominion Status after the war.* What emerged was the flaccid August offer of 1940, rejected by all Indian parties. The All-India Congress of the INC pretty accurately concluded that Britain 'had no intention to recognize India's independence, and would, if they could, continue to hold this country indefinitely in bondage'. Linlithgow sharpened his ordinance and waited for any unrest to appear, whilst the INC contemplated a civil disobedience campaign. Though Gandhi launched an individual *satyagraha* for the right to speak freely against the war, some INC leaders did not want to impede the fight against fascism or make a move that would appear exclusively Hindu. In the year following the August offer, 23,000 people were arrested under the provisions of the Defence of India Act. As a gesture to the moderates in May 1941 the Viceroy proposed to establish an advisory National Defence Council and to appoint more Indians to his Executive Council. In the summer Indians came to form the majority on this council for the first time, but such tinkering did not amount to the substantial political concession that the INC leadership was demanding. So the British decided to sit it out, to impose direct rule in the provinces vacated by the INC, and to rely more than ever before on Muslim cooperation.[19]

All of the advances towards consultation and shared government since the First World War were threatened by this reversion to old-style imperialism. The cost of this imperial intransigence, and the suppression needed to quell the civil disobedience that was to come, would be great. It might not have been this way, and India might have enjoyed an easier war-time career, with less reliance placed upon it as an imperial military stronghold, if it had not have been for the imperial defeats in Malaya and Burma. These catastrophic defeats brought Britain's reputation to an all-time low, and India's security to its most precarious pass since the British themselves had marched across the subcontinent forging the Raj in the century between 1760 and 1860. The reorganization of the War Cabinet in London that followed imperial disasters in the East brought the Labour Party leader

---

* Amery was one of the most influential imperial politicians of his age, and a friend of Churchill since schooldays at Harrow. He had served as Secretary of State for the Colonies and Dominions in the 1920s, and with his All Souls fellowship, and membership of the Round Table movement, was an apostle of imperial federation.

Clement Attlee to prominence as Deputy Prime Minister, and Sir Stafford Cripps to a senior ministerial position. Cripps wasted no time in revisiting the Indian question that he had grappled with at length in the 1930s. The rise of Japan from December 1941 signalled a new period of bargaining and posturing by both sides. America also developed an interest in this prime area of imperial real estate, though Roosevelt trod carefully following Churchill's angry reaction on the subject of India's political future when it was broached at their Washington meeting over Christmas 1941. In February 1942 Chaing Kai-shek also stuck his oar in whilst on a visit to India. Churchill's reaction to this intervention, from a leader he considered to be grossly inflated beyond his or his country's significance by virtue of American foreign policy alone, can only be imagined.

The real breakdown of collaboration between the INC and the British came in 1942. Imperial disasters against the Japanese led the British government to attempt to gain solid INC backing for the war effort at this critical juncture in the Empire's history, and to derail international, domestic and nationalist criticism of British policy in India. To do this the British needed to buy Indian support and to show the Americans that all was being done to advance India's cause, as America was putting increasing pressure on Britain to 'do something' for India. Though British eyes rolled heavenwards at this thought, something at least cosmetic had to 'be done' to satisfy their well-meaning though self-seeking, ignorant yet powerful, Atlantic ally. America identified its own interests with those of human progress, and those of the British Empire with the obstacles to that onward march. Furthermore the Labour Party, now powerful in the British War Cabinet, had an Indian agenda of its own that it insisted be investigated when India began to appear increasingly on the Cabinet agenda.

These various pressures – American, British, Indian and Japanese – did indeed lead to something being done. The arch enemy of Indian advancement, Winston Churchill, allowed an unprecedented offer of post-war independence to be made, along with the war-time association of Indian politicians with the central government of the Raj. Indians were given an offer to frame their own constitution and decide for or against an independent future, within or without the Commonwealth. The very making of this offer was, of course, revolutionary, and whatever the tortuous political manoeuvrings that were to follow, this alone spelt the end of British rule in India, sooner rather than later. The offer was taken to India by Sir Stafford Cripps in the spring of 1942. He was authorized to offer Indian leaders immediate Dominion status or secession from the Empire at the end of the war (provided that no part was forced to join a new state, a nod in the direction of Muslim anxieties as well as those of the Princely States), in return for support for the war effort in the meantime. More seats on the Viceroy's Executive Council were held out as an immediate prospect. Major sticking-points included whether or not there would be Cabinet-style government with Indians exercising genuine responsibility, and whether or not Indian politicians would have a voice in defence matters. On the latter, of course, the British were unlikely to budge with the Japanese knocking at India's eastern doors, and the Commander-in-Chief India, General Wavell, was adamant that this could not happen. Cripps's efforts were hampered by the opposition of the Viceroy, who enlisted the support of Churchill and his Conservative Cabinet colleagues to limit what he could offer the Indians. Cripps was left feeling that he had been at least partially deceived as to the amount of negotiating room he actually enjoyed, and that his powers were inadequately explained to the Viceroy. Many Indians were left underwhelmed by the offer, Gandhi allegedly calling it 'a blank cheque on a crashing bank'. On 2 April 1942 Churchill signalled Cripps to spell out the fact that this was the final offer. A late American flourish saw Roosevelt's personal representative, Colonel Louis Johnson, arrive in Delhi. His meetings with Cripps and Nehru, however, led to exasperation in London, and Roosevelt was obliged to limit Johnson to his initial role as assessor of India's need for American war materials. Harry Hopkins in London had to extricate Johnson and the President's name from a potentially embarrassing situation, and Churchill was able to signal Cripps, one imagines with some relish, to say that Johnson had in fact no presidential backing beyond the munitions issue.

The Cripps Mission failed because of INC immobility and, it is claimed by some, Churchill's conservatism when it came to all matters Indian (and his fear of splitting the Conservative Party). Fundamentally, neither he nor Linlithgow would accept the fact that the end of the war would bring the end of the Raj. As Wavell, Linlithgow's replacement as Viceroy in 1943, recorded in his diary, 'the Cabinet is not honest in its expressed desire to make progress in India'.[20] Casting Churchill and his Viceroy as the villains, however, may well attribute more influence to them than is their due. In the end, the Cripps Mission failed because the offer was not considered attractive and secure enough for the INC to risk taking the chance of their demands being met after a war-time interlude.

On the most immediate level the Cripps Mission failed, and this was not entirely to Churchill's displeasure as a lot of capital could be made of the saga in the wider world. To the rest of the world, most importantly to America, it seemed as if the British had made a reasonable offer that had been unwisely rejected by the Indian leaders. As a result, Indian 'freedom' was off the Anglo-American agenda, for the duration at least. Churchill, whose views on India were notorious amongst those who did not share them, resisted major change to the way India was governed, even though other members of his Cabinet, including Cripps and Amery, had more modern views. Despite its failure, however, the Cripps Mission radically altered the Indian agenda. It had conceded independence in the very near future, and there was little likelihood of Britain being able to remain, even should it wish to, for long after the conclusion of hostilities. Other things had changed too, making it easier for the British to countenance Indian independence. For decades the British and Indian economies had been drifting apart, the Indian Army had ceased to be an imperial cost-free benefit, and by the end of the war Britain owed India well over a billion pounds. In proposing Indian independence, however, the British government still believed that India would remain in a loose orbit of British influence, even if it decided to leave the Commonwealth, and it was hoped that defence agreements would give the British a continued say in India's defence and security, and the base facilities to match.

Cripps's visit to India was set against the backdrop of the Japanese army's advance in Burma and the Japanese navy's raid on Ceylon, the Bay of Bengal and the west coast, internal disorder in India, a growing tide of refugees from the east, mounting unemployment, food scarcity, a growing sympathy for Japan and diminishing respect for Britain. Given India's apparent rejection of as reasonable an offer as it could expect to get in the middle of a war crisis (including even an offer to appoint an Indian to be Defence Coordination Member), it was not hard to justify vigorous repression of INC opposition that inhibited India's ability to aid the Allied war effort thereafter. And at the time, with India choc-a-bloc with British as well as Indian soldiers, the instruments of repression were close at hand, and the civil authorities were not afraid to use them in a way that would have been almost unthinkable in peacetime.

The British were ready when the 'Quit India' movement was launched shortly after the rejection of the Cripps offer. INC leaders were imprisoned, and the upsurge in civil disobedience was ruthlessly suppressed. Nearly sixty battalions took part in this, up to 2500 people were killed and 66,000 imprisoned. The INC was left leaderless with the imprisonment of the Working Party, the outlawing of all committees and the seizure of funds and offices. Not all in the INC favoured its tactics of uncompromising opposition, especially given the proximity of the Japanese army. Others, however, thought that the British presence made Japanese attack more likely, and were in favour of *any* means of getting the British out. Gandhi demanded that the British leave, but was prepared to see British troops remain to defend India. Of course, the INC stance exasperated many British residents and officials. It was plain stupidity, given the peril of a Japanese victory; it was also clearly disloyal to an imperial connection that was supposed, many thought, to be duly appreciated by the majority of right-thinking Indians. The 'Quit India' movement was not particularly well organized and was relatively easily suppressed. It was a movement of lower leaders, of the disaffected and of students. The communications infrastructure of the Raj – police stations, post offices, railways – was attacked at many points. The worst affected areas were Bihar, United Provinces and Bombay, and in some areas government temporarily lost control or was cut off – Tiger Moths of the Bihar Flying Club, for example, being employed to keep the Bihar administration in touch with one of its outlying districts. (Bihar was of particular concern because it was important in maintaining communications with the front line in Burma.)

British repression and the imprisonment of the INC leadership alienated many Indians who might otherwise have remained acquiescent, and support for the INC became more solid. One result of the alienation and imprisonment of the

INC leadership was an increasingly close relationship between the Government of India and the Muslim League. The isolation of the INC allowed the League to capture the Muslim majority provinces and do some telling spadework for the cause of a separate Pakistan (it became the party of government in Sind, Bengal, North-West Frontier Province and Assam). The British could ill afford to alienate the Muslims as well, especially given the fact that Muslims supplied most of the Indian Army's recruits. Wishing to retain Muslim support, Britain promised that Muslims would not have to endure rule by an all-India government of which they disapproved. The Cripps Mission had confirmed this by stating that no part of India would be forced into an independent state in whatever form of rule emerged in India after the war, dealing a blow to INC hopes of a federal – but united – independent India. Thus the foundation of a separate state for Muslims entered the world of real politics for the first time. Incredibly, the Muslim League's call for an independent Pakistan was first officially enunciated as late as 1940, during a speech by Mohammed Ali Jinnah in Lahore, a mere seven years before Pakistan came into being. There was also a Sikh campaign for regional autonomy, and the fears of Britain's oldest allies, the Princely States, were graphically demonstrated when the Standing Committee of the Chamber of Princes resigned in 1944. The Viceroy Lord Wavell promised that Britain would not abandon them, but the writing was on the wall. Thus the British held India firmly to the Empire by tackling the INC head on, though in doing so it stored up political troubles that would well once war imperialism ended when peace broke out.

In 1941 Burma had hardly any roads and was dominated by terrain intrinsically difficult to traverse. The Burmans were the colony's main ethnic group (about ten million) and during the war some of them were actively anti-British and willing to work with the Japanese. Many of Burma's people appeared simply indifferent to the war. Elements of some ethnic groups, however, were loyal to the British, or opposed to Japanese or Burman influence, and therefore prepared to support them. These ethnic groups included the four million Karens of the south and the hill peoples of the north, and the central plains population of about a million hill people, the Chins, Kachins and Nagas. There was also an immigrant population of about a million Indians, many of whom fled to India in 1942 as the tentacles of Japanese power spread across the country. The Burmans had ruled before the British conquest, and the Karens, mainly in the region of the Irrawaddy delta, were generally well disposed to British rule because it had removed Burman rule. The hill peoples were generally pro-British, and had for long provided the lion's share of the recruits for the territory's militia and police forces.

Burma was a low-priority British colony until it became one of the Empire's major battlegrounds in the Second World War and the key to defending India and halting the rapid Japanese advance that had swept Britain out of Malaya. Even if for little else, the Burma campaign is still remembered because it gave rise to two of the most renowned supply efforts of the war, one bringing succour to the beleaguered forces of Chiang Kai-shek in southern China, the other enabling Japan's Burma Area Army to import supplies overland from its South-East Asian conquests. On the former count the Burma Road was the only supply route linking the Chinese nationalist forces with the outside world, and its closure in 1940 led to the American airlift that throughout the rest of the war connected bases in Assam and Burma to Chunking, Chiang Kai-shek's capital. On the latter count, the infamous Burma–Thailand railway was constructed in order to supply the Japanese army fighting in Burma, and was to lead to the deaths of tens of thousands of Asian civilians and Allied servicemen in conditions that in many cases can only be described as barbaric.

Burma had traditionally been a feature on India's political and military map, not Britain's. Until 1937 Burma had been ruled by India, whose governors-general and viceroys had supervised its conquest between the 1820s and 1880s. In 1937 it became a separate colony administered by the new Burma Office in London. Therefore, administratively Burma fell between two stools in the late 1930s, no longer a part of India, its natural protector, and barely established on the White-hall scene or the mental map of imperial decision-makers in London. The same was also true in the sphere of strategic and military thinking. In 1940 Burma was divorced from India Command, its traditional military home, and made a respon-sibility of the newly-formed Far East Command, headquartered in distant Singapore. With the position in Singapore and Malaya considered impregnable, Burma's defence received little consideration, and Far East Command, in its brief history, had more pressing problems to worry about much closer to its Singapore home. No one, of course, expected Burma to be anywhere near the fighting until it was far too late to do anything about it. Before Japan entered the war, even though India Command had lost Burma, London informed the Commander-in-Chief in Delhi that it recognized that Burma would remain a vital concern of India, and that he should cooperate in the defence of Burma and the Bay of Bengal with his counterpart in Singapore, Commander-in-Chief Far East Air Chief Marshal Sir Robert Brooke-Popham. As soon as he became Commander-in-Chief India, General Wavell concluded that the arrangement was flawed, and in September 1941 went so far as to visit London to try and get Burma returned to India Command, without success.

Burma never had much of a chance, therefore, once the Japanese expansion of 1941–42 had proved so successful and Singapore had fallen. It was at the bottom of the pecking order for supplies and reinforcements from Britain, preoccupied as it was with the war in Europe, the Middle East and, third on the list, the defence of Malaya. Until 1941 the defence of Burma ranked lower than the defence of the West Indies, an extraordinary fact given the mighty scale of the fighting front that was to develop in Burma, involving millions of imperial, American, Chinese and Japanese servicemen. Strategically Burma was not viewed as important before the Japanese rampage began, and its resources were not particularly prized, except for its rice and oil production, the former of imperial significance, the latter regional (a vast range of colonies, from the Far East to the West Indies, suffered food shortages directly because of the loss of Burmese rice imports).

Late in the day Burma began to be viewed by regional commanders as of some strategic value. The Singapore Defence Conference of October 1940 acknowledged the importance of its resources, its significance as a staging post on the air route from the Middle East and India to Malaya and Singapore, and the enormous importance of Rangoon and the Burma Road for the supply of China (a factor which meant that Burma was also on Washington's map). This did not lead to any striking review of defence forces stationed in Burma, however, as it was not considered to be under particular threat until the Japanese occupied sites in French Indo-China in July 1941, and then it was far too late. Burma had become a strategic responsibility of Far East Command upon its creation in 1940, the worst possible time for such a move. With the extinction of that command following the fall of Singapore, and the quick death of its successor, Wavell's ABDA Command, India Command (Wavell's responsibility as well, despite his ABDA position) regained responsibility for its erstwhile eastern buffer province with precious little time to do much about adequately defending it. Burma had been caught between imperial stools: responsibility was tossed to Singapore a year before it was conquered, and then tossed back to India months after the Japanese crossed the border from Thailand into Burma. It was an imperial dog's dinner, born of Britain's overall failure to appreciate the scale of the Japanese threat, and Whitehall's unfamiliarity with the fledgling Burma colony, for so long part of the Raj.

Burma's military unpreparedness was shared by the general population. Late in the day air raid shelters were constructed and an ARP network organized, though many people had already begun to flee. On the military side, wireless sets, stores and the telephone network, as well as available air power, were wholly inadequate. The roads that existed were frequently blocked by refugees and non-combatant soldiers when the retreat of Burmacorps began, and there were no arrangements in place for military control of the railways and inland water transport. Burma was never supposed to be a war zone, so when, at the eleventh hour, it was recognized that it might become one, it had to join the back of the queue of imperial locations clamouring for divisions, squadrons and anti-aircraft guns. In that queue, Singapore was far ahead, and yet even that intended fortress and long-anticipated war zone could not get the modern machines it so desperately needed.

Despite Burma's lowly military status, some belated attempts were made to improve Burma's defences as the menacing Japanese threat to South-East Asia developed in the year before Pearl Harbor. If the position at Singapore had held, those military preparations, given the mushrooming demand for imperial defence assets all over the world, would almost certainly have been considered impressive. Given the call on the Empire's stretched military resources, the reinforcements sent were considerable. Although they were not enough to stem the

Japanese tide, they did go on to form the nucleus of the army that was eventually to drive the Japanese back from where they had come. Given the strategic
importance ascribed to Burma by the Singapore Defence Conference of 1940, it
was decided to provide some air cover, and as a result the Burma government's
Public Works Department constructed airfields, though, without an early
warning system like radar, they were to be of limited use. No. 221 Group RAF
was formed in Rangoon (later evacuated to Bengal) to organize these airfields
for emergency use, commanded by an Australian, Group Captain E. R. Manning.
On the army front, General William Slim arrived to take over in Burma as corps
commander in March 1942, having recently led the 10th Indian Division in Iraq
and Iran following his stint in East Africa. As part of Far East Command's
responsibilities from November 1940, Burma was a rather distant and unknown
province. Certainly from the RAF point of view, the Air Officer Commanding in
India would have been better placed to view the value of Burma's new airfields
than his counterpart in Singapore. To occupy the new airfields a squadron of
Blenheim bombers and a squadron of Brewster Buffalo fighters were sent, as the
imperial warehouses were emptied to cater for military shopping lists all over
the world. No. 60 (Blenheim) Squadron arrived at Mingaladon airfield near
Rangoon early in 1941. It later left for Malaya, leaving only No. 67 Squadron and
sixteen Brewster Buffaloes in Burma at the time of the Japanese attack. These
reinforcements were wholly inadequate given the scale of the Japanese assault
that was to come. This was little surprise at a time when Malaya and Singapore,
let alone less prioritized regions, were unable to get anything like the number or
the quality of aircraft that the local RAF commanders put as the bare minimum
necessary for a successful defence of the peninsula.

Not sufficient to tilt the scales in Britain's favour, but showing the right spirit
nonetheless, the Burma Volunteer Air Force threw the weight of its eleven Tiger
Moths behind the RAF. A fascinating American aspect to the air defence of Burma
was the formation of the American Volunteer Group, a force of one hundred
Curtiss P-40s (Tomahawks to the British) dedicated to the defence of the Burma
Road from Japanese aggression.[21] In June 1940 the British were compelled to close
the road from Rangoon through Mandalay and Lashio to Chunking. With the
closure of the Burma Road, the supply line to China could only exist by air, and
so the 10th USAAF was assigned to the theatre, with its headquarters established in
Delhi. Though Britain always had more aircraft in the India–Burma theatre than
America, the American build-up in the region was massive, and in one crucial
category – transport aircraft – American strength dominated. Not only were most
of the transport aircraft on the RAF's strength American-built, but the RAF and
the Fourteenth Army often needed help from American transport squadrons. (At
a crucial juncture in the battle for Imphal, Mountbatten, the Supreme Allied
Commander, was told by Churchill to keep hold of a number of borrowed
Dakotas that the Americans were asking to be returned.)

One of the most notable features of Burma's war role revolved around the issue of supply. British imperial victory in Burma in 1945 rested squarely on the ability to supply large concentrations of troops not accessible by overland supply routes. The Burma campaign became justly known as one in which the air supply of Allied forces proved decisive. It had been the issue of supply that had caused the Japanese to invade in the first place. Burma – via the port of Rangoon, the railway to Mandalay and Lashio, and then the Burma Road opened by the British in 1937 – was the only supply line between Chiang Kai-shek's Chinese government and the outside world. The Japanese wanted to occupy Burma to sever this line of communication via Rangoon and Lashio and thereby, it was hoped, destroy the last supply route between China and its distant supporters. The Japanese finally succeeded in cutting the Burma Road in May 1942.[22] Burma then became – again because of the issue of supply – an important theatre of Allied operations. Though Britain's main concern was to evict the enemy from Burma and defend India, America's substantial commitment to the region was entirely due to its desire to continue supplying Chiang Kai-shek's regime, and with the loss of Burma this had to be done by air from India. American ground forces, including the famous Merrill's Marauders, also served with Chinese and British imperial forces in China and northern Burma, and the American general Joe Stilwell commanded Chiang Kai-shek's forces on this front. When the situation permitted a new overland supply route to China was opened up. This was the Ledo Road, built at American insistence as part of Allied support for Chaing Kai-shek. It was a supply route and oil pipeline stretching for 478 miles from Ledo in India to Myitkyina in Burma, on to a connection with the old Burma Road terminating at Kunming in China. It took 17,000 Allied engineers to build, starting in late 1942, and was opened in early 1945.

It was the issue of supply that led to the Burma campaign's most tragic and most infamous episode, the use of Allied prisoners of war and conscripted indigenous civilians from across South Asia and South-East Asia for the construction of the Burma–Thailand railway (immortalized in British film history in *The Bridge on the River Kwai*, about the bridging of the Mae Klong river). Burmese, Indonesian, Malayan and Thai labourers were conscripted for its construction, and of their number approximately 90,000 out of 270,000 perished. Most of imperial prisoners of war destined to work on the railway were drawn from the 130,000 imperial troops captured during the Malayan campaign, though some came from camps in Java and Sumatra. Of the 64,000 Australian, British, Dutch and Indian prisoners employed on the railway, 12,000 failed to return to their homes after the war. Half of the 64,000 Allied troops were British, the largest contingent being from the 18th Division, an East Anglian Territorial Army unit which had arrived in Singapore just before its surrender.

The Japanese embarked upon the ambitious Burma–Thailand railway project because of the need to supply their extensive forces in Burma. Plans were first tabled by the headquarters of Southern Army in February 1942, receiving approval from Tokyo in June 1942. Between July 1942 and October 1943 the railway snaked north from Nong Pladuk in Thailand, through 260 miles of mountainous jungle to Thanbyuzayat in Burma. Though renowned for its horror and the death of a worker for every sleeper laid, experiences on the Burma–Thailand railway were not entirely uniform. For example, conditions in base camps were generally much better than those in jungle camps, and not all Japanese commandants and their staff were brutal. The relationship between Allied officers and their Japanese captors were very important in determining conditions. In negotiating a way of living in these most trying of conditions, the line between cooperation and collaboration was always a thin one. The Burma–Thailand railway was only the most notorious form of pressed labour in Japan's new Asian empire, and it is estimated that in the Burma–Thailand–Malaya region up to 100,000 women and girls became sex slaves.

As was the case in India, the Japanese attack from the east was not seen by British commanders until the eleventh hour. Before the Japanese arrived in French Indo-China, indeed, the focus of the Burma Rifles was upon possible service in Egypt and East Africa, following the traditional Indian Army practice of looking to aid an imperial war effort by deployment to the region of greater Suez. At headquarters in Mandalay officers even began to study mechanized operations in the desert. The outbreak of war caused little change in the tempo of life in Burma, and it was not until well into 1940 that events elsewhere began to affect the daily lives of the majority of Europeans or indigenous people in the country. The Burma Rifles was Burma's only fighting force at the start of the war against Japan, organized on Indian Army lines. The land forces in Burma were separate from the Indian Army and the British Army, as the territory had recently become responsible for its own defence. Because Burma was never considered a candidate for an attack by a major power, only small forces were maintained there, intended for little more than internal duties. Of course, the whole basis of defence in the region was the 'impregnable' Singapore. Japanese forces, should they ever be foolhardy enough to go to war, were not supposed to get anywhere near Burma.[23]

Expansion of the Burma Rifles began in 1940 when the 5th and 6th Burma Rifles (BR) were formed from cadres provided by the four existing battalions. An Officers Cadet School was established at Maymyo to train young British, Burmese and Anglo-Burmese men, many of them drawn from the territory's teak firms and the Burmah Oil Company. A seventh battalion was raised from the Civil and Military Police and an eighth from the Burma Frontier Force (the Burma Frontier Force was formed by six battalions of the Burma Military Police upon Burma's separation from India. Other units of the force were assigned to defend the principal airfields). The 9th BR was raised to train and hold reinforcements, the 10th BR as a depot establishment. The 11th and 12th battalions were territorial formations for line of communication duties and the 13th and 14th battalions were raised from the Shan states for the defence of those petty principalities. So expansion was considerable, though the Burma Rifles – known collectively as the 1st Burma Division from July 1941 – were paper tigers when compared with the seasoned Japanese infantrymen they were to face, and the rapid formation of new battalions had debilitated the strength of the original four. Burma's home-grown forces also lacked strength in essential departments like artillery. What artillery there was was manned by the European, Anglo-Burman and Anglo-Indian Burma Auxiliary Force. It operated the examination battery at the mouth of the Rangoon river with eighteen-pounder field guns and six–inch coastal defence guns, and also formed a heavy anti-aircraft regiment. Ethnic differences limited the effectiveness of some units of the Burma Rifles. Britain had recruited mainly from among the non-Burmese peoples of the country, who generally disliked the Burmans, their pre-British rulers. This meant that Chins, Kachins and Karens formed the martial stock on which recruiters traditionally drew. This state of affairs led to demands for more Burmans in the armed forces. So Governor Sir Reginald Dorman-Smith formed two new territorial battalions, and Burmans made their first appearance in the Burma Rifles.

Though the 7th Indian Division was transferred to Burma in February 1941, it did not represent anything like adequate reinforcement. At the time, however, it appeared impressive and the military establishment in Burma did not lack confidence in its ability. Furthermore, the message from London was that there was very little chance of the Japanese ever being foolish enough to go to war with the British Empire. Because of this confident assessment, the scale of the attack that was to fall on Burma in early 1942 was not even remotely forecast. In the light of British confidence that there was little chance of Japan going to war, the reinforcements sent to Burma seemed substantial, though their lack of appropriate training and organization was to be exposed by the size and the efficiency of the Japanese invasion when it came, as well as by Japanese air superiority and control of the seas. The newly-arrived Indian division, like the Burma Rifles, had been preparing for war in the desert. More land forces were despatched to Burma after Pearl Harbor and the sinking of HMS *Prince of Wales* and *Repulse*, as commanders and policy-makers finally grasped the scale of Japan's threat to the integrity of the British Empire. The 17th Indian Division was rushed in in January 1942, though it had also been training for war in the Western Desert. It is probably fortunate that Churchill did not succeed in persuading the Australian Prime Minister to allow the Australian divisions returning home from the Middle East to be diverted to reinforce Burma, because it is unlikely that their presence would have tipped the balance in Britain's favour.

In February 1942 the British 7th Armoured Brigade arrived as the last-minute build up continued, and Slim arrived fresh from Iraq to take over as commander of Burma Corps the following month. He and his superior, General Sir Harold Alexander, were charged by the Commander-in-Chief India, General Wavell, with ensuring that the army in Burma was not cut off, maintaining contact with the Chinese and securing the road from Assam to Burma via Imphal. On its official formation in April 1942 the Order of Battle of Burma Corps showed a fighting strength of 13,700 British, 37,000 Indian and 12,300 Burmese soldiers. At sea, Burma fell within the area of the Eastern Fleet, though, since its main capital ships had been sunk in December 1941, its Ceylon-based ships were not in a position to dominate in the Bay of Bengal and Burma's coastal waters. Control of the sea had passed to the Japanese, who were therefore able to use Burma's ports, particularly Rangoon, to build and supply their forces.

The Japanese 15th Army crossed from Thailand into Burma in December 1941 and took airfields in Tenasserim from which fighters were able to accompany bombers on raids over southern Burma. Air raids over Rangoon in January 1942 brought the port to a standstill. Two thousand civilians were killed over the Christmas period, and 100,000 fled overnight. Panic was fuelled by stories of fifth columnists and by clever Japanese radio broadcasts that mentioned the names of individuals known to be serving with the British forces and promising retribution on their families. These things had a devastating effect on civilians and the inexperienced troops that formed the majority of the newly-constituted Burma Army's ranks. Desertion was rife and it was tacitly accepted that a man could resume his civilian status if he so chose. The Japanese attacking force was superior in numbers to a Burma Army split between Tenasserim and the Shan States. The British rushed troops to defend Rangoon, which the Japanese reached on 8 February 1942, a prime target for capture as this major port city would effectively close Burma to the outside world, given the rudimentary state of communications in the India-Burma border region. Four extra brigades arrived in the six weeks before the city fell on 8 March 1942. The Japanese captured the bridge over the Sittang River intact. When they blew it, most of the 17th Indian Division was caught on the wrong side. The destruction of the 17th Indian Division doomed Burma's capital and with it went any hope of holding Burma. Burma Army retreated to the Irrawaddy valley in the centre of the country, the longest retreat in British military history. The Japanese pressed their attack in central Burma using forces released following victories in South-East Asia. The Japanese were able to develop their attack in the mountains and captured Lashio on 28 April 1942, closing the Burma Road. Four days later, after severe bombing, Mandalay was captured, and with it went control of central and northern Burma.

The formal decision to leave Burma and retreat to India was taken on 25 April 1942, though the codeword 'Caesar', signalling evacuation, had been broadcast in early March. Thus began the chaos of the retreat north, hundred of miles of jungle pathway, road and river to be traversed by demoralized troops and frightened civilians, most of it on foot. As many as 600,000 civilians fled by land and sea to India, perhaps 80,000 perishing on the way. On its journey to Imphal in India the army covered a thousand miles in three and a half months, first by road and rail to Prome and along the Irrawaddy valley. The RAF provided what cover it could for the retreating columns, as what remained of No. 221 Group moved by successive stages towards India. In contrast to the generally road-bound Burma Army, the Japanese moved across country at astonishing speed, and the Japanese advance was smoothed by almost total air superiority. Hunger, fear, dysentery, malaria, narrow mountain tracks and monsoon conditions were constant travelling companions for the soldiers and civilians fleeing north into India. As one of the soldiers who endured the British exit from Burma wrote:

> The Burma retreat was in a class of its own. It was horrible to witness a beautiful country being ravaged; to see innocent men, women, and children dying by the roadside; to experience the total collapse of a civilized administration; and to have the feeling that so many of the Burmese were glad to see the backs of us after more than half a century of British rule.[24]

Deserted villages were a common sight, and upon reaching Mandalay it was only to see that four-fifths of the fabled city already lay in ruins as a result of Japanese bombing. The British added to the destruction, smashing up or burning anything that might be useful to the advancing Japanese. The great oil wells at Yenangyaung were destroyed, thus closing off a valuable source of fuel to the imperial war effort and obliging India to rely ever more heavily upon Iranian production. Though this was headlong retreat on the part of the Burma Army, it was not quite defeat, and the administrative excision of the force from Burma demonstrated a great deal of clever improvisation. The front-line forces commanded by Slim, keeping in touch with the rearguard and fighting delaying actions, retreated in good order, though this was in contrast to some of the rearguard forces, which disintegrated into groups of roving brigands.

Contact with the Japanese was finally broken at Shwegyin, and the retreat took on the character of a race up the Kabaw valley towards Tamu in the face of the advancing Japanese and the approaching monsoon. On 19 May 1942 Burma Corps crossed into India at Tamu. About 4000 of the imperial troops who had begun the campaign had died. A further 9000 were missing, mainly Burmese soldiers who had deserted. The main strength of the 17th Indian Division had been captured on the Sittang River. Only one Burmese battalion – about a thousand men – arrived in India, and the battered survivors of the Burma Army finally concentrated at Hoshiapur in the Punjab. Slim's 45,000 had been reduced to 25,000, and all but twenty-eight of his 150 guns had been lost. The indigenous Burmese soldiers were given the option of staying in the army or returning home, and about half decided to leave (later in the war the 2nd BR was to provide reconnaissance units for the Chindits). The treatment of the remnants of the Burma Army when they reached India was shocking, and many men suffered the indignities of being left without adequate billets or being cold-shouldered at the bar: for many armchair soldiers still sitting comfortably in India, these men were a disgrace to the British Empire, and a scruffy one at that. As ignominy closed in upon the remnants of the Burma Army, most of Burma itself settled down to over two years of Japanese occupation and sporadic, but steadily mounting, bombing and fighting as the Allies sought to reverse the decision of March-April 1942.

Once in India, the monumental task of rebuilding, retraining and expanding the army for the return match began. This saw the build up in India of hundreds of thousands of men, aircraft and all necessary equipment and supplies, along with the transformation of India's transport network. It took time, which inevitably brought pressure from Whitehall and Downing Street to 'do something'. A premature Anglo-Indian offensive took place in the Arakan region of coastal Burma between October 1942 and May 1943, though the Japanese drove the imperial forces back and defeated the 14th Indian Division. Slim was prevented from taking part in this campaign by his superior, General Irwin, though on 10 March 1943 he was sent by him to report on the situation and, on 5 April when Irwin finally appreciated how bad the situation was, Slim was ordered to Chittagong to supervise the orderly retreat of the defeated imperial forces. Slim, subsequently placed in operational command of all land forces dedicated to Burma's recapture, had the initial task of securing the Indian border before a renewed offensive could be contemplated. Wavell had appointed him commanding officer of Fifteenth Corps under General Irwin's Eastern Area Army (which eventually became Fourteenth Army), responsible for the seaward defences of Calcutta. At that time naval and air defences were extremely weak and offensive power on land, sea and air incapable of ejecting the Japanese. There was also a major supply problem to overcome as all rail and road links to the Burma front were centred on Calcutta in the Bengal province, where the worst nationalist outbreaks were to take place. As the British mustered their forces following the exit from Burma, and looked to the security of India's eastern border, they were also compelled to deploy an astonishing fifty-seven battalions on internal security duty as the 'Quit India' movement got under way following the failure of the Cripps Mission of March–April 1942.

There were many complicated plans for British operations in the South Asia and South-East Asia theatre, which consumed a great deal of time at SEAC and India Command headquarters, as well as in Whitehall among the Prime Minister, Chiefs of Staff and the service departments of state, and at the numerous Top Two meetings between Churchill and Roosevelt and their respective top brass. Some favoured amphibious attacks in Malaya, others cherished the idea of a landing in Sumatra, some backed a Burma only strategy, and others thought that Asia should be de-emphasized and British efforts be concentrated upon a re-entry into the Pacific, a proposal to which some, notably powerful American naval commanders, were hostile. In these plans, American voices had to be considered, for reasons of alliance cooperation, but also because America was dominant in the war against Japan, and by 1944, Britain was dependent to a large extent upon American economic and military aid around the world. In many respects America had the final say in shaping British planning because of this dependence, for example, in its control of so much of the merchant shipping in the eastern theatres. Many of the British plans, despite the resources lavished on them, came to nothing, or faltered on irritating but decisive details, like the perennial absence of (American manufactured and controlled) landing craft with which to mount large-scale amphibious assaults. Complicating all planning was the divergent perspectives of powerful individuals involved, and the politicking that surrounded such strategic decision making.[25]

To a large extent, despite the planning deliberations, Britain's main actions in the Asian theatre in the last years of the war were shaped by events beyond British control, in particular the decision of the Japanese to launch a major offensive in Burma and the American use of atomic weapons. Throughout 1943 British strength in India grew, in the air and on land, depending for its growth on continued British control of the Indian Ocean's convoy routes and the massive infrastructural development taking place on the Indian home front. A new command structure was created to relieve India Command of the burden of planning and sustaining operations in Japanese-occupied Burma and South East Asia whilst also keeping India's society, economy and huge army at the highest possible pitch of war efficiency. In June 1943 the Chiefs of Staff decided to separate Burma from India Command so that a separate commander could have charge of all offensive operations in the region, including the reconquest of Malaya. Thus in October 1943 South East Asia Command (SEAC) was formed, charged with the task of increasing pressure on Japanese forces and compelling Tokyo to move troops eastward from the Pacific, of maintaining the supply route to China and opening a land supply route through northern Burma and ejecting the Japanese from their conquered possessions. Mountbatten, the man chosen to become the region's supreme Allied commander, soon moved South-East Asia Command's headquarters from Delhi to Kandy in Ceylon. He was not only responsible for the war in Burma but also for the reinvasion of Malaya, the Dutch East Indies and French Indo-China.

Mountbatten, whether as a destroyer commander, Chief of Combined Operations, Supreme Allied Commander, Viceroy of India or Chief of the Defence Staff, always invoked opposites of passion. One thing he did for SEAC was to go to great lengths to improve morale among the troops under his command, famously through his planned 'impromptu' soapbox addresses to men in the field, by his attention to medical improvements, his determination to beat the Japanese at their own game, to fight through the monsoon and through initiatives like the publication of the troop newspaper SEAC News. He also managed to work well with General Stilwell, the acerbic and irascible American officer appointed as his deputy, who also commanded American and Chinese forces. Augmenting his suitability for this top job, Mountbatten played well to Americans back home because of his looks, charisma, modernity and vaunted royal connections. Naturally, he was not to everyone's taste. His naval commander, Admiral Sir James Somerville of the Eastern Fleet, left his position in the summer of 1944 (to become head of the British Admiralty Delegation in Washington) after warring with

Mountbatten for months. Somerville – in terms of age, length of service and experience very much Mountbatten's naval superior – found it difficult to respect him and some of his command methods, and vigorously defended his position as an independent Commander-in-Chief reporting direct to the Admiralty, not subordinate to Mountbatten's command and the Chiefs of Staff committee to which it reported. (The problem faced by Somerville was that the region's senior commanders – the Commander-in-Chief India as well as Mountbatten – erroneously believed Somerville to be their subordinate. He was, however, only answerable to them in certain circumstances, whilst in others he remained a proper commander-in-chief answerable only to the Admiralty in London). More generally, many naval officers found it very difficult to appreciate Mountbatten's rise to full admiral and supreme commander when he had had no experience of commanding anything larger than a destroyer flotilla, and that with equivocal results. General Bernard Montgomery, not a fan of Mountbatten either, wrote that he 'was, of course, quite unfit to be a Supreme Commander. He is a delightful person, has a quick and alert brain and has many good ideas. But his knowledge of how to make war is really NIL'. In men like William Slim, however, Mountbatten had wise heads around him, and he was an efficient administrator, planner and public relations expert. In order to accomplish the tasks given to SEAC upon its creation, three new offensives were planned: a fresh push in the Arakan; a thrust into central Burma from Imphal in India; and in the north a Chinese, American and British attack to try and open a land route to China. (Stilwell commanded two Chinese divisions, the American brigade known as Merrill's Marauders and several brigades of Chindits.) [26]

The biggest of these planned operations – the thrust into central Burma – was overtaken by the decision of the commander of the Japanese Burma Area Army, Lieutenant-General Kawabe Masakuza, to strike into India in the hope of precipitating a civilian revolt against British rule, whilst also capturing the major British supply dumps around Dimapur. Thus began the decisive phase of the Burma campaign. The first major battle developed in the Arakan, where the planned Anglo-Indian offensive was getting under way. The Japanese mounted what was supposed to be a diversionary attack (Ha-Go) in February 1944, and met for the first time with determined resistance that did not crumble when surrounded. Supplied by air, two Indian divisions defeated the Japanese attack and enabled the Allied attack to resume, a significant defensive victory known as the Battle of the Admin Box.

The main Japanese thrust towards India began in March 1944 when the 15th Army under Lieutenant-General Mutaguchi Renya headed for Imphal and Kohima (U-Go). Imperial forces in front of Imphal avoided being surrounded, and superior numbers and superior firepower, air support and supply, lifted the Japanese siege. The small hill town of Kohima commanded Imphal's supply routes, which the Japanese were trying to cut and which they anticipated capturing in order to ease their own supply difficulties and sustain the campaign against the British in India. General Slim welcomed this attack, for it would permit his forces to engage the enemy on a field of their own choosing. The Imphal plain had been marked as the killing field, and there the Fourteenth Army could stand and meet the Japanese charge, with one of the world's biggest supply complexes at its rear. The Japanese, by contrast, were at the very end of a lengthy supply line snaking back into South-East Asia and even further afield, across the seas to the home islands themselves. To compound the difficulties that the Japanese had to face, the Allies had increasing air superiority in the region and became adept at maintaining units in the field by air drops alone. At this stage in the war at sea, the Eastern Fleet was ceaselessly hunting for the increasingly rare Japanese ships and coasters that attempted to supply or evacuate Japanese troops. What developed was a battle in which the Japanese army slowly expended itself in increasingly desperate attacks. Slim reinforced the Kohima garrison and a defensive box was formed nearby. Crammed into it were thousands of imperial troops holding out against the waves of Japanese attacks. These battles were characterized by the most bloody and enclosed type of fighting, men unable to raise their heads above foxhole level without being shot at, living for weeks amongst rotting corpses and incorporating them into defensive construction work, and mounting and repelling bayonet and sword charges. This massive battle was fought across a miniature battlefield, where things like the local district commissioner's bungalow and tennis court became egregious landmarks to be fought over, and then fought over again. Both Kohima and the box were surrounded by the Japanese, but supplies were maintained by air. On 14 April 1944 the box was relieved, and on 18 April relief for Kohima arrived when an entire division was flown in following the Fourteenth Army's defensive victory in the Arakan. In vicious fighting the Japanese were driven back, until against orders they began to withdraw from Kohima at the end of May 1944. Imphal was then relieved on 22 June 1944 by an advance from Kohima.

Further hampering Japanese operations was the fact that by this time the naval situation in the waters around Burma, and connecting this Japanese theatre of operations to main bases like Singapore and the home islands, was far less favourable. Fewer and fewer Japanese warships were available to operate in this area, and Japan's merchant marine had been decimated. In 1943–44 the strength of the Royal Navy's Eastern Fleet grew substantially and was better placed to assist British land forces and harry what Japanese shipping there was. With its fortunes improving, the Eastern Fleet was able to hunt Japanese ships attempting to supply or evacuate its forces, and to aid Fourteenth Army's operations, for example in the Arakan offensive of early 1944. In the final year of the Burma campaign the Eastern Fleet was dominant at sea and Japanese vessels reduced to coastal creeps and optimistic dashes as they tried to keep scattered Japanese forces provisioned and in touch. With hardly anything left of its merchant marine, the Japanese made use of small wooden vessels as they tried desperately to keep a trickle of supplies flowing between garrisons and battle fronts in the region, though British submarines in particular took a heavy toll of such craft. Contributing to British naval forces in the region, the Burma Royal Naval Volunteer Reserve manned five motor launches and a few auxiliary vessels. An Arakan Inshore Flotilla was formed by the Royal Navy, and an Inland Water Transport Service was started on the Irrawaddy and Chindwin rivers.

On land, generals Mutaguchi and Kawabe agreed that no further offensive operations were possible. The Japanese 15th Army had been effectively destroyed. Kohima severely undermined Mutaguchi's planned offensive, whilst at the same time helping Slim. In the course of the attack 53,000 of the Japanese invading force of 85,000 had become casualties, 30,000 of them killed. The way was clear for Slim to advance into Burma, and British imperial forces were from that point on sure of victory. Meanwhile in the north Chindits were athwart the Japanese lines of communication, and on 17 May 1944 the Americans took Myitkyina airfield, from where supplies could be flown to China. Chinese troops advanced into Burma from Yunnan Province. From April 1944 the Japanese had been engaged in a major offensive (Ichi-go), aimed at taking Allied airfields in southern China. The offensive was called off in January 1945, however, and the Chinese began counter-offensives which were to drive the Japanese back to the South China Sea.

The Fourteenth Army crossed the Chindwin river in December 1944, and in the same month Ramree Island was captured in a combined operation. General Slim commanded more than six divisions in a fighting force totalling 260,000 men. In early 1945 Slim crossed the Irrawaddy in central Burma in pursuit of the 15th Army, recently defeated at Imphal. Japanese forces were pinned down in Mandalay after a British deception measure created a bogus headquarters and the belief that imperial forces were about to move to capture the city. Instead, Slim feinted and made for Meiktila, the heart of the Japanese army's communications and supplies, opposed only by INA units. Meiktila fell on 4 March 1945 and over 20,000 Japanese bodies were counted. This attack was supported by amphibious operations in the Arakan that secured airfields from which to support the assault on Rangoon. With Katamura's army pinned down around Mandalay, the Burma area commander ordered Meiktila to be recaptured. Though Indian Army troops were cut off at Meiktila, they were supplied and reinforced by air, and on 28 March 1945 the Japanese withdrew. This battle opened the way to Rangoon, which was recaptured on 3 May 1945. The recrudescence of British naval power in the Bay of Bengal was illustrated during the assault on Rangoon when the landings were covered by the battleships HMS *Queen Elizabeth* and *Richelieu*, the carriers HMS *Shah* and *Empress*, the cruisers HMS *Cumberland*, *Suffolk*, *Ceylon* and *Tromp*, and the destroyer HMS *Venus*. The Japanese army in Burma had been crushed, and approximately 190,000 Japanese soldiers had died in the region. Given that Burma was not even on the initial wish-list of the Japanese Greater East Asian Co-Prosperity Sphere, the Burma campaign represented a classic case of imperial overstretch.

For the British it was ironic that victory in Burma should have come via a major overland offensive, because Mountbatten and his SEAC planners had for long envisaged the major assault on the Japanese as being launched from the sea, with amphibious landings in Burma and Malaya. Rather than dragging a debilitating land campaign from India towards Rangoon, the simple option had appeared to be an amphibious assault. It was thought that the only way to reconquer Burma was a holding operation in the north, reconquest of the Arakan to provide forward bases and airfields, amphibious landings in Rangoon and a final battle to the death in central Burma against a surrounded foe. Arguments about operations in this region bedevilled British strategy. Whitehall and the Chiefs of Staff could not decide on a plan. British and American visions differed, Churchill insisting on defeating Japanese forces in South-East Asia to expunge the stain of earlier imperial defeats, whilst the Chiefs of Staff were just as keen to send significant forces to help the Americans in the Pacific. Churchill preferred to concentrate on South-East Asia, because the Americans could take the Pacific alone, though the Chiefs of Staff's idea was that as an ally Britain was bound to help America in the Pacific, thereby retaining some strategic influence in the region in the inevitably American-dominated post-war world. For Churchill, America was a threat to be guarded against, whereas for the Chiefs of Staff it was an ally to be supported and, where possible, influenced. Though the British political and military leadership was unable to decide on a coherent overarching strategy for Britain's part in the war against Japan, at the theatre level an amphibious invasion of South-East Asia was hamstrung by more practical considerations. Sufficient numbers of landing craft were never available, as the demands of first the Mediterranean and then Normandy took priority; so a land campaign came to the fore by default. SEAC's centrepiece was for long supposed to be the amphibious reconquest of Malaya, known as Operation Zipper. This invasion went off rather half-cocked, however, because the atomic bombs brought about a precipitate Japanese surrender. By the end of the war the forces under Mountbatten's command were enormous. In April 1945 SEAC commanded a military force of 1,304,126 men, including a military labour force of 11,000 from India and Ceylon. This was supplemented by 413,000 civilian workers.

A significant Burmese military force came into existence to fight the British, though, like the Indian National Army, large sections of it changed sides late in the war and fought against the Japanese, its erstwhile sponsors. Unlike in India, however, the Japanese and their collaborators had the chance to experiment with new political institutions, given the fact that they were the dominant power in a colony denuded of British personnel and therefore British authority, apart from in a few remote border regions. The Japanese found ready collaborators from among sections of the Burmese population that had never approved of British rule. Some groundwork had been accomplished well in advance of the Japanese conquest. Ba Maw, the Prime Minister of Burma until March 1939, maintained contact with the Japanese until arrested by the government in August 1940 and gaoled for sedition. Ba Maw's main crime had been to form, together with numerous Thakins (students of Rangoon University), the anti-war Freedom Bloc. Similarly, in early 1941 young dissidents led by Aung San visited Japan for training in resistance to British rule. Aung San had, since the outbreak of war in Europe, been touring the country and India talking to nationalist associations and ordinary people. The Thakins were trained on Hainan Island, a Chinese possession 300 miles south of Hong Kong occupied by the Japanese, and were to return to Burma with the Japanese as the 'thirty heroes'. Also in 1941, like counterparts in other imperial territories, Prime Minister U Saw had invoked the Atlantic Charter in calling for immediate self-government. In December 1941 he visited London in an effort to negotiate post-war independence. On his return journey British intelligence decrypts revealed 'inappropriate' discussions with a Japanese diplomat in Lisbon, and upon arrival in Burma he was arrested and interned in the Seychelles. In February 1941 a Japanese officer named Colonel Suzuki Keiji formed a secret organization, Minami Kikan, to prepare for armed insurrection with the object of closing the Burma Road. The young nationalist leader Aung San fled to Japanese-occupied China in August 1940, and three months later met Colonel Suzuki in Tokyo. They then worked together on the formation of a military force, the Burma Independence Army (BIA), which came into being in December 1941 and numbered about 18,000 a year later. On returning from exile Aung San placed the BIA at the disposal of Japan. So, even before Japanese troops crossed into Burma in late December 1941, the British administration was faced with an array of moderate and extreme forms of political, ideological and paramilitary opposition.[27]

Thereafter small BIA columns led the Japanese invasion into Burma and Thailand. About 1300 BIA fought against the retreating British imperial forces, suffering significant casualties and losing about 300 to desertion. After this the BIA followed behind the Japanese and attempted to establish civilian administrations in some parts of Burma. This amounted to little more than mob rule. Atrocities were common, irritating the Japanese because they did not want petty Burmese self-rule squabbles making their occupation any more difficult. The BIA was not successful in garnering nationalist support, as most of its operations were in the south among minority populations who did not share the indigenous Burmans desire for independence from the British. The Japanese eventually tired of the ineffectual BIA and in July 1942 it was dissolved. Aung San, given the rank of major-general in the Japanese army, headed a new 3000-strong Burma Defence Army, trained and equipped by the Japanese. This became the 10,000-strong Burma National Army (BNA) when Burma became 'independent' in August 1943. Aung San duly became the Minister of Defence in the new government. Many of the deserters from the Burma Army during its retreat towards India responded to Aung San's call to join the BNA and fight under the Japanese against the British. Illustrating the kind of 'equality' new subjects could expect to enjoy in the Greater

East Asian Co-Prosperity Sphere, all ranks of the BNA were required to salute all ranks of the Imperial Japanese Army, no matter how lowly, and the penchant of Japanese soldiers for face slapping extended to their new allies, as well as their imprisoned enemies, and did little to endear them to the Burmese collaborators.

The Japanese had ended Ba Maw's sojourn behind bars when they invaded Burma, and appointed him head of the country's civil administration, continuing the logical Japanese policy of trying to rule newly-conquered territories through groups that the defeated imperial power had sought to suppress. In May 1942 Thakin Tun Oke, a dissident trained by the Japanese, had been appointed head of a central government, but he was replaced in August 1942 by a more extensive civil administration headed by Ba Maw. In June 1943, anticipating difficult times ahead in the face of Allied counter-offensives, the Japanese Prime Minister declared his government's intention to delegate responsibility for civil administration in parts of the new-found empire. Thus on 1 August Burma duly became 'independent' under Ba Maw. He promptly declared war on the Allies and formed a one-party state. Specialists suggest that Japanese state-building was probably furthest advanced in Burma because in that country they found sympathetic collaborators from among the Burman population, and because many of the people who identified with British rule had fled the country and made for India. (As an Indian province until as recently as 1937, many of the people involved in ruling Burma were Indians anyway; a further weak point in Britain's hold on the colony.) The grant of 'independence' deserves its inverted commas, for the Japanese did not relax their grip on the levers of power and their intentions were to extend the Japanese Empire, not to create genuinely independent nation states from the ruins of the European empires. Ministers in Burma's new government had little else to do but dream, order stationery and send telegrams on the birthdays of prominent Axis leaders. They could, nevertheless, accomplish a lot of work at the local level. Ba Maw developed fascist-style youth leagues and got the country's Buddhist leaders to appoint 1500 preachers to tour Burma lecturing against the return of the British.

Japanese political initiatives were aimed squarely at gaining and keeping the indigenous collaborators upon which any type of empire depends. In doing this, the Japanese were compelled to make do with the tools to hand, and there were numerous left-overs from the years of British rule that they did not have time to change. Ba Maw's government rested on personnel and administrative methods from the British period, and indirect rule continued in the more remote districts. The occupation of Burma by a Japanese army limited this experiment in self-government for the people of Burma. In fact, having sampled the mixed blessings of Japanese occupation and nominal Burmese rule, by 1944 many Burmese people who had actively sided with the Japanese were secretly working against them, and in August of that year Aung San formed the Anti-Fascist Organization (AFO). This was an amalgamation of the BNA and the Burma Communist Party, dedicated to fighting the Japanese. With SOE encouragement, the AFO switched sides and took part in numerous operations against the Japanese in the latter stages of the war. At end of the war Aung San was a significant nationalist leader, certainly not a Japanese puppet. When he shifted sides in March 1945, he brokered a deal with Mountbatten whereby the BNA (now Patriotic Burmese Forces) were to be incorporated into a new Burma Army. Mountbatten told Sir Oliver Leese, Commander-in-Chief Allied Land Forces South East Asia, to rescind the order prohibiting the arming of Burmese anti-Japanese forces. Given the status afforded Aung San and his BNA supporters by Mountbatten, it was no surprise that returning colonial officials viewed him with ill-disguised contempt, considering him a war criminal for aiding the Japanese war effort. But his movement was a genuine threat to the return of British authority, and the colonial government would quickly learn that it had to meet and come to terms with Aung San; he could not be ignored or sidelined. This was acknowledged when the new Governor gave him considerable power through the Executive Council.

The colonial government of Burma remained in existence throughout the war, in exile in the Indian hill station of Simla. For as well as planning for the return of the British to their conquered domain, the colonial administration still had a job to do administering the parts of Burma not occupied by the Japanese. This meant border regions like the Chin Hills, the Upper Chindwin and the Naga Hills District, where the deputy commissioners of the Government of Burma went about their normal civil duties. The Chin Levies were organized by colonial officials, and the entire frontier region was placed under the charge of a commissioner with headquarters in Assam, ruling a stretch of country containing about 300,000 inhabitants. A major challenge for the British administrators in the region was the need to develop it so that supplies could make their way over the hills from India into areas normally only accessible from the Burma side of the border.

Another part of Burma where British administration continued to operate after the withdrawal of the Burmacorps and the advance of the Japanese was in the coastal Arakan region. This was because British counter-offensives in the Arakan temporarily cleared the Japanese out of areas that then required the reconstitution of civil administration. This area was heavily marked by the advance–retreat pattern of combat in the region, and the removal of the rule of law meant that communal violence was liable to erupt. In June 1942 the Burma Independence Army, advancing into the region with the Japanese, reached Buthidaung and looted the treasury for distribution to the poor. Communal violence and looting had accompanied the original British withdrawal. Arakanese Buddhists massacred Chittagonians, and Chittagonian Muslims massacred Arakanese. The Chittagonians fled north towards India, while the Arakanese moved further south. In northern areas, where Muslims predominated, all Buddhist pagodas and monasteries were destroyed. In the absence of civilian administration Chittagonian communities established Peace Committees, with a central committee at Maungdaw.[28]

The British military administration that came to operate in this region made contact with these committees as the army re-entered the Arakan and tried to re-establish order. The British needed local labour and local produce. For the region's many refugees camps were built, as well as roads and airstrips for the forces increasingly transiting in the region. In April-May 1943 there followed in the wake of the army at least 30,000 Chittagonians who were hoping to return to their homes as the Anglo-Indian forces advanced down the Mayu peninsula. Bringing turmoil upon turmoil, when these forces again retreated later on as the first Arakan offensive failed, the people fled for a second time towards India, aided by the military administration. In this heyday of improvised military administration attention was given to civil intelligence, public health and criminal justice, as Civil Affairs (Burma), created by the Commander-in-Chief India in February 1943, attempted to get to grips with its tasks using sixty-eight officers spread across the Arakan. Meanwhile, back in Simla, the Governor of Burma, Sir Reginald Dorman-Smith, and his staff busied themselves with plans for the eventual return of British rule. The constitutional plans being drawn up, however, which envis-aged offering Burma Dominion status, were out of date before the ink was dry, and the anticipated post-war withdrawal of Britain from India meant that London was going to be keen to find a smooth exit from Burma too.

The war had been a disaster for many people in Burma, uprooted as the country was fought over twice, once when the Japanese swept northwards and again when imperial, American and Chinese forces turned them back. In some outlying districts, where fighting did not take place and to which the exactions of the Japanese occupation did not extend, life was able to continue with a semblance of normality. The effects of Japanese occupation were somewhat less-ened by manpower shortages and the fact that Japan's military position began to deteriorate almost as soon as its forces had secured Burma. The Japanese army in Burma found itself at the end of a very long supply route stretching back to the centres of Japanese power and the home islands. Therefore the Japanese had less energy and fewer resources for setting about Burma as enthusiastic new colonial masters. With Japan lacking the means to transport many of Burma's exports, the domestic economy was neglected, leading to economic dislocation even in areas spared the full horrors of fighting and occupation. The loss of Burmese rice was felt far and wide throughout the Empire. Mauritius, Ceylon, East Africa, India, the Middle East and the West Indies were among the regions that had imported food from the Empire's biggest rice bowl.

As it happened, Burma was reconquered before Britain's South-East Asian jewels, Malaya and Singapore, were freed from Japanese rule. It had, of course, been the breathtaking imperial defeat at Singapore in February 1942 that had thrown open the door to Burma and India itself.

13

South-East Asia and the Far East

'Awful news from Singapore – can't quite understand why we are doing so badly', wrote the Chief of the Imperial General Staff, General Sir Alan Brooke, days before the island surrendered to numerically inferior Japanese forces. 'I have during the last ten years had an unpleasant feeling that the British Empire was decaying and that we were on a slippery decline! ... We are paying a heavy price for failing to face the insurance premiums essential for security of an Empire!'[1] The failure to keep up with imperial insurance premiums in the years of collective security and naval disarmament that followed the First World War meant that, when Japan threatened war against the Eastern Empire, Britain could only send two battleships as a deterrent. The new and inexperienced battleship HMS *Prince of Wales* and the ageing battle cruiser *Repulse* were sent to the bottom by Japanese bombers within days of their arrival at the great Singapore naval base from which they were supposed to operate in order to see off the enemy, the whole point of the Singapore strategy. Britain's abject defeat in the East, culminating in the surrender of Singapore, showed more than just a failure to pay the premiums for effective imperial defence. It revealed a poverty of strategic thinking and an ostrich-like ignorance of the capabilities of this new, non-European enemy, and of the revolution in warfare that had been brought about by the aircraft carrier that Britain, typically, had pioneered in order for others fully to develop.

Like Cairo and Delhi, Singapore was a major imperial power centre, but one that failed. Fortunately, the British could fall back upon Ceylon as a base from which to defend their vital imperial sea routes, but this was never supposed to have been the case. Singapore was designed to be the beacon of eastern imperial strength, the base from which a powerful Royal Navy squadron could defend far-flung imperial responsibilities in the Indian Ocean, the Pacific and the Far East, and see off all challengers.[2] The loss of the battleships in December 1941 and the surrender of 'Fortress' Singapore and its huge garrison of imperial troops two months later define the popular memory of Britain's war in South-East Asia and the Far East.[3] Given those two massive events – redolent with symbolism at the time and charged with extra meaning by the false wisdom of hindsight – accounts of British strategy in the East before the war are dominated by the rights and wrongs of the 'Singapore Strategy', and the painful ruminations about the size of the fleet that Britain would be able to send to Singapore if Japan turned to war. After the loss of Malaya and Singapore, historical attention tends to turn to the post mortem, an assessment of why the British and their imperial allies did quite so badly in the face of a numerically inferior enemy that, at the time of the surrender, had passed its offensive peak. Inevitably, focus on culpable individuals takes a central role here, and attention is switched variously from Churchill to Air Chief Marshal Sir Robert Brooke-Popham (Commander-in-Chief Far East), Lieutenant General Arthur Percival (GOC Malaya), Sir Shenton Thomas (Governor of the Straits Settlement and High Commissioner of the Federated and Unfederated Malay States) and Duff Cooper (Cabinet-ranking Resident Minister for the Far East).[4]

Singapore was *not*, however, the be all and end all of the imperial war effort in the East. There were other British territories in the region, notably Hong Kong, Labuan, Brunei, Borneo and Sarawak, and British imperial interests had for a century been lodged in Chinese mainland enclaves like Shanghai and Tientsin. Here, as in the Malay peninsula, crushing defeat was to be the imperial experience, followed by years of Japanese occupation and an eventual British return, triumphant but to a landscape irrevocably altered by war. At the end of the war British forces under Mountbatten's South East Asia Command (SEAC) also assumed responsibility for the transfer of power from the Japanese in French Indo-China and the Dutch East Indies. With so much attention focused on Britain's imperial defeats in the Eastern Empire in 1941–42, it is important not to forget that all of Britain's territories in South-East Asia and the Far East contributed for over two years to the Empire's global war effort prior to the commencement of hostilities with Japan in December 1941, and that, once lost, British attention and British forces were concentrated on regaining them. Prior to the fall, like their colonial peers around the world, these imperial territories supplied valuable resources, personnel for the armed forces and military and intelligence-gathering facilities. Even after Japan had conquered this Eastern Empire, stretching from Burma to Shanghai by way of Borneo, behind-enemy-lines resistance continued, and in places like Malaya a popular guerrilla movement developed which sought any means by which to kill Japanese soldiers and thereby hasten the end of their hated occupation. Meanwhile Britain's regional commands in India and Ceylon, constantly harried by that impatient human superpower in Downing Street, made their plans for a British reconquest. A war in Malaya was supposed to be the centrepiece of Britain's triumphant involvement in the defeat of the Japanese war empire, though, as things turned out, Burma was to provide the venue for this process of revenge and reconquest. Whilst giving all due attention to the sorry story of the fall of Malaya, it is also important to consider the other territories of Britain's Eastern Empire, and their contribution to the war effort before the lights went out from Hong Kong to Sarawak to Singapore, their trials under Japanese occupation, and British attempts to reconquer them.

The fall of Singapore was an intrinsically imperial disaster. Its surrender marked the most dramatic loss in British imperial history since Yorktown in 1782, meaning as it did that Britain's Empire east of India had become a part of the new empire of Japan. It massively increased the prospect of enemy attacks on India and Australia and exposed Britain's vital sea routes to the Imperial Japanese Navy. Singapore had been vaunted as the greatest naval base of them all. Played for propaganda purposes again and again in an inter-war period characterized by disarmament and the fear of another world war, reference to 'Fortress Singapore' was a way of reassuring the world that some things never changed, and that Britain's guardianship of the sea lanes of the world was one of them. Even as the Japanese prepared the *coup de grâce* from across the Johore Straits, imperial troops continued to pour into Singapore, the nine East Anglian battalions of the British 18th Division barely getting off the ship before capture. Until the last moment Movietone newsreels set to the sound of strident music and stiff upper-lip English voices showed the awesome defences of the island prepared for anything the foolhardy Japanese could throw against them. Typical was the news film entitled 'Imperial Forces for Malaya's Defence' which pictured smiling, waving and grinning Australians embarking for Singapore, as well as smartly-uniformed and well-drilled Indians manning anti-aircraft guns, and Brewster Buffaloes and Vickers Vildebeeste flying high over Singapore docks. Of course, to a city that had never seen a modern fighter before, the newly-arrived Buffaloes conveyed a sense of security, no one at the time realizing their inferiority to the Japanese aircraft that they were to take off against. A well-publicized symbol of America's involvement in Britain's imperial war even before America became a belligerent, the Buffaloes began arriving from American factories in February 1941. Amounting to 170 in total, they were an answer to Malaya's lack of fighters and Britain's inability to spare any Hurricanes or Spitfires to plug the gap. Such were the ways and needs of alliances and global prioritization in this greatest-ever war that Churchill had in August 1941 promised Stalin 200 Hurricanes. Demonstrating Britain's rock-solid commitment to the Russian cause in the face of the Barbarossa invasion was a strategic priority; the Commander-in-Chief Far East, Air Chief Marshal Sir Robert Brooke-Popham, could whistle for such bounteous reinforcements, though they might have made all the difference. But of course, Malaya's defence rested first and foremost with the navy, and the battlefleet that was to sail to Singapore if war looked likely.

As even the most feckless armchair historian now knows, the big problem with the Singapore strategy was that it was largely a façade, a show with plenty of pzazz but little substance, a well defended base without any major warships, its guns unsuited to the full range of defensive tasks they might be called upon to perform (all but one could fire landward, but other problems, like a lack of high-explosive ammunition, made them ill-suited for this role). The impregnable fortress was as reassuring before the outbreak of hostilities, and as useless once they had commenced, as the Maginot Line was for France. The Singapore strategy had been conceived as an imperial defence alternative, given the absence of a powerful Empire Pacific Fleet, and the unlikelihood of Britain paying for one in the inter-war years or getting the Dominions to contribute ships to one when it was proposed. It had also been conceived when Germany was on the floor and Japan and Italy allies, and became a cover for fundamental British weakness in a period when imperial overstretch was being challenged by aggressive powers seeking imperial spoils. Worst still, the Singapore strategy had been talked up to such an extent that it had almost become a strategic fact that Singapore would ensure imperial defence in the East. This had become fatally intertwined with a racially prejudiced view of Japanese fighting potential that, frankly, dismissed them as a martial joke right up until the storm broke over the heads of the complacent or ignorant European majority in offices, clubs, plantations and military headquarters throughout the eastern colonial world. The fact that the Royal Navy had placed so much emphasis on Japan as a likely future enemy in the inter-war years, that British admirals like Sir Geoffrey Layton (variously Commander-in-Chief China Station, Commander-in-Chief Eastern Fleet and Commander-in-Chief Ceylon) had viewed the Imperial Japanese Navy at close quarters and that intelligence reports about Japanese capabilities and intentions were not unknown, make this collective failure even more depressing to contemplate. For example, it was known that Japanese Zeros had been used against Chunking in the spring of 1940. Reports had reached the Air Ministry and been forwarded to Far East Combined Bureau in Singapore in September 1941. The information was not, however, transmitted to air headquarters, and when Japanese Zeroes appeared over Malaya, everyone was stunned by their superiority over the RAF's aircraft. Even in October 1941 the Admiralty was assuming that Japanese vessels would be inferior to British ones (even old ones), and that other factors, like morale, would make things extremely difficult for the Japanese. Overconfidence and arrogance was much in evidence, though there was more than a little of the 'it'll be all right on the night' spirit for which the British were renowned.

It must also be remembered that the Singapore strategy had been hatched at a time when Britain could still lay claim to having a navy that was on a Two-Power standard if the American navy was excluded from the equation. In short, in the 1920s the Royal Navy was still superior to the next two biggest navies, those of Japan and France, and it could be safely assumed that Britain would not be fighting both of those powers at the same time (indeed, the chances of fighting France, or of America siding with Japan in a conflict, were remote enough to be discounted). This situation, of course, had entirely changed by 1941, in particular because of the existence of six German battleships that were able to inflict upon the Royal Navy a greater degree of strategic paralysis than that inflicted during the Great War by the twenty-three dreadnoughts of the High Seas Fleet. In facing the threat of German and Italian naval power in Europe, Britain was also facing for the first time a first-class naval power *in the east*, operating close to its home base. Not so much by their strength as by their great distance from one another, the German and Japanese fleets placed the British Empire in an appalling dilemma.

Fundamental to the Singapore strategy was the assumption that Britain would be capable of sending adequate resources to the region, should war with Japan break out, or at least that Singapore was adequately defended to be able to hold out until significant naval reinforcements arrived. But in December 1941 Britain and its military resources were fully occupied, indeed perilously overstretched, elsewhere. There was simply nothing left in reserve with which to counter the Japanese threat, certainly nothing capable of doing so successfully. A major problem was that London's attention was focused closer to home, and as late as 1941 Churchill said that there was little chance of war with Japan and that the Middle East was the major overseas priority. Until the last, most British imperial forces preparing for a possible deployment overseas were training for desert warfare. The RAF was insufficiently equipped to meet its responsibilities in the Far East, and plans for reinforcing the region did not leave the desk. Having said all of that, it is also true that at the beginning of December 1941 Singapore's guns stood ready to counter an assault from the sea, the Malayan peninsula was packed with imperial troops and quite modern fighters, and the promise of a fleet for Singapore was in fact fulfilled with the arrival of HMS *Prince of Wales* and *Repulse* and their escorts (even if it was too small and lacking in air cover). The 'R' class battleships were on their way east too. From this point of view, given the pressing demands of desperate fighting fronts in Europe and the Middle East, distant colonies like Burma and Malaya actually did rather well in gaining the substantial military resources that they did. But they were to prove entirely inadequate, given their training, equipment, organization and leadership, to deal with the Japanese forces sent against them.

Various governments throughout the Empire had contributed to the costs of constructing the Singapore naval base, and any anxieties about Britain's capacity to answer Japan, should it threaten the Eastern Empire, were to be answered by its mighty guns and the battlefleet that its new naval base would accommodate. The appearance of confidence, security and longevity projected by Britain in the East was of course largely based upon past reputation and a good deal of bluff, and for the ill-informed majority a basic unawareness of Britain's relative weakness compared to its potential enemies' strengths. Furthermore, Britain's alliances with collaborative elites in the region were weak, and there was no plan for coordinated resistance in the event of a Japanese attack between Britain and the other colonial powers in the region – America, France and Holland. Plans that did exist went unfulfilled – after Pearl Harbor, for example, the British admiral commanding the Eastern Fleet fully expected to be joined at Singapore by the numerous American cruisers, destroyers and submarines of the Asiatic Fleet. There was little that could have been done to ameliorate some of these factors, given the fact that for years Japan had been planning for war and expansion, whereas Britain had been planning for peace, disarmament and the maintenance of the global territorial status quo, and had never given Japan the military credit that it deserved. Blame can be liberally apportioned when discussing an epic military defeat such as that which swept the Eastern Empire away in 1941-42, but it might, equally, be seen as just one of those things. The British public in the 1930s would not have countenanced expensive additional rearmament 'just in case' Japan went to war; the use of nearby French Indo-China as a base for massive Japanese forces had never been foreseen; nor had the crippling, at a stroke, of American offensive power at Pearl Harbor.

By the time the blow fell in the East, Britain was massively distracted by the war in Europe, which loomed far, far larger than a conflict in what was little more than a distant colonial sphere to most British people, habitually parochially-minded yet accepting global Empire as a natural part of the world order. Doubts about the Singapore strategy existed from its inception but, given the circumstances, acknowledging the doubts became more and more politically dangerous. By the late 1930s, furthermore, Britain had come to repose its hopes for Far Eastern security, if all else failed, in American naval power in the Pacific. In early 1941 talks between the British and the Americans acknowledged that, should Japan convert a European war into a global one, American power would inevitably predominate in the Pacific region, and the Dominions would then become vital bases that could not be permitted to fall to the enemy. So, unsatisfactory though it was to be talking in terms of 'worst case scenarios', from before the outbreak of the Pacific war, the Dominions had at least acquired a defence guarantee – even if that meant a liberation guarantee in the event of their conquest by Japan in the meantime – to underwrite Singapore in an imperial defence system that, it was hoped, would be sufficient for their protection. It is difficult to escape the conclusion that the British government, setting the tone in the East, hoped against hope that Japan would desist from war; having no resources to spare, there was little left but hope. In turn, when it became obvious that the likelihood of Japanese attack was great, the British, like rabbits caught in the headlights, were paralyzed, by denial and a simple inability to think of something useful that could be done.

There was plenty of opportunity to question the wisdom of the Singapore strategy because the base took nearly two decades to complete, a victim of the budgetary and political stop-go cycle of democratic politics in an age of disarmament. It was predicted initially that the base would need to hold out against attack for up to forty-two days until the battlefleet arrived, though this was extended to seventy days in 1937. At the Pacific Defence Conference, held in Wellington in April 1939, the Dominions were told that a battlefleet might not be available for dispatch to Singapore at all, if the situation in Europe and elsewhere was bad. In June 1939 the Chiefs of Staff declared that it was now impossible to predict the timing or the size of the fleet that would be sent, and in the following month the arrival period was raised to 180 days. Not surprisingly, this sounded alarm bells in the Pacific Dominions, and the Australian Prime Minister asked for assurances. He was told that the size of the fleet would depend on when Japan entered the war and on what losses the Royal Navy had sustained, and what its commitments were elsewhere. This was hardly a reassuring answer.

Despite this knowledge, both Dominions were prepared to maintain their commitment to dispatch forces to the Middle East. It is important to note the level of awareness in Canberra and Wellington about these bleak pre-war assessments of the Singapore situation. This is because after its surrender the idea that the British government led Dominion leaders up the garden path concerning the capacity of the Singapore strategy to protect them, and that the British not only misled them in order to get them to commit forces to the Middle East but then failed utterly to fight adequately when the Japanese attacked the Eastern Empire, has gained currency. This has been compounded by the British-Australian mudslinging that took place at this moment of greatest peril, born of frustration and the stress of an imperial war going – in most parts of the world in 1941 and the first half of 1942 – badly wrong for the British world. Australia had gripes about London's failure to consult in what it considered to be a sufficient manner, and there were grave reservations about the competence of British military commanders. In return Britain griped about Australia's failure to see the war in global terms, and doubts were sometimes expressed about the disciplinary standards of the Australian infantryman. These were petty squabbles between partners in an enviably successful alliance, but serious matters in the heat of battle.

Pre-war concerns about Singapore's capacity to bear the weight of expectation placed upon its harbour and its guns were compounded when in 1938 it was revealed that the jungles of Malaya were not, as was commonly thought, as impenetrable as a wall of steel. Attack from the north had been considered highly unlikely given the jungle barrier, and certainly ruled out the use of tanks. Singapore's great strength was facing seaward, where its fifteen-inch guns could devastate an enemy invasion force. In July 1938, however, General W. G. S. Dobbie, the General Officer Commanding Malaya, warned that an enemy landing in Johore, followed by an attack on Singapore from the north, should be regarded as the greatest potential danger to Singapore. As a result of this warning it was agreed by the British Cabinet's Committee of Imperial Defence that an Indian battalion normally stationed at Taiping should remain in Malaya. But there was not the urgency in this warning, nor the slack in the global deployment of imperial forces, to allow much to be done to rectify this possible deficiency.

Given the ever-rising estimate of the time that it would take for the battlefleet to arrive at Singapore, the knowledge that it would probably only possess two capital ships when it did, and the new assessment of the ineffectiveness of the jungle barrier, in July 1939 Dobbie's successor, Major-General L. V. Bond, told London that he needed at least twenty-six battalions and 556 front-line aircraft to guarantee the defence of the peninsula. At the outbreak of war in 1939, however, the air strength in Malaya consisted of twenty-four Blenheims, ten flying boats, twenty-four Vildebeestes and a handful of Fleet Air Arm Walruses and Swordfish, hardly a formidable air armada (though quite impressive when set against India's paltry air force). By the time of the Japanese invasion, Malaya was still four hundred machines short of Bond's target.

Another gaping capability gap was the absence of tanks in Malaya, although over 400 had been sent to Russia from British factories. The Japanese brought their own. The 1930s had seen the development of air bases at Alor Star, Butterworth, Kahang, Kota Bharu, Kuantan and Sembawang. By December 1941 twenty-seven air bases had been completed by the government of Malaya. The air reinforcement route to the Far East, which ran from Britain to Gibraltar–Malta–Egypt–Habbaniyah–Basra–Sharjah–Karachi–Allahabad–Calcutta–Mingaladon (Rangoon) to Victoria Point in Singapore, remained, however, worryingly uncongested. British and Middle Eastern airfields had first call on British production and aircrews. Australia was asked for help, and sent a Wirraway squadron and two RAAF Hudson squadrons in August 1940. At the turn of 1940–41, what was now known as the Far East Air Force possessed eight squadrons of old aircraft and not a single modern fighter. Indicating where Malaya was positioned in the pecking order in the minds of imperial decision-makers, in the summer of 1941 Britain possessed ninety-nine squadrons of modern fighters. None were to be sent to the Far East, though Churchill was at the time pressing to have twenty squadrons sent to Iraq and Syria. What this all meant was that there were insufficient air forces available to protect the capital ships at sea, to interdict Japanese landings or to support British imperial troops in the field. The Japanese won air superiority very early in the campaign and, already in control of the seas, there was little hope for the defending land forces.

Whilst the number of imperial and locally-raised troops in Malaya was considerable, too few adequately trained units could be spared to reinforce the peninsula against a full-scale enemy invasion. A trickle of army reinforcements began when two battalions were transferred from Shanghai in August 1940, and the Malay states expanded their volunteer forces. In August 1941 the new General Officer Commanding Malaya, Lieutenant-General Arthur Percival, demanded forty-eight battalions and two tank regiments as a minimum for the peninsula's defence if the naval shield were to fail and should responsibility for securing Malaya devolve upon the army. At the time, he had thirty-three battalions, little heavy artillery, few anti-aircraft guns and no tanks at all. What is more, the troops that did begin to arrive in increasing numbers from Australia, Britain and India were often inexperienced and had trained for war in the desert. Nevertheless, outnumbering the Japanese by nearly four to one, questions were inevitably asked about the way in which these troops were led.

Lack of the right type of resources – jungle-trained troops, aircraft carriers, tanks, modern fighters, thicker jungles – could not, however, disguise the fact that poor leadership also played a major part in the scale and the nature of Britain's defeat in the east. This leadership deficit was not just at the local level, with the local army commander, Lieutenant-General Percival, left carrying the can, but stretched to the apex of British government. When he arrived to take up his command in May 1941, Percival's freedom to influence strategy or the deployment of his troops was already limited. The deployment of his troops had been decided by the need to guard static positions, particularly exposed RAF airfields in the north; to provide a force capable of seizing the Kra isthmus should Japanese aggression be definitely proven to have taken place; and to cause as little disruption as possible to the Malayan economy.

The fact was that hardly anyone – at least, anyone with a powerful voice – believed that Japan would go to war. Even if it did, few doubted that the British would have too much about them to be defeated, lack of resources or not. Assessments from London continued to encourage the people of Britain and Malaya to believe that the Japanese would not be foolhardy enough to attack, reinforcing the Singapore strategy balloon. Churchill's confidence in the summer of 1941 that a new but inexperienced battleship, an ageing battlecruiser and a carrier would strike terror into the hearts of the Japanese was entirely misplaced, but revealed the confidence in Britain's ability to outface Japan, as well as the Prime Minister's ability to override the Admiralty. Further revealing the intelligence blind-spot so startlingly demonstrated by Britain and America in their approach to Japan and the prospect of war with its armed forces, British commanders believed that the Brewster Buffalo fighters obtained under Lend-Lease provided adequate air defence in a region bereft of Hurricanes and Spitfires. In fact, it was inferior on almost every count to the Japanese aircraft against which it would operate. The confidence of Britain's Prime Minister and Minister of Defence, Winston Churchill, was reflected in public opinion, and in the attitudes of British service personnel. The Japanese fighting forces and the racially stereotyped Japanese male were dismissed, and complacency was a state of mind in Malaya and Singapore. Indeed, some commanding officers lamented the fact that enemies more worthy than the Japanese could not have been found for their men. With such blind confidence on the part of the military, and the ubiquitous fear of doing or revealing anything that might dent general morale, it was no wonder that Malaya's civilians believed the peninsula as unlikely to be invaded as the American mainland.

Thus British defeats in South-East Asia and the Far East were the result of bad luck, poor leadership, inter-war disarmament, inadequate resources, the distraction of simultaneously facing invasion at home and Rommel in the Middle East, and an assessment of the potential of the Japanese armed forces that bordered on the negligent and was not a little informed by racial arrogance. In South-East Asia Britain suffered an ignoble defeat; planters and European civilians running away, soldiers giving up, binge-drinking, looting and an unseemly scramble to escape, prestigious warships pointlessly sunk, armies thrown into embarrassing retreat, and discipline disintegrating as Singapore took on the air of an island of the damned. The Governor and his sick wife were bombed out of Government House, the cathedral became a hospital, whisky by the crate load was downed at the cricket club to prevent it falling to the enemy and – finally signalling the end of colonial civilization – even the signing of chits, the credit system of Empire, became impossible, as native businessmen knew full well that the Europeans would not be in a position next week, never mind next month, to honour them.

Japan conquered the Malayan peninsula in a textbook military progress in the face of blunders and disarray on the part of their opponents. With the fall of Singapore the sea lanes to the great Australasian Dominions, and the very security of those Dominions itself, were imperilled as never before. The sinking of the British capital ships sent to outface the Japanese challenge marked the end of the Royal Navy's protection of the British lands in the east, and the formal beginning of America's assumption of ultimate responsibility for the security of the region. The failure to defend the Malay peninsula was therefore a hammer blow to the system of imperial defence that had for so long formed the basis of British strategic thinking and the bedrock of global security. The Royal Navy ceased to be a power east of Singapore, and its main task east of Suez became that of safeguarding the Indian Ocean supply routes and waiting for the time when victories elsewhere would allow it to gather sufficient strength in order to launch a new British Pacific Fleet.

British prestige was battered by the loss of Malaya, a significant problem because prestige was a vital buttress of imperial rule. Britain manifestly failed to defend the millions of British subjects who lived within its imperial domains and depended on Britain for their protection. British power in a major corner of the imperial world evaporated or was swept away, to be exchanged for Japanese occupation and its concomitant atrocities (particularly against the Chinese inhabitants) and an irreparable downturn in respect for the white colonial bluffers of the Eastern Empire. Britain's shame was plain for all to see, though the Japanese showed great expertise when it came to extracting every last drop of humiliation from the tens of thousands of white soldiers and civilians interned in the territories that they once ruled, from Stanley Camp in Hong Kong to Sandakan in Borneo and Changi in Singapore. Of greater immediate concern, as well as losing face, Britain also lost one of the world's great sources of highly-valued raw materials, for South-East Asia was one of the richest treasure troves of Empire. In 1941 Malaya produced 38 per cent of the world's rubber and 58 per cent of its tin, and £93 million pounds worth of its £131 million pound export business was conducted with foreign, mainly American, companies, making Malaya the Empire's premier dollar-earner. Defeat in the East also meant that Britain lost its major stake in foreign investment in China, centred on Shanghai, the great imperial banking and commercial centre of the Far East.

The Malayan peninsula ran from Singapore in the south to the southern extremities of Burma and Siam. Britain's interests in South-East Asia had grown as a result of the sea route to the east and its protection, and later because of the commodities of the peninsula itself, first tin and then rubber. Penang had been leased by the East India Company in 1786, and Singapore purchased by Stamford Raffles in 1819, himself an employee of the East India Company. Malacca was exchanged with the Dutch in 1824 in return for recognition of an exclusive Dutch sphere in Sumatra, another territory in which British private endeavour had sowed the seeds of Empire and in which Britain fought, in the Revolutionary and Napoleonic Wars as well as the Second World War. British forces had occupied Java during the Napoleonic period, beginning a strategic interest in the territories of the Dutch East Indies that was to be rekindled in the Second World War. Malaya was very much an extension of British expansion in and from India, and of Britain's determination to be the paramount power on the trade and shipping route between South Asia and the Far Eastern entrepôts of Empire. Commercial and strategic interest also witnessed the expansion of formal British rule in the area of north Borneo from the middle of the nineteenth century, as trading and strategic interests hardened into Empire.

In terms of administration the British Empire in Malaya and Borneo contained many variations. The settlements of Penang, Malacca and Singapore – including Christmas Island, Labuan and the Cocos Islands – formed the Crown Colony of the Straits Settlements. Elsewhere in Malaya the British for some time maintained the policy of suppressing piracy but not assuming political responsibilities, but the trade in tin and other products was growing in importance in the late nineteenth century and brought forth political intervention in its defence. The states of Perak, Selangor, Negri Sembilan and Pahang were separately induced to negotiate treaties with Britain, and became the Federated Malay States in 1897. In the north, the former Siamese provinces of Kedah, Kelantan, Perlis and Trengganu (ceded in 1909), along with the southern state of Johore, became the Unfederated Malay States. In these Malay states, officially protectorates as opposed to colonies, sultans governed with the advice of British residents and advisers. Brunei was also ruled by a Sultan, and at the time of the Second World War his former province of Sarawak was still being ruled by the descendant of Sir James Brooke, whom he had installed as its ruler a century before. In 1841 James Brooke had helped the Sultan of Brunei suppress a rebellion in Sarawak, and as a reward was made Raja of this district of the Sultan's domains. Brooke asserted his province's independence in 1853, and actually expanded his domains at the expense of Brunei. From 1881 Sarawak, North Borneo and Brunei became British protectorates.

Four-fifths of Malaya was covered with evergreen rainforest, the remainder cleared for plantations, mines, towns and villages. The tin industry had developed rapidly since the 1870s, leading to significant Chinese immigration. The native Malay population, little involved in tin production, had taken advantage of the growth of the rubber industry since the 1890s and developed smallholdings, though it was largely Indian immigrants who worked on the large rubber plantations, as well as a further influx of Chinese. Thus by the Second World War only about half of Malaya's population of 5,500,000 were indigenous. The remainder were Indians (700,000) and Chinese (2,400,000), the overwhelming majority of whom had not been born in Malaya and therefore maintained intimate ties with their homelands. There were about 30,000 Europeans in Malaya, 30,000 aboriginal Sakai, 20,000 Eurasians and 60,000 members of other races, including about 7000 Japanese (many of whom were evacuated from Singapore on ships like the *Asamu Maru* in the final days before Pearl Harbor). Given the diverse composition of the population of Britain's richest colony, it was understandable that during the war there was little unity amongst them. The Chinese community was the most violently opposed to Japanese occupation, no surprise given the suffering of the mother country since 1937. The Chinese made natural allies for the British. In arming and allying with Malaya's Chinese community, however, the British were to store up trouble for themselves in the post-war world, for it was to be these very Chinese allies, recast as 'communist terrorists', who fought the British in the Malayan emergency of the 1950s, largely with British weapons.

Throughout the 1930s and 1940s imperial subjects in South-East Asia became increasingly susceptible to politicization as powerful Japanese, Chinese and Indian nationalist voices arose. Japan's invasion of China in 1937 drew the British territories of South-East Asia and the Far East into a growing regional conflict long before the British Empire became involved in the Second World War. Given China's proximity, and the large Chinese diaspora in the region, British territories could not help but be affected by this Sino-Japanese maelstrom, particularly on the political and ideological levels. None of this augured well for stable colonial rule, as the peoples of Britain's Eastern Empire were exposed as never before to conflicting racial and ideological currents. There was Japan's appeal to all Asians to free themselves from European domination, as well as the rousing militarism of this inspirational non-European industrialized empire. Then there was the appeal of China to its overseas communities, for the defence of the motherland from Japan and the propagation of communist ideas. There was also the cry of Indian nationalism travelling clearly across the seas to the Indian diaspora in South-East Asia and other places with large Indian populations, such as Fiji and Mauritius. Also heard were Islamic reformers and leaders aiming to end European colonial domination.[5] Further denting British prestige in the East was the Japanese policy of undermining Western interests in China and the East whenever they could. As with Hitler's Germany in the run up to hostilities, the Japanese appeared determined to flout the rules of the international game as the Western powers had framed them, and every time these petty humiliations went unanswered by Britain, employing appeasement as its major diplomatic tactic, Britain's prestige dropped another notch on the barometer of public opinion.

Before war broke out Japan was able to capitalize on Britain's pressing European preoccupations, the lack of a coordinated Anglo-American defence plan for the Far East and Pacific regions, and the disagreements between the two powers on the question of China policy. Japan was able to exploit Britain's desire to do all that it could to keep the peace by forcing the closure of the Burma Road, the main supply line to China, and was able peacefully to strengthen its position vis-à-vis South-East Asia by gaining bases in French Indo-China, another disastrous and unforeseen result of the fall of France. Though the Malayan campaign and the capitulation of Singapore are commonly seen as testament to massive

British political and military failure, Japan's considerable strengths should not be overlooked. Japan's preparation for war before December 1941 was impressive. The Japanese had worked hard diplomatically to secure Russian neutrality, as Russo-Japanese clashes in the north of China in May–September 1939 had led to severe Japanese losses (Russia was Japan's traditional great power rival in the region). The April 1941 neutrality pact enabled Japan to stop worrying about the northern situation and to concentrate on the southern regions of China. Germany's invasion of Russia in 1941 further relieved this particular pressure on Japan. Japan exploited American isolationism to their advantage, and their military preparation for campaigns in the region was excellent, after years of fighting in China. Japanese use of carrier aviation was unparalleled. Japan had also done its homework as regards its target, using intelligence and photographs supplied by informers resident in Malaya as effectively as it had done in Hawaii, fuelling all sorts of rumours about fifth columnists. The Japanese use of its overseas communities was excellent, and overseas residents, particularly businessmen and traders, were extremely useful in gathering information of value to the military planners. In Malaya espionage was run by the Press Attaché in Singapore, submarines visited remote ports, military intelligence was gathered by the British officer Captain Patrick Heenan of the 3/16 Punjab Regiment and there was intensive aerial reconnaissance prior to the campaign.

Most of these things were known about, but no one had a firm enough grasp of the big picture, coupled with sufficient influence, to do anything about it. Massive intelligence regarding Japanese intentions poured into British headquarters, though nothing was done about it. The tactics adopted by the Imperial Japanese Army on landing in Malaya must also be credited. They were innovative relative to those of the British imperial troops facing them. And, of course, in sinking Britain's two capital ships at the start, they deprived Britain of the big stick with which it planned to stop any Japanese assault before it had even started (when the warships were sunk they were searching for Japanese transports full of troops bound for Malaya). It was a rare experience for British land forces, used always to taking control of the sea for granted.

When Japan finally went to war with the Western powers in late 1941 it invaded and conquered colonies belonging to all of them – the American Philippines, the Australian Mandates of New Guinea and New Britain, British Borneo, Brunei, Burma, Dutch Borneo, the Dutch East Indies, French Indo-China, Malaya, Portuguese Timor and Sarawak. In the months between December 1941 and March 1942, Japan brought ninety million people under its rule and gained rich oil fields, nearly 90 per cent of the world's rubber and over half its tin, and 30 per cent of the world's rice. This breathtaking imperial grab was bought at the bargain price of 15,000 men, 400 aircraft and about twenty minor warships. But Japan was not to be permitted the time in which to coordinate this empire and adapt its productive potential and mould it to its own imperial needs. This was because of the sturdy Allied response and Japan's growing inability effectively to link the territories of the new empire and the armies and garrisons fighting over its huge area. The merchant vessels required to link such a sprawling empire were sunk at an alarming rate, as, too, were the warships needed to protect them.

When war came to South-East Asia's the imperial response was severely hampered by an awkward command structure. First, the government of Malaya was not effectively subordinated to military authority, and so a kind of dual rule persisted in which the military went about its business whilst the civilian rulers continued to pursue theirs. Thus the government of Malaya under Governor Sir Shenton Thomas considered that its first duty was to keep Malaya producing its rich products for the greater imperial good, and not to go worrying the civilian population unduly by talk of invasion. In taking this policy line the Governor was following the instructions of the Colonial Office and doing what every other Governor in the far-flung Empire was doing – contributing to victory in the most effective way possible by stoking the productive powers of his domain. Whilst often criticized for this attitude, he was only taking his cue from the administrators of Empire in London, and taking Churchill's reassurances at face value. Singapore was impregnable. Malaya would not be invaded. Producing tin and rubber should remain a priority.

On the outbreak of war the Colonial Office instructed Sir Shenton Thomas that the production of rubber and tin were to be his top priorities. Much is made of the planters of Malaya and the businessmen of Singapore going about their peace-time business and resenting any inconvenience brought by the war, but they were doing what they had been told to do: run their estates and continue making Malaya a dollar-earner of the first order. As for the rest, the fifteen-inch guns and battlefleet would take care of that. Against the view of a Malaya well and truly caught napping when the Japanese arrived, it can be claimed that, until the calamities of December 1941 to February 1942, Malaya was successfully pulling its weight by supplying the Empire with vital war materials. Furthermore, it is open to question how much more the government of Malaya could have done to prepare its territories for the Japanese onslaught, especially how much more it could have done that would have been of any *use*. The regime was a limited government geared to peace-time and to consensus politics involving numerous indigenous rulers, operating in a historically fragmented and artificially constructed territory. It was also one in which the *Pax Britannica* had become a part of the furniture, to such an extent that invasion was not considered a serious threat by the vast majority of people, even if Japan were foolhardy enough to attack.

The second aspect of the awkward command structure afflicting the eastern Empire was purely military. In October 1940 Far East Command (FEC), head-quartered in Singapore, was formed under Air Chief Marshal Sir Robert Brooke-Popham, a former Inspector-General of the RAF and Governor of Kenya (replaced as Commander-in-Chief Far East in November 1941 by Lieutenant-General

Sir Henry Pownall). Whilst in charge of all land and air forces in the region, the command structure was complicated by the Royal Navy's separation with its own Commander-in-Chief in Singapore reporting direct to the Admiralty, and the fact that Brooke-Popham had no authority over the civil administration. Even in the case of the army and the RAF, ultimate command was not his and the local army and air force commanders remained responsible to their own service chiefs in London. In late 1941 the East Indies Station and the China Station were taken over by the newly-formed Eastern Fleet when Admiral Sir Tom Phillips arrived with the two battleships sent to deter Japan from a warlike course. Far East Command's territorial responsibilities stretched from Hong Kong to Borneo, Malaya and Burma, the latter detached from India Command in 1940 and presenting a new and unwelcome defensive headache for this ungainly new command (FEC also controlled air forces in Ceylon and the Indian Ocean). At the last moment, in early 1942, a new cog in the wheel was introduced when General Sir Archibald Wavell was given overall command for the entire Malaya–East Indies region with the creation of American-British-Dutch-Australian Command, headquartered in Java. The command structure in Malaya and Singapore was seriously flawed, and was further undermined by the appointment of new personnel in the crucial final months (Cooper, Pownall and Wavell).

The command structure was not aided when a new big-wig entered the equation in the months before the start of war with Japan. Illustrating the great strategic and economic importance of South-East Asia to the British world system, a Resident Minister Far East was appointed late in 1941. As in West Africa, French North Africa and the Middle East, this was a Cabinet-ranking appointment intended to coordinate the civil and military efforts of the region, and to maintain direct contact with London. The incumbent, Duff Cooper, was in position for barely a month before the imminent Japanese attack forced his evacuation. He was in Singapore long enough, however, to note the disarray that seemed to have infected its government and the conduct of the peninsula's defence, which he considered to be ramshackle. Brooke-Popham was one whose abilities were questioned, and Cooper also severely criticized the colonial government of Sir Shenton Thomas, whom he regarded as a blunderer ('one of those people who find it impossible to adjust their minds to war conditions', as he told Churchill in a letter of 18 December 1941). But if Singapore was a self-satisfied city awash with racial condescension towards the Japanese and a surfeit of Colonel Blimps, it was not entirely the fault of the men on the spot. The government of which Cooper was a senior member, and its predecessors, had allowed the people of Singapore and their rulers to feel relaxed by reassuring them, for nearly two decades, that they were sitting on top of one of the most unconquerable places on earth.

The debate about the awkward power structure in Singapore and the relative merits of the men involved will probably never end. The extremely variant accounts of who was to blame for what are illustrated by a comparison of the major biographies of Duff Cooper and Shenton Thomas. Cooper's biographer, especially having had the advantage of reading Thomas's biography before going to press, seems to adopt every possible criticism of Thomas in championing his subject. Thomas's biographer highlights the fact that most subsequent written accounts, including the official history of the war against Japan, take it for granted that the Governor and Malaya's entire civil administration were totally unhelpful in preparing for war. Yet Thomas emerges as a humane and selfless man, and clearly one who believed that he had done all he could to support Malaya's preparations for war, especially given the parameters of his instructions from Whitehall. He was also steeped in the responsibilities of his position, particularly in his concern for the people of Malaya when war came, and both he and his wife were extremely dignified in their long years of captivity.

Duff Cooper was, in all fairness, put in an unenviable position when Churchill sent him to Singapore. He was to go as an observer and report on the situation and what could be done to improve it. It has been suggested that he was sent to Singapore as a political exile, keeping him out of the way at a time when Churchill was susceptible to a leadership challenge. Descending on Singapore as a roving reporter in the last months before the Japanese invaded proved, in the end, to be a useless mission; dispatched a year earlier, he might have made a difference. Cooper had been appointed Chancellor of the Duchy of Lancaster in July 1941 after resigning as Minister of Information. He was waiting, it would seem, for a better job in government to turn up, biding time on the sidelines as senior politicians often have to do. This was not a useful background before becoming involved in the many complexities of the civil and military situation in Malaya, of which he knew virtually nothing. Cooper arrived at Singapore with Diana, his famously beautiful wife, on 11 September 1941. Inevitably, given that he had no official position, he was regarded with reserve by the Governor and the Commander-in-Chief, both of whom were responsible directly to the British government in Whitehall, not to its roving proconsul. Given that Cooper had a commission to report to Churchill, it was a classic case of power without responsibility, for his reports painted a bleak picture of the atmosphere and the personnel in Singapore. With almost comic timing, Cooper was given a specific position in the Singapore structure on the day that the Japanese invaded, being created Resident Cabinet Minister for Far Eastern Affairs. It was not a job that Cooper relished, suggesting other names that might be more suitable to the post. Having done all that he felt he could do now that war had actually come, Cooper and his wife left Singapore on 13 January, a month before the surrender.

The defence of the South-East Asian Empire was not aided by the use of forces brought together for the first time. In Malaya the Indian Army served alongside the British Army, locally raised forces and Australians. Many of these units were extremely inexperienced, and few had trained for war in the jungle; pre-war planning had identified the sands of the Middle East as the most likely theatre in which the imperial legions would be called upon to fight. As elsewhere, efforts were made to recruit military formations in South-East Asia that would supplement imperial forces and help resist an invasion, usually by expanding small military forces established before the war. The Malay Regiment, based at Port Dickinson, took over responsibility for beach defences in the west of Singapore, though it began expanding at the eleventh hour, in the very month of the Japanese invasion. Founded in 1933, the regiment's second battalion came officially into existence less than a week before Pearl Harbor. At this time the regiment's total strength was 1400, including fifty-nine British and nineteen Malay officers. The Sultan of Johore maintained a small regular force, and there were a number of volunteer units in the Straits Settlements, Federated Malay States and Unfederated States. The combined strength of the volunteer forces in the Straits Settlements and Federated Malay States was about 6000 men. There was, however, no rapid expansion of these pre-war forces. With the Japanese threat seen as remote, it was considered that the best use of local manpower was in support of the tin and rubber industries. Nevertheless by 7 December 1941 the total strength of these volunteer forces stood at 10,500, of whom 2430 were Europeans. Of this total, one-quarter fell into enemy hands. There were also over 33,000 people involved in various civil defence organizations.

Even before the British Empire went to war with Japan, the growth of Japanese power in the region was having an adverse effect in Malaya. By September 1941 it was estimated that there were around 200,000 Japanese troops in Vichy Indo-China; and, with bombers in places like Saigon, they presented a serious threat to Malaya's security. Malaya had to limit exports to the as-yet-undeclared enemy without provoking a Japanese reaction, a continuation of the pretence and posturing that characterized appeasement diplomacy in the West as well as the East. Japan's influence in the neighbouring kingdom of Siam affected Malaya, as most of Siam's tin and rubber was processed in Malaya, and Siam was the main source of Malaya's rice imports. Given Japanese influence in Siam and Indo-China, it was hoped that Ceylon, Hong Kong and Malaya, which had previously imported rice from these two countries, could become a market for Burma's exportable surplus. It wasn't possible, however, simply to break off trading relations in order to reflect diplomatic differences. Malaya depended on Siam's fish and other food supplies, and the Governor considered the maintenance of trade with Siam of great importance. Indo-China had been a source of anthracite coal for smelting, creating another import headache for the government of Malaya when Indo-China became a Japanese proxy. Increasing Japanese influence in these neighbouring territories made it necessary to tighten restrictions on exports, and from November 1941 there was a long list of commodities which were not to be granted export licences for Japan or Japanese-influenced territories. Some of the products thus debarred from their natural destinations could be consumed locally, whereas others languished for want of an alternative buyer. In 1940 58,000 tons of bauxite had been exported from Malaya to Japan, but Malaya now needed as much as it could get for the manufacture of aluminium for the rubber industry and defence services. It appeared that all of Malaya's bauxite mines were owned

THE BRITISH EMPIRE AND THE SECOND WORLD WAR

by Japanese people, encouraging rumours of fifth column activity and pre-war Japanese planning, though exports to Japan were stopped regardless (Malayan iron mines were also largely owned and operated by Japanese). Singapore's position as a regional entrepôt for the produce of the Dutch East Indies also gave rise to some difficult questions as to which re-export destinations were acceptable, given the war conditions affecting trade links. So, from the point of view of government and regulation, the headaches started long before the first shots were fired and Japan officially became Britain's enemy.

Like most other parts of the Empire and Commonwealth, Malaya formed a civil defence organization along the lines of Britain's Local Defence Volunteers (later the Home Guard), though perilously late as was the South-East Asian norm. Established in the autumn of 1941, the Local Defence Force, intended to help the police in an emergency, came to number 3400, Johore alone raising a thousand-strong contingent. A passive air defence organization centred upon 6000 ARP wardens was formed a little over a month before Japanese bombers first droned over the undarkened Singapore skyline. A further 2800 people were recruited into the auxiliary medical service, and 930 into the auxiliary fire service. The Malayan continent of the Royal Navy Volunteer Reserve was responsible for minesweeping trade routes to and from Singapore and keeping patrol boats in coastal waters. The Malayan Volunteer Air Force, founded in 1936, had 150 members. The RAF employed 800 locals for ground duties, and in 1940 a Government Flying Training School was opened in Singapore. All semblance of martial preparation was thus in place come December 1941. Without adequate imperial soldiers, aircraft, battleships or tactics capable of forestalling a Japanese invasion attempt, however, they were all doomed.

From a British perspective the story of the Malayan campaign makes grim reading on every count.[6] Conversely it must be a favourite of Japanese readers thrilled by stirring stories from their country's past. A theme of this dispiriting imperial campaign was the inability to concentrate superior forces at crucial points, and the reluctance of the army high command in Singapore to allow commanders on the ground to take up locally tenable positions. Adequate air cover was lacking throughout Far East Command, and the naval force which was supposed to see the Japanese off was sent to the bottom at the very beginning of hostilities. The positions of British troops were repeatedly outflanked, and the Japanese moved armour and bicycle-borne infantry down the peninsula at speed (each Japanese division had been issued with 6000 bikes). Though outnumbering the Japanese by nearly two to one, the imperial forces on the ground lacked tanks and artillery, as well as decent tactics. One result of the reluctance of civil and military authorities to back the work of Special Operations Executive was the lack of an effective scorched earth policy as imperial forces retreated. On the west coast, Japanese soldiers were even able to use British boats to outflank retreating imperial units.

British forces were on the back foot from the start, having failed to make pre-emptive incursions into Siam for fear of being the first to break that country's neutrality (despite the existence of a plan, Operation Matador, to do this in the event of war). The Japanese, of course, had no such diplomatically inspired compunctions, and gained a tactical advantage by putting forces into Siam at the outset when General Yamashita's 25th Army began its Malayan campaign. The British alternative, defensive lines established around Jitra, was not ordered until after the Japanese made their first landfall on Malayan soil. Intelligence authorities at Singapore's Far East Combined Bureau received the first definite news of the departure of a Japanese invasion fleet on 6 December 1941. Japanese troops invaded northern Malaya and southern Siam on 7–8 December 1941, making unopposed landings at Singora and Patani. What adequate air cover might have achieved was briefly demonstrated on that first day when RAF and RAAF aircraft terrorized Japanese landing craft, but this success was not repeated. Over the course of the campaign the RAF and RAAF lost most of their original strength, including 122 Buffaloes and forty-five Hurricanes. RAF reinforcements had arrived too late. On 17 December fifty-one Hurricanes at sea off South Africa destined for Iraq were diverted, and No. 258 Squadron was delivered from HMS *Indomitable* via Java and Sumatra. On 13 January 1942 a full squadron of twenty-four pilots and fifty-one Hurricanes arrived. After collecting the aircraft at Port Sudan, *Indomitable* flew off No. 233 Squadron from a point near Christmas Island, which progressed to Singapore via Java and Sumatra. The confidence of the pilots reflected the dangerous misapprehensions about the enemy that had matured over the years and which had still not been dissipated even with the sinking of Force Z. As one pilot put it, they were going to 'knock Japanese wooden biplanes out of the skies', a bit of a jolly for experienced British airmen and their well-regarded Hurricanes.

British naval power, of course, was extinguished at the start of the Malayan campaign. The vaunted Eastern Fleet assembled in early December 1941 under Admiral Sir Tom Phillips, a notorious unbeliever in the power of aircraft over capital ships at sea and a surprising choice of leader both to his colleagues at the time and naval historians since. When the Japanese attacked from Indo-China with aircraft from the 350-strong 3rd Air Division, the capital ships were not ready for action. The carrier HMS *Indomitable* did not escort the battleships because it had run aground in Jamaica. The fact that this was not seen as a major problem reflected the still unresolved debate within naval circles about the significance of the battleship versus the carrier. For men like Phillips the battleship still reigned supreme, and he was one of the many who believed that a battleship properly equipped with anti-aircraft defences could not be sunk from the air. Until December 1941 air attacks against battleships, no matter how heavy or closely pressed, had failed to do more than slight damage. So confidence in the ability of well-defended ships to see off the threat from the air was common, in America as in Britain. The final voyage of the ships was to hunt for Japanese transports. When

Prince of Wales and *Repulse* were spotted at 1710 on 9 December by submarine I-65 they were investigating reports of Japanese landings off Kuantan, having originally been on course to return to Singapore. Contact was lost until the following day when at 1140 a naval reconnaissance aircraft relocated them, and their position was reported to aircraft at bases in the Saigon area. Phillip's maintained radio silence, expecting an earlier signal to naval headquarters to result in the appearance of air cover from the peninsula's bases. British aircraft arrived on the scene, however, only to witness the final moments of the two ships and observe the hundreds of men in the water. Phillips went down with his ship, and a naval calamity entered the British record books, more for the fact that it destroyed a generations old system of imperial defence that pledged to shield Asia and Australasia as well as the Empire in the West, than because it cost Britain two of its precious capital ships.

The Japanese commanding officer in Malaya, General Yamashita, had 60,000 troops, several regiments of artillery, eighty tanks and forty other armoured vehicles. He was supported by the Imperial Japanese Navy's Malaya Force, 158 naval aircraft and 459 machines of the Air Division flying, like those that had put paid to the Royal Navy's main strength in eastern waters, from bases in nearby Indo-China, an earlier fruit of Japanese expansion and the malleability of the Vichy regime. The British were ill-prepared to defend Singapore from the peninsula approach, had lost control of the sea on the first day of action, and their air bases were poorly defended as well as poorly stocked. Even more difficult to overcome was the in-built military ignorance about the peninsula and its defence and the crushing ignorance and misconceptions that clouded almost every judgement on Japanese intentions and capabilities. The British imperial forces were far more static than the Japanese, even though more numerous. The Commander-in-Chief, Air Chief Marshal Brooke-Popham, had nearly 90,000 Australian, British, Indian and Malayan troops at the start of the campaign, and reinforcements were continuing to arrive. There were no tanks, however (despite Malaya's excellent roads), and the Air Officer Commanding Far East, Air Vice Marshal C. W. H. Pulford, had only 158 mostly obsolete aircraft with an equally obsolete reserve of eighty-eight (compared to the October 1940 defence appreciation stating that 566 aircraft would be needed to defend Singapore). The army had to defend a growing number of airfields, sited where the RAF wanted them rather than where the army could best defend them, and the navy and air force did not come to an agreement over the air defence of the precious capital ships before their final voyage. The airfields were poorly camouflaged and their ground defence inadequate or non-existent. Only 17 per cent of the authorized scale of light-and heavy anti-aircraft guns had actually reached Malaya. Air superiority was lost in the first few days of the campaign, leaving the army wrongly deployed protecting now defunct airfields. The brunt of the initial air action had been born by the Buffaloes, mostly flown by New Zealanders of Nos 453 and 488 Squadrons RAF.

The Japanese, having established forces on the Kra Isthmus and gained airfields, began attacking British airfields near the front line. The Japanese benefited from the capture of the four large northern air bases, which they called 'Churchill aerodromes'. The Battle of Jitra was a disaster for the 11th Indian Division, large quantities of stores and equipment were lost and, together with the retreat that followed, morale was badly undermined. There then ensued a disastrous battle at Slim River, which destroyed the division and seriously weakened the overall defence of the peninsula. In the peninsula's western half Penang was evacuated, and on 11 December 1941 it capital, Georgetown, was attacked by eighty Japanese fighters and bombers. There were no anti-aircraft guns and few air raid shelters, and over 600 people died. A working radio station was abandoned, as were an oil refinery, petrol warehouses and boats. What particularly horrified the governor, Sir Shenton Thomas, was that the Asian population had been so wantonly abandoned in their hour of need whilst efforts had been made to evacuate the Europeans. Kuala Lumpur airfield was evacuated, and by Christmas Eve 1941 the RAF had only thirty-eight Buffaloes left. Percival was loath to send the 8th Australian Division north, as he feared a Japanese landing in the south. In the eastern half of the narrow peninsula the 9th Indian Division fought a separate campaign. On 5 January 1942 it was decided to evacuate Kuala Lumpur and form a new line at the northern border of Johore. Shortly afterwards a retreat was ordered to a line across central Johore. Here, between Bakri and Parit Sulong, Australian troops won a notable victory at Gemas on 14 January, one of the few military engagements on the credit side of the ledger during the whole campaign. Notwithstanding this, the loss of the mainland followed and the decision was taken on 28 January 1942 to make a final withdrawal across the narrow Johore Strait to Singapore Island, which took place on the night of 30–31 January. The causeway connecting Singapore to the mainland was blown up, though not beyond Japanese repair (and to the detriment of the defenders, it also carried Singapore's main water supply). Up to that point, Malaya Command had lost over 19,000 killed and wounded, and a great deal of equipment. The Japanese had lost about 4500 killed and wounded.

On Singapore Island itself little was done to build up the island's northern defences facing the mainland. Percival divided the island into three defence sectors: Southern defended by two Malay and one Straits Settlement volunteer brigades; Western by 8th Australian Division and 44th Indian Infantry Brigade; and Northern by 3rd Corps (11th Indian and the remnants of 9th Indian divisions). The newly arrived 18th British Division was added, and Percival had over 70,000 men and a further 15,000 administrative and unarmed personnel. Singapore was dangerously congested with military personnel, and hundreds of thousand civilians, many newly arrived from the mainland. The island was heavily bombed from the start of the campaign and the city's air defences were negligible (later it was bombed by the Allies, with forces of up to a hundred B-29s appearing overhead). The defenders also faced artillery bombardment from the mainland. Attempting to defend the entire coastline prevented concentration when the

Japanese landed, and mobile reserves were inadequate to drive them back. Most of the formations were under strength, newly arrived or inadequately trained. Many were demoralized and short of equipment. There were far too many inexperienced troops around, crammed into a small area, and discipline began to crack. Hordes of troops took to milling around the harbour, seeking alcohol and transport away from the doomed island. People knew that the writing was on the wall when air forces were withdrawn and the naval base evacuated. Morale wilted further as radar operators were evacuated and equipment destroyed. Large amounts of RAF stock was withdrawn from Singapore's congested docks, bombed and bereft of labour, to strengthen South-East Asia's last redoubt, Java, where plans were already afoot to base a new Allied composite command of all the military remnants from the wrecked American, British and Dutch eastern empires. General Percival vastly overestimated the Japanese troop strength opposing him, believing that he was faced by 150,000 men and 300 tanks (overestimations of the Japanese strength became the norm once things started to go wrong). The irony of the situation was that the Japanese forces had culminated by the time that they reached the tip of the peninsula, and their commander did not think that the island could be taken in the face of resolute British resistance.

On the night of the 8–9 February 1942 landings were made on Singapore Island itself. Imperial troops quickly fell back from their defensive positions on the coast, being too thinly spaced and having been prevented – until the very last moment – from building proper defensive positions where the Japanese were most likely to land. On 12 February Percival ordered the formation of a perimeter defence around the town, further diminishing morale and leading to more desertions and a flood of refugees moving inland. Surrender came on 15 February to avoid unnecessary slaughter. General Sir Archibald Wavell, now in charge of the new American-British-Dutch-Australian Command based on Java and therefore in overall charge of Singapore, had authorized General Percival to seek terms when he saw fit. 14,000 Australians, 16,000 Britons and 32,000 Indians were captured out of the total of 85,000 on the island (including 15,000 administrative and unarmed personnel). The Japanese had advanced the length of the peninsula in under two months, suffering only 10,000 casualties. Total imperial losses during the whole campaign were enormous: 18,490 Australian, 38,496 British, 67,340 Indian and 14,382 locally-raised troops (those of the numerous Malayan states' Volunteer units), including two Singapore battalions of the Straits Settlement Volunteer Force, and a last-ditch Chinese formation led by Special Branch officer Lieutenant-Colonel J. D. Daley and known as Dalforce. This force was an example of the successful mobilization of the indigenous population to resist the Japanese that, if adopted wholeheartedly by the authorities in Malaya well before the invasion, might have played an important part in making the Japanese advance much harder. As it was, for the sake of 'morale', the civilian population of Malaya was kept woefully uninformed during the campaign and was never effectively enlisted in the struggle against the invaders. Locally-raised forces that took part in the campaign included the Straits Settlements Volunteer Force, the Federated Malay States Volunteer Force, armoured cars of the Singapore Volunteer Force, the Kelantan and Kedah Volunteer Force, the Johore Infantry and the Sultan Idris Company. Of the total imperial strength of 138,708, over 130,000 were marched into captivity by the Japanese during the Malaya campaign, from which many did not return. White servicemen were imprisoned in the infamous Changi gaol on Singapore Island, which initially contained over 50,000 men, while Indians went to separate camps. Many of these prisoners were soon to be sent north through Malaya by rail, on foot and by lorry to Siam and Burma to work on Japanese construction projects including the Burma–Thailand railway. Camps in Singapore became transit facilities as later in the war Allied prisoners from Sumatra and Borneo were also channelled north.

The fall of Singapore did not signal the end of imperial and Allied resistance to the Japanese in the region. American-British-Dutch-Australian (ABDA) Command was established under General Sir Archibald Wavell in January 1942. (Wavell was Commander-in-Chief India as well at the time and surely ranks as the busiest senior Allied commander during the early stages of the war.) It was as a scratch measure proposed by Roosevelt to Churchill in Washington at Christmas 1941, intended to unite the remaining Allied forces in the region from South-East Asia to the western Pacific in the frenetic period after Pearl Harbor and the destruction of HMS *Prince of Wales* and *Repulse*. Headquarters were established at Bandoeng on 10 January 1942, as it was clear that Singapore, the natural choice, was unlikely to hold out. The Americans were keen for Wavell to have the job, though the Commander-in-Chief India himself, whilst far too dutiful a soldier to cavil, wrote 'I've heard about carrying the baby. But this is triplets!' Cynics believed that America was keen for a British general in this experimental supreme commander role so as not to associate an American with the defeat that was likely to follow. ABDA's prime task was to defend Singapore and the Dutch East Indies. In the absence of any better plan, it was also supposed to cover Burma, Malaya, Thailand, the South China Sea and the northern and western coasts of Australia. The Chief of the Imperial General Staff, General Sir Alan Brooke, thought ABDA was wrongly configured and that Burma should have been omitted from the command's responsibilities and Australia and New Zealand included (they were included in new American command spheres, a fact that they were not entirely happy about).

ABDA Command had little time to prepare anything properly, however, and the command was crippled by its scanty resources, above all by the lack of substantial naval forces. There were no battleships or carriers, and the British imperial contingent rested on ships like the cruisers HMAS *Hobart* and *Perth*, HMS *Danae*, *Dragon* and *Exeter*, and the destroyers HMS *Electra*, *Encounter* and *Jupiter*. Most of these ships, including the *Exeter*, victor of the Battle of the River Plate, would not survive the opening naval exchanges between Japan and the

Allies. Thousands of British imperial troops and airmen congregated in the Dutch East Indies, many of them having managed to get out of Singapore. They did what they could, harrying Japanese invasion forces from the air and sea, without ever being able to overcome their relative weakness in numbers and the fact that they were not replenished. Whatever the expressions of pride and encouragement emanating from distant capitals, it was quite clear that this was a last-ditch stand and that death or capture were the likely outcomes.

Almost as hastily as he had arrived, Wavell had to leave his headquarters. The decision was taken to disband the command on 25 February 1942. Before it was finally wound up, the major action of ABDA's brief life took place on 27–28 February, when its combined fleet, under the command of the Dutch admiral Karel Doorman, tried to disrupt incoming Japanese troop convoys. This led to the Battle of the Java Sea, the largest naval battle since Jutland. Most Allied ships were lost and the Japanese invasion delayed by a mere twenty hours. The battle that followed in the Sunda Strait on 28 February–1 March 1942 saw the remaining ships in action. Of the initial force of fourteen warships, only a handful of elderly British and American destroyers escaped. Imperial air forces fared little better. Wavell had ordered all but eight Hurricanes and six Buffaloes to leave Singapore for the new bases in the Dutch East Indies. No. 226 (Fighter) Group Headquarters had been formed in Sumatra and No. 151 Maintenance Unit on Java. There was also an improvised bomber group in Sumatra (No. 225). More Hurricanes arrived from the carrier HMS *Indomitable* late in January 1942. The problem in the air was the same as at sea – too few units. What might have been achieved in the Dutch East Indies and Malaya, had a large number of modern fighters been available, was shown when the RAF stopped Japanese troops landing at the mouth of the Palembang river, killing thousands. By 18 February the evacuation of the air force from Sumatra to Java had been completed, and over 10,000 men in a state of great confusion had arrived on the island. Of the fifty or so RAF aircraft in Sumatra few survived, those that did escaping to Australia or Ceylon. When the inevitable happened and Java fell 11,500 British and Australian servicemen were captured. General Sir Alan Brooke back in London was relieved that this awkward command had come to an end: 'ABDA ended – at last! We can now run the war on a rational basis – the Americans running the Pacific up to Asia, including Australia and New Zealand, a British sphere running the opposite way around the globe, including the Middle East, India, Burma and the Indian Ocean'.

Brooke's relief at ABDA's demise, however, should not stand as the last word on this awkward and ill-resourced Allied command. Though seldom present in British accounts of the war in the region, it should not be forgotten that the Dutch were major players, under British leadership, in this campaign, and that for years the Dutch defensive plans for their eastern empire had rested squarely on the Singapore strategy. Furthermore, even with the fall of ABDA and the Japanese conquest of Java and Sumatra, Dutch forces continued to serve with distinction as part of the Eastern Fleet, despite having legitimate grounds to feel that they had been let down by their British ally in the defence of the East Indies.[7] Rather than, as is sometimes assumed, putting up a weak defence of their eastern colonies, the story of the Dutch East Indies campaign is one of misplaced Dutch trust in British and American promises of support, though, of course, the British and Americans were as surprised as anyone when the events of December 1941 wiped out all of their previous strategic calculations in the event of war with Japan. When war came, the Dutch committed some of their best forces to the Malayan campaign, and gave facilities to the US Asiatic Fleet after it had fled from the Philippines. They also defended the British territories in Borneo from Japanese naval attack. Dutch aircraft were detailed to work with British forces in the aerial defence of Borneo, and reinforced Singapore with two squadrons of Glenn Martins and one of Buffaloes. Even before the first Japanese attack on the Dutch East Indies, the Dutch had lost four of their fifteen submarines, along with some of their best aircrafts and crew, in executing a joint defence of British territories.

British reinforcement of the Dutch East Indies was non-existent until the two weeks prior to the fall of Singapore. The Australians sent RAAF and army units to the outer Indies – Gull Force to Ambon, Sparrow Force to Timor – which were placed under the orders of the local Dutch commander. The hasty creation of ABDA Command did not reassure the Dutch about the defence of their land and, reflecting British and American attitudes, only the command of the land forces went to a Dutchman, under Wavell's supreme direction. Nevertheless, the Dutch readily submitted their not inconsiderable forces to British command. The Royal Netherlands Indies Army comprised 30,000 men with a militia that took its strength over the 120,000 mark, its air wing provided 120 aircraft to the ABDA air force, and the highly professional Royal Netherlands Navy brought three light cruisers, seven destroyers, thirteen submarines and numerous patrol and torpedo boats to the Allied force.

The British forces that reached the Dutch East Indies were either fleeing from Singapore, or intended for Singapore but diverted en route. Three cruisers, four destroyers and some smaller vessels were sent to Java, as were two RAN cruisers and seven corvettes. The advanced party of the 1st Australian Corps reached Java on 26 January. They were followed by 3400 troops of the 7th Division, and a squadron of British light tanks reached Sumatra on 12 February. Squadrons of RAF fighters arrived from Singapore, or were flown off of carriers that had intended delivering them to the beleaguered island. Despite some early successes in defending Sumatra – British and Dutch forces at Palembang, RAF and Dutch forces on the Moesi river – the giant island was given up on Wavell's orders. The Japanese were then able to cut Java off from reinforcements coming from Australia, as well as invading Bali on 18 February and beginning the conquest of the eastern islands of the Dutch East Indies. The Battle of the Java Sea sealed the fate of the remaining Allied forces.

The Dutch were left with the distinct impression, as Wavell flew to India and various forces tried to make it to Australia or Ceylon, that a 'fight to the last' spirit had not been shown, and that it had been a strategic mistake to transfer responsibility for the defence of the Dutch East Indies from the Dutch Governor-General to the new British Allied commander. Given the situation, however, perhaps the British and the Americans were wise not to invest more in the defence of the Dutch colonies. With precious few resources to inject, and with the Japanese clearly on the way in force, it is difficult to see anything other than defeat as the eventual outcome. Nevertheless, all of the Allies involved sustained considerable losses. During the defence of the East Indies, the Americans lost thirteen warships, about forty aircraft and a regiment. The British lost nine warships, forty aircraft, four anti-aircraft regiments and a tank squadron as well as thousands of troops. The Australians lost two warships, thirty aircraft and the equivalent of two brigades of troops. The Dutch lost fifty-two ships, 200 aircraft and all but a few hundred of their soldiers.

Because of the rash of imperial defeats in British South-East Asia and the Far East, the lost lands of the Eastern Empire became an important theatre of behind enemy lines operations by special forces and their indigenous allies. In January 1941 a team left Britain to establish a Special Operations Executive (SOE) Mission in the Cathay Building in central Singapore (later in the war SOE in this region became known as Force 136). The Secret Intelligence Service (MI6) was also represented in Singapore in the form of the Inter-Services Liaison Department. In June 1941 SOE opened Special Training School (STS) 101 at Tanjong Balai, a large private estate at the mouth of the River Jurong, and STS 102 was later established in requisitioned premises at the Chunjin Chinese School near Kuala Lumpur. One of SOE's primary tasks was to prepare stay-behind teams in parts of the Empire that might be conquered by the enemy. These teams would then be in place to begin the dangerous work of relaying intelligence to the British armed forces, of executing acts of sabotage, and of recruiting indigenous people willing to take part in operations against the occupying forces.

SOE's attempts to prepare Malaya and Singapore for resistance 'should the invader come' were hampered by the reluctance of civil and military authorities to arm and organize stay-behind networks in the run up to the fall of Singapore. To prepare for invasion was to acknowledge a threat that many did not believe existed and that – if acknowledged – might panic the population and detract from Malaya's ability to contribute materially to the imperial war effort. It was a vicious circle. Though subject to much criticism because of its ostrich-like approach to the tides of war buffeting the region, it was difficult for a regime fundamentally based upon its superiority – over all locals as well as all potential challengers – to swallow its pride before a potential fall, that might not even come, and take prudent precautions. Besides, this was surely the task of the military authorities, and one of the command structure's great failings in Malaya was that there was no supreme military commander placed above everyone else. This lesson was painfully learned by the British, and following the fall of Singapore it was expressly ordered that Rear-Admiral Sir Geoffrey Layton, Commander-in-Chief Eastern Fleet when Admiral Phillips went down with *Prince of Wales*, be made supreme military and civil commander of the next threatened imperial base, the island of Ceylon.

Psychologically, the mindset of colonial Malaya meant that the peninsula froze as the Japanese juggernaut approached, puffing its chest out to the last. To allow SOE – viewed by many conventional soldiers as a grubby upstart outfit anyway – to organize post-invasion resistance was seen as defeatist and as setting a bad example to the locals. In a sphere of Empire where so much stock had been placed in British bluff and prestige, to admit that conquest was a distinct possibility was considered most unwise, especially as few were willing to belief that conquest was even a remote possibility. It would also detract from the government's efforts to raise Malaya to the highest pitch of productivity, and thereby be detrimental to its war effort. Malaya in December 1941 was a booming colony struggling to fill the ships that queued at Keppel Harbour to take its precious commodities away to Britain and America. The newspapers told people not to be unnerved by all the talk of war – the Japanese would never attack Singapore, whatever they might do in neighbouring lands like Siam – and the department stores tempted shoppers with all the lights and luxuries of Christmas.

In August 1941 SOE presented Governor Sir Shenton Thomas with a plan for the organization of stay-behind parties throughout Malaya. Acting with alacrity, it was eventually rejected two months later. It was said that it would be too great a drain on European manpower, that white men would not in any case be able to move freely in enemy-held territory, and that employing indigenous people on such a scheme – explicitly acknowledging the prospect of successful Japanese invasion in the process – would be disastrous for morale. Furthermore, the Chinese should under no circumstances be armed because many of them belonged to the outlawed Malayan Communist Party (MCP), founded in 1935 by Ho Chi Minh before his departure for French Indo-China. The GOC Malaya, Lieutenant-General Percival, also objected on the grounds of civilian morale. His superior, the Commander-in-Chief Far East, Air Chief Marshal Brooke-Popham, backed him up. In November 1941, however, Percival changed his mind and instituted a stay-behind policy of his own. By then, it was far too late.

Fortunately, used to operating in the teeth of official opposition from all sides, SOE in South-East Asia carried on regardless, though on a smaller scale than would have been possible if official backing had been forthcoming. It was to Malaya's Chinese community that SOE looked for support in resisting any Japanese invader, as well as to European planters and businessmen. The Chinese community were already mobilized against the Japanese because of the ongoing war in their homeland. All Japanese goods were boycotted (between 1937 and 1939 Japanese exports to Malaya dropped by 75 per cent), and money flowed into the China Relief Fund (creating a worrying flight of capital from Malaya).

Organizations like the Anti-Japanese Backing-Up Society flourished among the overseas Chinese community, making full use of traditional Chinese secret societies such as the Triads to stiffen their campaigns. By 1939 there were hundreds of associations with tens of thousands of members. SOE officer Major Freddie Spencer Chapman made contact with the Chinese, and it was agreed that as many as could be accepted were to be enrolled in STS 101. This occurred less than a fortnight before the Japanese landings, though the 165 communists who went to STS 101 became the core of the Malayan People's Anti-Japanese Army (MPAJA). SOE discovered that all the anti-Japanese societies were united under MCP leadership and that they were prepared to take part in any schemes against the common enemy. The Malayan Special Branch had already penetrated the MCP at the highest level, and an agreement in December 1941 committed the British authorities to release their MCP detainees and send them to STS 102. The Secretary-General of the MCP, Loi Tek, was a double-agent working for the British during the war.

Freddie Spencer Chapman's war career illustrates the nature of the covert resistance that characterized what fighting there was during the Japanese occupation of the lost eastern Empire. In August 1941 he was posted to Singapore's STS 101, after having trained Australian and New Zealand forces in Victoria in the art of ungentlemanly warfare SOE-style. When he arrived at the school from Sydney Airport in September 1941 it had only been running for six weeks, and Chapman was not impressed by the torpor that seemed to embalm Singapore. The general defence plan for Malaya, as far as he could ascertain, was for the RAF and the fixed defences of the great Singapore naval base to sink the Japanese transports far out at sea, if the Royal Navy had not already done so, whilst the infantry manned the open beaches in order to kill any Japanese who managed to get ashore.

Spencer Chapman and his fellow SOE agents were in action during the Japanese advance down the Malayan peninsula. In a period of two weeks he and his small raiding party destroyed seven trains, fifteen bridges and forty vehicles, killing several hundred Japanese soldiers. So began a war which, for Spencer Chapman and others like him, was to be fought entirely behind enemy lines, cut off from people, supplies and news from the outside world until the last months of the war, moving from guerrilla camp to guerrilla camp and living off the land. The Chinese community supported the guerrillas to the limit, so deep and abiding was their hatred of the Japanese. Spencer Chapman and other SOE operatives, some from the British armed forces, others from among the European community of Malaya and recruited by SOE from units like the volunteer regiments, conducted night ambushes and sabotage missions, often with Chinese guerrilla forces. It was extremely dangerous work. Spencer Chapman was often very ill indeed, and ended the war with bullet wounds in an ear, an arm and a leg, and the lasting effects of a mortar blast directly beside him during one engagement with a Japanese patrol.

Because of his experience as a trainer, and as a man with 'live' experience of fighting the Japanese, Spencer Chapman was in demand to train Chinese guerrillas, travelling cautiously at night. This could mean, for example, taking two weeks to cover fifty miles in order to team up with the Perak guerrillas known as No. 5 Independent Anti-Japanese Regiment. Venomous creatures, leeches, jungle ulcers (deep enough for three sixpences to fit into each), sores, malaria, blackwater fever and grubs, and innovations like the use of fireflies in the reflector of a torch, form the backdrop of Spencer Chapman's fascinating account of Force 136's behind-the-wire campaign, *The Jungle is Neutral*. The title reflects the perception common among British imperial servicemen that the jungle was a hostile environment, which the Japanese could master but they could not. In fact, the jungle was neutral – an armed neutrality for sure – and could be used to advantage, providing food, fresh water and cover to those with the necessary skills. Dispelling the government of Malaya's theory that whites could not operate behind Japanese lines without being detected, Spencer Chapman found that lamp-black, iodine, potassium permanganate and coffee blackened his European skin most effectively.

Spencer Chapman stayed with the Menchis guerrillas for a year from July 1942, attached to No. 6 Independent Anti-Japanese Regiment. These regiments showed the worth of even the minimal amount of work that SOE had been able to conduct before the fall of Singapore, all five of them built up around the nucleus of men and weapons put in by STS 101. The Chinese guerrillas had also harvested an enormous number of weapons following the British imperial débâcle at Slim River in January 1942. The guerrillas created organizations and networks that the colonial government, upon its return, was bound to regret; and, whilst the actions of men like Spencer Chapman were important, the Chinese guerrilla organization ran its own show when it came to opposing the Japanese. Their political and military cadres came complete with their own crude systems of law and discipline, as Spencer Chapman discovered when he visited a traitor-killing camp deep in the jungle. The regiments were a part of the Malayan Peoples Anti-Japanese Army (MPAJA), the military wing of the MCP. In 1945 this organization numbered 7000. Towards the end of the war, with Japanese resources stretched, the MPAJA gained control of some rural areas. Japanese records indicate that the operations of the MPAJA and its SOE allies inflicted 2900 casualties on the regime's police force and the Japanese army. The MPAJA and other SOE-trained outfits were to be important when Mountbatten's South-East Asia Command launched its amphibious assault on Malaya, operating in the same way as SOE cells in occupied France on the eve of D-Day, harrying the occupier, cutting his lines of communication and reporting his movements, as the attack came in from the coast.

In 1944 the SOE/Force 136 agents in Malaya finally established contact with headquarters in Ceylon, and new agents were infiltrated by parachute and by submarine. The Malayan Country Section of Force 136 had been established in July 1942. Its first insertion in May 1943, Gustavus I, saw John Davis and five Chinese men embark from Ceylon on a Dutch submarine, from which they paddled ashore in folboats from a drop-off point in the Malacca Strait. Three more Gustavus insertions followed, and Spencer Chapman linked up with the new arrivals. Wireless contact was, very intermittently, maintained with Ceylon headquarters. News sheets were printed for distribution amongst the people, and the MCP published its own organ, the *Voice of Malaya*. As the operations of Chinese and Force 136 fighters gathered momentum in early 1945, and British bases like Ceylon penetrated behind enemy lines more effectively, it became possible to broadcast radio programmes. Force 136 and Chinese guerrilla forces were increasingly supplied by air drops. In June and July 1945, for example, 249 sorties over Malaya were flown from Ceylon. In August 1945 Nos 99 and 356 Squadrons, recently moved to the new RAF base on the Cocos Islands, were placed at the disposal of Force 136. In August and September 1945, 756 sorties were flown from this base and from Ceylon.

Many other behind enemy lines operations were carried out in the vastness of Burma, Indo-China, Malaya and Thailand. Terence O'Brien was an Australian pilot who had volunteered for service in the RAF. After serving in Europe, he was sent east to command a Special Duties squadron, one of the units specializing in operations over enemy occupied territory. In this role, O'Brien and the men of No. 357 Special Duties Squadron flew Dakotas and Liberators from Jassore in East Bengal, dropping agents, equipment, leaflets and dummy packages over a vast region. The British gained permission to mount operations as far afield as Indo-China and Laos, and O'Brien's crews flew many missions over this region as well as over Burma and South-East Asia. The deception schemes that O'Brien's men were involved in were usually the brainchild of D Division in Delhi, headed by Peter Fleming.[8]

The Japanese occupation was disastrous for the Malayan economy, and many of Malaya's people, particularly the Chinese community, experienced the Japanese at their very worst.[9] Some regions, however, were less affected, given their remoteness from the main centres of Japanese power and interest. During the actual campaign the Japanese had moved too rapidly down the peninsula to pay much attention to the civilian population, but they soon began to look around after achieving victory in Singapore. Brutality, particularly against the Chinese, was the order of the day. In the week before the capitulation six to seven thousand perished, and the leaders of the Chinese community estimated that thirty to fifty thousand died during the occupation. Atrocities were numerous, the British particularly remembering the Alexandra Hospital massacre of 13–14 February 1942. Throughout Malaya the Japanese occupation heralded the interruption of a vibrant economy. Shortages of consumer goods, unemployment, high prices, corruption and a thriving black market became commonplace, and the situation worsened as the occupation lengthened, particularly given the worsening military fortunes of the new imperial masters. By 1944 the effort to maintain pre-war standards of comfort had for many people given way to a grim battle for survival.

People were hungry, dressed in rags and falling victim to diseases for which treatment was no longer available.

Given its status as an economic and strategic jackpot, the Japanese had no intention of following the route taken in Burma and granting Malaya independence, even of the sham variety. Malaya was to be annexed and there was little room for encouraging independence movements and attempting to work through indigenous leaders enjoying the trappings of Bantustan power. The Japanese ruled Malaya as a military province from headquarters in Singapore. Japanese rule was characterized by cruelty, racial arrogance, corruption, forced labour and crop and raw material confiscations. Most Malayan people were genuinely glad to see the British return, even if some had different ideas about how long they wished them to remain.

Japan's usual rallying-cry of 'Asia for the Asians' did not translate well in the Malayan setting, even though some people welcomed the removal of British rule. This was because it was quite clear from the outset that all local interests were to be subjugated to those of Japan. The eradication of Western influences became a key feature of Japanese rule, and measures were taken to replace such influences with Japanese culture, language and emperor-worship. In January 1943 a list of a thousand banned British and American songs was published. The Japanese attempted to adapt the administrative structure left by the British for the purposes of their own administration, though all of its senior personnel had either left or been imprisoned and there was therefore a lack of experience. Although the Japanese limited the power of the sultans, they could not replace them as they still needed to work through them, and Malays in the administration kept their jobs, many being promoted to fill vacancies left by their departed British superiors. The Malayan radical Ibrahim Yaacob was released and attempted to mobilize grass roots support for the new regime. Some younger men were encouraged to join the administration, and some Malayans were sent for special training or joined Japanese-sponsored paramilitary units. For the sake of administrative convenience, if nothing else, the Japanese realized that senseless alienation of the local people would be extremely counter-productive, and with this in mind they also respected the Islamic faith.

A problem for the Japanese was that once they had conquered new colonies, they had to occupy and administer them immediately; the full extent of the economic benefits that had been the reason they were conquered in the first place took much longer to come on stream. What Japan really could have done with in 1942 was a decade's peace in which to digest its newly-acquired empire, before resuming the war against the Allies. In Malaya battle damage and damage resulting from scorched earth operations was extensive, disrupting the operation of rubber estates and the transport infrastructure. A greater problem was that Japan was rapidly losing control of the seas, and so was increasingly unable to protect its dwindling merchant marine, and therefore unable to export the produce of Malaya. The peninsula's riches, which after the war were to make it the British Empire's most valuable asset and a phenomenal earner of precious dollars, were observed by the unfortunate Japanese but largely untapped.

It was also unfortunate that the Japanese wanted coal and iron from Malaya when it was geared to the production of tin and rubber. An inability to absorb Malaya's rubber brought this booming industry to a standstill. The Japanese lack of merchant shipping greatly reduced their ability to supply the needs of their new territories as well as to extract resources from them, a basic duty of an imperial power, as abundant rice, for example, was stockpiled in Burma while rice shortages developed elsewhere. A lack of imports led to inflation, hoarding, rationing and food shortages requiring compulsory food production campaigns (common throughout the world at the time). The peninsula's rice production fell (Freddie Spencer Chapman noted that in October 1944 rice prices were one hundred times the pre-war figure), and, where food was short, disease followed. The disruption of Malaya's society and economy heightened communal tension, as did new political configurations. For example, the Japanese allowed Siam to annex territory in the north which had been ceded to the British in 1909. They attempted to strip the sultans – key collaborators in the system of British rule – of their powers, and encouraged a new Malay nationalism. Indians were encouraged to join the Indian National Army, which had its base in Singapore alongside Subhas Chandra Bose's provisional government of India. Nevertheless, 60,000 Malayan Indians were sent to work on the Burma–Thailand railway, two-thirds of them perishing in the process. Japanese efforts to alter the political landscape were blunted because of their worsening military position, their shortage of manpower and the general chaos left in the wake of Britain's withdrawal.

The violence of the war period, its strong ideological currents and the experience of dramatic regime change fostered heightened political awareness and nationalism in Malaya. Working counter to this, however, war exhausted some of the nationalist drive, as well as profoundly altering the setting in which nationalists operated; the war had 'shorn the rungs off the ladder they hoped to climb and damaged the citadel they aspired to take'. For some nationalists the occupation was a period for consolidating support rather than taking on a regime that clearly was not going to be beaten by non-military means. The Malayan Communist Party believed that Japan would eventually be defeated, so chose to oppose the new regime. Of course, communist activity had to be concealed. The MCP, supported mainly by the Chinese (though not by the supporters of the Kuomintang), formed the Malayan People's Anti-Japanese Army. The Union of Young Malays (Kesatuan Melayu Muda – KMM) initially tried to work through the Japanese and was allowed to raise a military force, but it was banned in mid-1942, leaving the Indian Independence League as the only legal political movement. The KMM thereafter kept in touch with the MPAJA.

Showing admirable spirit, as soon as they lost a colony the British began plotting for its return, the administration usually having a plan in place before their military counterparts had worked out how to find the resources with which to eject the enemy. The damage to the pre-war imperial structure was deep, however, and the Japanese conquest and ensuing years of harsh occupation expunged the economic, political and military realities of the pre-war era that had been the foundations of colonial rule. But planning for the post-war world went on regardless, and, despite opposition from nationalists, the Chinese and the Americans, Churchill and his ministers displayed a dogged determination to go back as rulers. Churchill insisted that only the British reconquest of the iconic Singapore would restore British prestige in the East, and throughout the lost empire the British government was adamant that British forces should affect the reoccupation. Exasperated by American attempts to undermine the British Empire or hinder its reconstitution in areas where territory had been lost, British policy-makers pointed to American self-interest and America's own colonial holdings, such as the Philippines and the Japanese islands that American forces were conquering in the Pacific and from which they would be unlikely to depart once hostilities ceased.

To make Britain's return to its Eastern Empire a viable proposition would require – even more so than in other parts of the Empire where new rhetoric and a new spirit of partnership and development was abroad – a reconfiguration of power and a new sharing of the benefits under colonial rule. Planning was conducted at the Colonial Office by the Malayan and Borneo Planning Units. Radical proposals envisaged a union of British territory in the region and the eventual formation of a self-governing Dominion of South-East Asia with Commonwealth membership. Approval was given for a union of the Malay states and the Straits Settlements of Penang and Malacca, for Crown Colony rule in Singapore, Borneo and Sarawak, and for a single Governor-General responsible for the whole region. As in Arabia, Australia, Canada, Central Africa, East Africa, South Africa and the West Indies, the British love of federations expressed itself in South-East Asia as a way of charting a viable post-war political future for the region.[10] Among other things, these changes were to end the rule of the Rajah Brookes in Sarawak, which, after a period of British military administration, assumed the status of a Crown Colony under a British Governor in 1948.

Despite the unmistakable force of nationalism that the war revealed in South-East Asia, a vibrant 'new imperialism' was designed to contest the future of South-East Asia in the post-war years, as Britain determined to hold this strategically and economically vital region to the British camp. Plans for the post-war reconstruction of Malaya had been gestating since May 1943, so as soon as the reoccupation had taken place, the British government was able to announce its new policy, involving far-reaching constitutional changes affecting administration in British territory – the Straits Settlements – and British treaty relations with the Malay sultans. The object of the policy, as announced by the new Labour Party Secretary of State for the Colonies, George Hall, on 10 October 1945, was to establish a constitutional union of Malaya and to create a common Malayan citizenship in which immigrant communities had equality of status with indigenous Malays.

The union would produce a strongly-centred federation, and the great hope was that a unified, British-orientated Dominion of South-East Asia would be born and would remain within the orbit of the New Commonwealth (a term popular after the war to describe the new, non-European member states of the Commonwealth club). Moreover, efficient planning meant that, when Mountbatten's troops reached the Malayan beaches in September 1945 during Operation Zipper (or sank on the beaches in the case of the armour), civilian administrators were ready immediately to begin the work of ensuring that the machinery of local government was restarted.

Journeying east from the Malay peninsula, significant British strategic and economic interests had come to roost in the giant island of Borneo. Here the British had carved out the colony of British North Borneo and put down commercial roots, and the island of Labuan had been acquired on behalf of the navy. The sultanate of Brunei entered into protected relations with Britain, and the Sultan ceded part of his territory, Sarawak, to an Englishman in the 1840s, his heirs retaining authority until the war. Collectively known as British Borneo, the region formed part of Malaya Command's sphere of responsibility. (Malaya Command was the army command under the general military framework of Far East Command.)

As in Hawaii and Malaya, Japanese interests were embedded in Borneo long before the war. Commercial activities, like the management of rubber plantations and trade, were favourites of the Japanese, and firms like Mitsubishi and Nissan were involved. Intelligence-gathering prior to hostilities was another common theme connecting Borneo to the other areas of Japanese conquest, as when the Japanese consul at Sandakan embarked on a tour of Borneo, Brunei and Sarawak in October 1940. This was quite obviously a mission to select suitable landing places for an invasion force. A Japanese think tank, the Institute to Promote Pacific Relations, highlighted Borneo's economic appeal in 1937, particularly the oilfields at Miri in Sarawak and Seria in Brunei.

The Borneo coastline was fringed with mangrove swamp, the interior with thick evergreen forests. The territory's three million inhabitants used the rivers as the main form of communication, and there were few roads. Borneo occupied a strategically important position on the main sea route to Malaya and Sumatra, Java and the Celebes. There were not the forces available, however, to defend it adequately, given Malaya Command's inevitable focus on protecting Singapore and the Malay peninsula. It was unfortunate therefore that the Japanese decided that, as a subsidiary to their Malayan campaign, they would attack Borneo in order to gain its oilfields, to guard their flank and to help prosecute their campaign against Sumatra.

British Borneo was to become another region of Britain's Eastern Empire that was lost to the enemy. Before that came to pass in January 1942, however, the territories of British Borneo spent over two years contributing to the imperial war effort. British sanctions against Japan before December 1941 adversely affected Sarawak and Brunei, as both territories had exported oil to the Japanese home islands. The limitation of exports to Japan also caused difficulties in North Borneo, where many properties cultivating staple products were Japanese-owned. The infiltration of Japanese settlers had been a cause for concern for many years, but had been commercially beneficial to the colony, and much of the rubber, hemp, copra and jute exported from British Borneo was Japanese-produced.

A strategic reconnaissance of Sarawak was carried out in March–April 1940. The report suggested that part of Sarawak was easily defended and the General Staff at GHQ Malaya therefore decided that a small detachment of troops could defend the colony's strategic objectives. Sarawak was to be fought for, whilst the almost indefensible North Borneo, Brunei and Labuan were not. The airfield of Kuching in western Sarawak was to be defended, part of a broader defence that also encompassed Dutch airfields at Sinkawang over the border in Dutch Borneo. This Dutch airfield, it was hoped, would be a strongpoint for RAF aircraft, though in the event only a small number of Buffaloes and Dutch Glenn Martins were available to operate from it. On 23 December 1940 a detachment of the 2nd Battalion The 15th Punjab Regiment ('C' Company, comprising about a hundred men) was sent to Miri to assist and protect the civilian demolition parties of Sarawak Oilfields Limited, and to cover their withdrawal to Singapore. On Christmas Eve 1940 'B' Company of 2/15 Punjab Regiment was sent to Kuching to assist 'C' Company in covering the withdrawal from Miri, should it be ordered. In the meantime, they were to organize and train a local defence force. On 12 May 1941 the rest of the regiment arrived at Kuching, billeted in specially constructed barracks at Batu Lintang, two miles out of the town. The regiment thus had an opportunity to redress its lack of jungle training, learning to move and live in the jungle and swamps, and to construct defences around Kuching and the aerodrome five miles from the town. Some training was done in operating with guerrilla units, and the guerrilla training of the Sarawak Rangers continued, along with the Sarawak Volunteers and the Armed Police. Other locally raised units, such as the ARP, the Auxiliary Fire Service, the Sarawak Coastal Marine Service and the Voluntary Aid Detachment, also continued their training. In August 1941 a partial denial scheme was put into effect and the production of the oilfields cut by 70 per cent.[11]

Thus by the eve of the Japanese attacks on Borneo a sound mobile defensive plan had been devised and rehearsed. All told, Lieutenant-Colonel C. M. Lane's SARFOR (Sarawak Force) consisted of seventy-eight officers and 2642 other ranks, including just over a thousand all ranks of the 2nd Battalion The 15th Punjab Regiment. The cost was borne by the Sarawak government. The GOC Malaya, Lieutenant-General Arthur Percival, flew to Kuching in late November 1941 to inspect the garrison. It had been decided that the south-western part of Sarawak only would be defended, based on the aerodrome at Kuching, with a second line of defence shared with the Dutch at Sinkawang on the west coast of Dutch Borneo (sixty miles south east of Kuching). Percival, despite objections, insisted on a static defence for the Kuching aerodrome, centralizing the troops and overturning their previous dispersion. All troops were to be concentrated within a three and the half mile perimeter of the airstrip. When he hurried back to Singapore on 30 November, SARFOR was left to move equipment into central positions and dig slit trenches and other defences around the aerodrome. Defensive mobility was to be sacrificed, simplifying matters for the Japanese when they arrived. All of SARFOR's defensive plans and training to date had been reversed in the space of an afternoon thanks to Percival's appraisal and subsequent orders.

Sarawak had been ruled for a century by the descendants of James Brooke, the first Rajah. An employee of the East India Company, he had quelled a rebellion in the region, and the Sultan of Brunei had rewarded him by making him ruler. The territories of Sarawak were extended, and in 1864 Britain recognized the country as independent, though in 1888 gave it protectorate status as a means of warding off the attentions of acquisitive European powers. The absolute rule of the Rajahs was drawing to a close as the Second World War approached. On 24 September 1941, acutely aware of the closeness of war and the lack of British resources to defend his country, Rajah Sir Charles Vyner Brooke celebrated the centenary of his family's rule, announcing that autocratic rule would end in Sarawak and a constitutional monarchy emerge. The new constitution was celebrated with speeches, galas, horse races and triumphal archways. Dyaks, Malays and Chinese paraded in ceremonial costume, and Kuching was a blaze of lights at night, and by day the river was crammed with flagged and garlanded boats. But this special moment in the country's history was very soon to be swept away by war, and the sighting of a Japanese squadron off Miri on 23 December 1941. Before that day, with the Japanese momentarily detained elsewhere, Sarawak had taken the prescribed steps in preparation for war.

On 8 December, with Pearl Harbor wreathed in smoke and HMS *Prince of Wales* and *Repulse* about to be sent to the bottom of the Gulf of Siam, the oilfields at Lutong, Miri and Seria were set alight and the firing parties evacuated to Singapore (a platoon of the Loyal Regiment, a section of the Hong Kong and Singapore Gunners and a few Royal Engineers). A result of the complicity of the Vichy regime, the Japanese base in French Indo-China was the launching pad for the assault on British Borneo, just as it was for the land and air assault on Malaya. Three days later the same was done to the oilfields in Sarawak. On 16 December a Japanese brigade landed unopposed at Miri, while a large part of the delivering convoy continued westwards and anchored off the Sarawak river. On the same day landings were made in Brunei. On 19 December Kuching bore its first air raid, suffering over a hundred civilian casualties. Between 20 and 22 December the Kuching runway was destroyed and SARFOR took up its defensive positions around the aerodrome's perimeter. Despite the success of a Dutch submarine in destroying four out of a group of six Japanese transports on 23 December, the following day eight troopships protected by five escorts, carrying about 4000 men, sailed up the Sarawak river and landed unopposed. On Christmas Eve 1941 five Blenheim bombers of No. 34 Squadron, flying from Tengah, attacked enemy shipping approaching Kuching. It was not, however, enough to reverse the decision. On the same day, after destroying all messages, ciphers and wireless equipment, the government of Sarawak's officers surrendered at 4 o'clock in the afternoon. They were promptly chained together and displayed in the main bazaar. Kuching was captured that afternoon, the Japanese being welcomed by a number of Japanese residents.

A Japanese battalion left at Miri secured Labuan Island on 1 January 1942. Labuan was home to 5000 Chinese, 3000 Malays and six British (including the manager of the cable and wireless station, the British Resident, the Customs Officer and the Harbour Master). The denial scheme allowed for the destruction of the cable and wireless equipment and stocks of oil. On 27 December a Japanese aircraft had flown over and machine-gunned Government House, the harbour, the hospital and the convent, and dropped leaflets portraying John Bull standing over prostrate Asians. Japanese troops arrived in the evening. Hugh Humphrey, the British Resident of Labuan, suffered because of his thorough enactment of the denial scheme, being hit repeatedly on the face by a Japanese officer shouting 'Bad prisoner, burn oil!' Japanese troops took Jesselton on 8 January. On 17 January two infantry companies landed at Sandakan, the seat of the British government of North Borneo. The Governor surrendered the state the following morning.

Thus within a few Christmas Days the Japanese had occupied British Borneo, Sarawak, Labuan and Brunei. There was, however, still nearly two months of fighting ahead for SARFOR as it abandoned static defence and returned to mobile warfare. The force dealt severely with a Japanese force at Sibu Laut near the mouth of the Kuching river, and then engaged the Japanese in defence of the airfield. It quickly became clear that it could not be held, so SARFOR withdrew towards the Dutch border. 'A' Company, covering the withdrawal, defended the crossing of the Sarawak river at Batu Kitang on Christmas Day. At the end of the fighting, 220 men of the 15th Punjab Regiment were captured and taken back to Kuching, being treated roughly, herded into the town gaol, and left unfed for five days (soon after they were transferred to Seria in Brunei to operate the oilfields). At Krokong the retreating force abandoned its heavy equipment and vehicles and disbanded the Sarawak Rangers, the Sarawak Volunteers and the Armed Police (as with the Burmese soldiers of Burmacorps and the indigenous soldiers in British Somaliland, their service had come to an end and they were free to return to their homes). Continuing without the protection of their guerrilla activities, the 2/15 Punjab Regiment reached the airfield at Sinkawang II on 29 December 1941. Unfortunately the airfield had already been visited by twenty-four Japanese bombers, its strategic significance thereby negated. The Dutch aircraft could not take off with a bomb load, and so were withdrawn to Palembang on Sumatra.

On New Year's Day 1942 SARFOR, now consisting solely of Punjabis, came under Dutch command and set up a defensive line twenty miles inland. The

Japanese landed more and more troops along the coast and forced the defenders further towards central Borneo. Eventually the commanding officer decided that his force's best contribution would be to try and escape to Java to rejoin any forces that might be resisting the Japanese there. They therefore split into two columns and followed different routes to the south coast. They arrived at south coast ports on 20 February and 1 March 1942 respectively, to find a confused situation and little chance of escape. The Dutch authorities surrendered formally on 9 March, and the two reunited columns of the 2/15 Punjab Regiment discussed the possibility of continuing resistance. They were, however, still formally under Dutch command, and the Japanese arrival at Kumai on 31 March decided the issue. Two days later the Punjabis marched to Kumai and handed in their weapons. The men were transferred to Kuching in October 1942, though some were sent to Changi camp in Singapore. At Kuching the officers and men were separated, as were the Indians from the Europeans. The Indians were abused in an effort to persuade them to join the Indian National Army. Like many other prisoners of war, captivity did not mean four years of sedentary hardship: the British and Indian prisoners in Borneo found themselves shipped around, for example to operate oil fields and build roads. Japanese brutality combined with a lack of anything like adequate rations or medical supplies meant that many prisoners died. Lieutenant F. E. Bell of the 48th Light Anti-Aircraft Regiment, Royal Artillery, arrived at Batavia in the Dutch East Indies on 3 February 1942, in time to meet the Japanese invasion on 1 March. Upon the surrender of all Allied forces, Bell was confined for a time in Batavia before being transferred to Changi in Singapore on 27 September 1942. On 9 October he was transferred to Jesselton in North Borneo as part of a group of 1886 prisoners. On 25 November 1942 he was moved again, this time to Sandakan on the Borneo coast. In August 1943 he moved to Kuching. When elements of the Australian 9th Division landed to liberate British Borneo in June 1945, one officer and about 150 men were all that remained of the thousand men of the 2/15 Punjab Regiment.

Borneo became one of the major prisoner of war sites in the new Japanese Empire. Thousands of British, Indian and Australian soldiers died on the giant island, and today the Sandakan War Graves Cemetery contains the graves of 2972 soldiers. The central Japanese camp was at Kuching, with lesser camps at Jesselton, Sandakan and Labuan. For civilian internees, there was a camp at Batu Lintang near Kuching (formerly the barracks of the 2/15 Punjab Regiment), where a form of self-government by committee operated among the internees. These camps did not just hold prisoners captured during the Borneo campaign. They were also used as transit camps as prisoners were shunted around Japanese territories for storage or labour purposes. For example, after the capture of Singapore 2750 military prisoners were shipped to Sandakan (about 2000 Australians of the 8th Division, the remainder from different British units). By August 1945 only half a dozen of these men remained alive. In October 1942 1800 British military prisoners were shipped from Java to Borneo, 800 being interned at Jesselton, the remainder at Kuching. In the same month, 1886 prisoners from Changi were taken to Kuching. Work for POWs in Borneo included the operation of the oilfields, construction of airfields, working rubber estates and constructing roads to the Tegora and Geding mercury mines.

British North Borneo, Brunei and Sarawak were governed as one military unit, divided into five divisions, by the Japanese 37th Army. The new Japanese military commander, Marquis Toshinari Maeda, was quick to put into action Tokyo's plan for 'the discovery and acquisition of resources'. That, after all, was why the new Japanese Empire had been acquired. The Miri oilfields and the Lutong refinery were revived. Crop production became a major concern of government, given the difficulty of obtaining imports. The achievement of self-sufficiency in food was a positive effect of Japanese rule. Timber resources were exploited. Lacking the resources to do otherwise, the Japanese sought to work with existing political leaders to the greatest extent possible, leaving people little touched in more remote parts of the territory, for example, using educated Ibans to run the Second Division territory. There was, however, plenty of evidence of standard Nipponization. Schools conducted Japanese language classes. There was every encouragement for anti-European sentiments among the indigenous population. A North Borneo Volunteer Corps was formed in October 1943, consisting of 850 men in three companies. Though Japanese rule in Borneo was not as harsh for the inhabitants as it was in other parts of the empire, the Chinese community had to be constantly on its guard, and by 1944 resentment against the Japanese was widespread. Food shortages, Allied bombing and news of Japanese setbacks compounded this public feeling. The Ibans expressed their resentment in open armed clashes from the latter half of 1944, cooperating with the soldiers of the Australian Inter-Services Reconnaissance Department.

An important feature of the British Empire's war effort was the delivery, to all corners of the globe, of mail from families at home in Britain, Canada, India or Australia, to their relatives based overseas.[12] The need for this contact only increased when men were taken prisoner, though of course the barriers to the successful delivery of mail increased a hundredfold. By April 1942 over 10,000 bags of mail for British soldiers serving in the East had accumulated at Durban. After the loss of most of these troops in the Malayan campaign, the decision was taken to return the letters to sender as undeliverable. The case of mail intended for British prisoners in Borneo illustrates the threads of Empire during a period of global war. From March 1940 all air mail in and out of Britain was handled by the Postal Censorship Office in London. Far East air mail was then carried on the civilian carrier BOAC's Poole (Dorset)–Shannon (Ireland)–Lisbon air link. From Lisbon the mail moved overland via Spain and Vichy France to Switzerland. From Berne it went via Trieste to Istanbul, thence on to Tehran. The mail bags then went into Russian hands for a transcontinental journey on the Trans-Siberian railway, via Harbin and Mukden, until reaching Pusan in Korea. The mail was then taken by sea to Tokyo, before being carried to Singapore for distribution across Japan's prisoner and internee network spreading from the Bay of Bengal to the Pacific. A less common route in this planetary marathon was for mail to be put on board a Neutral Exchange Ship which would meet a Japanese vessel in the Indian Ocean or at a Portuguese East African port.

It almost goes without saying that once in possession of the mail Japanese efforts to distribute it were poor. This only added to the anxiety of families at home desperate for news, though it made the arrival of a letter, in whichever direction, a most significant affair. Aircraftsman W. Hazel was captured at Singapore only days after arriving in February 1942. His wife was notified by a letter on 15 March 1943, though she did not receive her first communication from her husband until August 1943, written from a POW camp in Borneo. In the other direction, Hazel received no mail from anyone at home until September 1943.

The people of the territories of British Borneo, prisoner and native, endured three years of Japanese occupation. A small number of civil servants were recalled to continue their work in the administration, the treasury and other essential departments of government, and by the first quarter of 1942 essential departments were running and public services functioning at a minimum level. In some parts of British Borneo resistance against the Japanese continued throughout the war. On 10 October 1943, for example, the Kinabula Guerrillas began their activities against the Japanese in the Jesselton–Kota Belud area. The Japanese responded with brutal reprisals against civilians. Resistance obliged the Japanese to transfer troops from Kuching until they had about 25,000 men in the area, and headquarters was transferred from Kuching to Jesselton. Australian and British agents were parachuted into British Borneo, for example Major Tom Harrisson of the Green Howards. He was seconded to Z Special Unit and sent to Borneo in 1944 in command of Operation Semut (Malay for 'ant'). Z Special Unit was part of the Inter-Services Reconnaissance Department, Australia's SOE (Force 137). Z Special Unit was responsible for organizing the large-scale uprising throughout Borneo that was timed to coincide with the Australian invasion.[13] Numerous Australian units operated in British Borneo, including its SOE-trained Independent Companies, and British SOE units were sent to make contact with anti-Japanese forces. SOE began enlisting local mountain tribes to fight against the Japanese. The Japanese were detested by the mountain people, particularly the head-hunting Iban, who became staunch allies in SOE operations to clear the country. SOE personnel also gathered information on Japanese movements and conditions in the prison camps in Kuching. They were joined in August 1945 by Chinese-Canadian SOE operatives who spoke Cantonese and who had been trained at SOE schools in Canada.

As Allied fortunes improved, air strikes against Borneo were mounted, American bombers, for example, targeting the oil installations. These strikes, and the depletion of Japanese forces elsewhere, meant that by March 1945 Japanese surface transportation in the region was at a standstill, and all weapons, material, provisions and medical supplies sent to Borneo from Singapore remained stockpiled at

Kuching. By the end of 1944 inter-island transport and shipments from overseas had virtually ceased. Australian forces, with American naval support, were responsible for reconquering this corner of Britain's lost Eastern Empire. The distinction fell to elements of the 1st Australian Corps supported by the RAAF, working from New Guinea via Morotai and Tarakan. The reconquest of British and Dutch Borneo was to be very much an Australian operation, spearheaded by the 9th Division and an Australian tactical air force.[14] The US Navy gave crucial support, and the Royal Navy was represented by HMS *Shropshire*.

In June 1945 the main assault force sailed in convoy from Mortal, whilst supporting forces sailed in five separate convoys from ports in the Philippines and Halmaheras in the Moluccas. Simultaneous amphibious landings were made by 24 Brigade on Labuan Island, and by 20 Brigade at Brooketon, in both cases with three infantry battalions. The campaign that followed featured the use of tanks, rapid advances aided by the willing cooperation of the indigenous people, especially the Dyaks, and the capture of a large number of Japanese prisoners. Over a hundred Australians were killed in the reconquest, and 1234 Japanese corpses were counted. The Inter-Services Reconnaissance Department's teams estimated that, with the help of the Dyaks, their operations accounted for a further 1800 Japanese dead. There was much work to be done once the victory had been won. The Japanese had set fire to the major oil fields, and it took three months and 7600 man days to extinguish them, involving 2400 troops. There was also a great need for medical attention both for the liberated prisoners and the indigenous population. In August leaflets were air-dropped over the areas where the Japanese were still concentrated, telling of the end of the war and Emperor Hirohito's instruction to maintain order and hand over weapons when Allied forces arrived. On 19 August 1945 a leaflet was dropped over Kuching bearing a message from the Rajah of Sarawak, headed with his royal coat of arms, the Rajah's personal crest and the crest of Brunei, in order to establish the document's veracity. The official Japanese surrender in Sarawak took place on 11 September 1945 on board HMAS *Kapunda* at Kuching.

In attending to the thousands of internees the Australian Red Cross was essential. Those needing attention were taken on board a corvette, carried down river to the sea and the American destroyer *Barnes*, then on to Labuan on board a 'duck' amphibious vehicle to finally be delivered to an Australian hospital. There were two Australian general hospitals set up on Labuan, each with 600 beds, along with a 300 bed Casualty Clearing Station and a Convalescent Camp for 1600 people. When called upon to do so, the 2/1 Australian Hospital Ship *Manunda* transported freed prisoners to Singapore for onward movement home. After mopping up all Japanese resistance and supervising the repatriation of Allied prisoners of war, the 9th Australian Division handed over to SEAC's 32nd Indian Brigade in January 1946. In the following month the Australian air component, No. 81 Wing RAAF, was transferred to Japan and replaced by an RAF detachment. As was the case in Burma, planning for the restoration of British rule in British

Borneo had not been neglected, though the territories remained under SEAC military administration for many months after the reconquest. A British Borneo Civil Affairs Unit existed and worked with the occupying military authorities to restore order, and in 1946 indigenous rulers like the Sultan of Brunei and the Rajah of Sarawak returned from exile.

British interests in the Far East had grown in the modern period with the 'opening up' of China in the first half of the nineteenth century, accomplished by the force of Royal Navy and Anglo-Indian arms, but based upon commercial and trade interests. Britain and its offshoots like the East India Company had for long been engaged in trade with the Far East, by the overland route terminating in the Levant and by direct sea links. New interest in the region had been stimulated by the burgeoning new settlements on the eastern coast of Australia and Britain's growing interest in the Pacific region. The fact was that the Far East was now on the map for British seafarers and explorers of all descriptions, as well as armchair world experts back at home, as china, tea and silk joined the list of commodities that the European market could not manage without. Inevitably, imperial intervention followed, the tone being set by British-led wars against the Chinese Empire from the 1830s.

Britain annexed the island of Hong Kong at the end of the First Opium War in 1842 (the Kowloon peninsula was ceded in 1860 and the mainland New Territories leased from the Peking government in 1898). But Britain also gained rights in many Chinese ports, places like Tientsin and Shanghai becoming part of Britain's informal empire by virtue of its right to station troops in them (including the capital, Peking), its trade privileges, investments and the extra-territorial jurisdiction that made Europeans immune from the processes of Chinese law. Britain's presence in these coastal enclaves was pioneered by merchants and investors. Big companies like Jardine & Matheson and Butterfield & Swire dominated Chinese trade with Britain and came to play a major role in the upcountry trade, organizing and shipping local Chinese trade around the coast and on the inland rivers. These avenues to the interior provided further evidence of Britain's informal imperial presence, as they were patrolled by river gunboats of the Royal Navy right up until the fall of the Chinese branch of the British world in 1941. The British invested heavily in railways, and the Hongkong and Shanghai Banking Corporation (HSBC) was founded in the 1860s to finance British business in the region. British firms carried 42 per cent of the total of foreign coastal and inland shipping, and Britain controlled over half of all China's shipping. As well as dominating commerce and finance, Britain was also a major force in cotton mills, factories and insurance.

As befitted its position as the pre-eminent western power in China, it was to Britain that the Chinese government had turned in desperation for help in the face of Japanese aggression in the 1930s. Given Britain's military incapacity in the region, however, as it worried about the activities of the dictators closer to

home, a policy of appeasement had been pursued as the only practical substitute
for hard military power. For Britain's mammoth soft power stake in China – in
the spheres of business, transport and finance – was not shielded by sufficient
hard power in the form of warships, fighters and soldiers, though there were
many of these scattered throughout the region. British policy in the face of
Japan's manifest aggression against China had been to not rock the boat, and to
do all possible to try and preserve British interests by confining Japanese expansion and quietly offering what little financial and military succour it could to the
beleaguered Chinese state.

Whilst besting Chinese military forces in the field, and trampling on China's
people in their homes (as during the infamous rape of Nanking), Japanese power
entwined itself around Western interests in China like ivy slowly choking a tree.
Before 1941 Japan occupied many of China's coastal provinces and deprived the
Western powers of their historic privileges, humiliating them in the process. But
in this period, despite the hope China reposed in Britain as the major great power
in the region, there was very little in reality that could be done to resist Japan.
British prestige buckled and bent with each passing year. Of course, the problem
was the same as elsewhere; Britain was facing an aggressive and – judged against
the norms of international relations to which Britain held – a defiant and unreasonable military dictatorship that threatened British interests and refused to play
by the rules. Britain was militarily weak after decades of disarmament, did not
want a fight, and had everything to lose and nothing to gain from conflict. It had
long ago acknowledged the fact that it could not maintain a fleet powerful enough
in Far Eastern waters to deal unilaterally with a major industrial enemy when in
1902, needing to concentrate more warships in home waters to meet the challenge
of the German High Seas Fleet, it had entered into a defensive alliance with Japan.
All European regimes in the Far East and South-East Asia were militarily weak
and dependent on the status quo; Japan was militarily strong and itching to
expand. America was not keen to link arms with Britain and take a stand against
the Japanese. Standing alone in 1940–41 and facing challenges in different parts of
the world all at once, with its mainstay great power ally lying prostrate and Hitler
parading on the Champs-Elysées, British strategy was paralysed in the East.
Sufficient forces to deal with Japan – the Admiralty thought that its entire main
strength would be needed in the Far East if matters were to be contested with the
Japanese – were simply unavailable because of the threat to Britain itself and its
imperial position in the Mediterranean and Middle East. What British forces there
were in the China region – the destroyers, elderly cruisers and river gunboats of
the China Station, and the soldiers dispersed in the treaty ports – were there to
help maintain law and order and protect British trading and diplomatic interests.
They were quite incapable of fighting a high-intensity war against a determined
and well-armed opponent in its own backyard.

It was these factors that saw Britain's imperial presence in China, founded on
victory in the First Opium War, rudely brought to an end when Japan occupied

all of the key areas of British power and influence in the region, radiating outwards from Shanghai, the major beacon of British-led Western capitalism in the East. All of the unequal treaty privileges – including extra-territoriality and the right to appoint a British Inspector-General of the Chinese Customs – that Britain had held were formally relinquished in an agreement of 1943 with its new ally, the Chinese government of Chaing Kai-shek. Of course, by this time the British rights had been swept away, and, whatever arrangements the post-war world held in store, a return of British treaty rights along the Chinese coast was unlikely to be among them. As a result of American policy, the Chinese government became an equal with its erstwhile imperial superiors (which Churchill considered farcical). Whilst Britain was determined to retrieve Hong Kong after the war, there was no chance of it reclaiming its position in Shanghai and outposts like Tientsin. Colonial China had gone for good. The relationship between Britain and China as allies was always a difficult one, China, on the one hand, undervalued Britain's contribution against the Japanese in Burma and was determined to resist the reimposition of Britain's former imperial role. Britain, on the other hand, was unable to view China as an equal after a century of inequality, and was shocked by the prospect of China interfering in imperial affairs in India and South-East Asia and deplored Chiang Kai-shek's Asian nationalist, anti-imperialist, stance. This led to discord when Japanese defeat neared, for Britain insisted on retaking Hong Kong with its own forces and receiving the Japanese surrender, though, in terms of the carve-up of military commands in the region, it came under Chiang's China Area Command.

Nothing better captured the waning of Britain's imperial star in the Far East, and the unreal twilight period before the sudden rise of Japanese power in 1941, than the fate of the Royal Navy's China Station.[15] In the few years between 1937 and war with Japan in December 1941, the China Station suffered death by a thousand cuts as diplomatic relations with Japan time and again constricted the fleet's room for manoeuvre, as Japanese forces grew larger and larger, and as Japanese forces took advantage of any opportunity to humiliate Britons, damage British interests or cause a situation that would demand a humiliating apology. As has been seen, the force configuration of the China Station was in no way designed to go head to head with the navy of a first-class maritime power. There was only ever one or two modern units on station, no larger than cruisers, and most of the fleet's vessels were ageing destroyers, sloops, submarines and river gunboats designed specifically for work on China's coastal and inland waterways (like the 'Insect' class, including ships such as HMS *Bee*, *Gnat* and *Ladybird*). The China Station was a trade protection force and a visible and potent reminder of British prestige. Whilst a symbol of Britain's imperial heritage, by the 1930s it was a force for stability in the region appreciated by the Chinese as well as the citizens of other foreign powers with interests in China.

The China Station was one of those quintessentially imperial forces – not a simple alien imposition, but a force that had had the time to grow into and become a part of its habitat, rather like the King's African Rifles or the Arab Legion. Most ships' companies were half British and half Chinese, many men having been recruited in Hong Kong or Shanghai. Its shore bases in Shanghai, Tientsin, Wei-Hai-Wei and elsewhere were manned by locally-recruited men and women. In 1937 the Commander-in-Chief China Station had over a hundred vessels under his command covering ten thousand miles of coastline and navigable waterways. On the outbreak of war with Germany, however, many of his ships began to be transferred to waters where there was a more urgent calling, particularly for trade protection duties in the Indian Ocean and Persian Gulf. This greater need coincided with the increasing incapacity of the ships to work usefully in Chinese waters, given the parlous state of Anglo-Japanese relations. Following the Sino-Japanese incident of 1937, as Japan became more powerful and bullish throughout China, the warships of the China Station became less and less able to act freely, so that even conducting the most routine business became extremely difficult. As one junior officer later recalled, 'matters reached the pitch where we were told not to take photographs from our own ships for fear of offending the Japanese', and even the most minor incident involving a drunken sailor on shore-leave could escalate into a major incident

Like Singapore, Hong Kong was not supposed to be invaded by the Japanese. Despite the turmoil of the Sino-Japanese War raging so close at hand, European eyes in Hong Kong were fixed firmly on the situation in Europe. New Year 1939 was full of hope after the passing of the Munich crisis. The cabarets, weddings, parades, billiards, sports fixtures, receptions and dinners that filled everyday life in colonial Hong Kong continued as per normal. There was the annual St George's Society Ball, Burns Night for the colony's Scots, visits aboard warships and a New Year's Ball at the Peninsular Hotel hosted by the flagship's company. This was a façade of peace and order as the Royal Navy continued its difficult task in an increasingly hazardous environment, suffering more and more disputes with the Japanese, who, predictably, interpreted the Munich agreement as a sign of British weakness.

In the early years of the war in Europe the ships of the China Station had plenty of work to do. HMS *Falcon* was alongside at Chiang Kai-shek's Chunking headquarters acting as a floating radio station for the British Embassy. Most of the seagoing warships were employed in patrolling the waters of the Dutch East Indies in order to counter the German surface raider threat, and it was expected that German merchant ships sheltering in Japan would attempt to break out. Warships continued to be transferred to western theatres, however, as the European war showed no signs of spreading to the Far East. The China Station was viewed by the Admiralty as a reservoir of seasoned ships and men.

The larger units were the first to be transferred. A division of the 21st Destroyer Flotilla had left Wei-Hai-Wei at the time of the Nazi–Soviet Pact, and the rest of the flotilla followed in September 1939. The carrier HMS *Eagle*, together with the heavy cruisers HMS *Cornwall* and *Dorsetshire*, formed a raider hunting group in the Bay of Bengal, and soon the China Station submarines were also heading west. Sloops were needed to escort coastal convoys in the North Sea, so HMS *Kent* left to reinforce the Home Fleet. With virtually no riverine trade with China to be protected anymore, and given that they were a source of such great irritation to the Japanese, even the specialist river gunboats began a westward migration. Most were to be withdrawn to Singapore, where they could be converted into minesweepers or anti-submarine vessels. HMS *Aphis, Cockchafer, Cricket, Gnat, Ladybird* and *Scarab* were destined for the Mediterranean and Persian Gulf, and *Dragonfly, Grasshopper, Scorpion* and *Tarantula* got as far as the East Indies. The China Squadron had virtually become an Indian Ocean and East Indies force, a fact that was recognized when Admiral Noble moved his flag to Singapore. The cruisers HMS *Emerald* and *Enterprise* of the East Indies Fleet, together with the China Squadron cruisers HMS *Danae, Dauntless* and *Durban*, spent most of their time patrolling the trade routes searching for raiders or waiting to intercept blockade-runners. By September 1941 very few Royal Navy ships remained in Chinese waters. The hangers-on included two old destroyers (HMS *Thanet* and *Scout*), four gunboats, a handful of harbour craft, the immovable wooden depot ship *Tamar* at Hong Kong and the 2nd Motor Torpedo Boat Flotilla. HMS *Thracian* laid mines, shadowed Japanese convoys and intercepted radio traffic which, among other things, revealed the Japanese build up of forces in Siam and Indo-China. HMS *Petrel* was acting as a floating radio station for the British Consulate ashore in Shanghai.

Shanghai presents an intriguing example of a territory that, whilst not imperial pink on the map, was to all intents and purposes a part of the British world, in terms of buildings, businesses, lifestyle, policing and political control.[16] Of Britain's $963 million stake in China, three-quarters was invested in Shanghai, the sixth largest city in the world (38 per cent of all foreign holdings in China in 1931 were British). Shanghai's famous International Settlement was run by a municipal council dominated by Western property owners, mainly from Britain and America. The council was led by the heads of organizations like HSBC and the great British merchant houses like Jardine & Matheson. The two brothers who ran this company, Tony and John Keswisk, were also the heads of Britain's clandestine war effort against the Japanese, for Shanghai was 'the intelligence capital of the Far East'.

Even before the outbreak of war with the Western powers in 1941 and the ejection of their forces and personnel from all of their Chinese enclaves, the Shanghai of old was slipping away. Shanghai was in decline from the Japanese intervention in 1937, for Japanese forces remained in Greater Shanghai, took over the industrial sector of the International Settlement and devastated the countryside surrounding the city. Unchecked violence, inflation and business uncertainty and slow-down sapped the city's reputation and effectiveness. The Chinese government strung booms across the Yangstze in November 1937, which hampered the Japanese navy but also brought the city's lifeblood river traffic to a halt. Shanghai lost what had made it great; the Yangtse River and access to the interior. The Chinese Maritime Customs, for so long a British-organized revenue-earner for the Chinese government, was taken over by the Japanese (purely for their own purposes), as was the Chinese Telegraph Office and Wireless Administration. The foreign cable companies were made subject to Japanese censorship. All of these moves, like the gradual emasculation of the Royal Navy's China Squadron based on Shanghai, were a part of Japan's slow but sure strangulation of all things Western in China, and its rolling back, ever further into the interior, of the independent government of China. The British Western enclaves became isolated, ever-shrinking, surreal islands in a darkening landscape, surrounded by Japanese barbed wire, roadblocks and buildings cleared to give Japanese machine-guns a clear field of fire. Yet even into this choking environment, until recently a beacon for international growth, cosmopolitanism and migration, the more seasoned representatives of the damned of the earth continued to pour: between 1938 and 1941 18,000 German and 4000 Polish Jews arrived in the Hongkew region of the city (including the only complete Jewish theological college to escape from Hitler's Germany). As one woman in Germany wrote: 'I nearly took my life last week. Only this news, that one can get easily to Shanghai, kept me from doing it.'[17]

The Municipal Council, chaired by Tony Keswick, was in a difficult situation. The Japanese could, of course, at any moment have taken the whole of Shanghai, rather than gazing covetously at the Bund whilst allowing all to carry on apparently as normal. The council had fourteen members – five Chinese, five British, two American and two Japanese. The Japanese complained at the representational mathematics involved – 30,000 Japanese residents in the International Settlement to 10,000 British. An election was fought in April 1940, when both sides tried to win over new voters (particularly the recently-arrived Jewish community). The British told residents to subdivide property, and thus register more names, and won by a whisker. The next ratepayers' meeting was a highly-charged affair, in front of 2000 Japanese and 3000 Westerners, at which the Japanese taunted the Westerners, and the Westerners tried to get taxes increased to deal with the mounting law and order crisis resulting from Japanese activities and direct encouragement to crime in the name of status quo destabilization. During the proceedings, Tony Keswick was shot twice by a Japanese man. Surviving the incident, from that moment on Keswick drove around in a bullet-proof car once owned by Al Capone.

The Shanghai Municipal Police was British-run, and its Special Branch gathered information for MI6. There was a British wireless monitoring station able to read telegram traffic on the Shanghai–Berlin and Mukden–Berlin lines. Efforts were made to prepare Shanghai for war, though this was very difficult, given the fact that within the cocooned settlement life wore a veneer of reality, and because the only kind of war that could come to Shanghai could not be defended against. The city was at the mercy of the encircling Japanese. A Shanghai Volunteer Corps of 2500 was recruited, though there was no plan to resist should the Japanese come in force to take the International Settlement – the Western commercial and diplomatic heart of Shanghai – as it was recognized that the city was not defensible with the resources available. Upon first entering the city Japanese troops confined themselves to the Chinese quarter, though strangling Western business in the process and humiliating Westerners in any way possible. As well as surrounding it from the outside, Japan attempted to win Shanghai from the inside as well, by intimidation and guile and by using political and constitutional pressure. By September 1939 the Japanese had more voters for the Shanghai Municipal Council than the British did. In this phoney war period the main battlefields were flagpoles, newsprint and airwaves. Britain's position was on a knife edge.

On the outbreak of war there were 1496 British and 1234 American troops in Shanghai, and over 4000 troops belonging to the two powers stationed elsewhere in China. In August 1940, however, the British government decided to withdraw its troops from Shanghai, Tientsin and Peking, because if it came to war they would simply be lost, or forced to withdraw in the most humiliating circumstances by a Japanese leadership bent on picking a quarrel. A battalion based in the Tientsin concession had already been transferred to Egypt earlier in the year. It was the old dilemma familiar to Britain as it attempted to deal with the bully powers strung across the world from Europe to the Far East by way of the Mediterranean: to withdraw gave the appearance, to all concerned, of weakness; to remain might provoke the first blow, which inevitably, given the lack of forces, would be a knock-out one. Of course, these withdrawals only encouraged Japan to persist in its designs to oust all British and Western interests and dominate China. The Royal Navy had withdrawn from Shanghai, leaving only the gunboat HMS *Petrel*. This vessel put up a stiff fight on 6 December 1941, the day before Pearl Harbor, when the Japanese opened their war against the Western powers, Shanghai's first and last battle of the war. Refusing to surrender to the Japanese, her two Lewis guns failed to see off a sustained attack from a Japanese cruiser, destroyer, gunboat and shore batteries (her main three-inch armament was immobilized). On 8 December, as America awoke to the carnage of Pearl Harbor and Japanese troops landed on Malaya's coastline, Japanese forces attacked the settlements in Shanghai and Tientsin and interned all British nationals, amounting to over 6000 in Shanghai alone. Pregnant with symbolism, Japanese troops occupied the headquarters of HSBC and expropriated the premises of Western clubs. British citizens, along with those from other Western nations, were interned in eight camps. Some Britons continued at their posts for a time after the Japanese conquest (raising the issue of collaboration), for example in the Shanghai Municipal Council, the Municipal Police and the Hankow Light and Power Company. The statue of Sir Robert Hart, first British Inspector-General of the Chinese Maritime Customs, was dismantled, and street names were changed. The Shanghai of old was dead.

Shanghai under Japanese occupation suffered economically, food shortages were acute and factories closed down. The fall of Singapore was marked by a Japanese-organized Rally of East Asiatic People. But as was the case throughout Britain's lost Eastern Empire, the war behind enemy lines continued. SOE started its Oriental Mission under John Keswick, and before the outbreak of war MI6 had had an estimated 300 agents in Shanghai alone. The China sections of SOE and its American counterpart were 'like the Shanghai Club in exile', SOE also being said to resemble 'Empire trade in khaki' because of the number of local businessmen that it recruited. One aim of SOE was to create effective escape channels for Allied servicemen attempting to get to friendly lines. SOE's Oriental Mission was hampered from the start because Keswick fell out with Chiang Kai-shek's intelligence service, making British activities from Chinese territory difficult.

Shanghai was the only part of the British imperial world that the British did *not* intend to return to after the war. The British government realized that Britain lacked the economic power ever to regain its position in China, especially in the light of America's economic power and its attitude towards China and Chiang Kai-shek. China, therefore, would cease to be an area of operation for the British imperialists who remained to act upon the world, and would be replaced by the rise of Hong Kong. Furthermore, with the treaties by which British and Western interests had remained lodged in Chinese coastal towns officially terminated in 1943, the Chinese government had every expectation of itself taking over Shanghai once the Japanese had been ejected. The Foreign Office estimated that British wartime losses in China, excluding shipping, amounted to 11 per cent of the total investment in 1941 (about £135 million). Recognition of Chinese independence after the war, however, in no way signalled a British desire to 'give up' in the Far East. Power would simply be redeployed. Britain's intention was to retake Hong Kong and develop it as a major entrepôt between the China and the West – a new Shanghai and new capitalist powerhouse. This was why Churchill and the Chiefs of Staff, as the end of the war in the East hove into view, were so determined to get British forces to Hong Kong before the Chinese or Americans beat them to it.

Hong Kong had been affected by Japanese aggression in China throughout the 1930s, particularly because it was a major supply channel for goods destined for China. To try and avoid provoking the Japanese, arms supplies via Hong Kong had been stopped, as it was feared that Japan might mount a blockade of Hong Kong in retaliation (the Hong Kong–Canton route for supplying the Chinese government was cut after the Japanese occupied the latter city, leaving French Indo-China and the Burma Road as the only avenues of supply for Chiang Kai-shek's government). After the fall of France, the Japanese redistributed their forces in south China, meaning that Hong Kong became effectively cut off from the territory of the Chunking government of Chiang Kai-shek. Japanese spies had been operating in Hong Kong before the war, gathering intelligence about troop numbers, dispositions and communications. Reflecting the uncertainty with which Britain's Eastern Empire prepared for war, and the 'will they, won't they' attitude to the prospect of a Japanese attack, little was done to crack down on Japanese spies in the colony. Many British settlers, as in Malaya, refused to believe that the Japanese would dare to attack, others realized that there was little they could do whatever they chose to do, other than keep functioning as normal. Possible suitors for a defensive alliance, like the Chinese nationalists and the Chinese communists, were spurned until the eleventh hour, the British administration of Hong Kong as much aware of the potential pitfalls in such alliances as they were of their potential defensive benefits. Far too late in the day, the colonial administration teamed up with these anti-Japanese Chinese elements, and enlisted the support of the local Triad gangs for defence and to ensure public order in the event of war. Indeed, with powerful Chinese political and criminal organizations in Hong Kong and significant Japanese infiltration, the extent to which the British actually 'ruled' Hong Kong is open to question.[18]

Some visible defensive measures were taken, however, despite this unpromising background. A network of rice stores was formed should Hong Kong be cut off from external supplies. Before hostilities commenced 1646 service families, and over 1800 wives and children of European civilians, were evacuated from the threatened outpost. This move caused great anger amongst many non-European sections of the community, and a group calling itself the 'Bachelor Husbands' protested at having their wives sent away whereas many influential men had managed to ensure that their wives were allowed to stay because of 'essential' war work. Others had cause to complain that contracts for the construction of air raid shelters and other defensive works were unfairly awarded. These disputes, between communities and within the European community itself, reflected the divided and contentious way in which Hong Kong faced up to an attack as 1941 unfolded.

Hong Kong was supposed to be defended by the American Pacific Fleet at Pearl Harbor, and by the 'Singapore Strategy'. Indeed, the colony had contributed £250,000 to the construction of the base. As in the case of the fortress base, Hong Kong had most of its heavy guns facing out to sea, and planned to withdraw forces from the mainland onto the island in the event of an overwhelming attack. The idea was that the island could hold out for long enough until relief arrived from the sea. Adequate provisions for defence of the colony against a determined and sustained Japanese attack in detail were not made, reflecting belief in Singapore, the overall dearth of military resources in the East, the desire not to provoke Japan by an egregious military build up and the dilemmas surrounding the deployment of token forces. Furthermore, it was impossible to predict what the Japanese would do, and there was the widespread belief, from London downwards, that Japan would not go to war. The imperial cupboard was bare and the military potency of the Japanese soldier underrated. Modern defensive elements such as air reconnaissance and radar were lacking in Hong Kong, as were aircraft and major warships. Despite this, considerable, and under the circumstances impressive, efforts were made to defend the colony in the event of an attack. 50,000 sandbags were purchased and all Chinese of British citizenship invited to enrol in an emergency force. The Hong Kong Volunteer Defence Force had been established years before the war, and in 1938 numbered 1175, growing to 2400 in June 1941 (also known as the 'Hughesiliers' or 'Methuseliers' after Colonel A. W. Hughes of the Union Insurance Company, who raised it). Mobile artillery was provided by the mountain and medium batteries of the Hong Kong and Singapore Royal Artillery, one of the many imperial military units in existence at the time. As in other British colonies there were Civil Defence Services, such as the Auxiliary Quartering Corps that found billets for essential defence organizations. There was also a small Hong Kong naval force. The Hong Kong ARP had enrolled 12,000 people, mostly Chinese, before the outbreak of war in 1939. Looking seawards as well as to the air, the coastal defences had been modernized and minefields were laid to protect the sea approaches. Local naval defence consisted of four destroyers and a number of light craft of the Royal Navy's China Squadron, while the garrison included two British and two Indian infantry battalions, three heavy coast defence batteries, two anti-aircraft batteries, two mountain and two medium batteries and two fortress companies. As has been seen, by the end of August 1939 the Admiralty had begun to withdraw the major units of the China Station for the protection of convoys in the Indian Ocean and the strengthening of the Home and Mediterranean Fleets.

Kai Tak, the colony's air base, was hardly overstocked. Its air strength in December 1941 amounted to three Vickers Vildebeeste torpedo-bombers, rising to seven on the eve of the Japanese attack. There were two Walrus seaplanes at the seaplane station in Kowloon Bay. The defence of Hong Kong was in the hands of the army, which was represented more impressively than the navy and the air force. The Shing Mun Redoubt was the centrepiece of the colony's defence, guarding the most vulnerable route into Kowloon. This mini-Maginot Line consisted of a series of strong points, including seventy-two pillboxes, centred on the Redoubt and stretching from Gin Drinkers' Bay to Tide Cove in the New Territories. The plan in the event of an attack was to hold this line for long enough to allow an orderly evacuation of Kowloon and a build-up of strength on the island, which would then hold out until the arrival of relief forces from Singapore.

The garrison stood at 12,000 combat troops by December 1941, including Canadians, Indians and Scots. The surprising involvement of Canadian forces in the minor imperial disaster that was to unfold came about because of the Canadian government's eagerness to get its soldiers into useful war roles, and the service in Hong Kong of a high-ranking Canadian officer. Major-General A. E. Grasett, a Canadian, handed over command in Hong Kong to Major-General C. M. Maltby in July 1941 and returned to London by way of Canada. Whilst there he told the Chief of the Canadian General Staff that the addition of a battalion or two would make Hong Kong strong enough to withstand a prolonged attack. Thus on 27 October 1941 the Royal Rifles of Canada and the

Winnipeg Grenadiers, previously on garrison duties in Newfoundland and the West Indies, embarked for the Far East, there to join men from Royal Scots, Middlesex, Rajput and Punjabi regiments. What the Canadian government did not realize was that Hong Kong's defence rating by the British government meant that it was still classified as an 'outpost', and therefore unlikely to be strongly reinforced in the face of an attack. In their hurry to get Canadian troops into more prominent war roles, the Canadian government had inadvertently condemned hundreds of men to a very short tour of duty in Hong Kong followed by a very long stay in Japanese prisoner-of-war camps.

On 8 December 1941 Japanese units of the 23rd Army's 38th Division attacked Hong Kong as they were more or less simultaneously attacking Hawaii, Malaya and Shanghai. All British aircraft were wiped out by thirty-six Japanese fighters of the Takatsuki Aviation Squadron on the opening day, and thus – as in other theatres where Japan was to triumph over imperial arms – there was no capacity to dispute Japanese command of the air from the very start of the campaign. Japanese troops crossed into the New Territories of mainland Hong Kong and by 10 December had broken through the main defence lines, taking the Shing Mun Redoubt and forcing the garrison to retire to Hong Kong Island, where all forces had gathered by 13 December. The decision to evacuate the New Territories was not communicated to the Chinese community, causing great consternation. Refugees nevertheless fled to the island, and law and order broke down in Kowloon, the British enlisting the aid of Triad gangs to try and stop the looting and disorder. But by this time British control and effective defence was petering out. Soon the Japanese controlled the power and electricity sources for the island, as well as the main reservoirs, another premonition of Singapore. Resistance was spirited but ineffective. Even though the China Squadron had very few ships left in places like Hong Kong and Shanghai on the eve of the Japanese attacks, there were still considerable numbers of naval personnel on station. Naval forces in Hong Kong amounted to 1600 Royal Navy, Royal Marines and Hong Kong Royal Naval Volunteer Reserve personnel, including the one-armed commander of the gunboat HMS *Cicala*, destined to be the last ship put out of action in Hong Kong. Two destroyers at Hong Kong were ordered to Singapore on 8 December, leaving only the destroyer HMS *Thracian*, *Cicala* and eight motor torpedo boats. All performed gallantly, providing fire support for the army, intercepting Japanese landing craft, sinking merchant shipping and evacuating troops from untenable positions. HMS *Cicala* was eventually crippled on 21 December by three direct hits from dive bombers and sunk in the West Lamma Channel. She had been the subject of sixty dive bomber attacks. On the day that Hong Kong surrendered, Christmas Day 1941, the 2nd Motor Torpedo Boat Flotilla made a dramatic escape from the colony. About seventy British and Chinese personnel, mainly from the navy but including two Ministry of Information employees and three members of SOE, escaped. The boats were scuttled in Mirs Bay on China's Guangdong coast, and the men then made their way overland to safety.

In the fight for Hong Kong 2000 imperial servicemen were killed and 1300 wounded, the figures being considerably higher for the Japanese. Governor Sir Mark Young, recently arrived from the governorship of Barbados, announced the surrender. It was the first time that a British Crown Colony had ever surrendered. Young's number two, Colonial Secretary Franklin Gimson, had arrived in Hong Kong on the day the invasion began. The Japanese victory resulted in looting, torture and rape, and over 4000 civilians were killed. In a lawless period, Japanese troops sacked the city. An estimated 10,000 Chinese women were raped. As elsewhere, the Japanese indulged their penchant for bayoneting prisoners. In the emergency hospital at St Stephen's College, fifty-six mainly Canadian soldiers were bayoneted in their beds. In the grounds of the Victoria Hospital, thirty British soldiers were bayoneted and incinerated with petrol. When they had stopped the general and indiscriminate slaughter, Europeans were publicly humiliated before being interned.

After the surrender soldiers were imprisoned in Kowloon, civilians at Stanley Camp, where over 2500 were interned, including 350 Americans. All classes of Europeans were housed together, causing bitter social tensions. A Japanese military governor, Lieutenant-General Isogai Rensuke, arrived to rule Hong Kong, annexed outright to Japan, and much booty was sent to Japan during his period of office. Hard currency was raked in and new taxes imposed. Over 20,000 cars and buses were heaped up on the cricket ground to be cannibalized or dispatched to the fighting fronts. (There were only 150 cars left in the colony by the end of the war.) As much as possible was done to Nipponize things, including the removal of statues, the renaming of shops, theatres and buildings, and the renovation of Government House. Japanese public ceremonies were forcibly celebrated and the Japanese calendar was introduced. Measures were taken to reduce the Chinese population, which had swelled by hundreds of thousands in the weeks prior to the attack. Hong Kong's sole purpose was to support the army. The Japanese aimed to rule Hong Kong through the Chinese gentry upon whom the British had also relied, and aimed to keep elements of the old administration, including Indian policemen, willing to work with them. The press was given freedom to give vent to Chinese frustrations with the British colonial period, one of the many ways that the Japanese attempted to elicit acceptance of their rule, even if not active support.

Support for the Japanese waned, as elsewhere, the more that Japan's fortunes sank. From July 1943 Hong Kong began to endure incessant American bombing. Its connection with the wider world severed, the British Empire's third port sank into destitution. Fewer and fewer raw materials and supplies arrived from the south, as Japan's merchant marine was decimated. A black market run by the Triads became responsible for feeding the population, and food shortages were severe throughout the colony. A creeping disenchantment was noticeable in the ranks of the gentry, who quietly began to prepare for another change of rule in Hong Kong. 'With singular genius' the Japanese even managed to alienate the most supportive group in the colony, drawn from among the Indian community, more susceptible than other ethnic groups to the promises of Asian cooperation espoused in the name of the Greater East Asian Co-Prosperity Sphere.

Whilst Japanese rule settled upon Hong Kong, determination to recover the colony grew in London. This was in spite of recommendations from the Foreign Office that the Chinese be allowed to take the colony. This, it was argued, would win favour from Chiang Kai-shek's government, and also from the Americans, who were pressing for this concession. Other British forces, however, were determined to recover the island. From bases in China the British Army Aid Group (BAAG) ran spies into the colony and helped the prisoners in any way possible. BAAG was an offshoot of MI9.[19] SOE and its special Z Force was also present, operating from China under the direction of John Keswick. The Colonial Office in London were also keen for Franklin Gimson, the most senior civilian in Hong Kong after Governor Sir Mark Young's removal to Japan, to assume power whenever the Japanese defeat came about. Plans were also made to provide a naval task force for the island's relief, though all of these plans were dependent upon a final Japanese capitulation.

As the war entered its final phase Churchill again and again emphasized the importance of British imperial forces retaking the lost empire in the East. 'Rangoon and Singapore are great names in the British eastern world, and it will be an ill day for Britain if the war ends without our having made a stroke to regain these places and having let the whole Malay peninsula down until it is eventually evacuated as the result of an American-dictated peace at Tokyo', he declared. For Churchill, so aware of America's seemingly limitless power, but bent on having America in the war as an ally, the prospect of the entire British Empire being dependent on America for its relief and security was abhorrent.

The centrepiece of Mountbatten's South East Asia Command's war effort was to be the amphibious invasion of Malaya. Operation Zipper, however, had to be put off repeatedly due to a shortage of landing vessels, and was then pre-empted by the sudden Japanese surrender after the atom bombs were dropped in August 1945. With enough landing craft available at last following D-Day in Europe, the assault went in nonetheless on 9 September 1945, in order to reoccupy British South-East Asia, disarm the considerable Japanese forces in Malaya and begin the complicated process of liberating prisoners and repatriating them, and returning Malaya to peace-time conditions. Covered by two battleships, four cruisers, six escort carriers, fifteen destroyers, eighteen squadrons of RAF fighters and bombers and 180 naval aircraft, two divisions and a brigade landed south of Port Swettenham and north of Port Dickinson. The warships of the East Indies Station based on Ceylon had taken up position off Penang on 28 August 1945. The plan was to land 182,000 men, 17,700 vehicles, 2250 animals and 225,000 tons of stores and petrol within six weeks of the initial landings. British imperial forces in Malaya then began the task of supervising the transfer from military to civilian rule and maintaining law and order in a fluid situation whilst organizing the repatriation of 700,000 Japanese personnel. This was done without using Indian military resources and with a limited budget from London.

American, British and Australian forces throughout the East organized surrender ceremonies so that the world could see the defeat of Japanese military power. The Council Chamber of the Municipal Buildings in Singapore was the scene of the formal surrender ceremony in South-East Asia. Mountbatten was the natural focal point as Supreme Allied Commander South East Asia. An open limousine conveyed him to the imposing Municipal Buildings through streets lined with Royal Marines. His three Commanders-in-Chief awaited his arrival. Four guards of honour, drawn from the Marines, the Royal Navy, the Indian Army and Australian paratroops, were inspected, a seventeen-gun salute rang out and then the massed bands struck up 'Rule Britannia'. The Union Flag again flew in Singapore and throughout the Eastern Empire.

SEAC's responsibilities did not end in Burma and Malaya. In November 1945 the 5th Indian Division was deployed to the Dutch East Indies, part of SEAC's area of transitional responsibility. A task of immediate importance was to intervene in Java where the local population set upon Dutch civilians released from internment. To maintain order it was necessary to employ surrendered Japanese soldiers. Thus imperial forces returned to the scene of one of their early eastern defeats, as victors this time, in order to re-establish Allied rule in Java and Sumatra. (The British established their headquarters in Surabaya in a building that had been used to accommodate Dutch women and children awaiting transfer to internment camps.) Elsewhere, SEAC was responsible for supervising the transfer from Japanese to Allied control in French Indo-China, employing the 17th Indian Division for the purpose.

In the Far Eastern quarter of Britain's Eastern Empire there was a race to get British imperial forces prepared in time. On 8 August and again on the 22 August the Chiefs of Staff in London had decided that it was 'a point of urgency' that British forces get to Hong Kong before the Americans or the Chinese. The surrender had been read outside of the Hong Kong Hotel on 16 August, the most senior colonial civil servant released from Japanese internment taking the initiative in formally reconstituting British rule. This was the Colonial Secretary Franklin Gimson, who became Acting Governor upon the surrender. For the time being, Gimson relied on the Japanese, still with 20,000 troops in Hong Kong, remaining at their posts and ensuring public order. On 28 August 1945 Gimson broadcast to the world that Hong Kong was once again British. In line with London's wishes, Rear-Admiral Sir Cecil Harcourt was dispatched with a powerful force to liberate Hong Kong (Operation Lion), his fleet including the battleship HMS *Anson*, the carriers HMS *Indomitable, Venerable* and *Vengeance,* the cruisers HMS *Black Prince, Euryalus* and *Swiftsure,* a submarine depot ship, eight submarines, four destroyers and six Australian minesweepers. The Canadians, who had lost two battalions on the surrender of the colony almost four years before, sent the anti-aircraft vessel *Prince Robert*. The fleet steamed into Victoria harbour on 30 August 1945. Two parties of 550 men each, Brown Force and Kennedy Force raised from the ships' companies of HMS *Anson*, *Euryalus*, *Indomitable* and *Swiftsure*, went ashore to secure the various parts of the colony. A proclamation of 1 September placed Hong Kong under military administration, with Admiral Harcourt as Commander-in-Chief and Head of the Military Administration, and this remained in force for a further eight months. An RAF construction unit of 3000 men, on its way to build airfields on Okinawa for British long-range bombers in preparation for the anticipated Allied assault on the Japanese home islands, was instead diverted to Hong Kong. Arriving on 4 September, it immediately set to work to restore public services. Over 2700 prisoners had already been released.

Further east along the China coast in Shanghai, over 100,000 Japanese troops surrendered and remained on duty under Allied command. Three American fleets and a Royal Navy task force arrived at the mouth of the river and recreated Battleship Row on the Whangpoo, the British force including the carrier HMS *Colossus*, the cruisers HMS *Bermuda* and *Argonaut* and four destroyers. On the Japanese surrender British forces were dispatched to other key enemy strongholds that were to be returned, at last, to British Commonwealth rule. The carrier HMS *Glory* went to Rabaul, and the battleship HMS *Nelson* and escort carriers HMS *Hunter* and *Attacker* to Penang. In British Borneo, Australian force took the surrender of the Japanese occupiers.

Despite these victorious returns to Britain's Eastern Empire, they were hardly glorious affairs. The British had been beaten out of their South-East Asian and Far Eastern holdings, and a lot had happened to their people in the four-year absence of the Union Flag. Particularly damaging had been the nature of Britain's exit – a scuttling out before the enemy arrived in some cases, seemingly inept military reverses in others. A fundamental premise of imperial rule – the need to keep a military grip and a basic promise to defend the population from external aggression – had been broken. The British had manifestly proved incapable of this one simple task, and they would not be viewed in the same light again. As Freddie Spencer Chapman wrote when living a guerrilla life in Japanese-occupied Malaya, 'it was embarrassing to live with people who had lost every shred of faith in the British, considered that they had been badly let down by us and did not hesitate to say so. They questioned our military competence and our integrity and courage'.

Even further east, in the Pacific extremities of the British imperial world, similar sentiments were echoed after British rule melted away in islands taken by the southward-spreading Japanese in 1942. In this region, though the 'neo-Britains' of Australia and New Zealand were to survive the war undefeated, a new power arose that would change forever Britain's role in the region. Whilst laying the global military and economic foundations of its new superpower status as the war progressed, America made the Pacific its very own pond as it took up the challenge in the region so dramatically laid down by the Japanese at Pearl Harbor. Because of this, even though imperial rule and Commonwealth bonds in the Pacific would outlast the war by decades, America became the most important military and economic power for Australians, Fijians, New Zealanders and Tongans alike, and the distinctly *British* contribution to the war in the Pacific was limited. That said, the territories and peoples of the British Empire and Commonwealth in the Pacific were constantly to the fore in the struggle to repel the Japanese explosion set off in December 1941.

14

Australia and New Zealand

The global reach of British settler imperialism from the late eighteenth century had created major Anglo-Saxon communities in the Pacific, forming the eastern-most corner of the white Commonwealth world that went to war with Germany in 1939. Over the course of the nineteenth century traders, settlers, missionaries, explorers, soldiers and sailors had extended the imperial tide beyond the Australian and New Zealand centres of endeavour, creating an island empire in the region encompassing Fiji, New Guinea, the Solomons and Tonga and many other Pacific territories. When Japan brought war to the region in 1941, the defence of the Pacific Empire rested on the system of imperial defence provided by the Royal Navy, and this depended upon the successful functioning of the Singapore strategy and smooth cooperation with the American Pacific and Asiatic fleets. The failure of the British naval shield in the East brought war to the shores of the Pacific Empire, and caused American power to blossom across a region that Britain, for the foreseeable future at least, was unable to influence through mili-tary force. The distance of these two great settler states from the mother country was the root cause of the security dilemmas that they both faced between 1939 and 1945. On the one hand, as Australian Prime Minister Sir Robert Menzies said in April 1939, concerned at Britain's apparent lack of urgency in strengthening Singapore to deter Japan, 'what Great Britain calls the Far East is to us the near north'. On the other hand, Australia and New Zealand felt bound by a matrix of shared ties to help Britain fight Germany and Italy on the other side of the globe; as Menzies resolutely put it on the day that Britain went to war in September 1939, 'there can be no doubt that where Britain stands, there stand the people of the entire British world ... One King, one flag, one cause'.

Popular memory of the Pacific War is dominated by images of American power overcoming the increasingly desperate and bloody resistance of Japanese garrisons, after a period of startling Japanese expansion and a series of dramatic naval battles. Images of kamikaze attacks on American carriers and the iconic photograph of American marines raising a giant Stars and Stripes on Mount Suribachi after the bitterly-fought victory on Iwo Jima seem to sum it all up. From the often-shown images of burning battleships filmed on the 'day of infamy', when the Japanese raided Pearl Harbor, to the bright mushroom cloud towering over the stricken city of Hiroshima nearly four years later, to modern Hollywood films, America *is* the Allied war effort in the Pacific. Britain, its Commonwealth allies Australia and New Zealand, and the dozens of Pacific islands that were part of the British Empire and Commonwealth rarely get a look in.

Whilst there can be no doubt that American military and industrial power was the overwhelmingly decisive factor in defeating Japan, the territories of the British Empire and Commonwealth were well represented in the region's struggle in a variety of ways and must be brought into the frame of Britain's imperial war. Much of that struggle was conducted on imperial soil, as colonies and mandates in the Pacific felt the full and horrifying impact of world war. Guadalcanal was part of the British Solomons Island Protectorate, Papua and New Guinea were Australian territories, and Tarawa, where a thousand Americans and 5000 Japanese soldiers died, was part of the British colony of the Gilbert and Ellice Islands. These and many other Pacific islands were the scene of bitter fighting and the final resting place of tens of thousands of Japanese, American and Australian soldiers, and of innumerable local innocents powerless to escape the vortex of world war. Australian troops had their own experiences of the horrors of Pacific island warfare, Fijians, Maoris and Aborigines joined the armed forces, and carriers of the formidable British Pacific Fleet had their flight decks dented by kamikaze pilots as they took part in the Okinawa campaign. Australia in particular committed significant forces to the Pacific war, and there was always a distinctive imperial flavour including Spitfires committed to the defence of Western Australia and the slouch-hats fighting the Japanese over the Kakoda trail in New Guinea. In the latter stages of the war a major British fleet entered the Pacific for the first time since the loss of HMS *Prince of Wales* and *Repulse* had temporarily ended Britain's traditional presence in the waters beyond the Malacca Strait. Both Pacific Dominians were key strategic bases for America's war effort, and until 1944 Australia furnished most of the forces available to General Douglas MacArthur's South-West Pacific Area Command.

Emphasizing these strands in the Pacific war is not to deny that America was the region's colossus. All the territories of the Empire and Commonwealth in those seas depended on America for security and in many cases for liberation, once it became clear that Britain had nothing left over with which to turn back the Japanese tide in those fateful months of late 1941 and early 1942. Though political, economic and defence links between Britain and the territories painted red in the Pacific would carry through into the 1970s, the war saw a distinct changing of the guard in the Pacific as America came to the fore. But the imperial nature of the conflict in the Pacific should not be dismissed. The two Dominions and many islands acted as power bases for American and Allied forces fighting the Japanese, providing infrastructure and manpower and themselves often becoming battlefields. Furthermore, the Pacific Dominions, colonies and mandates contributed to the war against Germany long before they entered the front line themselves with Japan's unannounced irruption in December 1941, and long before America came to dominate their war efforts and assume the role of ultimate arbiter of their fates.

Territories of the Empire and Commonwealth in the Pacific region acted as vital Allied bases in the war against Japan. Auckland was the headquarters of Admiral Halsey's South Pacific Area, covering New Zealand, Fiji, New Caledonia and the Solomons. Melbourne and then Brisbane were headquarters for General MacArthur's South-West Pacific Area, covering Australia, New Guinea, Java, Borneo and the Philippines. Australian ports supplied Allied forces in New Guinea (transport being provided by, among others, ships of the British Merchant Marine, like the Holt Line's *Centaur*, *Charon* and *Gorgon*. These ships were specially designed to operate from north-western Australian ports where they had to lie on the mud at low water). American submarines were based at Brisbane, and American bombers at numerous airstrips in northern Australia for offensive operations in the Pacific. On a smaller scale there were also British bases, such as the ports used by the British Pacific Fleet, air strips such as those used by Spitfires at Fremantle, and a submarine base at Fremantle that was home to British submarines from 1942 to 1945 (in that period over thirty British submarines were based there, including the last one to be sunk during the war, HMS *Porpoise*).

Australia and New Zealand sent servicemen the world over, and less well-known Pacific units were raised like the Fiji Guerrillas, the Solomon Islands Defence Corps, the Pacific Islands Regiment, the Tonga Defence Force and the Torres Strait Light Infantry. Among the Allied nations only Russia and Britain enlisted a larger proportion of their people for military service than New Zealand, and the Dominion lost a greater proportion of its men dead than any other part of the Empire and Commonwealth. It also spent as much as Britain on the war as a proportion of its national income. British and Australian personnel played a significant role in breaking Japanese codes and in fighting the war behind enemy lines, as SOE sprouted an Australian branch and special forces were trained to meet Japanese landings, and also to provide an intelligence-gathering network in areas where Japan dominated. As well as fighting lengthy and bitter battles against Japanese forces, notably in New Guinea, Australia deployed thousands of airmen to Europe, sent destroyers to the Mediterranean and suffered significant naval losses in the Pacific. In some campaigns, like that mounted to conquer Syria in 1941, Australian soldiers were to the fore, supported by naval and air forces including Australian Tomahawks and destroyers. New Zealanders fought in the Solomon Islands, the Middle East and Europe, formed a major part of the garrison standing ready to defend Fiji, and New Zealand naval forces served in the Pacific and the Mediterranean. Both the Royal Australian Navy (RAN) and the Royal New Zealand Navy (RNZN) ended the war as part of the British Pacific Fleet fighting the Japanese under overall American command. Both Dominions sent valuable divisions to the Middle East, and Australian troops fought bravely in the Malayan campaign; and, on the fall of Singapore, many thousands marched into Japanese captivity. Long before Japan went to war German raiders and submarines were nosing around Australian harbours and sinking merchant vessels in Australian territorial waters. Precautions had to be taken to defend ports and harbours and provide adequate escorts for the merchant vessels upon which the territories of the region depended for their trade and communications with the wider world.

The war effort of Australia and New Zealand, as well as the war's impact upon them, was significant, as it was for the islands of the Pacific Empire. The two great antipodean Dominions and the galaxy of islands over which the Union Flag flew were battlegrounds, bases for enemy and Allied forces, providers of military personnel for service in the Pacific, South-East Asia, the East Indies, the Middle East and Europe. They also became vital reservoirs of food, raw materials and armaments to stoke the fires of the Allied war machine in the East. For the first time in their histories, the Pacific Dominions faced the threat of invasion and were attacked from the air and the sea. Territories of the Empire and Common-wealth in the Pacific experienced the mass movement of both hostile and friendly people that world war brought in its wake: New Zealand played host to 20,000 Americans and Australia to 100,000 (the total numbers of Americans who passed through the two Dominions was much higher). The Australian territories of Papua and New Guinea were visited during the war by 300,000 Japanese, 500,000 Australians and one million Americans. Fijian soldiers fought in New Guinea, 20,000 Italian prisoners of war found their way to Australia as labourers, Euro-peans from the Dutch East Indies were evacuated to Western Australia, and a batch of British evacuee children arrived in Tasmania.[1] Australia accepted 2000 Jewish internees of German and Austrian origin, and thousands of Japanese pris-oners of war were encamped in Australia (300 were killed in an attempted mass breakout-suicide at No. 12 Australian POW Camp in Cowra, New South Wales, in August 1944). Perhaps a million of Australia's seven million inhabitants served in some kind of military role, from part-time civil defence volunteers to professional soldiers, and many of them served overseas or were removed from their home areas and sent to undisclosed bases 'somewhere in Australia'.[2]

Australia became the main American base in the Pacific, and together with New Zealand, Fiji and other territories acted as a barracks and training ground for hundreds of thousands of American servicemen, and a home for countless Amer-ican warships and aircraft. The two Dominions became major producers of supplies for these American forces, and together with their exports to Britain and elsewhere their productive roles were arguably more important in winning the war than their relatively small military contributions. Certainly civilians in both Dominions experienced many of the 'home front' effects of the war common in Britain, including the dramatic increase in the number of women in the work place, the conscription of labour, industrialization, rationing and fund-raising and war-related work for organizations like the Red Cross.

The Pacific War was the central front in the struggle against Japan.[3] The war was fought in China, Burma, South-East Asia, the East Indies and the Pacific, as the forces of the British Empire and Commonwealth, China and America sought at first to contain and then beat back the protrusions of Japanese power that darted across the eastern world in the four months following the raid on Pearl Harbor and the sinking of HMS *Prince of Wales* and *Repulse*. China had been at war with Japan for some years before December 1941, from which date a period of rapid and barely-checked conquest saw the Japanese establish a new resource-rich empire populated by nearly one hundred million people, in Malaya, the Philippines, the Dutch East Indies, Borneo, the Celebes, Burma and numerous Pacific islands, with military and political power also extending to regions like Siam and Indo-China. Though campaigns against Japanese forces were fought in all these areas, it was in the Pacific that Japan had to be fought, and its forces exterminated or pushed back to the home islands, if Japan was forced to capitulate. The Pacific campaign developed in stages to capture or neutralize major Japanese concentrations and facilities – Guadalcanal led to New Guinea and New Britain, Makin and Tarawa in the Gilberts led on to the Marshall Islands, the capture of which opened the way to the Marianas. From there, it was on to Okinawa in the Ryukyu Islands, and then finally to the Japanese home islands themselves.

From January 1942 Japanese forces also made landings in Borneo, New Guinea, the Solomons, New Britain, the Celebes, Ambon, Sumatra and Timor, and in February raided Darwin in northern Australia, as well as many other Australian coastal towns. In April 1942 Japanese expansion reached its high-water mark with an attack on British naval bases in Ceylon, and serious interest was shown in an invasion of Madagascar, far away in the western Indian Ocean. Casting around for the next target after their astounding early successes, Australia was favoured by some in Japanese naval circles, but an attack on the continent was ruled out by the army because of its commitments in China and the need for shipping elsewhere, particularly to harvest the resources of the new empire. The army instead preferred an offensive in the India–Burma region. But Australia still loomed large in Japan's strategic thinking, if not as a must-have then as a base of potential importance that should be denied to the enemy. It was therefore intended to isolate the continent so that it could not serve as a base for American counter-offensive operations. This was to be effected by capturing territories able to provide an effective screen, hence the desire to capture Port Moresby in New Guinea, thrusts into the southern Solomons and the planned capture of Fiji, Samoa and New Caledonia.

A Japanese offensive to move into a position from which Australia could be isolated and potentially isolated was thwarted at the Battle of the Coral Sea (7–8 May 1942). This was the first naval engagement in history in which warships did not see each other, as air warfare at sea came of age. The Japanese lost two carriers, the Americans one. Japanese strategic thinking was predicated on the notion of building a defensive outer ring around the core territories of the new empire, and this explains the appearance of Japanese garrisons in surprisingly diverse outposts of limited intrinsic value. This defensive wall, so the argument went, would be almost impossible for the enemy to break through. This strategy failed for a number of reasons: the poor management of Japan's mercantile resources; the increasing inability of the Imperial Japanese Navy to link and supply all of its overseas bases because of growing American naval power and the loss of ships in action; and the American tactic of bypassing Japanese strongholds in order to work a way towards the jugular of the Japanese home islands themselves.

Though in retrospect it is easy to see the spring months of 1942 as the height of Japan's success, it should be noted that until mid-1944 the Greater East Asian Co-Prosperity Sphere, as the new empire was known, remained largely intact, despite two solid years of Allied fighting. Though not clear to those living life forwards at the time, from June 1942 and the famous Battle of Midway Japan lost the edge, and had already lost the war because it was simply incapable of making good its losses and augmenting its forces in the way that America, peerlessly, was able to do. From this high-water mark, the Allies started to stem – if not quite turn back – the tide, and began effectively to deploy forces in the region. Australian forces were crucial in this early period, being well trained, seasoned by two years of war and on the spot. Thereafter American and Allied forces mounted a two-fronted assault. Forces serving under General MacArthur's South-West Pacific Area (SWPA) advanced through the Solomons and then the eastern archipelago, landing on Leyte in the Philippines in October 1944. Meanwhile Admiral Nimitz's Central Pacific Command pursued an island-hopping course through the Marshall Islands, Guam and the Caroline Islands. Both forces were then ready for the assault on Okinawa and the Japanese home islands. The new command designations under overall American control came into being after the failure of the hastily composed and resource-weak ABDA Command to stem the Japanese tide in early 1942. Though Australia and New Zealand were not entirely happy to find themselves in an exclusively American command sphere, it was never likely to be any other way, given that they themselves were too thinly populated to recruit a strategically decisive military force, and given Britain's temporary inability to commit any significant resources to the theatre.

The first step in re-establishing a presence in the Pacific after the disasters of Pearl Harbor and Singapore was to build up American forces in the two antipodean Dominions in preparation for the offensives to come. In April 1942 bombers from USS *Hornet*, led by Colonel James Doolittle, raided the Japanese home islands, and there were raids on Japanese positions in the British Gilbert Islands and the Marshall Islands. The raids were strategically unimportant but signalled American intent, worrying the Japanese population and providing a much needed boost for Allied morale. Australian troops were deployed as the main force stemming the tide in New Guinea, one of the few major theatres where the enemy was actually being engaged on land. On the naval front the Battle of the Coral Sea (7 May 1942) enabled forces to be built up in New Guinea. It also left the Japanese one crucial carrier short when, a month later facing an armada of 185 ships, American aircraft from Midway and three aircraft carriers sank four

Japanese carriers to the loss of their own *Yorktown*. It was to be a turning-point of the war in the Pacific. Slowly, gradually, the Allies began to win telling battles, and to avoid losing them, and all the while Japanese merchant shipping was being sunk, primarily by American submarines practising unrestricted submarine warfare, whilst Japanese submarines deployed ineffectively and to little strategic effect. The blockade of the home islands began to tell. These factors, together with the gradual shift in air power towards the Allies and the blunting of the Imperial Japanese Navy's offensive power, laid the foundations needed for the Allies to go over to the offensive and begin the bloody process of conquering the Japanese fortress islands studding the Pacific, bypassing some, and pushing inexorably northwards towards Japan. American air power became overwhelming, in a war that relied on air drops to supply isolated island garrisons, and a strategic bomber offensive was sustained against Japan causing the mass destruction of Japanese cities. Meanwhile the build up of American naval power was unprecedented, to the point where eighteen battleships – larger than Britain's entire battleship strength at the start of the war – could be mustered to take part in the assault on Okinawa. Similar might was shown in the overwhelming size of America's aircraft carrier fleet.

Allied victories started to prevent the Japanese from pursuing their strategic objectives. The Battle of the Coral Sea had persuaded the Japanese to call off the attempt to take Port Moresby in Australian New Guinea by sea, using forces from their base at Rabaul in Australian New Britain (Rabaul was the main Japanese fleet base in the south-western Pacific). This was a major strategic blow, but the Japanese instead attempted to take it by land across the mountains. After Midway the Japanese postponed their planned invasions of New Caledonia, Fiji and Samoa, as the importance of capturing Port Moresby rose. Given losses and deployments elsewhere, however, a naval invasion was no longer possible, so the Japanese choose to go overland. This led to the battle back and forth across the Kakoda trail, the path across New Guinea's Owen Stanley mountain range. This battle was fought mainly by Australian troops of the 7th Division, later joined by the American 32nd Division. When the Allied forces had successfully fought the length of the Kakoda trail and emerged at the Japanese end of it, they then encountered the type of dug-in Japanese defences that were to be a feature of the Pacific war, and it took until January 1943 to clear them and end organized Japanese resistance. In this campaign, the Japanese lost 13,000 men, Australia 2000 and America 600. In Papua and New Guinea Allied forces received a lot of help from indigenous people, many of whom loathed the Japanese because of maltreatment and brutality. Some fought individually, others as part of organized units. They were particularly renowned as bearers, carrying food and ammunition to forward areas and bringing the wounded out.

The Allies mounted operations aimed at the recapture of Rabaul following the Midway victory, and embarked on the bloody struggle that began as an attempt to prevent the Japanese constructing an airstrip on Gaudalcanal in the British

Solomon Islands Protectorate. The American landing was successful, but the Japanese persisted in trying to reclaim the airstrip (named Henderson's Field by the Americans after a dead airman), not withdrawing until February 1943. There was also fighting in Buna in northern Papua as MacArthur sought airstrips to support his push for the Japanese stronghold at Rabaul. American landings, supported by New Zealand forces, took place on the Solomon Islands of Bougainville and New Georgia. The New Zealand 3rd Division had been formed specifically for service in the Solomons Campaign. Further campaigns were fought by Australian troops in New Guinea from March 1943, at Wau, Salamaua, Lae and Finschhafen. American landings took place on the Australian island of New Britain in December 1943. In late 1943 landings also took place on Tarawa and Makin atolls in the British Gilbert Islands. American attention then turned to the Marshall Islands in the Central Pacific. Meanwhile MacArthur was looking to the north west and the Philippines, to which he had famously vowed to return at the time of the Japanese invasion. In February 1944 MacArthur moved for Los Negros in the Admiralty Islands and made landings in northern New Guinea. Admiral Nimitz then began the massive American attack in the Marianas, involving fifteen carriers, 1000 aircraft, 535 ships, and an invasion force of nearly 130,000 troops.

From October 1944 Australian units began relieving Americans in Bougainville (where 518 Australians and 8500 Japanese were to die, and where 23,571 Japanese surrendered), New Britain and northern New Guinea, as the build up for the invasion of the Philippines was organized. The Battle of Leyte Gulf in the Philippines in October 1944 ended the effectiveness of the Imperial Japanese Navy at sea. The Philippines were retaken, the bloody battle for Luzon, beginning in January 1945, standing as the greatest of the Pacific war's land campaigns and the second largest American land campaign after north-west Europe. Anxious to release more American troops for the Philippines campaign, MacArthur sent Australian units to conduct peripheral mopping up campaigns, for example in the British possessions of Borneo, Labuan, Sarawak and Brunei. These campaigns, in which 1500 Australians died without doing anything to hasten the surrender of Japan, attracted criticism in Australia as MacArthur ensured that the final stages of the fight to Japan were as exclusively American as possible. The final stages of the Pacific war featured the American landings on Iwo Jima, and the Okinawa campaign commencing in April 1945. The invasion of Okinawa was mounted by 1300 ships, including eighteen battleships, forty carriers and one hundred destroyers, supported by the British Pacific Fleet. The next move was to be the invasion of the Japanese home islands, but the atomic bombs dropped on Hiroshima and Nagasaki supervened.

The Second World War belonged to Australia and New Zealand even when it was confined to distant Europe. This was because of their foundation by British settlers and their development as part of a global economic and military structure centred on Britain. In taking part in the war the antipodean Dominions were not doing Britain a favour. Though politically free, they were imperial creations and key components of a global economic and defence community, to which they contributed and from which they drew. Britain was the regulator of this imperial community, and its warships and merchant ships were vital factors in the economic prosperity of both Dominions. The collapse of Britain would have been a disaster for them, as they were intimately bound to Britain's fate, not just because of shared historical and cultural ties but through diplomatic, economic and military dependence. Though they both had regional interests, they also shared the global interests of Britain and because of this the war in Europe – in which both Dominions were heavily engaged two years before the Pacific war started – was as important for Australia and New Zealand as it was for the territories of the Empire lying closer to Germany and Italy. The Middle East theatre to which antipodean divisions were dispatched early in the war and through which passed that key highway of imperial trade and communications, the Suez Canal, was of as practical an interest to Australia and New Zealand as it was to Britain.

Although both Australia and New Zealand had been technically free and equal since the 1931 Statute of Westminster, and therefore independent members of the Commonwealth, neither country was a true nation state in 1939, despite the obvious strength of local nationalism in Australia. They were still tightly meshed to Britain on a number of levels, but in a way not incompatible with political autonomy and a regional perspective that might differ in emphasis from that of the metropole. Not least, they were dependent upon Britain for their security, and in training, equipment, and ethos their armed forces had evolved as a comple-mentary part of an imperial defence system. The defence thinking of both Dominions in 1939 was dominated by the policy of contributing to larger British formations in times of imperial war, for service overseas as well as for regional defence. Thus when war in Europe broke out the Australian Imperial Force (AIF) and the New Zealand Expeditionary Force (NZEF) were dispatched to Europe, the RAN was placed at the disposal of the Royal Navy (the RNZN was still a part of the Royal Navy) and antipodean soldiers took up defensive positions in imperial islands throughout the Pacific. In 1939, despite the fears that existed about possible Japanese aggression, both Dominions committed to war in Europe (though the Australian government thought long and hard before committing the AIF to France). At that time, there was still no clear indication of a Japanese onslaught, and no premonition that France would capitulate and British and American naval power would be so easily brushed aside in the Pacific.

Unlike fully-fledged nation states, neither country had unilaterally concluded any treaties or agreements with foreign countries, or maintained diplomatic representatives in non-Commonwealth countries (though an Australian legation was opened in Washington in February 1940.) Economically both Dominions were dependent on the system of imperial trade, and Britain was by far their most important source of imports and capital investment as well as their greatest export market. The Second World War's disruption of world trade was as much a problem for them as it was for Britain, and they too had enemy submarines lurking off the coast attempting to sink the merchant shipping on which they depended for their livelihood. At the start of the war Britain guaranteed that the Australian and New Zealand economies would not fail by promising to buy all its traditional imports, even if Britain were not actually able to take delivery. Because of the war at sea 60 per cent of Australia's exports went to Britain, as did 97 per cent of New Zealand's food exports. With no significant merchant marine of their own, they relied for their participation in world trade upon the British (and American) merchant marines.

So the antipodean Dominions either hung together with Britain or hung apart. The war was not forced upon them, nor did they participate grudgingly in order to do the Poms a favour. Australian and New Zealand politicians and their people reluctantly recognized – like their British and Canadian peers – that the refusal of the European dictators to limit their demands to the bounds of reason made war unavoidable. Distance from the Third Reich did nothing to diminish the fact that it was their war, and not a single Australian parliamentarian criticized their Prime Minister's declaration of war in September 1939. It is worth noting all of this because of the controversies that developed when the European war, to which they had devoted their resources, was suddenly overtaken by a Pacific war that began with stunning imperial and American defeats that totally transformed the security situation facing the Dominions. Whilst New Zealand continued to repose its faith in British leadership, Australia endured a great deal of anguish as it struggled to face the emerging military situation, to develop a strong regional standing and to renegotiate its relationship in the councils of Empire.

A major theme in the war history of Australia, at the time and in subsequent historical accounts, centres on its frustrated desire first effectively to influence British strategic direction of the war, and then to do the same with America when it became the power dictating military affairs in the Pacific region.[4] At the root of the problem was the fact that Australia at the time was not a fully-developed nation state. Despite its geographical size, its population, and therefore its military clout, its power was small relative to the power wielded by Britain and America. In the case of the tension between Australian aims and Britain's dominance in the Commonwealth setting, the issue was compounded by the belief – at the time and since – that Australia had been badly let down by Britain over the Singapore strategy and imperial provisions for Pacific and Far Eastern defence.

The idea that Britain abandoned Australia when Japan entered the war, while understandable to a degree, is both inaccurate and unfair. Inter-war imperial conferences and internal discussions had permitted Australia ample opportunity to consider to what extent it should develop a distinctively Australian foreign policy: whether or not it should contribute to the Singapore naval base, how much faith could be reposed in the Singapore Strategy, and whether Australia should build up its own forces. Australian governments could have shown more energy in criticizing and questioning Britain's Singapore Strategy; they possessed the information that would have enabled them to do so. As it happened (as was the case in Britain and the other democracies), Australians had taken the peace dividend, greatly reducing their forces after the First World War and backing Britain's policy of appeasement as a means of sating the dictators and preventing another war. In the inter-war years Australia was at liberty to devote more money to defence if it had so chosen and to develop strategic planning outside the traditions of imperial defence. America was of course a natural ally to look to in order to augment the protection afforded by Britain, but America was unwilling to commit itself. So in 1939 Britain remained the only defence option, even though there were obvious signs that, if war with Germany and Italy should break out, there was little chance of the Royal Navy doing the job alone in the East should the Japanese take the opportunity to strike. Australian political and military decision-makers were well aware of the potential defects of the Singapore strategy, and of the elementary fact that war with both Germany and Italy would severely curtail the Royal Navy's capacity to send substantial forces east. Of course, no one in Britain – let alone in Australia – foresaw the devastation of American Pacific power or the fall of France – both crucial factors contributing to the nadir of imperial security cover in the Pacific in 1942. Further more all of the Allies were stunningly blind to Japan's potential to make effective war using the most up-to-date military and naval technology. The lessons of the Russo-Japanese War of 1904–5, when a European military giant was humbled by an Asian power for the first time in modern history, had not been learned by the racially-blinkered whites of the western world, in both hemispheres.

Australia's situation was made more difficult by three factors. First, senior politicians were determined to transform the imperial relationship with Britain and achieve a more genuinely consultative Commonwealth, being particularly anxious to be involved in decision-making when it came to the deployment of Australia's own forces. Secondly, Australia was set on playing a more autonomous and leading role in the affairs of the post-war Pacific. Finally, from 1942 Australia steadily became an appendage of America's Pacific War, and America was to prove as frustratingly impervious as Britain when it came to hearing Australia's voice. With Britain and then with America Australia struggled to reconcile its own interests, and its desire for a voice in the councils of the higher direction of the war, with the fact that it was a peripheral power in an Allied war effort dominated by heavyweights. The simple fact that Australia was populated by seven rather than seventy million people was the reason for this.

Disputes with Britain about the deployment of forces, leading to Australia's eventual demand to have two divisions fighting in the Middle East returned for home defence, were quite understandable. Disagreements rarely came to the surface before the onset of the Japanese war, but did thereafter as successive

Allied reverses left Australia feeling increasingly exposed and unprotected. The British, it seemed, did not take the Far East seriously enough, though of course their resources were painfully inadequate for the tasks faced in Europe and the Mediterranean, let alone that distant region. The failure of imperial arms bred recrimination. Reverses against the Germans in the Middle East, compounded by the abject collapse at Singapore (where Australians, overall, fought best, but also experienced disciplinary problems – providing grist to both mills), led hitherto unvoiced accusations to find expression. For their part the British were sometimes exasperated by Australia's attitude, and rubbed up the wrong way by outspoken men like the Minister of External Affairs, H. V. Evatt (as later were the Americans). New Zealand's political leaders resolutely continued to place their trust in Britain's direction of the war. They bit their lips, though desperately concerned about the situation, and never questioned the 'Germany first' policy. In contrast, Australia's objections to British direction of the war often found voice. There was a strong force in Australian politics opposed to the form of British dominance within the Commonwealth. Curtin's government wanted to redefine – though not to break – the relationship with Britain, and make more of the supposed equality among Britain and the 'white' Dominions club that had found constitutional expression in the Balfour Declaration of 1926 and the subsequent Statute of Westminster of 1931. Evatt, in particular, was keen on this, and questioned the 'Germany first' policy. Not surprisingly, he was unpopular with the many British politicians and military leaders that he harangued. After a meeting with Evatt in London in May 1942, the Chief of the Imperial General Staff, General Sir Alan Brooke, confided to his diary that he was a 'thoroughly unpleasant type of individual with no outlook beyond the shores of Australia'. Evatt had tried to 'blackmail' Brooke by threatening to demand the return of the 9th Division from the Middle East and the RAAF squadrons in Britain, if MacArthur wasn't given all of the aircraft that he had requested for the Pacific theatre. In an afternote to the entry, Brooke wrote that Evatt was 'not interested in the global situation. It was quite impossible to make him realize that the security of Australia did not rest in Australia'.[5]

Certainly, at the start of the war in 1939 British politicians and commanders were habitually imperious in their attitudes to Australia. The Dominions' voices were heard – but rarely, it seemed, listened to. Despite the mechanisms that existed for Commonwealth consultation (regular imperial conferences, high commissions in all Commonwealth capitals and London, regular official war briefings by the British government, and other links) and the lip service that Britain paid to the need for more and more of it, it was clear that Britain expected to be allowed to get on with prosecuting the war, informing and involving the Dominions where necessary, rather than seeking their input and advice on every important matter. It also seemed to some Australians that Britain was prepared to offer defence guarantees whilst keeping its fingers crossed behind its back, or just telling fibs, as it sought to secure Australian deployments overseas and damn the consequences for Australian defence, should Japan choose to strike in the East. There was not enough consultation in the deployment of Australian forces, particularly in the campaigns in Crete, Greece and Syria. Even when there was consultation, it could be the wrong kind; Prime Minister Sir Robert Menzies agreed to Australian participation in the Greece campaign without consulting his Cabinet back at home. The Australian Lieutenant-General Sir Thomas Blamey claimed that he was not adequately consulted by senior British commanders before operations in Greece. He thought that the Australian government fully backed Australian involvement in the doomed operation; the Australian government believed that Blamey thought that the operation had a fair chance of success. In the East Australians were excluded from high office in the short-lived ABDA Command formed after the fall of Singapore. Menzies spent months in London hoping to be able to better put Australia's case, though there is little evidence that his presence, though reassuring to the British public, made much difference, except to damage his standing with politicians back at home and weaken his leadership of his country and his party.

The sojourns of Australian Prime Ministers in Britain during the war reveal a great deal about Australia's attitude to Empire: love and community on the one hand, but a frustration at the habits and actions of the family giant on the other. Robert Menzies spent four months in London from January 1941, and it says a lot about the genuinely cosmopolitan nature of white imperial society at the time that, in some quarters, he was seriously tipped as a replacement for Winston Churchill as British Prime Minister. Menzies was a firm believer in Empire, though an Empire that took account of its geographical responsibilities and sought to develop the coherence of its Commonwealth community. He had also been a champion of pre-war appeasement. Menzies believed that Churchill focused too much attention beyond the Empire, particularly in his frenzy to get America into the war. Menzies had gone to Britain to accelerate the dispatch of arms to Australia and Singapore, in which he largely failed. Whilst in Britain, however, he was popular, and his criticisms of Churchill in the spring of 1941 struck a cord with many powerful people.

A year later, despite the acerbic exchanges caused by the Australian decision to withdraw troops from the Middle East after Japan had gone on its conquering spree, it must be remembered that whilst Australia had legitimate defence concerns and a perceived need to 'take a stand', Britain and America had their reasons for wishing the Australian forces to remain, as part of a sensible allocation of resources on a global scale. Churchill personally intervened to ensure that Roosevelt committed American troops to Australian defence, and there is no sense in the argument that the Allies drained the Pacific of troops and in so doing revealed a cavalier attitude to Australian security. America had 80,000 troops in the region and nearly 300,000 more due to arrive by the end of 1942; and in February 1942 it had become official American policy to ensure that Australia did not fall. Two months later, American intelligence knew that Japan did not plan to invade the Dominion. Furthermore, despite the shock of Pearl Harbor, American naval forces in the region made a concerted Japanese attack on Australia unlikely to have succeeded.

Australian efforts to shape the higher direction of the war were promoted by the desire to gain a more powerful voice in the post-war Pacific, rather than simply becoming a platform for growing American dominance in the region. Continuing a tradition of regional sub-imperialism that had witnessed a rush for German colonies in the First World War, Australia favoured an international commission to supervise the post-war Pacific, in which its voice would be as powerful as that of America and Britain. (Britain did not consider the option of a commission very attractive, as it invited other countries to poke their noses into imperial affairs.) New Zealand, attacking the same issue from a typical New Zealand stance, wanted participation in any such arrangements in order to ensure a British imperial presence in a region that American might otherwise dominate.

Pre-war imperial defence arrangements meant that Australia and New Zealand provided garrison and reconnaissance forces in outer perimeter islands to the north like New Caledonia, the New Hebrides, Fiji and Tonga, viewed as forming a defensive line, or a grave security threat if occupied by an enemy. It was agreed at the Wellington Conference in 1939 that the two Dominions would carry out air reconnaissance in the region, and RNZN vessels conducted surveys for possible air base and anchorage sites. Reconnaissance missions were also mounted between Papua and the Cook Islands. On the outbreak of war, Australia dispatched garrison forces to Norfolk Island, New Guinea and the Solomon Islands. By August 1941 a battalion of the 8th Division was also at Rabaul in New Britain (part of the Australian mandate of New Guinea), and other units were dispersed in the island chain north west of New Guinea. Reflecting their wide-spread deployment throughout the region, in the first two months of 1942 Australian troops were captured on Ambon, New Britain, New Ireland, the Solomon Islands and Portuguese Timor. The Timor deployment began when 'Sparrow Force' – 2/40 Battalion and 2/2 Independent Company – was dispatched on 15 December 1941 from Dili in Dutch Timor. The Portuguese objected but could do little to prevent the Australian deployment. The Japanese began landing on 20 February 1942, meeting with strong resistance. Though some of the Australians had to surrender, the remainder, reinforced with another Independent Company, were able to tie down a Japanese force of over 30,000 troops. On 23 September 1942 HMAS *Voyager* was lost after she ran aground whilst landing supplies and reinforcements and had to be destroyed by her crew.

Australia and New Zealand's military forces were British trained and equipped and designed to complement British imperial military and naval operations in both peace and war. They were not designed for large-scale independent action or to operate without British naval hegemony behind them. When Japan decided to challenge the Royal Navy to deploy effectively in the East whilst simultaneously containing German and Italian naval power in the West, however, it was pushing at an open curtain rather than an effective naval shield. Britain's inability to take the field against, let alone defeat, the Imperial Japanese Navy left Australia, New Zealand and the Empire's Pacific territories desperately exposed. The sinking of HMS *Prince of Wales* and *Repulse* and the fall of Singapore ensured that they would depend ultimately upon American military power for defence or liberation. It must be remembered, however, that this was not a sudden and decisive break in Commonwealth defence arrangements; close cooperation remained, and the majority of Australia and New Zealand's armed forces continued to serve as part of Commonwealth formations. Britain, long into the post-war period, remained an integral feature in the Dominions' defence arrangements. The difference was that the events of 1941 brought America firmly and irrevocably into the club as the dominant power.

The armed forces of the two Dominions underwent massive growth during the war, initially in order to support the British war effort against Germany and Italy, and later in order to defend themselves against Japan in the Pacific. At the outbreak of war Australia's armed forces were tiny: 3500 soldiers supported by 80,000 part-time reservists. Australian forces peaked at 750,000, the army accounting for two-thirds of this number. When Japan entered the war three experienced Australian divisions were in the Middle East, two brigades of the 8th Division were in Malaya and the third was at Darwin. Also in Australia were 270,000 militiamen organized into eight divisions. By 1942 Australia had eleven divisions in Australia and in 1942–43 it was providing the majority of Allied land forces in SWPA, six divisions fighting in the south-western Pacific.

In September 1939 a division had been offered to the British government for service in Europe (the Australian Imperial Force – AIF). Recruitment for the army proceeded at first on a voluntary basis, and loyalty to the imperial connection and Britain was expressed after the fall of France by a surge of recruits presenting themselves for attestation. In July 1940 recruitment for the AIF was temporarily halted, so great had been the response. The fall of France also led to increased conscription for the militia (the Citizen's Military Force), its strength rising to 250,000.

The AIF consisted of the 6th, 7th, 8th and 9th Divisions and was intended for service abroad. The 6th Division AIF left for France in early 1940, though whilst training in Palestine the fall of France forced a change in final destination, and it remained in the Middle East theatre where there was soon plenty of fighting to be done. Part of the division sailed for Britain to form the nucleus of the 9th Division. The fall of France also radically altered the strategic picture, making eastern defence appear even more difficult than before, though the Australian government agreed to retain the 6th Division in the Middle East, and sent the 7th to join it. The 6th, 7th and 9th Divisions then formed the 1st Australian Corps for service in the Middle East under Lieutenant-General Sir Thomas Blamey.

Born in Wagga Wagga, New South Wales, Blamey was one of the numerous antipodean commanders who had fought in the Gallipoli campaign, and in the inter-war years he had served as Australia's representative to the War Office in London. In 1940 he was given command of the 1st Australian Imperial Force, and took them to the Middle East. Whilst there he supervised the withdrawal of imperial forces from Crete, and served briefly as Deputy Commander-in-Chief Middle East. Upon his return to Australia he was appointed Commander-in-Chief Australian Military Forces and Allied Land Commander under General Douglas MacArthur's South-West Pacific Area. Elements of the Australian 6th Division served in the Balkans and the 7th Division formed the backbone of the imperial force that conquered Vichy Syria, providing 18,000 of the 34,000 troops employed against the Army of the Levant. In Greece 2000 Australians were captured, and a further 3000 in Crete. For some time four Australian brigades from the 7th and 9th Divisions provided a significant proportion of the garrison of Tobruk commanded by the Australian Major-General Leslie Morshead, before pressure to fulfil the undertaking to keep all Australian forces in the Middle East together led to their withdrawal.

The rise of Japan presented Australia with a great dilemma. Should it continue to maintain its main army force in the Middle East, or bring it back for home defence, given the fact that it seemed increasingly unlikely that the Royal Navy would be able to protect it should Japan choose to invade? After the fall of Singapore, in which two brigades of the 8th Division were captured, the 6th and 7th Divisions returned to Australia, though two brigades were diverted to Ceylon for garrison duties on Churchill's request (he had wanted them to go to Burma, an idea favoured by the Australian representative to the British government). Three thousand men of the 7th Division were captured in Java when the Japanese took the Dutch East Indies. During the Malayan campaign Australia provided 14 per cent of the land forces, yet sustained 73 per cent of the deaths in battle. (The other brigade of the 8th Division was dispersed in New Britain, Ambon and Timor – from where most were evacuated after a successful guerrilla campaign.) Taken with the losses sustained in the Middle East, these were serious reverses for the Australian army and heightened the sense of exposure as Japan expanded, Australian troops remained overseas, the Royal Navy faded from the region and American naval power in the Pacific wilted. It caused Churchill to encourage Roosevelt to dispatch American troops to Australia, and led to the return of two Australian divisions from the Middle East. But the 9th Division remained in the Middle East, and the American 41st Division was sent to Australia to take its place (arriving on 6 April 1942). The return of the seasoned Australian divisions from the Middle East, the recruitment of new units and the reorganization of Allied command structures in the Pacific saw General Blamey assume command of all land forces under General Douglas MacArthur's new SWPA command on 26 March. These forces initially amounted to seven Australian militia divisions, the Australian 6th and 7th Divisions (rushed to the defence of Darwin upon its return from the Middle East) and the 32nd and 41st American Divisions. Blamey reorganized the Australian Army for better home defence. The First Army defended Queensland and New South Wales, the Second Army Victoria, South Australia and Tasmania. Western Command became 3rd Corps, the 6th Division became Northern Territory Force, and the 8th Military District became New Guinea Force.

From the start of the war with Japan Australian troops served extensively in the Pacific theatre. What amounted to a second army was also recruited, largely through conscription and liable for service on Australian soil (which included battle zones like New Guinea). Historically, tension existed within the Australian army between the regulars and the part-time soldiers. In October 1942 the strength of the Citizen's Military Force stood at 262,000, the regular army at 171,000. After much debate the area in which the former could be used was broadened to include Borneo, the (non-Australian) Solomons, Timor, Java and the Celebes. This was brought about by the passage of a Militia Bill in February 1943, mainly the result of American pressure. MacArthur's determination to minimize the use of Australian forces in his key Pacific campaigns, however, meant that there was no need to send many more men overseas, and indeed in the final two years of the war the army shed 100,000 men as the demands of the home front loomed ever larger in Australia's war effort.

By November 1942 the Australian 6th and 7th Divisions and two militia brigades were engaged in the New Guinea campaign. In New Guinea Australia was to achieve its most telling contribution to the Allied war effort in the Pacific. The two militia brigades were part of an Independent Company, the name given to army special forces formed at Britain's suggestion in 1940 and trained initially by Special Operations Executive soldiers. Anticipating war in the south-west Pacific, an SOE training camp had been established at Wilson's Promontory at the extreme southern point of Victoria. Freddie Spencer Chapman, later to gain a reputation as a behind-enemy-lines fighter in Malaya, volunteered to go to Australia and join the team, 'quite certain that the Japs were shortly coming into the war ... there seemed as much chance of getting some fighting from Australia as from the British Isles'. The team consisted of a commanding officer and experts in demolitions, field craft, weapons-training and signals (including Mike Calvert, later of Chindit fame). Independent Companies were to be used to mount raids against enemy strongholds and to form stay-behind networks in occupied territory, to keep Allied forces informed, and to conduct sabotage operations and encourage resistance among civilian populations. The training site at Wilson's Promontory was selected because it was a National Park, inhabited only by kangaroos, wallabies and emus. It was connected to the mainland by a twenty-mile isthmus of sand and scrub, making the provision of security easy. The promontory also included every type of ground likely to be encountered on deployment overseas, from the Libyan desert to the jungles of New Guinea. Each six-week course offered by the team included the officers and NCOs of one Australian and one New Zealand Independent Company, about sixty men in all. Spencer Chapman taught them 'how to get a party from A to B and back by day or night in any sort of country and to arrive in a fit state to carry out their task. This included all sorts of sidelines – a new conception of fitness, knowledge of the night sky, what to wear, what to take and how to carry it, what to eat and how to cook it, how to live off the country, tracking, memorizing routes and how to escape if caught by the enemy. The course culminated in a three day-and-night scheme in which the Australians "fought" the New Zealanders all over the Promontory'. In July 1941, having trained their successors, the British personnel handed the Special Training School (STS) over to the Australians.[6] Independent Companies served in Borneo, Bougainville (and other Solomon Islands), New Guinea, Papua, the New Hebrides, New Britain, New Ireland and in support of the Free French administration in New Caledonia. In 1944 the Independent Companies became commando regiments.

In early 1942 a new SOE Australia organization was established, and a Far East Liaison Unit was set up for propaganda purposes. SOE Australia conducted many operations in Japanese-occupied territory, including the Dutch East Indies and as far afield as Singapore. Another important behind-enemy-lines initiative was the supervision of the coast-watcher system, planned before the outbreak of war and used to provide intelligence from many different Pacific locations where Japanese forces were in occupation or in evidence. Coast-watchers gleaned intelligence and reported on movements of enemy shipping and aircraft. Most coast-watchers were employed by the Australian government as planters and civilian administrators, though many also came from the indigenous populations. Australians had pioneered the coast-watching system during the First World War, and at the outbreak of war in 1939 Lieutenant-Commander Eric Feldt of the Royal Australian Navy was asked to complete a network in the region.[7] By mid-1941 there were over a hundred stations with wireless transmitters covering 2400 miles from western Papua to the New Hebrides. Many coast-watchers were evacuated before the Japanese arrived, but others remained and provided invaluable intelligence. Indeed the system was expanded so that by March 1943 the Solomon Islands were also covered. Sometimes coast-watchers mounted operations against Japanese troops, aided by the civilian population. Like all behind-enemy-lines operations, coast-watching was a potentially hazardous activity. In October 1942 sixteen coast-watchers and five of their associates were beheaded in the Southern Gilbert Islands, most probably in retaliation after an American air raid during which an Allied prisoner had been shot trying to escape. Coast-watchers were particularly useful to the Americans prior to their landings on Guadalcanal, and they acted as guides on Tulagi and other islands. Coast-watchers and their helpers also performed rescue tasks. In 1942 coast-watchers in MacArthur's SWPA became part of Allied Intelligence Bureau, those under SPA remaining part of Australian Naval Intelligence. A North Australia Observer Unit was established in August 1942. New Zealand also had wireless operators and soldiers acting as coast-watchers in the Gilbert Islands.

The war service of Australia's Aborigines provides an illustration of the depth of imperial mobilzation for war.[8] Most of the 80,000 Aborigines lived in rural areas of Queensland and the Northern Territory, and there were also 5000 Aboriginal Torres Strait Islanders (the strait divides Australian from New Guinea). Over 3000 Aborigines and 850 Torres Strait Islanders served in the forces, leading to some political and racial difficulties. Most Aboriginal political organizations supported participation in the war, seeing the conflict as a chance to push for more equitable citizens' rights in a Dominion where non-whites were still disenfranchised and economically marginalized. There was much opposition to the recruitment of non-whites by the armed forces, and a colour bar required recruits to be at least 'threequartercaste', in other words, predominantly white. This stimulated protest, particularly as some Aborigines had already enlisted in the AIF. The Royal Australian Air Force (RAAF) was more liberal, particularly as it was keen to find ground crew for its bases and those of the British Empire Air Training Scheme. Torres Strait Islanders formed a light infantry battalion, coast artillery and two water transport companies.

The looming Japanese threat sharpened the minds of military policy-makers and led to the creation of distinct Aboriginal units and Aborigines began to be enlisted in larger numbers. By March 1941 approval had been granted for the formation of a Torres Strait Islanders unit that would come to number over 800 men. They were particularly useful when Darwin's strategic importance grew, and with it the Torres Strait which provided access from the east. To defend this bottleneck between the Cape York peninsula and New Guinea an air base was constructed on Horn Island, later moved on to the mainland. Torres Strait Islanders were used to provide garrison forces. Defending the vital sea approaches to Darwin, air strips were constructed to patrol shipping lanes. Aborigine civil labour was recruited to build them and an Aborigine guerrilla force was raised to defend them. As Japanese forces moved south to occupy Portuguese Timor, the role of the islanders increased, and recruiting parties scoured the islands for candidates for enlistment. Aborigines with unrivalled knowledge of the local waters were employed in a water transport operating company sailing small vessels between northern Queensland and Papua. Aborigines were also employed for reconnaissance purposes and to locate aircraft lost in remote areas of the outback.

The Admiralty requested that the RAN be placed under its direction on the outbreak of war, as previously arranged as part of imperial defence strategy.[9] Despite some misgivings, the request was granted on 30 August 1939, days before a state of war existed. The Australian government retained the right to say which ships should serve outside Australian waters and the right to call for their return. Australian naval forces were deployed far and wide during the course of the war. By the conclusion of hostilities the RAN had suffered considerable losses without having sunk many enemy vessels, though it had been transformed from an adjunct of the Royal Navy to an independent fighting force. At the outbreak of war Australia had two eight-inch cruisers (HMAS *Australia* and *Canberra*), four six-inch cruisers (HMAS *Adelaide, Hobart, Perth* and *Sydney*), five old destroyers and two sloops. These thirteen fighting ships and a few auxiliary vessels were manned by 5540 permanent personnel. Seventy-one months after the declaration of war, the RAN had grown to include 337 ships of all types and 40,000 personnel. This was an impressive record, though Australia's naval contribution to the war effort went deeper than this. An astonishing 20 per cent of the anti-submarine personnel who served in the Battle of the Atlantic were trained in Australia at HMAS *Rushcutter*. In the Pacific, it was often RAN vessels that conducted the hydrological activities that paved the way for Allied amphibious landings. They also surveyed the Torres Strait for a safe route for the British Pacific Fleet to use when it deployed from the Indian Ocean to its Australian bases. (For this work four vessels of the RAN Hydrographic Branch were joined by the British survey ship HMS *Challenger* and four RAN minesweepers.) In the first phase of the war, up until the entry of Japan, the RAN supported imperial defence efforts alongside the Royal Navy. In the second phase, Australian ships concentrated in the Pacific and were integrated with American naval forces, beginning with the brief appearance of ANZAC Force under an American commander, before April 1942 brought command reorganizations and the creation of MacArthur's South-West Pacific Area. The final phase was marked by the return of the Royal Navy to the Pacific, marking a renaissance for the RAN as it was able to secure new resources for operations against Japan and the development of a post-war fleet.

Australian naval forces were configured to conduct trade protection and local defence, and to provide reinforcements for the British fleet when it arrived at Singapore. At the start of hostilities HMAS *Hobart* and the destroyers were sent to aid the Royal Navy, initially sailing for Singapore but ending up in the Mediterranean. HMAS *Perth* joined the Royal Navy's East Indies Station. The RAN's heavier ships escorted the nine convoys that took Australian and New Zealand troops to the Middle East. HMAS *Sydney* and *Australia* were sent to European waters, and *Sydney* sunk the Italian cruiser *Bartolomeo Colleoni* off Crete in July 1940. In 1941 Australian sloops and an armed merchant cruiser played important roles in the British interventions in Iraq and Iran. In late 1941 most Australian naval forces were recalled to Australia or Singapore and placed under the American South-West Pacific Area command. In November 1941 HMAS *Sydney* was sunk in a to-the-death struggle with the German raider *Kormoran* off Western Australia. As the decimated Allied naval forces attempted to sink Japanese convoys approaching Java in February 1942, nine Allied destroyers and five cruisers, including *Perth*, were sunk. The destroyer HMAS *Vampire*, escorting the carrier HMS *Hermes*, was lost in April 1942 when the Japanese carrier fleet of Admiral Nagumo raided Ceylon. HMAS *Canberra* was sunk along with three American cruisers at the Battle of Savo Island during the Guadalcanal campaign in August 1942, as they attempted to screen Allied landings (*Australia* and *Hobart* also fought in this battle). It was here that the Allies learned of the superior ability of the Japanese to fight at night. *Hobart* was also lost in the Solomon Islands. Other Australian units took part in the invasion of New Britain, the Philippines, Burma and Borneo, and several passenger ships were converted to become armed merchant cruisers. Late in the war Australian naval forces served with the British Pacific Fleet during the closing stages of the assault on Japan. Finally, the surrender of the 3235-strong Japanese garrison of Dutch Timor took place aboard the sloop HMAS *Moresby* on 11 September 1945. Australian warships were also present at the surrender in Hong Kong, and HMAS *Diamantina* took the surrender at Ocean Island. Two RAN corvette flotillas, each consisting of nine vessels, served with the Eastern Fleet based at Ceylon before joining the British Pacific Fleet based at Manus.[10]

Australia's naval effort included the construction of sixty 'Bathurst' class corvettes as well as three 'Tribal' class destroyers and twelve 'River' and 'Bay' class frigates. The AMC *Kanimbala*, *Manoora* and *Westralia* were converted to Landing Ships Infantry. Australian dockyards were given the task of converting the huge Atlantic liners *Aquitania*, *Mauretania*, *Queen Elizabeth* and *Queen Mary* to troop ships. Like Ceylon, Hong Kong, Singapore and South Africa, Australia provided major facilities for naval and merchant vessels requiring repair or refit. During the course of the war there were 5127 dockings in Australia by naval ships undergoing major refit, maintenance or repair. Of this total, 4008 were RAN, 391 Royal Navy, 513 American, 171 Dutch and forty-four French. In the same period 11,987 merchant vessels were repaired in Australian dockyards.

The Dominion also provided massive support and hospitality for the British Pacific Fleet's bases. Contact between the RAN and the Royal Navy was maintained throughout the war through the extensive loan of vessels and exchange of personnel, and this limited the influence of the American Navy on the RAN. As well as taking part in or sinking outright numerous enemy warships, the RAN captured or destroyed 150,000 tons of enemy merchant shipping and was represented at all the major battles of the Pacific war from the first to the last. The 'Scrap Iron Flotilla' (another one of Lord Haw Haw's disparaging remarks that backfired) gave valuable service to the Mediterranean Fleet, centred upon HMAS *Stuart*, *Vampire*, *Vendetta*, *Voyager* and *Waterhen*. At one point the Commander-in-Chief, Admiral Sir Andrew Cunningham, formed an Inshore Flotilla to support operations against Italian forces on the North African coast. The Australian vessels were committed along with the monitor HMS *Terror* and River class gunboats HMS *Aphid* and *Ladybird*, under the overall command of Commander Hector Waller RAN. Australian naval forces played a major role in retaining control of the sea in the Pacific. It kept convoy routes open and defended, particularly those around Australia and between the mainland and New Guinea. In 1942, for example, there were 211 separate convoys involving 1505 ships that sailed between

Australian ports, and 41 convoys involving 167 ships between the mainland and New Guinea.

Australia began the war with 160 mostly obsolete aircraft, though during the course of the war the RAAF grew to a strength of fifty-two squadrons. When Japan entered the war the RAAF had 373 first- and second-line aircraft, though most were obsolescent trainers such as Whirraways, and it had only fifty-three Hudson medium bombers.[11] Its main air contribution to the war was the training and provision of pilots for the RAF through the British Empire Air Training Scheme (BEATS), as well as the direct enrolment of pilots and ground crew into the RAF. Thousands of Australians ended up serving with the RAF, as part of Bomber Command, Fighter Command and Coastal Command (to which an RAAF squadron was transferred on the outbreak of war). Many Australians also served in overseas formations like the Desert Air Force, supporting the war effort of the Eighth Army in the Middle East. The RAF formed seventeen distinct Australian squadrons, though these were not the same as the independent units that the Canadians developed and that were controlled by Canadian political and military decision-makers (the Canadians insisted on a distinct Canadian air group commanded by a Canadian air vice-marshal). Australian airmen in the RAF were dispersed throughout the Middle East, Europe and Burma. All together about 27,000 Australians served in the RAF, 6500 losing their lives in Europe, over half of them in the strategic bombing offensive against Germany. After the withdrawal of the 6th and 7th Divisions from the Middle East in 1942, two to three thousand RAAF personnel remained in the region. Four RAAF squadrons also took part in the Malayan campaign.

The integration of Australia's forces with those of Britain, and its war-time commitment of resources to the RAF, meant that the RAAF was weaker in the Pacific than it might otherwise have been. In 1942 the ill-equipped RAAF could offer little more than token resistance when Japanese forces raided Australian territory – Darwin, Broome and Wyndham on the mainland, Rabaul and Port Moresby overseas. From early 1942 the RAAF was placed under MacArthur's SWPA, joining with the United States to form the Allied Air Force. It took part in the Papua and New Guinea campaigns, flying American, British and Australian-built aircraft. For example, in New Guinea airborne strike coordinators were used by the RAAF. Using Commonwealth Whirraway tactical reconnaissance and liaison aircraft RAAF personnel observed and led strike flights onto ground targets. Australian aircraft supported American forces in the Battle of the Bismarck Sea in March 1943. By the end of the war the RAAF had enlisted 189,700 men and 27,200 women. The RAF also maintained a presence in the region, for example in the form of No. 54 Squadron, charged with defending western and northern Australia. The squadron moved to Morotai in the Dutch East Indies early in 1945, as it became the concentration point for the operations of the 1st Australian Corps against Japanese forces in Borneo.

New Zealand's inchoate fears about the 'yellow peril' took concrete and disturbing form in the 1930s and early 1940s as Japan went on its Asian rampage. All hope for New Zealand's defence reposed in the Singapore naval base (towards which it had contributed £1 million) and the umbrella of the Royal Navy. But the great geostrategic shift of December 1941, signalled by the attack on Pearl Harbor and the sinking of the British battle squadron operating from Singapore, revolutionized the strategic environment facing New Zealand. With American and British power temporarily crippled in the Pacific, a handful of raw New Zealand soldiers manned slit-trenches along the coastline of their homeland, shouldering old-fashioned rifles, secure in the certain knowledge that, if they chose to come, the Japanese would brush aside their opposition. So New Zealand's security came to rest on the ability of the American navy to blunt Japanese expansionism before going on the offensive and forcing the Japanese back to the home islands, and in mid-1942 thousands of American marines began landing in New Zealand, to use it as a base and a barracks for operations, and to reassure the New Zealand public that they were not defenceless.[12]

At the peak of its war effort 157,000 New Zealanders were in the armed forces, 70,000 of them serving overseas. New Zealand lost 11,671 men, a larger proportion than any other part of the Empire. In July 1940 New Zealand adopted conscription for overseas service, and in total 306,000 were called up for some form of military enlistment. Some New Zealand forces were dispersed in the Pacific region. A division was sent to the Solomon Islands and New Zealanders officered the Fiji Military Force (FMF), units of which also served in the Solomons. New Zealand troops were sent to garrison Fiji, Fanning Island (it had committed to take over this British responsibility in the event of war in 1930), New Caledonia, Norfolk Island, and Tonga, and aircraft were based in Fiji and the New Hebrides. New Zealand forces in Fiji were substantial, amounting to an infantry brigade, rising to two when Japan entered the war. This force was known as the Second New Zealand Expeditionary Force (NZEF – redesignated the 3rd Division in May 1942). The 3rd Division carried out three important operations to capture Green Island, Treasury Island and Vella Lavella. In 1943 there were 5000 New Zealanders in Fiji, along with an air reconnaissance squadron.

The main effort of the New Zealand army was the provision of the First NZEF (redesignated the 2nd Division in June 1942) for service in Europe and the Middle East. This was a course of military action that had been decided upon before the war, in keeping with the traditions of imperial defence. The Dominion's forces served in the Desert War, the defence of Crete and the Eighth Army's progress into southern Europe. At their own request New Zealand's Maoris formed an infantry battalion (28th Battalion) which served in the Mediterranean. The 1st NZEF was dispatched to the Middle East in early 1940 and remained as part of the Eighth Army for the duration of the war. It was decided not to send a second division to the Middle East, though after a good deal of internal discussion the decision was taken not to follow the Australian example and withdraw military forces in response to the Japanese victories of December 1941 to February 1942. New Zealand forces played a major role in Middle East Command's Greece campaign: by the end of March 1941 the New Zealand Division was in position on the Aliakmon Line north of Mount Olympus. Later in the year all New Zealand forces were concentrated together at Mersa Matruh, amounting to 20,000 men. In the Libyan campaign of late 1941 New Zealand losses were heavy: 671 killed, 209 died of wounds, 1699 wounded and 2042 captured by the enemy. In mid-1942 the 2nd Division in the Middle East was reduced from 20,000 to 13,000 soldiers, in order to supplement forces defending New Zealand and the Pacific islands for which the Dominion was responsible. The build up of American forces in New Zealand, with the arrival of units like the 1st Division US Marine Corps, assuaged concerns about home defence, and America further eased the defence burden by taking responsibility for garrisoning Fanning Island, Fiji and Tonga. New Zealand troops were sent in August 1942 to New Caledonia. The 3rd New Zealand Division deployed to Nissan Island in the Solomons in February 1942, and on 27 October 1943 it was sent to Mono in the Treasury Islands.

The 2nd NZEF started recruiting in September 1939, and in the following month it was announced that a Maori battalion for the 2nd NZEF would be formed. In that month the 2nd NZEF, commanded by Lieutenant General Bernard Freyberg, started training in Burnham, Trentham, Hopuhopu and Papakura. The first echelon of the 2nd NZEF arrived at Port Said on 7 January 1940, and five days later the unit's second echelon began training back at home. This second echelon left Wellington on 2 May 1940, arriving at Greenock in Scotland on 16 June 1940. The third echelon began training when the second left New Zealand's shore, as the antipodean contribution to the imperial gathering of force in the Middle East gathered pace. In June 1940 New Zealand began raising a battalion for service in Fiji, and an advanced party of what became the 8th Infantry Battalion arrived in Fiji on 10 September 1940.

The New Zealand war effort stretched the Dominion's manpower resources to the limit, and from 1943, with the Japanese threat receding and the need to feed the American forces in the Pacific growing, home front tasks became a more important call on manpower resources than the tasks of the fighting front. So much so, in fact, that men were released from the armed forces to help on the land. In early 1944 the New Zealand Prime Minister, Peter Fraser (he had replaced Michael Savage upon the latter's death in March 1940), informed Churchill that the effort to supply troops and foodstuffs for the war had forced the country to its manpower limits. To address this problem the 2nd Division, now serving in the Italian campaign, was further reduced, and the 3rd Division was disbanded to reinforce the home labour market.

Enemy naval forces operated in the waters around New Zealand and its overseas possessions. The German auxiliary cruiser *Orion*, for example, sank the steamer *Turikina* off Cape Egmont on 20 August 1940. Raiders also accounted for the steamer *Holmwood* off the Chatham Islands on 25 November 1940 and the steamer *Komata* off Nauru Island on 8 December 1940. As a result of the enemy threat blackout restrictions were gazetted in February 1941. On 8 March 1942 the reconnaissance aircraft from the Japanese submarine I-25 flew over Wellington and Auckland. New Zealand mariners served across the world during the war, 7000 alone serving aboard Royal Navy vessels. New Zealand's two cruisers, HMNZS *Achilles* and *Leander*, formed the New Zealand Division of the Royal Navy, though in October 1941 the Royal New Zealand Navy was officially established. Early in the war, *Achilles* took part in the famous Battle of the River Plate that saw the destruction of the German pocket battleship *Graf Spee* off Montevideo. Later, both cruisers were damaged in the Solomon Islands campaign. On 5 January 1943 *Achilles* suffered severe bomb damage off Guadalcanal, and on the night of the 12–13 July 1943 *Leander* was badly torpedoed off New Georgia. They had briefly formed part of an ANZAC Squadron in early 1942, and thereafter came under SPA when it was formed in April 1942. HMNZS *Leander* sunk an Italian auxiliary cruiser in the Indian Ocean, and served for a time with the Mediterranean Fleet. The RNZN was strengthened by two corvettes, sixteen minesweepers, twelve anti-submarine patrol boats and over a hundred harbour defence launches and other minor craft. RNZN minesweepers saw continuous service in tropical waters from December 1941 to the end of the war. On 29–30 January 1943 two of their number, HMNZS *Kiwi* and *Moa*, sank the Japanese submarine I-1 off Guadalcanal after a fierce fight. The end of the Pacific war saw both HMNZS *Leander* and *Achilles* operating in the vicinity of Okinawa and the Japanese home islands with the British Pacific Fleet.

In the air New Zealand's policy was to supplement the RAF in every possible way, rather than maintain a significant independent force. Thus New Zealanders served extensively in the RAF in Europe and the Middle East, whilst in the Pacific the Dominion contributed fourteen squadrons as well as extensive supply and support facilities for American forces. In 1939 there were already 550 New Zealanders in the RAF, but by the end of the war the figure stood at 12,078, of whom 3285 died. New Zealand produced numerous senior RAF figures, including Air Chief Marshal Sir Keith Park (a group commander during the Battle of Britain, commander of the RAF in Egypt and then in Malta at the height of the siege, and later commander of all air forces in South East Asia Command) and Air Marshal Sir Arthur Coningham (commander of the Western Desert Air Force). Unlike Canada, New Zealand was content not to have separate RNZAF squadrons, and instead six 'New Zealand' squadrons of the RAF were created. The first New Zealand squadron of the RAF (No. 75) was formed on 1 April 1940. A seventh New Zealand squadron was based in West Africa. In the Battle of Britain 103 New Zealand pilots participated, a figure bettered only by the British and the Poles. By the end of 1941 there were 300 New Zealand airmen serving in North Africa and 198 in Malta. The RNZAF's greatest strength was 45,000, a third serving in the Pacific. A quarter of the pilots on board the British Pacific Fleet's carriers in 1945 were New Zealanders. New Zealand played an important role in the British Empire Air Training Scheme (BEATS) by increasing the number of Flying Training Schools in 1940 and contributing financially to the cost of the Canadian branch of the scheme. New Zealand produced 7000 pilots through BEATS. New Zealand sent two squadrons and 400 air force personnel to Malaya, and New Zealand's No. 488 Squadron was in action over Singapore in January 1942. In July 1942 New Zealand squadrons were deployed to New Caledonia.

Australia experienced many of the effects of war on the home front familiar in Britain, from the threat of invasion to the appearance of military uniforms on every street and in every village, and the construction of numerous bases across the continent for the use of Allied military, naval and air forces. The war brought political change as Labour politicians came in from the inter-war cold and formed lasting governments. The need to place the economy on a war footing brought interventionist government as well as Keynesian economic policies, social planning and the expansion of government bureaucracy. A powerful War Cabinet was formed, petrol, clothing, foodstuffs and rubber were rationed, wages and prices were controlled, manpower regulation was instituted, and all Australians over the age of sixteen were issued with identity cards. Effective price controls and growing employment, however, meant that Australia was able to avoid demoralizing restrictions on the production and consumption of consumer goods.

The fall of Singapore was a major shock to Australia and the subsequent raid on Darwin created panic that had to be kept hidden from the general public. The American high command in Australia expected an attack on Darwin by three enemy divisions before the end of March 1942. For two months the Japanese Imperial General Headquarters debated the possibility of an attack on Australia, along with the merits of a strike against Pearl Harbor.* Together with air and naval attacks on other Australian towns, Japanese assaults in Malaya, New Guinea and Australia itself opened what the Prime Minister called 'the battle for Australia', which, given Japan's strategy of capturing territories to the north, came to focus on the struggle for Port Moresby. Early in 1942 civilians were evacuated from Western Australia, Northern Territory and Queensland in response to the Japanese threat, and elsewhere British evacuees arrived to begin new lives away from German bombing in Europe. In Western Australia Broome, Derby and Wyndham were bombed. The Broome bombing was the second worst to be suffered on Australian territory (behind the Darwin raid two weeks before), killing seventy people and destroying twenty-four aircraft. In Queensland, Townsville, the site of Australia's most important air base, was raided three times by flying boats stationed at Rabaul and Thursday Island. In New South Wales

---

* The Imperial Japanese Navy was very keen on an invasion of Australia, though, as was the case when other invasions, like that of Ceylon, were mooted, army opposition was strong. On 7 March 1942 the invasions of Australia and India were put aside, and a policy of isolating Australia by capturing territory to its north was decided upon.

Newcastle was shelled for twenty minutes by a Japanese submarine on 8 June 1942. On 31 May 1942 three Japanese midget submarines (each twenty-four metres long and weighing forty-six tonnes) entered Sydney Harbour in an attempt to destroy shipping. USS *Chicago* narrowly escaped being hit, a torpedo passed under the Dutch submarine K-9, and the depot ship *Kuttabul* was destroyed with the loss of nineteen Australian and two British naval ratings. HMAS *Yandra* and *Sea Mist* sunk one of the submarines (when raised it was discovered that the crew had shot themselves rather than be captured) and another became entangled in the submarine netting and destroyed itself with demolition charges. These incidents provoked debate about evacuation and the provision of public air raid shelters.

The most serious raid was that visited upon Darwin in February 1942. This disrupted Allied communications and supply routes, and was bad enough to be concealed from the Australian public by a federal government concerned about civilian morale at a time of general imperial calamity.[13] The raid was conducted by Admiral Nagumo's four fleet carriers, which launched seventy-one dive bombers, eighty-one torpedo bombers and thirty-six fighters, supplemented for good measure by fifty-four bombers from bases in the Dutch East Indies. Complete surprise was achieved. A troopship and a freighter were sunk, and the airport destroyed. After bombing the town, the aircraft concentrated on shipping, sinking an American destroyer and damaging another, and sinking eight other ships. Over 240 people died in less than one hour, and the raid caused panic, leading to the flight of both military personnel and civilians into the interior (afterwards known as the 'Great Darwin Handicap'). Much of the town was destroyed and commercial life stopped. The centre of the Northern Territory administration shifted to Alice Springs. The town remained under military rule thereafter, and there were fifty subsequent, smaller raids. Japanese invasion was a realistic prospect; like their peers in Ceylon and India in the aftermath of Japanese raids, there was no hindsight to comfort them, and as yet no Allied triumphs against Japanese arms to provide a glimmer of hope.

The threat to Australian security from the air and sea led to numerous civil defence initiatives as the war was brought home to Australians. People unable to join the regular armed forces felt the need to do something to provide for their country's defence in the event of a Japanese invasion. The Volunteer Defence Corps provided 5000 men for the defence of airfields, for coast-watching, anti-aircraft and guard duties, and the manning of coastal defence batteries. In performing these tasks regular soldiers were released for duties closer to the front line. The Volunteer Defence Corps peaked in 1942 at 100,000, though in May 1944 (around about the same time as the stand-down of the Home Guard in Britain), nearly half were released as the danger to Australia subsided. National security and a sense of war cohesion were encouraged through propaganda, especially that fostering the idea of an enemy within that could only be defeated by greater unity and common effort. Jehovah's Witnesses, communists and other 'suspect' elements in society were banned, and foreign nationals interned or kept under close surveillance. At its peak there were 7000 people interned. The press magnate Keith Murdoch became Director-General of Information, as nation-wide propaganda became an important instrument in the country's war effort.

The federal government gathered to itself a comprehensive set of controls in order to direct the Dominion's war effort at every level. As a result the state parliaments lost a degree of their power to Canberra. In particular, new powers of taxation accrued to the federal parliament, as well as power over the distribution of goods, services, manufacturing and transport. Federal control of transport was necessary because most of the trade among the Australian states was seaborne, calling for continent-wide coordination at a time of severe shipping shortages. As part of a global Empire, Australia and New Zealand keenly felt the shifts in the availability of merchant shipping. When, for instance, there was a massive withdrawal of merchant vessels from the eastern cross-trades to the British supply routes in the west in February 1941, a rapid fall in stocks in countries like Australia followed. Australia and New Zealand moved to cut petrol consumption to two-thirds of the pre-war level. With the loss of oil supplies from the Dutch East Indies, Australia had to look to the Persian Gulf and America.

An Allied Works Council was formed to direct labour towards war-related construction projects. There was also a Civil Construction Corps which by June 1943 numbered 53,500 men, 16,600 of whom were conscripts. The construction of military installations was their main task, for example naval facilities for the arrival of the British Pacific Fleet, and extensive air bases in northern Australia for Allied operations across the Pacific. The supervision of agricultural and industrial production was taken over by the government, as the age of the managerial state dawned in Australia as it did throughout the Empire. By 1942 half a million people had been redirected from civilian to war-related jobs, achieved by a variety of means. A Department of War Organization and Industry was established which directed distribution, commerce and finance, simplified clothing manufacture, restricted retail delivery transport, reduced packaging and zoned bread and milk deliveries. The use of iron and steel was limited, and the production of alcoholic drinks and cigarettes was reduced by about a third. After Pearl Harbor a Manpower Priorities Board and a Manpower Directorate was formed. In August 1944 it was decided that 30,000 men would be discharged from the army and 15,000 from the air force in order to boost food production.

War wiped out the unemployment of the inter-war years as effectively as it did in many other parts of the Empire, and accelerated urbanization as cities and towns attracted workers during a period of manufacturing boom. Women entered the work force in increasing numbers, joining military units such as the Australian Women's Army Service, the Women's Emergency Signalling Corps and the Women's Flying Club. By early 1944 there were 50,000 women in the forces. As in Britain, a Women's Land Army was formed for agricultural tasks. A shortage of men led in 1941 to the formation of the Women's Auxiliary Australian Air Force, and there was a naval equivalent as well. Women also formed the backbone of home front war organizations like the Australian Comforts Fund, the Victorian branch of which had 22,000 members by 1940, all participating in the production of woollen garments and other luxuries to be sent to the soldiers overseas.[14]

Causing a social flurry, creating job opportunities and speeding up cultural change through media like film and music, ships bearing American servicemen began to arrive at Christmas 1941. In March 1942 there were 30,000 Americans in Australia. On 6 April the 41st Infantry Division arrived, followed by the 32nd Infantry Division five weeks later. By July the 30,000 had become 89,000, including a thousand US Army female nurses. By the end of 1942, the number stood at 110,000. By July 1943 there were 200,000 Americans in Australia, and more than 300,000 by December of that year. This rapid build up put great strain on Australia's already overburdened support structure. This created an insatiable demand for American supply troops, which is what brought so many black American servicemen to Australia. As the major Allied base for the war in the South-West Pacific, a massive construction programme was required to build the logistics infrastructure required to underpin operations to Australia's north. This required sensible use of resources. Thus, for example, in the last half of 1942, Australia provided about 70 per cent of the food for American forces, rather than shipping space being occupied to bring it in from elsewhere. By 1943, 48,000 Australians were working on military construction projects. By June 1943 they had built over 300 airfields, and under the Australian government's Allied Works Council 4621 miles of road had been built or reconditioned. Over 179 petrol storage tanks had also been built, along with hospitals, warehouses, military camps and improved harbour facilities at Brisbane, Cairns, Darwin, Fremantle, Townsville and Sydney.

Up to a million Americans passed through Australia during the war, Melbourne alone playing host to 30,000 GIs. Many more were based in Queensland. As in Britain their material wealth provoked envy, especially from males unable to compete as successfully for female attention. Following the German example in the Middle East, this led to Japanese propaganda leaflets aimed at Australian troops fighting in New Guinea. Typically, they would show an Australian girl in an intimate embrace with an American soldier and draw attention to the fact that, whilst the Australian was facing death in an active theatre, the American 'ally' – smart uniform, full wallet and access to luxury goods – was having his wicked way with Australian womenfolk. Brisbane's population of 300,000 was almost doubled by the arrival of soldiers, mostly from America. Many residents in Brisbane considered the city under real threat of Japanese attack, and moved inland to safer locations. Slit trenches and air raid shelters appeared in suburban gardens, with sandbags outside public buildings. American forces took over numerous public buildings, the city was browned out at night and crime rates increased as a result of the large military population and the city's attraction to black marketeers and various small-time criminals. The large contingent of black troops was segregated along Ipswich Road, and blacks were confined to the south of the city. In November 1942 the 'Battle of Brisbane' occurred after some Australian soldiers took exception to an American military policeman beating a drunken serviceman. The brawl that ensued involved many people and American military policemen opened fire, killing an Australian.

Many black Americans were included in the large number of American personnel stationed in Australia, presenting problems for the government's 'White Australia' policy and all sorts of half-baked segregationist measures; black Americans, for example, not being allowed to cross the Victoria Bridge in Brisbane to the north side of the river.[15] Initially their deployment was resisted, but the American stance was that, given the absence of Australia's main body of fighting troops, the country should take what it could get. To placate the Australian government the Americans agreed to their black troops being based mainly in remote areas of Queensland and the Northern Territory (though it should be noted that it was in these areas that service troops were most needed to develop the Australian supply infrastructure). In those regions, black American servicemen came into contact with Aborigines; and, as in numerous Pacific islands, their impact upon the world view of isolated people was considerable. Aborigines were less aware of the fact that black servicemen were treated worse than their white colleagues, though they couldn't help but notice that they were healthy, armed, well-paid and proud non-whites.

The threat to seaborne trade caused by German aggression in the early years of the war jeopardized Australia and New Zealand's capacity to earn money, so Britain took action to shelter their economies from the potentially devastating effects of world war. One way of doing this was to guarantee the purchase of the entire wool clip, which accounted for 30 per cent of Australia's pre-war export income. Australia's economic health continued to depend on primary exports to Britain, and this guarantee was important, especially as it was extremely unlikely that Britain would be able either to ship or sell the wool. Britain also undertook to purchase other traditional exports like butter, cheese and meat (interpreted by some commentators as an attempt to secure Australian military assistance in the Middle East). Naturally the war also threatened Australia's imports, for which Britain accounted for nearly half in 1939. Britain's difficulty in fulfilling its traditional role as exporter meant that import-substitution for domestic and military goods had to develop in Australia. In several sectors of the economy Australia made great strides, including iron and steel, non-ferrous metals, textiles, chemical fertilizers, clothing and footwear. Small arms and ammunition were produced in abundance, and important advances were made in aircraft manufacture, motor vehicle assembly and ship-building. Australia's economic transformation saw output rise during the course of the war from £1819 million to £2935 million. Australians had to tighten their belts for the sake of the war effort, and the scale of cut-backs in private consumption was greater than that experienced in the First World War. Private consumption fell from around 70 per cent of Gross Domestic Product (GDP) to 40 per cent. Stabilization of wages and prices was introduced with the support of the unions and proved effective, prices rising by only 14 per cent during the war. The war marked the start of a phase of expanded economic growth based mainly on the secondary sector, as secondary and tertiary industry supplanted farming in terms of GDP and employment for the first time in Australia's history.

As the Pacific war developed, it gradually became clear that one of Australia's main contributions to the overall Allied campaign would be to increase agricultural production as opposed to devoting further resources to providing soldiers or munitions. With the notable exceptions of wheat and wool, the primary produce surpluses experienced before Japan entered the war quickly became shortages as Australia struggled to supply the domestic civilian market, New Zealand, various Pacific islands, the Australian armed forces, American forces in Australia and the south-west Pacific, as well as Britain. This transformation of Australia from a surplus to a deficit country by early 1942 necessitated a massive concentration on home front industrial and agricultural production. The manifold demands on Australia's produce were the main reason for the introduction of rationing. Agriculture was given the status of a war industry, and state-farming projects were established (including the world's largest rice paddy). Government-to-government trade between Britain and Australia replaced the pre-war system of trade. With it came government control over distribution and marketing. As part of the Eastern Group Supply Council (EGSC) formed in Delhi in 1940, Australia became a major source of supply for British imperial territories east of Suez. Australia and India were the powerhouses of this 'Eastern Zone', the imperial territories east of Suez that could manufacture war goods for use in fighting theatres around the world, thus reducing the burden on British industry.

The contribution of Australia's war industry was impressive. There had been moves towards rearmament before the war, as in Britain, reviving some sectors of the Dominion's defence industry. Cockatoo Island dockyard, for instance, more or less derelict since the 1920s, was put into operation and had completed two escort sloops before the war began. Australian shipyards built sixty anti-submarine and minesweeping corvettes of the 'Bathurst' class, designed for convoy protection and the clearing of contact and magnetic mines. Of the sixty, four went to the Royal Indian Navy, thirty-six to the RAN and the remainder to the Royal Navy's Eastern Fleet, from which eighteen were transferred to the British Pacific Fleet on its formation in November 1944. Australia also constructed thirteen Liberty ships. Australia's aircraft industry built 3500 machines, many under licence from British companies. There were small arms factories at Footscray in Victoria and Lithgow in New South Wales (where Vickers machine guns and rifles were made), and ordnance and explosive factories at Maribyrnong near Melbourne. (New defence ordnance facilities were opened in five other Victorian centres. The one at Bendigo employed 1400 people by the middle of 1943.) By June 1941 Australia had delivered to Britain 100 million rounds of small arms ammunition, 30,000 rifles and nearly 200,000 mortar bombs. An RAN Torpedo Factory was opened, and factories at Bendigo were capable of reconditioning large calibre naval guns.

From as early as 1942 the labour demands of the home front began to challenge and outrank those of the armed forces. Australia became most valuable to the Allies as a base and a reservoir of food and supplies for the war effort, particularly given the demands made by the presence in the region of American forces in their hundreds of thousands. By the end of 1942 the American high command believed the chance of an invasion of Australia to be virtually non-existent. In July 1942 6000 men were released from military service to help bring in the harvest, and partial demobilization was discussed. About 100,000 men were eventually released from the army.

As in the case of Australia, New Zealand's food contribution to the war effort was ultimately at least as important as its military contribution. As well as supplying significant military forces, New Zealand continued to export its traditional agricultural products and sought to meet the almost limitless demands of the American military machine in the Pacific. Petrol was rationed from the start of the war, and all 'pleasure motoring' was banned from the opening weeks of war. Demand for New Zealand's foods led to rationing on the home front and to the release of thousands of men from the fighting forces and the home defence forces in order to work on the land. In 1941–42 10,000 troops became farm hands. In 1943 home defence forces released 16,000 men and in the following year 9000 troops were released when the 3rd Division was disbanded. As happened in Britain, the war witnessed both a rise in the acreage under the plough and great leaps in the mechanization of agriculture. The number of tractors rose from 9600 to 18,900, the lion's share coming from American factories under Lend-Lease. By May 1942 rationing extended to sugar, clothing, boots, hosiery, knitting yarn, and, from March 1944, to meat. New Zealand also stepped up war production in non-agricultural sectors of the economy (the arms industry in particular). As a member of the EGSC, for example, the Dominion exported mortars, grenades and Bren gun carriers to Africa and India. Its shipyards produced over 500 vessels, many for the American forces in the Pacific. As in the agricultural sector, this economic war effort required labour redirection, and 176,000 people were drafted into essential war work. Unemployment disappeared, and 35,000 women were absorbed by war industries. The membership of women's voluntary organizations peaked at 75,000. Women also entered the armed forces, and the New Zealand Women's Army Auxiliary Corps numbered 4600 within a few months of its formation in 1941. For two years there were 20,000 Americans in New Zealand, and over 1300 New Zealand women returned to America after the war, having married American servicemen.

Effective measures were taken in New Zealand to prevent the levels of inflation that the demand for goods and services, coupled with import scarcity, threatened. Wages and prices were fixed. At its peak, the Dominion's war effort was costing two-fifths of its output, and in 1943 53 per cent of national income was devoted to defence expenditure. This was financed through taxation and internal borrowing as opposed to borrowing from the City of London, another sign of growing Dominion autonomy and a changing relationship with Britain. Throughout the war New Zealand made preparations in case of attack or invasion. A home guard was formed in August 1940 and, at the height of Japan's power in April 1942, evacuation plans were made for coastal cities. From August 1942 air raid drill was regularly practised in New Zealand's schools.

Unlike Australia, New Zealand territory did not experience direct enemy aggression (though Japanese reconnaissance aircraft did fly over Auckland and Wellington), and only a small number of New Zealand's 8000 prisoners of war fell into Japanese hands. In contrast, 22,000 Australians went into Japanese captivity, and of that number 8000 died. Consequently Australia has a much more developed awareness of the plight of prisoners during the war with Japan. Australians were captured in Singapore, Java, Ambon, Timor and New Britain. New Zealand troops had far less contact with the Japanese, whereas their Australian counterparts had extensive contact in Malaya, the East Indies and the Pacific. Of the Australian total of 22,000 men in Japanese captivity, 13,000 were employed on the construction of the infamous Burma–Thailand railway, along with thousands more American, British, Dutch and Indian servicemen and Burmese civilians. Prisoners were also employed constructing airfields, equally as important for a Japanese army attempting to connect its newly-conquered territories to the major battle front developing in the Burma–India theatre.

The trials of captivity, as well as the diversity of Australia's war effort, are well captured by the war experiences of Sir Edward 'Weary' Dunlop.[16] His experience was typical of many men: 'the real horror of army life ... idleness in fixed camps', interspersed with short periods of intense activity, terror and excitement, but rounded off by nearly four years of the harrowing challenges and dangers of captivity. Having trained in medicine in his native Australia, Dunlop was working in a London hospital when 'the ball was kicked off' by Neville Chamberlain on 3 September 1939. By the end of the year he had joined a contingent of 110 Australians bound for Palestine and the main Australian Overseas Base in Jerusalem, where Dunlop was wanted as a headquarters medical officer. He left Tilbury docks aboard the British India Line vessel SS *Mantola*, adorned with a single 4.7-inch gun and an anti-aircraft gun, and also carrying 'the whisky-bitten colonials with their grubby children' returning to Kenya and Tanganyika, a few journalists, and some Royal Naval Reserve officers bound for Aden and Malta. His first posting was to the 600-bed 2/1st Australian General Hospital near Gaza. Dunlop was to spend many months in Palestine as the 6th Division gathered strength and the 7th Division arrived, and as Australian forces were deployed in Greece, Syria and the Western Desert, including a spell in Tobruk. Dunlop established a daily clinic in Tobruk, patronized by Australian and British soldiers, as well as Palestinians, Cypriots and Libyans in the labour corps and Italian prisoners of war.

Soon after came the fateful shift to the east. The Australian Imperial Force had been deployed in strength in Malaya since February 1941, when the headquarters of the 8th Division arrived. Dunlop landed only in time for the tail-end of the fighting in Java. Here he ran No. 1 Allied General Hospital, where 1351 patients were treated in the eighteen days of its existence before surrender to the Japanese. Thus began years of imprisonment, during which Dunlop, though a medical rather than a combat officer, attained legendary status as a leader of men. Epidemics, overcrowding, underfeeding, forced labour, the attentions of the Japanese secret police, public bayoneting, and calculated brutality and humiliation were to characterize the Japanese camps, as well as the constant longing for homes and for loved ones from whom they heard nothing, and for news of the progress of the war from which they had suddenly been divorced.

Because of his physical stature and the esteem in which he was held by many of his comrades, Dunlop was put in charge of a camp of 1500 Allied servicemen in Bandoeng, where he found the friendship of Lieutenant-Colonel Laurens Van der Post of the British Army particularly helpful, before moving on with his men through camps in Java, Siam and Singapore. Known disparagingly as the 'Java Rabble' when they arrived in Singapore, before their capture his men had variously fought in the Battle of Britain, the Battle of the Atlantic, the Mediterranean, the Western Desert, Greece, Crete, Syria and, finally, in the battle for Java. Freedom eventually came with Japanese defeat, and the beginning of the complex tasks for which Repatriation of Allied Prisoners of War and Internees units were rapidly established. The Japanese army claimed that there were at that time 29,630 British, 11,334 Dutch, 4662 Australian and New Zealanders and 296 Americans in Siam alone. In Bangkok Dunlop worked with Lady Mountbatten, the wife of the Supreme Allied Commander South East Asia, as she visited the many camps holding Allied troops awaiting repatriation, before Dunlop himself, finally, boarded the last Australian flight out of Siam, bound for home and the lengthy process of 'reclaiming the lost years'.

Edward Dunlop's experiences reflected the movement of tens of thousands of young Australians and New Zealanders from one side of the world to the other and back again that resulted from their involvement in an imperial war. Margaret Stone experienced similar migrations, though was fortunate enough to avoid enemy captivity. She enlisted in the Australian Army Nursing Service in February 1940, and was sent to the Middle East with the 2/2 General Hospital, taking charge of a plastic surgery ward at El Kantara in Egypt. She worked alongside Benjamin Rank, performing reconstructive surgery on men with horrific battlefield injuries. After a year in Egypt, Stone returned to the military hospital at Heidelberg in Melbourne. She was then posted to 2/8 Australian General Hospital in

New Guinea, where she was awarded the Imperial Order of the Royal Red Cross for her work, finally being discharged from the army in 1945.

The Australasian Dominions and Pacific islands of the Empire and Commonwealth all played a part in the Allied propaganda intelligence war.[17] It was, for example, an Australian interception station that alerted the Americans to the fact that the Japanese had fallen for their ruse regarding the Midway garrison's apparent lack of water. When the Japanese reported this intercepted 'intelligence', the Americans were able to confirm the codeword used by the Japanese for Midway, thereby also confirming that the Japanese were planning to strike at the island. British and Australian brains had been important in pre-war codebreaking. An Australian contingent had been attached to the Bletchley Park outstation at Hong Kong since 1937, and early in 1940 the Australian General Staff established its own signals intelligence section, recruiting four academics who later joined a group at Melbourne led by Commander Eric Nave. Most of Australia's signals intelligence personnel were in the Middle East theatre, but intercept stations were built at Brisbane, Canberra, Darwin and Melbourne, and the group cooperated with the British Far East Combined Bureau at Hong Kong and with the Dutch in Java. (Despite all of this, not even the most general warning was given before the raid on Darwin in February 1942 involving 250 Japanese aircraft.) Commander Rupert Long, RAN, was instrumental in developing Australia's coast-watching network in Papua and New Guinea. He liaised with cryptanalysts in the FECB at Singapore, and provided the Chief of the Naval Staff with the ammunition to fight the government for approval to establish a RAN cryptanalysis unit (the Special Intelligence Bureau under Nave). This unit broke merchant shipping codes, the wireless code used in the Japanese Mandated Islands and Japanese consular codes in Australia. When an Operational Intelligence Centre was established in Britain, Long founded the Combined Operations Intelligence Centre in Australia. Long was also the Australian link for SOE in Britain and its Oriental Mission. The US Navy maintained a Fleet Radio Unit in Melbourne, to which the Australians had access.

As well as intelligence interception and decryption stations, individual operators were scattered across the Pacific to relay information by wireless. MacArthur created his own army and air force signals intelligence facility called Central Bureau, organized as a combined American, Australian and British decryption centre. It moved from Melbourne to Brisbane when MacArthur transferred his headquarters, and grew considerably; in May 1942, for example, there were forty American staff assigned to Central Bureau, and a thousand by the end of 1943. In addition there were over five hundred Australians, a couple of dozen British Army and RAF personnel, and two RCAF codebreakers. During 1942 and early 1943, before American experts and their equipment had arrived in strength, MacArthur leaned heavily on Australian codebreakers and traffic analysts as well as US Navy cryptanalysts. Field units were established across Australia and beyond. By early 1943 the Australian Special Wireless Group had deployed 51 Wireless Section to Darwin, where it picked up a good deal of military traffic, particularly from Borneo and the Philippines. It listened in on Japanese naval land-based air force communications, particularly from Timor, whose air-fields served as staging bases for air attacks against Darwin. 55 Wireless Section operated from Port Moresby in New Guinea. Women of the New Zealand Women's Royal Naval Service worked on interception, direction-finding and the radio fingerprinting of Japanese signals at numerous sites in the South Pacific, stretching as far as Suva in Fiji.

Since the fall of Singapore SOE had operated in Australia from suburban Melbourne under the title 'Inter-Services Reconnaissance Department' (later Force 137). It established training facilities near Brisbane and in Darwin, and in 1940 special forces instructors had been sent from Britain to train Australian and New Zealand Independent Companies. An SOE Special Training School was opened at Cairns in northern Queensland, known as Experimental Station Z. True to form, however, MacArthur was not prepared to accept SOE within his area of operations, so SOE Australia came to focus on the region to the north west of the Australian continent. An operational base was established at Morotai in the Moluccas, and two advance camps were established on Labuan Island, the British colonial territory just off the coast of Brunei and British North Borneo, and at Balikpapan Bay in Dutch Borneo, to support operations in South-East Asia. Among other operations in enemy-occupied territory, SOE Australia famously staged Operation Jaywick in September 1943. A small fishing boat with a fourteen-man (mainly British) crew sailed the two thousand miles from Exmouth Gulf on the north-west cape of Australia to Singapore, sank seven Japanese ships with limpet mines (totalling over 30,000 tons), and made it back home without sustaining a single casualty. The idea had been conceived in Delhi in May 1942 when Lieutenant-Colonel Ivan Lyon of the Gordon Highlanders talked to Brigadier Bernard Fergusson, ADC to Wavell. Lyon had escaped from Singapore and Sumatra and, navigating native craft, had brought a party of forty escapees to Ceylon. He now proposed to sail a small ship fro Australia to Singapore for destructive purposes. Thus the seventy-eight foot *Krait* travelled the 5000 miles there and back again to sink Japanese ships. A second attempt was an abject disaster, all the men being captured and subse-quently executed in Tokyo a month before Hiroshima. Australia also devoted considerable resources to the wireless war, beaming propaganda into enemy-held territories, and dropping millions of leaflets, for example, 'Japan man bugger up finish. Altogether Japan man fraid too much, now all e like run away', dropped over New Guinea.

An aspect of the British Empire and Commonwealth's war effort in the Pacific region that is usually overlooked is the creation and war service of the British Pacific Fleet (BPF).[18] This is surprising, as it was the most powerful fleet ever to have assembled under the White Ensign, comprising on VJ Day four battleships, five fleet carriers, four light fleet carriers, nine escort carriers, eleven cruisers, forty-one destroyers, 170 minesweepers and support vessels and thirty submarines. Nevertheless, it remains the case that, in Britain's naval war against Japan, the sinking of HMS *Prince of Wales* remains firmly etched in the popular memory rather than HMS *King George V*'s bombardment of Tokyo.* Though dwarfed by the colossal American naval force amassed by the time it arrived in Pacific waters for the last months of the onslaught on Japan, and though only to play a cameo role in the fighting, it was considered politically important for Britain to have a significant presence in this final chapter of the war, and to have fitting representation at the surrender ceremonies in reoccupied colonies and in Tokyo Bay itself. In particular the British government considered it essential that South-East Asia and Hong Kong be recaptured by British arms. The BPF was intended to accomplish this along with the forces of South East Asia Command (including its naval component, the reconstituted East Indies Station), as well as to contribute to the defeat of Japan, an enemy that was as much Britain's as it was America's. It was also considered imperative that Australia, New Zealand and the British Pacific islands saw British forces fully committed to defeating Japan in their neighbourhood. The commitment of the fleet decisively shaped American attitudes to Britain and its armed forces in the post-war world, and its dispatch represented a significant victory for those who had fought against Churchill's conviction that the British should stick to their own, almost exclusive victory over Japan in the Indian Ocean and South-East Asia theatres, rather than sending an inevitably junior force to the American-dominated Pacific theatre.

The commitment of such a force also represented continuity with the ideas and plans of the Admiralty prior to the outbreak of the Japanese war, when it had been determined to send forces to Singapore and Manila to forge an effective eastern fighting alliance with the American Navy. That said, British policy regarding the defeat of Japan was never particularly clear, with Churchill inclined to favour concentration on the Burma campaign and regaining Malaya, feeling that America did not need and would not welcome British help in the Pacific, whilst naval planners believed that a proper force commitment to the Pacific would redound in Britain's favour and help Britain retain a degree of influence in American councils. This was the view of the Chiefs of Staff, who on more than one occasion contemplated mass resignation in order to trump Churchill. For them, Britain's alliance with America was an asset as valuable as the Empire itself. There were also powerful American voices calling for a British presence in the region, indeed at one point in 1944 considering it essential if the Pacific war was to be

---

* On 29 July 1945 HMS *King George V*, in company with American forces, fired 264 14-inch shells at the Imperial Japanese Navy's fleet anchorage at Hammamatsu, south of Tokyo, the last British battleship ever to fire in anger.

ended by the target date of October 1945. It was also important to ensure that the American public did not consider that the British failed to put lives on the line in the Pacific theatre (the point of the 'We will pursue the war with Japan until the finish' posters published in Britain). Not only did this topic receive plenty of attention at a series of top-level Allied conferences, it was constantly revisited by the Chiefs of Staff and the War Cabinet. Churchill was still very keen on north Sumatra as the site of a major British offensive. For him British imperial policy for defeating Japan after Germany's demise should concentrate on operations based on India and carried out in the Indian Ocean by SEAC with the object of liberating Burma, Singapore and – possibly – Java, Sumatra and Borneo. The alternative consisted of operations based on Australia carried out by all three services in close cooperation with the Americans. The first option was the easier to stage, though limited itself largely to freeing British colonies without directly participating in the final defeat of Japan.

There were other reasons for a major British commitment to the defeat of Japan in the Pacific. One came from Australia, though in ambivalent fashion. The Australian government hated the fact that America called the shots in the Pacific war and excluded Australia from decision-making, though it was not anxious for a return to a bossy British direction of military affairs. On the one hand, some Australians objected to the suggestion that Britain should take over South-West Pacific Command; on the other, some Australians saw a British return in such a role as a way of counterbalancing the fact that America had increasingly sidelined Australia as the war moved further and further north towards Japan. It was felt by some that Australia had carried the Empire and Commonwealth's flag in the Pacific war in 1942 and that now it was time, as Australia grew progressively exhausted, for Britain to step in and take a hand. This fitted well with the thoughts of many senior British military planners. In 1944 the Chiefs of Staff planned to send six divisions to take part in the war against Japan once Europe had been won, forty RAF squadrons (Lancaster bombers, with other Lancasters converted for in-flight refuelling), and a fleet built around fifteen carriers and eight battleships. This impressive aim was not to be fully achieved; first of all, the strategic lift simply did not exist to get so many people and so much material to Australian bases. Then there was the fact that MacArthur objected to Indian troops serving in his command and was determined to minimize non-American participation in the attack on Japan. The task of garrisoning Europe also became a priority for the British Army as soon as the European war ended, meaning that sufficient British troops were not available for transfer east. That said, the fleet plan did go ahead, and when the atomic bombs were dropped the RAF was already moving east in strength.

It was quite natural that warships of a strong British fleet would again nose among the islands of the Pacific and visit Dominion ports in strength. Britain had been a major naval power in the region for a century and a half, and – though the naval shield had broken in the face of the Japanese onslaught – Britain's imperial defence commitments did not change as a result, and it was only a matter of time before Australia, New Zealand and the Pacific islands of the British Empire again witnessed the sight of British battleship grey. Ever since the loss of HMS *Prince of Wales* and *Repulse* the Admiralty had been plotting the return. As has been seen, the Indian Ocean and its Eastern Fleet became an assembly area for the naval force that in 1944 began to deploy to the Pacific.

The arrival of the BPF at its Australian bases was confirmation of the naval facts of the war as they stood at the time of the fleet's formation in November 1944. Since the loss of HMS *Prince of Wales* and *Repulse* and the fall of Singapore, Britain had had no significant naval force operating in the Far East, a result of these defeats and the fact that British naval forces were stretched to the limit in other theatres. Now that threats in those other regions had palpably lessened, for example, with Italy's defeat and the turning of the tide in the U-boat war, a return to the Far East was possible. Therefore from 1943 the Eastern Fleet based on Ceylon was strengthened, until it was able to give birth to the new BPF. The Eastern Fleet split in two in November 1944, and the larger segment became the BPF. Admiral Sir Bruce Fraser hoisted his colours as the Commander-in-Chief British Pacific Fleet aboard the new battleship HMS *Howe* on 22 November 1944. On the same day Admiral Sir John Power became Commander-in-Chief of the reconstituted East Indies Station.

On the voyage from Ceylon to its Australian home port of Sydney the fleet raided Japanese positions at Palambang in Sumatra at the request of Admiral Chester Nimitz, Commander-in-Chief Pacific. It arrived to a rapturous welcome in February 1945. The Australians had been preparing to host a major British naval presence for some time, the Australian Commonwealth Naval Board, for instance, beginning to stockpile canned and dried provisions for 20,000 men. In May 1940 the then Prime Minister, Robert Menzies, had announced the start of work on a graving dock at Garden Island to make Sydney capable of taking capital ships, and the new Captain Cook Dock opened in time to allow the city to serve as the main BPF base. At its peak, the dock was employing 4100 on its construction. Its first customer was the carrier HMS *Illustrious* in February 1945, after damage received during a kamikaze attack. Subsidiary fleet bases had been prepared at Adelaide, Brisbane, Cairns, Fremantle and Melbourne. After a fortnight in Sydney the BPF left for Manus in the Australian Admiralty Islands. On 15 March the BPF was allocated to Admiral Chester Nimitz for operations against Okinawa. The task was to neutralize airfields on Miyako and Ishigaki to prevent Japanese forces from staging air reinforcements from Formosa to Okinawa. Therefore between March and May 1945 the BPF operated against the Sakishima Gunto Islands west of Formosa, during which time ninety-eight aircraft were lost. The fleet also bombarded the Japanese home islands, the last British battleships ever to fire in anger letting fly at Hamamatsu on 29–30 July 1945. All six of the modern 'Illustrious' class carriers served with the BPF, and all six were hit in April-May 1945. Demonstrating the wisdom of building these carriers with heavy armour (with the narrow waters of the Mediterranean, threatened by land-based bombers, in mind), *Illustrious* and *Indomitable* continued to operate aircraft after being hit in kamikaze attacks. *Formidable* was out of action for only a few hours and *Implacable*, *Indefatigable* and *Victorious* were all repaired within one month.

The BPF was known as Task Force 57, and its Fleet Train as Task Force 113 (combined, they were Task Force 112). It operated as part of Spruance's American 5th Fleet. The Fleet Train was of great importance, because American naval authorities (Admiral Ernest King in particular) would not entertain the use of British warships unless they were totally self-supporting, as the Americans did not want to have to provide logistical support for British carriers. This stipulation required the British to maintain a host of support ships and base facilities in Australia. Among other things, it also necessitated the dispatch of a floating dock to Leyte in the Philippines. The BPF was operating 12,000 miles from home, and would operate between 3500 and 4000 miles from its main base at Sydney. The British would have to learn quickly about replenishing at sea. The Fleet Train carried supplies from the rearward base at Sydney to intermediate bases at Manus or Leyte, and the tankers went right forward to the operational areas. There were Victualling Stores Issue Ships, Air Stores Issue Ships and Amenity Ships. At its peak the BPF counted 125 ships manned by over 26,000 men, and the 1st Aircraft Carrier Squadron could field 238 aircraft. It was a remarkably representative Commonwealth force, like the Eighth Army or the Western Desert Air Force. The Australian and New Zealand navies were incorporated into the fleet, and many Commonwealth men served on its ships. The cruiser HMS *Gambia*, for example, was transferred to the Royal New Zealand Navy, and the cruiser HMS *Uganda* was manned by Canadians. Australia provided the 7th Destroyer Flotilla and many of the escort ships for the Fleet Train, and a disproportionate number of the fleet's pilots were New Zealanders.

At the end of the war, ships of the BPF, along with those of the East Indies Station, took Japanese surrenders throughout the region. Ships of the BPF were amongst the 250 vessels that gathered in Tokyo Bay on 2 September 1945 to witness the official Japanese surrender, which took place aboard the battleship USS *Missouri*. Admiral Sir Bruce Fraser put pen to paper on behalf of the British government, and representatives of the Australian, Canadian and New Zealand governments did likewise. That evening, on the quarterdeck of HMS *Duke of York*, Allied military leaders, including the American Admirals William Halsey and Chester Nimitz, gathered to witness the Royal Navy's traditional sunset ceremony. The band of the Royal Marines gathered under the fourteen-inch guns of the aft turret. The bugler sounded and slowly the ensigns of the Allied warships were lowered, *Duke of York*'s last. The guard presented arms and the band played the hymn 'The Day Thou Gavest Lord is Ended'. 'All around', recalled Lieutenant Ronald Neith, 'the great American ships were silent, their crews facing towards the British flagship, saluting'. HMS *Nelson* took the Japanese surrender off

Penang, and the cruiser *Cleopatra* took the surrender at Singapore before Mountbatten arrived for the official ceremony. The carrier HMS *Glory* and the frigates *Amethyst* and *Hart* went to Rabaul, the cruiser HMS *Cumberland* and a couple of frigates to Batavia. To reoccupy Shanghai, the BPF sent the carrier HMS *Colossus*, the cruisers *Bermuda* and *Argonaut*, and the destroyers *Quiberon*, *Tumult*, *Tuscan* and *Tyrian*. After the conclusion of hostilities, the Commonwealth forces that were left to take part in the occupation of Japan were commanded by an Australian general with a joint forces base in Melbourne, and the massed fleet melted away within a matter of weeks.

The story of Tasmania's war effort, like much of the rest of the island's history, lies marooned in the Tasman Sea, cut adrift from its giant northern neighbour and from the British Empire and Commonwealth. Reflecting general Australian ignorance about its island state, even official war-time recruitment and propaganda posters left the island off the map. Many Tasmanians, not least the state's war-time premier, felt at the time and have felt since that their war effort had not been properly acknowledged or incorporated into the story of Australian mobilization. Here it is featured as an example of Australia's war experience that illustrates particularly well the effects of war on the home front in a state which also sent over 10 per cent of its population to fight overseas.[19]

Tasmania's war effort reveals the extraordinary global mobilization of manpower and resources that Britain commanded on going to war in 1939. First of all, though so distant from Britain and the initial scenes of battle, Tasmania, like every other part of the Empire, was dependent upon British seapower for its economic livelihood and its security. So in one sense, right from the outbreak of war in September 1939, Tasmania was threatened. If the Royal Navy was to be defeated, or if Britain fell to German invasion, Tasmania would be at the mercy of Britain's enemies and would-be enemies. Furthermore, though much emphasis is placed on Australia's restless struggle for autonomy, for a voice in the highest councils of imperial strategic policy-making and on its sense of 'betrayal' following the fall of Singapore, loyalty to the British Empire and Commonwealth was far from dead in that Dominion and could easily coexist alongside a distinctive Australian national identity.

The outbreak of war was met by a loyal response in Tasmania. Royal visits left no doubt of the strength of feeling on this matter, and events like the fall of France and the onslaught of the Blitz in London and other British cities led to renewed efforts to demonstrate loyalty to Britain in its hour of need, and to energize the Tasmanian war effort anew. The island sent men and women into the armed forces and home defence formations, even before the Pacific war cast its shadow upon Australian security, and Tasmania was active in prosecuting the war against Germany and Italy. Towards the end of the war Hobart was identified as a potential main operational base for the British Pacific Fleet, along with Darwin. Tasmania's economy was geared for war, industrial and agricultural capacity stretched, home defences prepared and funds and 'comfort' items gathered in abundance for war-related charities and support organizations.

Tasmania abounded with voluntary organizations supporting the war effort with knitting needles, crepe bandages, cups of tea and the collection of pounds sterling. Whilst not part of the Empire's martial contribution to the defeat of the King's enemies, such war-related activities across the globe were healthy and important indicators of a home front fully mobilized for war and committed to the cause of victory, and the sound of those knitting needles clicking around the world – on Tasmanian farms, in Kalahari villages and in Canadian cities – should have caused Germans and Japanese alike to pause and think about the global community that they had undertaken to fight. The cardboard boxes marked 'From the Australian Food Front' that appeared in British kitchens were as much a part of the Empire's global war effort as the Bren gun carriers rolling off the production lines from Britain to India to Australia and New Zealand.

The war effort on the Tasmanian home front raised hundreds of thousands of pounds for the war and comforted thousands of servicemen and merchant sailors, as perhaps they docked briefly in Hobart to break a dangerous journey from America to the Middle East, fought to survive in a prisoner-of-war camp or struggled to stay warm in a Syrian winter. Special events and military spectacles banged the recruitment drum in Tasmania, for the island's contribution was to be in manpower and battlefield blood as well as in gifts and comforts. The first Australian-built Beaufort bomber visited to stimulate RAAF recruitment, and a British Lancaster bomber visited Hobart and other towns, the largest aircraft ever to have flown over the island. 'Win the War' rallies raised money, loans for the government and support for the armed forces. Tasmanians gave generously to the King George's Fund for Sailors, the Spitfire Fund, the Greek Relief Fund, the Relief Fund for Air Raid Victims in Britain and the Red Cross. The 160 branches – and 360 Junior Red Cross circles – of the Tasmanian Division of the Australian Red Cross raised £500,000, and in a special appeal in 1940 contributed fourteen ambulances to the armed forces. The Tasmanian division of the Australian Comfort Fund provided amenities for service personnel encamped in Tasmania, knitted comforts, provided an advice service for members of the armed forces, sent 11,000 hampers for distribution among troops overseas, maintained leave hostels and welcomed service personnel on their arrival as well as waving them off on their departure. By June 1945 it had raised nearly £230,000. Between the outbreak of war and June 1944 the Comfort Fund had provided 75,000 pairs of socks, 28,000 scarves, 11,000 pullovers, 20,000 pairs of mittens, 2000 pairs of underpants, 450,000 packets of cigarettes, 541,000 cakes of soap and 4,174,000 sheets of writing paper. Between 1942 and 1945 the Country Women's Association made nearly 3000 sheepskin vests, slippers and mittens for soldiers overseas. In Launceston, a Volunteer War Workers' Salvage Committee collected goods to be sold in a second-hand shop. School girls spent two hours a week knitting and sewing garments in case of a war emergency.

Voluntary Aid Detachment (VAD) membership in Tasmania had reached 850 by the outbreak of war in 1939. VADs raised funds for the Red Cross, underwent training in First Aid, nursing and stretcher drill and were all available for national service. More specialized, some VADs received training in areas like radiology and dentistry. During the war they served in military and private hospitals throughout Tasmania, were trained in bulk cooking, care and use of transport vehicles and the use of ambulances. They also collected salvage and made up medical packs for the Red Cross. In Hobart Voluntary Aids entertained servicemen at the Anzac Buffet, a basement facility in the city centre with dining space for a thousand people, and in the church hut. Detachment 610 at Devonport on the island's northern coast met every single troop train that arrived for onward shipment overseas, in order to serve coffee and sandwiches. It also provided field dressing stations for Volunteer Defence Corps exercises throughout the state. Some went to the Middle East and to military hospitals on the Australian mainland, others joined the Australian Army Medical Women's Service.

There were many other manifestations of Tasmania's engagement in the war against Germany, Italy and Japan. The grounds of Government House in Hobart were converted into a market garden as the Governor, the representative of the King, followed the monarch's example and led from the top. In early 1942 tea was rationed to one ounce per person per week, and controls introduced for supplies from butchers, bakers and the milkman. Petrol was rationed, and talk of clothes rationing led to panic buying. An RAAF training school was established at Western Junction, Noel Coward visited on his Red Cross tour, and at the end of 1940 the port of Hobart was closed to shipping as a result of German mine-laying at the mouth of the Derwent river. The culprit was the ubiquitous German commerce raider *Pinguin*, eventually run to ground and sunk by a British heavy cruiser in the Indian Ocean in 1941. She laid mines in Storm Bay, leaving when a minesweeper was dispatched to challenge her. Hobart's port defences were adjusted at the start of the war when the observation post and guns were moved from Fort Nelson to Fort Direction. The Bass Strait was closed in November 1940 when the British steamer *Cambridge* was sunk by a mine. (An Emergency Supplies Committee had prudently stockpiled essential goods in case the island was cut off from its import sources as a result of such a closure.) In March 1941 Hobart was visited by the liner *Queen Elizabeth*, set on a war-time career as one of the 'monsters', the five massive liners turned transatlantic and trans-Indian Ocean troop carriers. The liner was being converted for her war role in Sydney. Hobart was used extensively by Allied shipping during the war and was the main reason for Tasmania having a strategic profile. In the months following Japan's entry into the war over 120 Liberty ships put in at Hobart, usually in need of some form of adjustment or repair, as American supplies were delivered to the Middle East using routes calculated to avoid Japanese submarines.

Defensive preparations and ARP rehearsals became more intense with the entry of Japan into the war and the genuine threat of invasion that this entailed. Though a reconnaissance flight over Hobart in March 1942 was to mark the limit of Japanese interest in the island, in those days of apparent Japanese invincibility a lot more was to be sensibly expected. Military guards appeared at strategically important points throughout the island. Blackout (or brownout as it was known locally) was planned and practised in the Hobart and Launceston areas. Electricity supplies were cut and daylight saving introduced, along with early closing and the restriction of exterior lighting and neon signs. Screens were fitted to street lights to reduce visibility from the air. The Japanese reconnaissance flight came in March 1942 when Lieutenant Meiji Tagami, commanding the 2625-tonne submarine *I-25*, was ordered to reconnoitre Hobart. He launched his vessel's floatplane from the sheltered expanse of Great Oyster Bay on Tasmania's east coast. He had previously conducted similar missions over Melbourne and Sydney from the waters around King Island.[20]

Enemy submarines remained a threat in Tasmanian waters until near the end of the war. On 9 November 1944 the tanker *Ilissos* reported that it was being fired upon from a position 130 miles south of Adelaide. The aggressor was the only German U-boat remaining in Pacific waters, U-862, operating from Surabaya. Korvettenkapitän Heinrich Timm had been ordered to visit the Australian coast to disrupt its southern shipping lanes. He reached the Tasman Sea sailing around the southern coast of Tasmania to avoid the expected RAN concentration in the Bass Strait. On 14 December 1944 the submarine reached Storm Bay, the approach to the Derwent river and the city of Hobart, but took no further offensive action. The vessel was eventually captured, and scuttled off Singapore by the Royal Navy in 1946.[21]

As in other parts of the Empire and Commonwealth, war eradicated the unemployment that had dogged Tasmania during the depression years. War also led to migrations both inwards and outwards. Of a population of 247,000, 29,000 Tasmanian men and 2000 Tasmanian women joined the armed forces, and most served overseas at some point during the war.[22] Most Australian soldiers saw service in various parts of their own nation-continent, as well as in the Dutch East Indies, Europe, the Middle East, South-East Asia and the Pacific. Even before the Pacific war began Australian forces were deployed throughout the Pacific and the Dutch East Indies as well as in the Middle East. Many Australian garrisons were then captured when Japan began swarming across the eastern world. For example, Brian Gordon was a mortar platoon commander in the 2/40th Battalion, a Tasmanian infantry unit sent to Portuguese Timor before the Pacific War began. Most of the battalion was captured when the Japanese invaded Timor. Gordon spent the remainder of the war as a prisoner, moving to Changi camp in Singapore, working on the Burma–Thailand railway and ending the war in Japan. Another Tasmanian, Major Colin Bidgood, illustrates a typical history of wartime deployment. A pre-war Militia soldier, he was called up for full-time service with the 12th Field Ambulance unit when war broke out in Europe. Wanting to serve outside of his home state of Tasmania and take part in any Australian deployments overseas, Bidgood volunteered for the Australian Imperial Force (which unlike the Militia was to be deployed overseas rather than concentrating exclusively on home defence). In August 1940 he was accepted into the Australian Army Medical Corps as a quartermaster and was posted to the 111th Australian General Hospital, originally located at the rear of the Royal Hobart Hospital. With the onset of the Pacific war in the following year, the unit expanded and moved to Campbell Town in central Tasmania (the site of this once bustling military hospital has now reverted to farmland).

Bidgood left Tasmania when he was posted to a convalescent depot near Brisbane preparing for overseas deployment. The unit was moved to Morotai, an island in the Halmaheras group in the Celebes, where Australian forces saw a great deal of action as MacArthur employed them on mopping up operations. Morotai was captured by American forces and became an Advanced Headquarters for South-West Pacific Area and the base for Australian invasions in Borneo and the surrounding islands. This was why a large Australian Army Medical Corps presence was building up on Morotai. Despite the Allied invasion of Morotai and its subsequent use as a major regional base for Allied operations, part of the island was still held by the Japanese, as were the other islands in the Halmaheras group. The Japanese remaining on Morotai were not seen as a great threat to Allied forces, though American and Australian patrols were maintained. It was believed that there were about 2000 Japanese servicemen still on the island, though when the war ended many thousands more surrendered. Bidgood and his units remained on Morotai for months after the cessation of hostilities clearing patients and returning them to Australia.

Tasmania produced a proportionately large crop of war heroes. (Of Australia's current fleet of six 'Collins' class submarines, three are named after Tasmanian sailors, including the eponymous HMAS *Collins*.) Edward Sheean was on board the corvette HMAS *Armidale* when it was attacked by Japanese forces in the Arfura Sea ninety miles south east of Betano on 1 December 1941. *Armidale* was a 'Bathurst' class corvette that had left Darwin on 29 November 1942 to escort the troop carrier *Castlemaine*, ferrying Javanese troops of the Royal Netherlands East Indies Army to support guerrilla forces in Timor. After landing the troops, the Australian ships were to evacuate the women and children. The ships were attacked by five divebombers, nine torpedo bombers and three Zeros. Forty of *Armidale*'s crew were killed, along with sixty-one of the Javanese troops. Showing no regard for his own life, Sheean remained strapped to his Oerlikon anti-aircraft gun and was seen to go down with his ship.

By 1943 50 per cent of Tasmanian men aged between eighteen and forty were in the armed forces. On the home front 4200 men joined the Volunteer Defence Corps, the equivalent of the British Home Guard, and a further 400 served in the Allied Works Council. The Civil Defence Legion, specializing in ARP duties, came to number 14,000 volunteers. Women entered the work force as never before. The Women's Army Service rose to number 6000, as women were required to work as typists, intelligence and cipher staff, drivers, cooks, wireless telegraphists and draughtswomen. Hostels were established for women war workers all over the country, operated variously by the Catholic Church, the Country Women's Association and the Salvation Army. Other hostels and recreational establishments were opened to cater for the needs of service personnel, visiting merchant seamen and home defence forces. As well as the 30,000 or so Tasmanians who left the island as soldiers, sailors and airmen, war workers migrated to the factories of the mainland, particularly those in the neighbouring state of Victoria. On the other side of the equation, the island played host to about a thousand Italian prisoners of war (mainly working on vegetable farms), and in October 1940 it received a batch of child evacuees from Britain. One of the more unusual tasks accomplished by the Italians was the construction of an escape tunnel running from the Anglesea Barracks in Hobart to St David's Park in the centre of the city.

War brought economic prosperity to Tasmania, though the state premier and Tasmanian members of the federal parliament had to lobby the federal government hard to ensure that Tasmania received a share of the contracts for munitions and equipment created by the demands of the Allied war effort. The federal government eventually spent about twelve million pounds in Tasmania on munitions, defence works and materials for the armed forces, after federal experts had visited to assess Tasmania's suitability for such skilled war work (it was initially thought that Tasmania was not sufficiently industrialized to be of much use). Federal control and interference in the Tasmanian economy increased during the war, as Australia's central government took measures to control wages, to raise income tax and to establish bulk purchasing arrangements. The net output of primary production in Tasmania increased from £8.1 million in 1938–39 to £13.2 million in 1945–46. As a result of central government defence contracts allotted to Tasmania, the industrial and manufacturing work force grew. Between mid-1943 and mid-1944 employment in factories rose by 8 per cent and savings bank deposits by 27 per cent.

Tasmania produced important strategic raw materials, including cadmium, cobalt, copper, scheelite and wolfram. Tasmanian carbide production increased until it was sufficient to supply the industrial requirements of Australia and New Zealand, as well as those of the American forces in the Pacific. Tasmanian phosphate fertilizer production was important as the usual Pacific sources, Nauru and Ocean Islands, were cut off by Japanese occupation. The zinc works at Risdon in Hobart were considered vulnerable to air attack, so shelters were dug, ARP strictly enforced with the establishment of blackouts, wardens and first aid posts, an evacuation road was built and anti-aircraft batteries installed. Tasmania was the only part of the Empire bar Britain and Canada that produced electrolytic zinc, and it was called upon to supply the needs of the rest of Australia, New Zealand, India and South Africa. Paper pulp production at Boyer and Burnie came to employ 1400 people by the end of the war and the main purchaser, Australian Newsprint Mills, built nearly twenty miles of railway track. From 1941 the works were producing 30,000 tons of newsprint a year. Tasmania's shipyards built 300-ton wooden ships designed for use by the armed forces in the shallow waters around Pacific islands as well as harbour defence launches. Tasmania's oldest ship-building yard, Purdon and Featherstone of Battery Point, Hobart, carried out repairs on eighty American Liberty ships.

Tasmania's textiles and clothing industry produced, among other things, nearly 1,300,000 blankets, 147,000 khaki drill shorts and 250,000 pairs of army boots. The federal government's Department of Supply and Shipping spent £3.8 million on such items. Tasmania produced a remarkable amount of weaponry and war-related machinery and components. For example, the Hobart firm of Henry Jones & Company contracted to produce one million nuts and 320,000 bolts for the Department of Munitions, as well as one million primers for 25-pounder shells and millions of cans of preserved fruit, jam and whitebait for the armed forces. In a typical war-time division of costs and responsibilities, the Department of Munitions loaned the necessary machinery, the government paid the rent, and the company accepted the defence contract on a no-profit basis. Another company supplied provisions to over four hundred ships which docked at Hobart. On behalf of the federal government the state's Public Works Department conducted and supervised war work worth £1.5 million. This included the construction, improvement and extension of RAAF aerodromes in Tasmania and on King Island and Flinders Island. The £220,000 worth of naval work included the construction of fuel oil storage facilities at Hobart.

One of Tasmania's most remarkable war industries was the Waterworth Optical Annexe at the University of Tasmania in Hobart. Starting from scratch in what was a pioneering line of work, this unit produced prisms and gunsights, vital items of military equipment at the time unobtainable from other sources. In Launceston a tool annexe was established and tens of thousands of precision tools produced. The town was also home to an ammunition annexe which produced 15,000 25-pounder shells a week at its peak, totalling about a million over the course of the war. Government railway workshops in Launceston produced £1,150,000 worth of bridging equipment, pontoons, camouflage equipment, cruiser tank periscopes, cylinders for Cheetah aircraft engines, anti-aircraft and field gun shields, machine tools and firing platforms for 25-pounders. The annexe was also expected to produce 50,000 4.2-inch mortar bombs for Australian forces in New Guinea. An ammunition factory was built on the old Ascot racecourse in Hobart, employing 1350 workers by the end of 1943, the majority of whom were women. It produced nearly 600,000 mortar bomb cases as well as two-inch mortar tails, nearly a million twenty-millimetre cartridge cases, and 690,000 forty-millimetre cases. Foundries in Launceston turned their skills to the war effort, one producing manganese-bronze 'A' brackets to carry propeller shafts in naval harbour defence launches and ambulance launches, propellers for naval vessels, steam winches and steel girders and panels for military bridging equip-ment and pontoons for use in the Pacific war. The splendidly-named Alexander

Patent Racket Company of Launceston turned the hands of its workforce, reduced by 40 per cent by service enlistment, away from the manufacture of sporting equipment for civilians and instead began to supply the Amenities Branch of the armed forces, as well as turning out shell carriers, camping equipment and ammunition boxes. A small engineering shop in Launceston produced tools and gauges, training new employees and borrowing others from the Commonwealth Training Scheme. It also made crank shafts for landing barges, aircraft cylinders for Avro aircraft, cylinder locking rings for Cheetah aircraft, tools for the production of Mustang aircraft, the De Havilland factory in Sydney (which built 212 Mosquitoes) and valve seats for Rolls Royce Merlin engines (used in Spitfires and Hurricanes).

Educational establishments also contributed to the state's war effort. Tasmania's technical schools trained service personnel in fitting, turning and machining. For example, nearly 250 RAAF fitters and fifty-nine army fitters and armourers enrolled at the Hobart Technical School. The Launceston Technical School trained members of the Women's Air Training Corps in mechanics and Morse code transmission. The federal government's Allied Works Council provided additional labour when necessary, for example transferring members of the Civil Aliens Corps from the mainland to work on the Butler's Gorge Dam project.

Tasmanian agriculture was stimulated by war-time demand, benefiting especially from federal assistance and a guaranteed produce market. Agricultural output expanded during the war, and required the injection of new labour as demand increased and manpower drained into the armed forces. Italian prisoners of war were employed on farms, as were members of the Women's Land Army. War caused reform and reorganization of Tasmanian agriculture as government became more involved and mechanization sped up. Lamb and pork was purchased by the British Ministry of Food, and flax production increased because of British demand. Apart from feeding itself and supplying traditional export markets, Tasmania joined with the rest of Australia in supplying the Allied forces in the Pacific. Field pea crops were taken under federal control and were bought at fixed prices. Nearly all Tasmania's blue pea crop was reserved for army ration packs. All potato crops of more than one acre were controlled by federal authorities, and the industry boomed as mechanization increased and crates of potatoes were sent to American forces in the Philippines. In October 1944 Tasmania's food processing industry met an urgent demand for two million units of canned fish as emergency rations for Indian troops fighting in Burma. Tasmania's rabbits had a bad war as the price paid for their skins rocketed, leading to their capture in huge numbers. The apple and pear industries were saved from collapse by a federal acquisition scheme that bought the island's entire output. The forestry industry produced charcoal gas as a substitute for petrol, and demand for Tasmanian timber increased, largely through defence industry orders. Timber output rose by 26 per cent during the course of the war.

In addition to the Volunteer Defence Corps, the Civil Defence Legion and the various women's military units, Tasmania maintained an Air Training Corps formed in 1941 (of its 676 members, 156 went into the RAAF) and a Naval Auxiliary Patrol. The patrol was formed in December 1940, and a voluntary yacht patrol started operating in March 1941. Members of the Royal Yacht Club of Tasmania patrolled the waters around Devonport, Hobart and Launceston and elsewhere. Over 160 vessels – motor and steam launches, fishing vessels, auxiliary cruisers – were registered for use, and forty actually employed, five of them commissioned as His Majesty's Ships to patrol Hobart and Devonport, to transport naval personnel, mails and stores to and from the coast-watching stations at Tasman Island and South Bruny Island, and to the Port War Signal Station on South Arm. The patrol also provided close escort for visiting warships and troopships, inspected the swept channels, carried mine disposal teams when needed, and transported personnel to examine vessels entering port. They also towed targets for naval gunfire practice, and on several occasions assisted in salvaging damaged merchant ships.

It can be seen that even though it was so remote from Britain, Tasmania played an energetic part in the global war effort of the Empire and Commonwealth, both at home and overseas. This was the case for all of the states that made up the Commonwealth of Australia, and the war witnessed Australia's emergence as a regional power in its own right, whilst also redefining its relationship with Britain. Further east a galaxy of Pacific islands, also connected to Britain by the bonds of Empire, were similarly engaged in the struggle, many in its front line.

15

The Pacific

Church bells were to signal an invasion of Britain, and in Fiji the beating of drums was to pass the message of Japanese landings from village to village. Blackout procedure was practised in Suva, Fiji's capital, and Tongans contributed enough money to purchase three Spitfires for the RAF. There was no doubt that the war was a real if distant prospect for the people of the British Pacific islands from its commencement in September 1939, though its significance and proximity loomed much larger from December 1941 when Japan attacked American, Australian, British and French possessions throughout the region. Many Pacific islanders subsequently observed the unseemly haste with which some white settlers, administrators, missionaries and soldiers left islands threatened by the Japanese, often followed by massive influxes of military personnel from one side or the other, as the Pacific islands became the Second World War's most eastern battleground.

The galaxy of islands and atolls in the Pacific and the extent of the fighting in the region makes it difficult to envisage the course of the war. It can best be visualized as a sudden Japanese thrust outwards from Micronesia for the first half of 1942, extending Tokyo's control south and south east, over Guam, the British Gilbert Islands, Australian New Guinea and parts of the Australian and British Solomon Islands. Until May 1942 the Japanese met with no effective resistance, and the Greater East Asian Co-Prosperity Sphere encompassed not only most of South-East Asia, the Dutch East Indies and the Philippines, but also the Gilbert Islands, the Solomons, Australian New Guinea and parts of Papua. The Japanese were poised to capture the strategically important Port Moresby, and the people of Australia had every good reason to feel worried as the Japanese southern perimeter edged ever closer to their continental homeland. From May 1942, however, the Japanese began to meet resistance of a different order. At the Battle of the Coral Sea American naval power prevented the enemy from mounting a seaborne invasion of central Papua. In the following month the Battle of Midway saw the combined Japanese fleet under Admiral Yamamoto repelled and America retain possession of a vital submarine refuelling base on Midway Atoll north west of Hawaii. For a while Japan continued to expand, gaining two small islands in the Aleutians in June 1942 and the Australian and British phosphate islands of Nauru and Ocean in the central Pacific in August. But the high-water mark had been reached, and after this Japan suffered only reverses.[1]

Whilst Australia and New Zealand dominated the Empire and Commonwealth's war effort in the Pacific region, the islands of the Pacific were profoundly marked by the turmoil brought by war, and witnessed battles more bloody than those that scarred the colonial possessions of Africa and South-East Asia. Some societies, indeed, suffered what can only be described as a break-down after enduring invasion, occupation and bitter campaigns of Allied reconquest. Some islands, though not fought over, became important staging posts or bases for aircraft conducting bombing raids, for ships patrolling sea lanes and for soldiers preparing for the invasion of the next Japanese island stronghold. Such 'friendly' invasions, though not as deadly as invasion by the enemy and subsequent fighting when Allied forces arrived, were nevertheless extremely disruptive and opened insular communities to all manner of intrusions from the Western world, including its desire to maximize resource exploitation.[2] The nine Ellice Islands, for example, were occupied by neither side, though American air bases in parts of the group destroyed coconut trees and food gardens. The southern Ellice Islands hosted American servicemen from October 1942, bringing with them consumer goods, rampant capitalism, novel ideas and products, and a demand for all kinds of services, both military and personal.

Because of the intensity and proximity of the fighting in the region, the Pacific islands of the British Empire and Commonwealth might well lay claim to being the most dramatically affected parts of the Empire along with the conquered territories of South-East Asia. Not all Pacific islanders, of course, were affected in the same way. Many people saw little evidence of fighting, and like others in the new Japanese Empire of occupation, experienced the war as a withdrawal of external government which, in many places, had been light before the war anyway. Most, for the first time, were approached ideologically by competing contestants for their assistance and acquiescence; the Japanese peddled their version of non-European equality and the Great East Asian Co-Prosperity Sphere, the Australians dropped twenty-three million leaflets across New Guinea produced by the Far Eastern Liaison Office; and the Americans talked convincingly with cash and material goods and declarations of territorial disinterest.

The British Empire in the Pacific stretched far beyond the two Dominions as it grew to envelop a dense scattering of islands and atolls that, since the age of Captain Cook, had endured intrusion and sub-imperial expansion in the wake of missionaries, runaway convicts and deserters, labour-seekers, whalers and traders. Towards the end of the nineteenth century the British government had formalized and in some senses attempted to tame the damage done by unrestricted European interaction with Pacific societies by declaring a number of protectorates, starting with the regionally ambitious though resource-weak High Commission for the western Pacific centred on Fiji.

The two antipodean Dominions administered significant League of Nations Mandates that were a legacy of Germany's loss of empire in the region during the First World War. Then Australia and New Zealand had jumped at the chance to acquire nearby German territories that to their minds the British government should never have been allowed to fall to a rival power in the first place. The Australians administered Papua following its transfer from British administration, and also north-eastern New Guinea, one of the former German holdings. The Solomon Islands, a six hundred mile long archipelago that witnessed some of the Pacific war's bloodiest fighting, were divided between Australian and British administration. The British islands in the group (population 100,000) included Choiseul, New Georgia and Guadalcanal. Australian New Guinea extended to the Solomon Islands of Bougainville and Buka, and to New Britain, New Ireland and the Admiralty Islands (the last three, collectively known as the Bismarck Archipelago, were former German territories). All were occupied by the Japanese during the early stages of the Pacific war. Australia was also responsible for the administration of the phosphate island of Nauru (the other phosphate island, Ocean Island, was part of the British Gilbert and Ellice Islands colony).

Beyond the territories that they ruled in the Pacific, Australia and New Zealand had wider commitments in the region. Not only had they defence commitments of their own, but they were responsible for deploying garrison forces to certain British territories, and had to consider the interests of their own nationals, including the 7000 Australian civilians and other Europeans in Papua and New Guinea and the thousand New Zealand civilians in Fiji. Australia and New Zealand each controlled islands in their territorial waters, including Norfolk Island and Lord Howe Island (Australia) and Chatham Island, Bounty Island, Auckland Island and Antipodes Island (New Zealand). Some of the Pacific islands ruled by the Dominions had been handed over by the British government in the early twentieth century, as white-ruled colonies became colonial powers themselves.

New Zealand was responsible for Western Samoa (formerly German), the Cook Islands (transferred from British rule), Kermadec Island and Niue. The British administered the colony of the Gilbert and Ellice Islands, from where the Ocean, Phoenix and Northern Line Islands were also ruled (total population 37,000). British administration in the Pacific was centred on Fiji, and its Governor was also the High Commissioner responsible for administration in the outlying islands of which the Solomon Islands Protectorate and Gilbert and Ellice Islands colony were the most significant. He was also responsible for the British portion of the New Hebrides (population 5700), and relations with Tonga (population 56,000), not a British territory but in a special relationship with Britain since 1900. The New Hebrides were an Anglo-French condominium, jointly ruled by the two powers under an arcane system which involved the arbitration of the Spanish monarch in cases of dispute. Far out in the south Central Pacific Britain also ruled Pitcairn, Henderson, Oeno and Ducie Islands.

In 1939 the security of the Empire's Pacific islands, like that of the antipodean Dominions themselves, rested with the Royal Navy, which included New Zealand's warships which worked closely with those of the Australia Station. Some land forces were to be deployed, intended to hold up an enemy attack before the warships arrived, a basic tenet of imperial defence applied to other islands and enclaves of the Empire similarly exposed to seaborne attack yet at a distance from the main concentrations of British or Indian army troops. Long before the war it was agreed that Australian and New Zealand troops would garrison certain islands, should war seem likely. With British relations with Japan deteriorating between 1939 and 1941, there was an urgent concern for Pacific security as Britain appeared to be fully engaged in Europe. There was particular concern for Fiji and Tonga, regarded as vital links in the defence of sea and air traffic across the Pacific. Military responsibility for the area was transferred to New Zealand, though the Governor of Fiji remained in control of civil matters. America pressed for the region to be reinforced, but New Zealand's commitment of troops to the Middle East made this difficult. In the spring of 1942 responsibility was transferred to America, and it was agreed that America could maintain military bases on Fiji and Tonga for the duration. From this point American power began to flood the Pacific, a process made even more noticeable by the abject lack of British power in a vast region that, politically, was still under the Union Jack.

The Australian territories of Papua and New Guinea (including the Bismarck Archipelago and the Australian Solomon Islands) and the British Solomon Islands Protectorate were the major sites in the Pacific war of protracted land campaigns between Japanese and Allied forces. Of 300,000 Japanese troops who landed in New Guinea and the Solomons, only 127,000 survived, most of them dying in New Guinea (more from sickness than from battle). Rabaul and Port Moresby, the administrative capitals of New Guinea and Papua, were bombed, and Rabaul occupied by the Japanese from January 1942. At the time Australia had a force of about 3000 men between Rabaul and Port Moresby. In March 1942 the Japanese invaded northern New Guinea, occupying Guadalcanal and Tulagi in the Solomons two months later. Australian land defences and the Battle of the Coral Sea prevented the Japanese from taking Port Moresby and establishing a base on the south coast of Papua. Having been prevented from taking Port Moresby by sea, in late July Japanese forces began advancing overland towards the town across the Owen Stanley Range, but were halted by Australian forces. Six Australian battalions then defeated an attempted landing at Milne Bay. These reverses gave way to successful Allied counter-attacks, and by January 1943 13,000 Japanese had been killed or had died of disease. Having lost the government station of Kokoda in November 1942, by February 1943 the Japanese had been forced to retreat from the goldfields town of Wau and for the next two and a half years the 18th Army fell back westward along the New Guinea coast, from Salamaua, Lae, Finschhafen and Madang, its remnants pinned in the east Sepik area. All of the islands of the Bismarck Archipelago also witnessed fighting. The Admiralty Islands were occupied by the Japanese in April 1942, where they established air bases and used the harbour as a fleet anchorage. MacArthur needed to take them as part of his plan to capture Rabaul, and they were duly conquered in February to May 1944. In 1945 Manus in the Admiralty Islands became an advanced fleet base used by the British

Pacific Fleet. Manus, and in particular Seeadler harbour, was already a massive American military base, and over a million American troops passed through the Admiralty Islands during the war.

The island of New Britain was part of the Australian Mandate of New Guinea. The capital Rabaul was captured by the Japanese in January 1942 and became the major air and naval base for the Japanese South-East Area. The Allies dropped over 20,000 tons of bombs on the town, forcing the inhabitants to live in caves and tunnels. MacArthur decided to recapture Rabaul, but changed his plan in August 1943 and decided to bypass it. In late 1943 Allied forces landed on the island's western shores and the Japanese withdrew to Rabaul in the east, as over the next eighteen months the Allies fought the Japanese all the way along the coast to their heavily defended stronghold on the Gazelle peninsula. Indigenous people led by Australian special forces fought a guerrilla war against the Japanese occupiers. By March 1944, given the strength of the Allied threat to Rabaul, the principal Japanese air and naval units had withdrawn to Truk Island to the north, though tens of thousands of Japanese service personnel remained. In November 1944 the Australian 5th Division replaced American forces on the island, and when the war ended their offensive was found to have trapped 100,000 Japanese troops and naval personnel and 20,000 civilian workers in Rabaul. This ended nearly four years of occupation during which the indigenous Tolai population fell by a quarter, forced to feed the Japanese and endure constant Allied bombing raids.

The capital of New Ireland, Kavieng, was defended by an Australian Independent Company when the Japanese landed in January 1942. The defenders were soon overrun and the town became an important Japanese base, garrisoned by about 11,000 troops. In Bougainville, the largest of the Solomon Islands and part of the Australian Mandate of New Guinea, American and then Australian troops tried to clear the Japanese from their stronghold. At the end of 1943 American Marines established a beachhead at Torokina. The 2nd Australian Corps replaced American forces from October 1944, and spent the rest of the war attacking the dwindling units of the Japanese 17th Army. The other major Solomon Islands campaign took place on the British island of Guadalcanal, where bitter fighting occurred to decide which side would control its strategically-located airstrip. Having taken the western Solomons and northern Guadalcanal in the first half of 1942, the Japanese then faced a huge American counter-attack which ejected them within a year, leaving Guadalcanal and its airfield as a launching point for further American attacks.

The sixteen atolls forming the Gilbert Islands also saw extensive military action. Japanese forces overran Makin, Tarawa and Butaritari early in the war, the capture of the latter being seen as a possible prelude to an advance on New Zealand. After an American raid had wiped out the Japanese garrison on Butaritari, on 16 August 1942, Japanese forces occupied Ocean Island and Naura ten days later, followed by Tarawa, Abemama and Betio on 15 September. The last became Japan's most easterly fortress, garrisoned by 2500 solders with bomb-proof shelters and hundreds of gun positions. Measuring only 600 yards by two miles, the defences included fourteen coastal defence guns of five and a half-inch to eight-inch calibre, field artillery and machine guns. In the first seaborne assault on a heavily-defended coral atoll, a thousand Americans died attacking it. Of the defenders, only 146 were taken alive, 120 of them being Korean labourers. The Japanese occupation of the Gilbert Islands presented an air threat to the American-Australian sea route, and from late 1943 the Americans began their westward attack on the Japanese positions in the region from bases in the central Pacific. As hard-fought victories were won, Japanese bases became American bases, the people of the Gilbert Islands witnessing one kind of military occupation replaced by another.

Nauru was an Australian Mandate and Ocean Island was part of the British Gilbert Islands. They were both important for their production of phosphates for use as agricultural fertilizer, and had already attracted enemy attention when in December 1940 the German auxiliary cruisers *Orion* and *Komet* sank three of the Phosphate Commission's ships and shelled the islands' installations. In this bombardment the great loading cantilever on Nauru was badly damaged, reducing exports from one million tons a year to 150,000 tons in 1941. Japan bombed the phosphate facilities on both islands and then occupied them in August 1942 (leading to rationing of fertilizers in Australia and a boom in demand for Tasmania's output, as well as imports from Egypt). Over 1600 inhabitants of Nauru were moved to Truk (a Japanese stronghold in the Marshall Islands) as forced labour, and 400 were sent to Ocean Island. (HMAS *Diamantina* was the platform for the surrender of Ocean Island, the last outpost of the British Empire in Japanese hands, on 1 October 1945.) The Americans bypassed Ocean Island when they ejected the Japanese from the islands of the region, and the people of the island endured appalling atrocities. Of 160 islanders still there in mid-1943, only two survived.

The war brought near disintegration to the system of British administration in islands attacked and occupied by the enemy, particularly those in the Gilbert and Ellice and Solomon groups. This was partly because British civil administration melted away, leaving only a few missionaries and British officials staying behind to organize networks of coast-watchers reporting Japanese movements. In some cases the authority of indigenous government also broke down. The expulsion of the Japanese often led to a period of lawlessness, and a refusal to supply labour to the Allied forces. British withdrawal in these islands, prudent on the one hand but construed as abandonment by some of their people on the other, was in sharp contrast to the arrival of generous American servicemen. The American presence was sometimes enormous; for example, 200,000 Americans were based in the New-Hebrides in advance of the recapture of the Solomons. The scale of the American presence could not help but have a massive psychological impact throughout the region, offering, for example, a different view of white men from that presented by colonial administrators and missionaries, the Americans bringing an abundance of material goods, and presenting a novel view of the non-white man where black Americans were deployed. American prestige was great, and American bounty, it seemed, could reach the highest levels, causing the phenomenon of cargo cults in New Guinea and the Melanesian islands, in which islanders tried to communicate with the ancestors by using fake wireless and aircraft technology in imitation of American servicemen. These remarkable manifestations of the disruption brought by war, beloved of post-war anthropologists, were syncretic religious movements that eradicated pre-war religious practices. The vast amounts of war material dropped by air into these islands brought massive change to people's lifestyles and expectations as manufactured goods, food, tents and weapons appeared in abundance, much of which went legally or illegally into the hands of islanders. When the war moved on, and ultimately when it ended, this manna stopped appearing, the airstrips were shut down and the supplies dried up. In an attempt to get the cargo to return, either dropped by parachute or flown in by aircraft, islanders adopted the practices and equipment that had been associated with them. Headphones were carved from wood, aircraft built from straw, control towers erected and runways cleared, complete with beacons running along the edge and flight controllers waving signal bats. The theory was that the foreigners had had a connection with the ancestors, the only beings powerful enough to command such riches. By adopting the foreigners' methods, it was hoped that the ancestors would respond similarly and lavish gifts on the islanders. Given the bounty that American forces had trailed in their wake, it was no wonder that there was a petition in the Solomons to get sovereignty transferred to America; the chief of Little Makin Island asked a passing American admiral for a sovereignty transfer; and on Butaritari in the Gilbert Islands a man stood up at a meeting and said that the island should be placed under American control.

This must have pleased the Americans, for America attempted to get post-war base rights in imperial territories like the Fiji, the Gilbert and Ellice Islands, the New Hebrides, the Solomons and Western Samoa. As in the Caribbean, India, the Middle East and West Africa, America was inexorably moving in, in one way or another, to imperial preserves by virtue of its war-time involvement in these regions and as a manifestation of its global economic and military power. Even before the war America had sought base rights in the region. Some islands, especially in the Gilbert and Ellice Islands, had had their ownership questioned by America in 1937 when it was looking for bases, and in 1938 Britain agreed to allow joint control of two of them, Canton and Enderbury. The appearance of American military bases, of course, raised political questions, and often British administrators felt that the realities of American power and presence made them *de facto* rulers. For example, British wireless stations on Canton and Christmas Islands were placed under the control of American army signals. All telegraph communications to and from British officials had to pass through them, and Americans were responsible for coding and decoding messages. Given the situation of American military dominance and continued British political control that arose in places like Fiji, great sensitivity was demanded of administrators and commanders on the spot. In the case of Fiji, Sir Philip Mitchell, previously Governor of Kenya and then Chief Political Officer in charge of captured Italian colonies in Africa, was sent to Fiji as Governor and High Commissioner for the Western Pacific to sooth Anglo-American relations after some abrasive clashes.[3] On the whole the right people were found to fill such posts in a dexterous manner and to keep the remarkably strong Anglo-American alliance on track at every level of command and responsibility. But for the British in colonial outposts like Fiji and Trinidad there was no mistaking the sense of reduced British power that was abroad in the world at large.

The Anglo-French condominium governing the New Hebrides was difficult to operate during the war given the status of France and French overseas territory following the establishment of the Vichy regime. The French resident eventually opted to join General de Gaulle and the Free French after British pressure had been brought to bear. He was then persuaded to try and rally New Caledonia to the Free French, being taken to the capital, Nouméa, on board the cruiser HMAS *Adelaide* in September 1940. The mission was a success, largely due to the skilled naval diplomacy of *Adelaide*'s captain, Henry Showers, and by autumn 1940 Tahiti had also nailed its colours to de Gaulle's mast.[4] Australian and New Zealand troops served in several islands of the French New Hebrides and other parts of French Pacific territory like New Caledonia and Wallis Island. In the British New Hebrides, a major American base was established at Espíritu Santo, from where B-17s could reach the Solomons.

The Pacific island territories of the Empire and Commonwealth raised a number of military formations for combat, defence and labour tasks. Pacific Islanders also provided invaluable labour for Allied military operations; and, under occupation, they were called upon to do the same for the Japanese. By mid-1944 Australian forces in Papua New Guinea, for example, had over 37,000 local people working for them. In the Gilbert and Ellice Islands two military forces were raised during the war, the Ocean Island Defence Force (disbanded in March 1942 but resuscitated as the Gilbert Islands Defence Force), and a Gilbert and Ellice Islands Labour Corps. Its first task was to unload supply ships in the Gilbert Islands for the American invasion of the Marshall Islands, and some of its members were sent to work on Guadalcanal. By February 1944 it numbered 1800. The Tonga Defence Force numbered 2000.

Fiji was an important cog in the military wheel in the South Pacific, operating as a base for significant numbers of American and New Zealand troops.[5] Military forces drawn from among the Fijian population itself were substantial, particularly after Pearl Harbor, when Fiji became a centre of major military activity. A small naval force had been established before the war, and its strength rose from thirty to over five hundred. It was used to man shore signal stations and mount night patrols in Suva harbour. It also operated security ships in the harbour. The

Fiji Defence Force, established in 1923, became the Fiji Military Force (FMF) in December 1942. It grew from a small territorial force to a full-time professional including an infantry brigade group, a heavy artillery regiment and a large number of ancillary units. Its strength stood at over 6000 by January 1945, including 590 men seconded from the New Zealand Army. Fijians served as officers in the unit. By the end of the war 11,000 out of the total population of 220,000 Fijians had served in the armed forces, including about 1900 Europeans. The peak strength was reached in August 1943, when there were 8513 serving, including 1070 Europeans, 808 Europeans of the NZEF, 6371 Fijians and 264 Indians. Soldiers of the FMF also manned coastal defence batteries and anti-aircraft defences on the Suva peninsula. Over 2000 Fijians served in the Solomons.

Fijians had a long tradition of warfare, and in attracting men to fight in the Second World War traditional recruitment methods were employed, as was the still-extant association of fighting with things honourable, noble and brave (though this was not true among the more reluctant Indian community). There were many similarities between recruitment methods in the Pacific and in Africa, where tradition was to the fore and the experience of sending men to soldier in the First World War was also still present. The Governor of Fiji, Sir Philip Mitchell, captured the nature of the call to war that was relayed to colonial populations throughout the Colonial Empire by British officials and their indigenous political allies. On 16 September 1942 he told the Fijian people that the war was being fought 'to preserve for you the freedom to live your lives according to the traditions and ceremonies you so rightly value very highly'.[6] Fiji's loyal response to the imperial call to arms was rewarded by the British colonial administration, as it was in parts of the British African Empire, by the granting of more power to traditional political elites. Reforms in 1944 put control of the Fijian administration in the hands of the chiefs. A new Fijian Affairs Board, consisting of chiefs and presided over by Ratu Lala Sukunu, possessed central powers over the affairs of all Fijian villages.

Indigenous Fijians in the FMF formed three infantry battalions, and Fijian and New Zealand troops were attached to American forces in the Solomons for patrol duties in 1942. In May and June 1942 the American 37th Division arrived in Fiji, together with a host of ancillary troops, and the division was given control of the FMF, with which some of its members were to serve in New Georgia, New Guinea and the Solomons. The FMF served in the principal battles of the Solomons campaign, fighting and providing garrison forces on Guadalcanal, New Georgia and Bougainville, where its bushcraft and fighting qualities impressed the Americans. The Fiji contingent in the Solomons rose to number 200 men and was named 1st Commando, Fiji Guerrillas. A similar Fijian commando party, the South Pacific Scouts, which included men from the Solomons and Tonga, participated in the American landings on New Georgia in July 1943. At the end of 1942 the Fijian forces were reorganized as a brigade group, assisted and equipped by

New Zealand. The brigade was never employed as a separate unit, but at least two of its four battalions saw service overseas, for example in the battle for Bougainville in December 1943.

Soon after the outbreak of war HMNZS *Leander* arrived at Suva with dummy guns, replaced by real 4.7-inch weapons in December 1939. Six–inch guns and searchlights had arrived before the end of the year, manned twenty-four hours a day, and soon there were several batteries defending Suva. New barracks were constructed and coastal defence positions prepared. A proclamation called up all men between eighteen and thirty-six years old for territorial training. Fiji was selected as an advanced training base for the 2nd NZEF, accommodated in Samabula and Namaka camps. In 1942 Fiji was selected as a training ground and potential defence line by the American forces now responsible for the defence of the region, command passing from the New Zealanders to the Americans at the end of June. As a forward base for American forces, particularly for their first major operations in the Solomons, Fiji became even busier. Stevedores were needed for the rapid clearance of the ships arriving at Suva and Lautoka, leading to the creation of the Labour Battalion. Tens of thousands of Americans were based in Fiji until 1944.

For a long time Papua and New Guinea were in the front line of the Allied war against the Japanese. Some of the Europeans living or stationed there joined the Australian New Guinea Administrative Unit, an outfit established to administer the region when civilian government ended in the event of Japanese invasion. Others Europeans joined the coast-watchers or the Papua Infantry Battalion, which included indigenous Papuan volunteers as well. The formation of the Papuan Infantry Battalion was one of the final acts of the Lieutenant-Governor of Papua, Sir Hubert Murray, before the Japanese attack. When Japanese bombers first appeared over Port Moresby, in February 1942, the unit numbered 300 men. The force expanded over the following two months. In March 1944 it was joined with the indigenous 1st New Guinea Infantry Battalion, and in October 1944 this merger became the Pacific Islands Regiment, which soon acquired three more New Guinea battalions. By that time the indigenous troops had acquired a reputation in Australia as fighters skilled in jungle warfare, feared by the Japanese, and regarded with affectionate by the Australian troops alongside whom they served. Over 3500 Papuans and New Guineans served in the regiment, dispersed in Bougainville, New Britain and north of the Sepik river when the Japanese surrendered. The Royal Papuan Constabulary also played an active part in the fighting, and many Papuans laboured in support of Allied military forces. Over 3100 Papuan and New Guinean policemen saw action, and a further 955 served as medical orderlies.

In the Solomon Islands Protectorate there was no military force beyond an armed constabulary of one hundred men. The Solomon Islands Defence Force had been established in 1939, though it was decided to disband it in February 1942. This action, however, had not been carried through by time of the first Japanese landings on 10 March 1942. The force consisted of 680 men. Some British officers remained to organize a system of coast-watching and intelligence work, and after the American landings the district commissioner of Guadalcanal organized a local service battalion for intelligence work and patrol assistance for the Americans. A Solomon Islands Labour Corps was also formed under British supervision, employing 2500 men in support of American operations. These men were paid a pound a month, carrying heavy loads, building airfields and moving equipment behind American lines. The generosity of the Americans provided a contrast to the relatively low pay provided by the British. In 1943–44 general discontent became a movement centred in south Malaita. The Maasina Rule movement was to continue well into the post-war period and undermine the reimposition of British rule.[7]

Tonga's inhabitants, scattered across three island groups 994 miles north of New Zealand, had little need for an army before the outbreak of the Second World War. This changed when in September 1939 Queen Salote Tupou III declared that 'all of Tonga's resources are at Britain's disposal', and changed again when Japan entered the war two years later. From 18 September 1939 Tonga's privy council ordered the conscription of all Tongan males of military age, and the first hundred recruits were attested on 22 September.[8] Tonga's Minister of Police and Public Works, the Honourable Ahau'ola, an ANZAC veteran of the First World War, was instructed to build an army, and by early 1941 the Tongan Defence Force comprised 2700 regulars at its peak strength with an auxiliary of 10,000 trained Home Guards. Tonga's incredible response to Britain's war had other manifestations. By royal decree all public officials contributed 10 per cent of their salaries to the British war effort. Public subscriptions and events raised enough money to purchase three Spitfires (named Queen Salote, Prince Tungi and King Tupou I). The Queen made available 160 acres of valuable land for the construction of Tonga's first airfield. Coast-watchers were set in place to watch for German raiders, unpaid volunteers built new barracks, and Tongan women cut and sewed defence force uniforms. When Japan entered the war, Tongatabu, the main island, had beaches crisscrossed with barbed wire, trenches in the main streets and a dispersed civilian population. From May 1942 thousands of Americans began to arrive as they took over defensive responsibility for the region from Britain. From May 1942, until New Zealand's 3rd Division replaced them in late 1943, there were 10,000 Americans based in Tonga.

It is fitting that this study of the British Empire and Commonwealth at war should end with what, geographically, was one of the most distant and diverse regions painted red on the map. It is highly unlikely that there will ever be a repeat of the remarkable phenomenon that was the British imperial war effort of 1939–45, whatever the achievements of globalization and coalitions may be. The Empire at war attained a perplexing, paradoxical and wonderful homogeneity of political will and military purpose shaped, coloured and flavoured by the most monumental human diversity. This conclusion must surely be shared by those who choose to run up the flag and celebrate Empire as well as those who choose to associate it with the bleakest forms of human exploitation and the foundation of many of the world's current ills. A miracle of organization that lies just beyond the reach of full comprehension, it remains a humbling spectacle.

16

Epilogue

Thousands of Empire and Commonwealth troops of the Eighth Army had the opportunity to read a small printed piece of paper whilst serving in Italy in 1944. Its message read:

> What's it all about? What are we fighting for? England has already lost the war and she has lost it to her Allies, with the American Colonies gone to the States, Canada on the brink, Australia and New Zealand military bases of the United States, East India gone to the Japs and for good, India threatened by the Japs and the Soviets, South Africa for years under American financial control, the Mediterranean and the Way to India handed over to the Soviets ... Mastery of the Seas passed to the States, the Old Country bankrupt, indebted to the States for a hundred years, England occupied by the States, and now under continuous bombardment for more than four hundred hours.

It's impossible to know what Arthur Townshend made of this German propaganda leaflet dropped on his Royal Tank Regiment unit and brought home as a souvenir. As with other German propaganda windfalls, like that showing an American soldier intimately passing the time of day with a British woman whilst her husband was away doing the fighting, it was probably the source of some amusement as well as thoughts about friends and family back home and the long-term implications of the war.[1] The point about this crude propaganda litany is that it contains some prescient perspectives on the effects that the war would have on Britain and its global imperial position, though they might not have been readily apparent to an Eighth Army tank crew in 1944, living history forwards and with rather more urgent matters on their minds. Nevertheless it was indeed true that American power in relation to Britain and in relation to imperial policy was growing during the war; that the Japanese had indeed smashed the eastern Empire and threatened India; that British sea power and the vaunted notion of *Pax Britannica* had taken a battering in eastern waters; that Russia was looming as a political and military threat to the British Empire; and that ultimately Britain was unable to afford the political, military and financial costs required successfully to run a world Empire in the post-war period. A domestic population might survive on austerity rations for a number of years but, in the long run, an Empire could not.

In 1945, however, these things were not at all apparent, even to those reading the runes of the imperial future. If we avoid gazing into the future from the pinnacle of August 1945 and simply focus on the moment of ultimate victory it is to imperial strength and confident hopes that we must look. The bunting went up in Tasmania and in Mauritius as it did at street parties across Britain, and every corner of the Empire and Commonwealth celebrated the end of a gruelling six year conflict. (Some celebrations got out of hand, as in Halifax where a swollen wartime civilian population, and 25,000 service personnel, went on a binge that saw 200 shops looted and several people die of alcohol poisoning.) The Empire was triumphant, the lost colonies were recaptured and erstwhile enemies were sitting behind imperial razor wire in Borneo as in Berlin. Victorious imperial armies were spread the world over, a massive navy with over forty aircraft carriers was anchored athwart every far-flung sea lane, a Commonwealth force under an Australian general sat alongside the Americans in occupied Japan, and thousands of imperial bombers and fighter congregated around runways throughout the Empire. Africa and the Middle East had long been cleared of the enemy, as had the oceans of the world where British and Allied seapower was overwhelming. In Burma an entire Japanese army had been virtually wiped out, and there was no question of if, but simply of when, the triumphant Fourteenth Army threw the Japanese out of the rest of occupied Asia. The myth of the Japanese superman was now only a memory, and the confidence of the Cumbrians, Gurkhas, Nigerians and Sikhs of Fourteenth Army was sky-high and almost chilling. On the military level Britain was a power as never before.

The war had witnessed a coordinated global effort orchestrated by a medium-sized European polity, the like of which will never be seen again. Hundreds of years of British imperial history and tradition and the networks, infrastructure, contacts and institutions that it had forged were called to life by a decision taken at the imperial centre in London. This sent a current running throughout the overseas power centres of Empire from Cairo to Colombo to Canberra, and they sprang to life alongside Britain and mobilized their respective regions for war. It was a breathtaking spectacle, and remains so to this day. In 1945 it also appeared as a remarkable validation of Britain's unique role as an imperial state, and it was not a role that was about to be relinquished.

In terms of the imperial future the men directing British affairs from London in 1945 evinced confidence and an attitude of back to imperial business-as-usual, and this was shared by the men lower down the imperial order in regional military commands and governorships throughout the colonies. Costly imperial wars had been fought before, and the world had returned to a British-influenced normality thereafter. Despite greater challenges than ever before, there was no reason why it should not be the same again this time round, and the British Empire and Commonwealth emerge, with some modifications, to be a leading force in world affairs, even if it now had to share the limelight with two stronger powers who threatened to make the 'Big Three' into an adversarial 'Giant Two'. The men in whose hands Britain's future lay were not stupid. The British government and the departments of state knew full well how deep Britain had had to draw on its reserves, financial, political, imperial, psychological and military, to reach the pitch of global mobilization that had been achieved. They had seen the bank statements, and they had watched the awesome manner in which American industry slipped through the gears to hypermobilization. They had seen the growth of the American military from continental containment to a global presence reflected in its carrier groups and its sole possession of the atomic bomb, and they knew that American meddling in imperial affairs was an unpalatable new variable with which they would have constantly to deal in the post-war world. They had also recogized the looming threat in the East, the latest awakening of the old Russian enemy, and knew that a new ideological climate and new, bigger powers, would define the post-war world.

But still they firmly believed that there would always be room for the British Empire and Commonwealth. It would, indeed, be a modified Empire and Commonwealth. India had been guaranteed independence, though this by no means signalled the start of a general retreat, and it was fully expected that India would remain in the Commonwealth, provide Britain with military bases and remain within a British-directed orbit – still, to all intents and purposes, pink on the map, even if a little paler than of old. Yes, the Dominions would look to America for extra insurance in terms of defence, though this in no way broke the fundamentals of imperial defence policy and unity inherited from the nineteenth century, and Britain would remain central to the functioning of the Dominions' economies and their leaders would remain willing partners in the Commonwealth club, even if more intent on having a greater voice in the *arcana imperii*. Elsewhere, the British government and its servants on the ground in the colonies were confident that things could be returned pretty much to normal. They believed that the dire impact of war in the Eastern Empire, the growth in social mobilization, the circulation of ideas and increasing linkage of rural colonial subjects to global currents and the demands of educated elites wanting moves towards a greater share in colonial governance – all factors speeded by the war – could be managed, dealt with, answered and channelled in ways that would benefit Britain, the people of the Empire and its long-term survival. This was not to say that a return to the *status quo ante* was the only thing in the minds of these officials. Not only was there a new imperialism of development and ideological engagement abroad, but political advances, in the gradualist tradition, were also on the cards. The Colonial Office itself had already acknowledged that its eventual aim was for general colonial self-government. Even in the Middle East, where the Holocaust had brought an unpredicted challenge to Britain's capacity to keep all of the balls in the air at once, Britain intended to remain the ringmaster.

In 1945 there was, if anything, a heartening overconfidence on the part of British policy-makers in their own ability to restore, to manage and to reform in order to preserve. Indeed, given the 'financial Dunkirk' that the war represented for Britain, the colonies were to become key factors in British economic recovery, whilst also having a paler version of the 'New Jerusalem' extended to them as a mark of Britain's enlightened colonial rule, as a means of spiking the guns of those advocating a turn towards communist Russia or national independence, and a means of countering the more subtle forms of American imperialism. Showing amazing resilience – or, some would say, a startling reluctance to engage in the kind of root-and-branch reappraisal of Britain's world role justified by the results of the Second World War – British imperial defence policy remained the same as in 1900. New factors – including the rise of the Soviet Union, the loss of the Indian heartland of Empire and the advent of nuclear bombs – were simply tacked on to old assessments and dispositions. India it was assumed would remain in the Commonwealth defence club and Britain would still defend the subcontinent. Russia, of course, had been a traditional British rival against which policy in the eastern Mediterranean and Central Asia had been directed. The sense of things simply remaining the same is best captured in the 1947 Chiefs of Staff defence review prepared for the Cabinet. In it, the reader enters a familiar nineteenth-century British world of sea lanes, garrisons and naval bases, the importance of primacy in the Indian Ocean and Persian Gulf, the need to keep open the routes to India and on to Australasia, and the prime importance of British predominance in the Middle East, the old Eastern Question now posed in nuclear terms.

All of this might seem, with the wisdom after the event unavailable to the Churchills, Bevins and Montgomerys of the immediate post-war months, to have been a failure to come to terms with the deeper effects of the war. But America had not yet fully flexed its muscles vis-à-vis the Empire and Britain was determined not to be bullied into abandoning its world role. Most importantly, *it was not known* that economic recovery would elude Britain time and again, and that repeated financial crises, American attempts to weaken the Sterling Area and dashed industrial hopes would mean, simply, that Britain did not recover sufficiently to allow it to play the global imperial role that was considered its birthright, and that the policy-makers of 1945 so confidently looked forward to. The centre proved unable to play the role of a global imperial metropole, though it took many years for this to become clearly apparent, and a few more years for it to be applied in the form of national policy in the late 1950s and 1960s. In 1938 Britain's net overseas assets were worth £5 billion, in 1950 under £0.6 billion. The costs of the welfare state, the failure of the Empire to aid recovery as had initially been hoped, the mounting costs of imperial defence in terms of technological costs and the maintenance of large forces overseas, regular 'small war' interventions and the novel and huge costs associated with being an independent nuclear power, were to dash the hopes that burned brightly in 1945. Finally, the forces of nationalism, with new platforms like the United Nations, new legitimacy and public sympathy in the Western world, and a new era of intrusive media scrutiny, were to develop at an unforeseen pace. The ideological battleground of the Cold War made formal Empire an increasingly outmoded method of wielding international power.

The point has been made that in 1945, in the eyes of British policy-makers, strategic planners, colonial officials and the public at large, the Empire had been shaken, but not to the point of imminent collapse. Though it would be possible just to leave it there, it would be cowardly not at least to peep beyond the curtain of VJ Day and view the contours of the 'decolonization period' that the Second World War is usually seen to have both hastened and in some respects actually caused. The war is commonly seen as a major solvent of the British Empire, a regular departure point for books and educational courses examining the decolonization that marked a revolution in sovereignty across the globe between the 1940s and the 1960s. The war has been variously branded 'the prelude to decolonization' and 'the imperial destabilizer', and had up in the dock as the prime suspect for the fall of the British Empire even if longer-term economic, cultural and political suspects are detained for questioning for having egged it on.

In building the Second World War into our understanding of decolonization it is important not to jump the gun, not to elide events and subscribe to a domino theory of a pell-mell retreat once the war had ended, once the superpowers had arisen and once South Asia had achieved independence. We must also guard against telescoping time. In real time, 1945 was a world away from 1955, as 1955 was from 1960. The independence of India, promised in concrete form during the war, and therefore hardly a surprising event when it came to pass in 1947, by no means signalled the beginning of a general retreat as far as British policy-makers were concerned. The independence of Burma in the following year was perfectly natural, as it had always been an Indian colony and of no significance to London. The independence of Ceylon, also in 1948, left Britain with a strong defence agreement ensuring the future use of the naval base at Trincomalee and an excellent relationship with a new government determined to remain part of the Commonwealth. As in South Asia, the British did not see the immediate post-war years as signalling an abject imperial retreat, but rather an imperial redeployment. South Asia remained resolutely on the imperial map of the world. Similarly the decision to return the Palestine Mandate to the United Nations in 1948 in no way signalled a lack of commitment to a British-dominated Middle East; rather the unique and utterly intractable situation in that unhappy land, and an unwillingness on the part of the British to attract regional and international contumely no matter what stance it adopted on the white-hot Jew versus Arab question. Elsewhere in the late–1940s plans were afoot to rejuvenate the imperial nexus in the new jewels in the crown, Africa and South-East Asia. This was to enable colonial people to resist the blandishments of the Soviet Empire, to buy off moderate nationalists, to develop the Empire for the economic benefit of bankrupt Britain through the Sterling Area and Colonial Development and Welfare Act, and to improve the lives of imperial subjects, extending a version of the New Jerusalem and warding off American criticism of Empire in the process. In all the other areas of British imperial rule, from the Pacific islands, the Indian Ocean islands and Persian Gulf states, to the Atlantic islands and the West Indies, there were no plans, and apparently no serious demands, for British withdrawal. Nationalism there was to be sure, though this was not uniformly frightening, and in general it was felt that, with sound footwork, nationalism could be managed. Partnership was the way forward – a new inclusiveness that would stop people having anything to be 'nationalist' about, save for the odd agitator. It was to be the partnership of the horse and rider, as the famous comparison went, with Britain firmly in the saddle.

In the 'white' Dominions the imperial link also seemed secure, though there was no doubt that in the post-war world the 'big four' imperial territories would behave much more like the equal club members that legally they were. The war had greatly accelerated the development in each Dominion of the apparatus of mature sovereign statehood, including independent foreign policies, economic nationalism, armed forces and multilateral economic and diplomatic links, as well as forcing them to focus more closely than ever before on the challenges extant in their own geographical regions. Britain would never again get away with any hint of bullying, though it hoped that its influence would enable it to retain the position of *primus inter pares*. Despite the fact that America had become a political, economic and military factor of prime importance for each Dominion, Britain was not by a long shot displaced in any of these spheres in the post-war world. It remained the prime import and export market and a key military partner and senior political ally on the world stage long into the post-war period.

As it turned out, the war had speeded the British decline discernible in the pre-war years, as well as spurring both America and Russia to an early industrial, military and global political awakening. In short, whilst all of the sanguine assessments of the post-war world were quite understandable, what no one realized was the extent of the damage that the war had done to Britain, or the forces that it had unleashed on the world that would make colonial empires increasingly outmoded and dangerous things to possess. The war bankrupted Britain and made it increasingly difficult for it to afford the running costs of an Empire that, in a new ideological landscape and international relations environment, required ever more frequent interventions and justification, and was constantly under the microscope at home and overseas. What is more, it became apparent in the 1950s that the Empire was not the answer to Britain's economic problems and that – to the horror of those steeped in the grand imperial tradition – those answers might lie much closer to home. Britain was less able to shape the post-war international order than it had expected, and its failure to recover economically, along with the need to lavish resources on domestic rather than imperial and foreign matters, militated against unreserved commitment to formal Empire whenever the half-open door to independence was pushed.

The post-war problems preventing a return to the pre-war world of imperial calm and stability in most parts of the British demesne had been multiplied by the *manner* in which the imperial war had had to be fought. The Second World War saw Britain draw deeply on its reserves of imperial power in order to mobilize and coordinate a quite remarkable global war and production effort. More than any other event in history, the Second World War had been a globalizing experience for people across the world, and the war had been an *imperial* people's war.[2] In the Dominions the British government did not have the deciding voice in political direction; this was the preserve of their elected governments, though London did hold several control cards, including Dominion dependence on the imperial import-export market centred on Britain, defence guarantees, investment, control of shipping and control of vital resources like oil. In all other parts of the Empire, while Britain preferred to work with the cooperation of indigenous elites, it was the ultimate arbiter of political decisions. Though the tradition was of cooperation and accommodation with indigenous political elites, Britain was prepared to take the gloves off and assume direct and firm control during the war when normal circumstances did not prevail and Britain's back was to the wall. Though this might rupture the fabric of Empire based on cooperation and consent, and stir the muddy pools of nationalism, victory was to be achieved at any cost. There was much indignation amongst some Britons who thought it thoroughly bad form that nationalists should push for concessions when Britain was in such a position, because, whatever one's stance on the future, there was little doubt that the alternatives of German or Japanese occupation and colonial rule were not to be relished, no matter how anti-British their subjects might be. This was why many who otherwise might have baulked at such 'old-fashioned' imperial action were prepared to support the firm repression that the Indian National Congress encountered after the 'Quit India' campaign was launched.

In whipping the Empire into fighting shape in minimum time when the very existence of Britain as an independent state was at stake, Britain was forced to act with an expediency and imprudence that would never have been entertained in peacetime. In order to win the war and use the Empire's resources in prosecuting it, Britain had placed too much pressure on the structures of political cooperation and public consent upon which imperial rule rested. Not only had this agitated many people and aroused interest in an independent future, particularly in India, but the process had also exhausted Britain. By 1945 Britain's capacity to sustain a global imperial role had been greatly diminished. War imperialism worked for the moment but worked against the longer term retention of Empire. Arresting all Indian National Congress leaders, banning the organization and suppressing unrest with fifty-seven infantry battalions certainly sorted things out in India for a while. So too did the drama in Cairo when King Farouk had his palace surrounded by British armoured cars on the orders of the British Ambassador because he refused to appoint a less pro-Nazi government. But for the long-term future of colonial rule such treatment did not augur well, even if British authorities around the world saw no choice but to act in this way. As potential enemies the world over became actual enemies, as potential allies remained neutral and actual allies were defeated, the British Empire and Commonwealth had to learn on the spot how to conduct itself for maximum efficiency. The over-stretch of the imperial system became evident. There were simply too many imperial responsibilities, and not enough men or guns to defend them all in the face of three aggressive industrialized powers.

Though Britain had ruled with a rod of iron in some parts of the Empire because of the urgent demands of war and survival, there was no chance of this carrying over into general post-war imperial policy. The moral dimension of the war – a war of freedom versus tyranny, a war of peaceful nations against unsolicited aggression – heavily influenced the philosophy of post-war rule. Britain had to be seen, before its own people and those of the watching world, to be acting humanely and not resisting the increasingly legitimate aspirations of colonial subjects. Empire and mature liberal democracy sat ill together. At Berchtesgaden in 1938 Hitler had advised Chamberlain on how to iron out the problem of nationalism in India.

> Shoot Gandhi, and if that does not suffice to reduce them to submission, shoot a dozen leading members of Congress: and if that does not suffice, shoot 200 and so on until order is established. You will see how quickly they collapse as soon as you make it clear that you mean business.[3]

In the short term at least, Hitler's tactics were right for retaining imperial control, but they were completely out of kilter with the spirit of the mid-twentieth-century democracies. There was little chance of nationalism being met by brutal suppression in the post-war Empire (though the 'wrong' kind of nationalism, like that of the Mau Mau fighters in 1950s Kenya or the Chinese fighters in 1950s Malaya, might meet with an uncompromising armed response).

The world war brought about a fundamental shift in the tectonic plates of global power. The rise of America and the Soviet Union, and the global enmity between them, would ultimately leave no room for the British Empire as a 'third force', even if junior partnership with America caused it to underwrite continued British rule in regions that, if the British were to leave, would have required an immediate American presence to forestall the Russians filling the void. But this was support for Britain for American reasons, not support for the British Empire. In the battle for hearts and minds, sacrificing old-style Empire and attempting to replace it with a looser and more palatable form of influence was prudent, especially as the Cold War hotted up. In a world where the Cuban missile crisis led many people to think that nuclear destruction was about to occur, loosening the ties of Empire was, in many ways, small beer indeed.

The British Empire dissolved slowly, with each colony or territory having its own experience of decolonization but with a range of major background factors common to all. Some of these background factors may be listed: American internationalism and its fundamental suspicion of the British Empire; Russia's wish to destabilize any empire for the benefit of its own; the borderless post-war world of ideological ferment stimulated by the Cold War, the United Nations, Chinese communism, Indian nationalism and Nasser's pan-Arabism; an increasingly articulate nationalism of both the armed and constitutional varieties in a growing variety of colonial settings; the public opinion of an increasingly liberal democratic society in a new age of state welfare; and the scrutiny of all colonial affairs by an evermore powerful national and international media. All of these factors militated against maintaining colonial rule. So too did the fact, upon which empire-building and rule had been fundamentally based, that Empire required the mass of people in Britain, and in the other powerful states of the world too, to be supportive, disinterested or irrelevant when it came to imperial matters. When those people started to debate the rights and wrongs of Empire, to side with moderate nationalists or question the previously unquestioned right of whites to rule non-whites, and to wield the vote, the writing was on the wall. A liberal state that sends trades union advisers and cooperative society advisers to work amongst its colonial subjects as Britain did from the 1940s, that encourages electoral politics, that allows colonial elites to attend the best schools and universities and meet communists and Fabians at cocktail parties in London and Oxford, and that had already conceded that self-government was the ultimate goal of imperial policy, would be willing if pressed to deal across the table with any nationalist movement that had the right feel about it. This usually meant a collar and tie, an educated voice, enthusiasm for constitutional progress and the right noises about post-independence friendship and defence agreements.

Colonial rule had always needed to be simple and inexpensive to be borne by the state at all. When colonial rule became an international pariah and empire an increasingly pejorative word, when maintaining colonial rule began to require ever higher expenditure on military policing and political bargaining, and when Empire ceased even to be seen as a sensible economic option, its days were numbered, even if Britain's ambitions to play a global role in world affairs outlasted the Empire until finally dying, like the Empire itself, on the barren rocks of sterling devaluation, empty coffers, the unaffordable price of the latest weapons systems and the shift in global politics away from Empire to influence. After nearly 400 years, the irrevocable geographical and material logic of the British Isles had returned the nation to the status of a regional power, with a major presence in Europe, and a presence in the wider world, but not with a global Empire.

Notes

Notes to Chapter 1: Prologue

1. For Low see Joseph Darracott, *A Cartoon War: World War Two in Cartoons* (London, 1989). For Fougasse see Mark Bryant, *World War II in Cartoons* (New York, 1989). The Barbados quote comes from Lawrence James, *The Rise and Fall of the British Empire* (London, 1995), p. 480.
2. Anthony Clayton, *The British Empire as a Superpower, 1919–39* (London, 1986).
3. Christopher Somerville, *Our War: How the British Commonwealth Fought the Second World War* (London, 1998), is a collection of oral history recording the war experiences and perspectives of people from all over the Empire.
4. Patrick Bishop, *Fighter Boys: Saving Britain 1940* (London, 2003), p. 98.
5. *Hope and Glory*, directed by John Boorman (1987).
6. From 'Caribbean Participants in the Second World War', by Marika Sherwood, BBC (as at 14 June 2004), www.bbc.co.uk/history/war/wwtwo/colonies. There are a few websites that have some general information on the Empire and the Second World War. Look for BBC, Ministry of Defence and Imperial War Museum links in particular.
7. The opinion of a lady in the ITV series, *The British Empire in Colour* (London, 2002).

Notes to Chapter 2: The Approach of War

1. In fact only fifteen in number in 1939, thirteen of which dated from the First World War or before, though with five more, the 'King George V' class, soon to enter service.
2. Paul Kennedy, *The Rise and Fall of British Naval Mastery* (London, 1983).
3. David French, *The British Way in Warfare, 1688–2000* (London, 1990), p. 200.
4. Ibid., p. 176.
5. Nicholas Mansergh, *Survey of British Commonwealth Affairs: Problems of War-Time Cooperation and Post-War Change, 1939–1952* (Oxford, 1958).
6. W. Schmokel, *Dream of Empire: German Colonialism, 1919–45* (New Haven, 1964).

Notes to Chapter 3: Imperial War

1. Keith Jeffery, 'The Second World War', in Judith Brown and William Roger Louis (eds), *The Oxford History of the British Empire*, iv, *The Twentieth Century* (Oxford, 1999), p. 306. This volume of the *Oxford History of the British Empire* together with volume V (*Historiography*) contains many useful metropolitan and regional chapters containing information on the Second World War.

2. Walter Sellar and Robert Yeatman, *1066 And All That: A Memorable History of England, Comprising All the Parts You Can Remember, Including 103 Good Things, 5 Bad Kings and 2 Genuine Dates* (London, 1930). See Terry Deary, *The Barmy British Empire* (London, 2002), for a modern-day, humorous contrast, in which the Empire is portrayed as a wholly, and very very, Bad Thing.

3. The Irish leader Eamon De Valera, feared that Britain might try to seize the ports restored to its sovereignty under the Anglo-Irish Agreement of 1938. De Valera promised the British government that he would fight if invaded and call upon British help in doing so. The Admiralty was not too concerned, until Norwegian and French ports fell to the Germans, which transformed the situation. The Royal Navy's ability to extend protection to convoys was reduced by 200 miles owing to the lack of a refuelling base in Ireland. Bases on the west coast of Ireland would have considerably cut the advantage gained by the Germans through their occupation of the Channel ports. A united Ireland was put on the table by the British government in return for Irish participation, but this offer was rejected by de Valera. See Robert Fisk, *In Time of War: Ireland, Ulster, and the Price of Neutrality, 1939–45* (London, 1983); Ian Wood, '"Twas England Bade Our Wild Geese Go": Soldiers of Ireland in the Second World War', in Paul Addison and Angus Calder (eds), *Time to Kill: The Soldiers Experience of War in the West, 1939–45* (London, 1997). Hitler seriously considered an invasion of Ireland, and the British secret services were very active in the Republic, as were Nazi agents. See Mark Hull, 'The Irish Interlude: German Intelligence in Ireland, 1939–1943', *Journal of Military History*, 66 (2002). America took a stern line with Ireland, particularly its refusal to grant Britain base rights, and as a result refused to provide it with military equipment or wheat under Lend-Lease, arguing that doing so would not be making a contribution to American national security. See also Rollph Keefer, *Grounded in Eire: The Story of Two RAF Fliers Interned in Ireland during World War Two* (Montreal, 2001).

4. See H. Duncan Hall and C. C. Wrigley, *Studies of Overseas Supply* (London, 1956) and H. Duncan Hall and C. C. Wrigley, *North American Supply* (London, 1955). These books form part of the excellent History of the Second World War, UK Civil Series.

5. David Dilks, 'The Commonwealth Contribution to the Second World War', conference paper, St Antony's College, Oxford (1998). As David French similarly argues, 'without imperial and Dominion forces Britain could not have secured her interests in the Middle East and Mediterranean'. French, *The British Way in Warfare*, p. 198.

6. From Duncan Hall and Wrigley, *Studies of Overseas Supply*.

7. R. J. Moore, *Churchill, Cripps and India, 1939–1945* (Oxford, 1979). Important new material is considered in Peter Clarke, *The Cripps Version: The Life of Sir Stafford Cripps* (London, 2002). For differences on India between Churchill and his Secretary of State for India, Leo Amery, see William Roger Louis, 'The Second World War, India, and the Clash with Churchill', in *In the Name of God, Go! Leo Amery and the British Empire in the Age of Churchill* (New York, 1992).

8. D. French, *The British Way in Warfare*, p. 197.

9. Numerous books deal with this topic. The classic is William Roger Louis, *Imperialism at Bay, 1941–45: The United States and the Decolonization of the British Empire* (Oxford, 1977). On the Indian civil servant turned imperial thinker, scholar and spokesman see John Cell, *Hailey: A Study in British Imperialism, 1872–1969* (Cambridge, 1992), and

Suki Wolton, *The Loss of White Prestige: Lord Hailey, the Colonial Office and the Politics of Race and Empire in the Second World War* (Basingstoke, 2000).

10. References to Alan Brooke's diary come from Alex Danchev and Daniel Todman (eds), *War Diaries, 1939–1945: Field Marshal Lord Alanbrooke* (London, 2001). In fact Pound had a tumour growing on his brain and often kept his eyes closed, giving the impression that he was asleep. See Stephen Howarth (ed.), *Men of War: Great Naval Leaders of World War Two* (London, 1992).

11. Alan Bullock, *Hitler: A Study in Tyranny* (London, 1954), pp. 543 and 337.

12. Lord Baden-Powell of Gilwell, *African Adventures* (London, n.d.), p. 21.

13. Ibid., p. 37.

14. In 1937 Britain accounted for 32.5 per cent of the world's merchant tonnage.

15. Ships built in Britain during the war, bought from America or captured, had names beginning with the word *Empire*. Those built in Canada began with the word *Fort* or *Park*.

16. Britain lost more destroyers than any other belligerent nation during the Second World War (169, as opposed to America's 99, Japan's 134, Italy's 134 and Germany's 25). Other major British naval losses included five battleships, ten carriers and 31 cruisers.

17. Philip Goodhart, *Fifty Ships that Saved the World: The Foundation of the Anglo-American Alliance* (London, 1965).

18. For RAF Coastal Command see Christina Goulter, *A Forgotten Offensive: RAF Coastal Command and the Campaign Against German Shipping, 1939–1945* (London, 1995).

19. For an account of the Holt Line's war record set against the general war picture of global shipping and supply, see Stephen Roskill, *A Merchant Fleet at War: Alfred Holt and Co., 1939–1945* (London, 1962).

20. See D. J. Payton-Smith, *Oil: A Study in Wartime Policy and Administration* (London, 1971).

21. Lend-Lease was not just an American operation. $8 billion dollars' worth flowed in the other direction (from Britain to America), and a third of all aircraft delivered to Russia between 1941 and 1945 were British. (4283 to America's 9438. This included 2952 Hurricanes and 1331 Spitfires.)

22. Charles Eade (ed.), *Secret Session Speeches by the Right Honourable Winston S. Churchill* (London, 1946).

23. Resident Commissioner Aubrey Forsyth-Thompson, on tour in the Okavango Delta, quoted in Ashley Jackson, *Botswana 1939–1945: An African Country at War* (Oxford, 1999).

24. For war-time Colonial Office appraisals of the state of the empire and future reform, as well as its efforts to present its policies in the best light to colonial peoples and the watching world, see J. M. Lee and Martin Petter, *The Colonial Office, War, and Development Policy: Organization and Planning of a Metropolitan Initiative, 1939–1945* (London, 1982); J. M. Lee, '"Forward Thinking" and War: The Colonial Office During the 1940s', *Journal of Imperial and Commonwealth History*, 6 (1977); and Kate Morris, *British Techniques of Public Relations and Propaganda for Mobilizing East and Central Africa in World War Two* (Lampeter, 2000). See also Robert Pearce, *The Turning Point: British Colonial Policy, 1938–1948* (London, 1982).

25. The term 'the official mind' was coined in Ronald Robinson and Jack Gallagher's

seminal study *Africa and the Victorians: The Official Mind of Imperialism* (London, 1961) and refers to the government and administrative machinery in Whitehall and Westminster that was responsible for imperial policy and imperial governance.

26. Harold Macmillan, *The Blast of War 1939–45* (London, 1967), chapter 7, 'The Colonial Empire at War', p. 166. Macmillan wrote of the 'curious experience' of exchanging the bustle of Lord Beaverbrook's Ministry of Supply 'for the cool dignity of the old Colonial Office in Downing Street … The vast caverns of the Colonial Office building, where light seldom penetrated and ghostly steps echoed down the lofty corridors as in the aisles of some great cathedral'.

27. Ibid, p. 161.

28. Though the Australians had particular gripes about the system and extent of consultation between London and the Dominions, the other Prime Ministers were on the whole satisfied with it.

29. K. Jeffery, 'The Second World War', p. 307.

30. British National Archives, Kew, DO 35/4180, John Shuckburgh, 'Colonial Civil History of the War' (unpublished manuscript, 1949).

31. At the start of the war the Commander-in-Chief at Plymouth was responsible for protecting all Allied shipping approaching the British Isles. Western Approaches Command was created because German access to French ports meant that the south-western approaches became untenable, so all shipping had to be diverted around the coast of Ireland. Plymouth was unsuitable as an operational headquarters for the battle in this region, so Liverpool was chosen as the site for a new command. This went to Admiral Sir Percy Noble, replaced by Admiral Sir Max Horton in November 1942.

32. D. French, *The British Way in Warfare*, p. 205.

33. Ronald Lewin, *The Chief: Field Marshal Lord Wavell, Commander-in-Chief and Viceroy, 1919–1947* (London, 1980), p. 15.

34. P. Bishop, *Fighter Boys*, p. 241.

35. Figures from Roy Conyers Nesbit, *An Illustrated History of the RAF* (London, 2002). Distribution information from Denis Richards and Hilary St George Saunders, *Royal Air Force 1939–1945*, i, *The Fight at Odds* (London, 1953), appendix 4.

36. See *MI9: The British Secret Service that Fostered Escape and Evasion, 1939–45* (Oxford, 1979).

37. See Alan Stripp, *Codebreaker in the Far East: How the British Cracked Japan's Top Secret Military Codes* (Oxford, 1995), and Michael Smith, *The Emperor's Codes: Bletchley Park and the Breaking of Japan's Secret Ciphers* (London, 2000).

38. See Nigel West, *Secret War: The Story of SOE, Britain's Wartime Sabotage Organization* (London, 1992). The classic, though European focused, account is M. R. D. Foot, *SOE: The Special Operations Executive, 1940–46* (London, 1984). See also W. J. M. Mackenzie, *The Secret History of SOE: The Special Operations Executive, 1940–1945* (London, 2000); Charles Cruikshank, *SOE in the Far East* (Oxford, 1986); and *SOE Operations in Africa and the Middle East: A Guide to the Records in the Public Record Office* (Kew, 1998). For articles on SOE in East Africa, French North Africa, the Middle East and South Africa see the bibliography. For SOE in Mauritius, see A. Jackson, *War and Empire in Mauritius and the Indian Ocean*.

Notes to Chapter 4: The Home Front

1. D. Richards and H. St George Saunders, *Royal Air Force, 1939–1945*, ii, p. 66.

2. See Bob Moore and Kent Fedorowich (eds), *Prisoners of War and their Captors in World War Two* (Oxford, 1996); also Moore and Fedorowich, *The British Empire and its Italian Prisoners of War, 1940–47* (Basingstoke, 2002).

3. William Roger Louis, *Imperialism at Bay, 1941–45: The United States and the Decolonization of the British Empire* (Oxford, 1977).

4. A full examination of the economics of the imperial war effort is long overdue. See Nicholas Westcott and M. P. Cowen, 'British Imperial Economic Policy during the War', unpublished seminar paper (City of London Polytechnic, 1984); Westcott, 'The Slippery Slope: Economic Control in Africa During the Second World War', in Paul Kingston, R. G. Tiedemann and Nicholas Westcott (eds), *Managed Economies in World War Two* (London, 1991); and Westcott's chapter on the imperial economy in David Killingray and Richard Rathbone (eds), *Africa and the Second World War* (London, 1986). See also B. R. Tomlinson, *The Political Economy of the Raj, 1914–1947: The Economics of Decolonization in India* (London, 1979). See also Allister Hinds, 'Imperial Policy and Colonial Sterling Balances, 1943–56', *Journal of Imperial and Commonwealth History*, 19 (1991), Gerold Krozewski, 'Sterling, the "Minor" Territories, and the End of Formal Empire, 1939–58', *Economic History Review*, 46 (1993), and Krozewski, *Money and the End of Empire: British International Economic Policy and the Colonies, 1947–1958* (Basingstoke, 2001). See also Jorge Fodor, 'The Origins of Argentina's Sterling Balances, 1939–43', in Guido di Tella and D. C. M. Platt, *The Political Economy of Argentina, 1880–1946* (London, 1989), and K. Wright, 'Dollar Pooling and the Sterling Area, 1939–1952', *American Economic Review*, 44 (1954). Recent work has concentrated on trade relations among the Dominions and Britain, as well as American policy towards Commonwealth trade policy. See Francine McKenzie, *Redefining the Bonds of Commonwealth, 1939–1948: The Politics of Preference* (Basingstoke, 2002).

5. There is a wealth of home front information in John Shuckburgh, 'Colonial Civil History of the War', unpublished manuscript (London, 1949).

6. Raymond Dumett, 'Africa's Strategic Raw Materials During World War Two', *Journal of African History*, 26 (1984). This is a special issue of the journal dedicated to the Second World War.

7. Almost inevitably, some latter-day commentators and historians find it easy to ignore any such contemporary intentions or justifications, and choose to see bulk purchasing arrangements as just another form of colonial exploitation. Work looking at bulk purchasing includes David Meredith, 'State Controlled Marketing and Economic "Development": The Case of West African Produce during the Second World War', *Economic History Review*, 39 (1986), and David Meredith, 'The Colonial Office, British Business Interests and the Reform of Cocoa Marketing in West Africa, 1937–1945', *Journal of African History*, 29 (1988); David Fieldhouse, 'The Case of Gold Coast Cocoa', in Michael Twaddle (ed.), *Imperialism, the State and the Third World* (London, 1992). See bibliography for other titles.

8. There is a distinctive literature on the subject of post-war development policy, formulated during the war. See note 25 in the previous chapter. Also Havinden and

540 NOTES TO PAGES 50–59

Meredith, *British Colonial Development Policy*; L. J. Butler, 'Reconstruction, Development and the Entrepreneurial State: The British Colonial Model, 1939–51', *Contemporary British History*, 13 (1999); D. J. Morgan, *The Official History of Colonial Development: The Origins of British Aid Policy, 1925–1945*, 5 volumes (London, 1980); Ronald Hyam (ed.), *The Labour Government, 1945–1951*, British Documents on the End of Empire series (London, 1992); G. N. Parsons, 'Imperial "Partnership": British Colonial Development and Welfare Policy, 1938–1950', M.Phil. Thesis, University of Oxford (1985); and D. G. M. Rampersad, 'Colonial Economic Development and Social Welfare: The Case of the British West Indian Colonies, 1929–1947', D.Phil. Thesis, University of Oxford (1979). See also Joanna Lewis, '"Tropical East Ends" and the Second World War: Some Contradictions in Colonial Welfare Initiatives', *Journal of Imperial and Commonwealth History*, 28 (2000).

9. Extract from the British National Archives by James Noble, formerly of Balliol College, Oxford.

10. See Jessica Mann, *Out of Harm's Way: The Wartime Evacuation of Children from Britain* (London, 2005).

Notes to Chapter 5: The Atlantic

1. The fight in the Atlantic is famously captured by Nicholas Monsarrat in *The Cruel Sea* (London, 1951), as well as *Three Corvettes*, stories written during the war whilst Monsarrat was an RNVR officer serving aboard the corvettes about which he wrote so powerfully.

2. For an eyewitness account of the voyage, see H. V. Morton, *Atlantic Meeting: An Account of Mr Churchill's Voyage in HMS Prince of Wales, in August 1941, and the Conference with President Roosevelt Which Resulted in the Atlantic Charter* (London, 1943).

3. Ibid.

4. See J. T. Gorman, *George VI: King and Emperor* (London, 1937).

5. See Rob Holland, *Britain and the Commonwealth Alliance, 1918–1939* (London, 1981), on development of British-Dominions relations. Literature on Canada and the Second World War is vast and sophisticated and the bibliography contains numerous titles. For an all round survey, see W. A. B. Douglas and Brereton Greenous, *Out of the Shadows: Canada and the Second World War* (Toronto, 1977). Volumes of the *Canadian Journal of Military History* provide an introduction to the well-established and ever-growing field of Canadian war history.

6. During the war America's economic and military rise, and the relative economic and military decline of Britain, did not mean that one great power sponsor was swapped for another in the Dominions. Whilst American economic links grew, and America became the ultimate guarantor against invasion, binding links with Britain remained. America's economic rise was often incompatible with the economic interests of the Dominions, and America's military rise did not bring with it any obligation to intervene in defence of Dominion interests in the post-war world, though the British obligation to do so, for historical, political, cultural and economic reasons, remained. Hence, Britain continued to be on most scales the Dominions' most important trading partner, and an integral feature of their defence arrangements.

7. See Gordon Smith, *The War at Sea: Royal and Dominion Navy Actions in World War Two* (London, 1989).

8. See W. A. B. Douglas *The Creation of a National Air Force: The Official History of the Royal Canadian Air Force* (Toronto, 1986).

9. A. Danchev and D. Todman (eds), *War Diaries 1939–1945: Field Marshal Lord Alanbrooke.*

10. David Mackenzie, 'Canada, the North Atlantic Triangle and the Empire', in J. Brown and W. Roger Louis (eds), *The Oxford History of the British Empire*, p. 587.

11. See C. P. Stacey, *Arms, Men, and Government: The War Politics of Canada, 1939–1945* (Ottawa, 1970), and Stacey, *Canada and the British Army, 1846–1971: A Study in the Practice of Responsible Government* (Toronto, 1963). For conscription, see J. L. Granatstein and J. M. Hitsman, *Broken Promises: A History of Conscription in Canada* (Toronto, 1976). For the coming of war, see James Eayrs, *In Defence of Canada: Appeasement and Rearmament* (Toronto, 1965).

12. See Patricia Roy, 'The Soldiers Canada Didn't Want: Her Chinese and Japanese Citizens', *Canadian Historical Review* (September 1978), and Marjorie Wong, *The Dragon and the Maple Leaf: Chinese Canadians and World War Two* (Toronto, 1992).

13. See J. Summerby, *Native Soldiers: Foreign Battlefields* (Ottawa, 1966).

14. F. J. Hatch, *The Aerodrome of Democracy: Canada and the British Commonwealth Air Training Plan, 1939–1945* (Ottawa, 1983).

15. See Marc Milner, *The U-Boat Hunters: The Royal Canadian Navy and the Offensive against Germany's Submarines* (Toronto, 1994), and Milner, *North Atlantic Run: The Royal Canadian Navy and the Battle for the Convoys* (Toronto, 1985).

16. See William Stevenson, *A Man Called Intrepid* (Harcourt, 1976).

17. David Stafford, *Camp X* (Toronto, 1986).

18. See David Mackenzie, *Inside the North Atlantic Triangle: Canada and the Entrance of Newfoundland into the Confederation, 1939–1949* (Toronto, 1986), and Peter Neary, *Newfoundland in the North Atlantic World, 1929–1949* (Montreal, 1988).

19. Donald Bittner, *The Lion and the White Falcon: Britain and Iceland in the World War II Era* (Hamden, Connecticut, 1983).

20. See Galen Rozer Perra, 'Anglo-Canadian Imperial Relations: The Case of Garrisoning the Falkland Islands in 1942', *War and Society*, 14 (1996).

21. See Vivian Fuchs, *Of Ice and Men: The Story of the British Antarctic Survey, 1943–73* (Oswestry, 1982); Kieran Mulvaney, *At the Ends of the Earth: A History of the Polar Regions* (Washington, 2001); and Klaus Dodds, *Pink Ice: Britain and the South Atlantic Empire* (London, 2002).

22. Operation Tabarin, broadcast by Klaus Dodds, BBC Radio 4, 6/1/05.

Notes to Chapter 6: The Caribbean

1. See Aarón Gamaliel Ramos and Angel Israel Rivera, *Islands at the Crossroads: Politics in the Non-Independent Caribbean* (Kingston, 2001).

2. For the Caribbean and the Second World War see Jean Andre Baptisté, *War Cooperation and Conflict: The European Possessions in the Caribbean, 1939–45* (Westport, Connecticut, 1988); Brian Dyde, *The Empty Sleeve: The Story of The West India Regiments of the British Army* (St John's, Antigua, 1997); and Ken Post, *Strike the Iron:*

A Colony at War, 1939–1945, 2 volumes (New Jersey, 1981). Other works dealing with the Caribbean at war are listed in the bibliography.

3. See P. Goodhart, *Fifty Ships That Saved the World.*

4. See H. Duncan Hall and C. C. Wrigley, *Studies of Overseas Supply.*

5. See Bede Clifford, *Proconsul: Being Incidents in the Life and Career of the Honourable Sir Bede Clifford* (London, 1964).

6. There is a strong literature on this war-time migration, and conditions encountered by West Indians in Britain. See for example Sonya Rose, *Which People's War? National Identity and Citizenship in Britain, 1939–1945* (Oxford, 2003); Ben Bosquet, *West Indian Women at War: British Racism in World War Two* (London, 1991); and Marika Sherwood, *Many Struggles: West Indian Workers and Service Personnel in Britain, 1939–45* (London, 1985).

7. Marika Sherwood, 'Caribbean Participants in the Second World War', www.bbc.co.uk/history/war/wwtwo/colonies.

8. Ibid.

9. See Michael Pye, *The King Over the Water: The Windsors in the Bahamas, 1940–1945* (London, 1981); and Michael Bloch, *The Duke of Windsor's War* (London, 1982). For the Duke of Windsor's earlier visits to the region, see *The Prince of Wales' Book: A Pictorial Record of the Voyages of HMS Renown, 1919–1920* (London, n.d.), and *The Prince of Wales' Eastern Book: A Pictorial Record of the Voyages of HMS Renown, 1921–1922* (London, n.d.)

10. M. Bloch, *The Duke of Windsor's War,* p. 226.

11. See D. Gail Saunders, 'The 1942 Riot in Nassau: A Demand for Change?', *Journal of Caribbean History,* 20 (1985–86).

12. See Howard Johnson, 'The Anglo-American Caribbean Commission and the Extension of American Influence in the British Caribbean, 1942–1945', *Journal of Commonwealth and Comparative Politics,* 22 (1984).

13. The British had federated and unified territories around the world, most of which survive to this day as nation states. Disparate colonies in Canada and Australia had been federated in the nineteenth century. The political centralization of the diverse states of India had led to the creation of a vast state. The Union of South Africa was created from four separate colonies in 1910. The federated and unfederated Malay states became, along with Singapore, Sarawak and Borneo, the Malaysian nation. Territories in Arabia were merged into the South Arabian federation. Failed federations were created in Central Africa and the West Indies, and an East African federation was mooted but never actually created.

14. Claudio Meunier and Carlos Garcia, *Wings of Thunder.*

15. See R. A. Humphrey, *Latin America and the Second World War,* 2 volumes (London, 1981 and 1982): Raúl García Heras, 'World War Two and the Frustrated Nationalization of the British-Owned Argentine Railways, 1939–1943', *Journal of Latin American Studies,* 17 (1985); Jorge Fodor, 'The Origins of Argentina's Sterling Balances, 1939–43', in Guido de Tell and D. C. M. Platt (eds), *The Political Economy of Argentina, 1880–1946* (London, 1989); Guido de Tella and D. C. Watt (eds), *Argentina Between the Great Powers, 1939–1946* (Oxford, 1989); and C. A. Macdonald, 'The Politics of Intervention: The United States, Britain and Argentina, 1941–46', *Journal of Latin American Studies,* 12 (1980).

Notes to Chapter 7: The Mediterranean

1. Studies are legion. An accessible recent overview is Paul Collier, *The Second World War: The Mediterranean, 1940–1945* (Oxford, 2003). See also the official history I. S. O. Playfair, C. J. C. Malony and W. Jackson, *The Mediterranean and Middle East*, 6 volumes (London, 1954–88).

2. A classic study is Michael Howard, *The Mediterranean Strategy in the Second World War* (London, 1968). See also Bernard Ireland, *The War in the Mediterranean 1940–1943* (London, 1993).

3. Rommel was portrayed by James Mason in the film *The Desert Fox*. Not surprisingly, the Desert War produced more war films than any other front. For example, *Sea of Sand* (about the LRDG), *The Desert Rats*, *Ice Cold in Alex* and Ealing's *Nine Men*. Within the region, the war effort of Malta also attracted a fair amount of attention, for example *Malta Story* starring Alec Guinness.

4. Ronald Lewin, *The Chief: Field Marshal Lord Wavell, Commander-in-Chief and Viceroy, 1919–1947* (London, 1980), p. 30.

5. Mussolini's impatience to get in on the action meant that a third of the Italian merchant fleet was caught in neutral ports at the time of Italy's declaration of war and therefore lost to the Italian war effort.

6. A. Danchev and D. Todman (eds), *War Diaries, 1939–1945: Field Marshal Lord Alanbrooke.*

7. The subject of logistics is neglected, and even in the books on the subject attention to this vital colonial labour army is minuscule. See Martin van Creveld, *Suppyling War: Logistics From Wallenstein to Patton* (Cambridge, 1977), and Julian Thompson, *The Lifeblood of War: Logistics in Armed Conflict* (London, 1991). For better coverage, see the official histories of the RPC, E. H. Rhodes-Wood, *War History of the Royal Pioneer Corps, 1939–45* (Aldershot, 1960), and E. R. Elliott, *Royal Pioneers, 1945–1993* (Hanley Swan, 1993). See also Paul Collier, 'The Logistics of the North African Campaign, 1940–1943', D.Phil Thesis (University of Oxford, 2001). See also Ashley Jackson, 'Supplying War: The Military-Logistical Contribution of the High Commission Territories in the Second World War', *Journal of Military History*, 66 (2002). For the battle for Crete see Callum MacDonald, *The Lost Battle: Crete 1941* (London, 1993).

8. For the latest study of the course of the Desert War, see Niall Barr, *Pendulum of War: The Three Battles of Alamein* (London, 2004).

9. Frank Harrison, *Tobruk: The Great Siege Reassessed* (London, 1997).

10. Numerous books focus on Churchill's relations with his commanders. See for example John Keegan (ed.), *Churchill's Generals* (London, 1991); Barrie Pitt, *Churchill and the Generals* (London, 1981); Correlli Barnett, *The Desert Generals* (London, 1999); and Stephen Roskill, *Churchill and the Admirals* (London, 1977). Television documentaries often return to this theme, and it has also been visited by playwrights. See Ian Curteis, *Churchill and the Generals.*

11. This story, and the history of desert exploration and its application in the war, is most recently and effectively told in Saul Kelly, *The Hunt for Zerzura: The Lost Oasis and the Desert War* (London, 2002).

12. See David Lloyd-Owen, *The Long Range Desert Group, 1940–45: Providence Their*

Guide (Barnsley, 1980); W. B. K. Shaw, *The Long Range Desert Group* (London, 1945); Mike Morgan, *Sting of the Scorpion: The Inside Story of the Long Range Desert Group* (Stroud, 2000); Jonathan Pittaway and Craig Fourie, *LRDG Rhodesian: Rhodesians in the Long Range Desert Group* (Johannesburg, 2002); and Virginia Cowles, *The Phantom Major: The Story of David Stirling and the SAS Regiment* (London, 1958).

13. See David Brown (ed.), *The Royal Navy and the Mediterranean* (London, 2002).

14. See S. W. C. Pack, *Cunningham: The Commander* (London, 1974); Jack Greene Alessandro Massignani, *The Naval War in the Mediterranean, 1940–1943* (London, 1998); and Donald Macintyre, *The Battle for the Mediterranean* (London, 1964). An excellent account of the air campaign in the region is provided in Philip Guedalla, *Middle East, 1940–1942: A Study in Air Power* (London, 1944).

15. Richard Hallion, *Strike From the Sky: The History of Battlefield Air Attack, 1911–1945* (Shrewsbury, 1989), p. 161.

16. W. Roger Louis in J. Brown and W. Roger Louis (eds), *Oxford History of the British Empire*, iv, *The Twentieth Century* (Oxford, 1999), p. 24.

17. Jean Lugol, *Egypt in World War Two* (Cairo, 1945); and John Kent (ed.), *British Egypt and the Defence of the Middle East* (London, 1998).

18. Artemis Cooper, *Cairo, 1939–1945* (London, 1989), p. 86.

19. The position of Officer Commanding Troops Egypt was one of the subsidiary commands under the overarching Commander-in-Chief Middle East. In this unwieldy commands structure, a separate officer then commanded the Western Desert Force in the field.

20. Books on Malta and the war, and the convoys on which the island depended, abound. The latest popular account is James Holland, *Fortress Malta: An Island under Siege, 1940–1943* (London, 2003). See also David Thomas, *Malta Convoys, 1940–1942: The Struggle at Sea* (London, 1999), and Douglas Austin, *Malta and British Strategic Policy, 1925–1943* (London, 2004).

21. See Michael Budden, 'Defending the Indefensible? The Air Defence of Malta 1936–1940', *War in History*, 6 (1999).

22. The major reason for the RAF's gloomy assessment of Malta's chances of survival was the notion that the bomber would always get through. If it were claimed that the commitment of fighters to Malta could save it from enemy bombers, the whole argument for the strategic bombing of Germany would be questioned.

23. See Hugh Lloyd, *Briefed to Attack: Malta's Part in African Victory* (London, 1949). Lloyd was Air Officer Commanding Malta before Sir Keith Park took over. See Vincent Orange, *A Biography of Air Chief Marshal Sir Keith Park* (London, 1984).

24. H. Lloyd, *Briefed to Attack*, p. 66.

25. See George Kelling, *Countdown to Rebellion: British Policy in Cyprus, 1939–1955* (Westport, Connecticut, 1990).

26. For a general history of Gibraltar, see John Masters, *The Rock: An Epic* (London, 1971). Also see *Flying from the Rock* (Gibraltar, 1945). For Somerville, see David McIntyre, *Fighting Admiral: The Life of Admiral of the Fleet Sir James Somerville* (London, 1961), and the chapter on Somerville in S. Howarth (ed.) *Men of War: Great Naval Leaders of World War Two*. See also Air HQ, RAF, Gibraltar (Intelligence Section), *Flying from the Rock* (Gibraltar, 1945).

27. See Arthur Marder, *Operation Menace: The Dakar Expedition and the Dudley North*

Affair (London, 1976). For the raid on Oran, see Arthur Marder, *From the Dardanelles to Oran: Studies of the Royal Navy in War and Peace* (London, 1974).

28. A. Danchev and D. Todman (eds), *War Diaries, 1939–1945: Field Marshal Lord Alanbrooke*.

29. Ronald Hyam, in Robin Kilson and Robert King (eds), *The Statecraft of British Imperialism: Essays in Honour of William Roger Louis* (London, 1999), p. 43.

30. *To War with Whitaker: The Wartime Diaries of the Countess of Ranfurly, 1939–1945* (London, 1994); Freya Stark, *Dust in the Lion's Claw: Autobiography, 1939–1945* (London, 1961).

31. For Palestine, see Michael Cohen, *Palestine: Retreat from the Mandate. The Making of British Policy, 1936–1945* (New York, 1978); Ronald Zweig, *Britain and the Palestine Mandate during the Second World War* (London, 1986); and Y. Bauer, *From Diplomacy to Resistance: A History of Jewish Palestine, 1939–1945* (Philadelphia, 1970). For SOE in the Middle East see Saul Kelly, 'A Succession of Crises: SOE in the Middle East, 1940–45', *Intelligence and National Security*, 20 (2005). For the blowing up of the *Patria*, see Erich Steiner, *The Story of the Patria* (New York, 1982). For the movement of Jews to parts of the British Empire, see Bernard Wasserstein, *Britain and the Jews of Europe*. For Jewish detainees in Mauritius, see A. Jackson, *War and Empire in Mauritius and the Indian Ocean* (Basingstoke, 2001).

32. Morris Beckman, *The Jewish Brigade: An Army with Two Masters, 1944–1945* (Staplehurst, 1998), and Bernard Moses Casper, *With the Jewish Brigade* (London, 1947).

Notes to Chapter 8: Iraq, Iran and Syria

1. For Iraq see A. G. Dudgeon, *Hidden Victory: The Battle of Habbaniya, 1941* (Stroud, 2000); Christopher Buckley, *Five Ventures: Iraq, Syria, Persia, Madagascar, Iran and Dodecanese* (London, 1977); and Geoffrey Warner, *Iraq and Syria 1941* (London, 1974). Philip Guedalla, *Middle East, 1940–1942: A Study in Air Power* (London, 1944), also gives excellent coverage. For general background see Charles Tripp, *A History of Iraq* (Cambridge, 2000). For the massacre of Jews in Baghdad, see H. J. Cohen, 'The Anti-Jewish Farhud in Baghdad, 1941', *Middle Eastern Studies*, 3 (1966). See also Chris Shores, *Dust Clouds in the Middle East: The Air War for East Africa, Iraq, Syria, Iran and Madagascar, 1940–1942* (London). For the Arab Legion, see James Lunt, *The Arab Legion*; J. B. Glubb, *War in the Desert* (London, 1950); and Peter Young, *The Arab Legion* (Reading, 1972).

2. See works listed in note 1 and A. B. Gaunson, *The Anglo-French Clash in Lebanon and Syria, 1940–1945* (Basingstoke, 1987). For all aspects of the French Empire at war, see Martin Thomas, *The French Empire at War, 1940–1945* (Manchester, 1998).

3. See C. Buckley, *Five Ventures*, and Clarmont Skrine, *World War in Iran* (London, 1962) and the brilliant account provided in Richard Stewart, *Sunrise at Abadan: The British and Soviet Invasion of Iran, 1941* (London, 1988). See also G. Lenczowski, *Russia and the West in Iran, 1918–1948: A Study in Big-Power Rivalry* (New York, 1949).

4. See A. Danchev and D. Todman (eds), *War Diaries, 1939–1945: Field Marshal Lord Alanbrooke*. For an excellent account of the command and its tasks, see *Paiforce: The Official History of the Persia and Iraq Command, 1941–1946* (London, 1948).

5. Ibid.

6. See D. J. Payton-Smith, *Oil: A Study in Wartime Policy and Administration* (London, 1971).

7. See Martin Wilmington, *The Middle East Supply Centre* (London: London University Press, 1972); Paul Kingston, 'The Middle East Supply Centre, 1941 to 1945: Regional Economic Planning Attempted', in Paul Kingston et al. (eds), *Managed Economies*; and E. M. H. Lloyd, *Food and Inflation in the Middle East, 1940–45* (Stanford, California, 1956). For the UKCC, see Viscount Swinton, *I Remember* (London, n.d.), and 'Studies in War-Time Organization 1, The UKCC', *African Affairs* (July 1944).

8. See Saul Kelly, *Cold War in the Desert: Britain, the United States, and the Italian Colonies, 1945–52* (Basingstoke, 2000), and John Kent, *British Imperial Strategy and the Origins of the Cold War, 1944–1949* (London, 1993).

Notes to Chapter 9: Sub-Saharan Africa

1. See David Killingray and Richard Rathbone (eds), *Africa and the Second World War* (Basingstoke, 1986); Ali Mazrui (ed.), *UNESCO History of Africa and the Second World War* (Libya, 1981); and Michael Crowder, 'The Second World War: Prelude to Decolonization', in M. Crowder (ed.), *The Cambridge History of Africa*, viii (Cambridge, 1988).

2. British rule would have lasted longer if Ernest Bevin, Attlee's imperialist Foreign Secretary, had had his way. He wanted Britain to be granted a United Nations mandate over Libya. The UN, however, elected to make Libya an independent country in 1951, though British bases remained until Colonel Gaddafi came to power in the 1960s. See Lord Rennell of Rodd, *British Administration of Occupied Territories in Africa, 1941–1947* (London, 1948). As Colonel Francis Rodd, Rennell had been appointed in February 1941 to serve as Controller of Finance for occupied territories under Sir Philip Mitchell.

3. For German ambitions in Africa see W. Schmokel, *Dream of Empire: German Colonialism, 1919–45*, and Andrew Crozier, *Appeasement and Germany's Last Bid for Colonies* (New York, 1988).

4. See Robert Pearce, *The Turning Point: British Colonial Policy, 1938–1948* (London, 1982).

5. For bulk purchasing see note 10 in the 'The Home Front' chapter in this book; 'The Colonial Economy: Nigeria and the Second World War', in B. Ingham and C. Simmons, (eds), *Development Studies and Colonial Policy* (London, 1987); and L. J. Butler, *Industrialization and the British Colonial State: West Africa, 1939–51* (London, 1997).

6. See F. A. S. Clarke and A. Haywood, *The History of the Royal West African Frontier Force* (Aldershot, 1964); Timothy Parsons, *The African Rank-and-File: Social Implications of Colonial Military Service in the King's African Rifles, 1902–1964* (Oxford, 1999); Malcolm Page, *KAR: A History of the King's African Rifles* (London, 1998); and J. Moyse-Bartlett, *The King's African Rifles: A Study in the Military History of East and Central Africa, 1890–1945* (Aldershot, 1956). An interesting personal account is provided in John Nunneley, *Tales from the King's African Rifles: A Last Flourish of Empire* (London, 1998).

7. See R. A. R. Bent, *Ten Thousand Men of Africa: The Story of the Bechuanaland Pioneers*

and Gunners, 1941–46 (London, 1952); B. Gray, *Basotho Soldiers in Hitler's War* (Maseru, 1953); E. H. Rhodes-Wood, *War History of the Royal Pioneer Corps, 1939–45* (Aldershot, 1960); and E. R. Elliott, *Royal Pioneers, 1945–1993* (Hanley Swan, 1993).

8. Malcolm Muggeridge, *Chronicle of Wasted Time*, ii, *The Infernal Grove* (London, 1973).

9. Parsons, *The African Rank-and-File*.

10. See O. Shiroya, *Kenya and World War Two* (Nairobi, 1985); R. L. McCormack, 'Imperialism, Air Transport, and Colonial Development: Kenya 1920–1946', *Journal of Imperial and Commonwealth History*, 17 (1989); Ian Spencer, 'Settler Dominance, Agricultural Production and the Second World War in Kenya', *Journal of African History*, 21 (1980); and John Lonsdale's Kenya chapter in Killingray and Rathbone (eds), *Africa and the Second World War*.

11. Bent, *Ten Thousand Men of Africa*.

12. See A. G. Dickson, 'Studies in War-Time Organization, 3, The Mobile Propaganda Unit, East Africa Command', *African Affairs*, 44 (January 1945); Rosaleen Smyth, 'Britain's African Colonies and British Propaganda during the Second World War', *Journal of Imperial and Commonwealth History*, 14 (1985); Smyth, 'War Propaganda during the Second World War in Northern Rhodesia', *African Affairs* (1984); and Kate Morris, *British Techniques of Public Relations and Propaganda for Mobilizating East and Central Africa During World War Two* (Lampeter, 2000).

13. Philip Guedalla, *Middle East, 1940–1942: A Study in Air Power* (London, 1944), p. 109.

14. A. Mockler, *Haile Selassie's War* (Oxford, 1984), gives a good account of the East Africa campaign, as do the official histories.

15. Saul Kelly, 'Great Britain, the United States and the Question of the Italian Colonies, 1949–1952', Ph.D. Thesis, London School of Economics (1995). Also G. K. N. Trevaskis, *Eritrea: A Colony in Transition, 1941–1952* (London, 1960).

16. I. M. Lewis, *The Modern History of Somalia: From Nation to State* (London, 1965). The British also had plans here for desert revolt (as well as among the Senussi in Libya), something of a hobby for British officers and administrators. See Dawn Miller, '"Raising the Tribes": British Policy in Italian East Africa, 1938–41', *Journal of Strategic Studies*, 22 (1999).

17. Sir Philip Mitchell, *African Afterthoughts* (London, 1954).

18. James Fox, *White Mischief* (London, 1982). A film of the same name was also produced.

19. Harold Macmillan, *The Blast of War, 1939–45* (London, 1967), p. 220.

20. See Gardner Thompson, 'Governing Uganda: The Second World War and its Aftermath', in John Smith (ed.), *Administering Empire: The British Colonial Service in Retrospect* (London, 1999).

21. 'Message to the People of Uganda' (1940), in J. Shuckburgh, 'Colonial Civil History of the War', unpublished manuscript (London, 1949).

22. Shuckburgh, 'Colonial Civil History of the War'. Shuckburgh offers a case study of Uganda drawn from contemporary government reports.

23. See the Tanganyika chapter in Killingray and Rathbone (eds), *Africa and the Second World War*; Nicholas Westcott, 'Impact of the Second World War on Tanganyika, 1939–49', Ph.D. Thesis, University of Cambridge (1982); and John Iliffe, *A Modern History of Tanganyika* (Cambridge, 1979).

24. See John Paul Rozier, 'The Effect of War on British Rule and Politics in the Sudan

1939–45', D.Phil. Thesis, University of Oxford (1984); K. D. D. Henderson, 'The Sudan and the Abyssinian Campaign', *African Affairs* (Janury 1943); 'The Sudan Defence Force and the Italian East African Campaign', *African Affairs* (July 1942); 'The Sudan at War: The Composite Infantry Battalion of the East Arab Corps, Sudan Defence Force, in the Abyssinia Campaign', *African Affairs* (October 1943); and 'The Sudan's Service in a Global War: The Story of a Section of the Trans-African Ferry Route', *African Affairs* (January 1944).

25. Ronald Lewin, *The Chief: Field Marshal Lord Wavell, Commander-in-Chief and Viceroy, 1919–1947* (London, 1980), p. 25.

26. Ashley Jackson, 'The Mutiny of the 1st Battalion The Mauritius Regiment, Madagascar 1943', *Journal of the Society for Army Historical Research*, 80 (2001).

27. Lord Swinton, *I Remember*, p. 192.

28. Shuckburgh, 'Colonial Civil History of the War'.

29. See Arthur Marder, *Operation Menace: The Dakar Expedition and the Dudley North Affair* (London, 1976).

30. See Peter Clarke, *West Africans at War, 1914–18, 1939–45* (London, 1986), and G. Olusanya, *The Second World War and Politics in Nigeria, 1939–1953* (Lagos, 1973).

31. See Robert Pearce, 'Morale in the Colonial Service in Nigeria during the Second World War', *Journal of Imperial and Commonwealth History*, 11 (1983).

32. See John Flint, '"Managing Nationalism": The Colonial Office and Nnamdi Azikiwe, 1932–43', in Ronald Hyam, in Robin Kilson and Robert King (eds), *The Statecraft of British Imperialism: Essays in Honour of William Roger Louis* (London, 1999).

33. See the Cameroons chaper in Killingray and Rathbone (eds), *Africa and the Second World War*.

34. See Nancy Lawler, *Soldiers, Airmen, Spies and Whisperers: The Gold Coast in World War Two* (Athens, Ohio, 2001).

35. See Sierra Leone chapter in Killingray and Rathbone (eds), *Africa and the Second World War*.

36. J. F. Macdonald, *The War History of Southern Rhodesia, 1939–45*, 2 volumes (Salisbury, 1947 and 1950). See also Christopher Owen, *The Rhodesia African Rifles* (London, 1970), and. W. V. Brelsford, *The Story of the Northern Rhodesia Regiment* (Lusaka, 1954).

37. Ian Phimister, *Wangi Colia: Coal, Capitalism and Labour in Colonial Zimbabwe, 1894–1954* (Harare, 1994).

38. See David Johnson, 'Settler Farmers and Coerced African Labour in Southern Rhodesia, 1936–46', *Journal of African History*, 33 (1992); Johnson, 'The Impact of the Second World War on Southern Rhodesia with Special Reference to African Labour 1937–48', Ph.D. Thesis, University of London (1989); Kenneth Vickery, 'The Second World War Recruitment of Forced Labour in the Rhodesias', *International Journal of African Historical Studies*, 22 (1989); and K. Datta, 'Farm Labour, Agrarian Capital and the State in Colonial Zambia: The African Labour Corps, 1942–52', *Journal of Southern African Studies*, 14 (1988).

39. David Coe and E. Cyril Greenall, *Kaunda's Gaoler: Memoirs of a District Officer in Northern Rhodesia and Zambia* (London, 2003).

40. James Lunt, *Imperial Sunset: Frontier Soldiering in the Twentieth Century* (London, 1981), is very good on war-time African military formations.

41. Shuckburgh, 'Colonial Civil History of the War'.

42. Ashley Jackson, *Botswana, 1939–1945: An African Country at War* (Oxford, 1999), p. 147. The bibliography in this book contains many titles on Africa and the Second World War.

43. There are a few accounts. Bent, *Ten Thousand Men of Africa*; Gray, *Basotho Soldiers in Hitler's War*. See also Deborah Shackleton, 'Imperial Military Policy and the Bechuanaland Pioneers and Gunners during the Second World War', Ph.D. Thesis, Indiana University (1996).

44. For an introduction, see Ian Phimister's South Africa entry in I. C. B. Dear (ed.), *The Oxford Companion to the History of the Second World War*, and Bill Nasson, 'South Africa', in volume 2 of John Bourne, Peter Liddle and Ian Whitehead (eds), *The Great World War, 1914–1945* (London, 2001). See John Keene (ed.), *South Africa in World War Two* (Johannesburg, 1995), for a general overview; and official histories such as H. J. Martin and N. D. Orpen (eds), *South Africa at War: Military and Industrial Organization and Operations in Connection with the Conduct of the War, 1939–1945* (Cape Town, 1975); also J. A. Gray, 'Studies in War-Time Organization, 4, The Union's Supply Effort', *African Affairs* (April 1945), and J. Crwys-Williams, *A Country at War 1939–45* (Johannesburg, 1992).

45. See Brian Bunting, *The Rise of the South African Reich* (London, 1964), and A. Hagemann, 'Very Special Relations: The Third Reich and the Union of South Africa, 1933–1939', *South African Historical Journal*, 27 (1992).

46. J. M. Tinley, *South African Food and Agricultural Production in World War Two* (Stanford, California, 1954).

47. An excellent account of the naval struggle in South African waters is found in L. C. F. Turner, H. R. Gordon-Cumming and J. E. Beltzer, *War in the Southern Oceans, 1939–45* (Cape Town, 1961). See also C. J. Harris, *War at Sea: South African Maritime Operations during World War Two* (Johannesburg, 1991).

48. See Albert Grundlingh, 'The King's Afrikaners? Enlistment and Ethnic Identity in the Union of South Africa's Defence Force during the Second World War, 1939–45', *Journal of African History*, 40 (1999).

49. Ian Gleeson, *The Unknown Force: Black, Indian, and Coloured Soldiers Through Two World Wars* (Johannesburg, 1994).

50. See G. Visser, *Ossewabrandwag: Traitors or Patriots?* (Cape Town, 1976).

51. See Ronald Hyam and Peter Henshaw, *The Lion and the Springbok: Britain and South Africa since the Boer War* (Cambridge, 2003).

52. Ibid.

53. Colin Newbury, *The Diamond Ring: Business, Politics, and Precious Stones in South Africa, 1867–1947* (Oxford, 1989).

54. Interview, 10 April 1995. See A. Jackson, 'Motivation and Mobilization for War: Recruitment for the British Army in the Bechuanaland Protectorate, 1941–46', *African Affairs* 96 (1997).

55. W. H. Walton, 'Colonel Herbert Johnson, OBE, MC, TD, Leader of the Swazi Pioneers, 1941–1945: A Memoir', unpublished (1993).

56. Quoted in A. Jackson, 'Supplying War: The High Commission Territories Military-Logistical Contribution in the Second World War', *Journal of Military History*, 66 (2002), p. 736.

57. Both quotes are from interviews conducted by the author in 1994–95. See Jackson, *Botswana, 1939–1945*.

58. Hamilton Simelane, 'Labour Mobilization for the War Effort in Swaziland, 1940–42', *International Journal of African Historical Studies*, 26 (1993), and Hamilton Simelane, 'Women and the Second World War in Swaziland 1939–45', *University of Swaziland Research Journal*, 3 (1990). For Basotoland, see Mary Ntabeni, 'War and Society in Colonial Lesotho 1939–45', Ph.D. Thesis, Queen's University, Kingston, Ontario (1996).

59. Jackson, *Botswana, 1939–1945*.

60. Ibid.

61. J. Zaffiro, *From Police Network to Station of the Nation: A Political History of Broadcasting in Botswana, 1927–1991* (Gaborone, 1991), p. 5.

Notes to Chapter 10: The Indian Ocean

1. A. Danchev and D. Todman (eds), *War Diaries, 1939–1945: Field Marshal Lord Alanbrooke*, diary entry 14 April 1942.

2. Alfred North-Coombes, *The Island of Rodrigues* (Port Louis, 1971).

3. See Ashley Jackson, *War and Empire in Mauritius and the Indian Ocean* (Basingstoke, 2001). For an outstanding example of how an apparently insignificant island could become an important military base, see Peter Doling, *From Port T to RAF Gan: An Illustrated History of the British Military Bases at Addu Atoll in the Maldive Islands, 1941–76* (Bognor Regis, 2004).

4. See Jackson, *War and Empire in Mauritius and the Indian Ocean*, for consideration of the growth of British power in the region from Napoleonic times. Also see Jackson, 'The British Empire in the Indian Ocean', in Dennis Rumley and Sanjay Chaturvedi (eds), *Geopolitical Orientations, Regionalism and Security in the Indian Ocean* (New Delhi, 2002).

5. The designation 'Indian Ocean region' was used by the Merchant Navy during the Second World War, and stretched from Freetown to Western Australia. See C. B. A. Behrens, *Merchant Shipping and the Demands of War* (London, 1955).

6. For Ceylon, see Michael Tomlinson, *The Most Dangerous Moment* (London, 1976). Also see Hugh Campbell, *Notable Service to the Empire: Australian Corvettes and the British Pacific Fleet, 1944–45* (Garden Island, New South Wales, 2000). Campbell served aboard an Australian corvette and spent a great deal of time with the Eastern Fleet based on Ceylon.

7. For the operations of the Eastern Fleet see A. Jackson, 'Defence of Empire and the Sea Lanes: The Royal Navy and the British Indian Ocean World', in Jackson, *War and Empire in Mauritius and the Indian Ocean*. The finest works available are Arthur Marder, Mark Jacobsen and John Horsefield, *Old Friends, New Enemies: The Royal Navy and the Imperial Japanese Navy: The Pacific War, 1942–1945* (Oxford, 1990), and H. P. Willmott, *Grave of a Dozen Schemes: British Naval Planning and the War Against Japan, 1943–45* (London, 1996). The Indian Ocean also received due prominence in Stephen Roskill, *Churchill and the Admirals* (London, 1977).

8. The reason for the neglect of the Eastern Fleet, relative to the Mediterranean Fleet or the Home Fleet, is simple; it did its job without doing much actual fighting, certainly in terms of naval engagements with the enemy at sea. This fact constantly frustrated

Churchill, who often demonstrated the limits of his understanding of the use of naval power with enquiries about what the 'idle' Eastern Fleet was doing with its ships.

9. Probably the best account of the course of naval engagements in the Indian Ocean region is provided in L. C. F. Turner, H. R. Gordon-Cumming and J. E. Beltzer, *War in the Southern Oceans 1939–45* (Cape Town, 1961).

10. Naval Historical Branch, Ministry of Defence, London, Eastern Fleet War Diaries.

11. For Somerville, see Arthur Marder, *Old Friends, New Enemies: The Royal Navy and the Imperial Japanese Navy*, i, *Strategic Illusions, 1936–41* (Oxford, 1981); Arthur Marder, M. Jacobsen and J. Horsfield, *Old Friends, New Enemies: The Royal Navy and the Imperial Japanese Navy*, ii, *The Pacific War, 1942–45* (Oxford, 1990); Donald MacIntyre, *Fighting Admiral: The Life of Admiral of the Fleet Sir James Somerville* (London, 1961); Somerville entry in S. Howarth (ed.), *Great Naval Leaders*; and Michael Simpson with John Somerville (eds), *The Somerville Papers: Selections from the Private and Official Correspondence of Admiral of the Fleet Sir James Somerville* (Aldershot, 1995).

12. See Ben Warlow, *Shore Establishments of the Royal Navy: Being a List of the Static Ships and Establishments of the Royal Navy* (Liskeard, 1992).

13. For German raiders see H. J. Brennecke, *Ghost Cruiser HK33* (London, 1954); Ulrich Mohr, *Atlantis: The Story of a German Surface Raider* (London, 1955); Edwin Hoyt, *Raider 16* (New York, 1970); and Bernhard Rogge, *Under Ten Flags: The Story of the German Commerce Raider Atlantis* (London, 1955). Also see A. M. Saville, *German Submarines in the Far East* (Maryland, Annapolis, 1961).

14. See J. Rusbridger, 'The Sinking of the *Automedon*: The Capture of the *Nankin*: New Light on Two Intelligence Disasters in World War Two', *Encounter* (November 1980).

15. The story is told in James Leasor, *Boarding Party*, made into the film *The Sea Wolves*.

16. Dennis Gunton, *The Penang Submarines* (Penang, 1970).

17. See Marc Antonio Bragadin, *The Italian Navy in World War Two* (Maryland, Annapolis, 1957), and J. J. Sadkovich, *The Italian Navy in World War Two* (Westport, Connecticut, 1994).

18. See Brian Crabb, *Passage to Destiny: The Sinking of the SS Khedive Ismail in the Sea War against Japan* (Stanford, 1997), and 'With the Eastern Fleet: The Japanese Submarine', in G. G. Connell, *Fighting Destroyer: The Story of HMS Petard* (London, 1976).

19. See Henry Probert, *The Forgotten Air Force: The Royal Air Force in the War Against Japan, 1941–1945* (London, 1995); Peter Ward Fay, *The Forgotten Army: India's Armed Struggle for Independence, 1942–1945* (Ann Arbor, Michigan, 1993); John Winters, *The Forgotten Fleet: The British Navy in the Pacific, 1944–1945* (London, 1969); Christopher Bayly and Tim Harper, *Forgotten Armies: The Fall of British South Asia, 1941–1945* (London, 2004); David Smurthwaite (ed.), *The Forgotten War: The British Army in the Far East, 1941–1945* (London, 1992); and John Latimer, *Burma: The Forgotten War* (London, 2004).

20. See Ian Cowman, 'Main Fleet to Singapore? Churchill, the Admiralty and Force Z', *Journal of Strategic Studies*, 17 (1994).

21. A. Danchev and D. Todman (eds), *War Diaries, 1939–1945: Field Marshal Lord Alanbrooke*.

22. See Michael Smith, *The Emperor's Codes: Bletchley Park and the Breaking of Japan's Secret Ciphers* (London, 2000).

23. See A. Jackson, 'Refitting the Fleet in Ceylon: The War Diary of Walker Sons and Company', *Journal of Indian Ocean Studies*, 10 (2002).

24. See Michael Wilson, *A Submariner's War in the Indian Ocean, 1939–45* (Stroud, 2000).

Notes to Chapter 11: The Islands of the Indian Ocean

1. Winston Churchill in the House of Commons, 23 April 1942, in Charles Eade (ed.), *Secret Session Speeches by the Right Honourable Winston S. Churchill* (London, 1946). In the section that follows, material on Ceylon has been drawn from a range of personal correspondence with people living in Ceylon during the war. Thanks to Mahinda Abeykoon, Trevor Anghie, William Atkinson, J. D. N. Banks, Ralph Banks, Ronald Barber and the Ceylon Association, John Barron, William Barry Cameron, Peter Beauchamp, Ivor Ferdinands, Joan Gottelier, George and Patricia Hayley, Monica Hulme, Alistair Jackson-Smale, Bubbles Mullins, David Parker, Mavis Pereira, Gerald Robinson (quotes have been taken from his self-published 1998 book, *The Fading Edge of Empire*), C. Samuel, George Shepperson and Jack Thornhill. Some material has also been taken from Rodney Ferdinands, *Proud and Prejudiced*. Though general histories of Ceylon tend to focus very much on the politics of decolonization, some information about the Second World War can be gleaned. See E. F. C. Ludowyk, *The Modern History of Ceylon* (London, 1966); Ludowyk, *The Story of Ceylon* London, 1962); S. R. Ashton, 'Sri Lanka', in W. Roger Louis and J. Brown (eds), *The Oxford History of the British Empire*, iv, *The Twentieth Century* (Oxford, 1999); Charles Jeffries, *Ceylon: The Path to Independence* (London, 1962); K. M. de Silva, *A History of Sri Lanka* (London, 1981); and Chandra de Silva, *Sri Lanka: A History* (London, 1987). The late John Brown, formerly Director of the Naval Historical Branch, kindly gave me a copy of his paper 'Admiralty House and the Royal Navy at Trincomalee, 1810–1957' (1980).

2. A. Jackson, 'Refitting the Fleet in Ceylon: The War Record of Walker Sons & Company', *Journal of Indian Ocean Studies*, 10 (2002).

3. Eade (ed.), *Secret Session Speeches*.

4. See K. M. de Silva (ed.), *Sri Lanka*, ii, *Towards Independence, 1945–1948* (London, 1997).

5. See Philip Ziegler, *Mountbatten: The Official Biography* (London, 1985) and Philip Ziegler (ed.), *Personal Diary of Admiral the Lord Louis Mountbatten: Supreme Allied Commander South East Asia, 1943–46* (London, 1988).

6. See Charles Cruikshank, *SOE in the Far East* (Oxford, 1986).

7. See Arthur Banks, *Wings of the Dawning: The Battle for the Indian Ocean, 1939–1945* (Malvern Wells, 1996).

8. For the RAF in the Dutch East Indies, see Terence Kelly, *Hurricanes Over the Jungle* (London, 1977); Terence Kelly, *Battle for Palembang* (London, 1985); Terence Kelly, *Hurricane and Spitfire Pilots at War* (London, 1986); and Terence Kelly, *Hurricane in Sumatra* (London, 1991).

9. Kelly, *Hurricanes Over the Jungle*.

10. Noel Crusz, *The Cocos Islands' Mutiny* (Fremantle, 2001).

11. See Peter Beauchamp, 'Some Account of Ceylon's "Wavy Navy" between 1939 and

1945', *Indian Navy Association Journal* (1993). Thanks to the author for sending me a copy of this article.

12. See Gerald Robinson, *Fading Edge of Empire* (Sydney, 1998).

13. See E. M. H. Lloyd, *Food and Inflation in the Middle East, 1940–45* (Stanford, California, 1956).

14. For a full account see A. Jackson, *War and Empire in Mauritius and the Indian Ocean* (Basingstoke, 2001).

15. See Peter Doling, *From Port T to RAF Gan: An Illustrated History of the British Military Bases at Addu Atoll in the Maldive Islands, 1941–76* (Bognor Regis, 2004).

16. Useful information has been gleaned from Erik Gilbert, *Dhows and the Colonial Economy of Zanzibar, 1860–1970* (Oxford, 2004).

17. See J. Shuckburgh, 'Colonial Civil History of the War', unpublished manuscript (1949) and Cliff Lord and David Birtles, *The Armed Forces of Aden, 1839–1967* (Solihull, 2000).

18. For Madagascar see Martin Thomas, 'Imperial Backwater or Strategic Outpost? The British Takeover of Vichy Madagascar in 1942', *Historical Journal*, 39 (1996); Tim Benbow, 'Operation Ironclad: The British Invasion of Madagascar, May 1942'; and Woodburn Kirby, S., *The War Against Japan*, 5 volumes (London, 1957–69). Also see entries in the bibliography in Jackson, *War and Empire in Mauritius and the Indian Ocean*.

19. For FECB, see Michael Smith, *The Emperor's Codes: Bletchley Park and the Breaking of Japan's Secret Ciphers* (London, 2000), and Alan Stripp, *Codebreaker in the Far East: How the British Cracked Japan's Top Secret Military Codes* (Oxford, 1995).

Notes to Chapter 12: India and Burma

1. Books on the Indian Army abound. See Roger Beaumont, *Sword of the Raj: The British Army in India, 1747–1947* (New York, 1977), Bisheshwar Prasad (ed.), *Official History of the Indian Armed Forces in the Second World War* (New Delhi, 1953–60), and Daniel Marston, *Pheonix from the Ashes: The Indian Army in the Burma Campaign* (London, 2003). See also Martin Brayley, *The British Army, 1939–1945: The Far East* (Oxford, 2002).

2. George Macdonald Fraser, *Quartered Safe Out Here*, p. 139.

3. For India and the war see Judith Brown, *Modern India: The Origins of a Modern Asian Democracy* (Oxford, 1993). A comprehensive account of India during the war, written from an imperial rather than a national perspective, is required. See Johannes Voigt, *India and the Second World War* (New Delhi, 1987). For a brief overview, see the entry in volume 2 of John Bourne et al. (eds), *The Great World War* (London, 2001).

4. See John Masters, *The Road Past Mandalay* (London, 1967).

5. This notion is that of John Gallagher. See 'The Decline, Revival and Fall of the British Empire', in John Gallagher, *The Decline, Revival and Fall of the British Empire* (Cambridge, 1982), p. 139.

6. The Eastern Group Supply Council has attracted very little scholarly attention. See J. Shuckburgh, 'Colonial Civil History of the War', unpublished manuscript (London, 1949), for good coverage.

7. See M. S. Venkataramani, *Bengal Famine of 1943* (Delhi, 1973), and P. R. Greenough, *Prosperity and Misery in Modern Bengal: The Famine of 1943–44* (Oxford, 1982).

8. See Kent Fedorowich, '"Toughs and Thugs": The Mazzini Society and Political Warfare amongst Italian Prisoners of War in India, 1941–43', *Intelligence and National Security*, 20 (2005).

9. Though Churchill opposed the 1935 act, it was working well before war broke out.

10. See Ronald Robinson and John Gallagher, *Africa and the Victorians: The Official Mind of British Imperialism* (London, 1961). For India as a sub-imperial actor see Robert Blyth, *The Empire of the Raj: India, Eastern Africa, and the Middle East, 1858–1947* (Basingstoke, 2002).

11. There are many books on the Gurkhas. A basic introduction is provided in John Parker, *The Gurkhas: The Inside Story of the World's Most Feared Soldiers* (London, 1999).

12. See *Indian Air Force Over Burma* (New Delhi, 1944).

13. For an interesting account see J. H. Williams, *Elephant Bill* (London, 1950).

14. See Yousuf Choudhury, *Sons of Empire: Oral History from the Bangladeshi Seamen who Served on British Ships during the 1939–45 War* (Birmingham, 1995).

15. There are many books on the INA and its leader Subhas Chandra Bose (whom SOE tried to assassinate as he passed through the Middle East). See Peter Ward Fay, *The Forgotten Army: India's Armed Struggle for Independence, 1942–1945* (Ann Arbor, Michigan, 1993); P. S. Ramu, *Azad Hind Fauj (INA) and the Freedom Movement* (Delhi, 1998); Chandar Sundaram, '"A Paper Tiger": The Indian National Army in Battle, 1944–45', *War and Society*, 13 (1995); Sisir Bose and Sugata Bose (eds), *Azad Hind: Writings and Speeches of Subhas Chandra Bose, 1941–43* (New Delhi, 2002); and Rudolf Hartog, *The Sign of the Tiger: Subhas Chandra Bose and his Indian Legion in Germany, 1942–45* (New Delhi, 2001).

16. Excellent general coverage, well linked to the independence movement in Burma, is provided in C. Bayly and T. Harper, *Forgotten Armies: The Fall of British South Asia, 1941–1945* (London, 2004). For British propaganda efforts see Sanjoy Bhattacharya, *Propaganda and Information in Eastern India, 1939–45: A Necessary Weapon of War* (Richmond, Virginia, 2001).

17. See Charles Carfrae, *Chindit Column* (London, 1985); Richard Rhodes-James, *Chindit* (London, 1960); Shelford Bidwell, *Chindit War* (London, 1979); and James Shaw, *The March Out: The End of the Chindit Adventure* (London, 1953). For the story of one of Wingate's senior commanders, see Michael Calvert, *Prisoners of Hope* (London, 1971), and Michael Calvert, *Fighting Mad* (London, 1964). For discussion of the differing assessments of Wingate's talents and tactics, see David Rooney, *Burma Victory: Imphal and Kohima March 1944 to May 1945* (London, 1992).

18. See Ursula Graham Bower, *Naga Path* (London, 1952).

19. Almost all books covering the politics of Indian decolonization, and all books assessing Churchill's political career, give considered attention to the issue of British Indian policy during the war, and Indian reaction to it. For a particularly focused account, see R. J. Moore, *Churchill, Cripps, and India, 1939–1945* (Oxford, 1979). See also William Roger Louis, 'The Second World War, India, and the Clash with Churchill, 1940–1945', in Roger Louis, *In the Name of God Go! Leopold Amery and the British Empire in the Age of Churchill* (London, 1992). For American involvement, see Kenton Clymer, *Quest for Freedom: The United States and India's Independence* (New York, 1995).

20. Ronald Lewin, *The Chief: Field Marshal Lord Wavell, Commander-in-Chief and Viceroy, 1919–1947* (London, 1980).

21. See J. F. Parry (ed.), *Burma Volunteer Air Force, 1940–1942* (London, 1998). For Canadian participation in the air war in South-East Asia, see John Gwynne-Timothy, *Burma Liberators: The Royal Canadian Air Force in South-East Asia Command*, 2 volumes (Toronto, 1991).

22. See Donovan Webster, *The Burma Road: The Epic Story of One of World War Two's Most Remarkable Endeavours* (London, 2004).

23. The latest account of the Burma campaign is John Latimer, *Burma: The Forgotten War* (London, 2004). The number of previous accounts covering the same ground suggests that, among historians at least, the 'forgotten' tag is beginning to wear as thin as the ranks of the Burma Star Association.

24. James Lunt, *A Hell of a Licking* (London, 1986).

25. The rather dispiriting saga of British planning and plans, and the way in which they often foundered, is to be found in Arthur Marder, M. Jacobsen and J. Horsfield, *Old Friends New Enemies: The Royal Navy and the Imperial Japanese Navy*, ii, *The Pacific War, 1942–45* (Oxford, 1990), and H. P. Willmott, *Graveyard of a Dozen Schemes*.

26. Excellent discussion of SEAC and its tasks, problems and personalities is to be found in Arthur Marder, M. Jacobsen and J. Horsfield, *Old Friends New Enemies: The Royal Navy and the Imperial Japanese Navy*, ii, *The Pacific War, 1942–45* (Oxford, 1990). See also Philip Ziegler (ed.), *Personal Diaries of Admiral the Lord Louis Mountbatten*.

27. See Bayly and Harper, *Forgotten Armies: The Fall of British South Asia, 1941–1945*, for an excellent guide to the BNA and the Burma home front.

28. See F. S. V. Donnison, *British Military Administration in the Far East, 1943–46* (London, 1956). *Forgotten Armies: The Fall of British South Asia, 1941–1945* (London, 2004).

Notes to Chapter 13: South-East Asia and the Far East

1. A. Danchev and D. Todman (eds), *War Diaries, 1939–1945: Field Marshal Lord Alanbrooke*.

2. There are dozens of books on the Singapore strategy and the fall of Singapore. Two of the latest are Alan Warren, *Singapore, 1942: Britain's Greatest Defeat* (London, 2002), and Colin Smith, *Singapore Burning: Heroism and Surrender in World War Two* (London, 2005). See also J. Neidpath, *The Singapore Naval Base and the Defence of Britain's Eastern Empire 1919–1941* (Oxford, 1991); and B. Farrell and S. Hunter, *Sixty Years On: The Fall of Singapore Revisited* (London, 2003), and other titles in the bibliography.

3. An excellent account is Richard Hough, *The Hunting of Force Z: The Sinking of the Prince of Wales and the Repulse* (London, 1963).

4. See the competing accounts in John Charmley, *Duff Cooper: The Authorized Biography* (London, 1986), and Brian Montgomery, *Shenton of Singapore: Governor and Prisoner of War* (London, 1984). Percival's assessment of the subject is provided in his *The War in Malaya* (London, 1949), written after his release from captivity.

5. For the political, economic and social situation on Malaya before and during the occupation, see C. Bayly and T. Harper, *Forgotten Armies: The Fall of British South*

Asia, 1941–1945 (London, 2004). Also see Nicholas Tarling, *The Cambridge History of South-East Asia* (Cambridge, 1992).

6. See Brian Farrell, *The Defence oand Fall of Singapore, 1940–42* (London, 2005).

7. See Jack Ford, 'The Forlorn Ally: The Netherlands East Indies in 1942', *War and Society*, 11 (1993).

8. See Freddie Spencer Chapman, *The Jungle is Neutral* (London, 1949), and C. Cruikshank, *SOE in the Far East* (Oxford, 1986). Terence O'Brien, *The Moonlight War: The Story of Clandestine Operations in South-East Asia, 1944–45* (London, 1987). O'Brien flew Special Duties missions all over South-East Asia in support of SOE operations. For Fleming's role, see Duff Hart-Davis, *Peter Fleming* (London, 1974). See also Andrew Gilchrist, *Bangkok Top Secret: Force 136 at War* (London, 1960). Gilchrist served in SOE India Mission's Siam Country Section. See also Neville Wylie, *Politics of Strategic Clandestine War: Special Operations Executive, 1940–1946* (London, 2006).

9. See Paul Kratoska (ed.), *Malaya and Singapore during the Japanese Occupation* (Singapore, 1995); Paul Kratsoka, *The Japanese Occupation of Malaya 1941–1945: A Social and Economic History* (London, 1998); Cheah Boon Kheng, *Red Star Over Malaya: Resistance and Social Conflict during and after the Japanese Occupation of Malaya, 1941–1946* (Singapore, 1983); Jos Kennedy, *British Civilians and the Japanese War in Malaya and Singapore, 1941–1945* (Basingstoke, 1987); and Nicholas Tarling, *A Sudden Rampage: The Japanese Occupation of South-East Asia* (London, 2000)

10. On post-war planning in the region of the lost eastern empire, see Mary C. Turnbull, 'British Planning for Post-War Malaya', *Journal of South East Asian Studies*, 5 (1974); Nicholas Tarling, '"A New and Better Cunning": British War-Time Planning for Post-War Burma', *Journal of South East Asian Studies*, 13 (1982); Tarling, '"An Empire Gem": British War-Time Planning for Post-War Burma', *Journal of South East Asian Studies*, 13 (1982); A. J. Stockwell, 'British Imperial Policy and Decolonization in Malaya, 1942–52', *Journal of Imperial and Commonwealth History*, 13 (1984); and A. J. Stockwell, 'Colonial Planning during World War Two: The Case of Malaya', *Journal of Imperial and Commonwealth History*, 2 (1974).

11. Ooi Keat Gin, *Rising Sun Over Borneo: The Japanese Occupation of Sarawak, 1941–45* (Basingstoke, 1999). See also Robert Payne, *The White Rajahs of Sarawak* (London, 1960).

12. Neville Watterson, *Borneo POW Camps: Mail of the Forces, POW, and Internees*, 2 volumes (self-published, 1989 and 1994).

13. See Tom Harrison, *World Within: A Borneo Story*; Dick Horton, *Ring of Fire: Australian Guerrilla Operations against the Japanese in World War Two* (London, 1983); Ronal Hastain, *White Coolie* (London, 1947); Colin Simpson, *Six From Borneo* (Melbourne, 1947); Maxwell Hall, *Kinabula Guerrillas: An Account of the Double Tenth 1943* (Jesselton, 1949); and Betty Jeffrey, *White Coolies* (London, 1954). For prisoners of war, see H. A. Probert, *History of Changi* (Singapore, 1965); Agnes Keith, *Three Came Home* (London, 1948); Don Wall, *Sandakan: The Last March* (New South Wales, 1988); Rohan Rivett, *Behind Bamboo* (London, 1946); J. S. Cosford, *Line of Lost Lives* (London, 1948); G. S. Carter, *A Tragedy of Borneo, 1941–1945* (Brunei, 1958) and Brian Macarthur, *Surviving the Sword: Prisoners of the Japanese, 1942–1945* (London, 2005).

14. Gavin Long, *The Final Campaigns* (Canberra, 1963); Gary Waters, *OBOE: Air*

Operations Over Borneo 1945 (Canberra, 1995); and George Odgers, *Air War Against Japan, 1943–1945* (Canberra, 1957).

15. Martin Brice, *The Royal Navy and the Sino-Japanese Incident, 1937–41* (London, 1973).

16. See Harriet Sergeant, *Shanghai* (London, 1991), and Bernard Wasserstein, *Secret War in Shanghai: Treachery, Subversion, and Collaboration in the Second World War* (London, 1998).

17. David Kranzler, *Japanese Nazis and Jews: The Jewish Refugee Community in Shanghai, 1938–1945* (New York, 1976).

18. See Philip Snow, *The Fall of Hong Kong: Britain, China, and the Japanese Occupation* (New Haven, 2003), and P. J. Melson (ed.), *White Ensign-Red Dragon: The History of the Royal Navy in Hong Kong, 1841–1997* (Hong Kong, 1997).

19. Edwin Ride, *BAAG (British Army Aid Group): Hong Kong Resistance, 1942–1945* (Hong Kong, 1981).

Notes to Chapter 14: Australia and New Zealand

1. See Annette Potts and E. Daniel Potts, *Yanks Down Under, 1941–45: The American Impact on Australia* (Melbourne, 1985), and John Hammond Moore, *Over-Paid, Over-Sexed and Over-Here* (Melbourne, 1981).

2. Alan Fitzgerald, *The Italian Farming Soldiers* (Victoria, 1981), and K. Fedorowich and B. Moore, *The British Empire and its Italian Prisoners of War, 1940–47* (Basingstoke, 2002).

3. Literature on the antipodean Dominions and the war is excellent, particularly the official histories, and numerous titles appear in the Bibliography. For a guide, see David MacIntyre, 'Australia, New Zealand and the Pacific War', in William Roger Louis and Judith Brown (eds), *The Oxford History of the British Empire*, iv, *The Twentieth Century* (Oxford, 1999). General surveys include Joan Beaumont (ed.), *Australia's War, 1939–45* (Sydney, 1996), and Gavin Long, *The Six Years War: A Concise History of Australia in the 1939–45 War* (Canberra, 1973).

4. Useful general guides to the Pacific war include David Horner, *The Second World War: The Pacific* (Oxford, 2003), and H. P. Willmott, *The Second World War in the Far East* (London, 1999). For the British Empire and Commonwealth and the war against Japan, see the official history, S. Woodburn Kirby, *The War Against Japan*, 5 volumes.

5. A great amount of the literature on Australia at war focuses on high command disputes and dilemmas. See Christopher Waters, *The Empire Fractures: Anglo-Australian Conflicts in the 1940s* (Melbourne, 1995); David Horner, *High Command: Australia's Struggle for an Independent War Strategy, 1939–1945* (Sydney, 1982); David Day, *The Great Betrayal: Britain, Australia and the Onset of the Pacific War, 1939–42* (London, 1988); and Day, *Menzies and Churchill at War* (London, 1986).

6. A. Danchev and D. Todman (eds), *War Diaries, 1939–1945: Field Marshal Lord Alanbrooke.*

7. See F. Spencer Chapman, *The Jungle is Neutral* (London, 1949).

8. Eric Feldt, *The Coast Watchers* (Melbourne, 1946).

9. See Robert Hall, *Fighters from the Fringe: Aborigines and Torres Straits Islanders Recall the Second World War* (Canberra, 1995); Hall, *The Black Diggers: Aborigines and Torres*

Straits Islanders in the Second World War (Sydney, 1989); and *Journal of Aboriginal History* special issue on the Second World War.

10. See G. Hermon Gill, *The Royal Australian Navy, 1939–1945* (Canberra, 1985), and David Stevens, (ed.), *The Royal Australian Navy in World War Two* (St Leonards, 1996).

11. For an excellent account of these corvettes, see Hugh Campbell, *Notable Service to the Empire: Australian Corvettes and the British Pacific Fleet, 1944–45*.

12. Douglas Gillison, *The Royal Australian Air Force, 1939–45* (Canberra, 1962).

13. For New Zealand see H. L. Thompson, *New Zealanders with the Royal Air Force* (Wellington, 1953); S. D. Waters, *The Royal New Zealand Navy* (Wellington, 1956); and J. M. S. Ross, *The Royal New Zealand Air Force* (Wellington, 1955).

14. See Douglas Lockwood, *Australia's Pearl Harbor: Darwin 1942* (Sydney, 1966), and Richard Connaughton, *Shrouded Secret: Japan's War on Mainland Australia 1942–44* (London, 1994). The latter book also covers the breakout of Japanese POWs from Cowra camp.

15. See Patsy Adam-Smith, *Australian Women at War* (Melbourne, 1984); Ann Howard, *You'll Be Sorry! Reflections on the Australian Women's Army Service from 1941–1945* (Sydney, 1990); and Lorna Ollif, *Women in Khaki* (Sydney, 1981).

16. See D. McIntyre, 'Paragons of Glamour: A Study of the US Military Forces in Australia 1942–45', Ph.D. Thesis, University of Queensland (1989). Also see Edward Drea, '"Great Patience is Needed": America Encounters Australia, 1942', *War and Society*, 11 (1993).

17. Sue Ebury, *Weary: The Life of Sir Edward Dunlop* (Ringwood, 1994).

18. See Michael Smith, *The Emperor's Codes: Bletchley Park and the Breaking of Japan's Secret Ciphers* (London, 2000).

19. See John Winton, *The Forgotten Fleet: The British Navy in the Pacific, 1944–1945* (London, 1969); Peter Smith, *Task Force 57: The British Pacific Fleet, 1944–45* (London, 1969); Jon Robb-Webb, '"Light Two Lanterns, the British are Coming by Sea": Royal Navy Participation in the Pacific, 1944–1945', in Greg Kennedy (ed.), *British Naval Strategy East of Suez, 1900–2000: Influences and Actions*; Arthur Marder, M. Jacobsen and J. Horsfield, *Old Friends New Enemies: The Royal Navy and the Imperial Japanese Navy*, ii, *The Pacific War, 1942–45* (Oxford, 1990); H. P. Willmott, *Graveyard of a Dozen Schemes*; H. Campbell, *Notable Service to the Empire: Australian Corvettes and the British Pacific Fleet*; and Michael Coles, 'Ernest King and the British Pacific Fleet: The Conferences at Quebec, 1944: Octagon', *Journal of Military History*, 66 (2002).

20. See Matt O'Brien, *Tasmania's War Effort, 1939–1945* (Launceston, 1946); Lloyd Robson, *A History of Tasmania*, ii, *Colony to State from the 1850s to the 1980s* (Melbourne, 1991); A. L. Graeme-Evans, *Of Storms and Rainbows: Tasmania in the New Guinea Campaign*; and Barbara Sargent, 'A Change in Perspectives: Italian Prisoners of War in Tasmania, 1943–1946', B.A. Thesis, Tasmania State Institute of Technology (1990).

21. See *Tasmania 40-Degrees South*, 33 (winter 2004–5).

22. See David Stevens, *U-Boat Far From Home: The Epic Voyage of U-862 to Australia and New Zealand* (London, 1997).

Notes to Chapter 15: The Pacific

1. This paragraph draws heavily on Donald Denoon (ed.), *The Cambridge History of the Pacific Islanders* (Cambridge, 1997), p. 296. The book provides the best non-military overview of the Pacific islands' region during the war. See also *Among Those Present: The Official History of the Pacific Islands at War* (London, 1946).
2. See for example Judith Bennett, 'Local Resource Use in the Pacific War with Japan: Logging in Western Melanesia', *War and Society*, 21 (2003).
3. See Philip Mitchell, *African Afterthoughts* (London, 1954).
4. See David Stevens, '"Send for a Naval Officer": HMAS *Adelaide* at Noumea in 1940', in D. Stevens (ed.), *The Royal Australian Navy in World War Two* (St Leonards, New South Wales, 1996).
5. For Fiji see R. A. Howlett, *The History of the Fijian Military Forces, 1939–1945* (Suva, 1948), and Asesela Ravuvu, *Fijians at War, 1939–45* (University of the South Pacific, 1988).
6. Ravuvu, *Fijians at War*.
7. Hugh Laracy (ed.), *Pacific Protest: The Maasina Rule Movement, Solomon Islands, 1944–1952* (Suva, 1983).
8. See Laurie Barber, 'The Mice That Bit: Tonga and the Pacific War', *Army Quarterly and Defence Journal*, 126 (1996).

Notes to Chapter 16: Epilogue

1. The Japanese also used this propaganda ruse to agitate Australian troops, suggesting that American forces stationed in their country were wooing Australian women whilst they were at the front in New Guinea. The British were adept at this kind of psychological warfare as well, as witness Channel 4 television's recent documentary *Sex Bomb* (in the 'Secret History' series).
2. Angus Calder's classic, *The People's War: Britain, 1939–1945*, is a massive study of war on the home front. What this book has suggested is that many aspects of the home front in Britain can be extended to the home fronts of Empire.
3. Ronald Lewin, *The Chief: Field Marshal Lord Wavell, Commander-in-Chief and Viceroy, 1919–1947* (London, 1980), p. 184.

Bibliography

Patsy Adam-Smith, *Australian Women at War* (Melbourne, 1984).

Paul Addison and Angus Calder (eds), *Time to Kill: The Soldiers Experience of War in the West, 1939–45* (London, 1997).

Manzoor Ahmad, *Indian Response to the Second World War: A Political Study* (New Delhi, 1987).

Richard Aldrich, *The Key to the South: Britain, the United States and Thailand during the Approach of the Pacific War, 1929–1942* (Oxford, 1993).

Thomas Allen and Norman Palmer, *Codename Downfall: The Secret Plan to Invade Japan* (London, 1995).

V. Alhadeff, *South Africa in Two World Wars: A Newspaper History* (Cape Town, 1979).

Among Those Present: The Official History of the Pacific Islands at War (London, 1946).

Louis Allen, *Burma: The Longest War, 1941–45* (London, 1984).

—, *Singapore, 1941–1942* (London, 1977).

—, *The End of the War in Asia* (London, 1976).

David Alvarez (ed.), *Allied and Axis Sigint in World War Two* (London, 1999).

J. Ambrose Brown, *South African Forces in World War Two*, iv, *Eagles Strike: The Campaign of the South African Air Force in Egypt, Cyrenaica, Libya, Tunisia, Tripoli and Madagascar, 1941–1943* (Cape Town, 1974).

—, *The War of a Hundred Days: Springboks in Somaliland and Abyssinia, 1940–41* (Johannesburg, 1990).

E. M. Andrews, *Isolationism and Appeasement in Australia: Reactions to the European Crises, 1935–1939* (Canberra, 1970).

—, *The Writing on the Wall: The British Commonwealth and Aggression in the East, 1931–1935* (Sydney, 1987).

S. K. B. Asante, *Pan-African Protest: West Africa and the Italo-Ethiopian Crisis, 1934–1941* (London, 1977).

S. R. Ashton and S. E. Stockwell (eds), *Imperial Policy and Colonial Practice, 1925–1945*, 2 volumes (London, 1996).

K. Attiwill, *Fortress: The Story of the Siege and Fall of Singapore* (New York, 1960).

Douglas Austin, *Malta and British Strategic Policy, 1925–1943* (London, 2004).

C. O. Badham Jackson, *Proud Story: The Official History of the Australian Comforts Fund* (Sydney, 1949).

A. J. Baker, *Eritrea, 1941* (London, 1966).

J. V. T. Baker, *The New Zealand People at War: War Economy* (Wellington, 1965).

Ba Maw, *Breakthrough in Burma: Memoirs of a Revolutionary, 1939–1946* (New Haven, 1968).

Arthur Banks, *Wings of the Dawning: The Battle for the Indian Ocean, 1939–1945* (Malvern Wells, 1996).

Fitzroy André Baptiste, *War, Co-operation, and Conflict: The European Possessions in the Caribbean, 1939–1945* (London, 1989).

Noel Barber, *Africans in Khaki* (London, 1948).

—, *Prisoner of War: The Story of British Prisoners Held by the Enemy* (London, 1944).

—, *Sinister Twilight: The Fall and Rise Again of Singapore* (London, 1968).

Glen St J. Barclay, *The Empire is Marching: A Study of the Military Effort of the British Empire, 1800–1945* (London, 1976).

A. J. Barker, *The March on Delhi* (London, 1963).

Correlli Barnett, *Engage the Enemy More Closely: The Royal Navy in the Second World War* (London, 1991).

—, *The Desert Generals* (London, 1999).

Niall Barr, *Pendulum of War: The Three Battles of Alamein* (London, 2004).

John Baylis, *Anglo-American Defence Relations, 1939–1984: The Special Relationship* (London, 1984).

Christopher Bayly and Tim Harper, *Forgotten Armies: The Fall of British South Asia, 1941–1945* (London, 2004).

Y. Bauer, *From Diplomacy to Resistance: A History of Jewish Palestine, 1939–1945* (Philadelphia, 1970).

Joan Beaumont (ed.), *Australia's War, 1939–45* (Sydney, 1996).

Roger Beaumont, *Sword of the Raj: The British Army in India, 1747–1947* (New York, 1977).

Morris Beckman, *The Jewish Brigade: An Army With Two Masters, 1944–45* (Staplehurst, 1998).

C. B. A. Behrens, *Merchant Shipping and the Demands of War* (London, 1955).

Christopher Bell, *The Royal Navy, Sea Power and Strategy between the Wars* (Basingstoke, 2000).

R. J. Bell, *Unequal Allies: Australian-American Relations and the Pacific War* (Carlton, 1977).

Malcolm Bellis, *Commonwealth Divisions, 1939–1945* (Crewe, 1999).

G. H and R. Bennett, *Survivors: British Merchant Seamen in the Second World War* (London, 1999).

R. A. R. Bent, *Ten Thousand Men of Africa: The Story of the Bechuanaland Pioneers and Gunners, 1941–46* (London, 1952).

Anthony Best, *Britain, Japan, and Pearl Harbor: Avoiding War in East Asia, 1936–1941* (London, 1995).

Mark Bevis, *British and Commonwealth Armies, 1939–43* (London, 2001).

—, *British and Commonwealth Armies, 1944–45* (London, 2002).

Sanjoy Bhattacharya, *Propaganda and Information in Eastern India, 1939–45: A Necessary Weapon of War* (Richmond, 2001).

Shelford Bidwell, *Chindit War* (London, 1979).

Alan Birch and George Endacott, *Hong Kong Eclipse* (Hong Kong, 1978).

Ian Bishop, *Fighter Boys: Saving Britain, 1940* (London, 2003).

Donald Bittner, *The Lion and the White Falcon: Britain and Iceland in the World War Two Era* (New York, 1983).).

Michael Bloch, *The Duke of Windsor's War* (London, 1982).

Brian Bond, *British Military Policy between the Two World Wars* (Oxford, 1980).

Sisir Bose and Sugata Bose (eds), *Azad Hind: Writings and Speeches of Subhas Chandra Bose, 1941–43* (New Delhi, 2002).

Ben Bosquet, *West Indian Women at War: British Racism in World War Two* (London, 1991).

John Bourne, Peter Liddle and Ian Whitehead (eds), *The Great World War, 1914–1945*, 2 volumes (London 2000 and 2001).

Marc Antonio Bragadin, *The Italian Navy in World War Two* (Maryland, Annapolis, Maryland, 1957).

E. Bradford, *Siege: Malta, 1940–1943* (London, 1985).

Martin Brayley, *The British Army, 1939–1945: The Far East* (Oxford, 2002).

W. V. Brelsford (ed.), *The Story of the Northern Rhodesia Regiment* (Lusaka, 1954).

H. J. Brennecke, *Ghost Cruiser HK33* (London, 1954).

Martin Brice, *The Royal Navy and the Sino-Japanese Incident, 1937–41* (London, 1973).

Carl Bridge (ed.), *Munich to Vietnam: Australia's Relations with Britain and the United States since the 1930s* (Carlton, 1981).

David Brown (ed.), *The Royal Navy and the Mediterranean* (London, 2002).

Judith Brown and William Roger Louis (eds), *The Oxford History of the British Empire*, iv, *The Twentieth Century* (Oxford, 1999).

Christopher Buckley, *Five Ventures: Iraq, Syria, Persia, Madagascar, Dodecanese* (London, 1977).

Brian Bunting, *The Rise of the South African Reich* (London, 1964).

K. A. Busia, *West Africa and the Issues of War* (London, 1942).

L. J. Butler, *Industrialization and the British Colonial State: West Africa, 1939–51* (London, 1997)

Raymond Callahan, *Burma, 1942–1945* (London, 1978).

—, *The Worst Disaster: The Fall of Singapore* (London, 1977).

Michael Calvert, *Fighting Mad* (London, 1964).

—, *Prisoners of Hope* (London, 1971).

P. Calvocoressi, G. Wint and J. Pritchard, *Total War: Causes and Courses of the Second World War* (London, 1989).

Hugh Campbell, *Notable Service to the Empire: Australian Corvettes and the British Pacific Fleet, 1944–45* (Garden Island, 2000).

Charles Carfrae, *Chindit Column* (London, 1985).

G. S. Carter, *A Tragedy of Borneo, 1941–1945* (Brunei, 1958).

Bernard Moses Casper, *With the Jewish Brigade* (London, 1947).

R. Citino, *Germany and South Africa in the Nazi Period* (New York, 1991).

F. A. S. Clarke and A. Haywood, *The History of the Royal West African Frontier Force* (Aldershot, 1964).

Peter Clarke, *West Africans at War, 1914–18, 1939–45* (London, 1986).

Aileen Clayton, *The Enemy is Listening: The Story of the Y Service* (London, 1993).

Anthony Clayton, *The British Empire as a Superpower, 1919–39* (London, 1986).

Nicholas Clifford, *Retreat from China: British Policy in the Far East, 1937–1941* (London, 1967).

Kenton Clymer, *Quest for Freedom: The United States and India's Independence* (New York, 1995).

Gavriel Cohen, *Churchill and Palestine, 1939–1942* (Jerusalem, 1976).

—, *The British Cabinet and Palestine, April–July 1943* (Jerusalem, 1976).

Michael Cohen, *Palestine: Retreat from the Mandate. The Making of British Policy, 1936–45* (New York, 1978).

D. H. Cole, *Imperial Military Geography: General Characteristics of the Relation in Relation to Defence* (London, 1928).

Paul Collier, *The Second World War: The Mediterranean, 1940–1945* (Oxford, 2003).

John Colvin, *Not Ordinary Men: The Battle of Kohima Re-Assessed* (London, 1994).

Richard Connaughton, *Shrouded Secret: Japan's War on Mainland Australia, 1942–44* (London, 1994).

Roy Conyers Nesbit, *An Illustrated History of the RAF* (London, 2002).

Artemis Cooper, *Cairo in the War, 1939–45* (London, 1989).

Ian Copland, *The Princes of India in the Endgame of Empire, 1919–1947* (Cambridge, 1997).

Gerald Corr, *The War of the Springing Tigers* (London, 1975).

W. J. L. Corser, *The RAF Masirah Railway* (Pinner, 1994).

J. S. Cosford, *Line of Lost Lives* (London, 1948).

Dudley Cowderoy and Roy Nesbit, *War in the Air: Rhodesian Air Force, 1935–1980* (Alberton, South Africa, 1980).

Virginia Cowles, *The Phantom Major: The Story of David Stirling and the SAS Regiment* (London, 1958).

Ian Cowman, *Dominion or Decline: Anglo-American Naval Relations in the Pacific, 1937–41* (Oxford, 1996).

Brian Crabb, *Passage to Destiny: The Sinking of the SS Khedive Ismail in the Sea War against Japan* (Stanford, 1997).

Andrew Crozier, *Appeasement and Germany's Last Bid for Colonies* (New York, 1988).

Charles Cruikshank, *SOE in the Far East* (Oxford, 1986).

—, *The Fourth Arm: Psychological Warfare, 1938–1945* (London, 1977).

Noel Crusz, *The Cocos Islands' Mutiny* (Fremantle, 2001).

J. Crwys-Williams, *A Country at War, 1939–45* (Johannesburg, 1992).

Brian Cull, *Hurricanes Over Malta, June 1940 to April 1942* (London, 2001).

—, *Malta: The Spitfire Year* (London, 1991).

—, Nicola Malizia and Frederick Galae, *Spitfires Over Sicily: The Crucial Role of the Malta Spitfires in the Battle of Sicily, January 1943-August 1943* (London, 2000).

Alex Danchev and Daniel Todman (eds), *War Diaries, 1939–1945: Field Marshal Lord Alanbrooke* (London, 2001).

Peter Davies, *The Man Behind the Bridge: Colonel Toosey and the River Kwai* (London, 1991).

David Day, *Menzies and Churchill at War: A Controversial Account of the 1941 Struggle for Power* (London, 1986).

—, *The Great Betrayal: Britain, Australia and the Onset of the Pacific War, 1939–42* (North Ryde, 1988).

I. C. B. Dear (ed.), *The Oxford Companion to the Second World War* (Oxford, 1995).

Donald Denoon, *The Cambridge History of the Pacific Islanders* (Cambridge, 1997).

Guido de Tella and D. C. Watt (eds), *Argentina between the Great Powers, 1939–1946* (Oxford, 1989)

Peter Dietz, *The British in the Mediterranean* (London, 1994).

D. Dinan, *The Politics of Persuasion: British Policy and French African Neutrality, 1940–42* (1988).

Saki Dockrill (ed.), *From Pearl Harbor to Hiroshima: The Second World War in Asia and the Pacific, 1941–45* (Basingstoke, 1994).

Klaus Dodds, *Pink Ice: Britain and the South Atlantic Empire* (London, 2002).

Peter Doling, *From Port T to RAF Gan: An Illustrated History of the British Military Bases at Addu Atoll in the Maldive Islands, 1941–76* (Bognor Regis, 2004).

F. S. V. Donnison, *British Military Administration in the Far East, 1943–46* (London, 1956).

W. A. B. Douglas, *No Higher Purpose: The Official History of the Royal Canadian Navy in the Second World War* (St Catherine's, Ontario, 2002).

—, *The Creation of a National Air Force: The Official History of the Royal Canadian Air Force* (Toronto, 1986).

—, and Brereton Greenous, *Out of the Shadows: Canada and the Second World War* (Toronto, 1977).

Kenneth Dower, *Into Madagascar* (London, 1943).

—, *The King's African Rifles in Madagascar* (Nairobi, 1943).

I. Downs, *The New Guinea Volunteer Rifles, 1939–45: A History* (1949).

A. M. Dubinsky, *The Far East in the Second World War* (Moscow, 1972).

A. G. Dudgeon, *Hidden Victory: The Battle of Habbaniya, 1941* (Stroud, 2000).

H. Duncan Hall, *North American Supply* (London, 1955).

—, and C. C. Wrigley, *Studies of Overseas Supply* (London, 1956).

Brian Dyde, *The Empty Sleeve: The Story of the West India Regiments of the British Army* (St John's, Antigua, 1997).

Charles Eade (ed.), *Secret Session Speeches by the Right Honourable Winston S. Churchill* (London, 1946).

James Eayrs, *In Defence of Canada: Appeasement and Rearmament* (Toronto, 1965).

Sue Ebury, *Weary: The Life of Sir Edward Dunlop* (Ringwood, Victoria, 1994).

Bernard Edwards, *The Quiet Heroes: British Merchant Seamen at War* (Barnsley, 2003).

Samuel Eliot Morrison, *The Rising Sun in the Pacific, 1931–April 1942* (Boston, 1951).

Matthew Elliot, *Independent Iraq: British Influence from 1941 to 1958* (London, 1996).

W. Elliott and H. Hall (eds), *The British Commonwealth at War* (New York, 1943).

Edward Ellsberg, *Under the Red Sea Sun* (New York, 1963).

Peter Elphick, *Far Eastern File: The Intelligence War in the Far East, 1930–1945* (London, 1997).

—, and Michael Smith, *Odd Man Out: The Story of the Singapore Traitor* (London, 1993).

W. H. Elsbree, *Japan's Role in Southeast Asian Nationalist Movements* (Cambridge, Massachusetts, 1953).

J. Eppler, *Operation Condor: Rommel's Spy* (London, 1977).

G. Evans and A. Brett-James, *Imphal* (London, 1962).

T. E. Evans (ed.), *The Killearn Diaries, 1934–1946* (London, 1972).

Brian Farrell, *The Defence and Fall of Singapore 1941–1942* (London, 2005).

—, and S. Hunter, *Sixty Years On: The Fall of Singapore Revisited* (St Davids, Pennsylvania, 2003).

D. A. Farnie, *East and West of Suez: The Suez Canal in History, 1854–1956* (Oxford, 1969).

Kent Fedorowich and Bob Moore (eds), *Prisoners of War and their Captors in World War Two* (Oxford, 1996).

—, *The British Empire and its Italian Prisoners of War, 1940–47* (Basingstoke, 2002).

Eric Feldt, *The Coast Watchers* (Melbourne, 1946).

Bernard Fergusson, *Beyond the Chindwin* (London, 1945).

—, *The Wild Green Earth* (London, 1946).

Robert Fisk, *In Time of War: Ireland, Ulster, and the Price of Neutrality, 1939–45* (London, 1983).

Alan Fitzgerald, *The Italian Farming Soldiers: Prisoners of War in Australia, 1941–47* (Victoria, 1981).

Flying from the Rock (Gibraltar, 1945).

M. R. D. Foot, *SOE: Special Operations Executive, 1940–1946* (London, 1984).

—, and J. M. Langley, *MI9: The British Secret Service that Fostered Escape and Evasion, 1939–1945 and its American Counterpart* (Oxford, 1979).

Douglas Ford, *British Intelligence and the War against Japan, 1937–45* (London, 2006).

James Fox, *White Mischief* (London, 1982).

Norman Franks, *The Air Battle of Imphal* (London, 1985).

Henry Frie, *Japan's Southward Advance and Australia from the Sixteenth Century to World War Two* (Honolulu, 1991).

Vivian Fuchs, *Of Ice and Men: The Story of the British Antarctic Survey, 1943–73* (Oswestry, 1982).

Patrick Furlong, *Between Crown and Swastika: The Impact of the Radical Right on the Afrikaner Nationalist Movement in the Fascist Era* (Hanover, New Hampshire, 1991).

Claudio Meunier and Carlos Garcia, *Wings of Thunder* (London, 2005).

A. B. Gaunson, *The Anglo-French Clash in Lebanon and Syria, 1940–1945* (Basingstoke, 1987).

R. J. Gavin, *Aden Under British Rule, 1839–1967* (London, 1975).

Imanuel Geiss, *War and Empire in the Twentieth Century* (Aberdeen, 1983).

Lee Geok Boi, *Syonan: Singapore under the Japanese, 1942–1945* (Singapore, 1992).

K. K. Ghosh, *The Indian National Army: Second Front of the Indian Independence Movement* (Meerut, 1969).

Andrew Gilchrist, *Bangkok Top Secret: Force 136 at War* (London, 1960).

—, *Malaya 1941: The Fall of a Fighting Empire* (London, 1992).

Douglas Gillison, *Royal Australian Air Force, 1939–45* (Canberra, 1962).

Ooi Keat Gin, *Rising Sun Over Borneo: The Japanese Occupaton of Sarawak, 1941–45* (Basingstoke, 1999).

—, *The Prospect of War: Studies in British Defence Policy, 1847–1942* (London, 1981).

J. Glendevon, *The Viceroy at Bay: Lord Linlithgow in India, 1936–1943* (London, 1971).

Ian Gleeson, *The Unknown Force: Black, Indian and Coloured Soldiers through Two World Wars* (Johannesburg, 1994).

J. B. Glubb, *War in the Desert* (London, 1950).

Philip Goodhart, *Fifty Ships That Saved the World: The Foundation of the Anglo-American Alliance* (London, 1965).

A. L. Graeme-Evans, *Of Storms and Rainbows: Tasmania in the New Guinea*

Ursula Graham Bower, *Naga Path* (London, 1952).

J. L. Granatstein, *Canada's War: The Politics of the Mackenzie King Government, 1939–1945* (Toronto, 1975).

—, *How Britain's Weakness Forced Canada into the Arms of the United States* (Toronto, 1989).

—, *Victory 1945: Canadians from War to Peace* (Toronto, 1995).

—, and R. D. Cuff, *Ties That Bind: Canadian-American Relations in Wartime from the Great War to the Cold War* (Toronto, 1977).

—, and J. M. Hitsman, *Broken Promises: A History of Conscription in Canada* (Toronto, 1976).

—, and Desmond Morton, *A Nation Forged in Fire: Canadians and the Second World War 1939–1945* (Toronto, 1989).

Ian Lyall Grant, *Burma: The Turning Point* (Chichester, 1993).

Shelagh Grant, *Sovereignty or Security? Government Policy in the Canadian North, 1936–1950* (Vancouver, 1988).

B. Gray, *Basotho Soldiers in Hitler's War* (Maseru: Government Press, 1953).

Jack Greene Alessandro Massignani, *The Naval War in the Mediterranean, 1940–1943* (London, 1998).

P. R. Greenough, *Prosperity and Misery in Modern Bengal: The Famine of 1943–44* (Oxford, 1982).

Jeffrey Grey, *A Military History of Australia* (Cambridge, 1990).

Kevin Grundy, *Soldiers Without Politics: Blacks in the South African Armed Forces* (University of California Press, 1983).

Philip Guedalla, *Middle East, 1940–1942: A Study in Air Power* (London, 1944).

Dennis Gunton, *The Penang Submarines* (Penang, 1970).

P. S. Gupta (ed.), *Towards Freedom: Documents on the Movement for Independence in India, 1943–44* (Delhi, 1997).

John Gwynne-Timothy, *Burma Liberators: The RCAF in SEAC*, 2 volumes (Toronto, 1991).

Paul Haggie, *Britannia at Bay: The Defence of the British Empire against Japan, 1931–1941* (Oxford, 1981).

Maxwell Hall, *Kinabula Guerrillas: An Account of the Double Tenth 1943* (Jesselton, 1949).

Robert Hall, *Fighters from the Fringe: Aborigines and Torres Straits Islanders Recall the Second World War* (Canberra, 1995).

Richard Hallion, *Strike from the Sky: The History of Battlefield Air Attack, 1911–1945* (Shrewsbury, 1989).

—, *The Black Diggers: Aborigines and Torres Straits Islanders in the Second World War* (Sydney, 1989).

Ian Hamill, *The Strategic Illusion: The Singapore Strategy and the Defence of Australia and New Zealand* (Singapore, 1981).

John Hamilton, *War Bush: 81 (West African) Division in Burma, 1943–1945* (Wilby, 2001).

John Hammond Moore, *Over-Paid, Over-Sexed and Over-Here* (Melbourne, 1981).

Gerald Hanley, *Monsoon Victory* (London, 1946).

Kathleen Harland, *The Royal Navy in Hong Kong since 1841* (Liskeard, 1985).

C. J. Harris, *War at Sea: South African Maritime Operations during World War Two* (Johannesburg, 1991).

Mark Harisson, *Medicine and Victory: British Military Medicine in the Second World War* (Oxford, 2004).

Frank Harrison, *Tobruk: The Great Siege Reassessed* (London, 1997).

Tom Harrisson, *World Within: A Borneo Story* (London, 1959).

Rudolf Hartog, *The Sign of the Tiger: Subhas Chandra Bose and his Indian Legion in Germany, 1942–45* (New Delhi, 2001).

A. D. Harvey, *Collision of Empires: Britain in Three World Wars, 1793–1945* (London, 1992).

Paul Hasluck, *Australia in the War of 1939–1945* (Canberra, 1952–70).

Ronal Hastain, *White Coolie* (London, 1947).

F. J. Hatch, *The Aerodrome of Democracy: Canada and the British Commonwealth Air Training Plan, 1939–1945* (Ottawa, 1983).

Milan Hauner, *India in Axis Strategy: Germany, Japan and Indian Nationalists in the Second World War* (Stuttgart, 1981).

Ian Hawkins, *Destroyers: An Anthology of First-Hand Accounts of the War at Sea, 1939–1945* (London, 2004).

Ian Hay, *Malta, The Unconquered Isle: The Story of Malta* (London, 1943).

G. Hermon Gill, *The Royal Australian Navy, 1939–1945* (Canberra, 1985).

James Holland, *Fortress Malta: An Island under Siege, 1940–1943* (London, 2003).

Rob Holland, *Britain and the Commonwealth Alliance, 1918–1939* (London, 1981).

G. Hogan, *Malta: The Triumphant Years, 1940–1943* (London, 1978).

Richard Hough, *The Hunting of Force Z: The Sinking of the Prince of Wales and the Repulse* (London, 1963).

—, *The Longest Battle: The War at Sea, 1939–45* (London, 1986).

Eugene Hevesi, *Hitler's Plan for Madagascar* (New York, 1941).

F. H. Hinsley, *British Intelligence in the Second World War* (London, 1993).

—, and Alan Stripp (eds), *Code-Breakers: The Inside Story of Bletchley Park* (Oxford, 1993).

David Horner, *High Command: Australia's Struggle for an Independent War Strategy, 1939–1941* (St Leonard's, New South Wales, 1982).

—, *The Second World War: The Pacific* (Oxford, 2003).

Dick Horton, *Ring of Fire: Australian Guerrilla Operations against the Japanese in World War Two* (London, 1983).

Ann Howard, *You'll Be Sorry! Reflections on the Australian Women's Army Service from 1941–1945* (Sydney, 1990).

Michael Howard, *The Mediterranean Strategy in the Second World War* (London, 1968).

Stephen Howarth (ed.), *Men of War: Great Naval Leaders of World War Two* (London, 1992).

R. A. Howlett, *The History of the Fiji Military Forces, 1939–45* (London, 1948).

Edwin Hoyt, *Raider 16* (New York, 1970).

F. G. Hutchins, *India's Revolution: Gandhi and the Quit India Movement* (Cambridge, Massachusetts, 1973).

H. Montgomery Hyde, *British Air Policy between the Wars, 1918–1939* (London, 1976).

John Iliffe, *A Modern History of Tanganyika* (Cambridge, 1979).

Geoffrey Inchbald, *Imperial Camel Corps* (London, 1970).

Indian Air Force Over Burma (New Delhi, 1944).

David Innes, *Beaufighters Over Burma* (London, 1985).

Bernard Ireland, *The War in the Mediterranean, 1940–1943* (London, 1993).

A. Iriye, *Origins of the Second World War in Asia and the Pacific* (London, 1987).

Ashley Jackson, *Botswana, 1939–45: An African Country at War* (Oxford, 1999).

—, *War and Empire in Mauritius and the Indian Ocean* (Basingstoke, 2001).

William Jackson, *Britain's Triumph and Decline in the Middle East: Military Campaigns 1919 to the Present Day* (London, 1996).

James Jankowski, *Redefining the Egyptian Nation, 1930–1945* (Cambridge, 1995).

Charles Jeffries, *Whitehall and the Colonial Service: An Administrative Memoir, 1939–1956* (London, 1972).

Betty Jeffrey, *White Coolies* (London, 1954).

Alan Jeffreys, *The British Army in the Far East, 1941–45* (Oxford, 2005).

F. C. Jones, *Japan's New Order in East Asia: Its Rise and Fall, 1937–1945* (London, 1974).

Matthew Jones, *Britain, the United States and the Mediterranean War, 1942–44* (Basingstoke, 1995).

Robert Jones, *The Road to Russia* (Norman, Oklahoma, 1969).

Robin Kay (ed.), *The Australian–New Zealand Agreement, 1944* (Wellington, 1972).

John Keegan (ed.), *Churchill's Generals* (London, 1991).

John Keene (ed.), *South Africa in World War Two* (Cape Town, 1995).

George Kelling, *Countdown to Rebellion: British Policy in Cyprus, 1939–1955* (Westport, Connecticut, 1990).

Saul Kelly, *Cold War in the Desert: Britain, the United States and the Italian Colonies, 1945–52* (Basingstoke, 2000).

—, *The Hunt for Zerzura: The Lost Oasis and the Desert War* (London, 2002).

Terence Kelly, *Battle for Palembang* (London, 1985).

—, *Hurricane and Spitfire Pilots at War* (London, 1986).

—, *Hurricane in Sumatra* (London, 1991).

—, *Hurricanes Over the Jungle* (London, 1977).

Greg Kennedy (ed.), *British Naval Strategy East of Suez, 1900–2000: Influences and Actions* (London, 2004).

—, and Keith Neilson (eds), *Anglo-American Strategic Relations and the Far East, 1933–1939* (London, 2002).

—, and Keith Neilson (eds), *Far Flung Lines: Essays on Imperial Defence in Honour of Donald Mackenzie Schurman* (London, 1997).

—, and Keith Neilson (eds), *The Merchant Marine in International Affairs, 1850–1950* (London, 2000).

Jos Kennedy, *British Civilians and the Japanese War in Malaya and Singapore, 1941–1945* (Basingstoke, 1987).

Paul Kennedy, *Strategy and Diplomacy, 1870–1945: Eight Studies* (London, 1983).

—, *The Realities Behind Diplomacy: Background Influences on British External Policy, 1865–1980* (London, 1981).

—, *The Rise and Fall of British Naval Mastery* (London, 1976).

John Kent, *British Imperial Strategy and the Origins of the Cold War, 1944–1949* (London, 1993).

—, *Internationalization of Colonialism: Britain, France, and Black Africa, 1939–56* (Oxford, 1992).

—, (ed.), *British Egypt and the Defence of the Middle East* (London, 1998).

R. T. Kerslake, *Time and the Hour: Nigeria, East Africa and the Second World War* (London, 1997).

Cheah Boon Kheng, *Red Star Over Malaya: Resistance and Social Conflict during and after the Japanese Occupation of Malaya, 1941–1946* (Singapore, 1983).

David Killingray and David Omissi (eds), *Guardians of Empire: The Armed Forces and the Colonial Powers, c. 1700–1964* (Manchester, 1999).

David Killingray and Richard Rathbone (eds), *Africa and the Second World War* (London, 1986).

Robin Kilson and Robert King (eds), *The Statecraft of British Imperialism: Essays in Honour of William Roger Louis* (London, 1999).

Paul Kingston, R. G. Tiedemann and Nicholas Westcott (eds), *Managed Economies in World War Two* (London, 1991).

Clifford Kinvig, *River Kwai Railway: The Story of the Burma–Siam Railroad* (London, 1992).

George Kirk, *Survey of International Affairs, 1939–1946: The Middle East in the War* (London, 1952).

Chan Lan Kit-Ching, *China, Britain, and Hong Kong, 1895–1945* (Hong Kong, 1990).

Martin Kolinsky, *Britain's War in the Middle East: Strategy and Diplomacy, 1936–42* (Basingstoke, 1999).

David Kranzler, *Japanese Nazis and Jews: The Jewish Refugee Community in Shanghai, 1938–1945* (New York, 1976).

Paul Kratoska, *The Japanese Occupation of Malaya, 1941–1945: A Social and Economic History* (London, 1998).

—, (ed.), *Malaya and Singapore during the Japanese Occupation* (Singapore, 1995).

Hugh Laracy (ed.), *Pacific Protest: The Maasina Rule Movement, Solomon Islands, 1944–1952* (Suva, Fiji, 1983).

John Latimer, *Burma: The Forgotten War* (London, 2004).

Nancy Lawler, *Soldiers, Airmen, Spies, and Whisperers: The Gold Coast in World War Two* (Athens, Ohio, 2002).

J. C. Lebra (ed.), *Japanese-Trained Armies in Southeast Asia: Independence and Volunteer Forces in World War Two* (Hong Kong, 1977).

—, *Japan's Greater East Asia Co-Prosperity Sphere in World War Two* (Kuala Lumpur, 1975).

—, *Jungle Alliance: Japan and the Indian National Army* (Singapore, 1971).

Bradford Lee, *Britain and the Sino-Japanese War, 1937–1939: A Study in the Dilemmas of British Decline* (Stanford, California, 1973).

J. M. Lee and Martin Petter, *The Colonial Office, War and Development Policy: Organization and Planning of a Metropolitan Initiative, 1939–1945* (London, 1982).

J. Lee Ready, *Forgotten Allies: The Military Contribution of the Colonies, Exiled Governments and Lesser Powers to the Allied Victory in World War Two*, 2 volumes (Jefferson, North Carolina, 1985).

—, *World War Two Nation by Nation* (London, 1995).

G. Lenczowski, *Russia and the West in Iran, 1918–1948: A Study in Big Power Rivalry* (New York, 1949).

H. T. Lenton, *British Battleships and Aircraft Carriers* (London, 1972).

Ronald Lewin, *Slim: The Standardbearer. A Biography of Field-Marshal Viscount Slim* (London, 1976).

—, *The Chief: Field Marshal Lord Wavell, Commander-in-Chief and Viceroy, 1919–1947* (London, 1980).

Joanna Lewis, *Empire State-Building: War and Welfare in Kenya, 1925–1952* (Oxford, 2000).

Julian Lewis, *Changing Direction: British Military Planning for Post-War Strategic Defence, 1942–1947* (London, 1988).

Oliver Lindsay, *At the Going Down of the Sun* (London, 1981).

—, *The Battle for Hong Kong, 1941–1945* (London, 2005).

—, *The Lasting Honour* (London, 1978).

E. M. H. Lloyd, *Food and Inflation in the Middle East, 1940–45* (Stanford, California, 1956).

Hugh Lloyd, *Briefed to Attack: Malta's Part in African Victory* (London, 1949)

David Lloyd-Owen, *The Long Range Desert Group, 1940–45: Providence Their Guide* (Barnsley, 1980).

Douglas Lockwood, *Australia's Pearl Harbor: Darwin 1942* (Sydney, 1966).

Eric Lomax, *The Railway Man* (1995).

Gavin Long, *The Final Campaigns* (Canberra, 1963).

—, *The Six Years War: A Concise History of Australia in the 1939–45 War* (Canberra, 1973).

Cliff Lord and David Birtles, *The Armed Forces of Aden, 1839–1967* (Solihull, 2000).

Peter Lowe, *Great Britain and the Origins of the Pacific War: A Study of British Policy in Asia, 1937–1941* (Oxford, 1977).

Jean Lugol, *Egypt in World War Two* (Cairo, 1945).

James Lunt, *A Hell of a Licking: The Retreat from Burma, 1941–42* (London, 1986).

—, *Imperial Sunset: Frontier Soldiering in the Twentieth Century* (London, 1981).

—, *The Arab Legion, 1923–1957* (London, 1999).

Robert Lyman, *Slim, Master of War: Burma and the Birth of Modern Warfare* (London, 2004).

Callum MacDonald, *The Lost Battle: Crete 1941* (London, 1993).

George Macdonald Fraser, *Quartered Safe Out Here: A Recollection of the War in Burma* (London, 1992).

Dudley McCarthy, *South West Pacific Area: First Year – Kokoda to Wau. Official History of Australia in the War of 1939–45* (Canberra, 1959).

John McCarthy, *A Last Call of Empire* (Canberra, 1988).

—, *Australia and Imperial Defence, 1918–1939: A Study in Air and Sea Power* (St Lucia, Queensland, 1976).

—, and J. Robertson, *Australian War Strategy, 1939–1945: A Documentary History* (St Lucia, Queensland, 1985).

Gavan McCormack and Hank Nelson (eds), *The Burma–Thailand Railway: Memory and History* (St Leonard's, New South Wales, 1993).

Alfred McCoy, *Asia under Japanese Occupation: Transition and Transformation* (New Haven, 1980).

Ian McGibbon (ed.), *Oxford Companion to New Zealand Military History* (Auckland, 2000).

—, *Blue-Water Rationale: The Naval Defence of New Zealand, 1919–42* (Wellington, 1981).

M. McKernon, *All In! Australia during the Second World War* (Melbourne, 1983).

Malcolm McKinnon, *Independence and Foreign Policy, New Zealand in the World since 1935* (Auckland, 1993).

Donald Macintyre, *Fighting Admiral: The Life of Admiral of the Fleet Sir James Somerville* (London, 1961).

—, *The Battle for the Mediterranean* (London, 1964).

W. D. McIntyre, *Background to the Anzus Pact: Policy-Making, Strategy and Diplomacy, 1945–1955* (London, 1995).

—, *New Zealand Prepares for War: Defence Policy, 1919–1939* (Christchurch, 1988).

—, *The Rise and Fall of the Singapore Naval Base, 1919–1942* (London, 1979).

David Mackenzie, *Inside the North Atlantic Triangle: Canada and the Entrance of Newfoundland into the Confederation, 1939–1949* (Toronto, 1986).

Francine McKenzie, *Redefining the Bonds of Commonwealth, 1939–1948: The Politics of Preference* (Basingstoke, 2002).

Brian MacArthur, *Surviving the Sword: Prisoners of the Japanese, 1942–1945* (London, 2005).

J. F. Macdonald, *The War History of Southern Rhodesia, 1939–45*, 2 volumes (Salisbury, 1947 and 1950).

John Mackenzie (ed.), *Popular Imperialism and the Military, 1850–1950* (Manchester, 1992).

J. W. E. Mackenzie, *Third Battalion The Northern Rhodesia Regiment: Burma, 1945–1946* (Lusaka, 1946).

Harold Macmillan, *The Blast of War, 1939–45* (London, 1967).

A. F. Madden and W. H. Morris-Jones (eds), *Australia and Britain: Studies in a Changing Relationship* (London, 1980).

Nicholas Mansergh, *Survey of British Commonwealth Affairs: Problems of War-Time Co-operation and Post-War Change, 1939–1952* (London, 1958).

Arthur Marder, *From the Dardanelles to Oran: Studies of the Royal Navy in War and Peace* (London, 1974).

—, *Operation Menace: The Dakar Expedition and the Dudley North Affair* (London, 1976).

—, *Old Friends, New Enemies: The Royal Navy and the Imperial Japanese Navy*, i, *Strategic Illusions, 1936–41* (Oxford, 1981).

—, M. Jacobsen and J. Horsfield, *Old Friends New Enemies: The Royal Navy and the Imperial Japanese Navy*, ii, *The Pacific War, 1942–45* (Oxford, 1990).

Henry Martin, *Eagles Victorious: The Operations of the South African Forces Over the Mediterranean and Europe, in Italy, the Balkans and the Aegean, and from Gibraltar to West Africa* (Cape Town, 1977).

—, *South Africa at War: Military and Industrial Organization and Operations in Connection with the Conduct of the War, 1939–1945* (Cape Town, 1979).

John Masters, *The Road Past Mandalay* (London, 1967).

Ali Mazrui (ed.), *Africa and the Second World War: Reports and Papers of a UNESCO Symposium* (Libya, 1980).

P. J. Melson (ed.), *White Ensign-Red Dragon: The History of the Royal Navy in Hong Kong, 1841–1997* (Hong Kong, 1997).

L. D. Meo, *Japan's Radio War on Australia, 1941–1945* (Melbourne, 1968).

Martin Middlebrook and Pat Mahoney, *Battleship: The Prince of Wales and Repulse* (London, 1977).

T. B. Millar, *Australia in Peace and War: External Relations, 1788–1977* (London, 1978).

A. C. Millspaugh, *Americans in Persia* (Washington, 1946).

Marc Milner, *North Atlantic Run: The Royal Canadian Navy and the Battle for the Convoys* (Toronto, 1985).

—, *The U-Boat Hunters: The Royal Canadian Navy and the Offensive against Germany's Submarines* (Toronto, 1994).

Alan Milward, *War, Economy and Society, 1939–45* (Harmondsworth, 1977).

Anthony Mockler, *Haile Selassie's War* (Oxford, 1984).

Ulrich Mohr, *Atlantis: The Story of a German Surface Raider* (London, 1955).

Jacques Mondal and Paul Aupahn, *The French Navy in World War Two* (Annapolis, Maryland, 1952).

M. Monteith, *First Battalion The Northern Rhodesia Regiment, Ceylon to the Chindwin, 1944* (Lusaka, 1946).

Mike Morgan, *Sting of the Scorpion: The Inside Story of the Long Range Desert Group* (Stroud, 2000).

R. J. Moore, *Churchill, Cripps and India, 1939–1945* (Oxford, 1979).

Thomas Moreman, *The Jungle, the Japanese and the British Commonwealth Armies, 1941–1945: Fighting Methods, Doctrine and Training for Jungle Warfare* (London, 2005).

—, *The Jungle, Japanese and the Sepoy: British Armed Forces and Jungle Warfare in South East Asia, 1941–45* (London, 2002).

D. J. Morgan, *The Official History of Colonial Development: The Origins of British Aid Policy, 1925–1945*, 5 volumes (London, 1980).

J. W. Morley (ed.), *The Fateful Choice: Japan's Advance into South East Asia, 1939–41* (New York, 1980).

Kate Morris, *British Techniques of Public Relations and Propaganda for Mobilizing East and Central Africa during World War Two* (Lampeter, 2000).

J. Moyse-Bartlett, *The King's African Rifles: A Study in the Military History of East and Central Africa, 1890–1945* (Aldershot, 1956).

Malcolm Murfett, *Fool-Proof Relations: The Search for Anglo-American Naval Cooperation during the Chamberlain Years, 1937–40* (Singapore, 1984).

R. G. Neale et al. (eds), *Documents on Australian Foreign Policy, 1937–1949* (Canberra, 1976).

Peter Neary, *Newfoundland in the North Atlantic World, 1929–1949* (Montreal, 1988).

J. Neidpath, *The Singapore Naval Base and the Defence of Britain's Far Eastern Empire, 1919–41* (Oxford, 1981).

David Nelson, *The Story of Changi, Singapore* (Perth, 1973).

Hank Nelson, *Prisoners of War: Australians under Nippon* (Sydney, 1985).

Agnes Newton Keith, *Three Came Home* (London, 1948).

Thakin Nu, *Burma under the Japanese: Pictures and Portraits* (London, 1954).

John Nunneley, *Tales from the King's African Rifles: A Last Flourish of Empire* (London, 1998).

Balfour Oatts, *The Jungle in Arms* (London, 1962).

Matt O'Brien, *Tasmania's War Effort, 1939–1945* (Launceston, 1946).

Terence O'Brien, *The Moonlight War: Clandestine Operations in South-East Asia, 1944–45* (London, 1987).

George Odgers, *Air War against Japan, 1943–1945* (Canberra, 1957).

Lorna Ollif, *Women in Khaki* (Sydney, 1981).

G. O. Olusanya, *The Second World War and Politics in Nigeria, 1939–53* (Lagos, 1973).

David Omissi, *Air Power and Colonial Control: The Royal Air Force, 1919–1939* (Manchester, 1990).

Vincent Orange, *A Biography of Air Chief Marshal Sir Arthur Coningham* (London, 1990).

—, *A Biography of Air Chief Marshal Sir Keith Park* (London, 1984).

Ritchie Ovendale, *'Appeasement' and the English-Speaking World: Britain, the United States, the Dominions and the Policy of 'Appeasement', 1937–1939* (Cardiff, 1975).

—, *Britain, the United States and the End of the Palestine Mandate, 1941–1948* (London, 1989).

Christopher Owen, *The Rhodesia African Rifles* (London, 1970).

Frank Owen, *The Campaign in Burma* (London, 1946).

S. W. C. Pack, *Cunningham: The Commander* (London, 1974).

Malcolm Page, *KAR: A History of the King's African Rifles* (London, 1998).

John Parker, *The Gurkhas: The Inside Story of the World's Most Feared Soldiers* (London, 1999).

J. F. Parry (ed.), *Burma Volunteer Air Force, 1940–1942* (1998).

Timothy Parsons, *The African Rank-and-File: Social Implications of Colonial Military Service in the King's African Rifles, 1902–1964* (Oxford, 1999).

Peter Partner, *Arab Voices: The BBC Arabic Service, 1938–1988* (London, 1988).

Stanley Pavillard, *Bamboo Doctor* (1960).

D. J. Payton-Smith, *Oil: A Study in Wartime Policy and Administration* (London, 1971).

Robert Pearce, *The Turning Point: British Colonial Policy, 1938–1948* (London, 1982).

Arthur Percival, *The War in Malaya* (London, 1949).

Roger Perkins, *Regiments: Regiments and Corps of the British Empire and Commonwealth, 1758–1993: A Critical Biography of their Published Histories* (Newton Abbot, 1994).

F. W. Perry, *The Commonwealth Armies: Manpower and Organization in Two World Wars* (Manchester, 1988).

C. H. Philips and M. D. Wainwright (eds), *The Partition of India: Policies and Perspectives, 1935–47* (London, 1970).

Barrie Pitt, *Churchill and the Generals* (London, 1981).

Jonathan Pittaway and Craig Fourie, *LRDG Rhodesian: Rhodesians in the Long Range Desert Group* (Johannesburg, 2002).

William Platt, *Operations of East Africa Command, 1940–43* (Nairobi, 1943).

I. S. O Playfair, C. J. C. Malony and W. Jackson, *The Mediterranean and Middle East*, 6 volumes (London, 1954–88).

Ken Post, *Strike the Iron: A Colony at War, 1939–1945*, 2 volumes (New Jersey, 1981).

Annette Potts and E. Daniel Potts, *Yanks Down Under, 1941–45: The American Impact on Australia* (Melbourne, 1985).

Bisheshwar Prasad (ed.), *Official History of the Indian Armed Forces in the Second World War* (New Delhi, 1953–60).

S. N. Prasad, K. D. Bhargava and P. N. Khera (eds), *The Reconquest of Burma* (Delhi, 1958).

Lawrence Pratt, *East of Malta, West of Suez: Britain's Mediterranean Crisis, 1936–39* (Cambridge, 1975).

A. R. Prest, *War Economies of Primary Producing Countries* (Cambridge, 1948).

Henry Probert, *The Forgotten Air Force: The Royal Air Force in the War against Japan, 1941–1945* (London, 1995).

—, *History of Changi* (Singapore, 1965).

Michael Pye, *The King Over the Water: The Windsors in the Bahamas, 1940–45* (London, 1981).

P. S. Ramu, *Azad Hind Fauj (INA) and the Freedom Movement* (Delhi, 1998).

Asesela Ravuvu, *Fijians at War, 1939–45* (University of the South Pacific, 1988).

Trevor Reese, *Australia, New Zealand, and the United States: A Survey of International Relations, 1941–1968* (London, 1969).

Lord Rennell of Rodd, *British Military Administration in Africa during the Second World War, 1941–1947* (London, 1948).

David Reynolds, *In Command of History: Churchill Fighting and Writing the Second World War* (London, 2004).

Richard Rhodes-James, *Chindit* (London, 1960).

E. Rhodes-Wood, *War History of the Royal Pioneer Corps, 1939–1945* (Aldershot, 1960).

Edwin Ride, *BAAG (British Army Aid Group): Hong Kong Resistance, 1942–1945* (Hong Kong, 1981).

Rohan Rivett, *Behind Bamboo* (London, 1946).

Andrew Roberts, *Eminent Churchillians* (London, 1994).

M. Roberts and A. E. G. Trollip, *The South African Opposition, 1939–1945: An Essay in Contemporary History* (London, 1947).

John Robertson, *Australia at War, 1939–1945* (Melbourne, 1981).

K. G. Robertson, *War, Resistance and Intelligence: Collected Essays in Honour of M. R. D. Foot* (London, 1999).

Lloyd Robson, *A History of Tasmania*, ii, *Colony to State from the 1850s to the 1980s* (Melbourne, 1991).

William Roger Louis, *Imperialism at Bay, 1941–45: The United States and the Decolonization of the British Empire* (Oxford, 1977).

Anthony Rogers, *Battle Over Malta: Aircraft Losses and Crash Sites, 1940–1942* (Stroud, 2000).

Bernhard Rogge, *Under Ten Flags: The Story of the German Commerce Raider Atlantis* (London, 1955).

Jürgen Rohwer, *War at Sea, 1939–1945* (London, 1996).

David Rooney, *Burma Victory: Imphal and Kohima, March 1944 to May 1945* (London, 1992).

Sonya Rose, *Which People's War? National Identity and Citizenship in Britain, 1939–1945* (Oxford, 2003).

Eric Rosenthal, *Japan's Bid for Africa: Including the Story of the Madagascar Campaign* (Johannesburg, 1944).

Aviel Roshwald, *Estranged Bedfellows: Britain and France in the Middle East during the Second World War* (Oxford, 1990).

Stephen Roskill, *A Merchant Fleet in War, 1939–1945* (London, 1962).

—, *A Merchant Navy at War: Alfred Holt and Co., 1939–1945* (London, 1962).

—, *Churchill and the Admirals* (London, 1977).

—, *The War At Sea, 1939–1945*, 3 volumes (London, 1954–60).

—, *The White Ensign: The British Navy at War, 1939–1945* (Annapolis, Maryland, 1960).

Andrew Ross, *Armed and Ready: The Industrial Development and Defence of Australia, 1900–1945* (Sydney, 1995).

J. M. S. Ross, *The Royal New Zealand Air Force* (Wellington, 1955).

Gerry Rubin, *Durban 1942: A British Troopship Revolt* (London, 1992).

H. St George and Denis Richards, *The Royal Air Force 1939–1945*, 4 volumes (London, 1953–75).

J. J. Sadkovich, *The Italian Navy in World War Two* (Westport, Connecticut, 1994).

Beryl Salt, *A Pride of Eagles: The Definitive History of the Rhodesian Air Force, 1920–1980* (Johannesburg, 2001).

Kay Saunders, *War on the Home Front: State Intervention in Queensland, 1938–1948* (St Lucia, 1993).

A. M. Saville, *German Submarines in the Far East* (Annapolis, Maryland, 1961).

W. Schmokel, *Dream of Empire: German Colonialism, 1919–45* (New Haven, 1964).

B. B. Schofield, *British Sea Power: Naval Policy in the Twentieth Century* (London, 1967).

Chris Shores, *Dust Clouds in the Middle East: The Air War for East Africa, Iraq, Syria, Iran and Madagascar, 1940–1942* (London, 1996).

Anil Seal (ed.), *The Decline, Revival, and Fall of the British Empire: The Ford Lectures and Other Essays* (Cambridge, 1982).

Harriet Sergeant, *Shanghai* (London, 1991).

Aron Shai, *Britain and China, 1941–47: Imperial Momentum* (London, 1984).

Peter Shankland and Anthony Hunter, *Malta Convoy* (London, 1961).

James Shaw, *The March Out: The End of the Chindit Adventure* (London, 1953).

W. B. K. Shaw, *The Long Range Desert Group* (London, 1945).

M. C. Shepherd, *The Malay Regiment, 1933–1947* (Kuala Lumpur, 1947).

Marika Sherwood, *Many Struggles: West Indian Workers and Service Personnel in Britain, 1939–45* (London, 1985).

O. J. E. Shiroya, *Kenya and World War Two* (Nairobi, 1985).

Christopher Shores and Brian Cull, *Bloody Shambles: The Defence of Sumatra to the Fall of Burma, 1942*, 2 volumes (London, 1992).

Josef Silverstein (ed.), *Southeast Asia in World War Two* (New Haven, 1966).

Colin Simpson, *Six from Borneo* (Melbourne, 1947).

Kelvin Singh, *Race and Class: Struggles in a Colonial State, Trinidad, 1917–1945* (Mona, Jamaica, 1994).

Clarmont Skrine, *World War in Iran* (London, 1962).

Field Marshal Viscount Slim, *Defeat into Victory* (London, 1956).

Colin Smith, *Singapore Burning: Heroism and Surrender in World War Two* (London, 2005).

Peter Smith, *Task Force 57: The British Pacific Fleet, 1944–45* (London, 1969).

David Smurthwaite (ed.), *The Forgotten War: The British Army in the Far East, 1941–1945* (London, 1992).

Gordon Smith, *The War at Sea: Royal and Dominion Navy Actions in World War Two* (London, 1989).

Michael Smith, *Station X: The Codebreakers of Bletchley Park* (London, 1998).

—, *The Emperor's Codes: Bletchley Park and the Breaking of Japan's Secret Ciphers* (London, 2000).

Peter Smith, *Pedestal: The Malta Convoy of August 1942* (London, 1987).

R. B. Smith, *British Policy and the Transfer of Power in Asia: Documentary Perspectives* (London, 1988).

Philip Snow, *The Fall of Hong Kong: Britain, China and the Japanese Occupation* (New Haven, 2003).

Christopher Somerville, *Our War: How the British Commonwealth Fought the Second World War* (London, 1998)

Freddie Spencer Chapman, *The Jungle is Neutral* (London, 1949).

Tony Spooner, *Supreme Gallantry: Malta's Role in the Allied Victory, 1939–1945* (London, 1996).

C. P. Stacey, *Arms, Men, and Government: The War Politics of Canada, 1939–1945* (Ottawa, 1970).

—, *Canada and the British Army, 1846–1971: A Study in the Practice of Responsible Government* (Toronto, 1963).

David Stafford, *Camp X* (Toronto, 1986).

Freya Stark, *Dust in the Lion's Claw: Autobiography, 1929–1945* (London, 1961).

Statistical Abstract of the Commonwealth, 1936–1945 (Cmd 7224).

David Stevens (ed.), *Reluctant Nation: Australia and the Allied Defeat of Japan, 1942–45* (Melbourne, 1992).

—, *The Royal Australian Navy in World War Two* (St Leonards, New South Wales, 1996).

—, *U-Boat Far From Home: The Epic Voyage of U-862 to Australia and New Zealand* (London, 1997).

R. A. Stewart, *Sunrise at Abadan: The British and Soviet Invasion of Iran, 1941* (New York, 1988).

A. J. Stockwell (ed.), *Malaya, 1942–1947* (London, 1995).

—, and A. N. Porter, *British Imperial Policy and Decolonization*, i, *1938–64* (London, 1987).

Alan Stripp, *Codebreaker in the Far East: How the British Cracked Japan's Top Secret Military Codes* (Oxford, 1995).

Julie Summer, *The Colonel of Tamarkan: Philip Toosey and the Bridge on the River Kwai* (London, 2005).

Janice Summerby, *Native Soldiers: Foreign Battlefields* (Ottawa, 1996).

Arthur Swinson, *Kohima* (London, 1966).

Nicholas Tarling, *A Sudden Rampage: The Japanese Occupation of South-East Asia* (London, 2000).

—, *Britain, Southeast Asia and the Onset of the Pacific War* (Cambridge, 1996).

—, *The Cambridge History of South-East Asia* (Cambridge, 1992).

—, *The Fourth Anglo-Burmese War: Britain and the Independence of Burma* (Gaya, India, 1987).

Nancy Taylor, *The Home Front: The New Zealand People at War*, 2 volumes (Wellington, 1986).

Robert Taylor, *Marxism and Resistance in Burma, 1942–1945: Thein Pe Myint's 'Wartime Traveller'* (Athens, Ohio, 1984).

Alan Tennett, *British and Commonwealth Merchant Ships Losses to Axis U-Boats, 1939–1945* (Stroud, 2001).

The Colonial Empire, 1939–1947 (London, 1947).

David Thomas, *Malta Convoys, 1940–1942: The Struggle at Sea* (London, 1999).

—, *Japan's War at Sea* (London, 1978).

—, *The Battle of the Java Sea* (London, 1968).

H. L. Thompson, *New Zealanders with the Royal Air Force* (Wellington, 1953).

Christopher Thorne, *Allies of a Kind: The United States, Britain and the War against Japan, 1941–1945* (London, 1978).

—, *The Issues of War: States, Societies, and the Far Eastern Conflict of 1941–45* (London, 1985).

—, *The Limits of Foreign Policy: The West, the League and the Far Eastern Crisis of 1931–1933* (London, 1972).

Hugh Tinker (ed.), *Burma: The Struggle for Independence, 1944–1948*, 2 volumes (London, 1983 and 1984).

J. M. Tinley, *South African Food and Agriculture in World War Two* (Stanford, California, 1954).

To War With Whitaker: The Wartime Diaries of the Countess of Ranfurly, 1939–1945 (London, 1994).

B. R. Tomlinson, *The Political Economy of the Raj, 1914–1947: The Economics of Decolonization in India* (London, 1979).

Michael Tomlinson, *The Most Dangerous Moment* (London, 1976).

Richard Townshend Bickers, *The Desert Air War, 1939–1945* (London, 1991).

Ian Trenowden, *Operations Most Secret* (London, 1978).

Charles Tripp, *A History of Iraq* (Cambridge, 2000).

Patrick Turnbull, *The Battle of the Box* (London, 1979).

L. C. F. Turner, H. R. Gordon-Cumming and J. E. Beltzer, *War in the Southern Oceans, 1939–45* (Cape Town, 1961).

M. S. Venkataramani, *Bengal Famine of 1943* (Delhi, 1973).

G. Visser, *Ossewabrandwag: Traitors or Patriots?* (Cape Town, 1976).

Johannes Voigt, *India and the Second World War* (New Delhi, 1987).

Martin Wainwright, A., *Inheritance of Empire: Britain, India and the Balance of Power in Asia, 1938–55* (Westport, Connecticut, 1994).

Ronald Walker, *The Australian Economy in War and Reconstruction* (New York, 1947).

Don Wall, *Sandakan: The Last March* (New South Wales, 1988).

War History Branch, New Zealand, *New Zealand in the Second World War: Episodes and Studies* (Wellington, 1948–54).

War Office, *Paiforce: The Official Story of the Persia and Iraq Command, 1941–1946* (London, 1948).

Peter Ward Fay, *The Forgotten Army: India's Armed Struggle for Independence, 1942–1945* (Ann Arbor, Michigan, 1993).

Ben Warlow, *Shore Establishments of the Royal Navy: Being a List of the Static Ships and Establishments of the Royal Navy* (Liskeard, 1992).

Geoffrey Warner, *Iraq and Syria, 1941* (London, 1974).

Alan Warren, *Singapore, 1942: Britain's Greatest Defeat* (London, 2002).

Bernard Wasserstein, *Secret War in Shanghai: Treachery, Subversion and Collaboration in the Second World War* (London, 1998).

Christopher Waters, *The Empire Fractures: Anglo-Australian Conflict in the 1940s* (Melbourne, 1995).

Gary Waters, *OBOE: Air Operations Over Borneo 1945* (Canberra, 1995).

S. D. Waters, *The Royal New Zealand Navy* (Wellington, 1956).

Neville Watterson, *Borneo POW Camps: Mail of the Forces, POW and Internees*, 2 volumes (self-published, 1989 and 1994).

Donovan Webster, *The Burma Road: The Epic Story of One of World War Two's Most Remarkable Endeavours* (London, 2004).

Gerhard Weinberg, *A World At Arms: A Global History of World War Two* (Cambridge, 1994).

Catharine Wells, *East with ENSA* (London, 1998).

Nigel West, *Secret War: The Story of SOE, Britain's Wartime Sabotage Organization* (London, 1992).

Nicholas White, *Business, Government and the End of Empire: Malaya, 1942–1947* (Oxford, 1996).

M. J. Whitley, *Cruisers of World War Two: An International Encyclopaedia* (London, 1995).

F. A. Wigzell, *New Zealand Army Involvement Special Operations Australia, South-West Pacific in World War Two* (Edinburgh, 2001).

Martin Wilmington, *The Middle East Supply Centre* (London, 1972).

H. P. Willmott, *Empires in the Balance: Japanese and Allied Pacific Strategies to April 1942* (London, 1982).

—, *Grave of a Dozen Schemes: British Naval Planning and the War against Japan, 1943–45* (London, 1996).

—, *The Barrier and the Javelin: Japanese and Allied Pacific Strategies, February to June 1942* (London, 1983).

—, *The Second World War in the Far East* (London, 1999).

Michael Wilson, *A Submariner's War in the Indian Ocean, 1939–45* (Stroud, 2000).

Wings of the Phoenix: The Official History of the Air War in Burma (London, 1949).

Barbara Winter, *Stalag Australia: German Prisoners of War in Australia* (London, 1986).

John Winton, *Cunningham: The Greatest Admiral since Nelson* (London, 1998).

—, *Sink the Haguro!* (London, 1979).

—, *The Forgotten Fleet: The British Navy in the Pacific, 1944–1945* (London, 1969).

Suki Wolton, *The Loss of White Prestige: Lord Hailey, the Colonial Office and the Politics of Race and Empire in the Second World War* (Basingstoke, 2000).

Marjorie Wong, *The Dragon and the Maple Leaf: Chinese Canadians and World War Two* (Toronto, 1992).

F. L. W. Wood, *The New Zealand People at War, Political and External Affairs* (Wellington, 1958).

S. Woodburn Kirby, *The War Against Japan*, 5 volumes (London, 1957–69).

Peter Young, *The Arab Legion* (Reading, 1972).

Philip Ziegler, *Mountbatten: The Official Biography* (London, 1985).

—, (ed.), *Personal Diaries of Admiral the Lord Louis Mountbatten, Supreme Allied Commander, South-East Asia, 1943–1946* (London, 1988).

Ronald Zweig, *Britain and the Palestine Mandate during the Second World War* (London, 1986).

Articles and Book Chapters

Yoji Akashi, 'Japanese Policy towards the Malayan Chinese, 1941–1945', *Journal of South East Asian Studies*, 1 (1970).

Richard Aldrich, 'Imperial Rivalry: British and American Intelligence in Asia, 1942–46', *Intelligence and National Security*, 3 (1988).

R. G. D. Allen, 'Mutual Aid between the US and the British Empire, 1941–1945', *Journal of the Royal Statistical Society*, 109 (1946).

G. St John Barclay, 'Australia Looks to America: The Wartime Relationship, 1939–1942', *Pacific History Review*, 56 (1977).

Y. Bauer, 'From Cooperation to Resistance: The Hagana, 1938–1946', *Middle Eastern Studies*, 2 (1966).

Tim Benbow, 'Operation Ironclad: The British Invasion of Madagascar, May 1942', in A.Lovering, ed., *Amphibious Assults* (London, 2005).

Judith Bennett, 'Local Resource Use in the Pacific War with Japan: Logging in Western Melanesia', *War and Society*, 21 (2003).

Bernard Bourdillon, 'Nigeria's War Effort', *African Affairs* (October 1940).

G. Bouskill, 'Studies in War-Time Organization: African Line of Communication', *African Affairs* (July 1945).

Carl Bridge, 'The Malayan Campaign, 1941–42 in International Perspective', *South Asia*, 19 (1996).

Michael Budden, 'Defending the Indefensible? The Air Defence of Malta, 1936–1940', *War in History*, 6 (1999).

L. J. Butler, 'Reconstruction, Development and the Entrepreneurial State: The British Colonial Model, 1939–51', *Contemporary British History*, 13 (1999).

H. J. Cohen, 'The Anti-Jewish Farhud in Baghdad, 1941', *Middle Eastern Studies*, 3 (1966).

Michael Coles, 'Ernest King and the British Pacific Fleet: The Conferences at Quebec, 1944: Octagon', *Journal of Military History*, 66 (2002).

Terry Copp, '"If This War Isn't Over, And Pretty Damn Soon, There'll Be Nobody Left, In This Old Platoon ...": First Canadian Army, February-March 1945', in Paul Addison and Angus Calder (eds), *Time to Kill: The Soldiers Experience of War in the West, 1939–45* (London, 1997).

Ian Cowman, 'Defence of the Malay Barrier?' The Place of the Philippines in Admiralty Naval War Planning, 1925–1941', *War in History*, 3 (1996).

Robert Crawford, 'Nothing to Sell? – Australia's Advertizing Industry at War, 1939–1945', *War and Society*, 20 (2002).

Michael Crowder, 'The Second World War: Prelude to Decolonization in Africa', Michael Crowder (ed.), *Cambridge History of Africa*, viii, *1940–75* (Cambridge, 1984).

—, 'The 1939–45 War and West Africa', in J. F. A. Ajayi and Michael Crowder (eds), *History of West Africa*, ii (London, 1971).

John Darwin, 'War and Empire, 1939–45', in John Darwin, *Britain and Decolonization: The Retreat from Empire in the Post-War World* (Basingstoke, 1988).

K. Datta, 'Farm Labour, Agrarian Capital and the State in Colonial Zambia: The African Labour Corps, 1942–52', *Journal of Southern African Studies*, 14 (1988).

A. G. Dickson, 'Studies in War-Time Organization: The Mobile Propaganda Unit, East Africa Command', *African Affairs* (January 1945).

Gerald Douds, '"Matters of Honour": Indian Troops in the North African and Italian Theatres', in Paul Addison and Angus Calder (eds), *Time to Kill: The Soldiers Experience of War in the West, 1939–45* (London, 1997).

Edward Drea, '"Great Patience is Needed": America Encounters Australia, 1942', *War and Society*, 11 (1993).

Raymond Dumett, 'Africa's Strategic Raw Materials during World War Two', *Journal of African History*, 26 (1984).

Harold Evans, 'Studies in War-Time Organization: The Resident Minister in West Africa', *African Affairs* (July 1944).

Kent Fedorowich, 'Axis Military Prisoners of War as Sources for British Military Intelligence, 1939–42', *Intelligence and National Security*, 14 (1999).

—, 'Doomed from the Outset? Internment and Civilian Exchange in the Far East: The British Failure over Hong Kong, 1941–45', *Journal of Imperial and Commonwealth History*, 25 (1997).

—, 'SOE in South Africa', *Historical Journal* (2005).

—, '"Toughs and Thugs": The Mazzini Society and Political Warfare amongst Italian Prisoners of War in India, 1941–43', *Intelligence and National Security*, 20 (2005).

D. K. Fieldhouse, 'War and the Origins of the Gold Coast Cocoa Marketing Board, 1939–40', in Michael Twaddle (ed.), *Imperialism, the State and the Third World* (London, 1992).

Lynette Finch, 'Knowing the Enemy: Australian Psychological Warfare and the Business of Influencing Minds in the Second World War', *War and Society*, 16 (1973).

Sibylla Flower, 'Captors and Captives on the Burma–Thailand Railway', in Bob Moore and Kent Fedorowich (eds), *Prisoners of War and their Captors in World War Two* (Oxford, 1996).

Jorge Fodor, 'The Origins of Argentina's Sterling Balances, 1939–43', in Guido di Tella and D. C. M. Platt, *The Political Economy of Argentina, 1880–1946* (London, 1989).

Douglas Ford, 'British Intelligence on Japanese Army Morale during the Pacific War: Logical Analysis or Racial Stereotyping?', *Journal of Military History*, 69 (2005).

Jacks Ford, 'The Forlorn Ally: The Netherlands East Indies in 1942', *War and Society*, 11 (1993).

Raúl García Heras, 'World War Two and the Frustrated Nationalization of the British-Owned Argentine Railways, 1939–1943', *Journal of Latin American Studies*, 17 (1985).

John Gooch, 'Politics of Strategy: Great Britain, Australia and the War against Japan, 1939–1945', *War in History*, 10 (2003).

Andrew Gordon, 'The Admiralty and Imperial Overstretch, 1902–41', in Geoffrey Till (ed.), *Seapower: Theory and Practice* (London, 1994).

J. A. Gray, 'Studies in War-Time Organization: The Union's Supply Effort', *African Affairs* (April 1945).

J. E. H. Grobler, 'To Pay and What to Pay? South Africa and Lend-Lease in the 1940s', *Historia*, 40 (1995).

Albert Grundlingh, 'The King's Afrikaners? Enlistment and Ethnic Identity in the Union of South Africa's Defence Force during the Second World War, 1939–45', *Journal of African History*, 40 (1999).

Louis Grundlingh, '"Non-Europeans Should Be Kept Away from the Temptations of the Towns": Controlling Black South African Soldiers during the Second World War', *International Journal of African Historical Studies*, 25 (1992).

P. S. Gupta, 'Imperial Strategy and the Transfer of Power, 1939–51', in A. K. Gupta (ed.), *Studies in History and Society: Myth and Reality. The Struggle for Freedom in India, 1945–47* (New Delhi, 1987).

A. Hagemann, 'Very Special Relations: The Third Reich and the Union of South Africa, 1933–1939', *South African Historical Journal*, 27 (1992).

Ian Hall, '"Looking Skyward from Below the Waves": Admiral Tom Phillips and the Loss of the *Prince of Wales* and the *Repulse*', in Greg Kennedy (ed.), *British Naval Strategy East of Suez, 1900–2000: Influences and Actions* (London, 2004).

John Hargreaves, 'War and the African Empires, 1939–45', in John Hargreaves, *Decolonization in Africa* (London, 1996).

Ted Harrison, 'British Subversion in French East Africa, 1941–42: SOE's Todd Mission', *English Historical Review* (April 1999).

Glyn Harper, 'Threat Perception and Politics: The Deployment of Australian and New Zealand Ground Forces in the Second World War', *Journal of the Australian War Memorial*, 20 (1992).

Rita Headrick, 'African Soldiers and World War Two', *Armed Forces and Society*, 4 (1978).

K. D. D. Henderson, 'The Sudan and the Abyssinian Campaign', *African Affairs* (January 1943).

N. Hillmer, 'Vincent Massey and the Origins of the British Commonwealth Air Training Plan', *Canadian Defence Quarterly*, 16 (1987).

Carol Hills and Daniel Silverman, 'Nationalism and Feminism in Late Colonial India: The Rani of Jhansi Regiment, 1943–45', *Modern Asian Studies*, 17 (1993).

Allister Hinds, 'Imperial Policy and Colonial Sterling Balances, 1943–56', *Journal of Imperial and Commonwealth History*, 19 (1991).

Arnold Hodson, 'An Account of the Part Played by the Gold Coast Brigade in the East African Campaign, August 1940-May 1941', *African Affairs* (October 1941, January 1942).

—, 'The War Effort of the Gold Coast', *African Affairs* (October 1940).

David Horner, 'Defending Australia in 1942', *War and Society*, 11 (1993).

S. Horowitz, 'The Non-European War Recruitment in South Africa', in Ellen Hellman and Leah Abraham (eds), *Handbook on Race Relations in South Africa* (Cape Town, 1949).

Ashley Jackson, 'African Soldiers and Imperial Authorities: Tensions and Unrest during the Service of High Commission Territories Soldiers in the British Army', *Journal of Southern African Studies*, 25 (1999).

—, 'Refitting the Fleet in Ceylon: The War Record of Walker Sons and Company', *Journal of Indian Ocean Studies*, 10 (2002).

—, 'Supplying War: The Military-Logistical Contribution of the High Commission Territories in the Second World War', *Journal of Military History*, 66 (2002).

—, 'The Mutiny of the 1st Battalion The Mauritius Regiment, Madagascar 1943', *Journal of
the Society for Army Historical Research*, 80 (2001).

David Johnson, 'Settler Farmers and Coerced African Labour in Southern Rhodesia,
1936–46', *Journal of African History*, 33 (1992).

Howard Johnson, 'The Anglo-American Caribbean Commission and the Extension of
American Influence in the British Caribbean, 1942–1945', *Journal of Commonwealth and
Comparative Politics*, 22 (1984).

Saul Kelly, 'A Succession of Crises: SOE in the Middle East, 1940–45', *Intelligence and
National Security*, 20 (2005).

John Kent, 'Regionalism or Territorial Autonomy? The Case of British West African
Development, 1939–49', *Journal of Imperial and Commonwealth History*, 18 (1990).

—, 'The Egyptian Base and the Defence of the Middle East', *Journal of Imperial and
Commonwealth History*, 21 (1993).

David Killingray, '"If I Fight for Them, Maybe Then I Can Go Back to the Village": African
Soldiers in the Mediterranean and European Campaigns, 1939–45', in Paul Addison and
Angus Calder (eds), *Time to Kill: The Soldiers Experience of War in the West, 1939–45*
(London, 1997).

—, 'Labour Exploitation for Military Campaigns in British Colonial Africa, 1870–1945',
Journal of Contemporary History, 24 (1989).

—, 'Military and Labour Recruitment in the Gold Coast during the Second World War',
Journal of African History, 23 (1982).

Paul Kingston, 'The Middle East Supply Centre, 1941 to 1945: Regional Economic Planning
Attempted', in Paul Kingston, R. G. Tiedemann and Nicholas Westcott (eds), *Managed
Economies in World War Two* (London, 1991).

Chan Lan Kit-Ching, 'The Hong Kong Question during the Pacific War, 1941–45', *Journal
of Imperial and Commonwealth History*, 2 (1973).

H. Leggett, 'Britain's East African Territories and their Strategic Implications', *African
Affairs* (July 1940).

David Jordan, 'Surabaya', *Small Wars and Insurgencies*, 11 (2000).

Gerold Krozewski, 'Sterling, the "Minor" Territories and the End of Formal Empire,
1939–58', *Economic History Review*, 46 (1993).

Roger Lambo, 'Achtung! The Black Prince: West Africans in the RAF, 1939–46', in David
Killingray (ed.), *Africans in Britain* (London, 1994).

J. M. Lee, '"Forward Thinking" and War: The Colonial Office during the 1940s', *Journal of
Imperial and Commonwealth History*, 6 (1977).

Joanna Lewis, '"Tropical East Ends" and the Second World War: Some Contradictions
in Colonial Welfare Initiatives', *Journal of Imperial and Commonwealth History*, 28
(2000).

Peter Lowe, 'Britain and the Opening of the War in Asia, 1937–41', in Ian Nish (ed.), *Anglo-
Japanese Alienation, 1919–1952: Papers of the Anglo-Japanese Conference on the History of
the Second World War* (Cambridge, 1981).

C. A. Macdonald, 'The Politics of Intervention: The United States, Britain and Argentina, 1941–46', *Journal of Latin American Studies*, 12 (1980).

W. D. MacIntyre, 'Australia, New Zealand, and the Pacific War', in Judith Brown and William Roger Louis. *The Oxford History of the British Empire*, iv, *The Twentieth Century* (Oxford, 1999).

P. Marshall, 'British Commonwealth Air Training Plan', *The Round Table*, 89 (2000).

David Meredith, 'State Controlled Marketing and Economic "Development": The Case of West African Produce during the Second World War', *Economic History Review*, 39 (1986).

—, 'The Colonial Office, British Business Interests and the Reform of Cocoa Marketing in West Africa, 1937–1945', *Journal of African History*, 29 (1988).

R. Meyers, 'British Imperial Interests and the Policy of Appeasement', in W. Mommsen and L . Kettenacker (eds), *The Fascist Challenge and the Policy of Appeasement* (London, 1983).

Dawn Miller, ' "Raising the Tribes": British Policy in Italian East Africa, 1938–41', *Journal of Strategic Studies*, 22 (1999).

Jama Mohamed, 'The Evils of Locust Bacteria: Popular Nationalism during the 1945 Locust Control Rebellion in Colonial Somaliland', *Past and Present*, 174 (2002).

Ritchie Ovendale, 'Britain, the Dominions and the Coming of the Second World War, 1933–1939', in W. Mommsen and L. Kettenacker (eds), *The Fascist Challenge and the Policy of Appeasement* (London, 1983).

—, 'The Empire-Commonwealth and the Two World Wars', in Robin Winks (ed.), *The Oxford History of the British Empire*, v, *Historiography* (Oxford, 1999).

Nicholas Owen, 'War and Britain's Political Crisis in India', in Brian Brivati and Harriet Jones (eds), *What Difference Did the War Make?* (London, 1993).

Robert Pearce, 'Morale in the Colonial Service in Nigeria during the Second World War', *Journal of Imperial and Commonwealth History*, 11 (1983).

—, 'The Colonial Economy: Nigeria and the Second World War', in B. Ingham and C. Simmons (eds), *Development Studies and Colonial Policy* (London, 1987).

George Peden, 'Winston Churchill, Neville Chamberlain and the Defence of Empire', in John Hattendorf and Malcolm Murfett (eds), *The Limitations of Military Power: Essays Presented to Professor Norman Gibbs on his Eightieth Birthday* (London, 1990).

Henry Pelling, 'The Crisis of Empire', in Henry Pelling, *Britain and the Second World War* (Glasgow, 1970).

William Platt, 'Studies in War-Time Organization: East Africa Command', *African Affairs* (January 1946).

Sebastian Ritchie, 'Rising from the Ashes: Allied Air Power and Air Support for 14th Army in Burma, 1943–1945', *Air Power Review*, 7 (2004).

Jon Robb-Webb, ' "Light Two Lanterns, the British are Coming by Sea": Royal Navy Participation in the Pacific, 1944–1945', in Greg Kennedy (ed.), *British Naval Strategy East of Suez, 1900–2000: Influences and Actions* (London, 2004).

William Roger Louis, 'The Second World War, India and the Clash with Churchill, 1940–1945', in Louis, *In the Name of God Go! Leopold Amery and the British Empire in the Age of Churchill* (London, 1992).

M. Roth, '"If You Give Us Rights We Will Fight": Blacks in World War Two', *South African Historical Journal*, 15 (1983).

Patricia Roy, 'The Soldiers Canada Didn't Want: Her Chinese and Japanese Citizens', *Canadian Historical Review* (September 1978).

Galen Rozer Perra, 'Anglo-Canadian Imperial Relations: The Case of Garrisoning the Falkland Islands in 1942', *War and Society*, 14 (1996).

James Rusbridger, 'The Sinking of the *Automedon*, the Capture of the *Nankin*: New Light on Two Intelligence Disasters in World War Two', *Encounter* (November 1980).

Nicholas Evan Sarantakes, 'One Last Crusade: The US-British Alliance and the End of the War in the Pacific', *Royal United Services Institute Journal*, 149 (2004).

D. Gail Saunders, 'The 1942 Riot in Nassau: A Demand for Change?', *Journal of Caribbean History*, 20 (1985–86).

Kay Saunders, '"An Instrument of Strategy": Propaganda, Public Policy and the Media in Australia during the Second World War', *War and Society*, 15 (1997).

Rosaleen Smyth, 'Britain's African Colonies and British Propaganda during the Second World War', *Journal of Imperial and Commonwealth History*, 14 (1985).

—, 'War Propaganda during the Second World War in Northern Rhodesia', *African Affairs* (1984).

Andrew Stewart, '1939 British and Canadian "Empire Air Training Scheme" Negotiations', *The Round Table*, 93 (2004).

A. J. Stockwell, 'British Imperial Policy and Decolonization in Malaya, 1942–52', *Journal of Imperial and Commonwealth History*, 13 (1984).

—, 'Colonial Planning during World War Two: The Case of Malaya', *Journal of Imperial and Commonwealth History*, 2 (1974).

'Studies in War-Time Organization: The UKCC', *African Affairs* (July 1944).

Chandar Sundaram, '"A Paper Tiger": The Indian National Army in Battle, 1944–45', *War and Society*, 13 (1995).

Nicholas Tarling, '"An Empire Gem": British War-Time Planning for Post-War Burma', *Journal of South East Asian Studies*, 13 (1982).

—, '"A New and Better Cunning": British War-Time Planning for Post-War Burma', *Journal of South East Asian Studies*, 13 (1982).

'The South African Economy during the Second World War', in *Official Year Book of the Union*, no. 29 (South Africa, 1956–57).

'The Sudan at War: The Composite Infantry Battalion of the East Arab Corps, Sudan Defence Force, in the Abyssinia Campaign', *African Affairs* (October 1943).

'The Sudan Defence Force and the Italian East African Campaign', *African Affairs* (July 1942).

'The Sudan's Service in a Global War: The Story of a Section of the Trans-African Ferry Route', *African Affairs* (January 1944).

Martin Thomas, 'Imperial Backwater or Strategic Outpost? The British Takeover of Vichy Madagascar in 1942', *Historical Journal*, 39 (1996).

—, 'The Massingham Mission: SOE in French North Africa, 1941–1944', *Intelligence and National Security*, 11 (1996).

D. Throup and D. Anderson, 'Africans and Agricultural Production in Colonial Kenya: The Myth of the War as a Watershed', *Journal of African History*, 26 (1985).

Gardner Thompson, 'Governing Uganda: The Second World War and its Aftermath', in John Smith (ed.), *Administering Empire: The British Colonial Service in Retrospect* (London, 1999).

Kosmas Tsokhas, 'Dedominionization: The Anglo-Australian Experience, 1939–1945', *Historical Journal*, 37 (1994).

Mary C. Turnbull, 'British Planning for Post-War Malaya', *Journal of South East Asian Studies*, 5 (1974).

Kenneth Vickery, 'The Second World War Recruitment of Forced Labour in the Rhodesias', *International Journal of African Historical Studies*, 22 (1989).

Johannes Voigt, 'Co-operation or Confrontation? War and Congress Politics, 1939–42', in Anthony Low (ed.), *Congress and the Raj: Facets of the Indian Struggle, 1917–1947* (London, 1977).

D. C. Watt, 'Imperial Defence Policy and Imperial Foreign Policy, 1911–1939: A Neglected Paradox?', *Journal of Commonwealth Political Studies*, 1 (1961–63).

Nicholas Westcott, 'Closer Union and East Africa, 1939–48', *Journal of Imperial and Commonwealth History*, 10 (1981).

—, 'The Slippery Slope: Economic Control in Africa during the Second World War', in Paul Kingston, R. G. Tiedemann and Nicholas Westcott (eds), *Managed Economies in World War Two* (London, 1991).

Ian Wood, '"Twas England Bade Our Wild Geese Go": Soldiers of Ireland in the Second World War', in Paul Addison and Angus Calder (eds), *Time to Kill: The Soldiers Experience of War in the West, 1939–45* (London, 1997).

K. Wright, 'Dollar Pooling and the Sterling Area, 1939–1952', *American Economic Review*, 44 (1954).

Dissertations and Unpublished Papers

J. H. Bowden, 'Development and Control in British Colonial Policy, with Reference to Nigeria and the Gold Coast, 1935–1948', Ph.D. Thesis, University of Birmingham (1980).

Paul Collier, 'The Logistics of the North African Campaign, 1940–1944', D.Phil. Thesis, University of Oxford (2001).

Jean-Michel Domingue, 'The Experiences of the Mauritian and Seychellois Pioneers in, and Contribution to, the Egyptian and Western Desert Campaigns, 1940–43', MA Thesis, University of London (1994).

Marc Epprecht, 'Women, Class, and Politics in Colonial Lesotho, 1930–65', Ph.D. Thesis, Dalhousie University (1992).

Hoosain Faroqui, 'In the Shadow of Globalism: The United States, South Asia and the Cold War, 1939–53', Ph.D. Thesis, Cornell University (1986).

W. Gaskin, 'Economic Policy in Palestine, 1939 to 1945', D.Phil. Thesis, University of Oxford 1986).

Louis Grundlingh, 'The Participation of South African Blacks in the Second World War', Ph.D. Thesis, Rand Afrikaans University (1986).

Allister Hinds, 'British Imperial Policy and the Development of the Nigerian Economy, 1939–1951', Ph.D. Thesis, Dalhousie University (1985).

David Johnson, 'The Impact of the Second World War on Southern Rhodesia with Special Reference to African Labour, 1937–1948', Ph.D. Thesis, University of London (1989).

Saul Kelly, 'Great Britain, the United States and the Question of the Italian Colonies, 1949–1952', Ph.D. Thesis, London School of Economics (1995).

John Kent, 'The International Dimensions of British West African Policy, 1939–1949', Ph.D. Thesis, Aberdeen University (1986).

Joanna Lewis, 'The Colonial Politics of African Welfare, 1939–1952: A Crisis of Paternalism', Ph.D. Thesis, University of Cambridge (1993).

D. McIntyre, 'Paragons of Glamour: A Study of the US Military Forces in Australia, 1942–45', Ph.D. Thesis, University of Queensland (1989).

N. Mlambo, 'Arms Production and War Supply in Southern Africa, 1939–1945: Limitations of the Industrial War Effort of South Africa and Zimbabwe during the Second World War', Ph.D. Thesis, University of Cape Town (1999).

L. A. Nalana, 'The Second World War, 1939–45/6: Its Significance for Lesotho – Collaboration and Resistance', BA Project, National University of Lesotho (1986).

C. R. Nordman, 'Prelude to Decolonization in West Africa: The Development of British Colonial Policy, 1938–1947', D.Phil. Thesis, University of Oxford (1976).

Mary Ntabeni, 'War and Society in Colonial Lesotho, 1939–45', Ph.D. Thesis, Queen's University, Ontario (1997).

Ritchie Ovendale, 'The Influence of United States and Dominion Opinion on the Formation of British Foreign Policy, 1937–1939', D.Phil. Thesis, University of Oxford (1972).

G. N. Parsons, 'Imperial "Partnership": British Colonial Development and Welfare Policy, 1938–1950', M.Phil. Thesis, University of Oxford (1985).

D. G. M. Rampersad, 'Colonial Economic Development and Social Welfare: The Case of the British West Indian Colonies, 1929–1947', D.Phil. Thesis, University of Oxford (1979).

J. P. Rozier, 'The Effect of War on British Rule and Politics in the Sudan, 1939–45', D.Phil. Thesis, University of Oxford (1984).

Barbara Sargent, 'A Change in Perspectives: Italian Prisoners of War in Tasmania, 1943–1946', B. A. Thesis, Tasmania State Institute of Technology (1990).

Deborah Shackleton, 'Imperial Military Policy and the Bechuanaland Pioneers and Gunners during the Second World War', Ph.D. Thesis, Indiana University (1996).

John Shuckburgh, 'Colonial Civil History of the War', unpublished manuscript (1949).

D. N. Souter, 'Colonial Labour Policy and Labour Conditions in Nigeria, 1939–1945', D.Phil. Thesis, University of Oxford (1981).

Clare Thomas, 'Colonial Government, Propaganda, and Public Relations and the Administration in Nigeria, 1939–51', Ph.D. Thesis, University of Cambridge (1986).

Gardner Thompson, 'Uganda and the Second World War: The Limits of Power in a Colonial State', Ph.D. Thesis, University of London (1990).

Charles Tripp, 'Ali Mahir and the Palace in Egyptian Politics, 1936–1942', D.Phil. Thesis, University of London (1984).

Nicholas Westcott, 'Impact of the Second World War on Tanganyika, 1939–49', Ph.D. Thesis, University of Cambridge (1982).

—, and M. P. Cowen, 'British Imperial Economic Policy during the War', unpublished paper, City of London Polytechnic (1984).

Novels

J. Alan Thompson, *Only the Sun Remembers*, trilogy (Chagos Archipelago, Indian Ocean)

James Allen Ford, *The Brave White Flag* (Hong Kong)

Noel Barber, *Tanamera: A Novel of Singapore* (Singapore, Malaya)

J. G. Ballard, *The Last Emperor* (Shanghai)

H. E. Bates, *How Sleep the Brave: The Complete Stories of Flying Officer X* (Australia, Britain, Malta)

—, *The Purple Plain* (Burma)

—, *The Jacaranda Tree* (Burma)

—, *The Scarlet Sword* (India)

Dirk Bogarde, *A Gentle Occupation* (British-occupied Dutch East Indies)

Pierre Boulle, *The Bridge on the River Kwai* (Burma, Thailand)

Errol Braithwaite, *An Affair of Men* (Bougainville)

A. R. Channel, *The Forgotten Patrol* (Western Desert)

James Clavell, *King Rat* (Singapore)

Lawrence Durrell, *Alexandria Quartet* (Middle East)

J. G. Farrell, *The Singapore Grip* (Singapore)

Amitav Ghosh, *The Glass Palace* (Burma, India)

Graham Greene, *The Heart of the Matter* (Sierra Leone)

Gerald Hanley, *The Consul at Sunset* (ex-Italian Somaliland)

John Harris, *A Funny Place to Hold a War* (Sierra Leone)

J. Hewitt, *Three Men on a Bridge, Sometimes Four* (China, Hong Kong)

Laurent Joffrin, *All That I Have* (Indian SOE agent in France)

James Leasor, *Boarding Party* (India, Goa)

—, *Nothing to Report* (India)

Andrea Levy, *Small Island* (West Indies, Britain)

David Malouf, *Great World* (Australia)

Olivia Manning, *The Levant Trilogy* (Egypt, Middle East)

Ngaio Marsh, *Died in the Wool* (New Zealand)

Anthony Masters, *Tenko* (Malaya)

John Masters, *Bhowani Junction* (India)

Alan Moorehead, *African Trilogy* (Middle East, North Africa)

Nicholas Monsarrat, *The Cruel Sea* (Atlantic)

—, *Three Corvettes* (Atlantic)

Leonard Mosley, *The Cat and the Mice*

Michael Ondaatje, *The English Patient* (Mediterranean)

J. M. O'Neill, *Commissar Connell* (West Africa)

Douglas Reeman, *A Dawn Like Thunder* (Burma, Ceylon)

—, *A Ship Must Die* (Australia, Indian Ocean, Pacific)

—, *HMS Saracen* (Malta)

—, *In Danger's Hour* (Mediterranean)

—, *Rendezvous South Atlantic*

—, *Strike from the Sea* (Borneo)

—, *Sunset* (Hong Kong)

—, *The Pride and the Anguish* (Singapore)

—, *Winged Escort* (Indian Ocean, Pacific)

Paul Scott, *Johnnie Sahib* (Burma)

—, *The Raj Quartet* (India)

Nevil Shute, *A Town Like Alice* (Malaya)

Christopher Sykes, *Albert and Emerald* (Middle East)

—, *A Song of a Shirt* (Middle East)

—, *High Minded Murder* (Middle East)

Laurens Van der Post, *Merry Christmas Mr Lawrence* (Java, POW camp)

Evelyn Waugh, *Sword of Honour Trilogy* (Britain, Mediterranean, West Africa)

Index

British warships are indexed under His Majesty's Australian Ships, His Majesty's Ships and His Majesty's New Zealand Ships. Other ships are indexed alphabetically.